Sports in American Life

Cover illustration:
Joe DiMaggio, in a classic batting stroke, unleashes his second home run of the game on June 28, 1939, in Philadelphia, against Connie Mack's Athletics. The powerful New York Yankees hit eight home runs in this game, and five more in the second game of a double header. Both numbers remain in the record books.

Sports in American Life

A History

Richard O. Davies

© 2007 by Richard O. Davies

BLACKWELL PUBLISHING
350 Main Street, Malden, MA 02148–5020, USA
9600 Garsington Road, Oxford OX4 2DQ, UK
550 Swanston Street, Carlton, Victoria 3053, Australia

The right of Richard O. Davies to be identified as the Author of this Work has been asserted in accordance with the UK Copyright, Designs, and Patents Act 1988.

First published 2007 by Blackwell Publishing Ltd

3   2008

Library of Congress Cataloging-in-Publication Data

Davies, Richard O., 1937–
      Sports in American life : a history / Richard O. Davies.
            p.   cm.
      Includes bibliographical references and index.
      ISBN: 978–1–4051–0647–4 (hardback : alk. paper)
      ISBN: 978–1–4051–0648–1 (pbk. : alk. paper)
      1. Sports—United States—History. I. Title.
      GV583.D39 2007
      796.0973—dc22   2006023918

A catalogue record for this title is available from the British Library.

Set in 9.5/12 pt Photina
by The Running Head Limited, Cambridge, www.therunninghead.com
Printed and bound in Singapore
by C.O.S. Printers Pte Ltd

The publisher's policy is to use permanent paper from mills that operate a sustainable forestry policy, and which has been manufactured from pulp processed using acid-free and elementary chlorine-free practices. Furthermore, the publisher ensures that the text paper and cover board used have met acceptable environmental accreditation standards.

For further information on
Blackwell Publishing, visit our website:
www.blackwellpublishing.com

For Jayme, Mackenzie, and Katie

Contents

 9 **America's Great Dilemma**   **193**
    Racism Shapes American Sports   194
    The "Fight of the Century"   196
    Separate and Unequal: the Negro Leagues   199
    Out of the Cotton Fields of Alabama: Jesse and Joe   204
    Jackie   210
    In the Shadow of Jackie Robinson   215
    Gentlepeople and Sanctimonious Hypocrites   218
    The Baron and the Bear   221

10 **Television Changes the Face of American Sports**   **228**
    The Formative Years of Sports Television   229
    Tale of the Tube: Boxing   232
    Professional Football Comes of Age   235
    Pete and Roone   238
    The NFL and the AFL Make Peace   242
    Super Sunday and Monday Night   242
    ESPN: All Sports, All the Time   246

11 **College Sports in the Modern Era**   **252**
    The Sanity Code Is Scuttled   253
    Creation of a Cartel   254
    Emphasis and De-Emphasis   256
    Woody and the Bear   258
    Deceit and Deception: the NCAA and Gender Equity   263
    Criticism of Major College Sports   270
    Television and the Triumph of Commercialized College Sports   277
    The Knight Commission Report   280

12 **Play For Pay**   **283**
    A Tale of Two (Football) Cities   283
    Urban Rivalry, Redevelopment, and Promotion   286
    The Travails of Baseball   289
    Baseball's Labor Disputes   294
    Reaping the Spoils: the NFL and the World of Parity   298
    The Wondrous World of Magic, Larry, and Michael   304
    Always Turn Left: NASCAR Takes the Checkered Flag   309
    Struggling To Be Major League   316

13 **Do You Believe in Miracles?**   **317**
    The Cold War Shapes the Olympics   321
    Television Transforms the Olympics   329
    The Games Must Go On   334
    To Boycott or Not To Boycott   338
    The Triumph of Professionalism   343
    Athens and Beyond   345

Illustrations

Preface

During the early years of the nineteenth century, the word *sport* carried a much different connotation than today. To be a sporting man in the mid-nineteenth century was to be someone who flouted the rules of social acceptability by gravitating toward activities deemed inappropriate for a proper gentleman. The term *sport* was, in fact, used to identify men who embraced the bachelor culture of the tavern, where amid a haze of cigar smoke and the distinctive odor of stale beer and cheap whiskey, they watched cockfights and dogfights, bet on an upcoming horserace or baseball match, and won or lost money on the toss of the dice or the turn of a card. Upon special occasions they might even watch pugilists bloody each other in a bare-knuckle prizefight.

By mid-century, however, there emerged a group of men of stature called *sportsmen*. These men of good social standing found outlets from their pressing business and professional lives as participants and spectators in such activities as boating, swimming, horse racing, foot racing, rowing, and baseball. By century's end they likely had also gravitated toward popular new activities such as tennis, bicycle racing, football, golf, basketball, and volleyball. As these sports grew in popularity, sportsmen (now joined by a small but growing number of sportswomen) mimicked pronounced trends within the professional and business worlds by striving to achieve order and stability. They established amateur and professional leagues and associations, published statistics, developed and marketed specialized equipment, and enforced written rules governing athletic competition. While sports and games revealed a distinctly provincial quality in 1800, by the end of the century the once-dominant spontaneity and informality had been replaced by formalized structures, written rules, and bureaucratic organization. Befitting the growing specialization within the emerging complex national marketplace, a small number of skilled athletes were even able to work at play, earning their living as professional athletes. Several of the new sports provided women the opportunity to participate, although under carefully guarded conditions. In this rapidly changing environment, the word *sport* lost much of its negative connotation. Now, to be a sporting man or woman was to be involved in the robust new American lifestyle. By the early twentieth century, organized sports had assumed a prominent place in American life, reflective of the exuberant capitalistic and democratic spirit of a rapidly maturing society.

This book traces the evolution of American sports, from disorganized and quaint origins to the present time when sports have become fully integrated into the political, social, cultural, and economic fabric of the nation. The narrative is organized around the argument that sports, for good or for ill, have been a significant, if often overlooked, social force throughout much of the history of the United States. In recent years, historians have increasingly come to recognize that throughout the history of mankind, games have revealed many of the underlying values and tensions of society. Rather than being irrelevant diversions of little consequence, such activities provide important insights into fundamental values and beliefs. The games people play may have provided a convenient means of releasing tension or a way to escape the realities of the day, but have also provided the rituals that link generations and unite communities.

The essential assumption of this book is that throughout American history the form and purpose of sporting events have been closely connected to the larger society from which they arose. As but one recent example: during the days immediately following the terrorist attack upon the World Trade Center in New York City and the Pentagon in Washington, DC, on September 11, 2001, Americans found solace and reassurance in expressing their national unity and resolve through highly symbolic patriotic exercises conducted prior to the start of baseball and football games. National leaders urged the resumption of sports schedules as soon as it became apparent that no more attacks were imminent, viewing the games as an emphatic statement of national resolve that the terrorists would not disturb the rhythms of everyday life.

The Special Role of Sports in American Culture

Organized sports in the nineteenth century grew naturally with the new systems of transportation, manufacturing, and commercial organization. They took hold primarily in the cities that were created by the new modern America, and during the twentieth century they grew exponentially, propelled to prominence by the new communications mediums of radio, motion pictures, newspapers, and especially television. In contemporary America, sports have become an enormous multi-billion dollar enterprise. Professional football and baseball franchises are valued at between $150 million and $800 million, and nearly every major American city has in recent years spent hundreds of millions of dollars to build sports arenas and stadiums to accommodate professional teams. Most professional teams operate on annual budgets that exceed $75 million, and "major college" athletic programs have budgets ranging between $40 and $75 million. An oft-overlooked ancillary economic activity attests to the importance Americans place upon sporting events: conservative estimates are that gamblers bet at least $3 billion a year on sporting events, a figure larger than the gross national product of many third-world countries. At least 20 percent of the news reported in any daily urban newspaper is devoted to the activities of a small handful of that city's prominent residents who dribble basketballs, hit baseballs, or knock each other to the ground with intense ferocity. Radio and television networks provide 24-hour coverage of America's sports to a seemingly insatiable sports-fan base. A vast assortment of consumer items, from automobiles to beer, from cosmetics to clothes, are marketed in close relationship with sports teams and athletes.

In many ways, America's obsession with sports and the men and women who play the games has intersected in unsuspected ways with larger issues of public policy. For example, in the central areas of major metropolitan areas children attend public school in dilapidated buildings with leaking roofs and outmoded classrooms and laboratories, and are taught by underpaid teachers using tattered out-of-date textbooks. City streets go unrepaired, public libraries close, and public hospitals struggle to deal with their patient loads, but in these same cities, civic leaders eagerly cater to the demands of professional teams. The owners – multi-millionaires all – enjoy a special kind of public welfare through their lucrative agreements with local governments. Crucial social services might go untended, but time and again, taxpayers vote in favor of a tax increase to build a new arena or stadium and public officials placate team owners by granting tax breaks, sweetheart deals on rental fees, and parking and concessions revenue. In some instances they have even guaranteed the sale of tickets.

Between 1980 and 2005, nearly every major American city constructed lavish new sports venues for several professional teams, often to the serious neglect of basic community needs. Just as the citizenry of medieval European communities revealed their essential values by constructing imposing cathedrals in the town square, so too have modern American cities given expression to their priorities and values by erecting enormous sports facilities.

Sports and American History

The issue of stadium construction is but one example of how sports and larger community issues intersect. The pages that follow examine the role of sports within the broader context of the major themes of American history. This book is an extension of major trends of the last quarter century that have reshaped the way historians look at the history of the American people. The historical profession, which had long focused its attention on political, economic, and diplomatic themes, was turned on its head by the social upheavals of the 1960s. As part of the fallout of that turbulent period, the traditional historical approach that focused on the achievements and failures of a white, male political and economic establishment was called into question. A new generation of students, who were in the process of challenging many of the existing truths and myths about the "Establishment," demanded university-level courses in African American, Hispanic, and Native American history, classes on the history of environmental issues, and fresh perspectives on the American experience from the vantage point of the poor, women, and the working class.

It was within this period of intellectual ferment and change that scholars first began a systematic and serious examination of the role of sports in American history. The extensive body of literature upon which this book is based reveals that most of the writing on the history of American sports before the mid-1970s was done outside the academy, but within the last quarter century professional historians have produced a rich trove of books and articles that explore the relationship of American sports to larger social issues. In 1972, the first professional society devoted to the field of sports history was established, and several pioneering scholars made laudable efforts to provide a meaningful synthesis.[1] A few pioneering courses on the history of baseball had been taught previously, but now more-inclusive histories of American sports were introduced. Academic publishers began releasing a growing number of scholarly monographs on the subject of sports. History survey textbooks now included pictures of early baseball parks or college football games along with the more conventional images of soldiers, presidents, and reformers. By the end of the century courses on sports history had become part of the curriculum of many American colleges and universities.

The emergence of sports history as a serious scholarly endeavor is no small achievement, because within any college or university faculty will be found many who decry the existence of competitive intercollegiate sports on their own campuses. A national survey I conducted in 1999 indicated that the overwhelming number of specialized upper-division and graduate-level American social history courses still do not deal with any issue or theme related to sports. Many faculty members have rightfully objected to gargantuan athletic department budgets and the simultaneous exploitation and coddling of athletes on their campuses, and have been outraged by the many athletics-related scandals that have besmirched the image of American higher education. The reluctance of the historical profession to pursue sports as a serious scholarly topic can understandably be attributed in part to these negative attitudes, but it can reasonably be argued that if the social historian is to understand the life of the "common man," then he or she cannot ignore the role that sports have played in shaping American society and public policy.

On a superficial level, from the colonial period to the present, sporting events have provided a useful diversion from the pressures of daily life. Just as colonists tossed a ball or watched a quarter horserace as a diversion from their often difficult lives, so too do contemporary Americans follow the ups and downs of their favorite teams, put $5 in the office pool on the NCAA basketball tournament, and play on their church's co-ed slow-pitch softball team. On a more serious level, sports have long been used by parents, religious leaders, educators, and moral reformers to teach new generations the values of fair play, honesty, perseverance, and cooperation. Presidents from Theodore Roosevelt to George W. Bush have interjected themselves into the public debate over pressing sports issues. President Bush, in fact, was part owner and managing partner of a major-league baseball team, the Texas Rangers, before his election as governor of the Lone Star State in 1994. Sporting venues have often provided a stage on which Americans have dealt with the paramount issues of race and sexual discrimination. Students can learn much about the nature of American race relations by examining the Negro Baseball Leagues, the "fight of the century" between Jack Johnson and Jim Jeffries, the triumphs and tragedies of track star Jessie Owens, or the courage and resolution of Jackie Robinson in challenging the unwritten exclusionary racial covenant of organized baseball. Students interested in the dynamics of the women's rights movement can similarly draw insights from the struggles against entrenched sexism in both amateur and professional sports by such gifted athletes as Gertrude Ederle, Babe Didrikson Zaharias, Wilma Rudolph, and Billie Jean King. Political battles over the development of athletic programs for schoolgirls and college women during the past three decades have been, and remain, an integral part of a much-larger national struggle to overcome gender discrimination.

Many definitions of sport have been advanced over the years, but for the purpose of this book the word *sport* entails an organized competitive activity between participants that requires some combination of skill and physical prowess. Thus, such games as baseball, volleyball, and tennis are considered sports; chess, backgammon, and bridge are not. Some competitive games governed by rules but played primarily for pleasure or exercise, such as croquet, badminton, jogging, aerobics, and racquetball, are likewise excluded from this narrative, but stock car and marathon races fit comfortably within the definition. Professional wrestling, despite its popularity, is excluded because it is a loosely scripted entertainment spectacle rather than a competitive contest. Similarly, junk sports such as roller-derby and motocross are excluded, along with choreographed performance spectacles such as water ballet, figure skating, and ice dancing. Although hunters and fishermen refer to themselves as "sportsmen" and while professional fisherman sometimes engage in tournaments, those activities are considered here to be of a recreational nature.

This is a study of the world of sports as it intersects with the larger themes and issues of American life. American sports, at their best, have provided us with inspiring stories of courage, grace, drama, excitement, and accomplishment. Conversely, they have also brought out for all to see depressing examples of brutality, cruelty, racism, sexism, stupidity, intolerance, homophobia, xenophobia, nationalism, greed, and hypocrisy. Both extremes are on display in the pages that follow. In many respects, these pages present my personal take on the role of sport in American history, a culmination of a lifetime spent as a participant in and close observer of the American sports scene, and, for the past dozen years, a college professor testing the waters of sports history as a researcher and classroom instructor.

For better or for worse, sports have played an integral part in the history of the United States, providing Americans with a venue in which major cultural and social issues have been debated, contested, and, in some notable instances, resolved. In a sense, this book seeks to examine the American past through the prism of sports. It is not simply a story of the winners and losers, nor is it a chronicle of the individual achievements of athletes. This is a book intended for the serious student interested in examining the American past from the perspective of sports. Trivia buffs and memorabilia collectors should look elsewhere.

Richard O. Davies
University of Nevada, Reno
June 1, 2006

Acknowledgments

Many friends, colleagues, and students contributed to this book. I am indebted to the hundreds of authors – scholars, journalists, sports junkies – whose works I have consulted. Their contributions to our understanding of American sports have made my effort to write an interpretative history of American sports possible. During the preparation of this book, three chairs of the Department of History at the University of Nevada, Reno – C. Elizabeth Raymond, Scott E. Casper, and Dennis Dworkin – have provided unstinting support, encouragement, and much-appreciated student assistance. I express my gratitude to those student assistants, without whom I could never have brought this work to publication on schedule: Jennifer Valenzuela, Seth Flatley, Jayme Hoy, Eric Bender, and Yuliya Kalnaus. I am deeply indebted to Dee Kille, Frank Mitchell, and Margaret Dalrymple for giving the original manuscript a much-needed critical reading. The final product was substantially enhanced by the deft touches applied by two editorial and production professionals at The Running Head, Cambridge, UK: Annie Jackson and Roger Jordan. Gail Meese of Meese Photo Search guided me through the process of locating and securing permission to publish historical photographs. I am especially grateful for the editorial guidance of Peter Coveney of Blackwell Publishing; his enthusiastic support for the project and his good humor and helpful suggestions have made the process of bringing the manuscript to publication an enjoyable process. The book is much the better as a result of his efforts. I also acknowledge the confidence expressed in my project by Susan Rabinowitz, Elizabeth Frank, and Kenneth Provencher at Blackwell. The Board of Regents of the Nevada System of Higher Education granted an invaluable sabbatical leave during the spring 2004. I also express my appreciation to a very special group: the more than one-thousand students who have completed my course in the History of American Sports over the past decade. They have provided an invaluable sounding board for many of the ideas presented in this book. Most important of all is Sharon. Throughout the five years that were devoted to the writing of this book, she has been unfailingly supportive as I have burrowed myself in the library and my office, often during weekends and holidays. Writing a book on a subject as broad and complex as this is a long and difficult, sometimes frustrating, task, but Sharon has made that endeavor possible. For that, and so much more, I thank her.

This book is dedicated to my three granddaughters, whose lives I hope will be enriched by playing games they enjoy and supporting the teams and athletes they respect. May they learn the importance of competing hard within the rules, and understand that the inevitable setbacks they will encounter – in sports and beyond – must be only a prelude to trying harder and preparing for the next challenge. Would that they also keep in mind the oft-overlooked fact that never fails to produce a murmur of surprise from my students: in every contest, 50 percent of the teams will lose. Winning, of course, is not the only thing, but striving for victory with all the strength and desire that one can muster is a most important thing indeed. The time-honored lessons taught through sports remain meaningful in the twenty-first century just as they did centuries ago.

1 Games the Colonists Played

Although there is substantial evidence to demonstrate that folk games and contests were an integral part of everyday life in colonial America, it was not until well into the nineteenth century that games and contests took on the structure of organized, modern sports. This is not to say that physical recreational activities were absent from the colonies. Rather, colonists participated in a myriad of activities that can best be described as folk games. These games were characterized by their spontaneity and the absence of standardized rules. Colonial children and young adults played various games using sticks and balls, ran foot races, swam in rivers and lakes in summer time and skated on them during the winter, and participated in roughneck contests that were precursors to today's games of baseball, lacrosse, soccer, and football. Additionally, among young lower-class male adults, no-holds-barred fights, which combined wrestling, biting, bare-knuckle fighting, and even eye-gouging, were part of the colonial scene, primitive precursors to the popular sport of prizefighting that emerged in more-or-less organized form well before the Civil War.

Many and varied games were played in the English colonies, but the most popular sporting event in colonial America was horse racing, most of which occurred in the Tidewater region of Maryland and Virginia. These games and recreations were characterized by their casual nature, more or less governed by informal rules of local origin and subject to constant revision and argument. Team games were unheard of, and participation in any activity that included physical competition was limited to a small percentage of the colonial population. Although the many games and contests that absorbed the attention of colonial America incorporated many New World variations – including adaptation of Native American games – their roots could be found in rural England. Immigrants to the New World naturally brought with them the customs, values, and vices of the Old World. The Puritan leaders who came to Massachusetts Bay Colony, for example, were determined to build a new order – a shining "city on a hill," as John Winthrop eloquently expressed it in 1630 – that placed emphasis on the creation of a theocratic state in which pious men and women responded to God's calling to a life of discipline and productivity as farmers, seamen, and craftsmen. Similarly, the Anglicans who gravitated to the Chesapeake Bay area were equally determined to replicate the social norms of the landed gentry of rural England, replete with the pleasures of lavish balls and banquets, riding to hounds, the playing of billiards and card games, and hell-bent-for-leather quarter horseraces, all of which were accompanied by high-stakes gambling.

The English Heritage

The games that the colonists played were largely adaptations of those that they had experienced in the Old World. Everyday life in Britain in the sixteenth and seventeenth centuries revolved around extended periods of hard work, the tedium of which was alleviated by lusty celebrations on Sundays and the holidays that marked the yearly calendar. As historian Richard Holt has stated, during the reigns of King Henry VIII and Queen Elizabeth I there flourished a "festive life" that embraced a wide range of parties, games, fairs, feasts, hunts, festivals, dances, and general merriment.[1]

Sporting contests were often held within this broader context of the celebration of holidays. Sundays afforded the peasants a day's rest from their arduous labor, a much-welcome opportunity for relaxation and socialization, but so too did the holidays – many of obscure and ancient origin – that cluttered the English calendar. During the reign of Henry VIII in the sixteenth century, the Anglican Church officially recognized no fewer than 165 holidays in addition to the day of rest that was supposed to be Sunday; as commerce and manufacturing grew during the early modern period, this number necessarily shrunk, but it nonetheless stood at 78 in the mid-eighteenth century. These holidays usually featured public feasts, music and dancing, plays and puppet shows, animal shows, the consumption of large quantities of beer and liquor, and the playing of games, many of which were of the rough-and-tumble variety. Celebrations often fused the occasion of religious holidays with the memorialization of historical battles, and sometimes becoming commingled with ancient pagan rituals and customs related to planting and harvest seasons.[2]

One of the most prominent of these special events was May Day, which celebrated the arrival of spring. This was a day often characterized by unrestrained revelry whose origins rested with ancient pagan fertility rites. The celebration centered on exuberant dancing around a maypole. A large tree trunk, stripped of its branches and erected in an open area, and festooned with colorful ribbons was recognized for what it was: a not-so-subtle phallic symbol. May Day festivities celebrated the hopes and joys of spring, marking a time for rebirth, regeneration, and reproduction. Young men and women danced merrily, and often drunkenly, around the maypole; and befitting the underlying fertility theme, couples often departed the dancing area for the seclusion of nearby woods. Few of the participating maidens, sniffed one offended observer, returned from this festival "undefiled." Critic Christopher Fetherston wrote in 1582 that young men "doe use commonly to runne into woodes in the night time, amongst maidens, to set bowes, in so muche, as I have hearde of tenne maidens whiche went to set May, and nine of them came home with childe."[3]

Thus it is not surprising that among the many rules established by the early Puritan settlers in Massachusetts Bay Colony was one forbidding a maypole festival; this was one of many English traditions that they considered not only wanton paganism but an invitation to lewd and immoral behavior that would undermine their determination to build that "city on a hill." Historian Winton Solberg has aptly noted, "The Maypole festivities were to Puritans heathen idolatry and a source of debauchery."[4] Determined to create a social climate that focused on solemnity, sobriety, striving, and a life dedicated to hard work and earnest worship, the Puritans took a dim view of any behavior that included the pursuit of idle amusements or light-hearted frivolity.

May Day in the English countryside, however, was only one of many holidays that provided the peasantry with opportunities for revelry. Such Christian holidays as Easter and Christmas sparked community celebrations. Fairs and special market days held during the summer months provided yet another occasion for merrymaking. The arduous and impoverished existence of the commoners who lived and worked on the countryside of "Merry Olde England" was thus enlivened by a bevy of holidays, religious and pagan, both formal and informal.

Central to these events was the playing of games, many of which would evolve over subsequent centuries into the structured games of organized sport that we recognize today. On the milder side, participants, both male and female, ran foot races, attempted to toss iron rings over pegs, and played skittles (an early form of lawn bowling). However, the most popular games that engaged young males placed special emphasis upon the demonstration of physical strength and agility, often within a context that encouraged violent play and unrestrained mayhem. Many of the most popular games were related to the high value that the English attached to hunting and military combat. Among the popular remnants of medieval warfare that survived well into the early modern era were martial-arts contests, including jousting, tilting, archery, and fencing, and, with the spread of firearms, target shooting and the hunting of wildlife.

The Commoners at Play

By today's standards, Elizabethan England was a crude and often cruel society. The welfare of animals was seldom respected, and the contemporary reader winces while reading of the heartless, even barbaric mistreatment of helpless animals that occurred for the sake of public amusement. A resident of Chichester sadly noted in the early eighteenth century that his fellow townsmen were "much given to mean diversions such as bull-baiting, which was very frequent, and for which many bulldogs were kept in town to the great torture and misery of those poor animals."[5] Nearly every town had its cockpit, which were put to use with considerable frequency. Excited and often inebriated spectators excitedly watched – and bet heavily on – cockfights in which two roosters, outfitted with razor-sharp metal gaffs, fought bloody battles until one was killed. Samuel Pepys reported watching such an event in London in 1663, attended by "the poorest apprentices, bakers, brewers, butchers, draymen and whatnot . . . all fellows with one another swearing, cursing, and betting."[6] One cruel variation of this activity was "cock throwing," in which a rooster would be tethered by a short rope to a stake and contestants at public events would pay a small fee to throw a missile (often a rock or piece of wood) at the bird; if it were downed or suffered a broken leg the thrower was given the bird as a prize to take home for dinner. Historian Robert Malcolmson has sardonically noted, however, that experienced roosters became adept at dodging the missiles thrown their way and consequently "could earn good money for their master."[7] Such treatment of animals was generally not considered abnormal or even cruel, and it was not until well into the nineteenth century that reformers managed to bring a halt to such brutal entertainments.[8]

Bearbaitings were popular, wherein a pack of powerful bulldogs were tossed into an enclosure where a tethered bear was forced to defend itself, although the inevitable outcome was the bear's gory death. Bullbaitings likewise drew cheering, sadistic audiences, as the trained dogs were turned loose on a bull tied to a stake, their objective to grab the poor beast's testicles with their powerful jaws and hold on for dear life as the drunken crowd raucously cheered on the tenacious bulldog. On other occasions, however, the tide was turned on these ferocious dogs when they were paired against each other by their owners and forced to fight until one of the animals was killed. Given the popularity of this type of brutal entertainment, it is not altogether surprising that the English informally adopted the tenacious bulldog as a national symbol.

Animals were not the only species that suffered physical injury. In emulation of the man-to-man combat that was the stuff of warfare of the time, men engaged in a wide range of violent contests. These often were merely a crude form of wrestling or fisticuffs where there were few if any rules. The emphasis of these contests was usually on using brute strength to overcome the opponent. Sometimes one community would put forth its best brawler to take on the champion of a rival town, with many a bet riding on the outcome. The English especially liked cudgeling, in which the winner was the one who was able to draw blood from his opponent's head, using a shield to defend himself while attempting to smash his opponent's skull with a wooden stick. One seventeenth-century public notice of a forthcoming cudgeling match announced, "No head be deemed broke until the blood run an inch."[9]

Hurling, a game somewhat similar to modern-day lacrosse and field hockey was especially encouraged because it was believed to provide excellent preparation for the hand-to-hand combat of warfare. Unlike the Native Americans who played with a leather ball they tossed and caught with a leather net attached to a long stick, the English played with sticks that featured broad blades, which were routinely used to smack an opponent's shins as well as advance the ball toward the goal. It was believed that hurling helped young men develop the courage and verve necessary to achieve victory in armed battle. Hurling, like other fiercely contested contact sports, was also viewed as a means whereby young men could prove their manhood to the young ladies in the audience by demonstrating their athletic skills as well as their manly ability to deliver and endure severe blows.

By the early eighteenth century, as intensified commercial activity and the early stirring of manufacturing were spurring urban growth, the rough-and-tumble fighting of the rural areas began to be channeled into a more-structured format that included the use of referees to enforce established rules. Bare-knuckle fist-fighting, popularly called "pugilism," was the first English sport to have written rules. In 1743, one leading London pugilist, Jack Broughton, apparently distraught over having killed an opponent, established the first set of written rules and insisted upon their enforcement in his future fights. These rules, which were more or less enforced for more than a century in the informal circuit of prizefighting venues in the London area, mandated the use of a referee, forbade hitting an opponent below the waist, granted a man knocked down 30 seconds of rest, and halted the long-time practice of hitting or kicking a contestant who had been downed. Broughton also introduced the use of "mufflers" – the precursor to today's boxing gloves – for training sessions, although they apparently were occasionally used in some bouts.[10]

Prizefights, often organized by taverns or private clubs, drew large crowds, including many of the leading gentlemen – popularly called "The Fancy" – of London society, who bet heavily upon their outcome. The audiences at most sporting events were restricted to certain classes; however, the crowds drawn to pugilistic events and cockfights were inclusive of all levels of English society, including women who were not overly concerned about their reputations. "What a concourse of people of all ranks there was to see this fight and what gambling," one observer at a Norwich match in 1772 exclaimed.[11] The attraction of the brutality of pugilism seemed to cut across all class lines, because Broughton's rules notwithstanding, many a fighter died in these contests. As late as 1803, one visitor to Lancashire noted that fierce fights were frequently held there that included

> the right of kicking on every part of the body and in all possible situations, and of squeezing the throat or "throttling" to the verge of death. . . . Contests of this nature are watched by crowds of persons who take part on each side. . . . That death often occurs in such battles will not be thought extraordinary.[12]

Contests that pitted one man against another or the few men who played on each side in a hurling match, however, lacked the immense mass spectacle provided by the raucous free-for-all that was the primitive game of football. This precursor of today's formalized games of English football (soccer) and rugby and American football was played in an endless variety of formats, usually without the benefit of any rules or strategies. It was essentially a disorganized brawl with a leather ball as the focal point. Surviving documents indicate that in one form or another, contests that can be lumped under the general rubric of "football" were played as early as the thirteenth century. As the centuries went by, the game's popularity increased as annual contests became the center of rivalries between neighboring villages or rural parishes. The game was often played with a crude ball made from an inflated animal's bladder encased in leather, but other types were also not uncommon. Because a pig's bladder was the bladder of choice, it has led some historians to speculate that today's slang term of pigskin used to denote the aerodynamically designed football of today (actually covered with calfskin), is rooted in the crude games played centuries ago in England.

The game was rugged and simplistic. Tradition held that the game be played on Shrove Tuesday, the day before Ash Wednesday, although games were held at other times as well. Played on large meadows and fields, the range of action sometimes encompassed several square miles of rolling English countryside. Goal lines were often miles apart, sometimes merely designated by a stand of trees or clump of bushes, sometimes the main streets of competing towns. One report indicated that participants had to swim across a sizable pond. The size of the teams fluctuated wildly, usually including dozens of young men per side, but the count sometimes exceeded hundreds of participants. After an initial "scrum" in which both sides attempted to gain control of the ball, the bladder would be variously kicked, thrown, or carried toward the designated goal, with the opponents seeking to grab the ball and head the other way. In more sophisticated instances, the two teams would be limited to an equal number of participants, with crude strategies employed to use guile as well as brute force to advance the ball against the defenders. One popular deception was for a swift runner to conceal the ball under his shirt (a tactic used briefly during the early American football era until ruled illegal). In most instances, however, the contest merely pitted all comers from two rival villages in what amounted to disorganized mayhem orchestrated around advancing the inflated bladder toward the distant goal by whatever means possible.

With few if any rules, and definitely no officials throwing penalty flags or blowing whistles, play was unrestrained and usually devolved quickly into a pitched battle in which punches were thrown, kicks were aimed at sensitive areas, and knees and elbows were ruthlessly used with the intent to inflict pain and suffering. The result was typically broken bones, bloody cuts and bruises, and sometimes serious internal injuries, even an occasional death. One onlooker noted, "When the exercise becomes exceedingly violent, the players kick each other's shins without the least ceremony, and some of them are overthrown at the hazard of their limbs."[13]

As early as 1314, the English monarchy issued its first public decree prohibiting the playing of this violent game, but it and the several score of subsequent similar royal orders had minimal impact. Much later, at the turn of the twentieth century, several American college presidents, troubled by the death toll produced by the new game of football, would issue equally ineffectual decrees. Football was one of the most popular spectacles/games that not only provided a diversion from the grim and difficult life of the rural commoners of Elizabethan England, but served as a means of promoting community unity and pride. The more philosophically inclined opined that the game helped promote physical fitness and prepare young men for service in the king's army. When the contest was ended, custom had it that the local elite would award prizes to the winners and host all participants to a public feast while the injured consoled themselves with a pint of ale. Or several.

The Games of the English Gentry

These crude and dangerous games were played by commoners. The upper strata of English society – the hereditary nobility and the affluent landed gentry – gravitated instead toward games that required the use of horses and were associated with hunting and fowling. With time on their hands, they also found a satisfying diversion in the breeding and racing of horses, a popular activity designated in England as the "sport of kings." Hunting had long been a privilege reserved to the upper classes – only the wealthy were permitted to hunt, while severe penalties were imposed on poachers – and many variations of games and contests that involved hunting and riding across the countryside were popular. They usually included the use of horses. Often, as in the use of hounds and horses to chase a frightened fox, these events were held in conjunction with elaborate banquets, receptions, and related social activities. Younger members of the elite played a rudimentary game of tennis (with a ball stuffed with animal hair), attended dances and picnics, raced small oar-powered boats, with the more daring demonstrating their skills as horsemen in a variety of races and contests, a not-so-subtle anticipation of their possible future role as king's horsemen in time of war. Whatever their social class, however, the English had one thing in common: they played their games within a social context that emphasized the hefty consumption of alcoholic beverages and the placing of substantial bets.

By the early eighteenth century, cricket had become well established as a pastime for the upper classes, although its origins lay with the commoners. It enjoyed widespread popularity among the more fashionable members of society, in part because of an elaborate set of rules that controlled the behavior of participants. It was also a game conducive to the making of a side bet. However, its appeal to the gentry was that, as social historian Robert Malcolmson writes, "its structure of rules allowed for a nice blend of energetic activity and dignity of behavior, and in this way it satisfied the disposition to compete without infringing on the normal standards of genteel propriety."[14]

London emerged as a major commercial city when the medieval era gave way to the new currents of business during the seventeenth and eighteenth centuries, and in the process several sports that had once been identified with the countryside were given a distinctly urban stamp. In 1720, a visitor to London observed the widespread nature of games played by the "common sort," who "divert themselves at Foot ball, Wrestling, Cudgels, Ninepins, Shovelboard, Cricket, Stow-ball, Ringing of Bells, Quoits, pitching the Bar, Bull and Bear baiting, throwing at Cocks, and lying at Alehouses."[15] Innkeepers and tavern operators recognized that they could attract a steady clientele if they offered lively entertainment in the form of games that stimulated gambling and heavy drinking. Hence they hosted a wide variety of contests, including bearbaitings, bullbaitings, dogfights, cockfights, and for human participants bare-knuckle prizefights and wrestling matches. When Las Vegas hotel-casinos of today seek to attract a large crowd of "high-roller" gamblers by holding highly publicized championship boxing matches, they are but continuing a tradition begun four centuries earlier in the small smoky, dank taverns of Elizabethan England.

The Puritan Reaction

This culture of games and frivolity, however, did not sit well with the growing middle-class Protestant reform group commonly known as Puritans. Devotees of the teachings of John Calvin, they were in the vanguard of the development of a new urban-based commercial economy. Serious to a fault, the Puritans were determined to "purify" the Church of England, which they believed had not sufficiently eradicated the remnants of Catholicism following its break with Rome during the reign of Henry VIII. They viewed the lax moral codes under which so many Englishman lived as a threat not only to the establishment of a proper and moral society but also to their vision of a hard-working, productive capitalist citizenry. Although it is easy to lampoon these earnest reformers, their objectives were clear. One of their early and persistent targets was the excessive drinking and carousing that occurred routinely on the Sabbath. They found themselves embroiled in a prolonged struggle with both the lower classes and the aristocracy, because both groups quite openly preferred a day of merriment to one devoted to the solemnities of worship, Bible study, prayer, and quiet contemplation. The most dedicated of the Puritans, in fact, believed that no true believer should engage in sexual intercourse from sundown on Saturday until sunup on Monday.

The Puritan attack on the Church of England for its tolerant attitude toward enthusiastic celebrations of religious holidays, however, met stiff resistance. The lower classes simply continued their customary ways of recreation, but the upper classes were most put off by the relentless Puritanical reform crusade. Thus, in 1618, King James I issued a royal decree that he demanded be read from every pulpit in the land. Formally titled the "Kings Majesties Declaration to his Subjects concerning lawful Sports to Bee Used," the decree was usually referred to simply as *The Book of Sports*. This controversial document made the case for the playing of games and for the convivial social practices that accompanied them. King James's declaration stipulated that "no lawful recreation shall be barred to our good people, which shall not tend to the breach of our aforesaid laws and canons of our Church." This included "dancing, either of men or women, archery for men, leaping, vaulting or any other such harmless recreation." The king even approved of the sensuous merriment that occurred during "May Games" and "the setting up of Maypoles."[16]

Much to the consternation of "the precise people," as the Puritans were often called, the king specifically ordered that Sundays and holidays were to be considered a time for recreational and social activities, taking note of the fact that for many hard working peasants those were the only days available for relaxation: "For when shall the common people have leave to exercise if not upon Sunday and holidays, seeing they must apply their labour and win their living in all working days?"[17] Many puritan-inclined clergymen refused to read the decree and they were subjected to serious punishment, including censorship and termination. The king was concerned that the suppression of sports would reduce the quality of future armies. He believed, of course, that by encouraging the development of physical prowess he was helping to prepare his countrymen for future battle.

The Book of Sports, however, remained a contentious issue, and many Puritans in Parliament repeatedly sought to have it recalled. These reformers were determined to push England into a new era of commerce and manufacturing to increase the nation's ability to produce food and the new products necessary for a growing population. Among their goals was to replace inherited position and birthright with a new ruling class based on competition, economic success, and productivity.[18] They had already accepted as their guidebook a 1583 publication by Philip Stubbes entitled *Anatomie of Abuses* which decried the desecration of the Sabbath by feasts and the playing of games, as well as the merrymaking associated with Christmas, Easter, and other holidays. "Any exercise which withdraweth us from godliness, either upon the sabaoth or any other day else, is wicked, and to be forbidden."[19] One special target were so-called "church ales," festive days sponsored by local parishes loyal to the Church of England, which featured dancing, games, informal plays, puppet shows, and substantial consumption of locally brewed ales and beers.

The Puritans, naturally, were aghast as they observed such offensive and licentious behavior occurring under the purview of the established church. Their goal was not only to "purify" the Church of England of its many "Popish" practices but to bring a halt to the practices of self-indulgence, debauchery, and game-playing that they believed defiled the name of God and diverted the common man from a life of contemplative worship and the serious pursuit of his responsibilities as a member of the labor force. The Puritans thus viewed the playing of games within a larger context, their opposition firmly grounded in the view that games were a waste of time and energy, that they diverted men and women from their work and other communal obligations, that many of the games were designed to inflict pain and injury (on both men and animals), and that because most sporting events occurred on Sunday they detracted from proper observance of the Sabbath. Overall they were considered disruptive of the social order.[20]

Thus to the Puritans, the building of a new competitive capitalistic society required the fostering of a nation of skilled and dedicated workers. Individual thrift and commitment to one's calling would prove futile if discipline did not replace licentiousness and revelry among the working classes. The creation of a new ethos among workers demanded nothing less than a reform of the leisure ethic that had long reigned supreme among the populace. To the Puritans, as one of their spokesmen put it, any recreation "must tend also to the glory of God."[21] King James's contention that rowdy games helped prepare future soldiers for his armies was not persuasive to this dedicated group of emerging capitalists.

This cultural conflict ebbed and flowed throughout English society for decades. Allegiances frequently crossed social and class lines, although the emerging commercial urban middle class, landed middle classes, and urban shop-keepers and small manufacturers tended to side with the Puritans, while the traditional aristocracy, large land-owners, and the peasantry supported the Crown and the Church of England in defense of their right to enjoy the serious playing of games. The Puritans ultimately triumphed in 1649, following a civil war. King Charles I, the nephew of James, was beheaded after a brief trial, and the Puritan revolutionaries ultimately turned to the austere Oliver Cromwell for leadership. Parliament swiftly moved to rescind *The Book of Sports*, which the Puritans viewed as an endorsement of sin, and imposed a rigid regime upon what had once been "Merry Olde England." The playing of games was not completely abolished, of course, but it was definitely restrained. Following the counterrevolution that led to the restoration of the Crown in 1660, the English people returned to their traditional ways of celebrating the Sabbath and holidays, but observers noticed that a more restrained pattern of behavior took much of the lusty ardor out of the revelry.[22]

Games in Colonial New England

Although colonists to North America brought with them the games that they had learned in England, the harsh frontier environment they faced initially gave them little time for fun and games. Adapting to the severe climate they found in the wilderness of North America was the first order of business; mere survival during the formative colonial decades was a desperate fact of life, and even well into the eighteenth century the lives of most colonists were consumed with hacking out a subsistence type of living in a difficult natural environment. It was thus logical that a popular consensus placed primacy upon the importance of productive work and denigrated behavior that detracted from labor. Puritan skepticism about the intrinsic value of non-productive games was therefore inevitably intensified by the unrelenting frontier environment in which they found themselves. What they regularly referred to as the "howling wilderness" proved to be a powerful influence upon their thoughts and actions; in such an environment, the development of a substantial leisure ethic was necessarily circumscribed.

If a game encouraged participants to shirk their essential obligations for work and worship, then it definitely was deemed inappropriate. Focus on the serious nature of life was especially pronounced in New England, as well as in Quaker Pennsylvania. In these regions, powerful public pressure gave primacy to the importance of one's dedication to a life of meaningful labor and worship. To be certain, the Puritans did not abolish games and recreational activities, but they made clear distinctions between games and other diversions that tended to restore clarity of mind and refresh the body so that one could return to the field or shop reinvigorated. Actually, much of the Puritans' concerns about games and play grew out of memories of the Old World, where unseemly social behavior routinely occurred in conjunction with ball games and blood sports, in particular, rowdy behavior, excessive drinking, and gambling.[23]

The grim image that the Puritans brought to New England of the rowdiness and brutality often associated with ball games provided sufficient wariness of such activities sufficient to keep them to a minimum. Ball games, in and of themselves, were innocent enough, but it was the unseemly behavior that so often accompanied them that led to their widespread unpopularity. As historian Bruce Daniels concludes, "colonies did not pass laws against ball and blood sports; public contempt sufficed to bar them." As he notes, the pervasive lack of attention to ball games by New Englanders in their sermons, diaries, correspondence, and newspapers throughout the entire colonial period "speaks volumes" about their absence from the daily lives of colonists of New England.[24]

To their credit, the Puritans adamantly sought to suppress "butcherly sports" – the mistreatment and torture of animals that regularly occurred in England. Puritans struggled to control and even abolish animal baitings, cockfighting, and violent human competitions such as pugilism. However, Puritan leaders permitted practical activities that promoted fitness and health, such as hunting and fishing, which of course also provided food for the table. Whereas the English nobility had generally restricted the taking of game by the middle and lower classes, New England's massive forests contained a bounteous array of game birds and wild animals. However, the successful hunting of big game – bear, deer, moose – proved a difficult task due to the lack of accurate firearms, so New Englanders tended to focus their attention on the many ponds, lakes, and streams that teemed with fish. Fishing enjoyed widespread popularity as a sanctioned recreational activity; it was, in fact, one of a small number of recreations that Harvard College officially sanctioned for students. Given the enormous attention devoted to fishing in the writings of colonial New Englanders, it is safe to conclude that nearly all males at one time or another cast a line into the streams and bays of the region. And of course many adults made their living as commercial fishermen in the waters of the North Atlantic. Fishing was, as Daniels concludes, the "ideal pastime for men and boys" because of its utility and lack of association with untoward social behaviors.[25]

Horseraces – complete with wagering – were held with surprising regularity in eighteenth-century colonial New England. In fact, horse racing was the *only* organized sport in colonial New England. Initially, the most popular form was the quick quarter-mile dash down a country road by horses specially bred for this particular type of race. As early as the 1720s, however, organized races were regularly held in Newport, Rhode Island, and in the nearby Narragansett countryside in which a cluster of countrified gentry had taken up residence. In these two places, racing meets of several days duration were held and through extensive advertising attracted large crowds from considerable distances. On a given day, up to a dozen races were held, with professional jockeys riding their mounts garbed in the identifying colors of their owners; the primary attraction of the races, of course, was the opportunity to make wagers on the outcome. On a somewhat less-structured scale, racing also occurred outside Boston as early as the 1730s. Because the crowds were well behaved, authorities never moved to halt the meets. Within this decorous and relaxing context, gambling was not viewed as a social problem.

The children of New England were of course encouraged to play games as part of their educational and physical development. Historical evidence indicates they played stick and ball games, swam in the summers, and ice skated when the ponds froze over. Upon occasion, boys played a rough-and-tumble game of football, although local records indicate that authorities repeatedly sought to ban the game because of injuries. At an early age, boys were taught to hunt and fish while girls were encouraged to play with dolls and "play house" in anticipation of early marriage and the responsibilities of motherhood; widespread conceptions about the delicate nature of females led to a concerted effort to repress "tomboy" behavior and to severely restrict excessive physical exertion by even young girls.

To the south of New England, the relatively diverse and cosmopolitan population of the New York City region dictated a less-constrictive view of games and recreation. Originally settled by the Dutch, the city of New York provided an environment in which residents found time to relax and play games suggestive of modern-day croquet, cricket, tennis, lawn bowling, and badminton. Even a game that resembled golf was apparently played by some residents. Following the takeover of Manhattan in 1664 by the English, the Church of England was declared the official religion; soon thereafter, horse racing became part of the local recreational scene. Much to the anguish of Puritans, however, animal baitings and cockfights were also instituted – often at fairs and other community-wide social events – and they enjoyed widespread popularity in part because they were conducive to the making of bets.

The Quaker domination of Philadelphia and its environs resulted in the banning of most forms of leisure activity, including dancing, card playing, animal baiting, and maypole celebrations. Young people were encouraged to learn to hunt and fish as part of the continued struggle for subsistence in the rugged colonial environment, and such activities as running and swimming were seen as helpful to the physical development of young girls and boys. Like the Puritans, the Quakers viewed the playing of games within the larger context of whether the activity promoted general community welfare, economic growth, military skills, physical fitness, and spiritual growth.

Thus playing games and engaging in recreational activities in the colonies north of the Chesapeake Bay region generally had to be rationalized within the context of the larger issues of protecting the Sabbath, preventing cruelty to animals, responding to one's secular calling, providing food for the table, or maintaining health and fitness. Gambling in the regions controlled by the Puritans and Quakers was generally minimal and not a matter for serious concern; in fact, churches, schools, colleges, and other public agencies themselves encouraged a widely accepted form of gambling to finance major projects. Public lotteries were frequently offered by authorities to raise monies to build a new church, school building, or other public facility, a practice that local governments would abandon

Figure1.1 Choctaws play a game called baggataway as depicted by an unknown artist. The webbed sticks reminded French explorers of the bishop's crozier and they called the game "la crosse." © Bettmann/CORBIS

early in the nineteenth century after a wave of scandals discredited the honesty of such lotteries. In the latter half of the twentieth century, political leaders in 37 states would resurrect the lottery as a means of raising revenue for such purposes as funding public education as a subterfuge to avoid raising taxes.

In both New England and the Middle Colonies, the white colonists interacted regularly with Native Americans. This interaction, however, does not seem to have greatly influenced the development of games and recreations engaged in by the colonists, although some of the games played by Indians were similar to those enjoyed by the colonists, and included ample symbolism related to fertility, healing, and warfare. Often the games played by Native Americans included preparation by elaborate rituals, dances, and sacred chants intended to ward off evil spirits and to help ensure victory in the upcoming contest. The most common of the games played by the natives was a game involving the use of a small ball and sticks equipped with small leather nets. The Cherokee called their version of the game "the little brother of war" because it involved hundreds of players engaged in advancing the ball over several miles over rugged terrain. Some games could last for days. Because of the vast numbers it was difficult for many players even to get close to the ball, so they contented themselves with attempts to injure their opponents with their sticks. In what is now upper New York and Ontario, early French explorers witnessed a similar game being played by the Iriquois, although typical sides numbered about 20 with two goals set up about 120 feet apart. The French thought that the sticks resembled a bishop's crozier, spelled *la crosse* in French, so the name of the game that remains yet today an important sport in the eastern United States carries the name given to it by the French.

Games of the Southern Elite

In 1686, an aristocratic Frenchman visited Virginia and recorded his observations of everyday life in his diary. Durand of Dauphine noted that in Jamestown many members of the House of Burgesses began to play high stakes card games immediately after dinner. About midnight, one of the players noticed the visitor from France intently watching the action and suggested that he might want to retire for the evening: "For it is quite possible that we shall be here all night."[26] Sure enough, the next morning, Durand found the same card game still in session. As historian T. H. Breen has explained, what Durand observed was certainly not an aberration but rather a routine aspect of life among the Virginia elite. In sharp contrast to social norms in the North, the planter class that controlled life in colonial Virginia and Maryland was strongly committed to high-stakes gambling as a primary form of entertainment; gentlemen regularly and heavily bet on cards, backgammon, dice, and horses.[27]

The tobacco planters in Maryland and Virginia found special meaning in their gambling obsession, which seemed to fit well into the culture in which they lived and worked. Gambling enabled them to translate into their lives the values by which they operated their plantations, where risk-taking, competitiveness, individuality, and materialism were paramount. During the seventeenth century, the first generations of planters utilized white indentured servants to help solve their need for unskilled labor in the tobacco fields, but that system proved unreliable. In order to assure an adequate and continual supply of field hands, they readily adopted the alternative of human slavery. The widespread use of black slaves – the first group of 19 being brought to Virginia in 1619 – changed the social order of the South forever, creating a complex social mosaic that commingled the emotionally charged issues of class and race.[28]

As a result of the increasing number of slaves imported from the Caribbean and Africa, white males assumed a social status that was determined by whether or not they owned slaves, and if so, how many. Whites who did not own slaves and were forced to work in the fields themselves were considered commoners with whom true Southern gentlemen – slave owners all – did not associate on a social basis. A gentleman of a high social level supervised the operation of his plantation and his slave labor force, but physical labor was considered beneath his dignity and social status. Thus this new Virginia upper class naturally gravitated toward a life that demanded expression of their social ranking – in their proclivity for large and richly appointed houses, their stylish clothes, their lavish entertainment style, and their expensive if sometimes impractical material possessions. Because both men and women of the elite were considered to be above the performance of manual labor, they were inevitably forced into a situation where they were expected to work very hard at serious leisure activities. For women this meant a constant social whirl of teas, receptions, and visits, while their men's lives were punctuated with high-stakes gambling, a widely accepted avocation that in and of itself connoted wealth and stature within Virginia society.[29]

These men were fiercely driven. Caught up in the immense uncertainties of the tobacco trade that was characterized by widely fluctuating markets, the planters often found themselves helpless pawns in an intensely competitive and turbulent economic environment. Simply put, in the tobacco-growing regions of Maryland and eastern Virginia, one could only improve one's social standing by increasing one's wealth. Truth be known, the planters' high status was often at risk, and their lives and financial well-being were often imperiled by forces beyond their control. Too much or too little rain often wreaked havoc with harvests; ships carrying their precious annual crops to European markets disappeared in bad seas; a succession of good harvests drove down the price of the commodity, but poor harvests also carried serious economic consequences; white indentured servants and black slaves remained an uncertain, unreliable, and often troublesome source of labor, prone to work slowdowns, their numbers often decimated by devastating epidemics and a short life expectancy. A prominent Virginia planter, William Fitzhugh, warned an English correspondent whose son was contemplating migrating to Virginia to take up the life of a tobacco planter, that even "if the best husbandry and the greatest forecast and skill were used, yet ill luck at sea, a fall of a Market, or twenty other accidents may ruin and overthrow the best industry."[30]

In such a precarious environment, gambling became a natural expression for men caught up in the system. For some of the more desperate, perhaps, it held out the hope of improving their financial status, but for most it was an essential form of social interaction that was consistent with the type of lives they pursued. Their willingness to risk large sums on horseraces, cockfights, or table games provided tangible evidence that they had sufficient affluence to withstand heavy gambling losses, as befitting people of their social status. While card and dice games provided popular indoor recreation – and many a fortune often hung on the turn of a card – it was horse racing that held the greatest fascination for the Southern gentry. In this rural environment, horses were held in very high esteem because they provided the essential means of transportation. Ownership of an elegant, high-spirited horse was not unlike ownership of an expensive, sporty automobile in twentieth-century America – it set a gentleman apart from the middling and lower classes. As a tangible extension of the planter's ego, a powerful and handsome horse was a source of pride and a symbol of lofty status. Virginians bred muscular horses with strong hindquarters that enabled them to run at high speeds for a relatively short distance. Popularly called the quarter horse, they were trained to run full-out in races measured to a quarter mile in length.[31]

While some races, such as those held in conjunction with fairs or the convening of the local courts, were scheduled weeks or months in advance, many were impromptu affairs that resulted from the offering and acceptance of a challenge between gentlemen. Stakes in these races were often high: sometimes an entire year's tobacco crop might ride on a single mad dash by two horses down a quarter mile of dirt road. Friends and invited guests eagerly flocked to these exciting events and made their own bets with others in attendance. While many commoners, as well as slaves, might attend, they were normally excluded from entering their own horses. For one thing, the high stakes involved usually precluded their participation. But more important, horse racing was a sport largely reserved from the country's gentry, and it simply was not acceptable for a gentleman to lower himself to compete with a commoner, let alone be the loser in such a competition.

In these intense, often violent, races, the gentleman rode his own horse, thereby intensifying the competitive factors at play while also producing psychological issues regarding the manhood and self-esteem of the participants. Devious tactics – attempts to bump a rival horse off his stride – were commonplace, or at least frequently alleged. The races were exciting events, with the two horses often crossing the finish line neck-to-neck, thereby producing many a dispute as to the winning horse. Because of such disputes and charges of illegal riding, the outcome of a race could be the beginning of a rapidly escalating argument. The accepted method of resolution, however, fortunately dictated that the dispute be settled without recourse to dueling pistols. Rather, the courts of Virginia developed a substantial body of case law regulating the payment of horse-race stakes and side bets. Custom required that wagers be made in writing, and colonial courts considered these documents legally binding. Often these agreements included promises by both parties to "fair Rideing", that is, the participants affirmed in writing that they would not attempt to bump the rival horse, unseat his mount, trip or cut off a rival's horse, or otherwise employ dangerous or devious tactics. As Breen observes, these high-stakes races provided an apt metaphor for the highly speculative business in which the tobacco planters found themselves.[32]

By the beginning of the eighteenth century, the racing culture had matured sufficiently that a few primitive oval race tracks began to appear on the Virginia countryside, and some of the most affluent sportsmen began to import thoroughbred horses of Arabian origin, which had become popular in England. During the nineteenth century, these elegant horses, which could run distances of several miles, slowly but surely replaced the quarter horse as the race horse of choice for Virginia's elite. These steeds were handled by skilled trainers, ridden by professional jockeys (not uncommonly slaves) wearing the bright-colored apparel signifying the owner, and raced at week-long events scheduled long in advance at the bustling colonial town of Williamsburg. Historian Elliott Gorn aptly summarizes the value system of the Southern gentry who "set the tone" for this "fiercely competitive style of living." In a constantly fluid social and economic system, he contends,

individual status was never permanently fixed, so men frantically sought to assert their prowess – by grand boasts over tavern gaming tables laden with money, by whipping and tripping each other's horses in violent quarter-races, by wagering one-half year's earnings on the flash of a fighting cock's gaff. Great planters and small shared an ethos that extolled courage bordering on foolhardiness and cherished magnificent, if irrational, displays of largess.[33]

Sporting Life of the Colonial Working Class

While the Tidewater gentry went about their gentlemanly pastimes of riding to the hounds, gambling, and horse racing, the lesser members of Southern society participated in a culture of fun and games that revolved around tavern life. These small establishments, located every few miles along country roads and in every crossroads town, offered shelter for travelers, hearty food, and plenty of drink. Here locals mingled with travelers for spirited conversation and played a wide range of card and dice games, pitched quoits, and displayed their talents at lawn bowling. The games were inevitably made more spirited by omnipresent wagering. As in England, blood sports were quite popular, and enterprising innkeepers promoted these events as a means of attracting business; most popular were cockfights and animal baitings, as well as an occasional bare-knuckle prizefight. The most popular sport by far was the cockfight, and these events often attracted an audience that saw men of all social stations lining the pit elbow-to-elbow, cheering, drinking, and gambling. During the eighteenth century, "gander pulling" enjoyed a surge in popularity; this particularly cruel contest, often held in conjunction with the Easter celebration, involved horsemen riding at a rapid pace past a greased goose helplessly dangling by a leg from a tree limb, and attempting to pull off the poor critter's head as they flew by. The prize offered by the sponsoring innkeeper to the successful rider was the carcass of the decapitated goose, to be taken home for roasting.[34]

Taverns were not merely a center of community life in the South. In fact, they exerted important social influence throughout all of the colonies. Because they encouraged the consumption of alcohol and provided various games that tended to lure workers away from their tasks, they were a frequent target for those elements of society that emphasized the importance of "industry" and "frugality" among the working classes. The ills that critics identified were inevitably gambling, drunkenness, and idleness. Some Northern colonial assemblies occasionally sought to attack the problem in a variety of ways – inevitably futile, as it turned out – by setting fines for innkeepers who permitted gambling, passing laws that would revoke the licenses of repeat offenders, even making it difficult in a court of law for individuals to recover money lost or loaned for gambling on events conducted in taverns. In 1760, for example, the Massachusetts General Court passed a resolution that stipulated, "Games and Exercises although lawful, should not be otherwise used than as innocent and moderate Recreations," and proceeded to outlaw gambling that occurred in taverns. Whatever the law, gambling on tavern-based games remained an integral part of the life of the American people of all social stations; the one variable seemed to be that the larger one's income, the greater amounts one was willing to wager.[35]

Figure 1.2 Men representative of different social classes watch roosters equipped with sharp gaffs fight to the death in New Orleans, circa 1820. Cockfighting was very popular in the South and West as a gambling venue. © CORBIS.

Along the colonial Virginia frontier and extending into the trans-Appalachian area of Kentucky and Tennessee during the early national period, the coarseness of daily life was reflected in the preference of games and contests. Shooting contests that determined local marksman champions were highly popular, reflecting the importance of hunting in securing meat for the dinner table. Local fairs and other social events often featured running and jumping contests. Of course cockfighting and dog-baiting contests were favorites, as was quarter horse racing. The southern back country, however, was uniquely known for its emphasis on a particularly violent form of human combat that was part wrestling, part fisticuffs, part pure mayhem, with a couple of particularly gruesome elements thrown in for good measure – eye gouging and attempts at severing various body parts. These gruesome hand-battles, called "rough-and-tumble," were occasionally held at community celebrations, but more often they occurred as a means of concluding an argument or obtaining satisfaction for a perceived personal insult. Spectators placed wagers on the combatants, and the contest was conducted with a pronounced absence of rules – any tactic to gain an advantage was acceptable – including hitting, biting, kicking downed opponents, kneeing in the groin, and scratching with sharply filed fingernails. In the rugged male-dominated environment of the frontier, personal "respect" was of great importance. For young men, historian Elliott Gorn concludes, "rough-and-tumble fighting demonstrated unflinching willingness to inflict pain, while risking mutilation – all to defend one's standing among peers."[36]

In the years after the American Revolution, this no-holds-barred form of fighting came to emphasize the gouging out of an opponent's eye as the ultimate objective of "rough and tumble," a rough equivalent of a knockout in modern boxing. Among those most likely to participate were uncultured young males who lived on the fringes of civilization along the trans-Appalachian frontier – hunters, trappers, stevedores, drifters, unskilled laborers, hardscrabble farmers. Rough-and-tumble fighting grew in popularity during the late eighteenth century and initially was prominent in the sparsely settled regions of western Virginia and the Carolinas, later moving into Kentucky and Tennessee. The emphasis of these fights was, Elliott Gorn writes, "on maximum disfigurement, on severing body parts." The primary objective was to extract an opponent's eyeball by the use of sharply filed and heavily waxed fingernails. Teeth were sometimes filed to severe points as another means of attack, although some local champions specialized in other tactics. One traveler noted, "these wretches in their combat endeavor to their utmost to tear out the other's testicles."[37] Travelers through the region well after the Civil War reported their shock at seeing a large number of aging men with missing eyes, or rough facial scars from fights held in the distant past. Rough-and-tumble – a natural phenomenon in a region where life was frequently harsh and brief – was a widespread practice that died out only slowly in the latter decades of the nineteenth century as a more genteel civilization slowly encroached upon the backwoods towns of the mountain country of the Southeast.

The Revolutionary Era

The patterns of informal sporting events and leisure activities that existed in colonial America continued essentially unchanged well into the mid-nineteenth century. These traditions, however, began to give way to a much more organized and formalized structure of sport as an expanding urban and industrial society began a fundamental restructuring of all facets of American life. This more formalized approach to sports and recreation began during the time of the American Revolution and the early national period. The emotional fervor associated with the Revolution tended to dampen interest in games and recreations because it was widely believed that the future of the new country depended upon a hard-working, serious-minded people who were not easily distracted by idle amusements. In fact, on the eve of the American Revolution the Continental Congress took official notice of this sentiment, urging the various colonies by resolution to "encourage frugality, economy, and discourage every species of extravagance and dissipation, especially all horse-racing, and all kinds of gaming, cock fighting, exhibition of shows, plays, and other expensive diversions and amusements."[38] In 1785, Thomas Jefferson, in a letter written from Paris, contrasted the importance of Americans dedicating themselves to their revolutionary cause to the dissipations of England, where young American male visitors would be seduced by the "peculiarities of English education," of which "drinking, horse racing, and boxing" were prominent, along with an attraction to "a spirit for female intrigue" that included "a passion for whores."[39]

Throughout the United States, the informal and localized nature of games and recreation continued well into the middle of the nineteenth century. However, powerful new forces – technological, economic, and social – produced a series of fundamental changes within American society, especially in the North. Following the War of 1812, the American economy entered a period of rapid expansion, fueled in part by the transportation revolution that saw the introduction of steam-powered shipping on internal waterways and the construction of a large network of canals and toll roads. The introduction of railroads during the 1830s set off a period of frenetic construction of new lines that saw more than 30,000 miles of track in use by the onset of the Civil War. What historians have often called the "transportation revolution" greatly encouraged the growth of manufacturing and other economic innovation. It also greatly reduced the time it took to travel to distant cities.

Following the War of 1812, the United States was poised on the cusp of a new era that would soon produce major new departures in mining and manufacturing, mass merchandising, heavy immigration, sustained urban growth, heavy expansion of international trade, and the establishment of companies that served regional and even national markets. It was within this context that sports – which for more than two centuries had been a largely localized and unorganized phenomenon – took on the appearance of the highly complex and organized structure that would be easily recognizable to the American sports fan of the early twenty-first century.

2 The Emergence of Organized Sports 1815–60

The surprising victory in January 1815 at the Battle of New Orleans, sparked by volunteers from Tennessee who rallied to the leadership of General Andrew Jackson, set off an extended period of patriotic celebration. This victory over a seasoned British military force provided a glorious transition into an extended period of national expansion and economic growth that would transform every aspect of American life.

By the eve of the Civil War, the foundation for the world's leading industrial economy had been established. New transportation systems provided the essential means of moving raw materials, finished products, and people. Steamships now traversed major rivers and the Great Lakes, and an expanding network of railroads – that reached 30,000 miles by 1860 – extended westward out of the major East Coast port cities, setting off heavy migration into the Midwest, and beyond. Contributing to this frenetic period of economic growth were major advances in machine technology that made mass production possible. The construction of a national telegraph system by 1860 provided a new means of rapid communication and proved to be an essential factor in the rise of modern American commerce.

All across the northern tier of states, from Massachusetts to Missouri, the forces of modernism were at work. Coal mines in Pennsylvania and West Virginia produced fuel to power trains, steamships, shops, and mills. On the eve of the Civil War, in northwestern Pennsylvania, the discovery of a new and promising source of energy – petroleum – held out even greater prospects for the future of economic growth. The lure of the cities, where economic and social opportunities beckoned, was strong. By 1860, 20 percent of the American people lived in cities, and the census of that year indicated that New York City contained a population of over one million. Although 53 percent of the American people still derived their income from agriculture, that figure revealed a startling 25 percent decline since Andrew

Jackson's presidency. Much of the South, however, lingered far behind, hamstrung by the anachronistic system of slavery that slowed innovation, the development of manufacturing, and the building of vibrant cities.

The new economy imposed a new order and rhythm upon the ebb and flow of daily life. Trains now ran on established schedules, and the shrill tone of a whistle at 6 a.m. summoned miners and factory workers from their homes. The time clock imposed a new sense of orderliness and efficiency on the workplace that contrasted sharply with work in rural areas, where sunlight and darkness and the passing of the seasons imposed a more natural sense of time and space. Thus did the United States enter the modern era, characterized by standardization, organization, hierarchical decision making, mass production, efficiency, and electronic communications. Life not only changed in the cities but also across the nation's farmlands. Subsistence agriculture gave way to commercialization as new and more efficient plows and reapers changed the way farmers went about their work. Wheat farmers in Kansas and Nebraska, beef and pork producers in Ohio and Illinois, and cotton and tobacco producers in the South now found themselves heavily dependant on the functioning of distant commodity markets and financial institutions. Just as the forces of industrialization and urbanization would in one way or another change the basic structure of American society – its organization, customs, and values – so too would they fundamentally change the way Americans played and watched sporting events. As a result of the economic changes occurring in the United States, the playing of games underwent a substantial transformation from what was largely an informal, unorganized, and localized leisure experience into a structured and formalized set of activities that became, in lock step with the larger economic and social order, standardized along national lines.

Sports in the Early National Period

Change came slowly but surely to the sporting world. It was not until the 1850s that a new era seemed to have arrived. Throughout the first half of the nineteenth century, informal quarter horse racing, animal-baiting, cockfighting, and bare-knuckle prize-fighting remained an integral part of the American sporting scene. Indications of changes in American leisure activities were increasingly in evidence by the 1830s, especially in Northern cities. Individuals interested in competitive games and contests were more often insisting on the use of agreed-upon standards and rules of play. These were frequently the product of committees working within the structure of sports clubs and other organizations designed to bring order and conformity to the rules governing a sports.

It was inevitable that the first major reforms leading toward standardization of rules and policies would apply to the most popular of sports – horse racing. Throughout the South and into the frontier West, informal quarter horse racing remained popular, but in and around New York City men interested in the turf introduced reforms that pushed the sport toward a modern identity. In 1802, the New York legislature – in a moralistic anti-gambling mood – passed legislation outlawing horse racing. Many racing meets were nonetheless conducted in the New York City area, especially across the Hudson River in New Jersey. In 1821, the state legislature reversed itself by a narrow majority and voted to permit horse racing once again. Legalization led to heightened interest in the turf, and horsemen joined together in formal organizations to push an agenda designed to bring consistency to the sport. Among the major innovations in the New York City area was the construction of oval tracks with wooden grandstands that permitted patrons to watch the entire race from an elevated seat.

Improved sources of information and means of communications were significant precursors of reforms to come. In 1829, the monthly *American Turf Register and Sporting Magazine* first appeared and soon was marketed along the entire East Coast. In 1831, there appeared a more important weekly magazine devoted to sporting life, especially horse racing. *The Spirit of the Times*, published by avid New York horseman William T. Porter, soon eclipsed the competition. Although he reported on many activities, Porter aimed his publication primarily at horserace bettors; he established and published odds, encouraged equitable betting policies, advocated the adoption of standardized rules regarding the conduct of races, promoted prominent racing meets, and, most important for bettors, reported in detail the times of individual horses and the level of opposition they had encountered in previous races. The growing popularity of the turf was revealed in the rapid increase in annual racing meets, which normally lasted for three days: 56 such events were reported in 1830, but 130 a decade later.[1]

Concurrently there emerged a movement to further advance standardization of the sport through the creation of jockey clubs. The premier antebellum organization was the New York Jockey Club, and its hefty $10 annual membership fee meant that only men of substantial social consequence applied for membership. In sponsoring its spring and autumn meetings at Long Island Union Course, the club went to great lengths to establish rules that would assure fair competition and prevent the sport from being subverted by "sharps."[2] The club's announcement of its fall 1842 meeting, for example, included a detailed list of 64 rules, including the appointment of four stewards who "shall wear an appropriate badge of distinction" and were responsible "to preserve order, clear the track, keep it clear, keep off the crowd of persons from the horses coming to the stand," and three judges who would approve the dress of jockeys and oversee the start and finish of each race. Even the uniform worn by jockeys was covered: Rule 35 stated that "No rider shall be permitted to ride unless well dressed in Jockey style. To wit, Jockey cap, colored jacket, pantaloons, and boots."[3]

This movement toward order and efficiency was championed by William T. Porter in his *Spirit of the Times*. He wrote at one point that it was the responsibility of "gentlemen of standing, wealth, and intelligence" to provide leadership of this sport so that it would not be overtaken by "lower-class ruffians and ne'er-do-wells."[4] One person who heeded Porter's clarion call to "the very Corinthian columns of the community" was the scion of a wealthy Hoboken, New Jersey, family, John Cox Stevens. In 1823, he and his brother Robert Livingston Stevens helped produce one of the first great sporting spectacles in American history, a match race between a powerful 9-year-old thoroughbred, Eclipse, which had for several years domi-nated the New York City racing circuit, and the leading southern thoroughbred, Sir Henry, a premier horse out of the stable operated by James J. Harrison of Peters-burg, Virginia. Each horse was backed by $20,000 raised by their sponsors. The nation's attention became riveted upon the upcoming challenge race. The loom-ing conflict between the slave and free states provided an emotional backdrop to this contest, coming as it did on the eve of a presidential election that produced four sectional candidates and just three years after Congress managed to avoid a showdown over the contentious issue of the westward expansion of slavery with the Missouri Compromise of 1820. The two horses ran three four-mile heats before a cheering crowd estimated by journalists present to exceed 50,000 at the Long Island Union Course, with Eclipse winning the third and deciding heat and taking home for his owner the prize. Substantial sums of money changed hands between bettors that exciting day – the *Niles Register* estimated $1 million – although that huge sum as well as the size of the crowd was most likely overstated.[5]

The strong sectional overtones that hovered over the race were palpable. Some saw the result of the race as a harbinger of the election of the northern presiden-tial candidate, John Quincy Adams, although one popular magazine cautioned northerners to celebrate in a restrained manner because "the safety of our union depends upon our moderation."[6] Northerners, however, were far from restrained as they reveled in a high-profile contest that witnessed proud southerners absorb-ing a crushing loss in what was their most prominent sport. Josiah Quincy, a spectator from Boston on that day, commented several decades later in his jour-nal about the symbolism of the race's outcome: "It seems to have foreshadowed the sterner conflict that occurred forty years afterwards. The victory resulted in both cases from the same cause – the power of endurance."[7] Following this thrill-ing event, Stevens threw himself into the affairs of the turf, providing substantial funding for the operation of the powerful New York Jockey Club. He maintained his own stable of thoroughbred horses and served as president or vice president of the club for more than two decades.

As tensions between the slave states and the North intensified, promoters took advantage of sectional feelings and promoted several more races with strong North–South overtones. One of the more memorable was the May 27, 1842, match between a Virginia horse owned by Colonel William R. Johnson, curiously named Boston, and the pride of the New York area, the inestimable filly Fashion. The first four-mile heat was close; Fashion won by less than a length and in the process set a world's record of 7:32.5 minutes. The second heat was close until the 9-year-old Boston showed his age and faded during the last mile, losing by some 60 lengths to the powerful filly. The Northerners' joy in their horse's victory, however, was muted by post-race criticism led by William T. Porter in his *Spirit of the Times*. He directed his ire at the Union Course promoters, who charged what Porter (and many others) viewed as an exorbitant $10 admission charge.[8]

In 1845, another North–South challenge occurred at the Union Course before a large and enthusiastic crowd "of race-going blades" who created a scene of "tumult, disorder, and confusion" according to one newspaper account. In addition, the *New York Herald* reported that the audience included a motley collection of "indescribable camp followers, sutlers, loungers, rowdies, gamblers, and twenty other species." Before a crowd estimated to number 30,000 (probably once more in substantial exaggeration, since the grandstands only seated 3,000), the Southern filly Peytonia narrowly defeated Fashion in two heats. Again, strong sectional sentiments provided a dramatic backdrop to the race, as reported by the *New York Herald*: "In addition to the sectional feeling and the strong rivalry of sportsmen, and in no sense partisans – the vast sums of money pending on the race, attached a degree of absorbing interest in the result."[9]

The Democratization of Racing: the Trotters

Although the general public took great interest in the occasional high-profile thoroughbred race, the sport was largely dominated by the wealthy – slave holders in Virginia and mercantile leaders of New York City. The less affluent found other outlets in which to engage their passion for speed and racing. Although it has received relatively little attention, thousands of Americans during the antebellum period participated in the new sport of harness racing. The sport of racing trotting horses began early in the nineteenth century in the Northeast, especially in the urban corridor between Baltimore and Boston. Informal races of horse-drawn buggies over distances between one and five miles became popular in northern cities, especially New York City. According to trotting historian Dwight Akers, the five-mile stretch of Third Avenue that ran northward from the Bowery was "consecrated ground" for the "roadites."[10]

The owners drove their own horses, and there soon developed a large, informal fraternity that raced their "roadsters" in the evening hours after work. The horses, which the men used for their daily business travel in the city, came from the common stock and lacked the bloodlines of the thoroughbreds. Central to the popularity of harness racing was that it permitted wide participation; anyone with a horse and buggy could try his hand, and unlike thoroughbred racing where professional jockeys were utilized, the owner and the driver were one and the same. Along Third Avenue, competition naturally grew, especially among the younger "blades" who enjoyed a spirited race. One lady observer, however, noted that many of these young men "spent their afternoons trotting from tavern to tavern along the highways." Apparently, she sniffed, "they live for alcohol and horses!"[11] Harness racing was open to all comers and most definitely was not an elitist sport. Oliver Wendell Holmes noted that the trotting horse served a useful purpose as an everyday source of transportation, while the thoroughbred did not: "Horse racing is not a republican institution; horse-trotting is."[12]

By 1850, harness racing had easily surpassed thoroughbred racing in popularity and had become the most popular of all spectator sports in America; not until baseball swept the nation after the Civil War would trotters lose their position as "number one." By 1815, a formal racing oval for trotters had been built in the rural area of Harlem on the north side of Manhattan. In 1824, the New York Trotting

Figure 2.1 Trotters Mountain Boy and Lady Thorn duel at Prospect Park in Brooklyn in 1869. During the mid-nineteenth century trotting races captured the imagination of working- and middle-class Americans as an alternative to thoroughbred racing, which was viewed as elitist. © Bettmann/CORBIS.

Club was established and an oval track was constructed on Long Island. Over the next quarter century, the sport continued to grow in popularity, but its middle-class roots precluded the magnitude of newspaper coverage reserved for thoroughbreds. Because the trotting horse came from common stock, rapid commercialization was feasible. Promoters recognized that the investment in such a horse was minimal when compared to the thoroughbred, a fact that enabled them to offer much smaller purses (often less than $50, sometimes as little as $10) and still attract a competitive field. The sturdy composition of the trotting horse also meant that they could be entered in races many more times a year than a thoroughbred. Since the trotters were culled from the common stock there were ample numbers of such animals available.[13]

Harness racing enjoyed widespread public interest. Its middle-class roots appealed to spectators who were put off by the snobbery and exclusiveness that surrounded thoroughbred racing. In 1856, with thoroughbred racing in a prolonged slump, a journalist observed that it "will never succeed in New York until it and its attended arrangements are put on a more democratic basis – something approaching the order of the first class trotting races. Then like the trots, it will get the support of the people." Oliver Wendell Holmes was struck by the bond between harness racing and everyday American workers:

> Wherever the trotting horse goes, he carries in his train brisk omnibuses, lively bakers' carts, and therefore hot rolls, the jolly butcher's wagon, the cheerful gig, the wholesome afternoon drive with wife and child – all the forms of moral excellence.[14]

The popularity of trotters spread rapidly across the United States. Seven tracks operated with regularity in the New York City area by the mid-1850s, and an additional 70 tracks had opened elsewhere. The operators of county fairs found harness racing an appealing attraction, and the affinity of the sport with state and county fairs remains an American tradition in the twenty-first century. The unlikely exploits of a four-year old grey mare, purchased by an Irish peddler in 1837 for $112.50, spurred the sport's popularity. For a time Lady Suffolk pulled David Bryan's butcher cart through the streets of New York City, but in 1838 Bryan entered her in a harness race on Long Island. She won her first race in a flat three minutes along with a purse of $11. Over the next 14 years, Lady Suffolk was entered in 162 races and won an estimated $50,000 for her owner, despite the fact that he was acknowledged to be an inept reinsman. She was eventually retired at the age of 19, but even then demonstrated her amazing strength by participating in 12 races during her final year on the track.[15] By the eve of the Civil War, in little more than a half century, harness racing had moved from an informal means of entertainment on the streets of New York to a successful commercial enterprise that was national in scope. As such, harness racing set the pace, so to speak, for many other commercial sporting ventures soon to come.

Racing by Land and Sea

Horse racing was not the only form of racing to capture the public's fancy. For several decades prior to the Civil War, long-distance human foot races captured widespread interest. Popularly called "pedestrianism," these races appealed to the proclivity for gambling among the American people. Between 1820 and 1835, several such races held in the New York City area received minor notice in the newspapers, but in 1835 the area's leading sportsman, John Cox Stevens (who had already made his mark as a leading figure in horse racing circles), attracted widespread attention when he announced a prize of $1,000 to any person who could run ten miles in less than one hour. On race day, nine men between the ages of 18 and 33 toed the starting line and took off to the cheers of a large crowd, many of whom had bets riding on the contestants. A 24-year-old farmer from Killingworth, Connecticut, Henry Stannard, was the only runner to cross the finish line under the one-hour mark, and he did so with only 12 seconds to spare.[16]

The novelty of that race inspired many others in the years to come, with promoters of the Beacon Course horserace track even holding foot race competitions as a means of recovering some of their financial losses from the lack of public support for their thoroughbred meets. One of the underlying themes of these races was the competition between Americans and runners from Ireland and England. An estimated 30,000 spectators turned out in 1844 at the Beacon Course to watch a field of 12 Americans (including a Seneca Indian named John Steeprock) fend off the challenges of three Englishmen and three Irishmen. America's pride was severely threatened as the runners approached the final mile with two Englishmen in the lead, but a New York carpenter, John Gildersleeve, took the lead during the final lap amid great cheers from the American spectators. One newsman, probing the reasons for the great interest in the race beyond its sheer novelty, found his answer in conversations with members of the audience: "It was a trial of the Indian against the white man, on the point in which the red man most boasts his superiority. It was the trial of the peculiar American physique against the long held supremacy of the English muscular endurance." As historian Melvin Adelman concludes, this particular race contained the dual attractions of racism and nationalism: "The excitement derived from the fact that the white man beat the red man and the American defeated the Englishmen."[17] Future promoters of sporting events would find racial, ethnic, and nationalistic rivalries to be a reliable gimmick to attract paying customers.

The interest in pedestrianism prompted many promoters to stage races, most of which were long distance affairs with men competing both against each other and against the clock for prize money. A few professional runners emerged who often put up their own challenge money before match races, and while Gildersleeve ended up accepting invitations to run in many parts of the country, most runners were content to compete in their own locale. The sport did not last, losing out to other more popular sports such as harness racing and baseball that increasingly captured the attention of the public. It ultimately fell victim to the rise of track and field as an amateur sport during the 1870s.[18]

Racing fans also showed considerable interest in various forms of rowing contests. As with other sports, informal contests had been held between locals in various American ports during the colonial and early national period; races between longshoremen and local boat owners, sparked by a wager or two, determined local bragging rights. But as early as 1824, a rowing contest with a $1,000 prize was held on the Hudson River between a group of young Americans organized into a rowing club called the Whitehallers and a crew from a British frigate. Newspapers reported that an assembly of upwards of 20,000 watched the four-mile race from the shoreline. An American victory produced a flurry of national pride and encouraged the conduct of races elsewhere.[19]

By the mid-1830s, more than 20 rowing clubs were active in the New York City area, and similar clubs were established in cities stretching from Boston to Savannah. Interest was particularly high in Philadelphia, where the normally placid Schuylkill River beckoned generations of dedicated oarsmen. Highly competitive meets were characterized by extensive wagering. The sport continued to flourish after the Civil War, primarily on an amateur basis, although contests among professionals for prize money occurred well into the twentieth century. However, the sport largely rested upon its strong embrace of the code of amateurism, in which men participated for the love of the sport and as a means of physical conditioning. In 1872, the National Association of Amateur Oarsmen was established with some 200 clubs existing around the country, and evidence of the sport's continuing popularity.[20]

Rowing appealed to a wide spectrum of men representative of the working and professional classes, but only the very wealthy could afford to participate in yachting. One of the first yacht races on record involved the omnipresent sportsman from Hoboken, John Cox Stevens, whose yacht *Wave* sped to victory over John Cushing's *Sylph* in a highly publicized race across the waters of New York Harbor in 1835. In 1844, Cox played a key role in establishing the New York Yacht Club for the express purpose of promoting "health and pleasure, combined with a laudable desire to improve our almost perfect naval architecture." Just as various jockey clubs asserted their goal in holding racing meets was to "improve the breed," so too did the yachtsmen seek to produce better ships. In 1846, the New York Yacht Club held its first regatta, producing great interest throughout the city.[21]

The New York Yacht Club soon became recognized for a membership representing the *crème de la crème* of New York society as one observer put it. Stevens constructed a large clubhouse in Hoboken at the Elysian Fields park and playing-field complex where club members and their spouses and friends enjoyed exclusive social events. The clubhouse was described by an former mayor of New York City, Philip Hone, as "a handsome Gothic cottage in a pleasant grove in the Elysian fields, presided over by that prince of good fellows, John Cox Stevens, who makes the punch, superintends the cooking and presides at the table."[22] During the immediate post-Civil War era, the club's annual regatta at exclusive Newport, Rhode Island, became a highlight of the annual social scene for New York City's high society.

The club attracted international attention in 1851 when Stevens formed a syndicate to build a ship specifically designed to challenge the best that England could put into the water. After Stevens retired from his role as a prominent owner of thoroughbreds in the late 1830s, he turned his attention to his "first love," the sea. The son of a wealthy entrepreneur, he had been raised along the water's edge and had swum and sailed since his youth, owning a long succession of private vessels, including *Trouble*, built in 1816 and of dimensions (56 feet in length) sufficient to be recognized as the first authentic American yacht. Now 65 years of age, Stevens had come to appreciate the talents of a young ship architect, George Steers, recently arrived from England. The result was the *America*, a low-slung vessel that was dispatched to Great Britain to challenge the best the English could muster. Initially the English yachting crowd held it in contempt because they "did not regard it as of the slightest consequence, or as at all likely to interfere with their monopoly of the glory." When *America* arrived at the Isle of Wight several days before the August 23 race date, however, its sleek profile made Englishmen nervous. One journalist noted that "she sits upon the water like a duck," but was possessed of "a

Figure 2.2 The sleek yacht *America* is pictured by artist J. E. Butterswortte leaving Boston Harbor on its way to England for the great race of 1851. Its stunning triumph over the best that the British could muster set off a long and loud outburst of American braggadocio. © Bettmann/CORBIS.

clean build and saucy raking masts." He feared that *America* "evidently looks bent on mischief."[23]

Indeed. After a slow start, *America* began to pass the competition, "leaping over, not against the water." Two hours into the approximately 60-mile race around the Isle of Wight, *America* had a two-mile lead against its nearest rival among 18 English challengers, and at the seven-hour mark it led the British favorite, *Aurora*, by seven miles! Queen Victoria and the royal family waited at the finish line aboard the Royal Yacht *Victoria and Albert*, and as the first sails came into view, she inquired of a signal master peering through binoculars, "Which yacht is first?" He replied, "The *America*, your majesty." "Which is second?" the Queen asked. "Your majesty, there is no second."[24]

The next day, the Queen boarded *America* to present John Cox Stevens and his crew with a hideously ornate cup that came to be called the America's Cup. It remains yet today the most coveted prize in yachting. In a most unsentimental move, Stevens soon thereafter sold *America* to English interests and returned to the United States aboard a steam-powered ship while American newspapers trumpeted the supremacy of Yankee shipbuilding. New York lawyer George T. Strong believed the exuberant nationalistic celebration disturbing: "Newspapers [are] crowing over the victory of Stevens' yacht which has beat everything in the

British seas," he wrote in his diary, "quite creditable to Yankee ship-building, certainly, but not worthy the intolerable, vainglorious vaporings that make every newspaper I take up now ridiculous. One would think yacht-building were the end of man's existence on earth."[25]

The Formative Years of Prizefighting

While a small segment of the population thrilled to yachting and a larger and much more diverse group followed the races of men and horses, bare-knuckle prizefighting also attracted widespread interest, especially among men. Eye-gouging rough-and-tumble contests remained a part of life in southwestern frontier regions, but in the cities a more "scientific" form of the "manly art" emerged. During the 1820s and 1830s, a group of professional pugilists began to put on exhibitions in public places, most often large saloons where the atmosphere was raucous, the air filled with cigar smoke, the language coarse, beer and whiskey flowed freely, and money changed hands as bets on the contestants were settled. Unlike the rough-and-tumble fights on the frontier, these bouts were conducted according to a few primitive rules. A downed opponent could not be kicked or hit. A round ended whenever a contestant was knocked or wrestled down. When that occurred, he had 30 seconds to resume the contest by "coming to scratch" or "toeing the mark," which meant resuming the fight by standing along a line drawn through the center of the ring. A bout ended whenever a fighter failed to toe the mark or conceded defeat. Consequently, bouts between evenly matched foes could go for scores of rounds; many a bout lasted for well more than an hour's duration.

Prizefight promoters found they could attract large crowds if they matched fighters representative of rival ethnic groups; pairing of an Englishman and an Irishman almost always assured a large and boisterous crowd. As with other sports, New York City became the center of American pugilistic activities, although prizefighting also flourished in such cities as New Orleans, Philadelphia, Baltimore, and Boston. It was in New York and its immediate environs, however, that most major bouts were held, in part because the existence of several small gyms provided opportunities for young fighters to develop their skills.

Although illegal, by the 1840s prizefighting had captured the attention of sports-minded New Yorkers. Public attitudes on pugilism were distinctly divided. As historian Elliott Gorn describes the situation, on the one hand boxing appealed to the democratic sensibilities of the nation: two men enter the ring with equal opportunity to achieve victory by dint of their skill, strength, endurance, fortitude, and guile. On the other hand, the fact that men engaged in a contest that could produce severe physical injury, even death, called into question the widespread belief that American society was one in which rationalism and civic responsibility were predominant. As one critic wrote in a New York magazine in 1806, pugilism produced "nothing but brutality, ferociousness, and cowardess" (sic) that served to "debase the mind, deaden the feelings and extinguish every spark of benevolence."

The violence of the sport stood in stark contrast to the widespread belief that democracy was capable of uplifting the moral character of the American people and in particular, eliminating violence from the social order. Consequently, as Gorn observes, boxing was a

> denial of mankind's moral progress. Even before boxing really existed in America, the republican ideology, with its suspicions of all things licentious and immoderate, gave men a frame of reference with which to judge the ring. . . . [I]t mocked the more optimistic ideologies ascendant in the early nineteenth century.

The ring seemed to contradict "romantic assumptions of man's reason triumphing over his passions, of the moral progress of humankind."[26]

Violence was only one of many factors that motivated pugilism's critics. They contended, long and loud, that prize fights encouraged public disorder, heavy drinking, and gambling. Further, it was a sport that appealed to man's basest instincts and it flourished among the lower echelons of urban society – especially Irish and German immigrants. Victorian middle and upper classes, intellectual descendants of the colonial Puritans, viewed the new urban working classes as dangerous, violent, and a serious threat to civic order. They believed prizefighting brought out the worst of man's nature – brutality, cruelty, passion, drunkeness, and gambling. They also connected the sport with the growing number of Catholic immigrants who had flocked to American cities in the wake of the 1840s potato famine in Ireland. In handing down sentences for three Irish in 1842 who had promoted a fight that led to the death of one contestant, Judge Charles R. Ruggles gave vent to this perspective:

> A prize fight brings together a vast concourse of people: and I believe it is not speaking improperly of such assemblages, to say that the gamblers, and the bullies, and the swearers, and the blacklegs, and the pickpockets and the thieves, and the burglars are there. It brings together a large assemblage of the idle, disorderly, vicious, dissolute people – people who live by violence – people who live by crime – their tastes run that way.[27]

These strong words of condemnation came at the sentencing of an Irish immigrant, Yankee Sullivan, who was the primary promoter for a notorious fight between Christopher Lilly and Tommy McCoy held on a bluff overlooking the Hudson River near the small town of Hastings, located 25 miles north of New York City on September 13, 1842. An estimated 2,000 spectators traveled by steamships to witness this bout, which had attracted considerable interest among fight fans in New York City. Both fighters weighed scarcely 140 pounds. For a time, the Irishman McCoy seemed to have the upper hand, but as the fight progressed past an hour's duration his endurance began to wane and his opponent carved his face into a bloody mess. Following the rules of the day that each knockdown ended a round, the match reached 70 rounds, but with McCoy enduring a merciless pounding: "both eyes were black – the left one nearly closed, and indeed that whole cheek presented a shocking appearance," one spectator wrote. "His very forehead was black and blue;

Figure 2.3 America's first famous pugilist Tom Molineaux was a free black, originally from Maryland, who lost a bloody 44-round bout with Englishman Tom Cribb in 1810 in London amid much controversy in what was billed as the world's first heavyweight championship fight. © Bettmann/CORBIS.

his lips were swollen to an incredible size, and the blood streamed profusely down his chest. My heart sickened at the sorry sight." As McCoy gasped for breath many spectators called out to the referee and McCoy's handlers to halt the fight as "blow upon blow came raining in upon him." The courageous Irishman refused to quit despite being knocked down 80 times, but at the end of Round 119 and two hours and forty-one minutes the fight ended suddenly when McCoy collapsed and died. The cause of death was later determined to have been from drowning in his own blood.[28]

No wonder Victorians were appalled by the popularity that pugilism commanded among the working classes – the "very dregs of society" as the critics were often prompted to say. One such proponent of Victorian sensibilities – Horace Greeley, publisher of the *New York Tribune* – denounced the "gamblers, brothel-masters and keepers of flash groggeries who had perpetrated this frightful spectacle." According to this famed journalist, the end of American civilization was in view unless the new urban working classes were brought under control.[29] Former New York City mayor Philip Hone took note in his diary that the sport of pugilism threatened American civilization: "The amusement of prizefighting, the disgrace of which was formerly confined to England . . . has become one of the fashionable abominations of our loafer-ridden city," he complained.[30] For critics such as editor Greeley and Mayor Hone, who spoke on behalf of the genteel elements of New York's population, the sport not only reflected the dangers posed by the new urban working class, but also undercut the essential truth of the enduring Protestant work ethic – with merely a lucky punch or two, a prize fighter could earn more money in one afternoon than a hard-working artisan or clerk could make in a year or more. Even more egregious, a gambler who bet heavily on that fighter could walk off with large sums without having to expend any effort, rewarded mightily for his endorsement of an antisocial activity that benefited saloon keepers and assorted other social misfits.

By the time of poor Tommy McCoy's demise, the Victorian element in the nation's leading cities had come to fear the steady growth and influence of what has been described as the "sporting fraternity," a highly visible segment of the larger urban bachelor culture that had developed in American cities. The sporting fraternity, sometimes called the "Fancy " – a popular English term for the same male culture – existed largely within the context of the many saloons that lined the streets of American cities. It was here that men could escape the control of wives and girlfriends and participate in an all-male subculture that focused on drinking, gambling, swapping stories, telling crude jokes, and discussing (and arguing over) matters of great import: sports, politics, and sex. Many of the saloons that catered to this crowd sponsored a variety of events to attract clients. These variously included such popular blood sports as dogfights, rat baits, and cockfights. Occasionally a prizefight was the feature attraction. Most professional fighters and their handlers were closely identified with saloons, and future bouts were often arranged at the bar. Cards, billiards, and dice games were a constant in this loosely organized urban brotherhood, and many an evening would be topped off with a visit to a nearby brothel. Participation in this urban subculture provided young men with a special sense of individual identity within the larger, impersonal urban complex, bringing with it a modicum of social status, a sense of belonging to a group where everyone knew one's name. Some of these young men also belonged to volunteer fire departments – exclusive male organizations often more recognized for their ability to drink large quantities of liquor rather than for their skill in extinguishing fires.

For several years, the highly publicized death of Tommy McCoy put a damper on prizefighting, but it made a comeback in the 1850s. Newspapers and magazines found a wide reading audience for their graphic stories about the pugilistic scene, and heavily promoted bouts between popular ethnic battlers again attracted large crowds. Such was the case when Yankee Sullivan challenged the top American

heavyweight Tom Hyer. In 1841, Hyer defeated Country McCleester and was popularly proclaimed the first American heavyweight champion, but the death of
Tommy McCoy had dimmed public interest. That hiatus ended in 1848, when Hyer
and Sullivan encountered each other in a New York City bar, got into an argument
that became a scuffle, which led inevitably to a challenge. Each man agreed to put
up $5,000 and went into training for the bout. For months, the forthcoming battle
was the talk of the town, and newspapers reported heavily upon the challengers'
training sessions. Betting on both sides was intense. At this time, when heavy
immigration from Ireland had unleashed strong anti-Catholic and anti-Irish passions in the United States, especially in those large eastern seaboard cities, the
ethnic context of the bout made it into an event of special significance.

Despite widespread public interest, only a few hundred spectators actually
witnessed the bout, which was held in a wooded area along Chesapeake Bay.
Maryland law-enforcement officials attempted to prevent the fight from taking
place, but while in pursuit of the boat carrying the pugilists and their entourage,
the police ship ran aground. Thus on a cold February day, with a dusting of snow
on the ground, a ring was hastily constructed from tree limbs and some rope,
and in mid-afternoon the much-hyped battle was on. It lasted less than ten minutes, as the much-larger Hyer knocked his opponent senseless with a barrage of
blows to the head. Although the fight was fought in near-isolation, in deference to
the authorities eager to arrest the participants, thousands in New York and other
major cities eagerly awaited news of the outcome. Foreshadowing the role that
communications would play in the growing popularity of sporting events, news
from Chesapeake Bay arrived in newspaper offices across the country by the new
technology of telegraph lines.[31]

The Hyer victory stimulated a demand for boxing matches, and many young
men, almost exclusively from the lower echelons of urban society, sought to fight
their way to fame and fortune. Most, of course, failed, but one marvelous Irishman
found that the sport provided his entree to a life of fame, power, and wealth. His
was truly a real-life example of the Horatio Alger myth of "rags to riches." John
"Old Smoke" Morrissey was born in Ireland in 1831 and brought to America by
his parents when he was three. Growing up in the small city of Troy, New York,
he became notorious for his violent temper, his frequent scrapes with the law, and
especially his ability to use his fists. He moved to New York City about 1850 and
quickly became an effective enforcer for local politicians who found his services
useful in breaking up opponents' meetings and in intimidating some voters to stay
away from the polls while making certain others got there. He soon had a street
reputation as a brawler and gang member. In one noteworthy saloon encounter,
he was knocked down and pinned atop a hot wood-burning stove by his adversary.
The resulting stench from his severely burned flesh led to his unusual nickname of
"Old Smoke."

On September 1, 1853, Old Smoke fought Yankee Sullivan at Boston Corners, a
tiny community where the state lines of Massachusetts, Connecticut, and New York
converge. The sponsors selected this site because they hoped the uncertainty about
the state in which the ring was actually located would prevent law-enforcement

officials from stopping the affair. A crowd variously estimated at 3,000 to 6,000 converged by railroad and horse and buggy on the little community. Serious money was wagered at ringside, but also in cities across the United States. One newspaper estimated that at least $200,000 rested on the fight's outcome, which predictably was controversial. By far the superior boxer, Sullivan bludgeoned Morrissey for 37 brutal rounds – Old Smoke's eyes were nearly shut from swelling and his face was a bloody mess – but then various allegations were shouted between the two men's supporters and a free-for-all brawl broke out among spectators, who spilled into the ring. When the referee called for round 38 to begin, Morrissey staggered to scratch but Sullivan was busily punching away at one of Morrissey's supporters. The referee awarded the bout to Morrissey.

Predictably, most prominent urban newspapers denounced the fight as immoral and the behavior of the spectators outrageous, but they also provided their readers with detailed descriptions of the event. Morrissey's greatest asset as a fighter, it was now clear, was his ability to take enormous punishment. The bizarre ending to the fight added to his growing reputation as a brawling but somehow romantic rogue, and he proceeded to win several fights over challengers of lesser ability than the now-retired Yankee Sullivan. His reputation as someone not to be meddled with was greatly enhanced when one of his associates shot and killed a rival, William "Butcher Bill" Poole (of English ancestry), who had once licked Morrissey in a street fight; this sensational shooting intensified anti-Irish sentiment in the city.

Morrissey fought his last formal prizefight in 1858 against John Heenan, a formidable up-and-coming boxer from San Francisco. Although both were of Irish descent, the intense pre-fight ballyhoo portrayed Morrissey as a near-savage Irishman while Heenan, himself no saint, was somehow made to be a respectable hard-working middle-class gentleman. The fight was held on a lonely spit off the Canadian coast of Lake Erie, with both men putting up $5,000 as prize money. Large numbers of sportsmen traveled by rail or boat to Buffalo, then boarded special excursion vessels to sail to the "secret" location near the town of Long Point. The entire nation waited to hear the outcome, because huge amounts of wagers rested thereon. Heenan almost won the bout in the first round, which lasted four and a half minutes; he demonstrated much greater boxing skill than Morrissey, and only when Heenan slugged a ring post and broke two knuckles was Old Smoke able to escape an ignominious first-round defeat. Relying upon his ability to absorb punishment, Morrissey slowly wore down the resistance of his opponent, who in addition to his injured hand was suffering from a leg infection. By Round 11, both men, exhausted and beaten to pulp, had to be helped to scratch. Only Morrissey had the strength to withstand a punch, however, and Heenan collapsed in a heap.

Thus ended the pugilistic saga of John "Old Smoke" Morrissey. But unlike so many professional fighters, upon retirement from the ring his life took an amazing upward trajectory. Throughout the decade of the 1850s, he had operated two popular saloons through which he became intimately involved with leading gambling and political figures in New York City. He became a gambling entrepreneur with

important political connections in the powerful Democratic Tammany Hall organization. When Morrissey opened a popular gambling hall at 8 Barclay Street that
attracted an elite clientele, his political connections and his willingness to grease
the palms of important men prevented the authorities from shutting down his
flourishing gambling operation. He also was part-owner of a city-wide numbers
racket that paid handsomely. Improbably, shortly after the Battle of Gettysburg
in 1863, he opened a racetrack in Saratoga to attract high roller customers to his
lavish red brick hotel and casino, the Saratoga House, that he had constructed.
This resort in the lower Adirondack Mountains soon became recognized as the
premier gambling establishment in the United States, often favorably compared to
the best that Europe could offer.[32] Morrissey's political career essentially ran parallel to his gambling enterprises; in 1866, he was elected to the United States House
of Representatives where he served two terms. Shortly before his death in 1878, he
served two terms in the New York State Senate, interestingly enough as an anti-
Tammany man after a major falling out with Tammany boss "Honest John" Kelly.
Morrissey's funeral was one of biggest the city had seen up to that time and was
reported on the front pages of city newspapers.

   The story of Old Smoke was truly amazing. What the *New York Times* called "a
checkered career" in its front page obituary illustrated the opportunities awaiting
immigrants to America in the nineteenth century. That few immigrants enjoyed
the success of John Morrissey is understood, but the connections he made between
his pugilistic, gambling, and political careers was an early and telling example
of an emerging pattern for American sportsmen. Not only did prizefighting open
up avenues to immediate financial success for those with the ability and willingness to make the sacrifices demanded by the blood sport, but pugilism's close
connections to urban politicos, gamblers, and the bachelor culture pointed in
the direction that organized sports would take in the decades to come. The main
thrust of the emerging pattern of American sports would be to counter the Victorian emphasis on self-restraint and social control with a heavy emphasis on
unrestrained masculine expression through blood sports, questionable political
machinations, and widespread gambling.

Baseball: the Creation of "America's Game"

Throughout much of the American colonial era young boys played a simple game
that utilized a small ball and a wooden stick. It was descended from the traditional English game of "rounders," that was popular among children. In colonial
America it had been variously called "base," "old cat," barn ball," "nine cat," and
probably many other long-forgotten names. The impromptu game was played
with an infinite variety of informal and ever-changing rules. Boiled down to fundamentals, however, a "feeder" tossed a small ball in an underhand fashion to the
"striker," who, upon hitting the ball ran in a counter-clockwise fashion around
four or five "bases," consisting of stone or stakes driven into the ground. The
runner sought to avoid being "put out," which occurred when his batted ball was

caught on the fly or first bounce, or when he was "soaked" by a defensive player, that is, hit with a thrown ball before reaching the safety of a base.[33]

By the 1850s, however, the game had been transformed by the strong drive for organization and structure that was a central driving force of the emerging modern era. Although still popular with youngsters, it now appealed to young male adults. Consequently, the informality of the timeless game gave way to written rules and policies, organized competition, statistical analysis of outcomes, eventually controlling regional and even national organizations. Especially in the cities along the northeastern seaboard, the game resonated with many members of the urban bachelor set. Young adult males who held positions in the expanding urban middle class – artisans, bankers, agents, lawyers, physicians, shopkeepers, accountants, clerks, salesmen, teachers, businessmen – sought social connections with like-minded men through organized clubs. Among the many activities sponsored by these clubs was playing the game that members recalled from their childhood.

In part, the game caught on so rapidly because of its inherent simplicity. It could be played in a corner of a city park or on a vacant lot in a few hours; the only equipment required was a wooden bat and a ball. Unlike the more complex English game of cricket, which enjoyed a brief spurt of popularity during the 1850s among a relatively small number of affluent urbanites, baseball did not require a lengthy time commitment (some cricket matches could last for several days), and it was not encrusted with complex rules and the snobbery of the English upper class. The new game could be played in a relatively short time, which fit busy schedules of upwardly bound urban professionals. As one commentator noted, as compared to the rival sport of cricket, baseball "comprises all the necessary elements for affording a pleasing and harmless excitement . . . yet can be regularly practiced and even played in the shape of formal matches without interfering unduly with business hours."[34]

The lively new game naturally grew out of the competitive nature of the emerging new class of hardy capitalists and it met the need for social structure and organization. Although the game came easily to those endowed with natural athleticism, it also rewarded hard-working, industrious individuals who strived to improve their limited skills with diligent practice. The more affluent clubs provided colorful uniforms for their ball teams, emulating the uniforms (or secret ritualistic attire) of competing fraternal organizations, in particular of members of private volunteer fire departments who rushed out in brightly colored uniforms to extinguish blazes.

For many years, rules were determined locally. When teams began to travel to other cities, the set of rules to be used became an issue. Knowledgeable followers of the game during its formative years understood that there was a distinct Massachusetts Game as compared to the Philadelphia Game. The number of bases and the distance between them fluctuated considerably, as did the specifications of the distance that separated the "bowler" or "feeder" from the "striker." The catcher usually stood ten feet or so behind the batter to catch the pitch after several bounces; no player used any protective equipment, including gloves or other forms of hand protection. The number of participants on a team also fluctuated, sometimes rising to as high as 14. In all versions of the organized game, however, the bowler was expected to help put the ball into play, and not deceive the striker; he was required to toss the ball gently in an underhanded fashion. Team captains normally arbitrated disputes over close calls, and the use of an umpire was resisted because the game was intended to be played fairly by gentlemen who adhered to the rules.[35]

The pioneering baseball club was the New York Knickerbockers, a fraternal group organized in 1845 to play the game and enjoy attendant social activities. Apparently some of its founding members had been playing for several years on a vacant lot at the corner of 27th Street and Fourth Avenue. Alexander Jay Cartwright, a young bookkeeper by trade, suggested the creation of a formal baseball club, complete with by-laws and a $5 annual membership fee. He also presented to his friends a written set of proposed rules for the game, which were readily accepted, probably in part because they incorporated many concepts already in use and because he had taken the time to write them down. With Cartwright's rules providing a foundation for play, the popularity of the game soared in the New York City metropolitan area; this particular form of the game spread rapidly up and down the Atlantic coast. By the eve of the Civil War, most teams had adopted the Knickerbocker rules for what had become commonly known as the "New York Game."

Cartwright's prescience is startling. All that he left out that is central to today's game, essentially, were the nine-inning rule, the use of umpires, and the base on balls. Cartwright placed four bases – now canvas bags instead of stakes – 90 feet apart in a unique diamond configuration, with the "bowler" required to release his stiff-armed underhand pitch from a distance of 45 feet. The bowler's responsibility was to give the batter a ball that could readily be hit, so that the pace of the game remained lively; it would take several decades of evolution of the rules before the role of the pitcher became one of getting the batter to make out with overhanded pitches thrown at high velocity. Cartwright established the size of each team at nine. A batter was declared "out" if his batted ball was caught on the first bounce or on the fly, if he swung three times without making contact, or if the ball arrived securely at base before he arrived. He also abolished the painful practice of "soaking." Cartwright also established that three outs ended a team's "at-bat" and that the first team to score 21 "aces" was the winner.[36]

In keeping with their intent to be seen as gentlemen, the Knickerbockers also adopted rules to encourage good sportsmanship, including fines for appearing at games intoxicated ($1), criticizing umpires (25 cents), and using profanity (6 cents). The Knickerbockers presented a sprightly appearance when they played their games, outfitted in blue and white flannel uniforms topped by a fashionable straw hat, making a sartorial statement consistent with their intent to be viewed as sportsmen of high moral character and important social standing. For a time the games they played were viewed as part of a pleasant social outing that would be followed by a picnic or a banquet, perhaps a dance.

It did not take long, however, for the American competitive spirit to kick in.

Within a few years, several rival teams had been formed, many of them dominated by young men drawn from the laboring classes, often lower-class German and Irish immigrants. Increasingly, teams played to win, even if it meant engaging in dubious tactics, and the language heard at games became anything but gentlemanly. The Brooklyn Eckfords, for example, became a top team by the mid-1850s and was composed of workers engaged in the shipbuilding trade. Baseball clubs sometimes had strong political connections; the powerful Brooklyn Atlantics (named for the street on which their clubhouse was located) was essentially a team comprised of players closely connected to the Democratic Party, and several members of the New York Mutuals were recognized as members of an aggressive volunteer fire department as well as enforcers for the growing political machine directed by the notoriously corrupt city "Boss," William Marcy Tweed.[37]

With incredible swiftness, the game took on a new level of seriousness. Competition became more intense and the importance of victory replaced the social aspects of the game. Encouraged by the speed and convenience of railroad and steamboat transportation, the best teams traveled considerable distances to play challengers – to Boston, Baltimore, Buffalo, and Philadelphia, and to many smaller towns in between. Improved communications provided by the telegraph also made it possible to send game results across vast distances. The true hotbed of the rapidly expanding game remained the New York City metropolitan region, perhaps because of heavy coverage by the local press. Several dozen teams now competed regularly for top billing, carrying such colorful names as the Eckfords, Atlantics, Eagles, Mutuals, Morrisianas, Gothams, Empires, Excelsiors, and of course, the Knickerbockers. The quality of play and the development of a spectator base led to the first enclosed field being established on a former ice-skating rink in Brooklyn in 1862.[38]

In order to ensure uniformity of rules and patterns of play, 14 prominent baseball clubs joined together in 1857 to form the National Association of Base Ball Players (NABBP). Its membership grew at an impressive rate as more teams joined each year. The organization adopted a standard set of rules (derived largely from the rules of Alexander Cartwright), but change was inherent as the game developed. The 21-"ace" rule was dropped in favor of a nine-inning contest, although it was not until 1864 that the organization acceded to the Knickerbocker club's new rule proposal that a one-bounce catch did not constitute an out. In 1858, the New York fans were captivated by a much-anticipated game featuring the best players from Brooklyn pitted against the best of Manhattan (New York, 22; Brooklyn, 18); excitement was so high that promoters for the first time in history charged an admission fee, and rumors abounded that some teams were engaged in the nefarious business of paying top players.

By the eve of the Civil War, the game had reached the cusp of becoming a competitive, modern sport, complete with a formal controlling national organization, compensation of talented players, written game rules and regulations, a team manager, and the keeping of formal statistical records of games, seasons, and individual player performances. Journalistic coverage continued to expand, and instructional manuals on playing the game sold well at newsstands. Businessmen naturally contemplated various approaches to exploit the game for financial profit and the idea of a professional league was not much distant. In just 15 years, the game had clearly outgrown the modest expectations of Alexander Cartwright and his pioneering band of Knickerbockers. Like other folk games that had been subjected to the powerful forces of modernism, baseball was becoming an integral part of the development of modern America.

3 "This Noble and Envigorating Game"

The American game of baseball has long been the subject of speculation and scrutiny. Some commentators, such as Mark Twain, noted its close relationship to the surging nineteenth-century economy, suggesting that the game was "the very symbol, the outward and visible expression of the drive and push and rush and struggle of the raging, tearing booming nineteenth century." Poet Walt Whitman famously described it as "Our Game, America's Game." Historian Allan Nevins commented that baseball is "a true expression of the American spirit." Others, such as A. Bartlett Giamatti, one-time president of Yale University and a distinguished Shakespearean scholar, and, for a brief time, commissioner of organized baseball, were fascinated with the "love affair between America and baseball that has matured and changed but never died." Giamatti wrote, "For so much of expanding and expansive America, the game was a free institution with something for everyone." A loyal Boston Red Sox fan, Giamatti understood the heartbreaks that baseball dealt those who took the game seriously. He was struck by the many disappointments the game inflicted upon its faithful, but was also drawn to its predictable rhythms:

> It breaks your heart. It is designed to break your heart. The game begins in spring, when everything else begins again, and it blossoms in the summer, filling the afternoons and evenings, and then as soon as the chill rains come, it stops and leaves you in fall alone.[1]

One scholar noted that baseball is a reflection of the aggressiveness of the American business culture, while another suggested that the game provided a symbolic transition from the rural America of Jefferson's time to the frenetic industrial and urban society of the modern era.[2] Others were drawn to the fact that baseball was a "timeless" game played without the constrictive influence of a clock, an essentially urban game heavily laden with symbolic rural imagery, and a "scientific" game in which technique and cerebral strategies were rewarded.

Throughout its more than 150-year history, America's special game of baseball has remained a simple game, easily learned, readily played. In its essential form, baseball can be reduced simply to throwing, hitting, and catching a small ball. It was a game adaptable to schoolboys in the backyard or vacant lot, a game laced with symbolism that fathers passed on to sons in an American version of the rites of passage. Over the years, baseball became intimately embedded in the American consciousness through the arts – poetry, theater, newspaper, song, film, radio, television, and novel. It also provided the medium for animated conversations (and arguments) in the daily flow of public and private discourse. One historian described it as "a complex of memories, associations, longings, focusing on things clean and aesthetically pure, things infinitely more pure, things infinitely more fun to think about, than the mournful political, economic, social realities, tensions, and discords afflicting the real world out there." Thus, most Americans have readily concurred with French scholar Jaques Barzun, who ventured this exaggerated observation: "Whoever would know the mind and heart of America had better learn baseball." Baseball, it seemed was, as the *New York Times* editorialized in the nineteenth century, "this noble and envigorating game."[3]

Baseball's special place in American life was indelibly established in 1907, when a commission charged with identifying the origins of the game went so far as to ignore obvious facts to create an enduring, if benign, mythology that still hovers over the game. The commission was recommended by one of the game's leading figures, former pitcher and now baseball entrepreneur, Albert Spalding, and was chaired by the commissioner of the National League, Abraham Mills. It sought to establish the pure American origins of the game and deny the contention of historians that the game had evolved from the English game of "rounders." The seven-man commission (whose membership included two United States senators) based its conclusion on the most dubious of evidence: a handwritten letter received from an elderly man who recalled an event that had occurred 68 years earlier in 1839 in the small upstate town of Cooperstown, New York. Abner Graves affirmed that his teenage friend Abner Doubleday had presented to his friends a written set of rules. Case closed. The commission declared that "Our Game" had no European roots and that Doubleday was its creator.[4]

This fabrication was accepted as Gospel because the American people wished it so. One of the compelling factors in accepting Graves's incredible recollection was that Doubleday had served as a general in the Union Army, thereby establishing for the game a symbiotic context of militarism and patriotism. However, when General Doubleday died in 1893, his obituary did not mention any role he might have had in creating the game of baseball. That is, of course, because he had none. In 1839, he was already a second-year cadet at West Point and presumably beyond playing childhood games, let alone having the time to invent a new game. Although several generations of historians have resolutely exposed the Doubleday–Cooperstown fable for the hoax it is, it has nonetheless maintained a strong hold on the American consciousness because it provides an aura of uniqueness to the nation's "pastime." On the 100th anniversary of Doubleday's imagined revelation, the Baseball Hall of Fame was opened in Cooperstown. Every year, hundreds of thousands of Americans make a "pilgrimage" to baseball's "Mecca" in that upstate sleepy tree-lined town to pay homage to the game's historical "legacy," where "immortal" players have been "enshrined" in the game's "pantheon."

The Early Professional Era

The Civil War did little to deter the spread of the game's popularity. During the conflict, many prominent New York clubs continued to play matches, although military obligations decimated the membership of some teams. Because it was relatively easy for military-age men to avoid the drafts that both the Union and the Confederacy eventually instituted, many of the better players managed to avoid military duty altogether. Large crowds continued to attend the games between the top clubs; in New York City, some 15,000 spectators watched the Atlantics and Excelsiors play on the same September day in 1862 that thousands of young men died at the bloody Battle of Antietam in Maryland.[5]

The war may have temporarily slowed baseball's growth, but in the last analysis it greatly stimulated the game's popularity. Union and Confederate soldiers played baseball to pass the time, and when they returned home after the war they took with them an enhanced knowledge of the game. These young men would become the heart of the development of "town ball," a phenomenon that swept the entire nation in the late nineteenth century. Employers saw the value in sponsoring teams for their employees as a means of healthy recreation during non-working hours; they also recognized the commercial benefits of sponsoring a winning nine, and competition for "amateur" players was often intense as employers in need of a catcher or clean-up batter would recruit one to his firm with the offer of salary bonuses. Shrewd employers recognized that the types of behavior that baseball required were consistent with those they desired in their employees, and as such the game became, as one historian concluded, "an ally in the constant battle to maintain a satisfied and productive work force." In the years following the war, the game, both strictly amateur and semiprofessional, spread rapidly throughout the United States; no longer was it a game closely identified with the East. Settlers moving west in Conestoga wagons played the game as a diversion, sometimes teaching the game to American Indians. Teams were formed as far west as California.[6]

Town ball flourished in the late nineteenth century, drawing upon the intense rivalry that developed between neighboring communities. It became a staple of life in the United States and would remain so until the 1950s, when the intrusion of national television seriously undercut the amateur local teams by broadcasting major league games. Competition often brought out the worst in many participants; towns routinely accused each other of hiring "ringers," using crooked umpires, and employing unruly and unsportsmanlike tactics on the field of battle.[7]

The most significant development of the post-Civil War era, however, was the establishment of professional teams as urban boosters and investors envisioned a winning team as a means of promoting civic pride and even economic development, not to mention profits to be made from ticket sales. Grown men now were openly paid to play a boy's game, and a new profession was created in the fast-paced modern economy, emulating changes occurring in the marketplace. Specialized skills and services were much in demand in all sectors of the expanding economy, including organized commercial recreations and amusements that saw the opening of vaudeville theaters, music pavilions, public beaches, amusement parks, and the like. Professional baseball filled a niche in the expanding entertainment business. The burst of popularity resulted from the impact of new technologies: railroads made possible efficient team travel; telegraph companies sent game results across the nation with incredible speed; and new printing presses ground out a massive amount of information that fed the hunger of fans for even more.[8]

For a time, the issue of paying players was debated. Founded in 1858, the National Association of Base Ball Players (NABBP) staunchly defended the concept of amateurism, and for a time enjoyed the support of most baseball journalists. The NABBP tenaciously clung to its view that "the custom of publicly hiring men to play the game of Base Ball [is] reprehensible and injurious to the best interests of the game." This position was probably grounded in the growing uneasiness about the increased numbers of professional players who were of Irish and German immigrant stock. As one sportswriter bluntly wrote, these players were "not men of moral habits or integrity of character."[9]

The construction of fenced ballparks encouraged the payment of players, who naturally demanded a portion of the gate receipts collected by promoters. In 1868, the *New York Times* reported that the nation's top eight teams had collected more than $100,000 in ticket sales. The drive for supremacy led clubs to search for top talent and to pay the best players for their efforts. Although only a handful of the estimated 100,000 adult ballplayers in 1870 were being paid directly for their ball-playing skills, several players were making in the neighborhood of $1,000 a year, about twice the annual income of a clerk or skilled manual worker. Any pretense about professionalism ended in 1869, when an upstart club in Cincinnati fielded the first all-professional team. Management hired one of the nation's best players and charged him with assembling a strong team. Born in England in 1835, Harry Wright initially became an outstanding cricket player for the Dragonslayers of the St George Cricket Club of New York City. He also became a leading baseball player for the Knickerbockers. In taking command of the Cincinnati club, Wright accepted the same salary he had earned playing cricket – $1,200 a year – and proceeded to sign several leading eastern players. In Wright's initial season at Cincinnati in 1868, his team won 41 and lost only seven games, touring the East and Midwest by train in search of competition.[10]

Wright introduced several innovations that would become a staple of the professional game. He conducted vigorous practices, schooled his team in various game strategies and tactics, demanded that they stay in good physical condition, preached the gospel of sobriety, and assumed complete control of the team. In so doing, he created a model for the position of team "manager." In addition to his on-the-field duties, Wright scheduled games and handled travel arrangements, routine business affairs, and even ticket sales. He also created the prototype of the team uniform that would be worn by millions of ballplayers thereafter. He outfitted his team in knee-length flannel knickers, with the calf covered by bright red woolen stockings. Wright also abandoned the popular brimmed straw hats in favor of more practical campaign caps with front bills, and placed a red *C* on the front of woolen shirts that featured stylish turned-up collars, to denote the team as representative of Cincinnati. Footwear featured black high-top shoes with metal cleats to increase traction. Reporters took to calling the team the Red Stockings, thus creating the tradition of teams being identified by a nickname. More than a century later, the uniform introduced by the Cincinnati Red Stockings had not changed much; the current Cincinnati Reds wear white home uniforms, red stockings, with a time-honored *C* embroidered on the shirt and cap. [11]

Wright's Red Stockings went undefeated in 1869, winning 57 games and tying one; many of the games were lopsided affairs as his professionals demonstrated not only good fielding skills but dazzled spectators with their well-honed ability to hit line drives and sharp ground balls called "daisy cutters." The star player was Wright's younger brother George, whose strong throwing arm enabled him to play as a deep shortstop rather than along the base path as was customary. George had been lured westward by his brother for the munificent annual salary of $1,400, at the time the highest salary ever paid a ballplayer. The Red Stockings traveled an estimated 12,000 miles by train that year in search of worthy opponents, at one point riding the new transcontinental rail line to show their stuff in San Francisco. President Ulysses S. Grant invited them to the nation's capital to play a local all-star team. An estimated 200,000 fans watched the Red Stockings play. When the team arrived home at season's end, appreciative fans hosted a dinner in their honor, which the *Cincinnati Gazette* termed "one of the most elegant ever seen" in the Queen City. Thrilled by the team's record, club president Aaron Champion proclaimed at the banquet that he would rather be president of the Red Stockings than of the United States.[12]

The following year, the mighty Red Stockings won their first 27 games before losing an extra-inning contest to the Brooklyn Athletics 8–7 before 15,000 New York fans who paid the substantial admission fee of 50 cents each to watch the game. The quality of the opposition had definitely improved, however, and the Red Stockings lost several other games that season. Because their home field could seat only 2,500 fans, the club lost money, and its stockholders (anticipating future trends in professional team management) rebelled against high player salaries and fired President Champion (who sadly learned that his was not the ideal job). The team was shredded. Manager Harry Wright, with several of his top players in tow, left town for a better offer – to create a new team, the Boston Red Stockings, for the 1871 season.[13]

Wright's leadership had radically transformed the game. Pious questioning about the correctness of paying men to play a boy's game largely disappeared from public dialogue. Once-skeptical journalists seldom thereafter questioned the propriety of play-for-pay. Wright left no doubt that this was a business, at one point writing to an aspiring young player, "Professional ball playing is business, and as such I trust you will regard it while the season lasts."[14] The nature of the game was transformed by the all-consuming factor of professionalism. Players commanding substantial salaries were expected by their employers to win games, an objective that managers and players interpreted as empowering them to use any means possible to that end. Clean, honest, fair play was for the naive. Instead, all types of cunning, intimidation, rough play, and skullduggery were encouraged, even to the extent of bending or breaking rules and physically and psychologically intimidating opponents and umpires. Tough, aggressive play became the norm as players sought to fend off challengers for their positions on a team as well as to defeat the opposition. Competition on the baseball diamond thus mirrored the cut-throat competition that raged in the business world of the Gilded Age.[15]

Henry Chadwick and a Game of Numbers

One individual who never played the game professionally stands out for helping produce the groundswell of popularity of baseball. Henry Chadwick was born in Exeter, England, in 1824, and emigrated to America with his parents when he was 12. Tall and slender, possessed of considerable natural athletic ability, he gained local fame as a talented cricket player on the Hoboken fields owned by John Cox Stevens. He became a newspaper reporter for several New York newspapers, initially covering local sporting events, and cricket in particular. One day in 1856, however, while leaving a cricket match, he came upon a baseball game being played by two top-notch teams, the Eagles of Brooklyn and the New York Gothams. He later recalled,

> The game was being sharply played on both sides and I watched it with deeper interest than any previous base ball match that I had seen. It was not long before I was struck with the idea that base ball was just the game for a national sport for Americans.[16]

Chadwick's conversion from cricket was indicative of the rapid decline of the traditional English game among the American people. In 1860, he wrote convincingly on the history of the new American game, noting that although it was clearly derived from the timeless English game of rounders (which he himself had played as a boy in England), it was a remarkable reflection of the American spirit. He went on to attest to the game's virtues as a molder of character and promoter of good health, proclaiming that "this invigorating exercise and manly pastime may be now justly termed the American game of Ball" despite that it was of "English origin."[17]

The new game became Chadwick's lifetime passion. Like other intellectuals of the Victorian era, he sought to find in sporting events a transcendent set of values that would help elevate a mere game to a position of social utility. He now proclaimed baseball "a moral recreation," and a "powerful lever ... by which our people could be lifted into a position of more devotion to physical exercise and healthful out-door recreation." As such, the game deserved "the endorsement of every clergyman in the country ... [as] a remedy for the many evils resulting from the immoral associations [that] boys and young men of our cities are apt to become connected with."[18]

Chadwick's contribution was twofold. Foremost, he championed reporting games by the extensive use of statistics. Over several decades he experimented with various methods to reduce each game and season to statistical analysis. By the late 1860s, he had devised the composite box score as a means of summarizing the story of a game that revealed in numbers the accomplishments of each player – runs scored, hits, walks, put-outs, wild pitches, passed balls, strike-outs, assists, and errors. His box score also presented an inning-by-inning line score. He introduced the batting average as a means of assessing a player's value. In Chadwick's world, even an entire season could be compressed into an assemblage of numbers detailing the accomplishments of teams and individual players.

Chadwick's statistical crusade was in tune with the times. Baseball, if it were to become truly the national game, had to meet the standards of the new age – comprehensive and precise rules and policies, standardization across the nation, a uniform method of statistical breakdown and analysis, and ways to chart and analyze trends over time. He thus devised a complex system of codes and shorthand that he demanded become the standard for scoring a game (including the ubiquitous use of the letter K to denote a strike out). His methods thus became the basis for the evaluation and comparison of the game over generations. "It is requisite that all first nine contests should be recorded in a uniform manner," he wrote in 1861 in explaining the manner in which his new score sheets should be employed uniformly across the entire United States.[19] Thus Chadwick created a means for fans to communicate (and argue) with each other, in real time and over the decades, about the game they love. The cold figures of a batting average thus compel fans to compare the relative merits of a Cy Young with a Sandy Koufax, a Wee Willie Keeler with a Maury Wills. What he helped create was similar to the innovations simultaneously occurring in industry, prompted by the preachings and teachings of time-and-motion expert Frederick Winslow Taylor. One scholar has noted,

> standardizing the rules of scoring was the equivalent of an industrial magnate's standardizing the weight, shape, and purity of a steel bar. If the statistics of performance were to have the meaning intended for them, it was absolutely essential that the playing situation for all teams and players be nearly comparable as possible.[20]

Chadwick's second contribution was to create through his extensive writings a national dialogue about the game and its merits. A Victorian moralist to the core, Chadwick in part used statistics to establish the value of each player and to hold him accountable for his efforts on the diamond. Repeatedly, however, his writings revealed him to be a scold. He continually argued for rules changes that placed value on "clean," "manly," and "scientific" play. His extensive and often intemperate writings urged the issuance of fines for players who argued with the umpire, used profanity, or spurned the instructions of their manager. In a typical Victorian revulsion against behavior that emphasized raw power or strength over the powers of the mind and social restraint, he railed against the innovation of fast pitches to overpower batters, and his ever-evolving box scores never quite found a place to record the singular event of a ball being knocked over a distant fence. Home runs were, to Chadwick, an aberration in a game that should be played "scientifically" – that is, with emphasis placed upon the use of the bunt, stolen base, hit-and-run, hitting behind runners, and the like. His moral sensibilities were never clearer than when he attacked the proclivity of many professional players – who tended to be young and unmarried – to gravitate toward gambling, drinking, and chasing women. In 1889 he wrote with consternation, "The saloon and brothel are the evils of the base ball world at the present day."[21]

Chadwick not only published his thoughts in New York newspapers but also contributed regularly to national journals. He was a regular contributor to Richard Kyle Fox's popular *National Police Gazette*, William Porter's *The Spirit of the Times*, *Beadle's Dime Base-Ball Player*, and Albert Spalding's *Spalding's Official Base Ball Guide*. Chadwick's 1868 book, *The Game of Base Ball: How to Learn It, How to Play It, and How to Teach It*, was the first serious published effort to describe the fundamentals, strategies, theories, and rules of the game. Although his strident moralism offended some, he maintained his role as critic-in-chief until his death in 1908, using his editorship of the unofficial baseball manual, *Spalding's Baseball Guide*, for the last 25 years of his long life to deliver his pronouncements on the state of the game. Although baseball historians have criticized Chadwick's work on many counts, his was a crucial role in creating a moral rationale and a statistical basis for the game that he believed held one of the keys to the nation's moral uplift.[22]

Growing Pains

During the 1870s, the game continued to change to meet the standards of the emerging modern era. It was now played by young boys and men in every town and city across the land. The game provided a common ground for conversations everywhere. As a product of modernity, it had yielded to the forces of standardization as national organizations supervised the establishment of rules and the maintenance of records and statistics. Fostered by the growth of the print media, including several national magazines, the game grew rapidly in popularity. No longer merely a pleasant game that boys and young men played for fun, baseball also had become the property of businessmen who created professional teams and leagues.

Rules were routinely changed to accommodate the special needs of spectators who wanted to watch an ever-more-exciting brand of ball. By the time the Cincinnati Red Stockings became the talk of the nation, the game had come to resemble today's game of fast-pitch softball. No longer was the "thrower" expected merely to lob up a fat pitch to the batter with a soft underhanded toss. "Throwers" were now were called pitchers, and managers expected them to employ all sorts of different speeds and other trickery to fool the batter. Among other things, they learned to snap the ball underhanded so that it would variously curve, drop, or rise. Until the 1870s, batters could request a pitch be tossed either "high" or "low." Umpires – usually local citizens willing to put themselves in harm's way – were now stationed off to the side from the batter and empowered to call a pitch as "strike" when the batter permitted a well-placed pitch to go by. Harry Wright became famous for his "dew-drop" pitch – a slow change-of-pace pitch intended to put the batter off balance after seeing several fast tosses. In order to keep the game moving at a rapid pace, the number of "balls" required to advance the batter to first base was reduced over the years from nine to four. The size of the ball – made with a hard rubber core, wrapped with woolen string, and covered with a sewn piece of horsehide – was reduced to about the size of today's ball – about five and a half ounces in weight and nine and a quarter inches in circumference, made of tightly wound string around a rubber core and covered by a thin leather cover. By 1880, standardized balls were being manufactured by several companies and marketed nationally through the first generation of sporting goods stores that were beginning to appear in larger cities. The nineteenth-century ball did not rocket off the bat like today's "juiced" balls, and because they were kept in play for several innings they lost even more of their bounce. These so-called "dead balls" would remain the standard until Babe Ruth's home-run spree in the 1920s produced the "live ball" era.

The ethics of the game had also changed dramatically. Whereas the games played by the early fraternal clubs were occasionally marred by arguments and a resort to fisticuffs, for the most part the early clubs sought to emulate the decorum and behavior standards expected of cricket players. "It isn't cricket," was a popular American expression indicating a lack of adherence to the spirit of the rules. Unlike the aristocratically minded sportsmen who played cricket, those who came to dominate the "American game" were mirror images of the hard-driving, conniving, unscrupulous men who were dominating the American business system. The dominant ethic of the baseball player was to find ways to bend, break, or otherwise subvert the rules to gain an edge on the opposition. Leo Durocher's famous comment of a later time, "Nice guys finish last," was a throwback to this era when mental and physical toughness, sharpened spikes, bean balls, and hard slides into basemen were hailed as "manly" play. Especially at the higher levels, winning was indeed everything, and it mattered little how victory was achieved.

With that ethic in place, the role of the umpire became crucial. The quality of umpiring presented league officials with a difficult problem that defied easy solution. In local town ball encounters, the umpire was usually picked out of the crowd and often lacked adequate knowledge of the rules or the mechanics of umpiring. At even the highest levels the quality of umpiring was not much better, with former players being hired as arbiters when their playing days were over. Physical intimidation of umpires occurred much too often. In 1876, the new National League sought to address the issue by mandating a substantial wage of $5 per game in hopes of securing quality umpires; but with only one man assigned to a game it was impossible for him to cover the entire field adequately. Umpires, of course, were expected to be fair and impartial in all their decisions, or as Harry Chadwick so eloquently put it, "the position of an Umpire is an honorable one, but its duties are anything but agreeable, as it is next to impossible to give entire satisfaction to all parties concerned in a match." Nonetheless, Chadwick said, "The moment he assumes his position on the ground," the umpire had "to close his eyes to the fact of there being any one player, among the contestants, that is not an entire stranger to him; by this means he will free his mind from any friendly bias."[23] But the truth was that the standards for selection and training were inadequate and the cost of multiple umpires prohibitive. Thus the tradition of baiting and intimidating the umpire became ingrained as a means by which players and managers would forever attempt to gain an advantage.

Enthusiastic spectators – aptly called "cranks" and later "fanatics" (later shortened to "fans") – joined in the fun and sought to assist their favorite team by seeking to distract the opposition and intimidate the umpire. In 1860, after working-class fans of the Brooklyn Atlantics peppered with rocks and epithets the opposition Excelsior team during a city championship game, the young writer Albert Spalding denounced them as "utterly uncontrollable . . . thugs, gamblers, thieves, plug-uglies, and rioters." In California, reports indicated that fans upon occasion even shot off a round or two into the air from a revolver when an opposing outfielder was settling under a fly ball. A *New York Times* writer observed in the early 1870s that the game had deteriorated from one "witnessed by crowds of ladies, and governed only by those incentives of an honorable effort to win the trophy," to

> [a] game patronized by the worst classes of the community . . . characterized by the presence of a regular gambling horde, while oaths and obscenity have prevailed and fraudulent combinations of one kind or another have marked the arrangements connected with some of the prominent contests.[24]

The general behavior of players and fans alike was disconcerting to the proper Victorians who cherished above all decorum, proper conduct, and suppression of antisocial behavior. One of the most disheartening practices associated with baseball to these right-thinking respectable citizens was gambling by spectators in the grandstands despite the posting of signs prohibiting such practice. By the late 1860s, gambling on baseball had become so widespread that some feared the game would be destroyed if it were not curtailed. Some gamblers preferred a sure thing to the thrill of watching a close game upon which they had money invested, and they were widely suspected of bribing players to throw games. This practice – popularly known as "hippodroming" – first hit the news in 1865 when it was learned that three players for the New York Mutuals had agreed to divvy up $100 offered by a gambler if they lost a championship series with the Brooklyn Excelsiors. In 1867, *Harper's Weekly* editorialized against baseball gambling, noting that the most respectable clubs in the country indulge in it to a highly culpable degree, and so common [are]. . . the tricks by which games have been "sold" for the benefit of gamblers that the most respected participants have been suspected of baseness.

In other words, the fix was in, and players were engaged in losing games in return for payoffs by gamblers.[25]

By the mid-1870s, baseball had developed a serious image problem. Gambling, rowdyness by players and fans alike, and the rough edges around many players who came from uneducated lower-class backgrounds, all tended to give the game a coarse, even corrupt image. It was under this substantial cloud that investors decided the time had come to create a professional league that would take on these substantial challenges.

Early Years of the Professional Game

The success of the 1869 Cincinnati Red Stockings essentially decided the issue. Amateur and semiprofessional teams and leagues would continue to thrive, but under the strong influence of the national print media, the attention of the average sports fan would be directed increasingly toward the exploits of the "major" professional leagues. The development of professional leagues was in no small way stimulated by intense competition between large northeastern and Midwestern cities to attract railroad lines and to encourage the development of industrial and commercial companies within their borders. These intense, no-holds-barred, economic and political urban rivalries helped fuel interest in fielding winning baseball teams as part of the larger urban competition. In the early 1870s, boosters formed clubs, often by issuance of stock, to field professional teams in hopes of emulating the glorious example of Cincinnati's triumph. Club managers raised capital to build wooden grandstands and enclosed fields and they hired a captain (increasingly now called a manager) to scour the country in search of the best talent. Perceptive observers of the juggernaut that was the 1869 Red Stockings took note that only one member of the team was a native Cincinnatian, the remaining players having been imported from distant eastern cities. Urban promotion, fired by urban economic and political rivalries, contributed heavily to the development of professional teams and the establishment of competing leagues in the late nineteenth century.

A case-in-point was Chicago. Leaders of this Midwestern railroad hub had looked jealously upon the publicity that the Queen City of Cincinnati had engendered from its undefeated Red Stockings, and they vowed to emulate that achievement. In late 1869, team founders induced investors to purchase $20,000 in stock, and the Chicago White Stockings was launched. With an eye on Cincinnati, they admitted they did not want to "see our commercial rival on the Ohio [River] bearing off the honors of the national game, especially when there was money to be made by beating her."[26] The importance of having a team "which would beat the world" was evident to these businessmen, whom the *Chicago Tribune* praised for "organizing a baseball club with the same energy as they would build a tunnel or construct a railroad."[27] These boosters, however, had assumed that the creation of a team would produce winning seasons and championships, bringing fame and fortune to the Windy City, along with new manufacturing and commercial enterprises. Thus there was introduced into professional sports at an early time the unproven contention that persists to this day, that a winning major-league team provides a stimulus for economic growth. That teams can lose as well as win was driven home to White Stockings fans in 1875, when their team lost out to the Browns, a team representing one of Chicago's primary urban rivals, the river city of St Louis. In the wake of that inglorious defeat, one Chicago newspaper sadly noted that "a deep gloom" now pervaded the city. In a substantial exaggeration, the reporter wrote, "friends refused to recognize friends, lovers became estranged, and business was suspended. All Chicago went to a funeral, and the time, since then, has dragged wearily along, as though it were no object to live longer in this world."[28]

The early years of professional baseball were not marked by high levels of financial success. Economic recessions, losing teams, disturbing reports of anti-social behavior by fans and players (both on and off the field), and the vexatious moral issues of Sunday play and the sale of alcohol all posed challenges to team owners. Teams played in the loosely organized National Association of Professional Base Ball Players (NAPBBP) that was dominated by Wright's Boston team. Several thinly capitalized teams were swept away in a tide of red ink. The effort to establish regional "minor league" teams was even more hazardous, and the early history of baseball was marked by the steady comings and goings of teams, even of entire leagues. As but one example, the Southern League had 18 different team franchises between 1880 and 1900, had seven seasons suspended prematurely due to financial exigency, and did not play at all in 1890, 1891, and 1897. Of all the professional teams established in the late nineteenth century, fully three-fourths lasted less than three years before folding.

That dismal record in large part resulted from the fact that well-established, respected businessmen of considerable wealth, viewed baseball – with its many rough edges – with contempt, leaving the field to marginal investors and individuals who did not take offense at having to deal with unsavory players and spectators. Prim-and-proper bank officials naturally viewed baseball teams seeking loans with justifiable skepticism. Thus it was not surprising that many of baseball's investors and team owners came from the shadowy edges of the urban business community, including gamblers, saloon owners, brewers, and machine politicians.

Although such marginal businessmen as these founded hundreds of professional teams during the late nineteenth century, much of the attention naturally focused on the so-called "major" leagues. The first of these leagues that sought to offer regular play of "America's Game" was fittingly created in 1876, the 100th anniversary of the Declaration of Independence. The driving force behind the creation of the National League of Professional Base Ball Clubs was Chicago coal magnate and civic booster William A. Hulbert, who had watched first hand the futile efforts of the NAPBBP as president of the Chicago White Stockings. A strong-willed man of considerable girth, Hulbert imposed his vision of the future of baseball upon his team and on the league that he controlled until his death in 1882. Comprised of eight teams representing the cities of Chicago, Boston, New York, Hartford, Cincinnati, Louisville, St Louis, and Philadelphia, the league easily displaced the poorly organized and inefficiently operated National Association of Professional Base Ball Players. With half of its teams located in the Midwest and the other half in the East, Hulbert's new league presented an image of a truly "national league."

Hulbert set the tone for the future, creating the first truly functioning league. A crafty businessman, he strictly limited the number of teams to eight and introduced a system to prevent the "revolving" of players from one team to another. Players could not negotiate a new contract with rival teams once a season began. Each member city was required to have a minimum population of 75,000, and no city could field multiple teams. All teams were owned by investors (individual or joint-stock), and players' cooperatives were forbidden. These crucial decisions, which set the pattern for the future merely emulated the confrontational pattern of management–labor relations of the time. Hulbert also championed policies designed to appease social critics who had attacked baseball for its lack of decorum. He banned Sunday games, prohibited the sale of beer and other alcohol at games, encouraged female attendance by offering reduced ticket prices for ladies on special days, and launched a strong anti-gambling crusade. In an effort to discourage the attendance of lower-class spectators most likely to engage in rowdyism, ticket prices were pegged at a formidable 50 cents (approximately one-half of an average laborer's full day's pay), which Hulbert hoped would entice "the better classes [to] patronize the game a great deal more." He even stipulated that weekday games begin at 3 p.m., a time when most laboring-class persons were still at work.[29]

Despite this strategy, the new league did not get off to an auspicious start. Several teams folded during the early years for financial reasons, and others were kicked out of the league for defying Hulbert's authority. Controversy and rumors about the influence of gamblers was endemic. Nonetheless, from the outset Hulbert demonstrated his toughness when confronted with a challenge to his authority. Near the end of the initial season, when the financially hard-pressed New York and Philadelphia teams, both having suffered through losing seasons, refused to make a scheduled late-season swing to the Midwest, Hulbert had the teams expelled from the league.

The following season, Hulbert responded decisively to the gambling issue when reports were published in the *Louisville Courier-Journal* that several leading players of the Louisville Grays had taken bribes to throw a series of games that cost the team the league championship. Four players were summarily banished from the league for conspiring with a New York City gambler to split his winnings (which amounted to about $300).[30] Despite Hulbert's decisive action, the dark specter of gambling lurked over the game for several more decades. It would not be adequately addressed until after revelations surfaced that Chicago White Sox players had taken substantial bribes from gamblers to lose the 1919 World Series.

In 1880, the club presidents, having adopted the point of view that players were mere employees and not skilled professionals, approved a policy designed to reduce greatly the practice of "revolving." Each team, the owners agreed, could identify five players whose services were "reserved" to a particular club for as long as that club wished to retain their services; the policy was soon extended to all team members. The "reserve rule" proved to be everything the owners wished, stripping players of the right to shop their skills on the open marketplace. This essentially eliminated any bargaining power the players might have used to increase their salaries. The "reserve clause" would remain a powerful tool of ownership until the 1970s. Until that time, salaries were kept in check, with even star players making salaries that today seem shockingly minuscule.

For many years, the White Stockings dominated the National League. Led by manager and pitcher Albert Spalding, Chicago easily won the first championship in 1876. Spalding was the compelling baseball figure of his time, and he shrewdly made successive career moves from star pitcher to team executive to sporting-goods entrepreneur and even to the role of leading baseball writer, historian, and publisher. After he retired from the field in 1878 due to a chronically sore arm, he devoted his attention to the commercial side of the game. His fledgling sporting-goods manufacturing business got a huge boost when he snagged the contract to provide all balls for the National League. By 1890, his sporting goods manufacturing and sales company had become the nation's largest. Spalding also established himself as the major spokesman for the National League, publishing its official annual handbook, which included team and individual records, official rules and league policies, and his own commentary on the state of the game. In a successful effort to co-opt a leading critic of the league, he appointed the opinionated Henry Chadwick as editor of *Spalding's Official Base Ball Guide.* Chadwick's criticisms were effectively silenced, and the annual publication became required reading for anyone seriously interested in professional baseball. Spalding also increased his financial investment in the White Stockings, and he not only assumed the presidency of the club when Hulbert died in 1882 but also became the primary spokesman for the league.[31]

During the 1880s, Chicago won several consecutive pennants, led by hard-hitting first baseman Adrian "Cap" Anson, who also served as manager. Standing 6' 2" and weighing 220 pounds, this rawboned Iowan towered above most players of his time. He was a powerful hitter, among the best of his generation. Although his managerial acumen was questionable, he won four consecutive championships because management provided him with the best talent in the league. As a player-manager, he set a high example on the field for his players, routinely leading the league in batting average and home runs. Over a 22-year career in the National League, Anson batted a stellar .334.[32]

While Anson provided the White Stockings with the necessary power, the colorful Mike "King" Kelly, who played every position but pitcher, produced the fireworks. Kelly was a flamboyant Irishman with a knack for stealing bases (he once stole six in one game), using exaggerated high-flying hook slides as one of his special crowd-pleasing ploys. Fans loved to chant "Slide, Kelly, Slide" as he cavorted on the base paths, and as the first great Irish-American ball player, he helped lure many Irish spectators to the ballpark. Even a popular hit tune entitled "Slide, Kelly, Slide!" swept the nation. He also found ways to frustrate his opponents, some of them quite humorous. He especially enjoyed outfoxing the solitary umpire (who had many things to watch simultaneously). Among Kelly's many tricks were holding opposing base runners, cutting inside bases to reduce the distance he had to run to beat an incoming throw from the outfield, and faking being hit by a pitch. In 1887, Spalding shocked the nation when he sold Kelly's contract to the Boston Red Stockings for the enormous sum of $10,000, a sensational transaction for the era. The sale provided a major statement about the power that owners now wielded over players through the reserve clause. Purchase of Kelly's contract delighted Boston fans, who raised funds to purchase for their new star player a pair of matching horses and a bright carriage as a demonstration of their affection. Unfortunately, Kelly could not control his serious drinking problem – he showed up for many games seriously hung over or even intoxicated – and his level of play deteriorated rapidly. This early fan favorite – arguably the first true "star" baseball player – died of alcohol-related symptoms a few weeks before he reached his 37th birthday.[33]

Emergence of the Modern Game

Despite its heavy emphasis on continuity and tradition, baseball has been a game that has undergone major changes in rules and techniques over the years. By the late 1880s, however, the type of play had become such that it would be quite familiar to fans in the twenty-first century. Of major significance were the changing rules regarding pitching. Over the years, the requirement that the pitcher softly lob an underhand toss to the batter was undercut by pitchers who began to throw the ball with considerable velocity, first three-quarter and then side-armed. One source indicates that the first overhand pitches were introduced in 1875, although that bit of trivia is open to question. In any case, the overhand pitch grew in popularity during the late 1870s and was formally accepted in the rule book by all professional leagues in 1885. In response to the increased velocity of pitches, the distance between batter and pitcher was lengthened from 45 feet to 50, and then to today's distance of 60 feet, 6 inches. Pitchers now had to throw with one foot planted on a rubber slab rather than, as had previously been the practice, of running toward the batter before releasing the ball, as was done in cricket. The size and composition of the official ball (it was of course the ball being manufactured and sold by the aggressive sports entrepreneur, Albert Spalding) were also standardized. New rules also called for a five-sided home plate made of hard rubber to replace the more dangerous metal plate.

It was during this period that gloves and other protective equipment were introduced. Previously, players had to handle sharply hit balls with their bare hands, which of course led to many errors and painful bruises. Games with ten or even 20 errors being charged were not unusual. Spalding recalls that the first glove he ever saw used was in 1875, but the player, Charles Waite, apparently was so

embarrassed by his "unmanly" use of a skin-tight glove to protect his hand that he had the glove colored in flesh tones. During the 1880s, an increasing number of players began wearing small gloves to protect their hands, and this early experimentation led to the creation of a rounded glove designed by Harry Decker, a player of modest abilities who appeared in both the National League and the American Association. His glove eventually was modified into the oversized mitts worn by first basemen and catchers, but the other fielders adopted a smaller model that featured padding at the thumb and heel and light padding on the four fingers. These original fielders' gloves were modest hand-sewn leather affairs – little more than eight or nine inches in diameter. For years, catchers suffered painful injuries from foul balls and wild pitches; broken fingers were a particular occupational hazard. To provide reasonable protection of catchers who were moving ever closer to the batter so that they could throw out base runners, chest protectors, shin guards, protective cups, and padded wire masks were introduced in addition to the larger padded mitt. With the introduction of the glove, the practice of using one's hat to catch fly balls was declared illegal.[34]

The venues from which spectators watched major league games were largely slap-dash wooden affairs, with most seating constructed

Figure 3.1 An overflow crowd packs the Baltimore ballpark in 1897 for a game with Boston. As was the custom, when the bleacher seats filled, fans were permitted to ring the outfield, sometimes creating havoc when a batted ball rolled into the crowd. © CORBIS.

of nothing more than unfinished wood planks that were bleached out by the sun (hence the term "bleachers"). The dry wood made the parks especially vulnerable to fires, and it was not unusual for play to be interrupted in at least one city each season while workers rebuilt burned-out grandstands. In 1871, as but one sensational example, the Chicago White Sox had to cancel their season when their stadium was leveled by the great Chicago Fire. Seating for the major league teams ranged normally from 7,000 to 10,000, although some clubs permitted fans to stand along the foul lines and to ring the outfield inside the fences, leading to exciting times when a deeply hit ball ended up in the crowd. Because most ballparks were constructed near the central city on whatever vacant lot was available, so that fans could walk or ride the trolley to games, the dimensions of the parks varied considerably. Distances to the fences, especially down the foul lines, were often relatively close to home plate, but distances in center field often reached 400 feet (an almost impossible range for even the most hefty of sluggers in the dead-ball era). On special days, red-white-and-blue bunting draped from the grandstand created a patriotic aura, and small bands provided entertainment between innings. If local laws were amenable, vendors hawked beer to the thirsty crowd, an influence that often intensified the fans' vocal support of the home team. Some clubs even offered a full-service bar for the convenience of fans.[35]

The 1880s: A Decade of Rancor

William Hulbert's drive to raise the image of baseball in the eyes of Victorian America created many problems for him in dealing with team owners. The policy forbidding the sale of alcoholic beverages at games became a major point of contention. Hulbert oversaw the expulsion of the Cincinnati franchise from the league in 1880 for its insistence on selling beer, and he resolutely prevented brewery owners from operating teams. In 1881, his critics rebelled against his dictatorial ways and formed a new league, the American Association of Base Ball Clubs, and proclaimed itself also a "major league." Franchises were awarded to clubs in Philadelphia, St Louis, Cincinnati, Pittsburgh, Baltimore, and Louisville. Brewery owners were prominent among the investors and were board members of four of the teams in the new American Association (AA). Supporters of Hulbert and his National League derisively denounced its rival as the "beer league," but the AA was determined to fill the vacuum created by Hulbert's morality crusade. Ticket prices were set at just 25 cents to attract working-class fans – most of whom viewed prevailing Victorian moral standards with disdain and were delighted to learn that not only would games be played on Sundays (where legal) but also that beer would flow freely at the ballpark. American Association teams secured the services of several of the top National League players with inducements of higher pay.[36]

For a time, the rival leagues seemed on the verge of a major fight when the National League reinstated a team in Philadelphia to challenge the Athletics of the rival American Association. Open warfare was avoided when the two leagues agreed to a "National Agreement" along with the Northwestern League, a respected minor league. Among other things, they agreed to respect each team's 11 "reserved" players, to pay each player at least a minimum annual salary of $1,000, to play the game by the same set of rules while using the same game ball sold by Albert Spalding's company. Shortly after the basic agreement was in place, managements of the two leagues also agreed to "blacklist" any player dismissed by another team, and they tacitly set salary classifications that in effect were caps upon players' compensation.[37]

On the playing field, the level of play in both leagues seemed about equal. The St Louis Browns in the American Association emerged as a team to be reckoned with under the strong ownership of Christopher Von der Ahe and the able field leadership of youthful manager and first baseman, Charles Comiskey. The Browns won four consecutive titles and defeated the National League champions in two informal post-season "World Championship Series," precursors to what would become the annual World Series in 1903. Meanwhile, under Cap Anson, the Chicago White Stockings continued their domination of the National League by capturing five pennants during 1880–6.

Anson was also a primary force in the development of an informal agreement that African American players would be barred from the National League. African Americans had embraced the game with the same enthusiasm as whites, and amateur and semiprofessional teams representing black urban neighborhoods were commonplace by the 1870s. However, in keeping with the racial standards of the day, the formation of interracial teams was discouraged. In 1867, the National Association of Base Ball Players issued a policy statement that it would not admit teams of color or bi-racial teams, ostensibly to reduce conflict on the field of play. In 1884, the Toledo team in the American Association signed a former University of Michigan player, Moses Fleetwood Walker, who became the first black to play for a major league team; he batted a respectable .263 in 104 games, but Toledo dropped out of the Association in 1885. By that year, leadership in both leagues had reached an informal "gentlemen's agreement" not to sign black players. Although a few African Americans played for various minor league teams until the mid-1890s, none was signed to play for a team in either the National League or the American Association.[38]

In 1887, Cap Anson refused to permit his White Stockings to take the field for an exhibition game against the Newark team if the hard-throwing George Stovey pitched. Newark's management capitulated to this threat, and the media was informed that Stovey was unavailable due to "illness." However, the highly publicized event was seen for what it was: a definitive statement by one of baseball's leading figures that racial segregation practices, now widespread in other sectors of American society, also extended to the national game. This informal and unwritten policy of racial exclusion would last for more than 50 years until it was challenged by the Brooklyn Dodgers with the signing of Jackie Robinson to a minor league contract in 1945.[39]

The National Agreement respecting rival league contracts helped keep the peace between the two major leagues, although many contentious episodes had to be contained as teams jockeyed for an advantage. Despite the soaring economy of the 1880s, teams in both leagues were locked in a difficult struggle for financial survival. Despite its best efforts, the National League found itself losing the battle to create a more wholesome, family-oriented image because of the behavior of many of its players who came from working-class backgrounds where heavy drinking, brawling, and general hell-raising were not uncommon. Management was frequently embarrassed by published reports of player misconduct. Mostly young and unmarried, players were often seen during evening hours frequenting saloons, brothels, and gambling halls. Despite the best efforts of management, the image of the game continued to suffer.

With the owners now fully in control of the game, players became increasingly dissatisfied with their conditions of employment. In 1885, the two leagues concluded another "National Agreement," this time capping players' salaries at $2,000 a year. This naturally produced outrage among the players, who now fully comprehended that when they signed an initial contract they placed themselves at the mercy of that team. Once a player signed a binding contract, he had few options if he was dissatisfied with a contract offer. Essentially, he could accept it, hold out in hopes of getting a more lucrative offer (an option realistically available to only a few top players), or quit the game.[40]

Consequently, when New York Giants third baseman John Montgomery Ward established the Brotherhood of Professional Base Ball Players as a self-help agency in 1887, the prospect of an all-out confrontation between management and labor loomed. In 1890, Ward's organization boldly formed a new Players' League, and more than one hundred National League or American Association players moved to the new circuit. Management of the Players' League made the fateful decision to challenge the National League directly, placing seven of its teams in cities already hosting National League clubs.

With players now distributed to 24 teams in three rival leagues, the quality of play naturally suffered, and fans went elsewhere for entertainment. Attendance slumped badly, and all three leagues suffered huge losses that year; investors who had funded the Players' League backed away from the possibility of another disastrous season and folded the league after only one season. As Spalding, who actively participated in the struggle against the Players' League, later wrote, the season of 1890

> caused serious financial loss to the moneyed backers of the Brotherhood. . . . It occasioned the utmost bitterness of feeling between players and club owners . . . and it utterly disgusted the public with the whole Base Ball business. It set Base Ball back from five to ten years in its natural development.[41]

One direct consequence was that the struggle devastated the financial base of the American Association, which unceremoniously folded in 1892. And so, following a decade of conflict, intrigue, and endless struggle, the National League found itself alone as a "major league." Club owners then did what came naturally – they slashed players' salaries and otherwise imposed their will upon their workers who had no other option than taking up a real job instead of playing a boy's game for pay. As the Brotherhood's adamant foe, Albert Spalding, euphemistically put it, the aftermath of the struggle of 1890 "settled forever the theory that professional ball players can at the same time direct both the business and the playing ends of the game."[42] Just as so many management–labor struggles of the late nineteenth century ended in a bitter defeat for labor, so too did the effort of John Montgomery Ward on behalf of baseball's version of the working man result in yet another triumph by the forces of capital and management.

Between the 1840s and the end of the nineteenth century, a simple child's game was transformed into a sophisticated professional game with which American society would be forever identified. Initially made popular as a pastime for young adults living in Eastern cities, following the Civil War baseball was played in towns and cities across the land. Its popularity led to the creation of professional teams and leagues and of a national game that captured the imagination of the American people. As historian Harold Seymour observed, by the onset of the twentieth century "baseball not only reflected American life, it had made an indelible mark upon it."[43]

4 The Formative Years of College Football

The American system of higher education is unique for its commitment to athletic competition. In no other country does anything even approach the massive sports enterprise that is supported by America's colleges and universities. Intercollegiate sports for those institutions competing at the highest levels of the National Collegiate Athletic Association (NCAA) command high visibility in the public eye. It is very big business, with individual campus budgets supporting a few hundred "student-athletes" reaching astronomical sums. Many major university athletic programs now have annual budgets that easily exceed $50 million.

Every March, American sports fans become fixated upon the annual NCAA basketball tournament, a made-for-television bonanza that annually produces in excess of $600 million in broadcasting rights, millions of dollars in ticket sales and ancillary enterprises, and generates an estimated $100 million in office bracket pools and in wagers placed with neighborhood bookies, and Nevada sports books. The Christmas and New Year's season has become a time for the playing of 25 college football bowl games – the culmination of a five-month season in which teams play an increasingly longer schedule – each of which generates millions of dollars for participating teams and their conferences. In addition to the 119 institutions that play football and the 327 that compete in basketball at the highest level (Division 1-A), there are some 3,000 community colleges, four-year liberal-arts colleges, and universities that field athletic teams for men and women athletes who compete throughout the academic year at lower classifications.

For more than a century, intercollegiate athletics have been an integral part of the life of American colleges and universities. In the process, college athletics have become intricately intertwined within the very fabric of American society. From their earliest days, intercollegiate athletics sparked widespread controversy, and it does so yet today. Although the size and scope of programs has grown enormously, the underlying issues remain essentially what they were a century ago. Over the years, critics and reformers have sought to eliminate, or at least reduce in scope and influence, intercollegiate athletic programs. With rare exceptions, however, these efforts have been repulsed. Although a wide range of sports has become part of the intercollegiate athletic scene, at the heart of the enterprise is the uniquely American game of football.

The Early Years of College Athletics

The earliest intercollegiate competition did not occur on a football field. Rather, the first instances of competition emerged among elite northeastern colleges that tested each other's mettle in rowing. Crew races became popular before the Civil War as rowing clubs were formed on several northeastern campuses. A highly publicized race between the rowing clubs of Yale and Harvard held on Lake Winnipesaukee in New Hampshire in 1852 drew a crowd of over one thousand spectators, including presidential candidate Franklin Pierce. By the end of the decade, the College Regatta Association had been formed, complete with written rules and regulations to guide its member institutions. Several of its regattas held in the late 1850s drew crowds estimated as high as 20,000.

College track and field teams were also organized, and spring meets became widespread during the post-Civil War decades. College men also competed in the nation's most popular team sport, baseball. The first recorded college baseball game was played in 1859 between Amherst and Williams, with the better-trained Amherst team (it actually held practices before the contest) recording a victory by the improbable score of 73–32. For much of the latter part of the nineteenth century, baseball was the most widely played game on American campuses until it was eclipsed by football. Baseball never caught on as a major college spectator sport because the game is best played in summer, a time when college classes have historically been suspended; thus, most nineteenth-century college teams played a modest spring schedule with their best players joining various amateur and semi-professional teams during the summer recess.

One of the striking characteristics of the early stages of intercollegiate sports was that they were organized and operated by the students with little if any interference or guidance from faculty or administrators. College sports grew out of campus competitions held between classes. Because most male students enrolled as freshman and graduated in four years, the symbolic importance of each class was great. For many decades, students had engaged in informal intramural games that casually mixed the rules of rugby and soccer. Upon occasion, these games turned into rugged physical contests that resembled more a barroom brawl than an athletic contest. These interclass contests were often held as part of the annual fall hazing of freshmen by upperclassmen during the so-called "rush" week preceding a new academic year.

When the game of football began to attract interest between 1875 to 1895, contests between classes were initiated, out of which slowly emerged the concept of the student body (and not the college administration) fielding a team to challenge nearby rival schools. Today's sports fans are accustomed to the dominant role played in college sports by the professional coach. The phenomenon of "coachers", as they were originally called, evolved slowly out of the growth of the college sports enterprise between 1880 and 1920. Originally, however, college teams were student-financed and operated affairs with an experienced student captain running the show. Elected by his teammates, the captain's responsibilities combined those of today's coach and athletic director, and included organizing the team, arranging a schedule, selecting team members, supervising drills and practices, and providing leadership during games.

It was under this informal, student-dominated structure that football made its appearance during the last two decades of the nineteenth century. According to most accounts, the first intercollegiate football game was played on November 6, 1869, when a group of Princeton students visited the College of Rutgers in New Brunswick. To ascribe to this event an important historical first as many historians have done, however, is a stretch. The game played that day scarcely resembled anything akin to today's American game of football, and the informality and lack of competitive zeal was a far cry from the emotion-laden spectacles of contemporary college contests. Instead, what transpired was merely a friendly game somewhat resembling a modern-day soccer match. Each side placed on the field 25 players who were cheered on by a few hundred spectators standing along the sidelines. The final score was 6–4 in favor of the home team; a banquet followed as each team toasted the other in a wholesome display of sportsmanship. Within three decades of the Princeton–Rutgers contest, however, this informal activity had evolved into a major spectator sport that trailed only horse racing and baseball in public appeal.

Football American Style

Following the Rutgers–Princeton encounter, during the next decade various forms of "foot ball" appeared irregularly on several college campuses, especially those of elite private colleges in the Northeast. Rules varied widely and were subject to constant revision. The game became increasingly physical, resembling today's game in which players use their hands to hold the ball and impede the progress of their opponents. Scoring systems changed frequently, but initially the largest number of points was awarded for drop-kicking the fat, somewhat oblong inflated ball through a goalpost, not by advancing it across the goal line for a "touch down."

From the beginning, the game stimulated controversy. Many of the issues about the college game today are not dissimilar from those of a century ago. As the game became increasingly physical, concerned administrators and faculty members sought its abolition because of the serious injuries absorbed by participants. Because of the lack of formal governing boards or conferences, player eligibility was left up to individual schools, leading to many flagrant abuses. It did not take long for skilled, physically adept "tramp" athletes to appear magically on a college campus in time for the fall season, then quietly disappear after the final game. "Proselytizing" (recruiting with financial inducements) of top players produced many a controversy. Occasionally, some itinerant athletes actually played for more than one school in the same season. Professors and deans questioned the dismal academic records of this migrant class of athletes, while also bemoaning the fact that many students exhibited far more interest in the games than they did in their studies.

The violent nature of the game – played initially without protective padding, governed by rules (or the lack thereof) that encouraged physical mayhem, and often poorly officiated by untrained referees – contributed to several highly publicized deaths and a long list of serious injuries each autumn. These highly publicized casualties predictably produced demands that the rules be modified to make the game safer, while others, often distraught professors, demanded the game be abolished. As an example, for many years one permissive rule stipulated that a player could be disqualified from a game *only after* he had slugged an opponent three times with his fist.

The new college game also had its legions of supporters. Some college administrators were pleased that the game was so physical in nature, a fact they believed helped dispel the widespread myth current at the time that male college students lacked adequate masculine attributes, that as a group they were sissified, effeminate souls who shunned physical challenges and cowered behind their books. At a time when the dominant Victorian culture was emphasizing the importance of "muscular Christianity" – a fusion of high levels of physical activity and religious devotion – football seemed to its advocates an obvious way to counter the notion that college men were not real men. Football demonstrated that its players were indeed men strong of body, fearless in the face of physical danger, and heroically willing to risk limb (and even life) on the football field for the glory of their alma mater.

College administrators also recognized that journalists devoted considerable attention to the game, providing a means of getting an institution's name before the general public on a regular basis. Journalists were pleased to provide that coverage because the game filled a major sports void after the baseball season ended in early fall. Campus administrators also recognized that a strong football team brought many benefits to their institutions, among them the ability to attract financial contributions from non-alumni (a practice elevated to a high art form by the University of Notre Dame) and a means of encouraging the continued loyalty and cash gifts from proud alumni.

On campus, the impact of football was palpable – at least to the game's supporters. The existence of a football team tended to decrease the often troublesome conflicts between classes because it created a common focus for all students. Campus leaders – students, faculty, and administrators alike – now stressed the importance of encouraging "school spirit." Administrators also noted the positive impact on student behavior; the rioting and drunkenness that had for so long plagued college campuses seemed to taper off during the football season (although later generations of deans of student life, confronted with the phenomenon of tailgating, would strongly disagree with this assessment).

For these and other reasons, by the 1890s many leaders of higher education had embraced football as a positive force on their campuses. When the founding president of the new University of Chicago set up shop in 1891, one of his first decisions was to hire Amos Alonzo Stagg, a former star end for the powerful Yale teams of the late 1880s, with the charge of building a winning team that would attract favorable publicity to the new institution. When it came to college athletic programs, President William Rainey Harper was enthusiastic: "I am most heartily in favor of them," he said. He assured Stagg that he would provide him with the physical and financial resources to build a powerful team. In return, Harper wanted immediate national recognition, something that normally takes decades to achieve if the emphasis is strictly upon the academic accomplishments of faculty and students.

At the same time, in a much different and more modest academic setting, the individual hired away from Ohio Wesleyan University to lead the small, struggling University of Nevada in Reno similarly turned to sports as a means of publicizing his remote institution. Early in his tenure, President Joseph Stubbs established a football team complete with a professional coach to help attract attention to the isolated campus. The editor of the student newspaper embraced Stubbs's vision, noting optimistically that it would soon be possible to send Nevada's teams to "Berkeley and Stanford to demonstrate our athletic supremacy." What presidents Harper and Stubbs perceived as a convenient strategy to help establish the foundation of a new university – fielding a powerful football team – provided a formula that would often be emulated by ambitious college presidents in the decades to come.

Yale and the Creation of Football

Today, the Yale Bulldogs play a modest Division 1-AA football schedule in the Ivy League. The few thousand spectators who show up for games rattle around the mammoth Yale Bowl with its seating capacity of 65,000. Completed in 1914, this was the first football mega stadium to be constructed. During the 1920s, similar monuments to the importance of football appeared on college campuses as football mania swept the nation. The construction of the Yale Bowl capped an incredible era of football domination at the New Haven campus beginning in 1876, during which time Yale's teams enjoyed several undefeated seasons and won over 95 percent of their games.

The primary factor in Yale's domination of the early college football scene was one man, rightly acknowledged as the "Father of American football." Walter Chauncey Camp's influence was not limited to his various roles at Yale as an outstanding athlete, team advisor, sometimes coach, and informal director of athletics. His influence extended to creating a set of rules that clearly distinguished the American game of "foot ball" from the English games of soccer and rugby. As had occurred during the formative years of baseball, the spirit of American nationalism militated the creation of a game unique to the United States. Beyond Camp's contributions to creating an unquestioned Americanized game, he helped to popularize the new sport by writing several books on how to play and coach the game. He also stimulated general public interest by writing some 250 articles on college football published in such widely circulated national magazines as *Harper's Weekly* and *Outlook*. As but one example of his flair for public relations, in 1888 Camp personally selected and publicized nationally the first "All-American" team and did so each year until his death in 1925. That initial team was comprised of 11 players that he considered to be the best in the nation (all of whom played for Princeton, Harvard, Columbia, and Yale), but by the early 1900s Camp's annual selections included the top players from Midwestern powerhouses such as Chicago, Wisconsin, Michigan, and Minnesota.

Born to middle-class parents and raised in New Haven, Camp was already well known locally as a skilled teenage rugby and baseball player before he first took the field for Yale in 1876. By the time that he was a junior, he had been elected football captain and immediately began to implement concepts of play that he would continue to develop and refine throughout his lifetime. Essentially, Camp sought ways to encourage synchronized team play over individual skills and the spontaneous action that occurred in free-flowing games of soccer and rugby. Over the years, as captain, team advisor (never officially "coach"), rules maker, author, and lecturer, Camp spearheaded the transformation of English-style rugby into the uniquely American game of football in which the players became pawns controlled by the coach. It was Camp's influence that essentially made American football more of a coach's game than a player's game.

Camp became a successful business executive as manager of a New Haven clock factory, and was an unabashed admirer of the "time-and-motion" theories of scientific management and production analysis being preached by engineering/manufacturing guru Frederick Winslow Taylor. Just as Camp utilized the efficiency concepts of "Taylorism" in his clock factory, he also applied them to the game of football. As he wrote in his *The Book of Football*,

> the object must be to use each man to the full extent of his capacity without exhausting any. To do this scientifically involves placing men in such position in the field that each may perform the work for which he is best fitted, and yet not be forced to do any of the work toward which his qualifications and training do not point.[1]

Throughout his career, Camp emphasized such telling phrases as "scientific planning" and "strategy and tactics." Essentially, he wanted to create a game in which chance and spontaneity were sharply reduced by rules requiring team discipline and organized patterns of play. This was what he liked to refer to as "scientific football." As Camp influenced the evolving structure of the game, athletes came to be viewed merely as cogs in an organized human machine, doing what industrial manager Camp like to call the "work" of football.[2]

After his playing days ended, Camp continued to advise the team even as he developed his business career. He never held a position analogous to that of today's professional "coach." Instead, he served as an informal advisor to the team captain, occasionally showing up at team practices, but more often relying upon his wife to report the practice results to him. He regularly met with team leaders in the evening, during which time he suggested practice drills and strategies for an upcoming game. Between 1876, when he led Yale to its first football victory as a running back, and 1909 when he stepped away from his advisory coaching position due to demands of business (and his declining influence within the game), Yale lost only 14 games.[3]

Although Camp was the primary force behind the creation of a powerful football dynasty at Yale, his lasting influence on the game was as rules maker. Either as chair or merely the first among equals on the self-perpetuating Intercollegiate Football Rules Committee, Camp dominated the evolution of the game during its formative years. His concepts were often insightful, if not brilliant. For a quarter century, his ideas controlled the way the game was played. As he often said, his emphasis was upon "method not men," by which he meant that the game was best played when each member of the team carried out specific responsibilities as part of a larger whole. His views mirrored the transformation occurring within the American economy, in which highly structured and carefully planned systems of manufacturing and distribution were implemented by an hierarchical structure within corporations and the factories they operated. Just as the captains of industry wanted to leave nothing to chance in their factories and mills, in which each worker had a specific assignment in the production process, so too did Camp seek to reduce the spontaneity of the game and the uncertainty of free (or "open") play so that the coach could effectively control the flow of the game.

Even during his playing days, Camp was thinking about the larger issues of the game. As team captain in 1878, he first proposed the reduction in team size from 15 to 11, a reform that was implemented by other schools two years later. In 1880, his proposal to eliminate the rugby-type "scrum" was adopted. Instead of teams gaining possession after the referee tossed the ball into a frenzied melee of both teams who then attempted to kick it free to a teammate, Camp introduced the concept of the kick-off and line of scrimmage. The team in possession of the ball retained it unless the ball was fumbled, punted away, or the opponent's goal penetrated by a field goal or touchdown; after a fiasco in the 1881 Princeton–Yale game, when each team merely downed the ball throughout the entire two halves (both teams believed that a 0–0 tie would give them the championship), Camp introduced the premise that a team could retain possession only if it advanced the ball five yards in three "fairs" (a term later changed to "down"). This fundamental change in the rules led naturally to the necessity of marking the field with white lime at five-yard intervals, leading to comments that the playing field looked like a "gridiron."[4]

These innovations produced precisely what Camp sought – a much less spontaneous and more controlled, predictable game in which players became instruments for carrying out their coach's strategies. Consequently, there soon emerged the revolutionary concept of written, scripted plays in which each player on offense had a particular role to play. In 1888, Camp introduced a rules change that proved to be of major import. His new rule made it permissible to tackle the ball carrier below the waist, a change that Camp correctly believed would reduce wide-open running plays around the end of the line because such a technique would greatly reduce the ability of agile runners to avoid being brought down in the open field. With tackling below the waist in effect, what little "wide-open" play that existed gave way to a careful, methodical (many bored fans said "dull") game that placed primary emphasis upon what was called "mass momentum play" – which meant a heavy concentration of struggling and slugging players at the inevitable point of attack in center of the line. In an effort to grind out the necessary five yards in three attempts without fumbling, teams tended to concentrate upon moving the ball forward by sheer brute force. Players closed ranks, often interlocking their arms, and pushed and pulled the ball carrier forward through similarly massed defensive players.[5]

"Mass momentum" play reached its apex in 1892, when Harvard introduced the "flying wedge" formation against a surprised Yale team. The play was designed so that the offensive players lined up several yards behind the line of scrimmage in a V-shaped formation and simultaneously rushed toward one stationary defense lineman. When this mass of closely knit players neared the line of scrimmage, the center snapped the ball to a running back inside the wedge. The resulting collision with a stationary, isolated lineman produced many a concussion, broken bone, or worse. "What a grand play!" a *New York Times* reporter enthused. "A half ton of bone and muscle coming into collision with a man weighing 160 or 170 pounds."[6] The flying wedge lasted only two years before the outcry against its brutality led to its being declared illegal by Camp's rules committee in 1894. Nonetheless, for the growing band of critics of the game, the short-lived flying wedge became a convenient symbol of the high level of violence that the game had achieved. Although many criticized the brutal play, others found it to be reassuring; the new urban male was up to the challenge of rugged physical combat. Some saw the game as a reassertion of the "Anglo-Saxon" traits of bravery and strength in battle. In an age when Social Darwinism, with its emphasis upon "survival of the fittest," was influencing public policy and academic inquiry, the game became a symbol of a resurgent national strength and virility. One close observer of football said the game "furnishes good ideals of courageous manhood." Or, as the president of Notre Dame, John Cavanaugh, commented, he would rather see his students suffer "a broken collar bone occasionally than to see them dedicated to croquet." After the University of Pennsylvania won a hard-fought Thanksgiving Day game against Columbia played in a cold rain and a driving wind that made the field "a quagmire of ice-cold mud," the team physician was effusive in his praise: "Those frozen eleven, purple, shivering, chattering players, were to be praised because "every one of them loves manliness and courage."[7]

Thus even with the abolition of the flying wedge, the game remained particularly dangerous. Newspapers printed a "hospital list" of major injuries as part of their game reports. Concussions became routine as players collided at full speed without benefit of helmet or padding; most players took to letting their hair grow long as a means of providing some natural protection, but it was a sign of one's manliness not to wear a leather "head harness" after they were introduced at the turn of the twentieth century. (Curiously, it was not until 1939 that NCAA rules actually required the wearing of a helmet.)[8] Although athletes of a century ago were well conditioned, they were much smaller than today's gargantuan players. Seldom did even the largest of linemen weigh over 180 pounds, and most running backs weighed between 130 and 160 pounds. Walter Eckersall, the famed All-American quarterback at Chicago who completed his eligibility in 1905, played at 135 pounds, and even as late as the 1924 season no member of the famed Notre Dame "Four Horsemen" backfield weighed over 160 pounds.

Walter Camp's emphasis on mass play thus resulted in a game in which injuries were more or less commonplace and deaths not all that uncommon. The president of Cornell University, Andrew Dickson White, denounced the game as a "vestige of barbarity," and Harvard President Charles Eliot caustically identified the problem as being "deliberately planned and deliberately maintained" – that is, deaths and injuries resulted not by accident but from young men playing a violent game *according* to the rules. By permitting tackling below the waist, unprotected heads were thrust into hard-pumping knees. With the rules permitting teammates to push, pull, or even catapult running backs through or over the massed defense, the emphasis upon raw strength was magnified and the potential for serious injury high.[9]

By the mid-1890s, as the game spread rapidly across the country, several college and high-school players died each year. These deaths were widely reported in the media, producing a national controversy over the merits of the game that lasted for more than a decade. Although the rules permitted rough play, critics were also correct in their assertion that referees (often poorly trained for their task) were reluctant to issue penalties. With 22 players concentrated at the line of scrimmage, slugging, biting, kneeing, and gouging opponents was commonplace.

Fistfights often disrupted play, and it was not unusual for police to have to intervene during a game to restore order. Football clearly was no place for the faint of heart, and many coaches reputedly taught tactics to "take out" opposing players. In 1893, President Grover Cleveland, having studied a report on the injury list at the two military academies leading to missed class days, called off the 1893 Army–Navy game. Throughout the 1890s and well into the new century, the ongoing debate over the violence inherent in the game waxed and waned, depending upon the annual death rate.[10]

From the earliest days, it was evident that the game was played by young men intent upon one goal: victory. Critics wondered why, if the game supposedly built character and encouraged clean play and good sportsmanship as its advocates said, referees were required. If the game was played by fair-minded sportsmen, why were rules necessary to prohibit kicking, biting, or even choking the windpipe of one's opponent? Harvard President Charles Eliot, one of the game's consistent critics, never received an adequate response to his 1892 comments that the very nature of the game encouraged devious and dirty play, or as he elegantly put it, the use of "tricks, surprises and habitual violations of the rules . . . [that are] inordinate and excessive" in "an unwholesome desire of victory by whatever means." Three years later, Eliot was even less charitable to a game that he believed perverted the essential mission of his university. In a commentary to his alumni on "the evils of intercollegiate sports," he singled out football because it "grows worse and worse as regards foul and violent play, and the number and gravity of injuries the players suffer."[11]

Football Moves West

Despite its critics on and off the campus, football continued to grow in popularity. During the 1890s, it spread rapidly to colleges throughout the Midwest and the South. Even in the sparsely populated Far West, the game caught on at such small institutions as the state universities of Idaho, Montana, Arizona, Oregon, and Nevada. Two Bay Area schools, Stanford and California, were recognized as the strongest football powers in the distant Far West. Colleges large and small took up the game, in part as a means of identifying with the prestigious Eastern institutions and in part in response to student demands for the creation of teams, apparently resulting from the enthusiasm for the sport generated by the national press. By early in the twentieth century the dominance of the Eastern elite schools was being threatened by powerful "Western" teams, namely the Universities of Michigan, Minnesota, and Chicago.

There is a timeless joke told by college presidents that their primary goal is to build an academic reputation at their school worthy of the stature of the football team. That wry comment's origins undoubtedly rest with the University of Chicago and its ambitious founding president, William Rainey Harper. As a Yale professor of religious studies, Harper had watched Amos Alonzo Stagg perform as a star end for the undefeated Yale 11 of 1888. Harper also came to know Stagg as a deeply religious individual, someone who seriously considered a career in the ministry. Deciding against that option, the pious Stagg became an instructor and coach at the YMCA school in Massachusetts, where students were trained to spread evangelical Christianity through the medium of sports. The handsome, muscular Stagg – named by Camp to his inaugural All-American team – was the epitome of the "muscular Christian."[12] This hard-driving young man became one of the first professional college football coaches, and incredibly he worked continuously at his profession as a head coach until he was 83 years old, and then as an assistant until his mid-90s.

In order to secure Stagg's services away from other schools vying for his services (Pennsylvania, Johns Hopkins), Harper hired his new coach at a salary comparable to or even higher than that offered to the top professors he was luring to his new university (with the help of a heavy infusion of John D. Rockefeller's money). He also granted him an associate professorship with academic tenure before he ever set foot on campus. In making this appointment, Harper showed his fellow presidents the way to circumvent student control of athletics: he created the Department of Physical Culture and Athletics, one of the first of its kind in American higher education, and named Stagg as departmental director. This decision gave the struggling infant discipline of physical education the legitimate academic stature that it had heretofore lacked and simultaneously created a friendly academic environment to which Stagg could recruit top-flight prospective players.

Figure 4.1 Coach Amos Alonzo Stagg addresses his University of Chicago Maroons at practice in 1915. Stagg established the model for the role of the professional coach and enjoyed three decades of winning seasons. University president Robert Hutchins stunned the sports world in 1939 when he dropped football after the program endured 15 consecutive losing seasons. © CORBIS.

Harper believed that a great university required a great football team. "The University of Chicago believes in football," he said with emphasis in 1895. "We shall encourage it here." Writing to his new coach, Harper told Stagg, "I want you to develop teams which we can send around the country and knock out all the colleges," and in a prescient comment about the importance of financial and other incentives necessary to attract to the Chicago campus the quality of athlete necessary to accomplish that objective, he added, "We will give them a palace car and a vacation too."[13]

Although Stagg was theoretically under the control of a student-athletic control board, he operated much like Camp had done as athletic advisor at Yale – he made the decisions and implemented them with little interference from his athletic control board, or even from the president's office. It did not take Stagg long to assemble the powerful football team that his president envisioned. From the beginning, some faculty carped about the dubious academic qualifications of his athletes, many of whom took their courses in the Department of Physical Culture. As

Director of Physical Culture, Stagg determined their eligibility to play football, and he wielded absolute control over his academic department and its budget. Whenever his authority or his program was challenged, he successfully appealed to Harper for support; after Harper's premature death in 1905, Stagg used his many connections with alumni, boosters, and wealthy Chicago businessmen – such as the legendary meat-packer Walter Swift and department store magnate Marshall Field – to beat back repeated faculty efforts that threatened his empire.

It did not take the aggressive, innovative young coach long to demonstrate the public-relations potential that a big-time football program possessed. At the end of his second season, Stagg created a stir throughout the Windy City when he brought in the famed University of Michigan team to play his Maroons on Thanksgiving Day. The "big game" had arrived in Chicago. President Harper seized upon this opportunity to invite many prestigious citizens (and potential donors) to be his guests at the game. A series of receptions and dinners was arranged around the spectacle. "For the last week nothing but football has been discussed at the University on the South Side," one newspaper commented.[14] Michigan, coached by Fielding Yost, a brash football empire-builder in his own right, proved to be the dominant team in the West as it trounced Stagg's inexperienced squad 28–10. But that loss did nothing to dampen football spirit in Chicago; it only served to create increased interest, upon which Stagg capitalized. The following year, Chicago fielded a powerful team that capped a successful season with a much-publicized train trip to the West Coast that included the use of an elegantly appointed palace railroad car (as Harper had promised). The Maroons played Stanford on New Year's Day in Los Angeles, thereby suggesting the potential inherent in the concept of the post-season New Year's bowl game.

Stagg relentlessly built his program. He received a donation of land from Chicago mercantile giant Marshall Field upon which there arose a 25,000-seat stadium of bricks and mortar. President Harper's dream of football putting his young institution on the front pages of Chicago newspapers culminated in 1905. On Thanksgiving Day, two undefeated teams met at Marshall Field before an overflow crowd of 27,000. Fielding Yost's Michigan Wolverines came into the game reputed to be the top team west of the Appalachian Mountains, but Stagg's well-trained team led by shifty All-American quarterback Walter Eckersall, fought them to a standstill, ultimately winning the game 2–0 on a fourth-quarter safety.

For the next two decades, Stagg continued to produce powerful teams, but ultimately his program fell on hard times in the late 1920s. As late as 1924, Stagg seemed to be on top of his game; the Maroons tied Illinois 21–21 in an epic contest that featured the exciting play of Illinois running back George "Red" Grange, the famed "Galloping Ghost" of All-American fame, and captured the Western Conference (Big Ten) championship. Stagg took satisfaction in that attendance records had been set and net ticket revenue had never been higher. The future of football at the University of Chicago seemed incredibly bright. However, his program soon fell into a swift and sure decline. Faculty criticism of the academic quality of his players had intensified, ultimately resulting in the elimination of the academic program in physical culture; several competing college football programs in the

Chicago area (Illinois, Northwestern, Notre Dame) drew away fans, as did the popular new professional team, the Chicago Bears; perhaps most telling was that the faculty and a much-less sympathetic administration imposed more stringent entrance and eligibility requirements that made it increasingly difficult for Stagg to attract a sufficient number of top athletes.[15]

The result was a depressing series of losing seasons that began in 1925. Each year the number of lopsided losses mounted. Stagg recognized that the university's youthful new president, Robert Maynard Hutchins, was unenthusiastic about, perhaps even hostile toward, football. Burdened with nine consecutive losing seasons, and embarrassed by defeats to conference teams he had once dominated, in 1933 the 71-year-old Stagg resigned and moved to the College of the Pacific in Stockton, California, where he coached for 12 more years, producing several winning seasons. In 1939, in the wake of an embarrassing 85–0 pasting by Michigan, the upstart school that had become one of the nation's first football powerhouses stunned the sports world when President Hutchins announced that the University of Chicago was dropping football as an intercollegiate sport.

Football as Spectacle

During the first decade of college football, relatively few spectators bothered to watch the contests, but by 1890 the game had definitely begun to attract larger attendance. This interest soon stimulated the enclosure of fields, the construction of permanent seating, and (naturally) the selling of tickets. By the mid-1890s, attendance at important games between powerful Eastern rivals attracted crowds ranging between 20,000 and 40,000. The reason for this enormous growth in public interest can be attributed primarily to the changing nature of the newspaper business. With literacy rates increasing, profit-minded newspaper owners and editors sought dramatic stories that would sell newspapers and enable them to outpace their competitors. When horse-racing and baseball seasons ended in September, editors lacked much in the way of sports news. Thus they turned to the new sport of college football. To read accounts of the games of this period is to be transported into a romanticized world of heroic players, brilliant coaches, and superhuman accomplishment. Large headlines proclaimed the amazing deeds of bigger-than-life players, and reporters wrote breathtaking accounts of epic gridiron battles. Important games between major rivals were reported on the front pages of the newspapers, complete with pen drawings depicting some of the action. Literature professor Michael Oriard observes in his study of the early years of football that "by the mid-1890s, both the quantity and quality of the football coverage in the daily papers in New York, Philadelphia, and Boston were staggering: front-page, full-page, several-page accounts of the big games, accompanied by sometimes dozens of sensationalized illustrations." Oriard concludes, "The late nineteenth-century daily newspaper 'created' college football to an even greater degree [than television during the 1950s], transforming an extracurricular activity into a national spectacle."[16]

Newspapers also paid considerable attention to the social aspects of the game, reporting on famous persons in attendance, even describing the clothes worn by socially prominent ladies at the exclusive receptions and parties they attended before and after the game. Hard-charging rival newspaper publishers Joseph Pulitzer and William Randolph Hearst created separate sports sections for their New York newspapers, the *World* and the *Journal*, and staffed them with specialized reporters and columnists in a furious drive to expand readership with a brash and sensational form of journalism. The extensive coverage of football stimulated increased newspaper sales, which boosted attendance, which in turn created a demand for even more newspaper coverage. Well before 1900, football had become more than a game played by a few college students. It was now one of the nation's most popular spectator sports. Surrounding it there coalesced a public spectacle and social scene that gave football high public visibility and widespread acceptance.

The ripple effect was staggering. Almost overnight, important traditions were established. Organized student cheering sections were formed, and cleverly scripted cheers rang out along the sidelines. Sometimes students were coerced into participation. Prior to a big game with Indiana in 1901, the *South Bend Tribune* reported that on the Notre Dame campus "rooter preparations are on a strong scale. Every student will be there whether he likes it or not and take part in organized cheering."[17] To be elected a "cheer leader" became a mark of distinction, almost as important as being a star player on the varsity. At some institutions, separate seating sections were established for men and women; on many campuses, only men could be elected to the cheer squad (a tradition that only slowly broke down in the decades following the First World War). Pep bands added to the festivities, and soon each school had its own "fight song"; such widely recognizable songs as "On Wisconsin," "Across the Field" (Ohio State), "Hail to the Victors" (Michigan), and "The Notre Dame Victory March," are among many such memorable pep tunes written during football's formative years.

The tradition of homecoming was also established during this period. Fearing a slender turnout for the big game against arch rival Kansas University scheduled in the small college town of Columbia, coach C. L. Brewer of the University of Missouri in 1911 issued an urgent public invitation to all alumni to "come back home, Tigers" to help cheer on his team against the Jayhawks. Much to his surprise, a record-setting overflow crowd of 10,000 showed up to watch a hard-fought 3–3 tie game. Shortly thereafter, the Missouri alumni director reported on the benefits of the event to a convention of his peers, and within a few years homecoming had become a signal autumn event on campuses across the country. Elaborate week-long "homecoming" events were held, including parades, dances, banquets, receptions, song-fests, fraternity and sorority parties, decorated dormitories, and bonfire rallies. All of these events were capped off with the Saturday afternoon football game. Campus leaders had discovered that the football homecoming week provided an effective way to maintain sentimental connections between alumni and their alma maters.[18] It also helped if the home team won the homecoming game.

Football thus became much more than a game, providing an important connection between students, alumni, community leaders, and the university. For prominent businessmen and politicians, it was considered advantageous to become recognized as a prominent "booster" of the local university team (no matter if one was an alumnus or not), a supporter who contributed generously to the athletic fund and bought a block of tickets to distribute to business or political associates. For their wives, it was important to be seen at games and to host pre- and post-game social events. For students, it provided an exciting diversion from studies and a focal point for many student social events.

Other parts of the unfolding spectacle naturally fell into place. For example, there was the simple matter of the color of uniforms that would distinguish one team from another. Student bodies held contests to select school colors for team uniforms, nearly all of which have remained unchanged to the present day. Similarly, students adopted various mascots or nicknames by which their team would be known. Ferocious animals were among the most popular (the Tigers of Missouri, Louisiana State, and Princeton; the Bulldogs of Georgia, Yale, and Mississippi State; the Wildcats of Kentucky, Northwestern, and Arizona; the Bears of Maine, Baylor, and California). Other schools sought to establish an identity with their state's heritage (the Tennessee Volunteers; the Ohio State Buckeyes; the Virginia Cavaliers; the Tar Heels of North Carolina; the Indiana Hoosiers; the Texas Longhorns; the Sooners of Oklahoma; the Rebels of Ole Miss; the Mountaineers of West Virginia; the Florida Gators). Less-imaginative team monikers were derived from school colors: The Syracuse Orangemen, Alabama's Crimson Tide, the Green Wave of Tulane, and the Crimson of Harvard.

Conversely, some mascots were simply puzzling or even humorous: the Ephs of Williams College named after its founder Ephraim Williams; the Sage Brushers and/or Sage Hens of Nevada (changed to a more ferocious Wolf Pack by a student vote in 1921, although no wolves lived in the desert state); the Blue Hens of Delaware; the Golden Gophers of Minnesota; the Bug Eaters of the University of Nebraska (later renamed Cornhuskers in a nod to the state's dominant agricultural economy). Several land grant institutions with prominent agricultural colleges naturally became the Aggies (Texas A&M, New Mexico State, Oklahoma State College, University of California, Davis). As a reflection of the widely accepted racial stereotypes popular at the time, many student bodies opted for scalp-taking Native Americans: Miami (Ohio) Redskins, Fighting Illini of Illinois, Fighting Sioux of North Dakota, Running Utes of Utah, Marquette Warriors, St Johns Redmen, and more simply, the Stanford Indians. Other racial or ethnic stereotypes also were employed, the most famous being the Fighting Irish of Notre Dame, a name that only gained acceptance during the 1920s after an often-critical press corps had conjured up many different names, some of them reflecting searing anti-Catholic prejudice.[19] During the 1990s, these racial images produced significant backlash and many were changed, often over the strenuous opposition of tradition-bound alumni. More benign, politically correct names were now in vogue – Miami became the Redhawks, St Johns the Red Storm, and Stanford the Cardinal (the color not the bird) with a generic tree as its curious environmentally sensitive mascot. The decision at Illinois to keep the "Fighting Illini" moniker reached epic emotional proportions in 2003 as a band of reformist students battled unsuccessfully with determined tradition-bound alumni over "Chief Illiniwek," brought to life by a white male student dressed in stereotypical Native American garb who did war dances at midfield before games. In 2005, the NCAA responded to critics and informed 21 member institutions with various North American related mascots believed to be insensitive that they would not be permitted to participate in future post-season play unless they changed their traditional mascot symbols, most of which had been in place for over a century.

Football in Crisis

In 1884, a New York reporter included this vivid description of the Yale–Princeton game staged at the Polo Grounds: "The elevens hurl themselves together and build themselves in kicking, writhing heaps." Spectators cheered as they witnessed

> a general vision of threatening attitudes, fists shaken before noses, dartings hither and thither, throttling, wrestling and the pitching of individuals headlong to earth. . . . They saw real fighting, savage blows that drew blood, and falls that seemed as if they must crack all the bones and drive the life from those who sustained them.

Finally, there "came a crush about midway of the field. All the maddened giants of both teams were in it, and they lay there heaped, choking, kicking, gouging and howling."[20]

Given the level of violence that characterized early play, it is surprising that football managed to survive as a college sport. Clearly, the socializing forces described above helped the game survive a major crisis that threatened its very existence when the matter became a national issue in 1905–06. As the game became increasingly popular among students and alumni during the final decade of the nineteenth century, it simultaneously attracted an increasing number of critics. Some wanted the game abolished, but the majority were content to demand widespread reforms on two fronts: first, changing (and enforcing) the rules to eliminate the dangerous mass momentum style of play, and, second, establishing rigorous controls on the process of player recruitment and the assurance that only bona fide students took part.

The most prominent person to step forward was the distinguished president of Harvard, Charles Eliot. He was both deeply concerned about the violent nature of football and fearful that the heavy emphasis upon victory threatened the integrity of higher education. In his crusade to abolish the game, Eliot found many allies among his own faculty and elsewhere, but he was ultimately thwarted by a combination of student support for the football program and pressures from prominent alumni and the general public. Twice between 1886 and 1906, the Harvard faculty succeeded in abolishing the sport for single seasons, but the game's popularity eventually overcame on-campus opposition. One of the primary reasons Harvard eventually opted for reform and not abolition was that two of its major competitors, Yale and Princeton, continued to encourage the game's development and in so doing attracted to themselves considerable public support and the dedicated loyalty of wealthy contributors.

At Princeton, a popular political science professor and faculty leader, soon to become president of the university, used his considerable prestige on campus to promote the game. A devout Presbyterian who enthusiastically embraced the doctrines of muscular Christianity, Professor Woodrow Wilson firmly believed that the game built character by teaching players important lessons about discipline, teamwork, perseverance, and dealing with adversity and pressure. In a telling comment about the repeated failure of Harvard to defeat Yale or Princeton, he once caustically observed that Harvard had instituted an academic program built around elective courses, which he said implied a lack of rigor, organization, and discipline – particular ingredients he believed important to a successful football program. As Princeton's president between 1902 and 1910, Wilson was known upon occasion to leap out of the stands to lead cheers during games; as one historian has written of the man who would become President of the United States, "Wilson glorified victory, lambasted those who failed to support athletics, criticized the team's failures, and carped about victorious rivals."[21]

Eliot, who built Harvard into a major academic powerhouse during his long tenure as president between 1875 and 1909, was dedicated to the premise that the university was a place where academic values must be paramount. In his drive to make Harvard into the nation's preeminent private institution, he repeatedly confronted the negative influence of football, whose values he believed were a denial of all that his academic reform agenda sought to accomplish. In a highly publicized report released in late 1894, Eliot condemned the concept of an institution of higher learning becoming engaged in entertaining the public. "The evils of the intercollegiate sports . . . continue without real redress and diminution," he said.

> In particular the game of football grows worse and worse as regards foul and violent play, and the number and gravity of injuries which the players suffer. It has become perfectly clear that the game as now played is unfit for college use. . . . The state of mind of the spectators at a hard-fought football match at Springfield, New York, or Philadelphia cannot but suggest the query how far these assemblages differ at heart from the throngs which enjoy the prize-fight, cock-fight, or bull-fight, or which in other centuries delighted in the sports of the Roman arena.[22]

Eliot's perspective was that of an academic elitist who viewed athletics through a prism that emphasized amateurism, fair play, sportsmanship, and character building. That football teams (and their professional "coaches") routinely sought dubious ways to win games – relying as he said upon "tricks, surprises and habitual violation of the rules" – indicated to him that the game did not build good character but actually produced the opposite effect. Noting that some reformers wanted to increase the number of officials on the field from the current one or two, he sniffed:

It is often said that by employing more men to watch the players, with authority to punish instantly infractions of the rules, foul and vicious playing could be stopped. The sufficient answer to this suggestion is that a game which needs to be so watched is not fit for genuine sportsmen.

And in a comment about the integrity or competence of game officials that would routinely resonate throughout the years to come, Eliot noted that "experience indicates that it would be hard to find trustworthy watchers."[23] Ultimately, Eliot came to focus his critique upon what he perceived to be an excessive emphasis upon winning at all costs. Not only did football present a misleading impression to the public about the nature of university life, it also diverted students from their primary role as scholars.[24]

Although many faculty emphasized the baleful impact of the game upon the academic mission, the general public focused upon the media reports detailing serious injuries and the occasional death. Eliot was of course appalled as well, especially when they occurred even when the rules were enforced:

The rules of the game are at present such as to cause inevitably a large number of broken bones, sprains, and wrenches, even during trial or practice games played legitimately, and they also permit those who play with reckless violence or with shrewd violations of the rules to gain thereby great advantages.[25]

This is not to say that Eliot was opposed to all sports. He supported the playing of games for their own sake in a manner that would enhance the academic atmosphere of the Harvard campus – for fun, physical health, and the joy of participation. Reflective of a widespread perception of the time, Eliot also believed that healthy exercise and sports competition offered the college man "a new and effective motive for resisting all sins which weaken or corrupt the body" – that is, premarital sex.[26]

President Eliot's reform efforts in 1894 failed to produce tangible results, but public discussion of the issues he raised grew in intensity during the next decade. Despite mounting criticism, football continued to grow in popularity, its proponents greatly outnumbering the opponents. University administrators, taking due note of the gate receipts being collected by student sponsors and aware of the public-relations benefits that could accrue in terms of student recruitment, alumni relations, and fund raising, began to take over control of the programs, hiring professional coaches, creating new departments of athletics, inserting physical education courses into the curriculum to help ease the academic burden of players, and making the football season an important aspect of campus social life.

In 1905, the long-simmering debate over rough play came to a head. That year three college players and 18 high-school or sandlot players died in highly publicized football accidents, and 167 collegians suffered serious injuries. A leading University of Chicago professor of divinity, Shailer Mathews, summarized the criticism as well as any when he denounced the game as "a social obsession – a boy-killing, education-prostituting, gladiatorial sport."[27] Despite a decade of mounting criticism, everyone recognized that the game had changed very little. It remained as violent as ever since the notorious heyday of the flying wedge. It was not without significance that one of the players who sustained a painful injury that season was the son of the President of the United States, Theodore Roosevelt Jr. "Teedie," who at 5' 7" and less than 150 pounds played on the line for the Harvard junior varsity, received a severely broken nose during a hard-fought game with Yale that required reconstructive surgery. Spectators reported that the Blues concentrated their attack on the president's son, who bravely held his ground; some said the Bulldogs massed their attack at Teedie because of his famous father, while others simply noted that he was the smallest man on the Harvard line.[28]

Whatever, this particular shattered nose helped focus the President's attention on the issue of rough play. The game of football – with its rigorous physical and psychological demands – naturally appealed to this rambunctious president who often spoke glowingly of those brave men who chose to demonstrate their mettle in the "arena." What seems to have bothered Roosevelt most about the state of the game were persistent reports of unsportsmanlike play by "muckers." The President never had anything but praise for the rugged nature of the game; his concern was that it be properly played by gentlemen and good sports, and that it be played by the rules.[29]

Roosevelt had little argument with the style of hard-hitting line play championed by his friend Walter Camp. His political conversations and correspondence were often punctuated with comments about "hitting the line hard" on behalf of a particular issue. Although it was widely believed that Roosevelt threatened to abolish the game if substantive reform did not occur, there is no evidence to support that contention. He had, in fact, no direct authority to force its abolition. What he did was to capitalize on public concerns and called a conference at the White House on October 9, 1905, to which he invited representatives from three major football schools – Harvard, Yale, and Princeton. The coaches present agreed to work to see that the rules against illegal play were enforced and expressed interest in pursuing some limited rule changes. Roosevelt declared himself satisfied and considered the matter closed. At no time did Roosevelt suggest that he wanted the game abolished; in fact, his efforts seem primarily motivated by his concern that reformers would succeed in abolishing the game.[30]

The following year, the major football schools created the Inter-Collegiate Athletic Association (ICAA), the name changed in 1910 to the National Collegiate Athletic Association (NCAA), and charged it specifically with revamping the rules to greatly reduce mass momentum play. Many coaches, especially those in the Midwest, were anxious to create a more exciting brand of football in order to attract more spectators. They advocated a more "open" game, that is the use of offensive plays other than the power run into the middle of the line. The result was that the new rule book made it illegal for teammates to push or pull the ball carrier through the defense, required the offense to begin each play with a minimum of seven men on the line of scrimmage (to eliminate linemen from lining up several yards behind the line of scrimmage and gaining momentum before crashing into a defensive player), and eliminated the use of interlocking of arms by blockers.

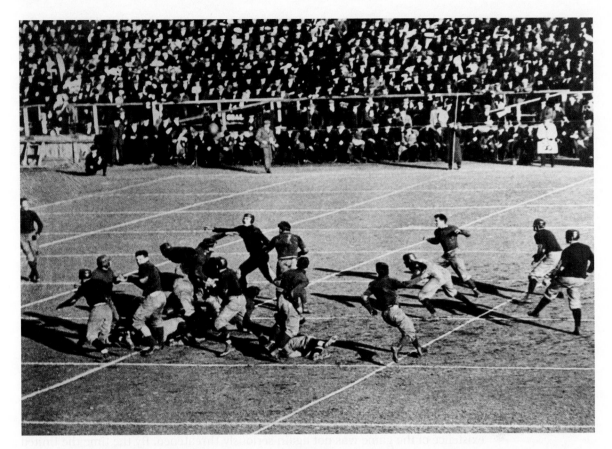

Figure 4.2 Harvard and Yale play on the "gridiron" marked by lime about 1910. For many years forward passes had to be thrown downfield within the narrow vertical lines. Note that only a few players have elected to wear helmets, use of which was widely derided at the times by the more "manly" players. © Oscar White/CORBIS.

To encourage the use of running plays around the end of the line in the open field, they lengthened the distance required to make a first down from five to ten yards. Most significantly, the committee introduced the forward pass as a means of reducing the emphasis upon mass momentum play at the line of scrimmage. Two years later, as but another means of encouraging the forward pass, the committee required that the ball be "tightly inflated" and changed its shape to make it more elongated so it could be thrown further and with greater accuracy. The committee also outlawed one of the major sources of excessive violence: the pushing or pulling of a ball carrier through the line by teammates. The ball carrier would now have to rely upon his teammates' skill as blockers.[31]

A new and exciting era was at hand. The emphasis of the game was now moving toward an emphasis upon speed, deception, timing, and well-designed, well-executed plays designed to make long yardage; the traditional line plunge, emphasis upon brute strength, and the tactics of the crude brawler were substantially diminished, although definitely not eliminated. Changes in the rules continued during the nineteen teens: the length of the field was established at 100 yards, with 10-yard end zones added (to encourage passes into touchdown territory), the value of a touchdown was increased to six points, and the one-point extra-point kick after a touchdown was introduced. Protective head gear and shoulder padding were added to team uniforms, and officiating became more standardized with major conferences requiring training, rules testing, and evaluation of the performance of game officials.

A most conservative lot, the coaches approached the new rules gingerly. They were reluctant to abandon time-tested techniques, but innovative younger coaches forced their hand, making their strategies obsolete with new formations and strategies. The impact of the new rules was forcefully made clear in 1913, when the obscure University of Notre Dame from South Bend, Indiana, traveled east to stun the football world when it upset a powerful Army team 35–13 by using the forward pass combination of quarterback Gus Dorias and end Knute Rockne to befuddle the Cadets. These two athletes had spent the previous summer working at Cedar Point resort along Lake Erie and had perfected their pass-and-catch timing on the wide expanse of sandy beach. In the wake of this startling upset, coaches began to incorporate the forward pass into their offenses, and fans responded enthusiastically. The potentials of a completed forward pass or a long run around end for a long gain produced a new level of excitement at games: touchdowns could be made on any play from any place on the field. Stories of entire games spent with both teams slogging away in the middle of the line became a thing of the past.

Despite the rules changes, the game remained a game of controlled violence. But the crisis was over. When eight college players died in 1909, no concerted effort to abolish football emerged. Between 1910 and 1950, more than five hundred high school and college players died from injuries sustained playing football, but the existence of the game was not again seriously threatened. By the time the United States entered the Great War in 1917, football was firmly entrenched on the campuses of American colleges. A few Western schools that had abandoned football for rugby under the misconception that it was a less dangerous game (Stanford, California, Oregon, Nevada) reinstated football. Within little more than a quarter-century, an indigenous American game that had great spectator appeal had become an important part of the popular culture. The stage was thus set for the rapid growth of the game during the 1920s when big-time college football became the focus of enormous public interest and spectator enthusiasm.

5 Sports and the Emergence of Modern America 1865–1920

Organized sports became an increasingly important part of American life during the late nineteenth century. Urban living created a need for new forms of physical exercise, and spectator sports provided new forms of public entertainment. Employers found in sports a subtle means of controlling worker behavior, and politicians and social workers believed organized play a useful tool to help "Americanize" immigrant children. Religious leaders encouraged sports that provided wholesome outlets for unmarried urban males, and a powerful evangelical movement called Muscular Christianity accelerated the acceptance of sports. Spectator sports became an important part of the urban popular culture, and heavy coverage of baseball, boxing, and football by newspapers and magazines fanned that interest. Affluent urbanites were attracted to new private clubs that offered gymnasiums and swimming pools, as well as to country clubs built on the urban fringe that offered golf, tennis, swimming, and equestrian activities.

Between 1860 and 1920, the United States embraced the modern age. Driven by heavy immigration from Europe and Asia, the population increased from 31 million to 120 million. Major technological advances in manufacturing and transportation contributed to the spectacular growth of cities. By 1920, over 51 percent of the American people lived in urban areas. On the farm, major advances in mechanization as well as breakthroughs in crop and animal science meant that the average farmer produced 15 times the amount of food or fiber in 1920 than his predecessor did 50 years earlier. This agricultural revolution drove marginal farmers off the land and into the towns and cities in search of new forms of employment. Those who remained on the land found themselves inextricably caught up in a complex and ruthless economic system of distant banks, commodities exchanges, foreign competition, and national railroad systems. America had left its agrarian past behind and had entered the modern age. As a consequence of this reality, American sports similarly took on a distinctly modern hue.

Boxing Enters the Mainstream

Prizefighting fell into sharp decline in the years after the Civil War because public officials felt the heat of Victorian moralists. Offended by the brutality of the blood sport, and concerned about its impact upon social values because of its image of immigrant and lower-class influences, excessive drinking, disorderly behavior, and gambling, these guardians of public morality insisted upon the enforcement of anti-prizefighting laws. By the 1870s, however, in Eastern cities, exclusive men's athletic clubs provided instruction in "the manly art of self-defense." These clubs scored favorable publicity when they conducted "public exhibitions" under the new rules announced in 1865 by the Marquis of Queensberry, which featured padded gloves, three-minute rounds, 10-second knockouts, a limit upon rounds, and the abolition of wrestling, hitting below the belt, holding, and gouging. Boxing began to make a comeback under the guise of a "scientific" exhibition rather than a brutal display of atavistic mayhem.

The popularity of prizefighting received a major boost when the *National Police Gazette* began to publicize the illegal sport. In 1877, the struggling weekly was taken over by a young immigrant from Ireland, Richard Kyle Fox. He was bright and brash and built circulation by featuring stories that emphasized sex and sin. Fox loved the bizarre and lurid, and so did his rapidly expanding national male readership. Printed on garish pink newsprint, the *National Police Gazette* was often called "the Bible of the Barber Shop." At a time before photographs could be reproduced in newspapers, he published many a woodcut portraying sensuous women. *The National Police Gazette* became ubiquitous, seen everywhere that men gathered – saloons, hotel lobbies, pool halls, tobacco shops, gambling dens, barber shops. Fox turned the weekly into one of the great financial success stories of the publications industry. The *Gazette* might have set a new low for racism, nativism, and anti-Semitism, but it provided a model for circulation-building for such up-and-coming newspaper magnates as William Randolph Hearst and Joseph Pulitzer.[1]

Along with sleazy stories about murders, sex crimes, bank robberies, and lynchings, Fox relentlessly promoted prizefighting. In part, Fox took up the cause because he enjoyed bedeviling ministers and social reformers, but most important he recognized that heavy coverage of "the manly art" would increase readership among males. In 1880, he learned its potential when the *Gazette*'s coverage of the Joe Goss–Paddy Ryan fight pushed circulation up from 150,000 to 400,000. Fox became not merely a reporter of boxing news, but a maker of the news he reported. He created six weight classifications and put up handsome championship belts for each. He sponsored bouts, negotiated with fighters and their managers, challenged anti-boxing laws in the courts, and imported pugilistic talent from Europe. His reporters cranked out an endless stream of enthusiastic accounts of major prizefights and the men who took part in them. Some of the best woodcut images that Fox printed were his artists' impressions of action in the ring.

Fox anticipated the key role that journalism and promotion would play in molding the future of American sports. His crusade on behalf of boxing was intricately intertwined with the career of the "Boston Strong Boy," John L. Sullivan. Throughout the 1880s, Fox carried on a controversial feud with the popular fighter, regularly belittling his pugilistic ability and futilely promoting one unsuccessful challenger after another who might topple the popular champion. Although Fox feigned personal animosity toward Sullivan, he knew that the public quarrel sold newspapers. Fox's petulance helped create America's first sports "star."

Legend has it that the Fox–Sullivan feud began one spring evening in 1881 in Harry Hill's Saloon, a popular New York City watering hole for the sporting crowd. As Fox took his seat, he noticed a boisterous group at a nearby table where the up-and-coming Irish heavyweight and well-known binge drinker John L. Sullivan was surrounded by a fawning entourage and a cluster of empty bottles. Fox reportedly said to the waiter, "Tell Sullivan to come over here. I want to talk to him." Well into his cups, Sullivan loudly retorted so everyone in the club could hear, "You tell Fox, that if he wants to see me he can goddamn well come over to my table." Angered by this public embarrassment, Fox spent the next decade attempting to teach the ill-mannered Bostonian a lesson in propriety by finding someone who could defeat him in the ring.[2]

Fox may have been truly offended by Sullivan's boorish behavior that night at Harry Hill's Saloon, but he also saw in the charismatic Irish brawler an intriguing foe made in heaven. Thus just a month after the confrontation at the saloon, he sent reporters to cover the championship fight between Sullivan and a barrel-chested longshoreman by the name of John Flood. The fight was held on a barge floating in the Hudson River to avoid the authorities. Much to Fox's dismay, Sullivan easily dispatched his opponent. Fox was soon promoting a new challenger in the person of Paddy Ryan. He posted a $2,500 purse on Ryan's behalf and then trumpeted the challenger's skills to his readers. Fox published on-site reporting for weeks from training camps. No prizefight had previously received such build-up. The fight was scheduled for New Orleans but was moved to Mississippi City, Mississippi, when Louisiana authorities threatened to arrest the participants. The *Gazette* even published a supplement on the fight, calling it the "Battle of the Giants," with Ryan being proclaimed (prematurely as it turned out) "Champion of America."[3]

Sullivan easily defeated Ryan, requiring fewer than 11 minutes before his "sledgehammer smashes" toppled the challenger. The best Fox's writers could say was that Ryan demonstrated "vigor and gameness." In the ninth round, Sullivan knocked Ryan senseless. "When Sullivan struck me," a woeful Paddy later said, "I thought that a telephone pole had been shoved against me endways." Disappointed, perhaps, but undaunted, Fox recognized that the man he despised was nonetheless his meal ticket. Fox thereupon put up $5,000 for a rematch with Ryan in 1885 (which produced a similar result). Fox had even commissioned a glittering diamond-studded championship belt for the winner, but Sullivan dismissed it as merely "a dog collar," and departed on an eight-month carnival tour during which

Figure 5.1 The popular John L. Sullivan squares off with an unknown opponent, circa 1890, in a bareknuckle bout held outdoors in a crudely constructed "ring." This makeshift venue was typical during an era when prizefighting was illegal throughout much of the United States. © CORBIS.

he fought any local challenger willing to take his chances for a $1,000 prize if he lasted four rounds against the champion. Few did.[4]

Ever determined to unseat the man now known as "The Great John L.," Fox came up with yet another challenger. Jake Kilrain had defeated several prominent fighters and seemed to be Fox's man. When Sullivan refused to agree to a match, Fox proclaimed that Sullivan had forfeited his crown and that Kilrain was the new champion. Sullivan's Boston fans retaliated by raising $10,000 to purchase an enormous gold studded championship belt that contained 397 small diamonds and images of Sullivan, an American Bald Eagle, and an Irish harp. No dog collar this garish belt! Sullivan took off for a six-month exhibition tour of Europe, and upon his return, went on a prolonged drinking and eating binge that saw him balloon up from his trim 195-pound fighting weight to 240 pounds of flab. His health deteriorated, and the *National Police Gazette* breathlessly reported that Sullivan was at death's door while simultaneously goading him with barbs that he was using his alcohol-induced illness to avoid Kilrain. Finally, Sullivan agreed to the fight, which was set for July 8, 1889, giving Sullivan six months to get back into fighting shape. For months, Fox's reporters informed readers of the "advance dope" from the training camps, much of which focused upon Sullivan's poor conditioning, and Kilrain's apparent strength and endurance.[5]

The nation's attention was glued to the upcoming confrontation as the melodrama unfolded in comic proportions. Louisiana authorities proclaimed their intention to arrest and prosecute the fighters and promoters, and the state police of Alabama, Mississippi, Louisiana, and Texas went on alert as rumors spread that the fight would take place in those states. For two months, the promoters sold tickets even though they did not know where the fight would be held. On the day before the scheduled fight, Mississippi sawmill operator Charles Rich had a crew assemble a makeshift wooden grandstand of newly cut pine in a clearing on his heavily wooded 30,000-acre spread near the town of Richburg. The fight promoters had three chartered trains at the ready, and when they gave the word ticket-holders piled aboard and headed for parts unknown.

The original plan was for the fight to occur shortly after dawn, to avoid the oppressive heat and humidity, but the start was delayed to permit all of the fans to get to their places on the freshly cut boards, which were now ominously oozing pitch in the hot Mississippi sun. By fight time, the temperature neared 100 degrees. A future mayor of New Orleans, John Fitzpatrick, served as referee, and precisely at 10:13 a.m. drew a line in the dirt and called the fighters to scratch. What would be the last bare-knuckle championship fight thus commenced. It proved to be an epic struggle. Within the first 15 seconds, Kilrain tossed Sullivan to the ground; end of round 1. It soon became evident that Kilrain's strategy was to take advantage of the perception that Sullivan had not recovered from his illness by wearing him down in the hot sun that poured down on the makeshift ring. Round 4, which lasted 15 minutes, however, revealed that it was Kilrain who was not in the best of condition as he absorbed a barrage of powerful blows. It became evident that Kilrain was outmatched, but he bravely persevered despite absorbing a terrific pounding, somehow managing to prevent Sullivan from landing a knockout blow with his famous right hand. By Round 30, Kilrain had to be carried back to his corner after each round and pushed out to the scratch line when Fitzpatrick shouted "time." During the 30-second intervals between rounds, Sullivan gulped down copious amounts of whiskey, which apparently produced a violent vomiting spell in the midst of round 44 that would become the subject of considerable press commentary. By round 60, Sullivan's eyes were nearly swollen shut, but an exhausted Kilrain could barely stand. Both men were bloodied, their ribs red and swollen, their faces splotched with ugly bruises, their skin bright red from the blistering sun. Finally, the carnage ended after round 75, during which Sullivan pounded Kilrain senseless with a flurry of powerful blows. Kilrain's manager tossed a sponge into the ring signaling defeat. The brutal contest had lasted two hours and 16 minutes.[6]

Controversy surrounding this historic match would remain in the nation's newspapers for more than a year. Both fighters were arrested on the East Coast and extradited to Mississippi to stand trial. Separate trials in the small town of Purvis led to convictions, substantial fines, and jail sentences (one year for Sullivan, two months for Kilrain). But the Mississippi justice system proved lenient. For one thing, several of the jurors had attended the fight, public sentiment supported the two fighters, and the judge seemed star struck in the presence of the famous

John L. Convoluted legal reasoning from the bench made a mockery of Mississippi's anti-prizefighting statute, and upon appeal both defendants evaded jail time. The epic battle between two men who slugged it out for more than two long hours in the midst of a steamy Southern summer's day became an instant legend that grew ever larger with the passage of time. It was also the last bare-knuckle championship fight. A new age of "scientific" boxing was at hand, complete with padded gloves and rules according to the Marquis of Queensberry. Consequently, over the next three decades, prizefighting moved into the mainstream of American society, becoming recognized as merely another form of entertainment. It was not unusual for crowds at ringside to include individuals representative of the best of American society, men in their tuxedos, their lady friends in fancy gowns.[7]

After escaping the clutches of the Mississippi legal system, Sullivan lost interest in fighting and did not defend his crown for three years. He spent time on the stage, touring the United States and Australia as the male lead in the melodrama *Honest Hearts and Willing Hands*, and for a time flirted with the idea of running for Congress. He also continued his life-long love affair with alcohol, and his body bloated to well over 250 pounds. In 1892, at age 34 and faced with financial problems, Sullivan returned to the ring once more to defend his crown for a big payday. He did so in his typical flamboyant style by issuing a national challenge to anyone (excluding African Americans he was quick to make clear) willing to put up a $10,000 side bet and fight for a winner-takes-all purse of $50,000 offered by New Orleans promoters eager to take advantage of a new city ordinance permitting boxing under the Marquis of Queensberry rules.[8]

Sullivan's last title defense produced the transition from one era to another. It was fought under bright electric lights in a public arena before an audience of 10,000 of New Orleans' leading citizens. It was the first gloved championship bout. The man who challenged Sullivan was a young San Franciscan, "Gentleman Jim" Corbett, who had defeated Jake Kilrain in 1890. Sullivan trained sporadically for the bout and continued his heavy drinking. Meanwhile, Corbett reduced his smoking to just two cigars a day while getting himself into fighting trim. Following months of pre-fight hype, the actual bout was anticlimactic, as the 26-year-old Corbett systematically took apart the aging champion. In round 3 he broke Sullivan's nose with a solid left jab, blood spurting spectacularly across the ring. By round 10, Sullivan was barely able to defend himself as Corbett toyed with his hapless opponent. Finally, in round 20, Gentleman Jim decided it was time to end the one-sided contest and he caught John L. with a vicious right cross. Sullivan fell to the canvas "like an ox," where the referee counted him out as the crowd roared its approval. The next day, Sullivan met the press, suffering from a broken nose, a closed eye, and badly swollen lips and tongue. His black and blue face was laced with ugly stitches. He also suffered from a severe hangover, the result of a long night of drinking to console himself on the loss of his crown.[9]

Thus boxing entered a new era. The defeat ended Sullivan's professional boxing career, and he headed back to the vaudeville stage. Clearly the most popular sports star of the nineteenth century, he remained a national icon until felled by a heart attack in 1918. His boxing career had spanned two distinct eras. The ability of the

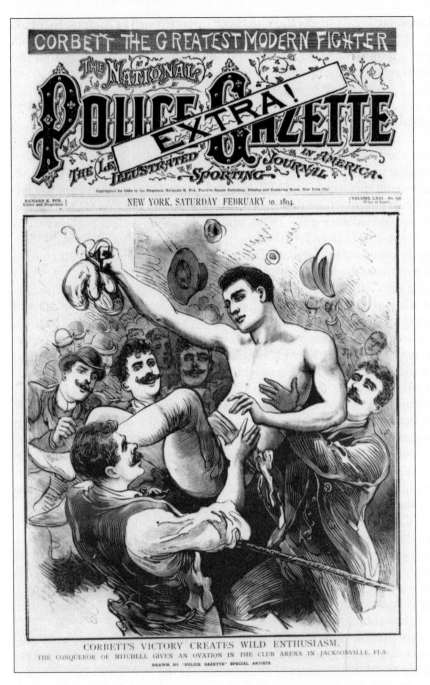

Figure 5.2 "Gentleman Jim" Corbett is featured on the cover of the nation's leading men's magazine after a knockout victory over Charley Mitchell in Jacksonville, Florida, in 1894. © Bettmann/CORBIS.

national media to create sports stars had been demonstrated by Richard Kyle Fox. When Fox died in 1922, the headline atop his lengthy obituary in the *New York Times* identified him as a "Patron of Sports," although the text conceded that "he knew nothing of any game or sport, except boxing."[10]

Sports and Social Class

Well before the Civil War, men from the upper strata of New York City society held memberships in exclusive "athletic clubs" that provided good food and drink, where they could play cards and billiards, and engage like-minded men in conversation while puffing on an expensive cigar. The prominent Union Club in New York City was opened during the 1830s, and by the 1850s similar exclusive clubs had been established in most large Northern and Midwestern cities. By the 1850s, a growing awareness of the importance of exercise prompted these private clubs to construct gymnasiums, running tracks, and swimming pools.[11]

Following the Civil War, the number of clubs grew, attracting young and middle-aged men who were building business and professional careers. In the vanguard of this movement was the New York Athletic Club (NYAC), created in 1868 by three young businessmen initially to provide a gymnasium where members could exercise. Its major contributions were in track and field, and over the years the club provided national leadership in standardizing weights and distances for various events, established an official record book, and created a program to train certified officials. In 1882, William Travers was elected president with a clear mandate to build a suitably luxurious facility, and in 1885 the club opened an elaborate structure in midtown New York that housed a rifle range, an indoor swimming pool, gymnasium, bowling alley, and billiard tables, along with commodious dining and drinking facilities. In 1888, the NYAC acquired land outside of the city, where it built a boathouse, an outdoor running track, and tennis courts. Membership in the NYAC became a tangible sign that a man had arrived at a high level of New York society.[12]

The NYAC was but one of several such clubs that operated in New York City, and across the country, similar clubs were established. By the late nineteenth century, nearly every American city of 100,000 or more residents boasted of at least one athletic club that offered members social exclusivity along with athletic facilities. With a few exceptions, however, the athletic club movement came a cropper during the economic hard times of the 1890s, and the numbers and influence they had within their communities tapered off substantially.

Before most of these clubs fell into decline, however, they championed a philosophy of sports that would greatly influence the future direction of American sports by embracing the British concept of amateurism. As the New York clubs engaged rival clubs in athletic competitions, the more aggressive clubs began to admit members whose social standing and income level was suspect but whose athletic talents exceptional. Others found it expedient simply to pay outstanding performers to represent them in competitions, or they granted them free memberships. These efforts meant that young men of working-class status were often representing exclusive social clubs in their track-and-field competitions. This development naturally came into conflict with sentiment within the membership to foster social exclusivity. This led to the adoption, at least in principle, of the British concept of amateurism. This ideal emphasized the principle that the true sportsman was one who participated in sports for the sheer joy of the competition, who never cheated or sought unfair advantage over an opponent, and who even played the game without much attention to physical training or practice. The best sportsmen were those who could win without much exertion, and who looked upon athletics as but one means of preparing for a professional career. Only men of lower-class standing would consider playing for pay. Walter Camp, the football pioneer at Yale, put it bluntly: "You don't want your boy 'hired' by anyone. If he plays, he plays for victory, not for money. . . . And he can look you in the eye as a gentleman should."[13] In 1876, the NYAC adopted a policy restricting its track meets to "any person who has never competed . . . for public or admission money, or with professionals for a prize . . . nor has at any period in his life taught or assisted in the pursuit of athletic exercises as a means of livelihood."[14]

Three years later, several athletic clubs joined together to form the National Association of Amateur Athletics of America (commonly referred to as the N4A), which adopted the NYAC amateur policy almost verbatim. But rancor and controversy revolving around various interpretations of the amateur code continued, and in protest the NYAC resigned its membership in N4A in 1886 and founded the Amateur Athletic Union. This organization would exert enormous influence over the domain of American track and field competition until well after the Second World War. Until the 1970s, the NYAC's annual indoor track meet held at Madison Square Garden was considered the premier event of its kind in the country. The long-term impact of the adoption of the amateur code was to restrict opportunities for minority and lower-class youth to participate in many sporting events. The amateur concept thus served to foster the exclusivity impulse endemic in the men's athletic club movement.

In reality, seldom did the NYAC or other clubs live up to their commitment to the code of amateurism. Too many members were hard-driving businessmen who lacked the detached perspective and social self-assuredness of the hereditary British elite. Few had inherited their wealth but rather had obtained it in the competitive environment of American capitalism. They tended to apply the same "win at any cost" attitude toward sports as they did in the roughneck business environment in which they operated. Nonetheless, they invoked the amateur concept when it suited their needs, and thus amateurism became deeply imbedded in the fabric of American sports. It would play an enormous role in how American sports evolved during the twentieth century. In particular, the amateur code dominated the leadership of the American Olympic Committee, and colleges and universities employed it as a means of avoiding paying athletes to perform; the "student-athlete" myth – a clever spin-off of the amateur code – underpinned the development of intercollegiate athletics in the United States and became the cornerstone upon which a multibillion dollar enterprise was created in which the athletes who did the work did not receive compensation.

Paralleling the urban men's clubs was the development of the suburban private country club, designed to provide affluent families with social separation from the middle and working classes as they pursued new sporting interests in tennis and golf. The first clear example of the new "country club" was the Myopia Club, which was established in the 1870s, built on a 200-acre private estate eight miles north of Boston. A clubhouse was built to provide card and billiard rooms, dining facilities, and sleeping quarters; several lawn tennis courts were constructed, along with a baseball field; but the primary interest of members was horseback riding and foxhunting. The Myopia Club set the pattern for future developments by providing a wide range of activities in a bucolic setting. However, commuting by train from Boston was inconvenient, so several members, having resettled in the elite suburb of Brookline on the west edge of Boston, organized a new country club at Clyde Park in Brookline. The prospectus released by founder J. Murray Forbes in 1882 stated that the Brookline Club's "general idea is to have a comfortable clubhouse for the use of members with their families, a simple restaurant, bed-rooms, bowling-alley, lawn tennis grounds, etc." In addition, his statement suggested that the intent was "to have race-meetings and, occasionally, music in the afternoon."[15]

Similar clubs sprung up around major cities in the next three decades. On the East Coast, several emphasized tennis, a popular game recently imported from England. In Newport, Rhode Island, several wealthy families built their own private tennis courts in the 1880s. Here, at the location of the future National Tennis Center, the well-manicured grass courts provided tangible evidence of the club's exclusivity. The new game fitted well into an outdoor setting; significantly, it was a game that women could play despite the restrictions on movement imposed by long dresses and corsets. Because these pioneering women tennis players could not move with ease, they tended to play doubles, gently tapping the ball across the net. Tennis was a game suitable for both men and women, and it tended to provide a family atmosphere the new clubs sought to encourage. However, tennis did not become the primary focus of the new country clubs. Only a few – such as Maidstone and Westchester in the New York City area – were established as primarily tennis facilities. Tennis proved to be more adaptable to play within the cities, and besides, the country clubs had discovered another game open to both men and women that was perfectly suited to the leafy suburban environment.

Although examples of its existence can be traced to earlier times, golf swept across America during the 1890s. Its appeal was complex, but it clearly was rooted in class and social attitudes. After overcoming early attitudes that the game was for the weak and effeminate (women, after all, played the game), it became associated in the public mind with a healthy outing in the sunshine and fresh air. It also appealed to those who held negative attitudes toward such violent sports as boxing – raw strength was not an advantage in golf – but ultimately it was embraced because it provided moderate exercise. The first country club to establish a golf course has long believed to have been St Andrews Golf Club of Yonkers, New York, in 1888, although it has been demonstrated that a few primitive courses existed in South Carolina and Georgia as early as the late 1700s. A private course was apparently built in Foxburg, Pennsylvania, in 1885, but it was the St Andrews Golf Club,

opened in 1888, in Yonkers that set the mold and established the compelling environment wherein an exclusive country club could flourish. During the next ten years, many country clubs featuring golf were opened, and the rapid growth in popularity of the ancient Scottish game is indicated by the fact that by 1900 there were 1,040 courses in operation across the United States; 165 of these were in New York, although 43 had made their appearance in California. The number of holes varied widely, from four to 12, but by the late 1890s, following the leadership of the Shinnecock Hills Country Club of Southampton, New York, the normal course offered a nine-hole challenge. During the early decades of the twentieth century, many nine-hole courses were increased to eighteen, which became the standard by the 1920s.

Golf was a game that could be played by both men and women of all ages with a wide range of skills. It provided moderate exercise in the open air, held out a variety of mental as well as physical challenges, was conducive to handicapping and betting, and seldom produced serious physical injury.[16] There also developed around the game a special mystique that contributed to its appeal, an emotional attraction that only those smitten with the game can fully appreciate.

The appeal of the country club to those who could afford its costs

Figure 5.3 Early in the twentieth century, golf provided women with a new opportunity to develop their athletic skills at private country clubs. This unknown lady was captured by a cameraman at the Portrush Club in New Jersey in 1911 hitting a fairway wood. © Hutton-Deutsch Collection/ CORBIS.

was great. Membership usually established one's elite social status and provided opportunities for socialization and conducting business on an informal basis. They also provided members with a clear social separation from the common citizen, as Robert J. Moss has observed: "Getting into a club became important not so much as because it constituted a positive accomplishment in itself but because it gave the new member the right to participate in the exclusion of the unworthy. Country clubs . . . existed to create unequal access, to draw a boundary between the elect and the unwanted."[17] The physical appearance of the course, with its well-manicured fairways and greens set among trees and ponds and streams, appealed to the agrarian-frontier nostalgia that percolated in the American subconscious. Golf provided relief from the congestion of the city in which members lived and worked. As the movement spread, some critics naturally worried that the clubs were exacerbating social divisions within communities; others simply condemned the snooty elitism of the clubs. Consequently, both golf and tennis acquired an image of elitism that would only slowly dissipate during the twentieth century.

During this formative period, however, a few perceptive social commentators took notice of the tendency of the country club to provide greater avenues for growth and participation in sports for women. As one writer, perhaps looking through rose-colored glasses, noted, "the Country Club has brought our women out of stuffy houses and out of their hopeless, aimless selves, has given color to their cheeks, vivacity to their movements, charm and intelligence to their conversation." However limited its impact upon society at large, the county club nonetheless helped advance the role of women in sports. "The country club has taken its legitimate position in the social cosmos. A place has been found outside the restricted possibilities of the home where men and women may meet on equal footing."[18] This, of course, was not correct. Although women were accepted, in many instances their presence and participation on the golf course was barely tolerated. Men controlled the boards of directors and set the policies, hired the staff, and often decreed that women could play only on designated "ladies days" (scheduled mid-week when the men were in their offices). Equality of the sexes would remain an issue in some private clubs in the twenty-first century.

Without the galvanizing influence of golf, most of these institutions would not have survived. Clubs originally planned for equestrian sports, hunting, or cricket learned that by adding golf that they could attract many new members. Journalist E. S. Martin aptly summarized the essence of the movement:

> Country clubs are the result of the centralization of population, the increase of wealth, and the discovery of the game of golf by America . . . . Country clubs could hardly flourish in great numbers without golf. To a majority of the active male members golf is the great attraction. Golf keeps up the membership and makes the club strong.

Another writer put it more succinctly: "If sport has not been the raison d'être of every club's establishment it is at all events, with extremely few exceptions, the chief means of their existence."[19] It was not until the 1920s that the game of golf gained momentum with the general population as local governments began to construct and operate public courses. By 1930, there were 5,856 courses in the United States, the majority operated by city parks and recreation departments.

The Early Years of Women's Sports

Modern America confronted many new social issues. Among these was pressure from feminist leaders on behalf of fundamental changes in prevailing attitudes toward accepted gender roles. Although various terms were used to describe this phenomenon, the most widely used was "the new woman." Their demands included the right to vote, increased economic freedom, wider educational and employment opportunities, entree into traditional male professions, and the right to hold public office. The growing popularity of outdoor recreations and competitive sports naturally produced increased interest among the new women of America's emerging modern age. These demands challenged nearly every prevailing Victorian standard relative to the role of women. At stake were the traditional views that women must at all times remain in control of their actions and behavior, that they should not exhibit "manly" traits, and that their delicate bodies were incapable of withstanding vigorous physical activity. In particular, it was widely believed that excessive exercise could damage female reproductive organs. As early as the 1840s, such pioneering women as Catherine Beecher had begun attacking such stereotypes. She lamented that while parents of young girls sought to educate their minds, they tended to discourage active play and exercise: "They have done almost every thing they could do to train their children to become feeble, sickly, and ugly." She urged parents to insist upon healthy exercise for their girls as an essential step to the development of healthy adult women. "Next to pure air," she wrote in 1855, "healthful exercise and amusements are the most important remedies."[20]

Beecher's ideas boldly challenged accepted gender roles, and did not produce immediate results, but during the 1880s a small number of normal schools that had a primary responsibility for the preparation of public school teachers began to offer courses in women's physical education. Inspired by the teachings of Harvard professor Dudley Sargent, a new generation of teachers began to implement programs of regular exercise for young women. Taking the leadership in this movement was the Sargent School and the Boston Normal School of Gymnastics. Universities and colleges followed their example, and by the early 1900s courses in physical education had become an integral part of the curriculum in American colleges and universities. Graduates of these programs took the message into the public schools where they taught physical-education classes and put girls through a regimen of exercises and games. In 1911, *Lippincott's Magazine* published a probing article entitled "The Masculinization of Girls," which explored the pros and cons of the new "athletic girl." The magazine reported, "She loves to walk, to row, to ride, to motor, to jump and run . . . just as Man walks, jumps, rows, rides, motors, and runs."[21]

Not everyone accepted the new woman or the new athletic girl. In fact, an enormous ambiguity hovered over the entrance of women into the world of rigorous exercise and competitive sports. Not everyone agreed with *Lippincott's Magazine*, which concluded that the new "athletic girl" was a positive development: "with muscles tense and blood aflame, she plays the manly role." And that was the nub of the unanswered question. Did female athletes have to become "masculine" in order to participate in competitive athletics? Was a finely honed competitive instinct "unfeminine?" Would competitive sports unleash repressed sexual desires? Or worse, would girls become too "manly" and lose their femininity? Fears abounded of a new generation of "muscle-bound" women who no longer accepted traditional roles as submissive wives and nurturing mothers.

During the latter decades of the nineteenth century, women slowly began to show interest in games. Among the upper-class women, these games included archery, lawn bowling, horseback riding, tennis, golf, and croquet. A few women began to take these games seriously, and national championships were held by fledgling national organizations in archery (1879), tennis (1887), and golf (1895). But these events were severely limited to only a small group of affluent women who played the games with proper "refinement." This country-club-style elitism, however, was overwhelmed by the bicycle craze of the 1890s, which saw an unknown but substantial number of women take to the streets and roads on the bicycle. Breakthroughs in technology, especially the pneumatic tire and brakes, made cycling a safe new form of transportation as well as a source of amusement and exercise. Women and men found the new craze equally appealing. "Wheelmen" clubs sprung up across the country and even vaudeville songs were written about the nation's new fascination with two-wheeled mobility. The impact was seen almost immediately in women's clothing styles. Long flowing skirts tended to get caught in the spokes and chain drive, and soon women were seen wearing stylish new types of riding pants or shorter, divided skirts. As *Life* magazine noted lightly in 1897,

> Be it recorded that a large proportion of the bicycle girls look exceedingly well in bicycle clothes. Whether they wear stockings or leggings, whether they wear divided skirts, they adorn creation. Not the least good thing that the bicycle has done has been to demonstrate publicly that women have legs. Their legs are unquestionably becoming to them. So are their shirt-waists. Long may they wave.[22]

Although the cycling craze faded before the onslaught of the automobile culture during the early years of the new century, it definitely helped create a new mindset regarding women and exercise. However, the major breakthrough occurred with the introduction of the new game of basketball. First played at the YMCA Institute in Springfield, Massachusetts in 1891, the game gained popularity with amazing rapidity. From the beginning women were fascinated by the game. They formed class teams in schools and colleges, and by 1900 women's teams were challenging those of other colleges. Girls high-school teams were equally popular. Women found that on the court they could play with a freedom and abandon that enabled them to express themselves in ways not normally accepted. However, such free-flowing play on the court led to physical contact and contortions that challenged accepted conventions for girls and young women. School and college administrators sometimes felt the need to decree that their games and practices be played behind closed doors so as to exclude wide-eyed male spectators. Such established gender roles were readily evident in 1904 in the village of Camden, Ohio, when the high school put its first girls' team on the floor. The town's weekly newspaper reported that the school's "fair maidens" were defeated because their "feminine sweetness" was no match for the "rough and tumble" visitors from a nearby city school who "used other than lady-like tactics."[23]

The result was that various proposals for rules changes were put forth that made the girls' game less aggressive than that played by males. One modification made it illegal to steal the ball from the possession of an opponent. Another restricted a player's participation to either the offensive or defensive end of the court to prevent excessive running. In Iowa, a special variation of the game that required three girls to play on the defensive end of the court and three on the offensive end became a state obsession; it was a game that had special appeal in the small rural schools that were prevalent throughout the state. The popularity of this particular form of girls' basketball remained high in the state throughout much of the twentieth century; in many communities, the girls' teams attracted more interest than the boys', and would persist until the standard five-on-five game was imposed by the Iowa Girls High School Athletic Union amid a firestorm of controversy in 1993.

Despite public discussion of the "new woman," most had little opportunity for meaningful participation in the expanding sports world. Except for those young women who could play basketball, the opportunities were essentially restricted to younger wealthy women along the Northeastern seaboard where private country clubs were most prominent. It was this small slice of the American female population that caught the attention of popular social artist Charles Dana Gibson, whose stunning drawings of tall, attractive upper-class young women were popular from 1895 until the First World War. His popular "Gibson Girl" sketches were frequently published in such magazines as *Collier's Weekly*, *Cosmopolitan*, and *The Outlook*. Gibson often took his subjects outdoors, where they would be seen astride a bicycle, on the tennis court, swinging a niblick on the golf course, or driving an automobile. When she managed to go into the water, the Gibson Girl was amply covered with a decorous bathing suit and stockings. The stunning Gibson Girl was tall and slender, of ample female form, smartly dressed, her upswept hair impeccably set, her face attractive but haughty. Clearly Gibson was not advocating an independent woman. To the contrary, he seemed preoccupied with romance and courtship, and his subjects were subtly portrayed as discreetly but resolutely flirting with handsome men. The message was clear: these attractive new-age women were headed in the direction of marriage and motherhood. Whenever they appeared holding a tennis racquet or golf club, a suitably handsome male companion was somewhere in the picture. In one of Gibson's most popular drawings, entitled "Is a Caddy Always Necessary," a couple is pictured seated unhappily on the side of a sand trap while their teenage caddy stands by, oblivious to their desire to be alone on the wooded back nine. When the Great War broke out in 1914, Gibson became infatuated with military subjects and largely abandoned his popular Gibson Girls. Within a few years, the alluring, and bewitching, somehow aloof

Gibson Girl gave way to the raucous flapper of the 1920s, wearing a short dress and short bobbed hair and dancing the frenetic Charleston or Black Bottom.[24]

Strong Bodies and Devout Souls

When Englishman Thomas Hughes published *Tom Brown's School Days* in 1857, few Americans had ever considered that there might be a powerful relationship between strenuous exertion on the playing field and the development of devout Christian youth. But shortly after Hughes captured the imaginations of young boys on both sides of the Atlantic with his sparkling story of young Tom's heroic behavior on the playing fields of Rugby School, educators and clergy were enthusiastically championing the connection between effective religious education and healthy athletic endeavor. Hughes's book had a profound impact upon middle-class America; it sold nearly a quarter million copies in the United States within a year of its publication. Hughes book contributed substantively to the powerful educational-religious movement that came to be called "Muscular Christianity." Its central message was quite simple: participation in vigorous sports competition would produce a young man who understood the values of fair play, good sportsmanship, and an appreciation of the Ten Commandments. In the next half century, many Amercian writers sought to emulate Hughes's message of the importance of fair play on the playing fields, including such popular writers of novels for teenagers as Gilbert Patten, who cranked out more than two hundred books and short stories detailing the breathtaking feats of the heroic Frank Merriwell on the football and baseball fields at Fardale Academy and Yale University. When he was not triumphing over poor sports on the playing field, running track or basketball court, he was touring the world to find adventure, even helping a horse win the English Derby.

Muscular Christianity appealed to a wide range of Americans because it addressed serious questions that concerned American leaders. Middle- and upper-middle class men now labored behind counters or desks rather than doing strenuous outdoor physical labor. It was widely feared that as a consequence the office-bound American male was becoming less "manly." Some medical professionals even believed that the middle-class male was suffering from a newly discovered disease called "neurasthenia," a modern-day malady that sapped urban males of their vitality and virility. The perceived existence of neurasthenia led many to believe that the American male had become a liability in the competitive world in which Darwinian struggles for survival were believed to be a constant.[25]

Even more threatening was the perception that modern city urban life was undermining future generations of American men. Young boys were now required to spend up to nine months a year sitting at a school desk, as compared to as little as four a few generations earlier; this, it was believed, deprived them of opportunities to build their physiques. Fears grew that young boys were being "feminized" by overly protective mothers who assumed greater responsibility for child rearing in the cities as their husbands spent much of their time attending to business. Other dangers to the future of American masculinity also lurked in the cities: the morals of young men were under attack by the urban bachelor subculture with its alluring but unsavory amusements. The consensus solution as to how to resist these threats was regular, vigorous exercise conducted in a wholesome Christian atmosphere. The influential Presbyterian minister Henry Ward Beecher was convinced that there existed a close connection between a vigorous life and moral development. He argued that activities such as swimming, rowing, horseback riding, gymnastics, and baseball were conducive to moral as well as physical development, and he urged religious and civic leaders to "give to the young men of our cities the means of physical vigor and health, separated from temptations of vice."[26]

Beecher's appeal was emulated by a rising chorus of voices from the nation's intellectual elite and the Protestant clergy. Ralph Waldo Emerson, Henry David Thoreau, Oliver Wendell Holmes, Nathaniel Hawthorne, and Henry Longfellow were but a few of the prominent individuals who encouraged boys and young men to pursue a vigorous life. As this movement gained momentum, no voice was heard more clearly than that of the Reverend Thomas Wentworth Higginson, a graduate of Harvard Divinity School. Writing in *Atlantic Monthly* in 1858, he denounced the perception that "physical vigor and spiritual sanctity are incompatible." Higginson argued that good health was "a necessary condition of all permanent success" because it enabled men to confront the challenges of life. He expressed his fear that in the new urban environment, young boys were greatly influenced by overly protective mothers because their fathers were off to office or factory; the result was a growing softness, sentimentality, even effeminacy, among young American males. He chided parents whose sons were "puny, pallid, sedentary" for naturally pushing them toward a career in the ministry or other nurturing professions. Acknowledging that girls also benefited from exercise, Higginson nonetheless said that only strong men could build a strong nation and that protective mothers could do lasting damage to their sons by sheltering them from the dangers of childhood:

> As the urchin is undoubtedly physically safer for having learned to turn a somerset, and fire a gun, perilous though these feats appear to mothers, – so his soul is made healthier, larger, freer, stronger, by hours and days of manly exercise and copious drought of open air, at whatever risk of idle habits and bad companions.[27]

Muscular Christianity enjoyed substantial growth in popularity with the passing of the years. By the onset of the twentieth century, it had picked up a full head of steam. One tangible result was to increase the role and scope of physical education and competitive sports programs in the public schools and to sustain the creation of such new institutions as the Young Mens' Christian Association (YMCA) and the Boy and Girl Scouts. The YMCA movement was founded in England in 1844 and spread to the United States before the Civil War. Initially, its primary target was young men who had immigrated from Europe or had left rural America in search of better opportunities. The "Y" offered inexpensive housing in a Christian atmosphere as an alternative to the seductive influences of working-class boardinghouses and tawdry amusements of the city. It was believed that the gymnasium and swimming pool provided positive alternatives to the many immoral activities that might tempt unmarried young men. An interdenominational organization, the YMCA movement spread rapidly across the United States after the Civil War. By 1900, some 350 separate facilities were operating in cities large and small, teaching the virtues of self-control, mental toughness, personal discipline, and good personal hygiene, concepts widely assumed to be prerequisites to success in America's competitive economic system. The organization's needs for professional leadership were so great that a special school was established in Springfield, Massachusetts. As the YMCA movement expanded, it increasingly focused on physical fitness and less on religious education; its clientele also became more diverse as well-established business and professional men were attracted to its swimming pools, squash courts, gymnasiums, and running tracks rather than its moral instruction.[28]

A parallel movement to establish a Young Women's Christian Association (YWCA) naturally occurred, but its emphasis lay largely outside of the Muscular Christianity movement. The YWCA emerged out of a confluence of many parallel and sometimes rival organizations, all aimed at elevating the morals of young urban women. This organization tended to shy away from working with young girls to focus on adult women living in urban areas. Consequently, the heavy emphasis of the YMCA upon physical fitness was not reflected in the YWCA, which tended to focus instead on educational and career programs for its adult membership. Consequently the burden of working with young girls fell to the Camp Fire Girls and the Girl Scouts.[29]

Like the YMCA, the Boy Scouts movement had its origins in England, and was established in the United States in 1910. The Boy Scouts movement developed its program upon a common-sense set of desirable personal traits (honesty, trustworthiness, reverence, cheerfulness, obedience, bravery, etc.) and used the great outdoors as the environment in which to instill those traits in its young charges. It was believed that teaching the skills of survival in the great outdoors was an ideal way to develop the young Muscular Christian. The Scouts' emphasis upon hiking, climbing, boating, swimming, camping, and wilderness survival skills met with widespread approval, prompting Theodore Roosevelt to become an active advisor. Roosevelt praised the program's potential for "the development of efficiency, virility, and good citizenship," because he believed it essential that future leaders "be men of strong, wholesome character, of unmistakable devotion to our country, its customs and ideals." In short, vigorous sports and related outdoor activities provided growing boys with the necessary preparation for success in business, politics, and the military, enabling them to become vigorous leaders with sound moral principles firmly ingrained.[30]

By the early twentieth century, the several ideological strands of Muscular Christianity had permeated American life. Although many scholars, educators, social commentators, and clergymen contributed to the cause, no one person better symbolized the movement than Theodore Roosevelt. His own life was a testament to the importance of physical conditioning. As a child, he was asthmatic and endured other debilitating illnesses. He was near-sighted and had to wear thick glasses, which made the frail son of socially prominent parents ripe pickings for neighborhood bullies. When he was 14, after he was roughed up by two young toughs, his father introduced him to physical training, telling him that it was time to "build your body." The youngster received instruction in the manly art from a former professional boxer and under the watchful eyes of a personal trainer enthusiastically plunged into a regimen of weightlifting and calisthenics. Summers were spent on the family's estate on Long Island where he exuberantly took to hiking, horseback riding, and swimming. By the time he entered Harvard, Roosevelt had transformed himself into a sturdy young man possessed of considerable physical prowess and an enormous enthusiasm for rigorous physical activity. At Harvard, he boxed, wrestled, and rowed on class teams, and during the summers took long arduous backpacking trips into the backwoods of Maine and upstate New York. In 1883, in an effort to escape the concurrent personal tragedy of the deaths of his young wife and his mother, he bought a ranch in the Badlands of South Dakota and spent a year working the line with regular cowboys. Among other adventures, he had the delightful experiences of singlehandedly capturing at gunpoint a gang of rustlers and in a barroom fight thrashing a thug who made the mistake of poking fun of TR's thick eyeglasses.

As Roosevelt began his rapid ascendancy in the political world, he boistrously advocated "the strenuous life." Greatly influenced by the doctrines of Social Darwinism, Roosevelt believed that enemies abroad and softness at home imperiled America's future. In 1895, he confided to Walter Camp his fear that "we are tending steadily in America to produce in our leisure and sedentary classes a type of man not much above the Bengalee baboo."[31] He feared that men did not become warriors by attending college and working behind a desk, and he lamented the decline of the rural population because fewer soldiers would have the benefits of growing up in the outdoors with a rifle in their hands. What was needed, he said, were strong men who understood that a leader "in the arena" required the traits of courage, endurance, and strength that came from a vigorous life. Strenuous sports, such as boxing, rowing, and football, provided the training and experiences necessary for leadership. In 1893, Roosevelt wrote that in modern America it was natural to place

> too little stress upon the more virile virtues – upon the virtues which go to make up
> a race of statesmen and soldiers, of pioneers and explorers by land and sea, of bridge
> builders and road-makers, of commonwealth builders – in short, upon those virtues
> for the lack of which, whether in an individual or in a nation, no amount of refinement and learning of gentleness and culture, can possibly atone.[32]

The solution, he said, was "the very qualities which are fostered by vigorous manly out-of-door sports." In 1902, in his book *The Strenuous Life*, Roosevelt noted that during his own childhood it was acceptable for boys born to wealthy parents to ignore their physical development, but that the new thinking to which he had greatly contributed now required that they participate in "the rough sports which call for pluck, endurance, and physical address." In his widely read essay on "The American Boy," TR urged parents and educators to focus upon both the physical and moral development of boys:

Now, the chances are he won't be much of a man unless he is a good deal of a boy. He must not be a coward or a weakling, a bully, a shirk, or a prig. He must work hard and play hard. He must be clean-minded and clean-lived, and able to hold his own under all circumstances and against all comers.

Because today's boys will become tomorrow's soldiers and statesmen, "A boy needs both physical and moral courage," and he emphasized that the traits that boys develop in their youth would shape their conduct as men "in the field." Roosevelt concluded his message to the young men of America with an oft-quoted exhortation: "In short, in life, as in a foot-ball game, the principle to follow is: Hit the line hard; don't foul and don't shirk, but hit the line hard!"[33]

America's Greatest Athlete

Because of the emphasis that intellectuals and public leaders now placed upon physical conditioning and the important lessons to be learned from sharp athletic competition, most Americans did not know how to react to the accomplishments of Jim Thorpe. As a student at Carlisle Indian School he demonstrated his superior talent on the football field, earning All-American honors. He could run, he could tackle, he could kick, and he did so in competition with the best of the powerful eastern teams. In 1912 he achieved world acclaim for his unprecedented triumphs at the Stockholm Olympics. Because he was a Native American, however, the mainstream media treated him courteously, but as somewhat a curiosity. Thus when his status as an amateur was called into question, white America was quick to condemn him.

In 1879, the United States government established a small school in Pennsylvania that was named the Carlisle Indian Industrial Training School. The intent of its founder, Richard Henry Pratt, was to educate Native Americans about the dominant white culture and to prepare them for jobs in industry. Although such a concept is repugnant in today's society because the intent was to eradicate traditional Indian culture, Pratt believed that only by so doing could the Native American people avoid extinction. It was from this educational environment that Jim Thorpe burst onto the American consciousness in the early twentieth century as a phenomenal All-American football player. Descended from Native Americans who belonged to the Sac and Fox, Potawatomi, and Kickapoo tribes, Thorpe was born in 1887 and grew up in Oklahoma on the Sac and Fox reservation east of Oklahoma City. In 1904, he was sent to Carlisle, where he came to the attention of the famed coach Glenn "Pop" Warner. His prowess as a member of the school's track and field team soon attracted attention, but Warner was reluctant to play Thorpe on the football team for fear of injuring his top track star. Large for an athlete of his time, Thorpe stood 6' 1" and weighed a muscular 190 pounds. In 1911, however, he became the focus of the media when he led the football team – naturally called the Indians – to an upset victory over unbeaten Harvard. His punting ability – he kicked an 83-yard punt against Brown – and his skill as a running back and sure-handed tackler led

Figure 5.4 Jim Thorpe is shown in the shotput competition during the decathlon at the 1912 Olympics in Stockholm. Thorpe was voted the top American male athlete of the first half of the twentieth century. © Bettmann/ CORBIS.

to All-American honors. The American people became infatuated with what the press called "the Indian" and portrayed him as somehow replicating on the football field the military engagements between American tribes and white settlers and the Army.[34]

In 1912, Thorpe became the focus of the Western world when he won both the pentathlon and the decathlon at the Stockholm Olympics. In the five-event pentathlon he won four first places (broad jump, 200-meter dash, javelin throw, and 1,500-meter race), and in the 10-event decathlon he scored 8,413 points out of a possible 10,000, some 700 points ahead of his nearest competitor. King Gustav of Sweden told him upon presenting his gold medals, "Sir, you are the greatest athlete in the world." Thorpe reportedly responded, "Thanks, King."[35] Upon returning to the United States, Thorpe found himself a top media attraction and was greeted in New York City with a ticker-tape parade. He immediately enhanced his reputation as a multisport phenomenon by leading Carlisle's football team to a consensus national championship with a 12–1 record against the top teams in the East. He was again named an All-American by Walter Camp. The American people, always fascinated by Native Americans, made Thorpe into a national treasure, but in a way that emphasized his ethnicity in a curious way.

Thorpe's high standing with the public did not last for long. In 1913, a Massachusetts newspaper revealed that during the summers of 1909 and 1910 he had played for a Class-D minor-league baseball league in Fayetteville, North Carolina, where he earned between $2 and $5 a game. The all-white male members of the American Amateur Union (AAU) and the American Olympic Committee (AOC) decreed that Thorpe had to return his Olympic medals and trophies and that his name and records be stricken from the Olympic record book. Public opinion on this harsh and arbitrary decision to uphold a pristine concept of amateurism was sharply divided. Some felt betrayed by Thorpe's violation of the strict amateur code, while others, including his coach Pop Warner, contended that he was being singled out as an example because he was Native American. A white champion, they suggested, would have been treated much differently. This controversy brought into sharp public focus the relationship between sports and race. In his letter of apology to the AAU, Thorpe subtly pointed to the double standard by which he had been summarily judged:

> I was not very wise to the ways of the world and did not realize that this was wrong and it would make me a professional in track sports, although I learned from the other players that it would be better for me not to let any one know that I was playing.

Pointing out that most of his professional baseball teammates were college athletes who maintained their amateur standing, he noted, "I did not know that I was doing wrong because I was doing what I knew several other college men had done; except that they did not use their own names."[36]

Thorpe's sudden decline in the eyes of many of his fans led him to leave Carlisle in 1913 without having graduated. He moved on to play professional baseball and football. Although baseball was not his best sport, he was good enough to play sparingly for the New York Giants, Cincinnati Reds and Boston Braves; he hit .327 in 156 at-bats in 1919 with the Braves, but like so many with baseball aspirations, he could not hit the curve ball. He thus became a pioneer in the early days of professional football, playing for low pay with several teams in the American Professional Football League (reconstituted into the National Football League in 1922) at a time when most players went the full 60 minutes on offense, defense, and special teams. Again he was a standout, thrilling the small crowds of a few thousand who turned out in such Ohio towns as Canton, Dayton, and Columbus with his enthusiastic brand of play. He began with the famed Canton Bulldogs in 1915 and concluded with the Chicago Cardinals in a brief appearance in 1928.

Thorpe's playing days were over in 1928. He was already engaged in what proved to be a losing battle with alcoholism and supported himself doing odd jobs that included deck hand, painter, carpenter, barroom bouncer, factory guard, and ditch digger. He died in southern California living alone in a small trailer in 1953. He was named by various media organizations as America's top athlete of the first half-century, and in 1999 some experts picked him over Muhammad Ali, Babe Ruth, and Michael Jordan as the leading athlete of the entire twentieth century. In 1955, the NFL named their annual Most Valuable Player award for Thorpe, and he was among the initial class admitted to its Hall of Fame in 1963.

Organized Play for the Modern Era

As America strode into the modern era, the necessity of a reformed education system was evident. America's new industrial and business systems needed managers and workers, men and women with skills that could only be provided by extensive formal education. Legislatures in many states mandated increased regular school attendance until age 16, and state education boards established a network of teachers colleges (originally called "normal schools") whose role was to produce professionally trained classroom teachers and administrators. Universities and colleges developed new curricula to prepare teachers, engineers, physicians, lawyers, and businessmen.

Central to this widespread movement was Dr Luther H. Gulick. While attending Oberlin College in the early 1880s, this serious young man fell under the influence of a pioneering professor of physical education, Delphine Hanna, whose inspired teaching led him to abandon his plans to follow in the footsteps of his parents and become a medical missionary. Instead, his new mission in life was to encourage the development of purposeful physical education, play, and dance programs that would encourage the simultaneous development of the physical and the moral dimensions of the individual. After obtaining his medical degree from New York University in 1887, Gulick joined the faculty of the International Young Men's Christian Association Training School in Springfield, Massachusetts, which provided formal training for all YMCA instructors and directors. Much of the curriculum originally focused on formal religious training, and it fell to Gulick to increase the emphasis upon physical education.

Joining Gulick on the faculty at Springfield were two other young men who had embraced Muscular Christianity, Amos Alonzo Stagg and James Naismith. They were equally committed to the "fourfold program of fitness: physical, social, mental, and spiritual." An All-American end at Yale, Stagg had decided that because of his stutter he could better serve his God on the football field rather than in the pulpit. Naismith, an ordained Presbyterian minister recently graduated from McGill University in his native Canada, had arrived in 1890 as an instructor and part-time student after completing three years of theology. Both men saw a close relationship between matters of the spirit and the body. Stagg won the attention of the sports world when he molded a new football team out of the Springfield student body and faculty and nearly upset his alma mater. His star center on that team that lost to Yale 16–10 was the 160-pound Naismith, who upon inquiring as to the reason he was selected to anchor the center of the line, was told by Stagg: "Jim, I play you at center because you can do the meanest things in the most gentlemanly way."[37]

Stagg soon departed for the green pastures of the new University of Chicago where he would build a national football powerhouse, but Naismith remained on the Springfield faculty for several years. During his first year at Springfield, Naismith volunteered to teach a class of 18 adult males who were in the final stages of their two-year training course to become YMCA administrators and physical education directors. Although they gladly took to fall football and spring baseball, they found the mindless routine of winter calisthenics a terrible bore and expressed their dissatisfaction in such vigorous fashion that senior instructors refused to teach the class. When Naismith volunteered to take over the class, Gulick told him what his challenge was:

> This new generation of young men wants the pleasure and thrills of games rather than the body-building benefits of exercise. They rebel at tumbling, push-ups, working out with Indian clubs, and other calisthenics. I want you to come up with a game that will give them the exercise they need in the gym during the winter months when we can't go outdoors for football or baseball.[38]

For two weeks, Naismith labored at solving the challenge, presenting indoor versions of soccer and lacrosse, which led to too many bruises and bloody heads, and various forms of leap-frog and tag that the students scorned as childish. Then one evening he recalled a game he had played as a child called "duck on a rock," which had emphasized tossing a rock at a target. The next day, he nailed two peach baskets to serve as targets precisely 10 feet above the floor at each end of the gym. When his 18 students arrived for their class one cold December morning, they were met by their instructor bouncing a soccer ball. He proceeded to explain to them 13 basic rules that he had personally typed out before class. Twelve of these rules still exist in modified form more than a century later. The young men soon learned that throwing the ball into the 10-foot-high peach basket target was much more difficult than they had believed, and within 30 minutes their happy shouts had echoed down the hall and a crowd of curious students and faculty had assembled to watch the action. With 18 men maneuvering around the small floor, it became evident that finesse, good passing, skilled marksmanship, and sound physical conditioning were essential qualities to this new game.[39]

Unlike other major American sports, which have obscure origins and have evolved for several centuries, the game invented by James Naismith had no historical roots and was inspired by the conditions of the new modern era of American life. The tenets of Muscular Christianity, with its emphasis upon formal education, the obsession for control by written rules and regulations, and a national movement called the YMCA had come together to create a game that would rapidly gain widespread popularity throughout the country. It appealed to adults and youngsters, males and females alike. Basketball with its emphasis on agility and skill rather than on pure physical strength was the ideal indoor winter game for modern America. By 1895, important changes had already been made in Naismith's rules: dribbling enabled players to avoid close guarding, and the number of players on each team was set at five to encourage the speed of the game over cumbersome mass play. As one enthusiast wrote in 1902, in playing it comes the joy of a quickened pulse and fast-working lungs, the health-giving exercise to all our muscles, the forgetting of all troubles. There is no game which requires more wind or endurance nor which needs greater agility and deftness."[40]

Naismith would never benefit financially from his invention of the game. He left Springfield in 1895 to attend medical school in Denver, and upon graduation in 1898 took a position as the first professor of health and physical education at Kansas University, where he would remain on the faculty until his death in 1939. He seldom played the game himself, although he was the first basketball coach at KU. Ironically, with a nine-year record of 55–60, the inventor of the game of basketball compiled the only career coaching losing record in the school's history. Dr Naismith was much more interested in teaching health and exercise science to undergraduate students and in encouraging participation in the intramural program than in promoting intercollegiate athletics.

The inspiration for Naismith's game, of course, was the department of physical education head, Luther Halsey Gulick. In 1895, Gulick encouraged another instructor to come up with a new indoor sport, which produced the game of volleyball. In 1900, Gulick became principal of Pratt High School in Brooklyn, where he introduced physical-education classes into the formal curriculum; in 1903, he became director of physical education for the entire New York City school system, where he introduced physical-education classes and created a system of competitive athletic leagues. Gulick's message that daily physical activity encouraged better learning by relieving muscles cramped from long hours of sitting at a desk and by stimulating blood flow to the brain was widely hailed as a major advance in progressive education theory. His Public Schools Athletic League (PSAL), founded in 1903, was the nation's first competitive sports league for schoolboys. He added a comparable program for girls in 1905. The PSAL was a model for interscholastic sports that would be emulated across the nation.[41]

Interscholastic Sports

It was only a matter of time until public schools began to field teams and form leagues. Having learned from the leaders of the progressive education movement the importance of fostering the physical as well as the intellectual lives of their charges, school administrators rushed to create competitive team sports programs in football, baseball, and track and field. Most surprising, however, was the rapid spread of basketball, which became by the 1920s the most popular sport at the high school level. Basketball simultaneously developed deep roots in the urban cores of American cities and in the nation's rural areas. In thousands of small rural high schools that lacked sufficient number of boys to field a competitive football team, basketball became the most important school activity, one that bonded the school with the community, whose members packed small gymnasiums on Friday nights to cheer the local five. Even the smallest rural schools could field a team of five boys relatively adept at the game. Following the First World War, state athletic associations were established to create eligibility standards, game rules, and conduct championship tournaments. At the end of the regular season in February, county school districts held tournaments, the winners advancing sequentially to district, regional and state championship tournaments.

High school football also flourished throughout the United States. In some smaller schools, six- and eight-man team conferences were formed for schools whose student bodies could not produce squads sufficiently large enough to support an 11-man team. Just as Indiana and Iowa formed a strong bond with basketball, the states of Pennsylvania, Ohio, and Texas became known for their strong support of high school football. Widespread introduction of high-school physical education and sports programs provided the logical conclusion of advocacy of the strenuous life as an antidote to the conditions of modern society where machine was replacing muscle. Argued for on a lofty moral and intellectual plane by advocates such as Luther Gulick and Theodore Roosevelt, who saw in competitive sports intrinsic values essential for national reform and perhaps survival, in reality the competitive nature of the American people turned those arguments aside in quest for the gratification of winning, even at considerable ethical cost. Just as college football from its very inception was riddled with corruption among players, coaches, administrators, trustees, and alumni, so too did the same victory-at-any-price ethic surface in high-school sports. Academic eligibility requirements were often subverted by compliant teachers and administrators; coaches were paid higher salaries than other faculty; and public opinion often forced well-meaning coaches intent on teaching sportsmanship as well as winning games to resign. Although physical education was trumpeted as an integral part of education reform, in reality these classes were often given short shrift by teachers and administrators alike, with the real emphasis on fielding competitive teams in major sports. And within the social structure of the schools themselves, a special elite status was reserved for skilled athletes while outstanding academic achievers were frequently scorned if they were not also an athlete. Had Luther Gulick not died an early death in 1917, it is altogether conceivable that he would have led a national movement to reverse these trends.

6 Baseball Ascendant 1890–1930

Between 1890 and 1930, baseball was unquestionably the most popular sport in America. The game attracted millions of amateur participants and even the smallest of communities proudly fielded a "town team," complete with colorful uniforms paid for by local merchants. In the cities, YMCA leagues and semiprofessional leagues were popular. Employers sponsored teams to play in industrial and commercial leagues, often hiring employees whose primary function was to win ball games for the company team. In an age of pervasive racial segregation, African Americans formed their own amateur and semiprofessional teams and leagues and only on special occasions played white teams in "exhibition" games. Wherever there was a vacant city lot or an open field in a small town, boys of all ages "chose up sides" and played informal games to their hearts' content.

The game's popularity was evidenced by the construction of modern new stadiums for major league teams that seated between 20,000 and 35,000 spectators. Because many wooden stadiums had been destroyed by fire over the years, double-decked structures of brick, concrete, and structural steel were erected in their place. The first of these new stadiums, Shibe Park, was constructed in 1909 in Philadelphia, and in the following year a similar structure opened at the other end of the state, Forbes Field in Pittsburgh. Within the next five years there appeared Navin Field in Detroit (later named Briggs and then Tiger Stadium), League Park in Cleveland, Redland Field in Cincinnati (later renamed Crosley Field), Ebbetts Field in Brooklyn, National Park in Washington, DC (renamed Griffith Stadium in 1920), Braves Field and Fenway Park in Boston, Weeghman Park in Chicago (renamed Wrigley Field in 1926), and on the south side of the Windy City, Comiskey Park. The New York Giants replaced their burned out Polo Grounds in 1911 with a new horseshoe-shaped double decker that seated 35,000, the largest seating capacity of the new stadiums. In 1923, however, the across-town rival Yankees opened the most famous ballpark in America that eclipsed that capacity. Located in the lower Bronx, Yankee Stadium had a capacity of nearly 70,000, a monument to the game's increased popularity (and management's vision of a prosperous future).

Unlike most sports venues built since 1960, these ballparks were not financed by local governments, but were paid for by team ownership. Nearly a century after they were constructed, three of these venerable ballparks remain in use and enjoy the nostalgic affection of fans: Wrigley Field, Fenway Park, and Yankee Stadium. Efforts by short-sighted urban planners or greedy owners to replace them with modern facilities have thus far been rebuffed. These structures are precious historical landmarks, symbols of the special place that baseball enjoys in American life and culture, providing connections to teams and players of years gone by. Baseball's hold on the American mind has been repeatedly revealed in literature and the theater. Schoolboys for the past one hundred years have listened to eloquent readings of Ernest Thayer's famed poem, "Casey at the Bat," and in 1908 the American people first heard a song destined to become an American favorite: "Take Me Out to the Ball Game" was first sung on the vaudeville stage by a young lady imploring her male friend to escort her to a game. Over the years baseball has been featured in hundreds of Hollywood films and it has even entered our everyday conversations: everyone knows the meaning of "strike out," "can't get to first base," "home run," "grandstander," "out in left field" "grand slam," and "booted that one."

The 1890s: Years of Discord

The demise of the Players' League after only one year of operation in 1890 left the National League unchallenged as the nation's only true "major league." The American Association made a feeble effort to continue, but disbanded after the 1891 season, with the franchises in Washington, St Louis, Louisville, and Baltimore joining the National League. This meant, however, that the surviving circuit had swollen to 12 teams. No longer confronted by competition from other leagues for players or fans, the owners demonstrated the arrogance and power consistent with the best of America's robber barons of the day and put a tight lid on salaries. But the monopoly they now controlled did not guarantee financial success. Attendance fell to just 1,800,000 in 1894, due largely to a severe economic downturn.

The Baltimore Orioles and Boston Beaneaters were the undisputed best teams of the 1890s, with the two teams winning each championship until the Brooklyn Superbas broke their domination in 1899. The Orioles set the standard with their refined system of "scientific" or "inside" baseball. This style of play emphasized low-scoring games, sacrifice bunts, base stealing, hit-and-run, squeeze plays, slapping ground balls through holes in the infield, solid pitching, and strong defense. The scientific game was crafted to take advantage of the "dead" ball with which they played. A home run was an infrequent occurrence. The Orioles also played the game with a raucous attitude that pushed beyond the limits of good sportsmanship. They routinely employed roughhouse tactics in an attempt to intimidate their opponents. Spikes were sharpened and used as weapons on the base paths against vulnerable infielders. Holding base runners when unobserved by the single umpire and catcher interference with batters were routine tactics. A veteran Boston sportswriter commented that the Orioles played "the dirtiest ball ever seen in this country," and did not hesitate to "maim a fellow for life." Umpire baiting was also a given. Under player-manager John McGraw, the Orioles used every tactic possible – including physical attacks and verbal assault and intimidation – to sway the umpires their way on close calls. McGraw frequently encouraged Baltimore fans to unleash a barrage of verbal abuse upon the umpire when a call went against the home team. [1]

The prim and proper Connie Mack once commented that there were "no gentlemen" on the feisty Baltimore team, and umpire John Heydler (who later became a president of the National League) said that their brand of play was destructive to the game:

> They were mean, vicious, ready at any time to maim a rival player or an umpire. The worst of it was they got by with much of their brow beating and hooliganism. Other clubs patterned after them and I feel the lot of umpire never was worse than in the years when the Orioles were flying high.

Turbulence on the field was not restricted to the Orioles, however. As historian Charles Alexander points out, rowdy behavior was endemic in a game that was dominated by poorly educated young men who came from working-class backgrounds. He suggests that the brawling Cleveland Spiders under the leadership of Oliver "Patsy" Tebeau might have been even more notorious than the Orioles; in one notable brawl-marred game in Louisville the entire Cleveland nine was arrested for disturbing the peace and thrown into jail. Games were frequently punctuated by violence: beer bottles were thrown out of the stands at umpires or opposing players; angry players physically assaulted the lone umpire; foul language spewed out of the stands and the dugouts; fights between players were frequent, and occasionally players would charge into the grandstands to punch a fan whose criticisms became too personal. Even the umpires sometimes got into the action. In 1892, umpire Tim Hurst smacked a fan seated on a front row seat with his mask after being called "a monkey-faced dub." When a policeman came to the fan's assistance, he too was flattened. Critics of the game feared that unless the incessant umpire-baiting, foul language, and brawling were controlled, the game would never win over the middle-class fan.[2]

Perhaps the players had good reason for taking the field with a sour outlook, because the team owners, fortified by the reserve clause, responded to falling attendance by slashing salaries. By 1895 players' paychecks had fallen on average 30 percent from the days of the Players' League. In 1893, the owners put in place an unwritten policy limiting team payrolls to $30,000 and $2,400 for any individual player. Players grumbled but had no viable option other than to accept what management was willing to pay or quit the game. Despite the cuts in payrolls, most teams lost money during the Depression years. Although no firm evidence was forthcoming, the low salaries led to repeated rumors that some players sought to improve their income by consorting with gamblers to throw games, as well as betting on games in which they themselves played.[3]

Ban Johnson and the American League

The precarious condition of the game, exacerbated by insensitive and shortsighted owners, virtually invited the intervention of a dynamic and progressive leader. That person proved to be a hard bitten, hard-drinking, chain-smoking, overweight (300 pounds) journalist from Cincinnati, Byron Bancroft Johnson. A college drop-out, the humorless and imperious Ban Johnson had learned the intricacies of the game as a sports writer for the *Cincinnati Commercial Gazette*, and then as a successful chief executive of the Western League, a top minor league that consisted of teams located across the Midwest. In 1899, he took advantage of the patriotic fervor produced by the Spanish–American War and announced the establishment of an American League. In 1901, he approached the National League asking that his new league be recognized as a co-equal major league organization. He was predictably rebuffed.[4]

Johnson thereupon declared war, announcing that he would no longer respect the National League's reserved players and added new franchises in major Eastern cities. Johnson's success was made possible for the constant internal feuding and inept management by the National League's hierarchy. By offering a mere $500 more per player, the American League was able to lure more than 100 players away from its rival; among the more prominent of the defectors to the new league were three future Hall of Famers, all popular members of the Philadelphia Phillies: second baseman Napoleon Lajoie, slugger Ed Delahanty, and the reliable outfielder/high-percentage hitter Elmer Flick. With the economy booming, Johnson had little difficulty in finding good leadership for his league's franchises. Clark Griffith established a team in Washington, wealthy Philadelphia businessmen Ben and Tom Shibe joined with Connie Mack to create the Athletics, and Charles Comiskey agreed to head the White Sox in Chicago. Comiskey's friend, Cleveland coal magnate Charles Somers, not only provided crucial financial support for several franchises, but agreed to establish a team in his home city. Although the amount of Somers' investment is unknown, the best estimates are that he put up somewhere approaching $5 million to jump start Johnson's new league. In return, Johnson fondly referred to his financial angel as a man "of the daring soul, courageous heart, and a vast fortune." As Johnson's biographer, Eugene Murdock concludes, "Ban Johnson built the American League, but Charles Somers paid the bills."[5]

The American League did well at the box office, attracting more than 1,600,000 fans its first year of operation in 1901, just 5 percent behind the National League. The National League hierarchy responded to the challenge by sulking and filing an occasional law suit, none of which went far. The 1902 season made even the most obdurate National League owner recognize that Johnson's new league was for real.

While the National League was dominated by the Pittsburgh Pirates, which had finished a boring 27 games ahead of second place Brooklyn, the American League tantalized fans with a close pennant race ultimately won by Connie Mack's Philadelphia Athletics. Not surprisingly, the Athletics outdrew the Phillies by 140,000 spectators and the American League attracted 237,000 more fans than its rival.[6]

It was now clear that the National League had to make peace with its upstart rival. With big money at stake, that occurred with unexpected swiftness during winter 1902–03. It took only a few weeks for the two leagues to negotiate a peaceful resolution to their differences; most importantly, they agreed in principle to "co-exist peacefully and to abstain from signing the other league's players." They also agreed that both leagues could field teams in Chicago, Philadelphia, New York, and St Louis and that the two leagues would be considered equals as major league teams. A National Commission was created to supervise operations, consisting of the presidents of the two leagues and a third person whom the two leagues could mutually accept. That person turned out to be the politically well-connected Garry Herrmann, the jovial owner of the Cincinnati Reds. Herrmann, however, was not equal to jousting with the determined and domineering Ban Johnson, and neither was the president of the National League, Harry Pulliam. From the beginning, Johnson dominated the policy-making and administrative decisions of the National Commission.[7]

It did not take long for Ban Johnson to be recognized as "Baseball's Czar." With Johnson calling the shots, the Commission established a stable and orderly climate in which the game became the focus of the fans' attention rather than distracting legal struggles, player defections, labor disputes, franchise moves, and the collapse of entire leagues that had characterized the previous quarter-century of professional baseball. The two leagues entered into a 50-year period where there were no franchise moves and relatively little turnover in team ownership.

Consequently, the game enjoyed a half-century in which it was the unchallenged premier professional sport in the United States. To his credit, Johnson focused upon establishing the game's integrity. He pushed hard for "ladies day" games whereby women would be admitted at reduced charge, in hopes that their presence would help reduce antisocial behavior in the stands and on the field. He cracked down hard on players or managers who abused umpires, and launched a determined anti-gambling crusade. His effort to eliminate the influence of gamblers ultimately failed because many team owners did not share his apprehension, but his instincts were definitely on target.

One of the first innovations Johnson orchestrated was the creation of a postseason playoff between the champions of the two leagues. In October 1903, the National League champion Pittsburgh Pirates, an aggregation of skilled players led by shortstop Honus Wagner, took on Boston, then known variously as the Americans, Pilgrims, and Puritans. Wagner was clearly the best player of his generation, awkward and ungainly in appearance, but who fielded his position with grace and flair seldom matched thereafter. He also hit for high percentage, winning eight batting titles, retiring in 1917 after 21 seasons in the major leagues with a handsome .327 average. The vaunted Wagner batted only .222 in the World Series and the upstart American Leaguers triumphed five games to three. Historian Louis Masur concluded his absorbing study of the first World Series by noting that

> Ban Johnson took special joy in the victory. By force of will he had created the American League and went to war against the National. He had helped fashion a peace that looked as though it would last, and a circuit that attracted fans and played, in the parlance of the times, "a fast game."[8]

The last echoes of that war, however, had not completely faded. The following year, the New York Giants won the National League pennant but manager John McGraw refused to play the American League champions from Boston. McGraw absolutely hated Ban Johnson because of events that occurred in 1901 and 1902 when McGraw managed the American League Baltimore Orioles. Johnson had suspended McGraw several times for his ruthless umpire baiting, and gave him an indefinite suspension in July 1902. McGraw then moved on to the Giants but his hatred of Johnson endured until Johnson died in 1931. The hiatus of 1904 would not be repeated until a prolonged players' strike forced organized baseball to cancel the 1994 "fall classic."[9]

The following year, however, McGraw felt compelled to play the World Series because his players remained upset that they had lost out the previous autumn on a post-season payday. The 1905 confrontation between two excellent teams established the World Series as an important event in the minds of baseball fans everywhere. McGraw's Giants played his patented style of scientific baseball behind pitcher Christy Mathewson to win the Series. The enormous national interest this Series created removed any doubts but that it had become an important part of the national sports scene.

The Cyclone and the Georgia Peach

Under the leadership of Ban Johnson baseball became respectable. Exciting pennant races and the emergence of a large number of outstanding "star" players lured spectators to the ballparks in ever increasing numbers. In 1909, attendance exceeded seven million paid admissions. Fans easily reached the new parks which were located near subway or trolley lines. (It would not be until the 1920s that management had to deal with the headache of providing adequate automobile parking.) The Brooklyn club even changed its name from the Superbas to "Trolley Dodgers" as no less than nine trolley lines converged within a short walk of Ebbetts Field.

The value of individual franchises escalated as the game grew in stature and attendance soared. In 1906, the Boston National League franchise sold for $75,000, but five years later it was resold for $187,000, a very large sum for the day. The Chicago Cubs were purchased for $105,000 in 1905 but resold for $500,000 in 1915. When John McGraw went to the Giants in 1902, the team had just been purchased for $125,000, but in 1919 investment broker Charles

Stoneham paid the astounding sum of $1,820,000 for the team. That the new generation of owners were often civic leaders, with strong local political connections and deep roots in their communities, did not hurt the image of baseball either. League stability meant that strong loyalties were established with fans, producing an era of stability and public acclaim that even an occasional scandal or labor dispute could not destroy.[10]

One of the surest signs that baseball had achieved a special place in American life occurred on opening day in 1910, when President William Howard Taft – all 310 pounds of him – threw out the first ball of the season from the presidential box that Washington Senators owner Clark Griffith had installed by the team's first base dugout. Taft is also credited with creating one of baseball's important traditions; during the middle of the seventh inning of a game he was attending, he stood up to stretch, and the entire stands, in deference to their president, also rose. The seventh inning stretch was thus, at least according to this tale, added to baseball's timeless traditions. In 1915, Woodrow Wilson, an inveterate sports fan, became the first President to attend a World Series game when he traveled to Philadelphia to watch the Phillies tangle with the Boston Red Sox.

The improved quality of on-the-field play did not hurt either. Each team had its own "star" players, and the reputations of several have endured. One of those whose career spanned the change from the disputatious 1890s and the new era of public acceptance, was pitcher Denton T. "Cy" Young. Born and raised on a farm in northeastern Ohio, as a teenager Young developed a local reputation as a hard throwing righthander – earning him the nickname of "Cyclone" because of the velocity of his intimidating fastball. In 1890, at the age of 23 he reached the major leagues as a pitcher for the Cleveland Spiders. He proceeded to pitch in the major leagues for 22 years – an amazing feat for a time when pitchers were not pampered, conditioning programs and therapy treatments were virtually non-existent, with expectations that starters pitch every four days and sometimes in relief in between. Young stood an imposing 6' 2" and weighed about 180 pounds. As his career unfolded, Young expanded his repertoire of pitches by developing two distinct curve balls and a change-of-pace. Like his contemporaries, he also used a spitball upon occasion, which when properly loaded and thrown, would veer wildly as it approached the plate. (The spitball would not be declared an illegal pitch until 1920.)

Young pitched for ten seasons with the National League Spiders, winning more than 20 games each season; three times he recorded 30 or more wins. In 1901, Young was one of the more than 100 players who joined the Boston club of the American League, more than, doubling his $3,000 salary. Although he was one of the oldest pitchers in the league, Young registered back-to-back 30-win seasons. In 1904, Young pitched 24 consecutive hitless innings – a record still unmatched – and threw the first perfect game from the longer pitching distance of 60' 6" against Connie Mack's potent Philadelphia Athletics. Despite his years, Young continued to pitch effectively, eventually retiring at age 45 in 1911 with a career won–lost record of 511–316 (both totals remain all-time records and surely will never be equaled).[11]

Figure 6.1 The Georgia Peach, Ty Cobb, flies around third base on his way to home plate. His flashing spikes intimidated many an opponent, and his mastery of the "scientific" or "inside" game epitomized baseball during the early decades of the twentieth century. © Bettmann/CORBIS.

The unquestioned superstar of the prewar era was a center fielder for the Detroit Tigers, the tempestuous Tyrus Raymond Cobb. Beginning with his first at-bat in August 1905, when he slapped a double to right-center field, the "Georgia Peach" proceeded to dominate the game like no other player of his era. His play was the epitome of the "scientific" game. As he later commented, he relied upon "brains over brawn," which meant "the hit-and-run, the steal and the double-steal, the bunt in all its varieties, the squeeze, the ball hit to the opposite field and the ball punched through the openings in the defense for the single." A native of a small town in northern Georgia, Ty Cobb was intensely driven to succeed at his chosen craft. Not blessed with great natural ability, he drove himself to become the game's top player. Everything about Cobb was in excess – his ferocious base running, sliding into base with spikes flashing, continual verbal warfare with teammates, opponents, umpires, and even fans in the stands that featured an unending flow of vulgarity and venom, an icy intensity in the batter's box. As he once told a young player,

> Always have a belligerent, take-charge attitude up there. You can cultivate quite a "mad on" while awaiting your turn at bat, a cold determination to ram the ball down the pitcher's throat. You'd be surprised how effective it is. It will show up in your walk, in your eyes, in the way you hold your head, the stance you take. Now the pitcher is fearing *you*.[12]

As his many confrontations with teammates, opponents, and everyday citizens revealed, Cobb feared no one and, holding an exaggerated sense of personal honor tinged with a mean streak of racism, was always ready for a fight. His many on-the-field scrapes led to frequent fines and suspensions by league president Ban Johnson, who deplored his behavior. In more than one instance he beat adversaries senseless; in one notable fight in a hotel room with a teammate, he beat him unconscious by repeatedly banging his head against the bed headboard. In several instances he went into the stands to attack his hecklers, and in one embarrassing encounter he even beat up a physically handicapped taunter seated 12 rows from the field. He later recalled, "When I played ball, I didn't play for fun. . . . Its no pink tea, and mollycoddles had better stay out. It's a contest and everything that implies, a struggle for supremacy, a survival of the fittest." When he retired as a player at age 43 in 1928, Cobb held an incredible 43 major league season or individual records. He won 12 American League batting titles, including nine in a row, and had a lofty .367 lifetime batting average that has never been equaled and his career number of base hits (4,191) was not exceeded until 1985 by Pete Rose. Blessed with above average speed, Cobb terrorized the opposition with his cagy and aggressive base running, leading the league in stolen bases six times; in 1915 he stole 96 bases, a record that stood until Maury Wills of the Los Angeles Dodgers eclipsed it in 1962.

Cobb's personal life was almost a mirror reflection of his on-the-field ferocity. Clearly racist, he seemed to single out African Americans for personal abuse. He repeatedly got into scrapes with private citizens – bellmen, laborers, whomever. In more than one instance he even hit an African American women whom he felt had not shown proper respect to him. In 1914 he made the headlines when he pulled a revolver – he routinely carried a pistol when off the field – on a neighborhood butcher whom he felt had shortchanged his wife. Cobb was detested by his teammates, some of whom demanded trades to get away from him. He returned the disdain, usually skipping most of spring training just to stay away from them. On the road he preferred to live and eat alone. His behavior did not change after he retired in 1928. His two marriages failed. His children shunned him and he lived out his life alone and angry as his mental problems become more pronounced. He compounded his personal troubles with excessive drinking. When Cobb died in 1961, only three persons associated with baseball bothered to attend his funeral. Yet his impact upon the game was fundamental; one of the initial five players elected to the Hall of Fame, he garnered more votes than any other candidate, including Babe Ruth. As biographer Charles Alexander concludes,

He was never an easy man to know, never easy to get along with in or out of uniform, never really at peace with himself or the world around him. Ty Cobb was the most volatile, the most fear-inspiring presence ever to appear on a baseball field.[13]

Calling the Shots: the Manager

The role of manager evolved steadily after Harry Wright created the position with the Cincinnati Red Stockings. Although there were several notable mangers during this period, two men with distinctly different personalities stand out – the pugnacious John J. McGraw and the gentlemanly, unflappable "tall tactician," Connie Mack. Both men enjoyed extraordinarily long tenures in their positions; McGraw managed the New York Giants from 1902 until he retired in 1932, while Mack sat quietly on the bench orchestrating the play of his Philadelphia Athletics from 1901 until 1950; despite many losing seasons, Mack was never fired. That undoubtedly was because he also owned the club.

McGraw had begun his career as a third basemen in 1891 with the notoriously rowdy Baltimore Orioles, and quickly became recognized as someone who would use whatever means necessary to win a game. One journalist condemned him as "the toughest of toughs and an abomination of the diamond," while another said he was a

rough, unruly man, who is constantly playing dirty ball. He has the vilest tongue of any ball-player. . . . He has demonstrated his low training, and his own manager knows that, while he is a fine ball-player, yet he adopts every low and contemptible method that his erratic brain can conceive to win a play by a dirty trick.[14]

From the beginning of his professional career, McGraw was recognized as a special student of the game. This prompted his being named manager of the Orioles in 1899 at the age of 26. Throughout his career, the aptly named "Muggsy" (a name he detested and no one dared use in his presence) approached the game as if his very life depended upon winning. Among many talents, he became a master at intimidating umpires. They were his natural enemy and he used every tactic possible to make them bend to his will. Although he never hit an umpire, he did become a master of what he called "judicious kicking" during his many nose-to-nose confrontations with his adversaries in blue. One umpire once said that he "eats gunpowder every morning and washes it down with warm blood."[15] His teams reflected the personality of their manager, and his record spoke for itself: 10 league championships, 11 second place finishes, and three World Series championships. Pitcher Christy Mathewson, his favorite player, summarized his impact when he said, "The club is McGraw."[16]

Frustrated with the suspensions handed down by Ban Johnson, McGraw abandoned the American League in 1902 and assumed the reins of the Giants. He was a perfect fit for New York, his temperamental Irish personality readily embraced by Giants fans. When the Giants defeated the Philadelphia Athletics in the 1905 World Series, fans stormed the field at the old Polo Grounds and carried the players and manager off on their shoulders. The *New York Times* reported that the crowd's cheering following the final out was a "deafening, reverberating roar" that "lifted Manhattan's soil from its base."[17] The hard drinking McGraw would become one of New York's most popular residents, and when not at the Polo Grounds ripping the umpires, could be found at one of the several nearby race tracks, where he engaged his love of wagering, or at one of his favorite watering holes buying a round for the boys.

If ever there was a polar opposite of McGraw, it was Connie Mack. Born in 1864 to Irish immigrant parents, Cornelius McGillicuddy grew into a tall, slender man with a talent for baseball. He changed his name to Connie Mack, perhaps in deference to the strong anti-Irish sentiment of the day, but according to baseball lore to assure that his name fitted into newspaper box scores. Although he played at every position but pitcher, he was primarily a catcher with the Washington club of the American Association. In 1901, Mack joined the new Philadelphia Athletics as general manager, purchasing 25 percent of the ownership. Over the years, Mack acquired all outstanding shares, thus becoming sole owner. For 50 years, Mack served simultaneously as owner, general manager, and field manager. His half century produced a record that included nine pennants but 17 last place finishes; he won 3,776 games and lost a record high 4,925. He built two powerful teams that won seven pennants and four World Series (twice during 1911–1915, and twice again during 1929–1932), but both times after building championship teams, he systematically dismantled them by selling off the team's star players to remain financially solvent.[18]

Connie Mack was a picture of calmness and control, sitting quietly in the dugout, using his scorecard to move players into proper fielding position. Tall and slender, he eschewed the tradition of the manager wearing a uniform, invariably wearing a three-piece suit with a tight white collar and necktie held neatly in place by a stickpin. Instead of the traditional baseball cap, he wore a derby or straw sailor hat. Unlike McGraw, who prided himself on controlling every move on the field, Mack tended to permit his players to make decisions and assumed that as professionals they knew what to do. Throughout his career he was widely respected, win or lose, as a man who embodied the best of baseball's virtues as he expected clean play on the field and good behavior off the field. He was an ideal leader in the eyes of Ban Johnson, the very antithesis of the tempestuous McGraw. Mack rarely swore but could command obedience from even the most arrogant player with a harsh stare or pointed comment. He insisted that his players call him "Mr Mack" while he always addressed them as "Mister." He rarely argued with or shouted at the umpires, and off the field he was the cautious, quiet businessman who did not swear, smoke, gamble, or drink, four traits common to players and managers of the day. Mack's quiet demeanor and personal integrity would become his hallmark.

In 1922, the United States Supreme Court would rule that organized baseball was a sport and not a business and thereby exempt from federal antitrust statutes, but to Connie Mack baseball was all business. It was his sole source of income and he had to rely upon gate receipts and concession sales to pay the bills. At one point he revealed his businesslike approach to the game:

It is more profitable for me to have a team that is in contention for most of the season but finishes about fourth. A team like that will draw well enough during the first part of the season to show a profit for the year, and when they don't win you don't have to give them a raise for the next year.[19]

Immediately after taking over in Philadelphia in 1901 with a war raging with the established National League, Mack signed star second baseman Nap Lajoie away from the across-town Phillies. John McGraw sarcastically commented that Mack's team would soon be a big money loser, or in the parlance of the day a "white elephant." Mack playfully seized upon McGraw's comment and adopted the elephant as the team's mascot, putting a cute pachyderm on the team's uniform (where it remains to this day in Oakland). He even acquired a live elephant that for years cavorted around the ballpark to the fan's delight. In 1905, Mack and McGraw met head on in the World Series, complete with one elephant. Powered by Christy Matthewson's pitching, McGraw prevailed in their first meeting, but he would lose to the Athletics in the World Series of 1911 and 1913. During Mack's early years, the Athletics were a dominant force, winning six of the American League's first 14 pennants, before the team fell on hard financial times due to the salary wars created by the Federal League in 1914–15.[20]

Mack's second run at baseball fame occurred when he was nearing the age of 70 and many sportswriters were questioning his ability to manage in the new age of power baseball. Featuring catcher Mickey Cochrane, slugger Jimmy Fox, hard-hitting outfielder Al Simmons, and one of baseball's all-time great pitchers, Robert "Lefty" Grove, between 1925 and 1933 the Athletics finished no lower than third, dethroning the powerful New York Yankees in 1929–30–31 and defeating the Chicago Cubs and the St Louis Cardinals in the World Series of 1929 and 1930. Once again, financial problems forced Mack to sell off his team's stars. This time the culprit was the Great Depression; despite successes on the field, the Athletics home attendance dropped by more than 200,000 between 1929 and 1932. Things never got better for Mack and his Athletics. Over his last 17 years, until he retired at age 86 in 1950, the Athletics had only one first-division finish, a distant fourth in 1948.

The Federal League Challenge

Under the leadership of Ban Johnson baseball became a stable and profitable enterprise and its popularity grew apace. Between 1903 and 1914, player salaries gradually inched upward, while the profits of team owners improved substantially. In 1910, the average major league player earned about $3,000, which compared favorably to the annual salary of a factory worker of $700 or a skilled laborer of $1,200. Nonetheless, the players looked at the large crowds in the grandstands and concluded that they were not getting their fair share of the profits. They also harbored resentments over the behavior of tyrannical managers, petty team regulations that often produced fines and suspensions, the power of owners to trade them against their wishes, and the lack of a uniform player contract. But they were severely constrained in their freedom of action by the reserve clause. They had few viable options: quit the game (which for most would have meant earning that $700 annual income), or accept what management offered. A few brave souls each year attracted sports page coverage by "holding out" during spring training in hopes of obtaining a more lucrative offer. When that occurred, the owners easily stirred up negative fan reaction against the recalcitrant player for being disloyal. Even such stars as Ty Cobb had little leverage. In 1913, the owner of the Detroit Tigers bluntly told him during a holdout, "You will play for Detroit or you won't play for anybody."[21] Cobb caved shortly before the season began.

The profits being earned by successful franchises naturally attracted the attention of big investors interested in cutting themselves in on the action. Thus there appeared yet another new league in 1914–15. The short-lived Federal League contributed to a financial disaster for the management of all three leagues while giving players only a temporary boost in pay. In 1913, the Federal League was organized but it initially seemed of little significance since it pledged not to sign any player who was reserved by an existing team. But before the 1914 season, wealthy Chicago businessman James Gilmore agreed to take over the struggling league; he had big plans that resulted in an eight-team league that included franchises in four cities directly challenging major league teams (Brooklyn, Chicago, St Louis, and Pittsburgh), while franchises in Kansas City, Indianapolis, Baltimore, and Buffalo slugged it out with top minor league clubs. His request to be included in the National Commission and to have the Federal League designated as a third major league was summarily rebuffed by Ban Johnson who took to the field of battle in defense of his empire like a medieval baron. He bluntly told Gilmore, "There is no room for a third league," and tenaciously attacked the new league for what it was – a significant threat to the peace and prosperity of the Nationals and Americans. Some thought Johnson guilty of hypocrisy; it was he who had created a new league a decade earlier, but now he set out with determination to destroy the Federal League in its infancy.[22]

Between the 1914 and 1915 seasons, Gilmore's league signed 81 players away from the two established leagues along with 140 top minor leaguers with the bait of substantially increased salaries. The turbulence created by the heavy turnover in team rosters greatly alienated fans, who stayed away from the parks of all three leagues. This put the owners in a squeeze; just as their labor costs were more then doubling, their income was in free fall. In 1914, only 1.7 million persons paid their way into one of the three leagues' parks, a figure that compared unfavorably with the benchmark year of 1903. It is estimated that at least half of the teams lost money in 1914, and those that had a profit were only marginally in the black. Connie Mack lost an estimated $80,000 despite winning the 1914 American League pennant; consequently, shortly after running the championship flag up the Shibe Park flagpole, he held his famous fire sale that resulted in his either selling or releasing outright his star players. In 1915, attendance improved only marginally and remained below the 1903 level.

For a time it seemed that the situation would be resolved in the courts when the Federal League brought suit alleging that organized baseball constituted a cartel in restraint of trade. The case ended up in the court of a federal district judge whose future would be intricately intertwined with baseball – Judge Kenesaw Mountain Landis. At the formal hearing, Landis left little doubt that his sympathies lay with the game itself and neither adversary. Instead of issuing a ruling, Landis simply sat on the case as the season of 1915 unfolded, giving off not-so-subtle hints that he preferred the two sides to come to a mutually agreeable settlement. That is essentially what eventually happened.

Escalating salaries dictated that the impasse could not be permitted to continue, and after the disastrous season of 1915, common sense prevailed. Complex negotiations resulted in the folding of the Federal League, whose owners lost an estimated $10 million. However, the wealthy Chicago restaurant owner Charles Weeghman, who had operated the Chicago Whales, was permitted to purchase the National League Cubs and he moved them into his new stadium on the north side of the city, where they remain to this day. Federal League president John Gilmore ruefully commented upon the conclusion of this turbulent episode of baseball history: "I thought there was plenty of room for three major leagues. I admit I had the wrong perspective. . . . There is no room for three major leagues."[23]

Although most parties were reasonably satisfied with the complex settlement, it left the owners of the Baltimore franchise of the Federal League out in the cold. They thereupon filed suit in federal court alleging a violation of the Sherman Antitrust Act. The case eventually ended up before the United States Supreme Court, resulting in one of the most curious decisions ever handed down by the high court. In 1922, the Court handed baseball unprecedented "umbrella" protection from antitrust provisions of federal law. Associate Justice Oliver Wendell Holmes wrote the majority decision that proclaimed that although baseball was a for-profit business, it nonetheless was not "trade or commerce in the commonly accepted use of those words." Players did not produce a product, only "effort," and the court ruled that this "product" was only "incidental" to interstate commerce. Although millions of dollars were tied up in the overall enterprise and although the 16 teams played in seven states and the District of Columbia, the tight cartel that was now organized baseball was nonetheless declared exempt from federal antitrust laws. As a result of this incredibly friendly decision, baseball became, and remains yet today, the only professional sport to enjoy such an extraordinary exemption from federal oversight, an advantage that its leadership has exploited ever since.[24]

Crisis: Gamblers fix the World Series of 1919

With peace restored, owners moved swiftly to cut players salaries back to pre-Federal League levels. Although the players groused over their reduced income, they put on a good show in 1916 with two close pennant races. Attendance jumped 30 percent. The Brooklyn Robins (briefly so named after their corpulent manager Wilbert Robinson), brought the first league championship to Flatbush since 1899, but lost the World Series in five games to the Boston Red Sox. The Bostonians were led by a rising star, left-handed pitcher George "Babe" Ruth, who won 23 games during the regular season. In the second game of the World Series the 22-year-old phenomenon pitched all 14 innings in a tense 2–1 Red Sox victory.

The season of 1916 restored baseball's popularity, but two major crises loomed around the corner. The first of these was what stance to take after the United States entered the Great War in Europe in April 1917. Should the season be cancelled? Baseball was a game played by young men, most of whom were of prime military age, and baseball's leadership found itself in a quandary. Would the teams be so depleted by player departures for military duty that the 1917 season would be imperiled? Those fears proved unfounded and the season was completed without serious difficulty as mobilization occurred relatively slowly. By the time the Chicago White Sox defeated the New York Giants in the 1917 World Series, only 40 players had been lost to military service.

As the first among equals on the governing National Commission, American League president Ban Johnson responded shrewdly to public opinion, making several popular patriotic gestures. He ordered that the US flag be flown at all games, required that bands be on hand to play the national anthem, plastered stadiums with posters urging fans to purchase war bonds, and granted free tickets to all men in uniform. He even required his American League teams to take part in military drill training, offering a prize to the league's best marching team. While National League players enjoyed a good laugh at their expense, the American League teams underwent regular instruction from an army sergeant in close-order marching drills that culminated in late August with a much-hyped patriotic marching contest. The sixth place St Louis Browns walked off with the grand prize of $500, one of the few triumphs in their long and dismal history.[25]

The season of 1918, however, was a disaster. The departure of 227 major leaguers for military duty or for conscripted work in defense factories, made a shambles out of the season. Older players, many of them retired and others with diminished skills, were hustled back onto the field of play. In May 1918, Secretary of War Newton Baker further complicated things for baseball with his order that all able men between the ages of 18 and 45 had to serve either in the military or work in a defense factory or shipbuilding yard. Ban Johnson considered canceling the season in July but the owners overruled their "czar", although agreeing to shorten the season to 140 games. Few Americans got excited when the World Series was played in early September with the Boston Red Sox defeating the Chicago Cubs in a widely ignored World Series. Had the war continued, the 1919 season would undoubtedly have been cancelled, but when an Armistice went into effect on November 11, 1918, it meant that the 1919 season would proceed on schedule.[26]

In retrospect, it might have been best had Johnson cancelled the season, because 1919 became the year that baseball fans would like to forget. The World Series of that year pitted the heavily favored Chicago White Sox against a gritty but clearly underdog Cincinnati team. The Reds, however, romped to a 5–3 game triumph (the World Series had reverted to a best-of-nine format for this and the next two seasons), but the glory of that upset victory was to be dashed when it was revealed that eight Chicago players had pocketed $110,000 from two different sets of gamblers to assure that their large wagers made on the Reds at attractive odds would pay off. The American people did not learn about this fraud until a year after the fact, although one dogged newspaper man, Hugh Fullerton, had published in the *Chicago Herald and Examiner* a series of inflammatory allegations shortly after the Series ended. Fullerton had long been considered by baseball men as a hopeless gadfly, and so his charges were dismissed as unsubstantiated sensationalism. But Fullerton, whose suspicions had been fueled by comments made to him by ex-pitcher Christy Mathewson who covered the Series as a reporter, continued publishing his speculations during the 1920 season, charging a cover-up and demanding a thorough investigation.[27]

In October 1920, Philadelphia gambler Billy Maharg created a major stir when he was quoted in the *Philadelphia North American* under the sensational headline, "Gamblers Promised White Sox $100,000 to Lose." The next day two rattled White Sox players, star slugger Joe Jackson and ace lefthander Eddie Cicotte, admitted to throwing the Series under oath before a federal grand jury in Chicago. They also implicated several teammates. Maharg was part of a small group of Philadelphia gamblers that had promised the players $100,000 to dump the Series, although they only managed to fork over $10,000. In two hours of testimony, with tears streaming down his face, Cicotte described how he had made two defensive errors in one inning that gave Game Four to the Reds and how he had "grooved" the ball down the middle of the plate in the Game One so that the Cincinnati batters could "read the label on it." He and other witnesses then explained how pitcher Claude Williams had lost Game Two with an uncharacteristic streak of wildness, and why the normally reliable outfielder Happy Felsch managed to botch two easy plays in the sixth inning of Game Five. When star hitter "Shoeless Joe" Jackson entered the federal court house to testify before the grand jury, a young boy reportedly said, "Say it ain't so, Joe! Say it ain't so!" And Jackson is reported to have quietly responded, "I'm afraid it is, son." Indictments were handed down by the grand jury charging the eight Chicago White Sox players with conspiracy, but legal maneuvering prevented the trial from taking place until August 1921.

Baseball executives quickly went into full-scale damage control, expressing both incredulity and outrage. They denied any knowledge of gambling influences in their game, a tale that many insider baseball men found amusing. Baseball executives plaintively pointed out that even the best of hitters have slumps, that top pitchers sometimes get shelled, and that excellent fielders occasionally bobble a ground ball or make a bad throw. Detecting whether a player is deliberately attempting to make a misplay is no easy task. As Ban Johnson later recalled, he watched every game and had no inkling that the fix was in:

> It all unfolded naturally to us in the grandstand. It seemed just hard luck that the great southpaw [Claude Williams] should be visited by a streak of wildness in two vital innings when all the remainder of the game he was steady as a clock.[28]

The truth is that Johnson had long warned of the dangers of gambling but team owners had not responded to his concerns. For years, as historian Charles Alexander has established, the corrosive influence of gamblers had been bubbling near the surface, especially in games that involved the notorious gambler-fixer Hal Chase, who played first base for the Reds and the Giants. Charles Seymour concludes along the same vein as Alexander: "The evidence is abundantly clear . . . that the groundwork for the crooked 1919 World Series, like most striking events, was long prepared." The scandal, he writes, "was not an aberration brought about solely by a handful of villainous players. It was a culmination of corruption and attempts at corruption that reached back nearly twenty years."[29] Apparently it was easier for most of baseball's executives to ignore the many warning signs; fearful that if they cracked down hard the resulting publicity would damage ticket sales, they preferred to leave well enough alone. The result was a public relations disaster that for a time seemed to have the potential for destroying organized baseball.

The sordid details of the corruption of the 1919 World Series are incredibly complex and the complete story probably will never be known. Suffice it to say that the episode is replete with enough duplicity, corruption, double crosses, and broken trust to fill many a book – as indeed it has. However, the essential story is relatively simple. Chicago pitcher Ed Cicotte hatched the idea to sell the series for about $100,000, and he made contact with two separate groups of gamblers. Several of his teammates agreed to participate, apparently angry about their low pay checks handed out by the unpopular, autocratic White Sox owner, "Old Roman" Charles Comiskey. One group of gamblers was headed by Abe Attell, a former featherweight boxing champion and co-conspirator with Billy Maharg. The other group was headed by the infamous New York City gambler and underworld figure, Arnold Rothstein, who was in cahoots with a few big-time gamblers from Boston. Two days before the Series began, unknown to the Philadelphia crowd, Rothstein's agents met with the players in a south side Chicago hotel and handed over $40,000 with the remaining $60,000 to be paid after the deed was done. The plan called for the White Sox to throw only selected games so as to cover their tracks, with Rothstein placing his bets on the outcome of the Series and individual games accordingly. He even bet in a very public manner on the White Sox when he knew the fix was in so as to cover his tracks. Rothstein's biographer estimates that after all expenses were paid, New York's premier gambler pocketed about $350,000.[30]

On November 6, 1920, a grand jury filed indictments against the "Chicago Eight" along with three gamblers. Notably missing from the list was Arnold Rothstein, who professed complete innocence. He cleverly had associates do his dirty work while keeping to his residence in New York City.[31] The subsequent trial was a farce. Shortly before it opened, the District Attorney discovered that all of the grand jury records and physical evidence in the case had been stolen! Even transcripts of the players' confessions before the grand jury had been lost. Inspired by this development, Cicotte and Jackson recanted their confessions and developed serious cases of amnesia. Without evidence or credible witnesses, the District Attorney dropped the case in February 1921. Several months later, new indictments were handed down and the trial finally occurred in mid-July, 1921. Once again the fix was in. The essential evidence was still missing and several new witnesses had fled to Canada, where they successfully fought extradition. Other witnesses contracted cases of serious memory loss and the judge was forced to issue a narrow set of instructions to the jury, which made the jury's decision inevitable and easy. It declared everyone innocent and the much relieved Chicago Eight spent that evening celebrating.

Even before their hangovers had lifted, however, they learned that organized baseball now had a new sheriff in town who was determined to mete out his own special form of frontier justice. His name was Kenesaw Mountain Landis, a former federal judge, whose legal acumen was highly suspect but whose reputation for personal honesty and love for baseball was unquestioned. In November 1920 he had accepted an invitation to become baseball's first Commissioner at the lofty salary of $50,000 per year (his salary as federal district judge was $7,500). In the wake of the White Sox revelations, the owners believed that baseball desperately needed a new leader to assure the public that its house was clean; the irascible Landis was that person. Thus the Chicago Eight awoke the day after their acquittal to learn that the Commissioner had little confidence in the Chicago system of justice. He had banned them from baseball for life. Landis declared,

> Regardless of the verdict of juries, no player who throws a ball game, no player who undertakes or promises to throw a ball game, no player that sits in conference with a bunch of crooked players and gamblers where the ways and means of throwing a game are discussed and does not promptly tell his club about it, will ever play professional baseball.

Landis even tossed third baseman George "Buck" Weaver out of the game despite the fact he took none of the gambler's money and did not participate in throwing any of the games. His sin? He had originally agreed to the scam but changed his mind before the first game. His crime was that he should have reported the conspiracy. "Birds of a feather flock together," Landis told the press. "Men associating with gamblers and crooks should expect no leniency."[32]

In appointing Landis, the owners had dumped the three-man Commission that had run things since 1903, empowering baseball's first commissioner with virtually unlimited authority to take action for "the good of baseball." They agreed that he would have absolute power to take action against any person or any club he "suspected" of doing anything "detrimental to the best interests of the national game." The two league presidents would have subordinate authority. The owners agreed "to loyally support their commissioner" and to "acquiesce in his decisions even when they believed them mistaken," and not to criticize him or his actions publicly. Armed with these unlimited powers, and superbly confident in his own judgment, Landis sacked the players and won widespread public acclaim. The scandal was put to rest. Soon baseball was soaring to new heights of popularity.

The Babe

Historians have often referred to the 1920s as the "Golden Age" of American sports. Millions of fans flocked to stadiums to watch their favorite teams and "star" players perform. Even such heretofore overlooked sports – the Olympics, tennis, golf, swimming, and boxing – became the stuff of stunning headlines. Sports became, seemingly overnight, very big business. This so-called "Golden Age" coincided with major advances in communications. Motion pictures, radio, and a greatly expanded print media both benefitted from and contributed to this growing sports frenzy. Thus as the United States returned to what President Warren G. Harding called a time of "normalcy," the stage was set for the coronation of George Herman "Babe" Ruth as the most popular sports figure of the twentieth century.[33]

Ironically, the man who would be known for his home run hitting prowess had first attracted the attention of serious baseball fans as a young pitcher with the Boston Red Sox in 1916 when he won 23 games. However, his ability to handle a bat could not be ignored, and so manager Ed Barrow began inserting him in the lineup at first base or in right field when he was not on the mound. Up until he burst on the baseball scene, the home run was not only an infrequent event, but most baseball purists disdained it, preferring the scientific game of well placed singles ("hit 'em where they ain't" as Wee Willie Keeler used to say), stolen bases, and well-executed hit-and-run plays. Now fans flocked to see the powerfully built Ruth swing from his heels, thrusting his 6' 2" frame into the ball with enormous power. That he had overcome a difficult childhood in Baltimore that included spending several years in a home for delinquent boys, only added to his public persona. Nineteen-nineteen was his last year with the Red Sox and his last season as a pitcher. Although listed as a pitcher, he set a major league record of 29 home runs. Despite the fact that his team finished far down the standings, Ruth's pitching and hitting, coupled with his youthful exuberance and flamboyant personality attracted large crowds. Reporters loved his accessibility and his willingness to say something funny or even provocative. In his truncated career as a pitcher, Ruth won 85 games and had a sparkling career earned run average of 2.70.

The owner of the Red Sox was the heavily indebted Harry Frazee, who regularly seemed to lose large sums producing bad Broadway musicals and making erratic stock investments. When Ruth demanded a doubling of his salary to $20,000, Frazee sold his contract to the New York Yankees for $100,000 and promptly lost it in another bad Broadway musical that closed after a two-week run. Ruth's pitching and hitting had enabled the Red Sox to defeat the Chicago Cubs in the lackluster 1918 World Series, and it would be the last such triumph to be enjoyed by the baseball fans of New England until the fall of 2004. Ruth's trade to the Yankees created one of baseball's most popular and enduring myths – Frazee, it was contended by generations of disgruntled Red Sox fans, had imposed the "Curse of the Bambino" upon one of baseball's most storied franchises. After the sale of Ruth, the Red Sox went into a tailspin, finishing in last place in nine of the next 11 seasons. And although the Sox won four American League pennants between 1946 and 1986, they failed to win the World Series. Finally, after 86 long seasons, the Sox exorcised the curse in fall 2004 with a decisive four-game sweep over the St Louis Cardinals.

Babe Ruth thus landed in the nation's largest and most exciting city at the very time when sports were in ascendancy. In 1920, he became the unquestioned toast of New York when he smashed 54 home runs while batting an astronomical .376.

The Babe was the biggest show in the town that was the center of the growing entertainment business and hub of the national media. His on- and off-the-field exploits made him seem bigger than life, swatting towering home runs by day and enjoying the city's night life afterwards. His hearty appetite for vast quantities of food and alcohol became the stuff of legend, and his sexual appetite was equally prodigious as he spent many a night with a seemingly endless parade of willing women. On the road, roommate (and Hall of Fame pitcher) Waite Hoyt seldom saw him until the sun came up in the morning.

Shortly after arriving in New York, Ruth hooked up with a former sports cartoonist turned publicist, Christy Walsh, who helped mold Ruth's public image as benefactor of the downtrodden and friend of children. Not content with merely telling the Ruth story, Walsh set out to make his client a national icon of mythic proportions, and in the process help satisfy Ruth's unrelenting thirst for vast amounts of money. Walsh's efforts often made it difficult to separate fact from fiction. He especially played up Ruth's many visits to children's hospitals – an activity that Ruth in fact enjoyed. Soon Walsh had Ruth appearing in motion pictures, earning $8,000 a week on the vaudeville circuit telling corny jokes, endorsing an endless line of products (Babe Ruth Gum, Babe Ruth baseball caps, Babe Ruth Home Run Shoes, Bambino Smoking Tobacco), and publishing how-to-play baseball books, children's stories, and a long running weekly syndicated newspaper column, all ghost written by the creative Christy Walsh or one of his associates. Ruth saw nothing wrong with simultaneously endorsing Reo automobiles in St Louis, Packards in Boston, and Cadillacs in New York. At one point Walsh had four ghost writers working overtime cranking out the Babe's many publications. (Ruth once cryptically commented that one of those men, Bill Slocum, "writes more like me than anyone I know.")[34]

With the cagy Walsh calling the shots and prudently managing Ruth's investments while putting words in his mouth, Ruth amassed a substantial nest egg despite his penchant for spending money as prodigiously as he consumed food and beer. Thus he easily survived the Great Depression and lived comfortably until his death from cancer in 1948. Ruth was the first of the great sports celebrities of a celebrity-saturated era. As historian Jules Tygiel aptly summarized Ruth's life,

> He symbolized not only the exuberance and excesses of the 1920s, but the emergent triumph of personality and image in a modern America suddenly positioned to glorify these attributes. Lavishly chronicled on radio and in print, memorialized in photos and film, elevated to a new form of adoration in testimonial advertising, and molded by shrewd public relations, Ruth fulfilled people's fantasies and embodied their new reality.[35]

His performance on the field was equal to his public image. In his second year in New York, taking advantage of a more lively ball, Ruth hammered 59 home runs – an astounding number for the time – and drove in 170 runs while leading the Yankees to their first World Series appearance. His salary jumped to an unprecedented $52,000, a fact that only intensified public adoration in this materialistic age when the self-made man myth reached its apex. He had an "off season" in 1922

Figure 6.2 Babe Ruth uncorks a home run late in his career as a member of the Boston Braves during the early season of 1935. He retired a few weeks after this picture was taken. © Bettmann/CORBIS.

when he sat out a 39-game suspension imposed by Landis for playing in unsanctioned post-season exhibition games, hit "only" 35 home runs, and began to show sizeable girth. Publicly chastised for his poor showing by Mayor Jimmy Walker for "letting down the kids," Ruth showed up for spring training in 1923 in top shape. It was only fitting that in the inaugural game played at Yankee Stadium he smashed a home run in the ballpark already being called "the House that Ruth Built." Before record crowds, Ruth hit 41 home runs and enjoyed a .544 on-base percentage. He was selected unanimously as the American League's most valuable player. He capped off that glorious year by hitting three home runs in leading the Yankees to their first World Series championship in an exciting cross-town match-up with the Giants.

Ruth continued his assault upon American League pitching throughout the rest of the decade, averaging 49 home runs a season and 152 runs batted in, while batting 353. The Yankees continued their domination of baseball during that time, winning four pennants and three World Series championships. Ruth's salary continued to escalate and he earned a salary of $70,000 in 1927 when he hit 60 home runs, a record that would last for 34 years. In 1930 his salary topped out at $80,000, which was more than double that of any other major league player. Many Americans marveled that his salary that year was $5,000 higher than that of President Herbert Hoover. Asked how he could justify making more than the depression-besieged President, Ruth responded, "Why not? I had a better year than he did."[36]

By the early 1930s, however, Ruth's excessive weight and legendary all-night binges had taken their toll. He did rise to one final myth-making moment. Facing pitcher Charlie Root of the Chicago Cubs in the 1932 World Series, with presidential candidate Franklin D. Roosevelt sitting in a first base box, he stepped out of the batter's box and, according to legend, pointed toward the right-center field stands where he promptly hit the next pitch. Few persons at the time recalled this gesture and it was not widely reported until several days afterward. But in the days and years to follow, many versions of that dramatic moment made their way into print. Whether or not the "called shot" actually occurred is beside the point; once it was reported it became part of the bigger-than-life aura that surrounded the Babe. Pitcher Charlie Root later insisted that Ruth never pointed to the stands: "Ruth did not point at the fence before he swung. If he had made a gesture like that, well, anybody who knows me knows that Ruth would have ended up on his ass."[37]

Ruth's home run in the 1932 World Series, however, was a prelude to his rapid decline as a player. His performance on the field fell off rapidly during the following two seasons and he was traded to the Boston Braves for the 1935 season. But he was now 40 years old, out of shape, suffering from a bum knee and an assortment of other ailments. When he realized that the Braves were not about to make him their new manager and had signed him only to boost attendance, he slugged three home runs in one game against Pittsburgh in late May, and promptly retired. He had the satisfaction of hitting his last home run – a seventh inning blast of monumental proportions – off a long-time rival and one of his more proficient hecklers, Guy Bush. The ball was the first ever to be hit over the second deck of the right field stands in Forbes Field; the head usher attempted to measure the distance and concluded Ruth's last home run had traveled 600 feet. Although the measurement was imprecise, Pittsburgh baseball fans still claim that it was the longest home run in the history of the town. Even pitcher Bush, who loved to tweak the Babe from the bench, was amazed at the homer he had given up:

> I never saw a ball hit so hard before or since. He was fat and old, but he still had that great swing. Even when he missed you could hear the bat go swish. I can't remember anything about the first home run he hit off me that day. I guess it was just another homer. But I can't forget that last one. It's probably still going.[38]

That blast – number 714 – fittingly was the last hit of The Babe's incomparable career.

Baseball's Golden Age

Babe Ruth towered like a colossus over the game during the 1920s, his spectacular exploits often obscuring the substantial accomplishments of many other outstanding players. During the 1920s, the Yankees were clearly the dominant team, but they always had strong competition. Yankee owner Jacob Ruppert and his shrewd general manager Ed Barrow assembled a powerful supporting cast to complement their superstar. Hard hitting first baseman Lou Gehrig joined the team in 1925 off the campus of Columbia University, and along with Earle Combs, Bob Meusel, Tony Lazzeri, and Ruth, formed one of the most formidable batting lineups in baseball history. The press aptly called it "Murderers Row." However, at decade's end, this powerful juggernaut was surpassed by the great team Connie Mack assembled in Philadelphia. Over in the National League, John McGraw's Giants were always in the pennant chase, winning the flag four times in succession (1921–24), but gave way to the talented teams that general manager Branch Rickey assembled in St Louis. In 1926 the Cardinals, led by pitcher Jesse Haines and the league's best hitter, second baseman Rogers Hornsby, defeated the Yankees in a dramatic seventh game of the World Series when the aging (and alcoholic) pitcher Grover Cleveland Alexander strolled in from the bullpen to strike out Lazzeri with the bases loaded in the seventh inning and shut out the Yankees in their last two at-bats. Hornsby led the league in hitting for six consecutive seasons and averaged an incredible .397 during that stretch; but indicative of the new style of play, Hornsby also hit for power, including 42 homers in 1922.

Over the next two decades, the Cardinals won nine pennants and six World Series championships. Cental to their success was the leadership of general manager Branch Rickey. He was a former catcher possessed of modest major league skills, a graduate of Ohio Wesleyan University, and held a law degree from the University of Michigan. When injuries and tuberculosis cut short his major league career with the New York Highlanders (later renamed the Yankees), he assumed the position of general manager of the St Louis Browns in 1913 and in the next two seasons also served as field manager. He emphasized proper off-field conduct by his players and drilled them in the fundamentals of the game during spring training. His sessions on the fundamentals of hitting, fielding, sliding, base running, and game strategies earned him the title "Professor of Baseball." Over the years, he introduced such innovative teaching tools as batting tees, sawdust sliding pits, and batting practice cages. In 1917, he moved to the other St Louis team as field manager and moved into their front office that same year as general manager. Although holding several different titles, he ran the Cardinals' front office until 1941.[39]

Burdened by low budgets, Rickey realized he could not build pennant contenders the traditional way by buying the contracts of top minor league prospects. To assemble a pool of young player talent, Rickey created a feeder system of minor league teams. The concept was to sign large numbers of young prospects at low cost, give them a thorough grounding in fundamentals, and carefully monitor and evaluate their progress, promoting the successful players up the ladder toward the major leagues, cutting loose the others when they had lost their value. Rickey reasoned that over the years this "farm" system would provide the Cardinals with a steady stream of major leaguers. And indeed it did. Rickey later commented that his farm system was not so much the work of a creative baseball executive as it was "the result of stark necessity."

Other teams had tinkered with the concept, but Rickey perfected it. In 1919, the

Cardinals purchased the contract of future Hall of Fame pitcher Jesse Haines for $10,000, but would not buy another player contract for nearly 30 years. Rickey began building his system in 1919 when the Cardinals purchased the Class D Ft Smith, Arkansas, club, and in 1921 he purchased the Syracuse franchise of the International League and Houston of the Texas League. As the years went by, more teams were added to the point in 1940 that the Cardinals owned 32 minor league franchises and had working agreements with eight more teams. The Cardinals had affiliated teams playing at the lowest Class D level all the way to AAA. The result was that the Cardinals received a continual flow of talent that made them a perennial contending team. Between 1930 and 1949, the Cardinals finished in first or second place 15 times. The Cardinals also were able to make a large profit by selling players' contracts to other teams. Because his own contract called for him to receive 10 percent of those sales, Rickey amassed a considerable personal fortune in the process.

Rickey's farm system, however, did not meet with the approval of Commissioner Landis, who believed it kept many players with major league talent tied up in the Cardinal farm system. He viewed it as a means of stifling competition and undercutting the independence of minor league teams. His several efforts to dismantle the Cardinals farm system, however, were rebuffed. During the depression years of the 1930s, hard-pressed minor league teams discovered that an affiliation with a major league team helped stabilize their finances and they were not about to permit Landis from cutting them loose in tough economic times. Further, several other teams, most notably the Yankees, began to emulate the Cardinals and created their own network of feeder teams. Insider baseball people enjoyed watching the ongoing feud between the two headstrong men who detested each other.[40]

As Commissioner, Landis continued to fight the influence of gamblers, but his actions revealed a man whose policies were neither consistent nor always in the best interests of baseball. Although he made headlines by forbidding some prominent owners to own stock in race tracks, he never took decisive action against Giant owner Horace Stoneham who was indicted on federal charges of bribery and mail fraud in the mid-1920s and who was a close friend of fixer Arnold Rothstein. The high-stakes gambler and World Series fixer was frequently sighted sitting in Stoneham's personal box at Giants games. Although Landis banned an additional 12 players for gambling indiscretions after concluding the Black Sox episode, he wavered in dealing with top name players. Landis reportedly had in his possession strong evidence that implicated Ty Cobb and Cleveland's Tris Speaker of gambling on baseball games, but he did not take action, permitting them to retire quietly while issuing a public statement exonerating them of all allegations. Likewise, he refused to act on information pointing toward the dumping of games between Detroit and Chicago in 1917 and later issued a statute of limitations on any impropriety that might have occurred prior to his taking office in 1921. But he did ban for life base-stealing whiz Benny Kauff, charged (but found innocent) of involvement in a car theft ring. His real crime seems to have been jumping to the Federal League in 1915.[41]

In 1923, several of the owners, now sorry that they had given Landis vast power over their game, had become disenchanted with his imperial attitude and arbitrary decision-making. Landis then confronted them with a well-publicized demand: either support him or fire him. The rebellion fizzled because by this time Landis had already won over the media, which repeatedly praised him as the staunch defender of America's Game. As the historian Eugene Murdock sardonically puts it, "In the annals of 'lost opportunities' the failure to accept Landis at his word and terminate his contract must rank near the top."[42] With his opposition in full retreat, Landis consolidated his control and seldom did the owners mount the gumption to challenge his decisions, inconsistent and arbitrary that they frequently were, until he died in office in 1944 at the age of 78. He truly was the "czar" of baseball, a game that during his time came to rightfully enjoy the sobriquet of the National Pastime.

Historian Harold Seymour accurately concludes that by the end of the 1920s, a strong bond – what he calls a "close association and identification" – had developed between the millions of baseball fans and their favorite teams as well as with the game itself. Fans everywhere took their baseball seriously. Baseball's appeal, Seymour concluded, had produced "a profound emotional grip on the public that gave the game genuine vitality."[43]

7 "An Evil to be Endured"

Sports on Campus, 1920–50

From the time he assumed the presidency of the University of Chicago in 1929 at the age of 28, Robert Maynard Hutchins was skeptical about the value of athletic programs as part of the American system of higher education. After a decade-long dialogue over the merits of this elite private institution fielding a football team in the Western Conference (Big Ten), in 1939 Hutchins convinced his board of trustees to drop the sport. Despite his many qualms about the negative aspects of college football, however, Hutchins was able to take this drastic step only after a long and contentious dialogue. He made his decision at a propitious time: after humiliating 61–0 defeats administered by Ohio State and Harvard, and an 85–0 pasting by Michigan. These lopsided losses contributed to the school's 15th consecutive losing season.

As expected, Hutchins was widely criticized by many male alumni, football fans, and sports journalists, but he also received widespread praise. Despite accolades from academics for placing educational values above athletics, no other major football institution followed his lead. Hutchins explained that his presidential peers "could not stand the pressure" that fans, coaches, boosters, alumni, legislators, and the sports media created on behalf of the game.[1] Hutchins believed that "education is primarily concerned with the training of the mind, and athletics and social life, though they may contribute to it, are not the heart of it and cannot be permitted to interfere with it." He once quipped, "A college racing stable makes as much sense as college football. The jockey could carry the college colors; the students could cheer; the alumni could bet; and the horse wouldn't have to pass a history test."[2] Hutchins took heart when University of Missouri professor W. E. Gwatkin wrote him a letter of congratulations and pointed out that most university presidents had to tolerate football "as an evil to be endured for the sake of a rather vaguely defined greater good."[3]

The Essential Myth of Big-Time College Athletics

The template for intercollegiate athletics was established before the Great War. As they built their intercollegiate empires, coaches and athletic administrators embraced the English model of amateurism, while university presidents preached the gospel that athletics helped mold good character and moral habits while providing a strong complement to their institution's academic mission. Both rationales were at best wishful thinking, at worst hypocritical. Although the amateur idea was widely presumed the basis for American intercollegiate sports, in fact those schools which played "big-time" football or basketball schedules opted for a professional sports model that placed the highest priority upon winning.

When administrators took control of athletics away from the students between 1890 and 1910, they insisted that athletics had to be funded outside of the regular institutional budget. They hired professional coaches who replaced elected student "captains," their job being to produce winning teams and sell tickets. They also hired "business managers" – the precursor to today's entrepreneurial athletic directors – whose role it was to oversee the athletic programs and to help raise the funds necessary to produce winning teams. The arrival on campus of the paid professional coach and the athletic director ended any pretext that the college programs were to be run on the English amateur model.

Instead, the working model was that of American capitalism. The principles that underpinned the rise of the intercollegiate sports were the same that guided the American system of capitalism: rugged competition and the primacy of profits. The British concept of amateurism had grown out of a stratified society in which the elite were born to their status and could exclude themselves from significant social interaction with lesser groups. Their social stature was assured by birth, and so the English elite did not have to prove themselves. In egalitarian America, where there was no royalty, where society selected its leaders based upon performance and merit, and where freedom of opportunity and competition were exalted, the amateur model made little connection. Only in a society where an hereditary upper class existed could the English amateur system work. But it served the narrow purposes of American college coaches and athletic directors extraordinarily well.[4]

Thus in the highly competitive economic environment of the United States, intercollegiate sports naturally reflected the nation's basic capitalistic creed. Rivalries were established between similar institutions, often through conference affiliation; tickets were sold; team boosters were solicited for large donations; athletes were granted tuition and fee waivers (in effect "paid") in return for their athletic performance; special facilities were provided for the exclusive use of athletes; a training table was established to provide the best nutrition; tutors were hired to help athletes meet modest eligibility standards; extensive recruiting programs sought out skilled athletes; and professional head coaches ran the business. Despite all of these examples of raw professionalism, colleges and universities continued to insist that they were engaged in amateurism. Thus the underlying dilemma, as sports historian Ronald A. Smith has aptly noted:

If a college had truly amateur sport, it would lose contests and thus prestige. If a college acknowledged outright professional sport it would lose respectability. ... Be amateur and lose athletically to those who were less amateur; be outright professional and lose social esteem.[5]

These policies were established without much, if any, discussion of the long-term implications. There was no comparable model that university presidents could study, and there was no national coordinating organization to provide guidelines. Although the National Collegiate Athletic Association (NCAA) maintained a national office, its scope of authority was severely limited. It would not be until the 1950s that the NCAA began implementing polices that produced the powerful body it is today. Prior to that time its responsibilities were restricted largely to producing rules for the playing of games and providing a national forum for discussion of topics of mutual interest among member institutions. Even the regional athletic conferences – just coming into their own in the 1920s as effective bodies – lacked adequate jurisdiction over their members in supervising recruiting, enforcing eligibility standards, and monitoring the financial subsidy of athletes. In effect, supervision and regulation of the college sports enterprise was left up to individual institutions, which were expected to supervise themselves. In this curious laissez faire environment, independent athletic departments naturally distanced themselves as far as possible from the academic side of the institutions they represented, essentially marching to the special beat of their own drummer. By 1920, faculties had largely given up any hope of abolishing big-time football, and had only dim hopes of effectively regulating their campus program. University presidents, who came to their responsibilities from a traditional academic background, were either caught up in the assumption that a winning team was essential for institutional well-being and/or lacked the ability to understand and therefore control the athletic department. Eight decades later, as the twenty-first century dawned, critics of big-time college athletics would continue to lament the same lack of "institutional control" by central administrations over intercollegiate athletic programs that they had decried in the 1920s and the 1930s.

Using the arcane process of academic accreditation as a guideline, wherein regional accrediting organizations interact with institutions on the basis of a common set of ethical standards and self-governance, the guiding assumption of college athletic conferences was that each campus would be guided solely by high standards of ethical behavior and academic integrity, and would operate internally to achieve those worthy objectives. As per the amateur code, the college athlete was presumed to be a student engaged in a serious process of intellectual development. The games he played were believed to provide an important activity according to the Greek ideal of the fusion of body and mind.[6]

The blatant hypocrisy of this system, however, was exposed on every campus where major college football programs existed. Financial incentives to lure athletes to campus – a major deviation from the amateur ideal – were crucial to the building of a successful program. Few big-time college athletes were willing to play simply for the joy of competition. A true amateur did not require professional coaching, but on the campuses the coach not only held a prestigious position, but also commanded a salary far beyond what was paid top professors (occasionally earning a salary higher than that of the president of the institution). According to the professional model, the more successful coaches expected ever-larger salary and benefit packages, and if these were not forthcoming, they felt impelled to move to another school eager to provide them. Unlike college faculty members, who usually spent an entire career on one or two campuses, football coaches often came and went with regularity – staying in one place about five to seven years.

Another important part of the amateur myth was that the athlete was a student first and an athlete second, devoting time to his sport only after his academic work was completed. Faculty oversight committees required that athletes had to be in good academic standing to represent their institution. In fact, however, faced with the expectation of producing winning teams, coaches were forced to recruit the best athletes they could find with only secondary attention paid to their academic interests or abilities; although the "tramp" athlete of the prewar era – the player who moved from campus to campus each year to play football and then just as suddenly disappeared when the season ended – disappeared during the 1920s, academic dishonesty remained a major problem that was never adequately addressed. Fabricated admissions documents, the funneling of players into special classes in which a professor was known to look kindly upon athletes, ghostwritten term papers, the maintenance of test files, and other fraudulent academic schemes abounded. In direct contradiction of the amateur code, boosters provided illegal financial assistance in the form of easy campus and summer jobs, compliant campus administrators reserved top-paying on-campus jobs for athletes, coaches operated slush funds from which cash gifts were made to encourage a recruit to commit to an institution, and secret payments made once he arrived. Recruiting and academic scandals were more common than not. In 1929, a special study funded by the Carnegie Foundation revealed that serious academic integrity issues existed in at least three-fourths of the 130 institutions it had examined.

During the early years of the twentieth century, several faculties attempted to abolish football – most notably at the University of Wisconsin under the leadership of prominent history professor Frederick Jackson Turner (on one notable evening in 1906, an angry mob of students surrounded his house and threatened his lynching in response to his effort to shut down Badger football). Except at the University of Chicago, these faculty efforts came a cropper because the game had too many important friends. Off campus, boosters and alumni were vociferous in their support, and on campus many non-athletes supported football because a wide range of campus social activities were connected to the game. The team fueled a campus-wide unity and a sense of identity, frequently identified as "school spirit." When Lawrence Lowell became president of Harvard in 1909, replacing anti-football crusader Charles W. Eliot, he conceded that football and other sports had their rightful place on campus because "such contests offer to students the one common interest, the only striking occasion for a display of college solidarity." University of Wisconsin faculty member J. F. A. Pyre, wrote in 1920 that sports provided "a tradition that fuses together all the forces of an institution in enthusiastic social consent." He continued:

> It is a mistake to suppose that the extravagant enthusiasm lavished upon athletes by students and the alumni implies a proportionate over-estimate of their intrinsic worth. It is a mistake that arises from a puritanic failure to appreciate the significance of a ritual. That "esprit de corps" amongst the undergraduates and graduates of a school that we call "school spirit" requires a rallying point or occasion for demonstration. Athletic contests and rivalries are convenient and pleasurable occasions for its manifestations.[7]

As Professor Pyre argued, college athletics – and football in particular – had become the one special conduit whereby strong connections could be made between the campus and the general public.

Football: Driving the Bus

Early in the twenty-first century, a new cliche entered the lexicon of sportswriters and athletic directors. Football, they said, "drives the bus." The bus in question was the large sports enterprise that most major universities felt compelled to offer for both women and men athletes, and income derived from football produced the bulk of the revenue that made it all possible. By the 1920s, football had already assumed the role of propelling the athletic department financial bus. During that decade, attendance more than doubled, and to accommodate the growing number of spectators eager to pay good money for a ticket, universities moved boldly to construct large stadiums in which teams could be showcased to large crowds of ticket-buying spectators. Seizing upon the patriotic fervor left over from the war, institutions encouraged wealthy alumni and state legislatures to cough up large sums to build "memorials" in the form of football stadiums to honor the 63,000 Americans who had lost their lives in the trenches of France. What they could not generate from legislative appropriations or private donations, they covered with the sale of revenue bonds. Yale had shown the way when the gigantic Yale Bowl was completed in 1914. By 1930, seven additional stadiums with seating capacity above 70,000 had made their appearance on campuses, and nearly all institutions with serious football aspirations boasted of stadiums with seating for 30,000 or more. In 1926, an American Association of University Professors committee condemned the stadium mania to no effect: "The sheer physical size of the stadium dwarfs the significance of the library, laboratory, and lecture hall."[8]

A tour of universities today reveals the centrality of football on the campus 80 years ago; nearly all the edifices constructed in the 1920s remain in use (expanded and modernized) and stand near the center of the campus, massive monuments of brick and concrete to the "golden age" of college football. In 1924, coach Amos Alonzo Stagg convinced the University of Chicago board of trustees to permit the doubling of the Stagg Stadium seating to 60,000, obviously envisioning days of pigskin glory to come. Ironically, 1924 would be the year of Chicago's last winning season. A planned second deck (to take the capacity to 80,000) was never added, and after the university dropped football in 1939, in what some observers have commented was a fitting epitaph for the stadium given the heavy military symbolism surrounding the game of football, the locker rooms underneath the stadium were converted to become the location of the nation's first nuclear pile. It was there in 1942 that the first self-sustaining nuclear reaction occurred, a decisive step toward the making of the atomic bomb that ended the Second World War.[9]

Football's Golden Age: the Twenties

The excitement that teams provided during the 1920s seemed to justify the construction of these huge facilities. Major rules changes produced a much more exciting game than Walter Camp ever envisioned. The day of boring mass play at the line of scrimmage was now history, and wide-open offenses were encouraged by rules changes. Most teams operated out of single-wing formations designed to produce long gains. These formations featured a direct snap of the ball to a fleet-footed halfback who usually ran or passed the ball. The wing formations also included the use of deceptive "spinner" plays in which the ball carrier would turn ("spin" sometimes a full 360 degrees) and either hand off the ball to another back or conceal it from defenders and run himself. The quarterback seldom touched the ball but was used as a lead blocker. The single-wing required intricate timing, precise blocking, and careful ball-handling, which made possible tricky misdirection plays, forward passes, sneaky reverses, open-field laterals, and exciting end sweeps. Fans now thrilled to open-field runs and long pass plays that occasionally produced a dramatic last-minute come-from-behind victory. Better-trained athletes and improved coaching contributed to the exciting action. What the coaches of the 1920s would only reluctantly admit, however, is that they had adopted a new style of play in response to spectator demand for a more wide-open, exciting brand of football. Even the rules of the game, it seemed, were prompted by financial incentives.

The most spectacular player of this era was unquestionably Harold "Red" Grange, a whirling dervish of a running back at the University of Illinois. At Wheaton High School he had set many state records while earning 16 letters in football, basketball, baseball, and track. Grange worked summers delivering large blocks of ice for a local company, a demanding task that helped build his physique in a day before athletes routinely engaged in off-season weight training. During his sophomore year he captured national attention when he scored three touchdowns and gained over 200 yards in his initial game against the University of Nebraska. He subsequently scored the winning touchdowns in close games against Ohio State, Wisconsin, and Chicago as he led the Fighting Illini to an undefeated season and the conference co-championship. He was named an All-American.[10]

Fans were enthralled by Grange's ability to break runs for long gains, twisting and turning sharply in the open field to avoid tacklers. His amazing display of speed and balance introduced the term "broken field runner" into the football

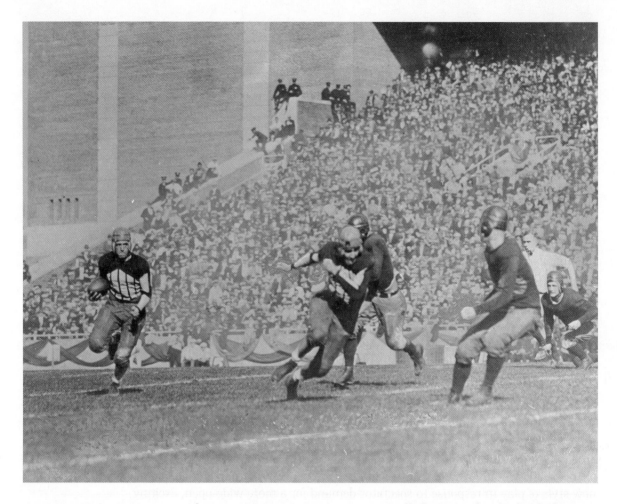

Figure 7.1 The Galloping Ghost, Red Grange, is loose on one of five touchdown runs for Illinois against undefeated Michigan in 1924. This was the first game played in the 67,000-capacity Memorial Stadium on the University of Illinois campus. Grange's speed and deception epitomized the new "open" style of play that became popular during the 1920s. © Bettmann/CORBIS.

lexicon. One sportswriter was compelled to note that he "picks his way through the line with infinite care," and another noted after one spectacular performance, "They knew he was coming; they saw him start; he made no secret of his direction; he was in their midst, and he was gone." One such performance came on October 18, 1924, when Grange helped inaugurate the 67,000-seat Memorial Stadium, dedicated to the students of the University of Illinois who had not returned from France. The opponent was Michigan, which came into the game with a three-year unbeaten record and with its venerable coach, Fielding "Hurry Up" Yost, boldly proclaiming that his team would "stop Grange cold." Unfortunately for the Wolverines, Red Grange had what is now termed "a career day." Taking the opening kickoff at the five-yard line, he swivelled his way through the Wolverines for a 95-yard return touchdown, and before the first quarter had ended he had scored on runs from scrimmage of 67, 56, and 44 yards. After sitting out the second quarter, he ran for a fifth touchdown in the second half and passed for yet another. He amassed 402 yards rushing and another 60 passing in an unprecedented individual performance. The hyperbolic wordsmith, sportswriter Grantland Rice, proclaimed him "The Galloping Ghost." Even this performance, however, did not satisfy skeptics in the East, where doubts still lingered about the quality of "Western" football. In Philadelphia, early in his senior season of 1925, Grange answered the unconvinced as he ran for 369 yards and three touchdowns while leading his team to a decisive 24–2 walloping of the pride of the East, a University of Pennsylvania team that had enjoyed an undefeated season in 1924.[11]

Media attention was overwhelming as the nation now had a new star who for a time came close to rivaling even the popularity of Babe Ruth. Unlike the voracious Babe, however, the fans saw in Grange the traditional qualities long esteemed by Americans – a strong work ethic, abstention from tobacco and drink, a wholesome determination to overcome financial disadvantages, and an "aw shucks" response to praise of his athletic accomplishments. Although few football fans had the opportunity to see Grange confound tacklers in person, millions thrilled to his darting runs on the weekly newsreels now being shown in motion picture theaters. The primitive film technology of the day – producing somewhat herky-jerky images as the black and white film flickered onto the screen – made Grange's runs seem even faster and more daring than they were in real life. Few fans doubted the verdict handed down in 1925 by Grantland Rice:

> A streak of fire, a breath of flame
> Eluding all who reach and clutch;
> A gray ghost thrown into the game
> That rival hands may never touch;
> A rubber bounding, blasting soul
> Whose destination is the goal.[12]

Public adulation turned to public disappointment, however, when he turned professional immediately after his final college game and well before graduation. After leading Illinois to a hard-fought 14–9 victory over Ohio State at Columbus before a record 85,000 fans, he announced that he had already agreed to a lucrative contract with the professional Chicago Bears. Advised by a shrewd agent, C. C. ("Cash and Carry") Pyle, Grange had agreed to drop out of college and embark immediately upon a nationwide barnstorming tour in which he would receive half of the gate receipts. At a time when most sports purists considered professional football a "dirty little business run by rogues and bargain-basement entrepreneurs," Grange had broken with the myth of amateur college sports. A college degree apparently meant little to this young All-American. His comments to the press did not help: "I'm out to get the money and I don't care who knows it." When critics denounced Pyle as "a notorious money-hungry promoter" who had misled the nation's collegiate hero, Grange retorted that his agent had merely followed his instructions and "was one of the finest people he had ever known."[13]

Fans nonetheless flocked to see Grange play professionally for the Bears during the winter months when, according to convention, he should have been completing his college studies. His professional career continued until 1935, but a series of injuries slowed his running ability. A spectacular catch of a touchdown pass while lying flat on his back in the 1932 NFL championship game against the Portsmouth (Ohio) Spartans added to his storied legend, and in 1933 he made a last-minute open-field tackle to preserve another championship for the Bears. Red Grange moved on to a lucrative post-playing career as a businessman and radio and television football commentator. His years of glory, however, were those at Illinois when he demonstrated the excitement that a college football star could generate. More than any other individual, Red Grange established the importance of big-time college football in American popular culture.

Grange might have exemplified the role of campus football hero, but the game had become the province of the professional coach. The head coach had the services of several assistants who taught specialized skills to running backs, lineman, kickers, and other position players. During the off-season, the coaching staff concentrated on recruiting a new crop of talented players and also supervised off-season fitness programs and spring practices. Head coaches established networks among alumni and boosters to provide tips on talented high-school players and employed scouts to watch upcoming opponents' games and report on their style of play and personnel so that an effective game strategy could be concocted. The intent of the coaching staff was to put a team on the field that would perform according to carefully designed plans. Just as America's corporations were attacking their competitors with finely tuned strategies and well-oiled operations, so too were football teams reflecting the same commitment. Little wonder that football became a special passion of many male business executives.

One point of contention among faculty was the salaries paid to the head coach. His salary was typically substantially higher than the best-paid professors, and his contacts in the community often provided additional remuneration. But unlike the tenured faculty, his status was tenuous, subject to his won-lost record and the whims of boosters and college administrators. For those who produced winning teams year after year, however, the enterprise could be rewarding indeed. The success of coaches such as Yost at Michigan, Stagg at Chicago, Glenn "Pop" Warner at Carlisle Indian School, Dana X. Bible at Texas, John Heisman at Georgia Tech, and Bob Zuppke at Illinois, were the stuff of campus lore. The coach who made the greatest contribution to the development of the game was Warner, who began his coaching career at Iowa State Agricultural College in 1894 after a successful playing career at Cornell. He went on to Georgia in 1896 and turned a humdrum team into an undefeated team in two seasons. After producing powerful teams at Carlisle between 1898 and 1914 (where he tutored the great Jim Thorpe), Warner's Pittsburgh Panthers teams won 33 straight games and laid claim to three national championships. During the 1920s and the early 1930s, he led Stanford to three Rose Bowl victories, and capped off his lengthy career with strong teams at Temple. Warner was considered the most creative among the coaching fraternity of the period and is credited with such innovations as the practice blocking dummies and the development of the spiral punt, the screen pass, and several other innovative offensive plays. Warner has also been credited with having major input into the development of such protective equipment as shoulder pads and helmets. To help spectators identify individual players, he placed numbers on the back of jerseys.

Knute Rockne and the Making of Notre Dame Football

Although Pop Warner's name would become a permanent part of football lore when a youth program was created in 1929 that still carries his name, he was upstaged by Knute Rockne of Notre Dame. Rockne's 13 years at the helm of the Fighting Irish set the stage for the fabled football tradition at the private university located 75 miles east of Chicago. He brought to his role the traits that helped produce an engaging public personality that featured a flair for the dramatic, a quick wit, and innovation (he introduced pre-game choreographed calisthenics and created the Notre Dame shift and box backfield formation). At Notre Dame, he almost single-handedly devised what Murray Sperber has called "the unique formula" that has enabled Notre Dame to reign supreme atop big-time college football for over three-quarters of a century.[14] Even on those infrequent occasions when the Irish have endured losing seasons, football fans everywhere have remained in awe of the mystique that encompasses Notre Dame football. The formula that Rockne produced during the 1920s would never quite be duplicated elsewhere. Rockne grew a national fan base that included not only former students, but also the so-called "subway alumni," dedicated fans who had neither attended the university nor even set foot on its campus. Because the institution shrewdly permitted radio stations free access to its game broadcasts, millions of fans across the country became hooked on Notre Dame football.

At the heart of the Rockne's fame was the fact that he lived the American Dream, beginning with his arrival in the United States at age 5 from his native Norway. At age 22, having saved some money from a job in the post office, he decided to enroll at the small college in South Bend, Indiana. Founded in 1844 by a small French religious order, the Congregation of the Holy Cross, the liberal arts curriculum attracted a few hundred students who were largely of Catholic immigrant stock. When Rockne arrived in 1910, Notre Dame had a modest academic reputation and was better known for the quality of its baseball teams than football. Rockne earned a degree with a major in chemistry, and played end on the football team while excelling as a middle distance runner in track.

One particular game began the Rockne mystique. During the summer before his senior year of 1913, while working at the Lake Erie resort at Cedar Point in Ohio, he and quarterback Gus Dorias practiced the forward pass on the resort's vast expanse of sandy beach. This helped Notre Dame confound a heavily favored Army team that autumn with a refined passing attack. The Irish pulled-off a 35–13 upset win over the baffled Army defenders who had seldom seen a forward-pass play before. Dorias rifled a first-half 40-yard pass to Rockne, who scampered into the end zone untouched, and by day's end, Dorias had completed 13 of 17 passes for more than two hundred yards. The next day the *New York Times* headlined the game story with "Notre Dame Open Play Amazes Army!" The lead sentence told it all: "Football men marveled at this startling display of open football, as the Westerners flashed the most sensational football ever seen in the East." It should have come as no surprise to the Army, however, because Notre Dame had utilized the forward pass since head coach Jesse Harper arrived from Wabash College in 1912. Several teams had experimented with its use ever since it was first legalized in 1906; the first forward passes were most likely thrown in 1906 by Marietta College and St Louis University. By 1913, the forward pass was no secret, as was later implied by Rockne myth makers.[15]

After graduation, Rockne assumed an assistant coaching position at Notre Dame, and for a time taught freshman chemistry laboratories and picked up spending money playing semi-pro football. In 1916, he got his first taste of being a head coach when Harper came down with a heavy chest cold; Rockne rose to the occasion when he fabricated a story that the opposing Wabash College team – certainly no powerhouse – had been strengthened with several mercenaries and, besides, harbored anti-Catholic sentiments. He concluded this, the first of a long series of pre-game histrionics, by shouting an apt metaphor befitting a religious institution: "Now get out there and crucify them!"[16] And indeed they did, to the tune of 60–0. In 1918, Rockne accepted the position of head coach of the Irish and quickly implemented his system, which emphasized guile, speed, and agility over sheer brawn. He had the pick of the best Catholic players throughout the Midwest, who naturally gravitated to what was rapidly becoming a football power. By the mid-1920s, building upon his team's success, he operated a recruiting system that utilized an informal national network of Catholic churches and organizations as well as the efforts of members of the Irish subway alumni.

Rockne shrewdly promoted Rockne. He found himself much in demand as an after-dinner speaker, and spent off-seasons traveling extensively to speak to church and alumni groups, always fusing his commitment to a winning football program with his university president's dream of making Notre Dame "the Yale of the West." By playing a national schedule – creating traditional rivalries with the Army in the East and Southern California in the West – he built not only Notre Dame's football reputation but also its national fan base. During Rockne's first three years, his star player was George Gipp, whose daring-do on the field pleased the fans but whose behavior off it dismayed faculty and administrators. After he lead Notre Dame to a 9–0 record in 1919, the All-American team captain was expelled for his lack of interest in the classroom. Dismayed Irish fans learned that the mercenary Gipp was about to depart to play for arch rival Michigan, where "Hurry Up" Yost was eagerly awaiting his arrival, or perhaps even worse, to West Point, where recruitment of football "tramps" was the norm. Ultimately, Notre Dame president Father James Burns reinstated Gipp in time for his senior season in response to plaintive appeals from the business community of South Bend, which had become convinced that Notre Dame football was essential to the health of the local economy.[17]

Gipp rewarded his supporters as he led the Irish to an undefeated season in 1920. He played little in the final two games, however, because he became infected with

the respiratory illness that would kill him shortly before Christmas. The 1920 season firmly established Notre Dame as a football giant, and its fans reveled in a national championship. That year the Irish had played before 90,000 fans, despite the limited capacity of Carter Field (replaced in 1930 with the stadium that lies in the center of campus today).

Year after year, Rockne's teams rolled to victory. His 1924 squad trampled its opposition by a combined score of 258–44. Among the most significant victories was a hard-fought 13–7 win at the Polo Grounds in New York City over the Army. This victory on a dark and dreary November day set the stage one of the most memorable moments in Notre Dame football history. Journalist Grantland Rice, was driven to hyperbolic heights when he began his game report with the most famous passage ever written by a sportswriter:

> Outlined against a blue-gray October sky, the Four Horsemen rode again. In dramatic lore, they are known as Famine, Pestilence, Destruction and

Figure 7.2 The Notre Dame backfield of (left to right) Don Miller, Elmer Layden, Jim Crowley, and Harry Stuhldreher, pose as the Four Horsemen after their big victory over Army in 1924. This famed backfield, immortalized by journalist Grantland Rice's florid prose, averaged barely 160 pounds. © Bettmann/CORBIS.

Death. These are only aliases. Their real names are Stuhldreher, Miller, Crowley, and Layden. They formed the crest of the South Bend cyclone before which another fighting Army team was swept over the precipice at the Polo Grounds this afternoon as 50,000 spectators peered down upon the bewildering panorama spread out upon the green plain below.[18]

These few words etched forever in the memories of football fans everywhere the legend of Notre Dame football. In reality, the exploits of the "Four Horsemen" were nothing spectacular – they were good but hardly great athletes – and their size (they averaged 160 pounds each) was relatively small even for this period of college football. There have been many backfields at South Bend more talented than the 1924–25 quartet, but Grantland Rice placed the Four Horsemen in a special identity that Professor Sperber says "floats through American sports history, assuming a mystified reality."[19]

Sports journalists became enamored with Notre Dame because of its success on the field, but also because of the accessability of the affable head coach, who was always ready with a humorous quip or a compelling story to fill tomorrow's column. Among the most memorable tale, of course, was the 1928 pep talk that Rockne gave to his team before they took the field against an undefeated Army team. Rockne reportedly recalled the last words of George Gipp, who died of influenza in December 1920. Lying on his deathbed, as Rockne recalled, "He turned to me. 'I've got to go, Rock. Its all right. I'm not afraid'." Rockne continued,

> His eyes brightened in a frame of pallor. "Some time, Rock, when the team's up against it; when things are going wrong and the breaks are beating the boys – tell them to go in there with all they've got and win just one for the Gipper. I don't know where I'll be then, Rock. But I'll know about it, and I'll be happy."

There is absolutely no evidence that Gipp – whose career at Notre Dame was distinguished by heavy gambling, drinking and a lackadaisical academic effort that ended far short of graduation – ever said anything approaching what Rockne relayed to his team in the locker room eight years later. One of his star players, Jim Crowley, kept a long list of fabrications and half-truths that the dramatic Rockne presented to his teams in order to stimulate their enthusiasm for the task at hand. "They were all lies, blatant lies," Crowley later said. "The Jesuits call it mental reservation, but he had it in abundance." Whatever, following the Gipper talk, the aroused Irish stopped the Cadets on the one foot-line as the game expired, preserving a 12–6 upset victory, and adding to the Notre Dame legend. Two weeks after the game, a ghost-written article about the pre-game oration appeared in *Collier's Magazine*, and it was reprinted in Rockne's posthumous autobiography in 1931. In 1940, this story of dubious origins took on even greater mythological proportions when young actor Ronald Reagan portrayed the Gipper in a popular motion picture that produced many a tear among sellout audiences during the deathbed scene. Of such fiction was the reality of Notre Dame football constructed.[20]

Even Knute Rockne's sudden death at age 43 in an airplane crash in 1931 added to the Notre Dame saga. Although it was later said he was on a trip to "help his boys" when the commercial airplane crashed in a snowstorm in western Kansas, in fact Rockne was en route to the West Coast to make lucrative personal appearances for a sporting-goods chain and to finalize a $75,000 motion picture contract deal with Universal Pictures, which planned to make a movie of his life. Rockne was the first American celebrity to die in a commercial airplane crash, and news of his death stunned a depression-mired nation. The ensuing mourning was truly a national event, and his funeral in the Notre Dame chapel added to the football legacy as the university choir ended the service by singing the fight song that had become familiar to millions of Americans, the "Notre Dame Victory March." Rockne's won–lost record of 105–12–5 would never be equaled. That record, coupled with his flair for public relations, enabled him to escape the criticisms that would have damaged mere mortals: his unwillingness to discipline outstanding players for their drinking, gambling, and carousing; his casual interest in academics; his frequent flirtations with other institutions to become their head coach as a means to obtain substantial salary increases; and his use of his position to earn large sums from speaking engagements and product endorsements that saw his highest university salary of $10,000 – extraordinary for the 1920s – eclipsed by the large sums that he earned externally (the greatest slice coming from promoting the South Bend-based Studebaker Automobile Company).

More than three-quarters of a century after his death, Rockne remains one of the nation's most famous football coaches. It was he, more than anyone else, who established the template for future generations of big-time college coaches. By his example, as John Thelin concludes, the many sides of Knute Rockne

> demonstrated that the big-time college football coach had drifted from the company of professors. . . . The activities of recruiting, promoting, and public speaking, along with the lures of endorsements, indicated that by the 1930s the role of the big-time college coach had evolved very differently from that of university faculty.[21]

The Second Challenge to Big-Time Football

Not even the vast public enthusiasm for football and the leadership of public luminaries such as Rockne could stanch the criticisms that the enterprise regularly generated. The game had escaped virtually unscathed from the crisis of 1905, but again in 1929 it encountered serious criticism. Even during the glory days of the 1920s, on the campus many faculty and administrators remained skeptical about the game's impact on academic quality and institutional integrity. They had a substantial number of allies in the world of journalism and business. With abolition no longer a realistic option, the focus was on broad-based reform. Thus in 1926, the Carnegie Foundation decided to fund an extensive three-year study that culminated in the publication in 1929 of a scorching indictment of big-time college football. The commission's findings were succinctly summarized in one blunt sentence: "Apparently the ethical bearing of intercollegiate football contests and their scholastic aspects are of secondary importance to the winning of victories and financial success."[22]

The person behind this investigation was the head of the Carnegie Foundation, the former president of the Massachusetts's Institute of Technology, Dr Henry Pritch-ett. Although the Foundation supported many causes, its focus under Pritchett was the elevation of the standards of higher education, especially in the emerging professional schools of engineering, law, and medicine. Pritchett was no anti-football fanatic, but he saw the college game being used by many institutions to emphasize non-academic programs as a means of improving enrollment fig-ures, thereby reducing the quality of intellectual pursuits. He was aware of many abuses, including the amount of time and effort demanded of college football play-ers that precluded "any serious intellectual effort" on their part. Although his criticisms were similar to those made earlier by Harvard president Charles Eliot, Pritchett did not present them in a context of a morality play. Instead, reflecting his engineering profession, he expressed concern about educational efficiency and academic quality.

Although the Foundation had earlier sponsored a small study of football at a select number of Southern institutions and another of sports at British univer-sities, the board was reluctant to support the large-scale study Pritchett desired. That reluctance, however, melted before a series of events in 1925, among them the revelation of Red Grange's abandonment of his education for the professional game the very same day that he played his final college contest. Shortly before the 1925 season began, a syndicated article appeared in many newspapers across the country, written by an anonymous "graduate manager" of football who claimed to be working at a big-time Eastern school. His story carried too many plausible accusations for it to be dismissed outright, although football's defenders made a determined effort. The author told of a large well-funded alumni-booster organi-zation that assisted the football program, beginning with paying a large network of scouts to identify potential recruits and bring them to campus for a lavish visit. Once the recruits were enrolled, the graduate manager oversaw their registration, provided tutors, hired handlers to make certain they attended classes, encour-aged faculty friendly to football to permit their enrollment in snap classes, and especially, looked out after their financial well-being. In a day before the introduc-tion of formally recognized "athletic scholarships," the manager would see that tuition and living costs were taken care of, often by the creation of non-work jobs that required the player only to show up to receive a pay check. Cushy summer jobs were also part of the financial subsidy scenario. The author even discussed a program to hide top recruits at remote summer camps as counselors, so that rival institutions could not entice them to their campus at the last minute.[23]

While football critics were mulling over the revelations of this insider expose, they also focused on the replication of William Rainey Harper's strategy of using football to gain instant recognition for the recently opened University of Chicago. Ironically, the new example was Northwestern University, located just a few miles north of downtown Chicago. President Walter S. Dill, a former college football player himself, launched an effort to make his institution a national power in foot-ball as a quick method of obtaining immediate national recognition. He funded a successful team, which he then used as a means of gaining access to big donors to support his dream of building an elite academic institution. Dill not only built the

enormous Dyche Stadium but also many academic buildings, created endowed faculty chairs, and established an impressive array of professional colleges on Chicago's affluent North Side. In 1925, the "Fighting Methodists" tied for the Western Conference (Big Ten) title, which was capped by an improbable 3–2 victory over Michigan in a game played before 100,000 spectators in Soldier Field. Suddenly the University of Chicago, which had long dominated the football scene in the Windy City, had a powerful local competitor, both academically and athletically. Chicago coach Stagg took particular umbrage over a new football endowment at Northwestern that would fund 50 part-time scouts to procure the top talent available; without a hint of the irony his words conveyed, Stagg wrote a letter to Fielding Yost of Michigan, "I am satisfied that Northwestern at the present is loaded with athletes who have been induced to go there by the offer of free tuition and in certain cases something additional."[24]

Figure 7.3 Seventy-three thousand fans jam Memorial Stadium at the University of California in Berkeley for the Big Game against Stanford in 1928 as the teams line up for the opening kickoff. Clearly visible are the student "card sections" located along the 50-yard line, popular at the time; on cue, participating students would flash spirited messages and images to the other side. © CORBIS.

Such examples as those witnessed in the graduate manager's story, and the heavy emphasis on football programs at institutions such as Northwestern, encouraged Pritchett to put the prestige of one of the nation's largest foundations behind a thorough and careful study. Although the scope of the project was intended to survey all of collegiate athletics, football naturally emerged as its central focus. During 1926–29, social scientist Howard Savage led a team of researchers in an intensive study of the athletic programs of 130 colleges and universities. They did not rely simply on documents submitted by the institutions, but visited each of the campuses for intensive interviews. Although the final report, issued during the midst of the 1929 football season, encompassed 12 chapters and 347 pages, the chapters on recruiting and financial aid to athletes received the greatest attention. Writing more than 20 years later, Savage took satisfaction in his accomplishment, calling it "encyclopedic in scope" and "unprejudiced in method." He noted that "its chief faults were its length and its detail and yet without sufficient preponderance of evidence it would have failed of its purpose altogether."[25]

The report contained few surprises as it documented the complex system that college football had become. In many respects, the report illustrated that the current system had merely evolved and expanded from that which was in place in the 1890s. What the Carnegie researchers discovered was that even at institutions that played football at a modest level, a sophisticated system of recruitment and financial subsidy was in place. Only a handful of schools were reported as operating completely clean programs – Tufts, Wooster, MIT, Reed – which only served to emphasize the extent of deception that occurred at such big-time football schools that were included in the study: Wisconsin, Northwestern, Illinois, and the Army. Even colleges that never dreamed of national recognition were singled out for improper practices – Lafayette, Rutgers, Lehigh, Grove City, Lebanon Valley, Carnegie Institute of Technology.

Perhaps the most sensational new revelation was that most institutions had quietly, with substantial subterfuge, created a new form of assistance that was considered at the time highly unethical – the athletic scholarship. Not that it was so identified. Instead students were given free tuition and fees through scholarship funds labeled under such nebulous categories as "student leadership." Up until this point, colleges had maintained that only athletes whose academic abilities were high could receive scholarships on a competitive basis with other students. Additionally, it was learned that many athletes also received "loans" from campus funds or from alumni and boosters, with the implicit understanding that the loans need not be repaid. Many schools also had in place a formal campus employment office that controlled many on-campus jobs, with higher pay rates for athletes than available to other student workers. A standard practice was for athletes to be given jobs on campus (waiting tables, handing out towels in the gym, lifeguarding, doing routine janitorial work) or working in the businesses of alumni. Many of these "jobs" were make-work positions requiring little or no actual work. The report also uncovered several secret slush-fund operations, usually controlled by the head coach or athletic director, which were used to pay players directly.

These subsides, of course, were directly related to the recruitment process. All football programs recruited in one way or another. Networks of alumni were formed to recommend talent to the coach. Recruiting was the lifeline of all football programs, and coaches pursued it with efficiency, often with one assistant coach being designated as the "recruiting coordinator." At the heart of the system was the fact that recruits would be promised various types of financial incentives to take part in a program that all the institutions claimed was based upon the precepts of amateurism.

The vociferous denials and protests from coaches and presidents of institutions identified with slimy practices served to confirm the accuracy of the report. Interestingly, the report identified four prestigious private Eastern institutions – Pennsylvania, Columbia, Brown, and Dartmouth – as conducting recruiting and under-the-table financial assistance in a manner no different from the most egregious of the practices it found at such public institutions as Michigan, Wisconsin, and Washington State. The report rightfully identified the professional coach as one glaring manifestation of the problem, but it also focused attention on the failure of campus presidents to insist on a clean program. Many coaches claimed they had been deceived by the visiting researchers. Presidents went on record denying they knew of the alleged practices, while others had made it clear that they did not *want* to know the facts. The report concluded that the presidents were unable or unwilling to challenge wealthy alumni, boosters with open checkbooks, college trustees, and powerful politicians who wanted a winning football team. The collective behavior of the presidents seemed to confirm one of the conclusions of the Carnegie study that the academic reputation of an institution had become secondary to the winning of football games.

Not surprisingly, however, after a brief flurry of media accounts and public discussion, the coaches went about their work with business as usual, knowing full well that if they did not produce a winning team their president would not hesitate to terminate their employment. In a telling commentary, Knute Rockne told a Buffalo audience in 1930 that the Carnegie Commission had got it all wrong: the problem with college football was that it was not commercial enough.[26] In the years that followed, despite the economic crisis, college football continued to expand upon the same *modus operandi* as before, while the Carnegie report collected dust on library shelves.

"Playing Nice": the Demise of Women's Athletics

While athletic programs for men gained in size and prestige on the campus during the 1920s, the opposite was the case for women's programs. From the perspective of the twenty-first century, the dominant philosophy of women physical education professors and coaches prior to the 1970s is surprising in the extreme. Although most colleges sponsored intercollegiate programs for women between the 1890s and the First World War, during the 1920s leading women educators led a concerted attack upon competitive programs to the point where most were abolished by the early 1930s. At the same time, most interscholastic programs for high-school girls also were axed. Neither would be re-established for almost a half-century.

The reasons for this movement against competitive athletics for women are complex and need be understood within the context of the times. At the heart of the issue lay a set of social values and attitudes that were central to nineteenth-century ideas about the different roles of men and women within American society.

The male was expected to be "manly" in thought and action. The dogma of "muscular Christianity" prescribed a regimen of physical activity that would enable him to develop his body while simultaneously restraining his natural sexual desires until marriage. The male was expected to maintain self-control and to follow an impeccable set of behavioral traits in his personal and business affairs. Women, however, were viewed as frail and unable to engage in vigorous exercise. The "cult of domesticity" restricted the "weaker sex" to the role of homemaker. Thus young women were largely denied access to higher education; reform-minded Oberlin College was the first to admit women in 1831, but few other institutions followed suit until a half century later. Only after 1880 were most colleges and universities opened to women, albeit grudgingly.[27]

These attitudes greatly influenced thinking about exercise and athletic competition for women. Physical culturalists generally prescribed a regimen of light to moderate exercise that would not overburden the female reproductive system, taking due notice of popular perceptions that women suffered chronic fatigue, wide mood swings, and dizziness that were assumed to be the product of the menstrual cycle. This line of analysis even led to a widely accepted theory that the human body possessed a set amount of energy and that the mental exertion required by a rigorous higher-education program would diminish a female's capacity for physical strength. Thus the denial of access to higher education and vigorous exercise was believed to protect young women from the possibility that they would not achieve "true womanhood." This outlook provided a clever rationale for men's desire to maintain social control and dominance by using traditional medical and scientific theories to rationalize and maintain traditional sex roles in a rapidly changing social order.

Such nonsense, of course, would not stand in the long run. But its influence was felt in the sphere of American sports well into the second half of the twentieth century. As early as the 1830s, the pioneering feminist Catherine Beecher drew skeptical attention with her call for rigorous exercise for women, and in 1861 the innovative and reform-minded philanthropist Matthew Vassar established a women's college that featured a rigorous physical-education program at the heart of its curriculum. The initial planning document for Vassar College emphasized that "good health is essential to the successful prosecution of study, and to the vigorous development of either mental or moral powers." One of the first buildings constructed on the Poughkeepsie, New York, campus was the "Calisthenium," where physical education and recreational activities could take place. It also housed the School of Physical Training, where faculty implemented Matthew Vassar's vision of fusing rigorous physical and intellectual activity for women students.[28]

Slowly Vassar's ideas were replicated elsewhere, especially in Boston at the

Sargent School and the Normal School of Gymnastics beginning in the 1880s. Graduates of these two pioneering programs greatly influenced the development of women's athletic and physical-education programs throughout the expanding world of higher education. Although appreciative of the importance of physical activity, these women educators nonetheless were greatly influenced by Victorian standards, so they emphasized the importance of "moderation" in their curricula. It was also crucial that female students should reflect the "proper behavior" expected of ladies and not engage in activities "in excess," which might encourage "manly" attributes. It was widely believed and taught that excessive exercise would produce undesirable unfeminine traits and appearance. Fears of "muscle-bound women" abounded. This cautious philosophy was implemented through routinized calisthenics and dancing classes, the playing of games such as badminton, croquet, bowling, tennis, and golf, and such activities as horseback-riding, boating, and skating. Weight lifting, long-distance running, and aggressive games definitely were not permissible. Females were expected to "play nice."[29]

The theory of moderation came under special challenge when the wildly popular new game of basketball swept the nation in the 1890s. High-school girls and college women took to the game with the same exuberance as their male counterparts. The response of educators to the vigorous level of play was predicable as they denounced the tendency toward rough play. Obserevers noted the "mad play," as participants often became "bitter in feeling and lose self-control." Senda Berenson, a physical-education professor at Smith College, took careful note of the lack of restraint. Writing in 1903, she expressed concern about the "rough and vicious play" that "seems worse in women than in men. A certain amount of roughness is deemed necessary to bring out manliness in our young men. Surely rough play can have no possible excuse in our young women." Because the game seemed to make the young women "rough, loud-voiced and bold," and prompted them to play with aggressive abandon, many institutions made their games off-limits to gawking male spectators.[30]

A leading physical educator, Berenson emerged as the major critic of spirited play by women on the basketball court. Her mantra was "sport for the good of all," which placed emphasis upon participation and enjoyment rather than the pursuit of victory. She expressed fears that lack of proper decorum on the basketball court would erode desirable feminine qualities. Reflecting popular assumptions about women's nature, Berenson wrote,

> It is a well known fact that women abandon themselves more readily to an impulse than men. ... This shows us that unless we guard our athletics carefully in the beginning many objectionable elements will come in. It also shows us that unless a game as exciting as basketball is carefully guided by such rules as will eliminate roughness, the great desire to win and the excitement of the game will make our women do sadly unwomanly things.[31]

Berenson introduced what became widely known as the "Smith Rules" for women's basketball. Members of the six-player teams were restricted to three separate areas on the court, physical contact was forbidden, and a player could dribble the ball only once. Defenders could neither "snatch" the ball from an opponent nor attempt to prevent an opponent from shooting for a goal. Although many girls' teams continued to play the five-person "boys' rules," the Berenson model stifled the development of rigorous female basketball. Berenson's leadership thus set the tone for a growing movement by leading women physical educators and coaches to abolish the competitiveness of women's sports on the campus. Fears about encouraging masculine traits and damaging reproductive organs were not the only factors influencing the thinking of college administrators. Adding to concerns about intercollegiate play was the recognition that the teams would have to travel, thereby raising concerns about proper chaperoning.

Women educators' emphasis upon "sports for all" led initially to the popularity in the 1920s of the "play day" movement. Instead of providing competitive athletic contests between rival schools, young women from several campuses would meet for a day of games and activities, without the benefit of prior practice or instruction in the games to be played. As Berenson explained, "The greatest element of evil in the spirit of athletics in this country is the idea that one must win at any cost – that defeat is an unspeakable disgrace." Certainly the "win at any cost" syndrome was corrupting men's programs, especially football, and women educators did not want to encourage its replication in their programs. The play day concept neatly fused the traditional – but declining – Victorian image of proper womanhood with prevailing medical theories on female physiology and a growing disgust over the reputation of college football. As Berenson said, "We [women] can profit by the experience of our brothers and therefore save ourselves from allowing those objectionable features to creep into our athletics." Thus the view prevailed that women were different both physiologically as well as morally from men.[32]

Play day precluded teams competing under their own school colors. Instead, teams were created that mingled students from the participating institutions and a day was spent playing basketball, softball, soccer, field hockey, volleyball, and tennis, perhaps even including track and field events in which individuals would indeed be winners and losers. The emphasis, however, was upon participation rather than competition. The concept of teamwork, training, practice, planning, and the implementation of strategies was downgraded in favor of enhancing the individuality of the participants. Play day was thus both anti-competition and anti-varsity; it was formalized in the 1923 Platform adopted by the Women's Division of the National Amateur Athletic Federation at a Conference on Athletics and Physical Recreation for Women and Girls, which emphasized the objective of "a sport for every girl and every girl in a sport."[33]

Although the great majority of women coaches and physical educators were firmly committed to this anti-competitive model, there were naturally some dissidents. The leader of this minority group was Ina Gittings, a physical education professor at the University of Arizona. "Play days," she wrote in 1931

> are extremely weak and offer little or none of the joy and values of real games played skillfully, willingly, intelligently, and eagerly by well-matched teams. I picture

the girls in a Play Day as sheep, huddled and bleating in their little Play meadow, whereas they should be young mustangs exultantly racing together across vast prairies.[34]

Gittings definitely presented the minority view among women physical educators during this time, but her strong critique of the anti-competitive model would resonate loud and clear in the 1970s when the women's rights movement discovered the great inequities in the college athletic experience:

> Have we not postponed this legitimate phase of physical activity and recreation long enough? There is nothing wrong with the games, competition, the girls, or travel, but there is something wrong with the Directors, who have phobias at the thought of making the same mistakes in intercollegiates (sic) as men have made. And there is something wrong with the physical education instructors who cannot coach and conduct such activities without letting them get beyond control. Why not graciously concede and be in on the inevitable – the return of intercollegiate competition for women?[35]

Thus, much to Ina Gittings' dismay, but largely at the behest of women physical-education professionals, all across the United States colleges and public schools dropped competitive athletic programs for women and girls; they would not return for nearly a half century amid much controversy and conflict that required the firm intervention of the federal government.

Hoop Dreams

During the 1930s, men's college basketball enjoyed substantial growth in popularity. Most teams played their games in cramped gymnasiums designed primarily for physical-education classes. The game was played conservatively, with an emphasis on zone defenses, slow-moving patterned offenses, with most field-goal attempts being of the two-handed "set shot" variety; coaching theories mandated that free throws be released underhanded. Until 1937, when a basket was scored the teams would return to center court for a jump ball. Scoring was limited, with games ending in the twenties being commonplace.

Interest in the college game resulted in large part from the effort of Madison Square Garden officials in New York City to generate revenues during the Depression years. Impressed by the enthusiastic standing-room-only crowds he often encountered at games held in small on-campus gymnasiums, a young reporter for the New York *World Telegram* proposed to Madison Square Garden officials that he promote college games in a double-header format that matched local teams against top teams from around the country. But even Ned Irish was surprised when more than 16,000 fans turned out on the evening of December 29, 1934, to witness New York University defeat Notre Dame and tiny Westminister College from Pennsylvania upset St Johns. Irish soon thereafter abandoned sportswriting and became the full-time director of basketball for the Garden.

Coaches and athletic directors of aspiring teams from around the country eagerly solicited invitations from Ned Irish to come to the Big Apple, seeking both the national spotlight and a hefty payday. Sometimes Irish even put on triple-headers when top teams were available. In 1938, he invited 16 teams to compete in a new tournament that he called the National Invitational Tournament (Temple defeated Colorado 60–36 in the final), and it would be the premier college basketball event for more than a decade. The following year, the NCAA responded by creating its own tournament, but it did not overcome the NIT as the premier postseason tournament until the 1950s.

It was during one of Irish's inter-sectional games in December 1936 that basketball would be forever changed. The game featured the nationally ranked Blackbirds of Long Island University, who came into the game with a 43-game winning streak. The opponent was Pacific Coast Conference defending champion Stanford University. In this game, 6' 3" Stanford forward Angelo "Hank" Luisetti stunned basketball-savvy New Yorkers with a revolutionary one-handed shot, launched from 15 feet from the basket while jumping. Traditionalists, familiar only with shots being launched two-handed with the feet firmly planted, gasped in shock. Luisetti scored 15 points against the befuddled Blackbird defenders, who had never encountered the jump shot before; even the thousands of disappointed LIU fans rose in a standing ovation when he left the floor. Players everywhere, to the exasperation of their hidebound coaches, began to experiment with variations of the Luisetti one-hander. Soon the two-handed set shot was history, and the same fate befell the once-ubiquitous underhand free throw. Innovative coaches began to experiment with a much more rapid-paced game, including full-court pressing defenses and the fast-break offense.

The Second World War proved to be a boon for college basketball. Whereas colleges had to cut back on football due to the loss of players to the military and restrictions on travel by large groups, it was not difficult for ten-man basketball squads and their coach to get permission to travel. The military also had a height restriction on recruits that worked to basketball's distinct advantage. Based on the standard size of military beds and uniforms, anyone who stood over 6' 6" was automatically exempt from military duty. Thus some of the best players remained in school, including the top basketball player of the first half of the century, the high-scoring 6' 10" De Paul center George Mikan. College basketball actually thrived during the war years by filling a void left when most football schedules were either canceled or sharply curtailed.[36]

Thanks to Ned Irish's efforts, college basketball became closely identified with New York City. Irish added stops in Buffalo and Philadelphia to his promotions and offered teams a three-game swing through the East. After the war, he was promoting about 25 events a season and attracting more than a quarter-million spectators. Irish drew large crowds by featuring local teams, such as New York University, City College of New York, Long Island University, Manhattan College, and Brooklyn College. Many urban Catholic universities that had shied away from football because of its high costs were not far behind in developing their own programs: De Paul and Loyola in Chicago, St Louis University, Xavier in Cincinnati, Villanova and La Salle in Philadelphia, Duquesne in Pittsburgh, St Bonaventure,

Niagra and Canisius near Buffalo, and Fordham, St Johns, and Seton Hall in the New York City area were among the top-notch college basketball programs of this era. Thanks to the lure of Madison Square Garden and the promotions of Ned Irish, New York reigned as the basketball capital of America, and area teams often rested atop the national rankings.[37]

Out in the Midwest, where the high school game had become a way of life in small farming communities, three public universities rose to prominence due to the presence of charismatic coaches who dedicated themselves to a long-term career at one institution. One of the first coaches to gain national visibility was Forrest "Phog" Allen of Kansas University. He had the unique opportunity of replacing the "father of basketball" as the Jayhawks' coach when Dr James Naismith stepped down from coaching in 1907. Allen had played for Naismith and took over the University of Kansas team for two years, then returned in 1920 and coached the Jayhawks until his retirement in 1956. Possessed of a booming "foghorn" voice, which led a Kansas City journalist to coin the nickname "Phog," Allen turned out teams year after year that dominated its opposition. He prided himself on his ability to mold Kansas farm boys into powerful teams, and they helped him compile a career won–lost record of 591–219. One of the few exceptions he made to his philosophy of recruiting players primarily from Kansas and nearby farm states was when he lured the high school phenomenon, 7' 2" Wilt Chamberlain from Philadelphia to Lawrence in 1955.

One of Allen's perennial competitors was Hank Iba, who began coaching at Oklahoma A&M in 1934. Known for a deliberate style of play that featured a weaving "swinging gate" offense and a tenacious man-to-man defense, Iba won back-to-back NCAA championships in 1945–46 using the shot-blocking talents of 7-foot center Bob "Foothills" Kurland. Although his slow-down style largely went out of style in the 1950s, Iba remained at Oklahoma State until 1970, when he retired with a 767–338 career record. The nation's growing number of basketball fans also admired the strong, up-tempo teams produced at the University of Kentucky by one of Phog Allen's former players. Adolph Rupp went to Kentucky in 1930 and immediately turned the state into a hotbed for college basketball. More than 80 percent of his players came from within the state. During his 42 years at Kentucky, the "Baron of the Bluegrass" captured 27 Southeast Conference championships and four NCAA titles en route to winning 875 games. Rupp's teams dominated the Southeastern Conference at a time when many of its football-happy members did not take basketball seriously, but nonetheless his teams became nationally famous for their use of a high-powered offense that featured a pioneering form of the fast break.

These basketball coaching giants in the nation's midsection, however, were dwarfed in the national basketball spotlight by the teams and famous coaches who operated out of the national media capital of New York City. Clair Bee not only won several national titles and produced incredible won–lost records at Long Island University, but he also established himself as the intellectual leader of the game by writing 21 books on coaching and conducting coaching clinics around the country. He also published for the teenage market 23 popular novels that featured a clean-living, multi-sport athlete named Chip Hilton who managed to overcome various adversities to help his team win championships fair and square against unsportsmanlike opponents. Bee had to share the New York spotlight with Nat Holman, an egocentric former professional star and longtime college coach who was called "Mr Basketball" by fawning sports journalists. Holman had learned the game on the streets of New York City and was the much-proclaimed star scorer and passing wizard of the first popular professional team, the New York Original Celtics of the 1920s, who had played before packed audiences of 4,000 in a city opera house. In addition to playing professionally, Holman began coaching the Beavers of City College of New York (CCNY) in 1919, where he taught a tough street-smart style he called "the city game." He introduced the concept of the pivot player and created the switching man-to-man defense; throughout the 1930s and the 1940s, his teams battled Long Island University for local bragging rights while also contending for national honors. In 1950 Holman reached the height of his profession when his team won both the NCAA and the National Invitational tournaments.[38]

Hoop Nightmares

The careers of several of these renowned coaches intersected in the early 1950s during the revelations of a massive gambling scandal that threatened to destroy, or at least greatly slow, the growth of major college basketball. On January 18, 1951, the *New York Journal American* broke a front-page story that District Attorney Frank Hogan was about to indict several top college basketball players for "controlling" the outcome of games by "shaving points." Within two months, his investigation had revealed solid evidence that some 49 games had been tampered with by gamblers who gave bribes to 32 college players from seven different universities. Insiders believed that far more games and athletes were actually involved and that the investigation was terminated prematurely under intense political pressure. What came to light, however, was that the attraction of major college basketball in the urban areas, and in New York City in particular, was not simply the high quality of play; many of the spectators at Madison Square Garden came to watch teams upon which they had placed bets. Although the scandal was centered in New York, its tentacles reached into the nation's heartland as players were implicated at Toledo, Bradley, and most shocking of all, Adoph Rupp's vaunted Kentucky.

The scandal broke in 1951, but it had been building for more than a decade. As early as 1945, Phog Allen had received headlines when he warned of the influence of gamblers at the Garden, but his warnings were ignored, even made light of by his fellow coaches. Betting on college football had become established during the 1920s. In the large cities of the Northeast and Midwest illegal bookies offered odds on college football and professional baseball, often in the form of "pool" cards that offered bad odds to fans who had to pick several winning teams in order to win. New York City's gambling chieftains naturally took note of the Madison Square Garden games promoted by Ned Irish and developed a flourishing trade during the 1930s. Although no solid evidence exists to that effect, the respected journalist-historian Charley Rosen insists that games were fixed by gamblers well before the Second World War. The attractiveness of basketball to corrupt gamblers was greatly intensified during the war years when Chicago bookmaker Charles McNeil introduced a new approach to betting on team sports – the "points spread" – in which the favorite team had to win by more than the number of points set by the bookmaker. By 1950, the points spread system had been widely adopted for betting on football and basketball. As one bookie told journalist Rosen, by replacing the awkward odds system, the points spread had generated much more "action" on games. This appreciative bookie considered the new betting format "the greatest discovery since the zipper."[39]

While the points spread made business more lucrative for the bookmaker, it created new headaches for coaches and athletic administrators. Under the odds system, unscrupulous gamblers had to bribe players to lose a contest; now they merely had to get them to win a game by less than the points spread. It was now possible to convince a college basketball player that he could earn several hundred or even a few thousand dollars by making a few misplays so as to keep the final score differential below the spread while still helping his team win the game. In February 1951, New York District Attorney Hogan announced the arrest of three of Nat Holman's top CCNY players and the *Sporting News* "College Player of the Year," LIU All-American center Sherman White for "shaving points." Hogan's investigation shocked the nation, especially when he subsequently indicted three players from the 1948 and 1949 national championship University of Kentucky Wildcats team. When news of the scandal first broke, the imperious Kentucky coach, Adolph "Baron" Rupp, arrogantly told the press, "Gamblers couldn't touch my boys with a ten foot pole." A few weeks later, he was stunned when two popular All-Americans, guard Ralph Beard and center Alex Groza, along with high-scoring forward Dale Barnstable, admitted taking bribes from gamblers throughout their college careers. Beard and Groza, who had led the 1948 United States Olympic team to a gold medal, even confessed to throwing a game in the 1949 National Invitational Tournament. At the time of their indictments, they were playing professionally for the Indianapolis Olympians in the National Basketball Association, from which they were summarily banned.[40]

Most of the players involved agreed to plea bargains or were convicted in New York Federal Court on charges of bribery, conspiracy, and illegal gambling. One of the several CCNY players involved, Norm Mager, recalled his participation more than 40 years after the fact:

> We were just dumb, naive kids, 19, 20 years old. We didn't know of any law that said you shouldn't shave points – we weren't throwing games, after all. And we thought, hell, the money looked pretty good. Even if it wasn't a lot, it seemed a lot to us, since we had almost nothing.[41]

Although a few players served short jail sentences, most received suspended sentences while a few took an option to serve in the military in lieu of jail. The major perpetrator of the fixes, however, New York City gambler Salvatore Sollazo, ended up doing 12 years of hard time in Sing Sing, and his associate, former LIU guard Eddie Gard, served three years.

Apologists for college sports argued that the scandal involved only a small number of athletes and that the system itself was sound. However, the federal district judge who presided at several of the trials saw much more than the moral failure of a few young athletes. In a scorching commentary, Judge Saul Streit laid the blame for the scandals at the feet of the culture of big-time college athletics, which he charged was infused with "a moral debasement." Streit called for fundamental reform of "this evil system of commercialism and overemphasis." The critics of college sports seemed to get a second wind from the scandals. Some asked a simple question: if colleges could pay players to *make* baskets, why would players not also take payments to *miss* them? Even the humbled Clair Bee understood: "Something must be done before all sports are discredited," he wrote in a national magazine. Echoing the words of the Carnegie Commission in 1929 and anticipating the criticism of future critics, he concluded, "Nothing will be accomplished until college presidents take aggressive action in cracking down on irregularities in their athletic departments."[42]

Thus the irony: while football had dominated the college sports scene from the inception of intercollegiate athletic programs and had been a continuing target of criticism, it would be a lesser sport that would illuminate the corruption that lay at the foundation of big-time intercollegiate athletics. Just as the headlines began to fade on the basketball point-shaving scandal during the summer of 1951, however, football once again gained the front pages when it was revealed that a widespread academic cheating scandal had been uncovered in one of the premier big time football programs. Shortly before the opening of fall practice, West Point, poised to make a run at a national championship under head coach Earl "Red" Blaik, dismissed 90 cadets for academic dishonesty under the Academy's strict honor code. Nearly half of the disgraced cadets were members of the vaunted Black Knights football squad. Once again the integrity of college athletics was on the front pages of the newspapers. President Harry S. Truman ordered a thorough investigation, and several US senators demanded the abolition of sports programs at the two military service academies. Newspaper columnists and editorial writers said all the obvious things as they pointed toward the obsession with victory that college athletics had become. Could it be, they collectively asked, that contrary to popular myth, sports did not build young men of good character but rather existed in an environment in which college administrators, coaches, and players were required to live a shameful deception? Could it be that the pressures to win actually imbued college athletes with negative values?

8 Sports in an Age of Ballyhoo, Depression, and War, 1920–45

Bounded by two world wars, the decades of the 1920s and the 1930s constitute a pivotal period in twentieth-century American history. However, the two decades have little in common and stand out for their sharp contrast with each other. The "Roaring Twenties" saw the emergence of both a consumer and a celebrity culture in which mass marketing, the growth of specialized professions, the routinization of work, and the introduction of myriad new products and services helped produce a significant rise in disposable income among an expanding middle class. This was the time when both radio and motion pictures came of age. By 1927, two national radio networks, NBC and CBS, were broadcasting the same profitable combination of drama, comedy, news, and music coast to coast.

The American people were thrust, willingly and eagerly, into a new age of mass production and mass consumption hyped by the mass media. A rapidly expanding economy lifted many boats, putting disposable income into far more hands than ever before. Chain stores, such as A & P grocery stores, Rexall Drugs, J. C. Penney and Sears Roebuck, invaded towns large and small, threatening the viability of local merchants. The urban department store, offering everything from cosmetics and clothing to refrigerators and wristwatches, became the Mecca of a nation of dedicated shoppers. The new automobile age, symbolized by the ubiquitous Model-T Ford, gave the American people a new sense of independence and freedom as distant places became readily accessible.

The Roaring Twenties, however, ended not with a loud roar but a dull thud. The crash of the stock market in October 1929 was prelude to the Great Depression. It shook the foundations of America's basic economic and political institutions. By 1932, the stock market had lost over 80 percent of its value, giving back all of the Dow Jones average gains made since 1910. When Franklin D. Roosevelt took the oath of office on March 4, 1933, fully 26 percent of the American workforce was unemployed. Soup lines and apple peddlers on street corners became a familiar scene in urban centers, as did the sheriff's sale on the countryside as millions of farmers suffered mortgage foreclosures. The price of agriculture commodities plunged 75 percent by 1932. Ironically, America's farmers suffered because they produced far too many foodstuffs and fibers for the marketplace to absorb, the burgeoning surpluses relentlessly driving down prices. No area of American life remained untouched, and historians consider it to have been one of the greatest challenges confronted during the two hundred years of life under the Constitution.[1]

The economic disaster would not end until the government began a military build-up in 1940 to prepare for the possibility of war with Nazi Germany and Imperial Japan. The economic malaise naturally affected American sports. Baseball endured a long winter of discontent, and the sparkling performances of athletes no longer seemed all that thrilling. The Golden Age of American sports gave way to a dour and disconsolate era that aptly reflected the tough times of the 1930s. The Great Depression seemed to cut even leading sports figures down to size. Popular writer John Tunis noted that "as business fell away, American [athletic] prowess also suffered. After 1930 our stream of super-champions ran dry, replaced by a turgid brook. The champions were now just ordinary mortals, good players but nothing more."[2]

Gee-Whiz: Sports Journalism During the 1920s

In 1931, veteran *New York Daily News* sportswriter Paul Gallico assessed the previous decade of sports reporting:

> Never before had there been a period when, from the ranks of every sport, arose some glamorous, unbeatable figure who shattered record after record, spread-eagled his field and drew into the box office an apparently unending stream of gold and silver. We have lived through a decade of deathless heroes.[3]

Gallico was describing the so-called "Gee-Whiz" school of sports journalism of the 1920s that emphasized and often greatly inflated the positive attributes of athletes while giving little attention to the negative.

The leading figure of the Gee-Whiz school was Grantland Rice, a pleasant Southerner possessed of a florid vocabulary and a passion for sports. He preferred to write about heroic effort and stunning victories than underachievement and defeats. He would have been very uncomfortable in the world of investigative and negative reporting that came to characterize the sports media in the intense, competitive-driven world of the late twentieth century. He considered the personal failings of athletes out-of-bounds; even their setbacks and failures on the field of play were treated with understanding. Rice summarized the approach of himself and his many imitators:

I give the other guy a break. That's because I've been an athlete and made mistakes too. In a 2–0 baseball game, for instance, I tend to give the pitcher credit for a good game, instead of belaboring the other team for poor hitting.[4]

Thus, under the protective shield of Grantland Rice and a small army of similar-minded journalists, the shameless off-the-field behavior of Babe Ruth was chalked up to "youthful exuberance," and the pathological behavior of Ty Cobb somehow was transformed into the rosy image of the "Georgia Peach."

During the 1920s, the sports "star" became a popular symbol of the new consumer culture. Historian Lynn Dumenil has observed that the sport idols "embodied the new culture" and also reassured a nervous people caught up in a time of rapid change because they

seemed to reaffirm older ideas about success. They represented a path to attainment outside the bureaucracy and regimentation of the corporation, and they held out the reassuring prospect that success was linked not just to hard work and individual discipline but also to the clear-cut rules of the individual sport and sportsmanship.

The new media-created sports stars endorsed consumer products and were celebrated in the pulp magazines and in the headlines of the newspapers; as such they symbolized the new era of a mass-media driven culture of consumption. It was, as Dumenil concludes, "an ethos of leisure and spending . . . that placed private, individual commodity-based self-realization at the center" of American life. That world came tumbling down with the collapse of the economy during the 1930s, giving way to the new outlook of pessimism and doubt that cut the once super heroes down to human size. Looking uncomfortably back upon his own work during the hyperbolic 1920s, Gallico admitted to "spinning a daily tale in the most florid and exciting prose that I could muster, part of the great ballyhoo, member of the great gullibles, swallower of my own bait." Now he would write articles that exuded skepticism and downright negativism.[5]

Rice was a friendly, caring individual who viewed sports as a metaphor for life itself; the strong moral sense he brought to his craft often surfaced in his writings. He believed that the contests that he reported were important as much for the struggle as for the outcome. A skilled wordsmith, Rice often inserted his own verse into his columns and game reports, including the famous stanza written early in his career in 1908 when he was a young reporter for the *Nashville Tennessean*:

For when the Great Scorer comes
To write against your name,
He marks not that you won or lost –
But how you played the Game.[6]

Born and raised in Tennessee by a prominent family, Rice graduated from Vanderbilt in 1901. Discouraged by his parents from pursuing a professional baseball career because of the game's soiled image, he gravitated to the emerging field of sportswriting. By 1912, he had secured a position with the *New York Herald Tribune*, and during the 1920s had become the nation's most widely read sportswriter. His daily column was syndicated in more than a hundred newspapers, and he also wrote a feature almost every week for *Collier's*. When Walter Camp died in 1925, he assumed the task of picking the All-American football team, and he produced Spotlight Films, a monthly 10-minute motion-picture newsreel on major sporting events. A generalist who covered all sports, Rice played an important role in making tennis and golf popular spectator sports, all the while writing extensively on the mainstream sports of college football and professional baseball. At the time of his death in 1951, it was estimated that he had written some 67 million words.

Rice set the standard for the sportswriting of the 1920s – florid, hyperbolic, emotional, as when he described Babe Ruth's three-home-run effort in a 1926 World Series game:

> After the manner of a human avalanche hurtling on its downward way from the blue Missouri heavens the giant form of Babe Ruth fell upon the beleaguered city of St Louis today and flattened it into a pulp of anguish. If another mighty planet had slipped its ancient moorings to come crashing through unlimited space against the rim of the earth it could not have left one sector in its path more dismantled or forlorn. . . . An enraged bull in a china shop of fragile bric-a-brac would be a mere kitten playing with yarn compared to the astonishing infant who lashed the ball over the stands into Grand Avenue twice and then hammered another home run into the center field seats 430 feet away . . .
>
>   It is just a picture of a large portly form taking a wild cut at the ball and then loafing along the open highway with a stunned and startled crowd wondering who let old Doc Thor or the bolt-heaving Jupiter into the show. It was smash-smash-smash and then a steady, even unhurried trot from the plate back to the plate with the ball bounding on its way down St Louis thoroughfares through brokenhearted crowds.[7]

When pioneering radio stations began experimenting with live broadcasts of sporting events, Rice decided to give the new medium a try. Consequently, during the 1922 World Series, Grantland Rice was seated next to the Yankee dugout for the subway series with the Giants. Station WJZ had a signal that reached 300 miles from New York City, and it was estimated that 1.5 million fans listened in. Rice, however, was not comfortable behind the microphone and permitted long periods of silence to fill the airways. One listener said, "I would hear the crowd let out a terrific roar and it would seem ages before I knew whether it was a single or a three-bagger that had been made or whether the side had been retired." Surprisingly, for a man for whom words flowed naturally through his fingertips onto his typewriter keys, Rice was too often left speechless before the microphone. "I didn't know what to say," he confessed. But he persevered and the following year signed on to broadcast the Series for another New York station, WEAF. He was assisted by station announcer and studio baritone singer Graham McNamee, but once again Rice discovered that the words simply did not flow into the microphone as when he was hunched over a typewriter. He abruptly quit in the fourth inning of the third game and turned the microphone over to McNamee, who made the most of his opportunity.[8]

Graham McNamee soon became the nation's leading sports broadcaster. His experience as a youth playing sports and boxing as an amateur enabled him to convey the drama and context of boxing matches and football and baseball games. He made a good impression announcing the 1923 Johnny Wilson–Harry Greb middleweight championship fight in which he was able to describe the many blows and defensive tactics while creating an "infectious excitement" among his listeners. McNamee, possessed of a staccato voice, became a leading announcer for championship boxing matches, college football games, and the World Series. Signing on with NBC, McNamee had the distinction of broadcasting the first game carried coast to coast: the 1927 Rose Bowl game between Stanford and Alabama. McNamee, according to one critic, had the ability "to take a new medium of expression and through it transmit himself – to give out vividly a sense of movement and of feeling." Rival network CBS developed its own broadcast star, Ted Husing, whose rich detail and comprehensive commentary seemed to put the listener inside the stadium. He was CBS's major sportscaster until after the Second World War. One commentator said that Husing may have been even more capable than the highly popular McNamee, because he "has given more complete information, more accurate and prompt news of the changing position of the ball and acute observations as to place, possibilities and potentialities of the teams and individual players on the field before him."[9]

Radio brought to millions of Americans the exciting feel and flavor of big games being held at distant locations and served to heighten public interest. It was a vital factor in the development of the so-called "Golden Age" of American sports.

Heroes for a Heroic Age

One of Grantland Rice's important contributions to the transformation of sports into mass spectacle was his role in increasing public interest in sports of limited mass appeal. Golf had arrived in America during the 1890s but play was largely restricted to private country clubs. Not surprisingly, the game was widely perceived to be one reserved for the elite. President William Howard Taft received considerable criticism when he permitted himself to be photographed swinging a club but it was not until Dwight Eisenhower was in office that another president permitted himself to be photographed playing golf. Even John Kennedy, a low-handicap golfer, never permitted his love for the game to become the stuff of media coverage. Until the 1920s, even the most important tournaments were small affairs with relatively little press attention. Tournament sponsors could offer only small prize monies for the professionals; many of the best golfers were amateurs. Such was the case in 1913, when the 20-year-old son of an Boston gardener and handyman, amateur Francis Ouimet, shocked the two dominant English professionals of the time, Ray Vardon and Ted Ray, in the US Open. The tournament was held in suburban Boston at the Country Club in Brookline, where Ouimet had once worked as a caddy. Playing in a three-way 18-hole playoff, Ouiment out-dueled the Englishmen, winning the championship by five strokes. Unlike the sparse crowds that had watched previous major American tournaments, an unprecedented crowd estimated to be over 3,000 trampled over the course following the three competitors.[10]

Ouimet's stunning victory swept golf onto the front pages of American newspapers. A working-class American had toppled the giants of the world of golf. Although Ouimet continued to play competitively for the next three decades, he never won another major tournament, but he had awakened the American people to the possibilities of golf. Middle-class American men and women began to take up the game in the 1920s as public courses opened in most cities. By 1925, an estimated two-and-a-half million Americans played the game. Many businessmen, confined to office or store, found relief from job pressures playing in the open air on well-groomed courses that blended grass, sand, water, and trees into beautiful (if not challenging) vistas. Businessmen discovered that the golf course was a perfect location for cutting deals and building relationships with clients. During the dry years of Prohibition, others discovered that the most hospitable place on the grounds was the "nineteenth hole," which featured a well-stocked bar located in a secure private club, safely hidden from the long arm of the law.

After the First World War, Ouimet was replaced in the national golfing spotlight by two men whose lifestyles and approach to the game contrasted sharply with the other. Walter Hagen was born into a middle-class family in Rochester, New York, in 1892. He became a golf professional at the Country Club of Rochester, which at the time meant that he was expected to earn his living overseeing the day-to-day operation of the golf course, supervising grounds keepers, giving lessons, assigning caddies, and managing the pro shop, club restaurant, and bar. In 1914, Hagen won the US Open and several other victories followed. His flamboyant, if not arrogant, personality, and sharp golfing skills led to the media-inspired nickname "Sir Walter."[11] Hagen made golf history in 1922 when he became the first American to win the British Open, and for several years he reigned as the world's greatest golfer, winning two more British Opens (1928 and 1929) and four consecutive Professional Golf Association (PGA) tournaments (1924–25–26–27).

The flamboyant Hagen attracted widespread public acclaim and helped to democratize the game of golf. Newspaper writers loved him for his celebrity and fans flocked to his exhibitions, where he bantered with members of the gallery and joined them at the bar afterwards. But the charismatic Hagen had to share the spotlight with another public favorite, the unassuming Bobby Jones, son of a prominent Atlanta family who was blessed with one of the most picture-perfect golf swings in history. Both men, in their own way, contributed to golf's growing popularity. Jones not only rose to the top of the golfing world but also simultaneously graduated from college and law school, passed the Georgia Bar, and launched a career as a practising attorney. At a time when many Americans still believed that the true sportsman was an amateur who played for the joy of competition rather than for hard cash, Jones became a public favorite because he refused to turn professional.[12]

In 1923, after gaining considerable attention as a teenage prodigy, Jones won the US Open golf tournament in dramatic fashion in an 18-hole playoff. Jones boldly ripped a two-iron out of the rough 190 yards over a water hazard fronting the green. The ball rolled within a few feet of the hole and he putted out for a one-stroke victory. Grantland Rice exulted:

> The red badge of courage always belongs upon the breast of the fighter who can break and then come back with a stouter heart than he ever had before. This crimson decoration of valor came to Robert Tyre Jones, of Atlanta, 21-year-old amateur, when he rode at last yesterday to the crest of the open golf championship of the United States on one of the greatest iron shots ever played in the game that goes back through 500 years of competitive history.[13]

Over the next seven years, Jones – who handled the wooden-shafted clubs of his day with both finesse and power – won 12 more major tournaments in a time when amateurs could enter only a handful each year. In 1930, even Grantland Rice had trouble finding the words to describe Bobby Jones's domination of the world of golf. That year Jones won golf's four most prestigious tournaments, the equivalent of today's Grand Slam – the US Open, the US Amateur, the British Open and the British Amateur – bringing his total major tournament victories to 13. His seemingly flawless game helped convert golf into a public spectacle. Unprecedented large crowds followed his every tournament round, and his name became a household word. When he came onto the scene, there were fewer than 500 courses affiliated with the United States Golf Association, but by 1930 there were 1,154 private member clubs, and the flurry of construction of public courses meant that there was a total of nearly 6,000 golf courses in the country. After winning the Grand Slam in 1930, Jones abruptly announced his retirement from competitive golf at the age of 28. Rice conceded that Jones had at least 20 good years left in him, but with no new "worlds to conquer" any future victories would be "nothing but anticlimax."[14]

The game of tennis had more difficulty in overcoming its elitist image, but during the 1920s Bill Tilden and Helen Wills attracted considerable attention in the mainstream media. Playing at a time when standard equipment was a small wooden racquet that would be dwarfed by the oversized high-tech titanium and composition weapons of today, "Big Bill" Tilden mastered every stroke like no one else of his time. Famous for his come-from-behind victories, Tilden's court behavior often pushed the outer limits of what was supposed to be a "game of gentlemen and ladies." A writer for the *New Yorker* described tennis's big star on the court:

> He will turn and glare at any lineman who dares give a decision against his judgment; before the thousands in the stands he will demand the removal of the offender; he will request "lets" at crucial moments, object when new balls are thrown out. When he mis-hit a shot he would stand with his hands on his hips and exclaim, "Oh, Peaches!"

Writing in 1953 upon Tilden's death, veteran sportswriter Al Laney recalled that Tilden was "arrogant, quarrelsome, unreasonable; very hard to get along with." All in all, Tilden's tantrums made him a favorite of the press, in particular Grantland Rice.[15]

Possessed of a slender body, Tilden appeared much taller than his 6' 1" frame, which led to his nickname "Big Bill." Biographer Frank Deford contends that "no man ever bestrode his sport as Tilden."[16] Indeed, after becoming the first American to win the singles title at Wimbledon in 1920 (a feat he repeated the following year), Tilden proceeded to win the US Open championship in six consecutive years (1920–25), while also leading the American Davis Cup team to the title for seven consecutive years. At a time when the tennis establishment would only recognize amateur players, Tilden played technically as an amateur although he, like other top players, demanded large payments to "cover their expenses." In 1928, the United States Lawn Tennis Association declared him ineligible because he was being paid $25,000 a year by a newspaper syndicate to write about tennis; the association contended that his tennis articles made him a professional. This shocking decision came on the eve of the Davis Cup matches with France, and the controversy for a time knocked the Herbert Hoover–Al Smith presidential race off the front pages. Reinstated at the last possible moment, he led the United States to victory with a dramatic five set victory over French star Rene LeCoste. Angered by the USLTA's petty ruling, and in need of money, Tilden announced the next year that he was turning professional, which meant that he played exhibition matches for pay for several years because the professional circuit was in its formative stages.

Women's tennis during the 1920s and the 1930s did not produce the drama and controversy that surrounded the mercurial career of Bill Tilden, but the superb skills of a young woman from California, Helen Wills, served the purpose of creating increased awareness of what women athletes could accomplish. After struggling with severe childhood illnesses, she turned to tennis as a means of enhancing her physical condition. Standing 5' 7", Wills cut a sharp figure on the court in her simple but stylish white skirts and always-present white sun visor. Seldom showing any emotion, she was dubbed "Little Miss Poker Face" by the press. Wills hit with incredible power and had uncanny accuracy in placing her shots. One leading tennis player and authority, Don Budge, recalled that he had never seen a woman with such power until Steffi Graf came on the scene in the 1980s.[17]

In 1926, Wills was just emerging as a top player when she traveled to France to meet the reigning Wimbledon women's champion, Frenchwoman Suzanne Lenglen. That match, held at Cannes, produced a great deal of public interest, and scalpers were getting the astronomical sum of $50 apiece for tickets. In a dramatic match, Wills ultimately lost by a 6–3, 8–6 margin, but the match was much closer than the score indicated, with many games going to multiple deuces and featuring very long, tense rallies. At a time when travel was much more time-consuming, these two giants never again met on the court; the possibility of great rivalry was unfortunately missed. Wills dominated American women's tennis from 1927 until the mid-1930s. Her record of six US Open singles titles would last until eclipsed by Chris Evert in the 1980s; she also won two championships on the clay courts of Rolland Garros at the French Open, and four Wimbledon titles. Between 1927 and 1933, Wills won 180 straight matches without losing a single set.

One of the more improbable sports heroes of the 1920s was the daughter of a

Figure 8.1 One of the first American sports heroines was swimmer Gertrude Ederle, shown here on August 26, 1926 slathered in lard and petroleum for protection from the cold waters of the English Channel. She became the first woman to swim the Channel, doing so in a time of 14 hours and 31 minutes, more than 90 minutes faster than any of the five men who had previously traversed the treacherous waters between France and England. © Bettmann/CORBIS.

New York City butcher. Gertrude Ederle learned to swim at an early age while spending summers on the Jersey shore. She later recalled that she was "a water baby" who was "happiest between the waves." When she was five, she developed a problem with her hearing after suffering a bout with measles. "The doctors told me my hearing would get worse if I continued swimming, but I loved the water so much, I just couldn't stop," she told a reporter. By her late teens, she was winning freestyle races ranging between 100 and 800 meters, setting several world records. On one day in 1922 she set seven world records in the waters of Brighton Beach in Brooklyn, between 1921 and 1925 she held 25 amateur national and world swimming records, and she attracted national attention when she swam 16 miles from the Battery to Sandy Hook, New Jersey, through turbulent waters. At the 1924 Olympics, which for the first time held limited competitions for women, she won a gold medal and two bronzes, despite suffering from a knee injury.[18]

On August 6, 1926, Ederle thrilled the world when she became the first woman to swim the English Channel. When she entered the water at Cap Griz-Nez, France, she noticed a warning sign about high waves and choppy water, but after a brief prayer she plunged into the cold waters, her body slathered with heavy grease. If she had been able to swim in a straight line, her distance would have been 21 miles, but the high winds and waves were so rough that it is estimated she swam 35 miles to reach the English coast.

Ederle immediately became a national sensation, and when she returned to the United States she was welcomed by a ticker-tape parade through the New York City financial district while an estimated two million people waved and cheered "Trudy! Trudy! Trudy!" She was even invited to the White House, where President Calvin Coolidge, not known for his social sensitivities and in typical form, laconically commented, "I am amazed that a woman ... should be able to swim the English Channel." For a brief time Ederle rivaled Bill Tilden, Babe Ruth, and Red Grange as a national sports figure, but she discovered that fame was fleeting. She made a Hollywood movie about her life, which paid her $8,000, took a stab at vaudeville, and was deluged with marriage proposals from unknown suitors. Her stint in Vaudeville fell flat: "I was just a bundle of nerves. I had to quit the tour because I was stone deaf." In 1929, she suffered what was then called a "nervous breakdown," and in 1933 she fell in an apartment stairwell, suffered a broken back, and was confined to a body cast for four years. She lived a long but lonely life, supporting herself during the 1950s and the 1960s giving swimming lessons at the Lexington School for the Deaf in New York City. Although the press would occasionally recall her Channel swim, she dropped out of sight and lived quietly in New York, her moment of glory during the 1920s long forgotten by most Americans. She died alone and forgotten in 2003 at the age of 98.

The triumphs of women such as Helen Wills and Gertrude Ederle raised concerns that they exhibited traits that exceeded the conventional image of femininity. Ederle's stout 5' 7" 145-pound physique drew some comment, but the fact that she had crossed the English Channel two hours faster than any of the five men who had previously made the arduous trip produced many questions. When the dominant European tennis player Suzanne Lenglen came to the United States in 1920 to play America's top women players, she startled the sensibilities of many when she told *Collier's Magazine* that she and other serious women players "are out to win. No mercy is shown. ... There is no such thing as 'ladies first'." Helen Wills's domination of her era of women's tennis produced considerable ambivalence. Tennis fans appreciated the speed, agility, and power that she exhibited, prompting journalists to use such terms as "killer," "ruthless," and "heartless" to describe the cold efficiency she displayed in relentlessly dispatching her opponents. Such women were pursuing athletic excellence by exhibiting the same traits as male athletes – strength, speed, endurance, agility. This appealed to feminists but disturbed traditionalists who feared that the new woman athlete portended the arrival of a generation of women who were neither fragile nor vulnerable and who would not need the protective care of men. Beyond question, the new female athlete as exemplified by these women no longer practiced the long-expected "moderation" that had long been expected of them.[19]

Boxing Becomes Respectable

The 1920s gave rise to the professional sports promoter. The prototype for this important role was the flamboyant George "Tex" Rickard, who concentrated his considerable abilities upon the long-derided sport of boxing. His creative flair for the dramatic enabled him to help move boxing from the shadows of public skepticism and dubious legal status to mainstream legitimacy. During the 1920s, he promoted five championship fights that grossed over $1 million at the gate and drew crowds that reached the unprecedented figure of 100,000.[20]

Rickard arrived on the scene at the right time. Boxing had been used by the army to help prepare soldiers for combat in the Great War, and changing public attitudes led to the legalization of the sport in many states, including New York in 1920. With intensive newspaper coverage, it became fashionable for politicians, business executives, and social leaders, often in evening dress, to be seen at championship fights in the company of their lady friends. Boxing no longer squirmed uncomfortably under the baleful stare of moral absolutists; the blood sport had become an integral part of the age of sports ballyhoo, and Tex Rickard was just the person to exploit it. Born in 1871 to itinerant Texas parents, Rickard worked for a few years as a cowpuncher, and at age 19 became a town marshal. In 1895, he migrated to the Klondike in quest of gold, but he soon discovered that it was more profitable to mine the miners than to undergo the duress of digging for gold himself. He operated a Dawson City saloon, installed gambling tables, and promoted boxing matches. He migrated westward to Nome, Alaska, where he pocketed a large profit from his Great Northern Saloon and the promotion of a series of boxing matches. After losing his fortune in South Africa, where he went in search of diamonds, in 1906 Rickard landed in Goldfield, Nevada, in the midst of a gold mining boom. There he established another saloon and became famous when he promoted a world championship fight between middleweights Joe Gans and "Battling" Nelson, putting the $30,000 purse on display in the window of his saloon in the form of stacks of $20 gold pieces. In 1910, he attacted world wide attention when he promoted the "fight of the century" in Reno, where Jack Johnson defeated the "Great White Hope" Jim Jeffries.

After losing his fortune once again, this time cattle ranching in Paraguay, Rickard returned to the United States and in 1916 resumed promoting boxing matches. Aware that his future definitely rested with boxing, Rickard went in search of a "killer" fighter who would become the next sensation. He found him out west in Jack Dempsey, a fighter of modest skills who had been earning a few bucks fighting local thugs in small-town Nevada saloons. Cursed with spindly legs and an unimposing physique, complete with a high-pitched effeminate voice, Dempsey was also saddled with an unspectacular record. But no matter. Rickard dubbed him the "Manassa Mauler" (after Dempsey's small Colorado hometown) and arranged for a match in Toledo with the aging "Pottawatomie Giant," the 6' 6" 245-pound reigning champion, Jess Willard, whose career was in sharp decline. Rickard placed Dempsey under the direction of skilled trainer Jake Kerns, and on July 4, 1919, he savagely beat Willard, knocking him down five times in the first round and finishing him off with a technical knockout in the fourth round. Standing barely six feet tall and weighing only 187 pounds, Dempsey was now, the press gleefully reported, "Jack the Giant Killer." Rickard had his meal ticket and was off to New York City and Madison Square Garden, where he signed a deal to promote boxing and other attractions.[21]

In the immediate postwar era the flames of patriotism still burned brightly, and Rickard had himself a powerful gimmick with which to promote Dempsey's fights. The new champion was considered by many a "slacker," the term applied to men who found a way to avoid military service in France. Dempsey had even faced federal indictment in 1920 for his failure to serve, but he won acquittal on the dubious grounds that his wife and mother had required his financial support. Rickard thereupon brought from France a decorated soldier, Georges Carpentier, to fight the man whom the American Legion wanted barred from the ring. After scheduling the bout for Madison Square Garden, Rickard had to move it across the river to Jersey City when political criticism of Dempsey grew too intense. It was not only war hero versus slacker, because Rickard also played upon images of perfumed Frenchmen, implying that Carpentier was an upper-class dandy, a handsome lady-killer and man-about-town who liked to dance and sing rather than fight. Conversely, he also portrayed Dempsey as a working-class Irish "mauler" and also an "abysmal brute" whose devastation of Willard was only a sign of worse things to come. Eighty-thousand fans paid good money to see the bout, including many of the glitterati of New York society. Rickard raked in $1,600,000 at the gate, and Dempsey lived up to his reputation, knocking out his outclassed and over-hyped opponent in the fourth round.

Dempsey grew in popularity as memories of war waned. Dempsey seldom defended his crown, and when he did it was against weak opponents whom Rickard somehow managed to portray to the gullible public as formidable challengers. In 1923, Dempsey's next victim was a working-class stiff from Argentina, Louis Firpo, whom Rickard dubbed the "Wild Bull of the Pampas." Actually, Firpo had last worked as dishwasher and had only marginal pugilistic skills; he came into the fight having won a few contests over opponents that Rickard had lined up to create an aura of respectability. Rickard again played the nationalism card, noting that this was an epic battle between North America and Latin America. Writer Bruce Blevin bluntly wrote, "We are here to see the Nordic race defend itself against the Latin." Once again, this time in the Polo Grounds before a crowd of

88,000, Rickard had another million-dollar gate. An estimated 35,000 additional would-be spectators were turned away after all of the seats were sold. It was a bizarre fight. Dempsey knocked the hapless Firpo to the canvas seven times in the first round, but as the round neared its end, Firpo somehow arose from the canvas and unleashed a wild swing that caught Dempsey flush on the jaw, knocking him completely out of the ring. The dazed champion got back on his feet and into the ring only with the help of ringside reporters and an obliging Western Union telegrapher. A dazed Dempsey managed to hold on until the bell, but 88,000 fans had just witnessed one of the most sensational rounds in boxing history. Firpo's lucky punch only served to enrage Dempsey, who finished him off with two more knockdowns in the second round. Firpo had been decked nine times in less than five minutes. An editorial writer for the *Brooklyn Eagle*, satisfied with the outcome, read a great deal into a mere prizefight: "One shudders to think what might have happened to the Monroe Doctrine if Firpo had won. To-day it is safe to say that South America has more respect for us than ever before."[22]

Despite his growing popularity, Dempsey did not defend his crown again for three years. He enjoyed his role as a celebrity and earned large sums from public appearances, motion-picture roles, and product endorsements. Rickard was busy making money with his various Madison Square Garden promotions, and was content to wait until the right opponent came along. For certain, he did not want Dempsey to fight the logical contender, Harry Wills, an African American from New Orleans. No one knows for certain the details, but despite demands from leading New York politicians for a title defense against "the Brown Panther," Rickard reported that he encountered stiff resistance to the fight from prominent public leaders. Some critics charged that Rickard harbored racist sentiments, but historian Randy Roberts concludes that Rickard, who had promoted the controversial Jeffries–Johnson fight in 1910, simply did not want to upset what he considered a "delicate balance of race relations in the United States."[23] Dempsey had fought African Americans in his early barroom brawls out west, and was willing to give Wills a shot, but most likely Rickard simply did not want to promote the fight.

Finally, in 1926, Dempsey agreed to defend against a relative unknown – and presumably another easy mark – Gene Tunney. The New York City native had learned to box as a teenager and was fascinated with the "scientific" aspects of the sport. He became a Marine Corps champion during the war and afterward worked his way up boxing's ladder as a light-heavyweight until he won the title in 1922, defeating "Battling" Levinsky. The following year, he lost the title to Harry Greb in a bout that saw him pummeled for 14 rounds, absorbing a beating so savage that he nearly died and had to spend a long time in hospital recuperating. But he decided that his beating was the result of bad strategy, so he plotted new tactics for the rematch, which he won on a decision. While in the military, he reportedly had read the major works of Shakespeare, and after he turned professional in 1919 he carried books with him everywhere he went. His love of reading was probably about half-true and half-fabricated, and he clearly used his erudition to irritate boxing writers and hype ticket sales. Tunney was naturally dubbed an effete intellectual, a "sissy" and a "snob" by the press and fight promoters.

Tunney appeared to be the perfect foe for yet another mismatch. He had amassed an enviable string of victories over quality opponents and, other than Wills, was the logical challenger. Although memories of the war had dimmed, Rickard nonetheless had himself a match between a draft dodger and a marine who had served in France. Nearly every boxing expert predicted a Dempsey victory, the consensus forecasting an early knockout. A record 120,000 fans turned out in Philadephia expecting to watch Dempsey knock another challenger senseless. But Tunney handily defeated Dempsey in a unanimous decision. As the bout unfolded, the impact of Dempsey's three-year layoff became apparent because he was unable to develop a rhythm and appeared in less than tip-top shape. Conversely, Tunney demonstrated impressive boxing skills as he forced the champion to miss frequently while peppering him with jabs and counter-punches. At the end of the tenth round, Dempsey's face had been cut in several places and both eyes were swollen shut. Dempsey did not win a single round. Rickard moved swiftly to set-up a lucrative rematch.[24]

That battle occurred in a packed Soldiers Field in Chicago on the night of September 2, 1927. In many respects it is one of the most memorable boxing matches ever staged. Tunney, who upon occasion had lectured reporters on their bad manners, had irritated them once more when he announced upon his arrival in Chicago, "I'm here to train for a boxing contest," he said, "I don't like fighting. Never did." Little wonder the *New York Times* had written that Tunney had "an unconcealed dislike for the sport."[25] An immense crowd estimated at 145,000 filled the football stadium, some sitting more than two hundred yards from the ring. Rickard kept the attendance figures secret, but the throng paid an astounding $2,658,660 dollars. NBC estimated that 50 million Americans listened to the description provided by an energized Graham McNamee. The fight began much like the first had ended, with Tunney controlling the pace and easily side-stepping Dempsey's wild swings while connecting with his counter punches. But then in the seventh round, events occurred that would create the most controversial moment in boxing history. Dempsey managed to connect with a powerful barrage of blows to the head and Tunney dropped to the canvas. An apparent knockout had taken place. The referee motioned to Dempsey to move to a neutral corner as specified in the rules of the Illinois Boxing Commission. But Dempsey ignored him, remaining in mid-ring and leering down at his helpless opponent. An estimated seven seconds passed before he finally retreated to a corner. The referee then began his count, which reached nine, at which time a wobbly Tunney rose to his feet and managed to survive the round. He then regained his senses and returned to his normal boxing style for the remaining three rounds, frustrating the wildly swinging ex-champion.

When the judges awarded Tunney a unanimous decision, outrage erupted at ringside and across the country. Dempsey, on the one hand, was now the sympathetic victim of a referee's insistence upon enforcing a rules technicality; Dempsey, the one-time slacker, was now transformed into the people's champ. Tunney, on the other hand, because of the "long count," was considered an accidental champion. After defeating Tom Henney in 1928, Tunney acceded to his wife's insistence that he retire from the ring, becoming the first heavyweight champion to vacate the title. Tunney's intellectual qualities proved to be real as he went on to a long and successful career as a business executive and writer, and served as a commander in the US Navy during the Second World War.

With Tunney's retirement and with Dempsey no longer active, Rickard was without a credible fighter to promote. But that problem became moot on January 6, 1929, when the master of ballyhoo died suddenly in a Miami hospital, the victim of an infection from a ruptured appendix. Tex Rickard died with his big meal ticket, Jack Dempsey, holding him in his arms. Boxing's heyday came to an unexpected end. During the Age of Ballyhoo of the 1920s, there had been five million-dollar fights – all promoted by the onetime cowboy from Texas. There would be only four million-dollar fights in the next 30 years. More than 20,000 admirers filed past Tex Rickard's casket as it rested on the floor of Madison Square Garden. The man Will Rogers said had a "Midas Touch" departed the sports scene as the sizzling twenties were winding down and the bleak years of depression lay just around the corner.

Babe: the Texas Tomboy

The Great Depression spread a heavy pall over the entire nation. Its devastating impact was felt in the once prosperous and proud cities, along the hard-hit main streets of some 10,000 small towns, and on the fertile countryside where farmers faced the loss of their farms to sheriff's sales and mortgage foreclosures. The exuberance and excess of the 1920s gave way to a somber and frightened mood as America became mired in the vortex of a devastating economic collapse. When President Franklin D. Roosevelt told a hushed and frightened nation during his first inaugural address on March 4, 1933, "The only thing we have to fear is fear itself," he poignantly touched a raw nerve of his people. The sense of frustration and despair extended to the world of American sports. The excitement and enthusiasm that had greeted America's athletes during the 1920s was replaced by a muted, even muffled public reaction. Promoters had great difficulty generating excitement for an event. When they sparked public interest, the hard times naturally depressed ticket sales. Even the best athletes received a muted public reception. In this baffling new economic environment, it was only to be expected that the Gee-Whiz school of sports writing fell into general disfavor as a new generation of tough-minded realist writers emerged. This new school of realists was led by a talented cadre of New York City sports journalists – Heywood Broun, W. O. McGeehan, Damon Runyan, Paul Gallico, Westbrook Pegler – and they produced more accurate, occasionally critical, assessments of the world of American sports. Grantland Rice would remain at his typewriter until 1951, but the world that he once ruled had passed him by. Gallico's acerbic comments in 1938 about the moral stature of one of the pre-eminent sports of the period is indicative of the new outlook of the new generation of writers:

> College football today is one of the last great strongholds of genuine old-fashioned American hypocrisy. . . . If there is anything good about college football it is the fact

that it seems to bring entertainment, distraction, and pleasure to millions of people. But the price, the sacrifice to decency, I maintain, is too high. As far as I am concerned, it is good-bye to college football and good riddance.[26]

The collapse of the American economy and widespread hard times forced the sports journalists of the 1930s to recognize that sports, first and foremost, were merely the playing of games. Even the greatest sports accomplishments were overshadowed by the harsh realities of mortgage foreclosures, the collapse of thousands of banks and savings institutions, the loss of family savings and investments, double-digit unemployment figures, and long lines of the unemployed workers and their families lining up in front of a Salvation Army soup kitchen for something to eat. Shattered dreams and uncertain futures thus produced a fearful wave of angry farmers and industrial workers who, upon occasion, took their frustrations to the streets in massive protests that some observers believed might be the early stirrings of revolution.

In such depressing times, it was difficult to get excited about a new home-run slugger or a record-setting Olympic runner. Thus when Mildred "Babe" Didrikson captured headlines with her record-shattering exploits in several sports, the public response was appreciative but definitely subdued. The muted public response to Didrikson was not simply the economy. It was also the result of the uncertainty of how to respond to a woman athlete of incredible strength and skill, whose multi sport accomplishments overshadowed even the best of the male athletes of her time. Didrikson powered her way onto the front of the nation's sports pages at a time when the role of women in American society was in the formative stages of a major transition, one that in fact would not run its full course by the end of the century. As biographer Susan Cayleff suggests, Didrikson "was caught in the midst of conflicting and rapidly changing notions of ideal womanhood" that were sweeping through American society. The new ideas were leading "to growing participation by women in the economy and politics, yet the dominant ideology asked them to remain housewives."[27]

The hesitancy with which the general public viewed Didrikson resulted in part from her refusal to conform to established standards. Her public comments about her lack of interest in boyfriends raised suspicions, which were accentuated by her physical appearance: a chiseled muscular body, what one journalist called a "hatchet face," and an unstylish short hairstyle produced apprehension about her femininity and gender orientation. One journalist elaborated, "This chin of the Babe's, the thin, set lips, the straight sharp profile, the sallow suntan, undisguised by rouge, regarded in connection with her amazing athletic prowess at first acquaintance are likely to do her no justice."[28] Many a writer referred to her as "freakish." Her exceptional physical strength and fluid body motions, her frequent participation in men's baseball and basketball games where her skill level was unquestioned, and her frequent use of profanity added to public discomfort. Paul Gallico criticized her repeatedly, giving her the unfortunate but lasting nickname of "muscle moll." He wrote that Didrikson's appearance and behavior raised the question as to whether she "should be addressed as Miss, Mrs, Mr, or It."[29]

Didrikson's undisguised disdain for things feminine and her overpowering athleticism naturally inflamed the fears of parents that their daughters would adopt her as a role model and become "tomboys." "My mother cried when I played softball," a women's physical-education professor at Lamar University later recalled. "I just don't want you to grow up to be like Babe Didrikson."[30]

Didrikson was born in 1911 to working-class immigrant Norwegian parents in the tough seaport town of Port Arthur, Texas. Although she would later claim that her nickname was given to her by boys who admired her ability to hit a baseball like Babe Ruth, it was more likely a knock-off of the Norwegian word *baden*, which means "baby." As a youngster, she exhibited a fondness for contests and hard-nosed play at which she excelled. Her parents actively encouraged her competitive nature, including her unusual practice of repeatedly jumping the front-yard hedge (a skill she later said helped her win an Olympic gold medal in the hurdles). When the family moved inland to Beaumont, Babe's raucous behavior soon led to the designation as "the worst kid on Doucette Street" because she got into frequent fights with neighborhood boys. In the ninth grade, she knocked cold a football player who challenged her to hit him on the chin. In high school, she became known as a multisport overachiever as she excelled in basketball, softball, volleyball, swimming and diving, tennis, and track.

Even before graduating from Beaumont High, Didrikson accepted a position to become a "secretary" for a Dallas insurance company at the munificent sum of $75 per month (a very high starting clerical wage for the depression era). She typed few letters and took no shorthand. Her job was to play on the firm's industrial women's basketball team that owner and sports enthusiast Melvin J. McCombs had assembled. She led the Employer's Casualty Insurance Company Golden Cyclones basketball team to national titles in 1930 and 1931. Before she joined the Golden Cyclones, a typical home-game crowd would number about 100. By 1932, the team was attracting 5,000. Didrikson added to her reputation as a rebel by disposing of the customary loose-flowing pantaloons for a skintight orange satin uniform that shocked everyone; her teammates soon adopted the same style, and other teams followed suit. In the summers, she played on the firm's softball team, slugging many a home run, and at McCombs's urging, competed on the company's track and field entry in Amateur Athletic Union (AAU) tournaments.

Didrikson pushed herself to excel, putting in long hours every day on physical conditioning and practice. In the summer of 1930, despite suffering from a badly cut foot, she set a US record in the high jump and won first place in the shot put, baseball throw, and javelin. She then set her sights on the 1932 Olympics, a dream she had held since childhood. At the 1932 AAU national meet, which also served as the Olympic qualifier, she was entered by McCombs as a one-person team, which enabled her to compete in all events – a daunting physical challenge. In a three-hour period, she won six of ten events, setting world records in the baseball throw (272'), the javelin (139' 3"), and the 80-meter hurdles (12.1 seconds), and national records in the shot put (39' 6.5") and the high jump (5' 3/16"), while also winning the long jump (17' 6"). She also finished fourth in the discus. This effort produced 30 points; the second place team chalked up 22 points.

Figure 8.2 A determined and focused Babe Didrikson cleanly clears a hurdle in practice prior to the 1932 Olympics in Los Angeles. She won three medals, one of them typically in a controversy over her "unfeminine" high-jumping style. © Bettmann/CORBIS.

Now a highly publicized sports figure, Didrikson was frustrated to learn that Olympic rules restricted women to just three events, a silly throwback to an earlier era when experts feared the dangers of over-exertion to the female body. She thereupon set two world records, winning the javelin with a 143' effort, and the 80-meter hurdles at 11.7 seconds. Her effort in the high jump also should have produced a gold medal, but she was "penalized" by the judges for using an unorthodox and unladylike jumping style, her own modification of the western-roll technique. The baffled judges delayed a decision for 30 minutes while they reviewed film of her jumps, and thereupon ruled that, although she and Jean Shiley had tied at 5' 5", Didrikson had committed a foul when her head crossed the bar before her feet. But instead of disqualifying her, they awarded Didrikson the silver medal. This strange turn of events aptly symbolized the controversy and confusion about gender roles that her superb athleticism provoked.

Didrikson proceeded to capitalize on her Olympic fame, receiving a nice raise from McCombs and earning substantial sums on the vaudeville circuit (telling corny jokes, singing, jumping hurdles, running a treadmill, and playing a harmonica). She appeared as a pitcher in two hundred games with the popular men's touring baseball team, the House of David, which required its players to wear long beards as part of their quasi-religious promotional gimmickry. She even pitched an inning of a 1934 exhibition game for the St Louis Cardinals against Connie Mack's Philadelphia Athletics (getting Hall of Fame slugger Jimmy Foxx to fly out), played professional basketball for a barnstorming team, Babe Didrikson's All-Americans, and would have taken up tennis competitively except for a chronic right shoulder injury suffered while making her world-record javelin toss. These activities, while bringing in much-needed dollars because she was now supporting her parents, were essentially gimmicks and smacked of hucksterism.

In search of a serious competitive outlet, Didrikson turned to a game she had played only casually a few times previously – golf. For several months, she hit an estimated 1,500 practice balls a day, quitting only when her hands were bleeding. She won the prestigious Texas State Women's Golf Championship in 1935, but on the top amateur circuit Didrikson found herself treated as a pariah by her fellow golfers, largely women from genteel social circles who found her plain appearance, penchant for self-promotion with the press, and questionable use of language beneath their expectations of a lady golfer. These criticisms stung, and Didrikson determined to undergo an image change. She wore more stylish clothes, had her hair done in the latest styles, began wearing makeup and high heels, and was even seen carrying a dainty monogrammed purse. In 1938, she met a leading professional wrestler at a golf exhibition in California, fell in love, and 11 months later married George Zaharias. The rumors about her sexual orientation diminished.

For several years, Didrikson's status as an amateur golfer was in question due to her having accepted pay to play with the House of David. Rumors had it, however, that some of her fellow golfers filed a protest with the United States Golf Association because they were unable to beat her. Beyond question, she had used her Olympic fame to earn money, had been paid well by the House of David, and had received part of the gate as a barnstorming basketball player. But she had never played golf for money. Nonetheless, she was given a three-year suspension with the understanding that her amateur status would be restored if she did not play any sport for pay for three years. She served the three-year suspension and returned to competition in 1943. In 1945, her victory at the Western Golf tournament began a 10-year streak of golf that has never been equaled. Her game featured long drives; she was routinely 225 to 240 yards off the tee (one day with a brisk wind to her back she nailed a drive 442 yards); she often out-drove top male professionals in exhibition matches. She played the game shrewdly and intelligently, although at times struggling on the green. She brought a strong desire for victory to the game. At times, she seemed to will herself to make a dramatic comeback, to hit a mid-iron pin high, even to sink a crucial putt. In 1946–47, she won 17 consecutive tournaments, and the following year captured the US Amateur. She was now earning $100,000 a year in product endorsements and, in a reversal of her earlier desire to preserve her amateur status, played a pivotal role in establishing the Ladies Professional Golf Association (LPGA). Despite many spats with her peers, Didrikson was elected president of the LPGA three times and did much to elevate public

Figure 8.3 Babe Didrikson never played golf seriously until she was 34 years of age, but after taking up the game she became the leading woman's golfer in America at a time when the LPGA was in its infancy, winning tournaments even after undergoing major stomach surgery for a cancer that would prove fatal in 1956. © Bettmann/CORBIS.

awareness of the women's game. Nonetheless, the prize money for the LPGA tour was paltry in comparison with the men's tour; the largest single payday she received for a victory was $2,100. In 1951, she won $15,087 when she won eight tournaments and finished second in five others; it was the largest annual amount won by a woman golf professional up to that time.

Didrikson continued her dominance of women's golf until spring 1953, when she was diagnosed with colon cancer. At a time when even the mention of the word "cancer" was avoided, she publicly announced the nature of her disease and devoted herself to raising monies for research and treatments. Incredibly, she returned to her golf four months after major abdominal surgery and quickly regained championship form, winning nine more tournaments and finishing high in the money in 20 others. She had to combat fatigue and pain, but her competitive fires still burned brightly. However, the disease returned, and in September 1956 the woman who was overwhelmingly elected the top female athlete of the first half-century succumbed to the disease at 45 years of age.

News coverage of the last 10 years of Babe Didrikson Zaharias' life should have concentrated upon her unprecedented success as a professional golfer. Her string of golfing triumphs, however, provoked an ongoing discussion about her transformation from "muscle moll" to a loving wife and homemaker who, the press never seemed tired of reporting, was an expert cook, loved to work in her flower garden, and slept in an eight-foot-square bed with her husband. *Life Magazine* announced her transformation into a "real woman" with a headline: "Babe Is a Lady Now: The World's Most Amazing Athlete Has Learned to Wear Nylons and Cook for Her Huge Husband." The fact that she eventually concentrated upon a sport with high social standing, one that seemed more "feminine" and did not require excessive strength, seemed to mollify her earlier critics.[31] The *Saturday Evening Post* proclaimed that although she was once rumored to be a male, she now definitely had large breasts and a slender waist. The article noted with approval her "cooking, interior decorating, curtain making, gardening and other housewifely arts." The once hypercritical Paul Gallico even commented favorably upon her "transition from the man-girl who hated sissies to a feminine woman." Even after her death, journalists such as Gallico were prone to say that she would be remembered not just for her many athletic accomplishments but "likewise in the hearts of all of us who loved her for what she was, a splendid woman."[32]

Thus, as the life and athletic career of Babe Didrikson Zaharias illustrates, even at mid-century the status of women athletes was tenuous at best. They could not be recognized simply as athletes but were subject to scrutiny for the level of their "tomboyishness," their attention to domestic responsibilities, and their athletic performances. As Cindy Himes concluded in a doctoral dissertation written at the University of Pennsylvania,

> Babe Didrikson Zaharias, more than any female athlete of her day, embodied the new female athlete. Zaharias changed cultural perceptions of the physical limitations of womanhood using her body as a weapon. . . . And, although she eventually knuckled under to society's dictates, for many years she stood in direct defiance of sex and class prejudice in the world of sport and in society at large. . . Babe Didrikson Zaharias became the standard for excellence in women's sports for several decades.[33]

Baseball's Long Slump

Like other American institutions, baseball also took its licks during the Great Depression.[34] The game remained popular with the American people, and fans everywhere continued to follow the fortunes of their favorite teams by listening to radio broadcasts and reading game accounts in the newspapers. But far fewer fans could afford the 50 cents general admission price or the top $1.75 ticket for field-level box seats. Attendance fell precipitously as the depression held America in its tenacious grip. In 1930, major-league attendance reached an all-time high of 10.1 million, but by 1933, the bottom year of the Depression, it had fallen 41 percent to less than six million. Minor-league attendance fell at about the same rate of 45 percent; five of 19 minor leagues folded during the 1932 season alone. The worst year for baseball, as well as for the national economy, was 1933; the St Louis Browns drew only 80,000 for the entire season, and the Cincinnati Reds, Philadelphia Phillies, and Chicago White Sox, along with the Browns, were all rumored to be on the verge of financial collapse. In 1932, the 16 major-league teams lost $1.2 million, and another $1.6 million the following year despite cost-saving measures, including slashing salaries by about 50 percent. In 1934, Babe Ruth earned only $35,000, a sharp reduction from his $80,000 salary of four seasons previous. Roster size of major league teams was reduced from 25 to 23 players, and the roster of umpires was reduced to ten in each league, which meant that many games were umpired by two-man crews rather than the usual three.

Although fans stayed at home, the product on the field was better than ever. Although most of the stars of the 1920s had fallen into the twilight of their careers, as symbolized by the rapidly deteriorating skills of Babe Ruth, a new generation of exciting players replaced them. In the National League, the shrewd management of Branch Rickey produced high-powered, exciting teams in St Louis that won two pennants in the late 1920s, two during the 1930s, and four more during the 1940s. Rickey's intensive scouting program and his elaborate farm system – which reached 30 affiliated teams in 1938 while controlling 750 player contracts – produced a bountiful crop of talented players, many of them poor farm boys from the South. In 1931, the Cardinals upset the favored Philadelphia Athletics in an exciting seven-game World Series, but only 20,000 St Louis fans turned out for the deciding seventh game, which the Cardinals won 4–2.

The 1934 Cardinals were an intriguing group of characters who would later be dubbed the "Gas House Gang." Damon Runyon called them "a warrior club, with warrior spirit."[35] Led by their fiery player-manager, second-baseman Frankie Frisch, they played in dirty uniforms, ran the bases with abandon, and partied long into the night. Popular third-baseman Pepper Martin epitomized the team. Not blessed with great talent, he went all-out on every play that featured his aggressive base-running and belly-flop of a slide. Possessed of a modest physique and perpetual unkempt appearance both on and off the field, Martin came to symbolize the "forgotten man" of the Great Depression who had to scratch and fight to survive. This native of Osage, Oklahoma, had spent seven long years in the minor leagues, but somehow managed to will himself to the major leagues. At shortstop, the Cardinals had the light-hitting but feisty Leo Durocher, a throwback to the early playing days of John McGraw, and in left field the power-hitting Joe "Ducky" Medwick, who led the team with 18 home runs while batting .319. Fans loved the barrel-chested Medwick because he would swing lustily at any pitch that came anywhere close to the plate. The heart of this zany team was the extraordinarily talented and free-spirited pitcher, Jerome "Dizzy" Dean. The son of Arkansas sharecroppers, Dean was irreverent and brash ("It ain't braggin' if you back it up"), possessed of a live fastball, nasty curve ball, and a tantalizing change-up, all of which he served up with pinpoint control to baffled hitters. Although he was the Cardinals' leading pitcher in 1932 with 18 wins, total innings pitched (286), and strikeouts (191), he nonetheless had his salary frozen the next year at $3,000 as the Cardinals retrenched. "This here depression ain't my fault," he plaintively

argued.[36] In 1934, Dean reached his prime, winning 30 games while losing just seven. Joining Dizzy Dean on the Cardinals pitching staff was his younger brother Paul, a phlegmatic 21-year-old who won 18 games without the fanfare that always surrounded his brother. In deference to his colorful brother, writers pinned the inappropriate nickname of "Daffy" on this quiet young man.

Despite their entertaining antics and a dramatic pennant race in which the Cardinals captured the pennant on the last day of the season, only 335,000 fans turned out in depression-riddled St Louis to see them play 77 home games. The 1934 World Series against the Detroit Tigers turned into an apt metaphor for the Great Depression as both teams represented cities that had been severely stricken; Detroit's industrial plants were operating on a limited basis, if at all, and St Louis had been devastated by a sharp drop-off in river boat traffic and the collapse of the Midwestern farm economy. Dizzy Dean was in his element – the center of attention. The Cardinals won the first game 8–3, although

Figure 8.4 Baseball was truly the National Game between the 1870s and the 1950s. Shown here in the late 1930s is a game of stickball, popular among boys in New York City. For many decades, informal ball games such as this were organized by the youth themselves, unlike the adult-supervised Little League that gained popularity during the postwar era. © Bettmann/ CORBIS.

Dean told the press, "I didn't have nary a thing on the ball. . . . It was a lousy, tick-flea-and-chigger-bite ball game." In the fourth game, Dean produced the winning run when, as a pinch runner, he failed to slide into second base during a double-play attempt and the second-baseman's throw smacked him flush in the forehead, knocking him senseless. As Dean collapsed in a heap, the ball bounced into left center field, permitting Leo Durocher to score the winning run. When he regained consciousness in the clubhouse, Dean announced that he was ready to pitch the next day: "You can't hurt no Dean by hittin' him on the head. I saw thousands of stars and all kinds of animals, but I still can't see them Tigers." A Detroit newspaper happily headlined: "X-Rays of Dean's Head Show Nothing."[37] Dizzy lost that game but came back in game 7 at Detroit's Navin Field to pitch the Cardinals to a lopsided 11–0 victory. In the sixth inning of that final game, Ducky Medwick knocked in the Cardinals' seventh run with a triple; in typical Gas House Gang style, he flung himself into third-baseman Marvin Owen with a hard slide, spikes flying high. A shoving match ensued, and when Medwick trotted out to his left-field position he was greeted by hostile Tigers fans in the bleachers with a barrage of beer bottles, vegetables, and anything else that they could heave over the fence. With the Cardinals far ahead, Commissioner Landis ordered Medwick to the clubhouse. Despite his productive 17-year career, Medwick is largely remembered as the only player ever removed from a World Series game by order of the Commissioner of Baseball.

The New York Yankees continued the domination that had begun in the early 1920s. Beginning in 1932 and concluding in 1943 under manager Joe McCarthy, they won eight pennants and seven World Series titles. In 1936, the Yankees purchased the minor league contract of a graceful center-fielder with a picture-perfect swing. Just 21 years of age, Joe DiMaggio became an immediate star. Dubbed the "Yankee Clipper" (named for the sleek, high-masted sailing ships of the early nineteenth century) DiMaggio gracefully roamed the vast spaces of center field in Yankee Stadium, running down hard-hit balls with apparent ease. During his 13 seasons between 1936 and 1951 (he sat out three seasons for military duty), he was an impressive clutch batter who not only hit for power but high average. DiMaggio led his team to 10 pennants and nine World Series championships (as compared to the figures of seven and four during Babe Ruth's 15-year tenure at Yankee Stadium). The Yankees won their four consecutive World Series in 1936–39 with an astonishing 16–3 record in games while winning the pennants by an average margin of 15 games.

The Yankees of this era were overpowering. After they beat the Reds decisively 4–0 in the 1939 World Series, the frazzled National League President John Heydler lamented, "Is this thing never going to change? No club can be as good as the Yankees have shown themselves to be in the recent Series against our teams."[38] But they were, and the Yankee juggernaut continued its dominance for next quarter century, winning 18 pennants and 12 World Series between 1940 and 1964.

Despite the difficulties presented by the sagging economy, baseball moved forward during the 1930s with three important innovations. The first of these was the establishment of the annual All-Star Game. Proposed by Chicago baseball writer Arch Ward, the game was played on July 6 in Comiskey Park, and 49,000 fans showed up. It was appropriate that the two teams were managed by Connie Mack, now 70 years of age, and John McGraw, whose health was rapidly deteriorating. It was also appropriate that Babe Ruth, now 38 and woefully out of shape, hit the first All-Star Game home run, a two-run blast into the upper deck in right field, and also made a spectacular catch while running into the right-field wall in the seventh inning to preserve an American League victory. While the game was conceived as a one-time event to coincide with the Century of Progress world's fair being held in Chicago, it proved so popular that baseball officials thereafter set aside a three-day mid-season break in which to hold the game. It became an important new event of the baseball season.

By the end of the 1930s, all major league teams had made their peace with the radio and signed contracts for most, if not all games, to be aired. Many owners feared that "giving the game away for free" would cut into ticket sales and only reluctantly agreed to permit live broadcasts in return for much-needed permission rights fees. Showing the way were the Chicago Cubs and the St Louis Cardinals, which saw an opportunity to build a larger fan base. By the early 1930s, the Cubs had established a network that reached far into the upper Midwest, while the Cardinals created millions of new fans in the mid-South and Southwest. When the worst of the Depression had passed, baseball's leaders recognized that radio had created new fans, which translated into increased ticket sales. In 1934, Commissioner Landis signed a four-year, $400,000 contract with Ford Motor Company to broadcast the World Series, and when Ford withdrew from the sponsorship, Gillette Safety Razor began a long and profitable relationship to advertise the qualities of its ubiquitous "blue blades." By 1936, all teams but those three located in New York City had some arrangement for radio broadcasts.

In most instances, home games were broadcast live from the ballpark, but economic constraints kept the broadcasters at home when the team hit the road. Announcers then sat in a studio and "recreated" the game based upon minimal information sped to them from a distant ballpark over Western Union telegraph lines. One of the popular broadcasters of this era was Ronald "Dutch" Reagan, who recreated Chicago Cubs games in the mid-1930s for Des Moines station WHO. One of the problems he and all "re-creators" faced was what to say when the telegraph lines went down. Speaking to a Baseball Hall of Fame luncheon in the White House in 1981, now President Reagan recalled one such episode:

When the slip came through, it said, "The wire's gone dead." Well, I had the ball on the way to the plate. And I figured real quick, I could say we'll tell them what happened and play transcribed music, but in those days there were at least seven or eight other fellows that were doing the same game. I didn't want to lose the audience. . . . so I had Billy foul one off . . . and I had him foul one back at third base and described the fight between two kids who were trying to get the ball. Then I had him foul one that just missed being a home run, about a foot and a half. And I did set a world record for successive fouls, or for someone standing there, except that no one keeps records of that kind. I was beginning to sweat when Curley [WHO's station telegraph monitor] sat up straight and started typing . . . and the slip came through the window and I could hardly talk for laughing because it said, "Jurges popped out on the first ball pitched."[39]

In 1935, the imaginative Cincinnati Reds business manager Larry MacPhail installed a young Southerner, Walter "Red" Barber, in the WLW studio to recreate all of the Reds' road games, but leery of giving away the product, permitted him to broadcast just 13 home games live from Crosley Field. He charged two local stations $2,000 each for the rights. In 1939, MacPhail moved on to Brooklyn as general manager and informed the Giants and Yankees that the Dodgers were withdrawing from their mutual agreement not to broadcast games. He had in hand a hefty $77,000 contract with station WOR to broadcast the Dodgers' games, a sum that would pay 40 percent of the Dodgers' salaries. MacPhail brought Red Barber and his soft Southern accent to Brooklyn, where he would remain the Dodgers' lead broadcaster until 1954, when he moved across town to join the Yankees' broadcast team. The Yankees and Giants quickly signed their own radio contracts, so by 1939 all 16 teams now had radio affiliations. Fourteen of the major-league teams – excluding only the two Boston teams – had the sponsorship of General Mills, which saw the advantage of promoting its Wheaties cereal as "the breakfast of champions." Many local breweries also joined in sponsorship as they sought to reach a predominantly male listening audience. Baseball had found a new source of revenue, with about 10 percent of all teams' budgets now being derived from the sale of broadcast rights.

Just as baseball's leaders had been cautious about the All-Star Game and radio broadcasts, so too did they approach gingerly the prospect of illuminating their fields for night games. The technology had been around since the 1920s, when many communities installed outdoor lighting for public recreational activities. In 1930 several minor league teams began night play and realized a significant bump in attendance. When Larry MacPhail became the general manager of the hard-pressed Cincinnati Reds in 1934, he pushed to have lights installed at Crosley Field. Owner Powell Crosley met staunch resistance from his fellow owners, who only reluctantly agreed to permit a few games in 1935 as an experiment. New York Giants owner Horace Stoneham abstained, explaining: "With pitchers like Dizzy Dean, Roy Parmelee and Van Lingle Mungo throwing at night we may have serious injuries to batsmen. Besides, baseball is strictly a daytime game."[40] At 9 p.m. on the evening of May 24, 1935, President Franklin Roosevelt flipped the switch in the White House and the bright lights came on in Cincinnati, where the lowly Reds met the equally lackluster Phillies. That season, the Reds averaged 18,700 fans for their seven night games, as compared to 4,300 for day games. By the 1941 season, only the Boston Braves and the Chicago Cubs did not have lights, although Cubs owner Phil Wrigley had purchased $185,000 worth of equipment to light the field for the 1942 season; when the war broke out, he donated it to the military. After the war, the Cubs took special delight in being the only team that played an all-day home schedule. Lights would not shine over Wrigley Field until 1988, 11 years after the chewing-gum magnate's death.

The 1941 season was conducted with the winds of war increasing in intensity, but despite the foreboding news that greeted the American people every morning, they found relief in following the hitting streak that "Joltin' Joe" DiMaggio began on May 15 when he hit a single off Edgar Smith of the White Sox. For the next 55 games, DiMaggio made at least one hit, while batting .408, hitting 15 home runs, driving in 55 runs, scoring an average of one run a game, and striking out just seven times. As his hitting streak grew, the American people watched with growing interest as the suspense mounted. On several occasions, DiMaggio got a hit in his last time at-bat, and there were, to be certain, a couple of scorer's decisions that went in his favor. After he passed the modern record of 42 games held by George Sisler and the "old-timers" record of 45 set in 1897 by Wee Willie Keeler, the American people embraced Joe DiMaggio as one of their new heroes. The streak finally came to an end in Cleveland on July 17 with 67, 000 fans looking on. Slick-fielding third-basemen Ken Keltner made two improbable backhand snags of hard-hit ground balls near the third-base foul line and followed them up with accurate throws to first base to end the string. Keltner and his wife were escorted out of Municipal Stadium by the police. "Joe had a lot of Italian friends in Cleveland," Keltner recalled, "and the club wanted to make sure I got to my car OK."[41] The next day, DiMaggio started another streak that extended for 16 games.

Once the worst of the Depression had passed, baseball fans returned to the ballpark. Beginning in 1935, attendance slowly began to increase, and in 1941 finally exceeded the record of 1929 with 10.5 million tickets sold. Although the Cardinals and Yankees were the dominant teams, other teams were also blessed with outstanding talent and exciting players who lured the fans back to the ballparks. Among these players was the hard-hitting left fielder of the Detroit Tigers, Hank Greenberg, who attracted more than his share of attention because he was Jewish. Anti-Semitism was alive and well in the United States during the 1930s, and one of its hotbeds was Detroit. The Ku Klux Klan had been active in this industrial city during the 1920s, and during the 1930s a local suburban priest, Father Charles Coughlin, presented weekly radio broadcasts to millions of avid listeners on a national network, routinely asserting that international Jewish conspirators and their banking allies had caused the Great Depression. As the 1930s unfolded, Coughlin's tirades became increasingly rabid and supportive of Adolf Hitler. Greenberg later recalled, "Being Jewish did carry with it a special responsibility. . . . If I had a bad day, every son of a bitch was calling me names so that I had to make good. I just had to show them that a Jew could play ball." Not only did Greenberg hear it from fans but also from the opposing dugout where, as he recalled, he was routinely called "a Jew bastard and a kike and a sheenie."[42]

Seabiscuit: Sport Star for the Depression Era

Despite the many top-notch athletes who performed during the Great Depression, it is intriguing to note that arguably the most popular sports figure of this era was a horse. During the latter years of the 1930s, an undersized, knobbly-kneed thoroughbred by the name of Seabiscuit captured the affection of the American people by overcoming many obstacles to win several memorable races. The improbable saga of the "people's race horse" has been eloquently captured by author Laura Hillenbrand and is the subject of a popular motion picture released in 2003.[43]

If attendance can be considered a determining factor, thoroughbred racing was arguably the most popular sport in America in the two decades between the wars. Attendance at race tracks during this period fluctuated between three and six million, outstripping baseball by several lengths. The primary attraction, of course, was the possibility of hitting a big payday on a two dollar bet. The reputation of horse racing had fluctuated over the years, remaining popular in the South but often becoming the target of anti-gambling crusaders elsewhere. Under relentless anti-gambling pressures, except for some notable tracks such as Churchill Downs in Louisville, and Pimlico Race Course in Baltimore, most race tracks had closed by the late nineteenth century. During the heyday of the progressive reform movement during the early twentieth century, matters got worse when legislatures in such prominent racing states as California, Illinois, and New York passed stiff anti-gambling laws. After the First World War, however, legislators took a careful look at a new betting system recently imported from France, the *pari-mutuel* system, which assured the authorizing government of receiving 16 percent of each and every dollar bet at the tracks. Legislatures recognized this innovative betting system as a means of increasing state revenues without having to pass new taxes. Horse racing thus enjoyed a major resurgence during the 1920s and its popularity was sustained throughout the Great Depression. Such legendary horses as Sir Barton, Man O' War, Gallant Fox, War Admiral, and Whirlaway added to the glamor and sparked intensive media coverage.

Unlike at the baseballparks, attendance at the races did not fall off significantly during the 1930s. It was in this context that the improbable story of Seabiscuit, "the little horse that could," became a major sports story of the depression years. In 1935, the 2-year-old Seabiscuit performed so poorly that his famous trainer, "Sunny Jim" Fitzsimmons, did not enter him in any of the Triple Crown races the following year. Despite his rich heritage – he was descended from the incomparable Man O'War and his sire was the handsomely sculpted Hard Tack – Seabiscuit was undersized and built on stubby legs that would not fully straighten, forcing him to run in a manner that many compared to a waddling duck. His stunted body, Hillenbrand writes, gave no indication of his special lineage and "had all the properties of a cinder block."[44]

In 1936, Seabiscuit was sold for a mere $7,500 to wealthy San Francisco automobile dealer Charles Howard, who had no prior experience in the unique culture of horse racing. He hired an unknown trainer, Tom Smith, whose career up to this point had been unspectacular despite his instinctive ability to get the best out of cantankerous horses. Smith hired Red Pollard, an unproven jockey with little big-time racing experience. Under Tom Smith's gentle prodding, Seabiscuit began to show promise, and soon he was winning races at California tracks. Racing fans began to take notice of this undersized thoroughbred with the ungainly stride but powerful finish. Seabiscuit's popularity spread as racing fans recognized that the

improbable team of Howard, Smith, Pollard, and an undersized horse no one wanted was a fitting metaphor for their own struggles during the Great Depression. In November 1938, this small horse with a big heart came out of the West to challenge the consensus top horse of the year in a one-on-one match race. War Admiral – also descended from Man O'War – exuded the perfect image of a thoroughbred – tall, sleek, glistening, perfectly proportioned, and high spirited. Few turf experts, most of them hidebound Easterners, gave the upstart from California with the funny gait any chance; each of the *Racing Form* handicapping experts picked War Admiral, the 1937 Triple Crown winner, as did 95 percent of newspaper writers.

The match race took place on War Admiral's own turf at Pimlico Race Course. Millions of Americans listened to the veteran announcer Clem McCarthy make the call. In what everyone conceded was an

Figure 8.5 The people's favorite, Seabiscuit, drives toward victory in his last race, the 1940 Santa Anita handicap. Jockey Red Pollard is aboard the "Biscuit," making a brave comeback from near-fatal injuries suffered two years earlier when he was thrown and dragged several hundred yards by a young thoroughbred during a morning workout. © Bettmann/CORBIS.

enormous upset victory, Seabiscuit won by four lengths going away, despite having a substitute jockey due to a life-threatening injury Red Pollard had suffered when thrown from a mount during a practice session. Like so many Americans who had braved the Great Depression with courage and determination, this horse and his handlers had overcome great obstacles. Their victory was one that the American people savored. In 1938, the small horse with the big heart received more news coverage than President Franklin Roosevelt.

In 1940, coming off a serious leg injury, Seabiscuit went to the starting gate for the last time in the $100,000 Santa Anita Handicap. A recovering Red Pollard was aboard despite his still-fragile condition. Doctors warned that merely the strain of riding in the race could splinter his still-mending leg. In a thrilling 12-horse race, Pollard expertly guided Seabiscuit from behind, bursting through a narrow opening in a cluster of horses bunched at the head of the home stretch to win a stunning victory before 85,000 enthusiastic spectators. It would be Seabiscuit's last race. As he was applauded and cheered on the way to the winner's circle, Seabiscuit pranced and preened for the crowd. Red Pollard later recalled, "Don't think he didn't know he was the hero."[45]

Baseball During the War Years

When the United States entered the Second World War following the attack on Pearl Harbor on December 7, 1941, the leaders of baseball recalled the difficult time they had encountered in 1917–18. Commissioner Landis seemed inclined to shut down for the duration, fearing that critics would say baseball lacked patriotism. However, concerns that seasons would be canceled were soon set aside when President Franklin D. Roosevelt urged organized baseball to stay on the field:

> I honestly feel that it would be best for the country to keep baseball going. There will be fewer people unemployed and everybody will work longer hours and harder than ever before. And that means they ought to have a chance for recreation and for taking their minds off their work more than before.[46]

Thus the game did go on, with full 154-game seasons being played; only the 1945 All-Star Game was canceled. Within days after Pearl Harbor, many ballplayers enlisted for military duty. By 1943, nearly one thousand major and minor league players had departed for the war. Management had to find players to fill the void.

The president's desire that baseball provide a diversion from the burdens of the war effort prompted two baseball executives, Branch Rickey and Phil Wrigley, to create a professional women's league. With the war going badly in 1942, they feared that subsequent seasons might be canceled, and so they organized the All-American Girls Baseball League. With women assuming non-traditional roles in the military and in defense factories, they reasoned, why should women not assume a role on the ball field? With the infusion of $100,000 from Wrigley, four franchises were established in small Midwestern cities – initially the Racine Belles,

Kenosha Comets, South Bend Blue Sox, and Rockford Peaches. Each team had a male manager (including some ex-major leaguers) and a female chaperone. In addition to playing in their home ballparks, they played games at military bases. The teams initially played fast-pitch softball, drawing upon a large pool of talent from urban industrial leagues. Players earned between $55 and $150 a week and played a 108-game season, providing inexpensive entertainment for more than 200,000 fans who paid small admission charges. While spectators came initially out of curiosity, many returned because of the high quality of play. The league – now called the All-American Girls Professional Baseball League – survived after the war and in 1948 had expanded to 10 teams, the most successful being the Ft Wayne Daisies. In that year, the league changed its rules to create a modified form of baseball, complete with overhand pitching and a smaller ball. That year attendance approached one million, the appeal being a tough brand of baseball complete with fast pitching, stolen bases, and plenty of injuries, especially skin abrasions from sliding into bases in short skirts. Although the women exhibited exceptional athletic skills, they were outfitted in one piece tunic-like skirts cut above the knee as a reminder to spectators that these were, indeed, female ballplayers. Make-up was required and hair could not be cut in a short bob. The first crop of players even had to endure a Helena Rubinstein preseason charm school where they were instructed in ladylike behavior. The league dissolved in 1954, victim of the same economic and social forces that killed town ball and most lower-level minor leagues.[47]

Television was a major factor in cutting into attendance and producing the demise of the league; it is possible that the league could have found a niche as a new venue for sports broadcasting. That, however, did not happen. The league also was victimized by postwar expectations that women should revert to traditional roles. Thus the idea that women played a hard-nosed form of baseball conflicted with societal standards. As historian Susan Cahn writes, "By continuing to see athletic ability as masculine skill rather than incorporating athleticism within the range of feminine qualities, the league's ideology posed no challenge to the fundamental precepts of gender in American society."[48]

While women's ball was presented as a patriotic effort to support the war effort, major league baseball had to make do with men that the military did not want. Teams found many older players in the minor leagues, and several retired ballplayers returned to the game. Some very young players were also hustled onto the field. The 1944 Brooklyn Dodgers played a 16-year-old, Tommy Brown, in 46 games, and that same year Cincinnati manager Bill McKechnie inserted a 15-year-old left-handed pitcher from nearby Hamilton, Ohio, into a hopelessly lost game against St Louis; although Joe Nuxhall would eventually enjoy a lengthy career as a journeyman pitcher for the Reds (and 35 more years as a Reds broadcaster), his brief appearance was beset by wildness as he gave up five walks and two hits while retiring only two batters. The St Louis Browns even played a one-armed outfielder, Pete Gray, although his signing was not the cheap publicity stunt many people made it out to be; Gray had commendable skills and previously had been selected as the Most Valuable Player in the Southern League. He hit .218 in 72 games for the Browns in 1945 before being released.

Some leading players – including Cleveland shortstop Lou Boudreau and Detroit left-handed pitcher Hal Newhouser – played throughout the war due to medical deferments, but most of the younger players ended up in the military by 1943. Star Cardinal hitter Stan Musial, given a family hardship deferment, did not leave for the Army until 1944 and helped the Cardinals win three wartime pennants and two World Series titles. Boston Red Sox hitting star Ted Williams signed on as a Marines pilot before the 1943 season, and his great American League rival, Joe DiMaggio, volunteered for the Army Air Corps, although he could have received another deferment. Few players actually saw action in battle; most ended up behind the lines, many spending the time playing baseball for military teams. Cleveland fireballing pitcher Bob Feller, however, saw action against the enemy in the Navy in both the Atlantic and the Pacific theaters. Only two men who had played in the major leagues died in combat: Harry O'Neill who caught for one inning in 1939 with the Phillies, was killed at the bloodbath of Iwo Jima, and Elmer Gedeon, who had played in five games for the Washington Senators, died when his aircraft was shot down in Europe. Perhaps the most important development for organized baseball during the war years was that Commissioner Kenesaw Landis died in 1944 and was replaced by former Kentucky Governor Albert "Happy" Chandler.

9 America's Great Dilemma

In 1944, Gunnar Myrdal, a distinguished Swedish social scientist, published a pivotal study of race relations in the United States. In the aptly entitled *An American Dilemma*, Myrdal and his research associates presented the essential argument that racial segregation was a denial of fundamental American values. Thomas Jefferson's introductory words in the Declaration of Independence succinctly summarized the American Creed: "We hold these truths to be self-evident: That all men are created equal; that they are endowed by their Creator with certain inalienable rights; that among these are life, liberty, and the pursuit of happiness." As Myrdal documented in exhaustive detail, that essential American belief was given the lie by a pervasive system of segregation and racial discrimination that lay rooted deeply within American history, and on an everyday basis adversely affected the lives of every African American.

Segregation, Myrdal demonstrated, denied millions of American citizens such basic constitutional rights as voting and equal protection under the law, and subjected them to inferior education, restricted access to employment and housing, and kept them repressed under a wide spectrum of laws, judicial decisions, religious doctrines, and social customs. The fact that Myrdal's book appeared in 1944 added a special poignancy to the issue, because the United States was then engaged in a great global war in defense of democracy against a totalitarian regime based upon a doctrine proclaiming the superiority of the "Aryan" race.

> In fighting Nazism, America had to stand before the whole world in favor of racial equality. It had to denounce Adolf Hitler's regime as a reversion to barbarism. It had to proclaim universal brotherhood and the inalienable human freedoms. The fact that the Japanese utilized anti-white feelings in Asia and elsewhere made it even more necessary to stress the racial equality principle.[1]

Myrdal's book had a galvanizing impact upon the future of American race relations; no longer could right-thinking Americans square their much-heralded political heritage with the brutal reality of a segregated society.

Racism Shapes American Sports

The emancipation of four million slaves in 1865 did not translate into equality for African Americans. Following the Civil War, well-established patterns of discrimination remained in place in the North, assuring that blacks had few of the opportunities available to whites. In the rural South, the freedman had little choice but to opt for a life of poverty as sharecropper, tenant farmer, or day wage laborer. Although emancipation had created great hope among African Americans, those aspirations and dreams were dashed by a pervasive system of white supremacy enforced by lynch mobs, the systematic disfranchisement of the great majority of Southern blacks, and everyday discrimination within their communities at the hands of white merchants, religious leaders, law enforcement officers, employers, and government officials. In the face of these realities, African Americans struggled to cope, even survive, by establishing community organizations that could provide hope and help. African American churches sprang up everywhere, soon to be followed by the creation of mutual-assistance organizations such as penny banks, life insurance companies, and community-action groups to provide for public health and other basic services. Support for poorly funded segregated public schools became a community-wide mission as the first generations of free blacks sought educational opportunities so their children could acquire the skills necessary to function as free people in a competitive society. Black colleges were founded throughout the South to provide future teachers, healthcare providers, journalists, businessmen, and lawyers.

The policies of segregation were rigorously applied to sports. During the age of Jim Crow, it was inevitable that most opportunities for African Americans in sports occurred within the context of the doctrine of "separate but equal." Poorly funded black public schools had to struggle to support varsity teams, but many managed to do so. Black colleges emulated their white counterparts by forming baseball, basketball, and football teams, and women were encouraged to take part in athletics as well as male students. Black educators embraced the view current in white America – that physical exercise was essential to the full development of the individual. As one black college catalog stated, "The best education is that which develops a strong, robust body as well as other parts of the human makeup."[2]

Black communities embraced baseball just as enthusiastically as white America. A notable early example was the Philadelphia Phythians club, established in 1866. Although forced to play many of their games against three other all-black teams in the City of Brotherly Love, they also entertained touring teams from Harrisburg, Washington, DC, and even distant Chicago. However, the Phythians and subsequent ball clubs of their high caliber wanted to compete against the best of white teams, and while they were occasionally permitted to do so in "exhibition" games, their entreaties to be admitted to white leagues were summarily rejected by those intent upon making certain that America's Game, like the larger society, remained segregated.

Between 1880 and 1930 throughout the United States, amateur "town ball" flourished in communities large and small. The number of black teams that participated is unknown, but it was large. At the top of the heap of town ball was the elusive phenomenon of semiprofessional teams. Located in larger cities, African American teams played in local and regional leagues, the more entrepreneurial becoming touring ball clubs that traveled far and wide, playing local teams in return for a percentage of the gate receipts. Pay was low but the talent substantial and the quality of play frequently sparkling. Teams came and went due to the vagaries of personalities and finances, but they played an exciting brand of baseball that attracted paying customers. Such outstanding players as pitcher Rube Foster, and the hard-hitting infielder Sol White, whose 25-year playing career also included a few brief interludes as a member of white semiprofessional teams, became famous within black communities. At least two efforts were made to establish a black professional league, in 1887 and 1907, but they never got much beyond the talking stages. Lack of adequate capital severely circumscribed the potential of a viable black professional circuit. These semiprofessional teams provide a vivid example of the effort of black businessmen – their primary backers – to counter the oppression of segregation.[3]

The sharp color line drawn through American society meant that most leading black athletes, no matter what their sport, were forced to compete only within narrow boundaries. However, there were some notable examples of individuals who proved themselves in competition with whites, although they had to endure the indignities of discrimination. Because some slaves had become jockeys during the antebellum period, it was only natural that several blacks became highly regarded jockeys in the growing thoroughbred racing circuit that developed during the late nineteenth century. One leading example was Isaac Murphy of Lexington, who became the first jockey to ride three Kentucky Derby winners (1884, 1890, 1891), and during a 20-year career won 44 percent of all of the races he entered, including notable victories at the prestigious American Derby and the Latonia Derby. Although he frequently had to deal with racial comments and clumsy efforts to exclude him from races, he managed to earn an income sufficient to enable him to assemble a portfolio of real estate holdings. As he once proudly wrote, his annual income was "as much as that of the members of President Harrison's Cabinet." In 1955 he was the first jockey voted into the Racing Hall of Fame in Saratoga Springs, New York.[4]

Although Murphy and other black jockeys had to struggle against discrimination, they did not face the obstacles that confronted cyclist Marshall "Major" Taylor, who was a leading "wheelman" at the turn of the century when bicycle racing enjoyed high national visibility. Between 1898 and 1900 he set seven world records at distances between one third of a mile and a mile and in 1899 was recognized as the national champion wheelman. However, as he related in his autobiography, he was frequently the victim of illegal bumping during races, and he learned to take the lead early in races or a group of white cyclists would block his way to the front. Upset at having to live and eat in segregated accommodations while on the road, and frustrated and hurt by physical attacks, he found solace by competing in Europe and Australia. When he retired from racing in 1910, he had earned $75,000 in prize money.[5]

The successes of Murphy and Taylor, however, were not widely known because they competed in sports that did not receive the attention of the masses. Thus the triumph of prize fighter Jack Johnson, who captured the powerfully symbolic world heavyweight championship in 1908 and then held it for seven years, was a major story of the time. Johnson was the first athletic figure to become a symbol of racial pride within the black community, and his open defiance of the racial conventions of the time endeared him to African Americans. Although prize fighting was one of the few venues that permitted black participation, the unwritten racial codes still applied. Many promising black fighters matched against a white opponent felt the sting of prejudice when white judges and referees rendered decisions. It was also very difficult for top-notch blacks to get a shot at a white champion. John L. Sullivan had occasionally said he would fight a black challenger if the money was sufficient, but he never did; in the late 1880s, he artfully ducked the formidable George Godfrey and the eminently qualified Peter Jackson, who in 1891 fought to a draw with Jim Corbett in a marathon 61-round four-hour bout. As Sullivan's biographer explains, John L. considered himself the "champion of white America." He was not about to provide any man of color an opportunity to take the crown. In his famous public challenge to take on "all comers" that preceded his famous match with Corbett, Sullivan said, "In this challenge I include all fighters – first come, first served – who are white. I will not fight a negro. I never have and never shall."[6]

The "Fight of the Century"

It was therefore fitting that when Jack Johnson successfully defended his heavyweight championship in Reno in 1910, Sullivan was in the audience. Born in Galveston, Texas, in 1878, Jack Johnson survived a rough childhood and dropped out of school after the sixth grade. As a teenager, Johnson fought in the East Texas bare-knuckle circuit, where he enjoyed considerable success. He moved on to the national level and by 1903 had defeated the best black heavyweights, enjoying the unofficial title of "Negro Heavyweight Champion." However, he was repeatedly rebuffed by leading white heavyweights when he attempted to arrange a challenge. Although it was permissible for blacks to contest white boxers in the lower weight divisions, the potent symbolism of the heavyweight crown militated that blacks could not aspire to the championship. [7]

Prevailing views of African American fighters in the lower divisions were mixed. On the one hand, there was the popular lightweight "Old Master" from Baltimore, Joe Gans. He won the championship from the defending champion, Frank Erne, in 1902 with no racial repercussions, and during the succeeding eight years, he won and lost the title several times. When he died in 1914 of tuberculosis, his death was widely mourned by fight fans of all colors. On the other hand, an editor of the New Orleans *Times-Democrat* commenting upon a bout in 1892 in which light-weight George "Little Chocolate" Dixon administered a fearful beating to a white opponent, noted, "The sight was repugnant to some of the men from the South . . . the idea of sitting quietly by and seeing a colored boy pommel a white lad grates on Southerners." The writer concluded that it was "a mistake to bring the races together on any terms of equality, even in the ring."[8]

Jack Johnson got his opportunity when reigning heavyweight champion, Tommy Burns of Canada, agreed to a match to be held in Sidney, Australia. Burns needed a payday and Johnson was available. The cocky but undersized Burns (he weighed only 175 pounds) believed that his Anglo-Saxon heritage would enable him to defeat his much larger challenger, who stood 6' 2" and weighed a trim 190 pounds. Johnson, however, dominated the fight, pounding the overmatched Burns at will until officials stopped the action in the 13th round. Johnson's victory set off a racial crisis for millions of white Americans who could not accept the fact that an African American now wore boxing's most prestigious crown. Johnson's persistent flaunting of prevailing racial customs greatly exacerbated the situation. He not only appeared in public in lavish clothing and expensive jewelry, and drove high-powered luxury automobiles, but also he violated the ultimate racial taboo by escorting attractive white women (he preferred blondes) in public places. During his life, Johnson was married to three different white women.[9]

With Johnson now the undisputed champion, a desperate search for a "Great White Hope" commenced in the United States. Much to the chagrin of white supremacists, the thin pool of talent failed to produce a challenger who inspired confidence. Ultimately the desperate quest focused upon James Jeffries, who retired as champion in 1905 and was now enjoying life on his northern California farm. Novelist Jack London perhaps best expressed the fears of millions when he urged Jeffries to abandon retirement to reclaim the championship for the white race. "Jeff, it's up to you," he implored. "The white race must be rescued." Jeffries initially refused, but eventually relented to the pressure and began a conditioning program that shaved off 75 excess pounds he had gained since retiring. Promoter Tex Rickard announced that the fight would be held in San Francisco, but progressive-inspired anti-prizefighting spokesmen there forced him to move the fight to Nevada, where the sport was both popular and supported by public officials. Rickard scheduled the bout for July 4, 1910.[10]

Rickard found a warm welcome in the small city of Reno. Both the mayor and governor of the state – recognizing a big payday when they saw one – had no qualms about hosting the match. In the weeks before the scheduled fight, both fighters set up training camps at Reno dude-ranch resorts, normally the temporary residences of wealthy women establishing a six-month residency requirement before appearing in a Reno divorce court. Pre-fight press coverage focused almost exclusively on the racial angle. Some Southern white editors grimly predicted a race war if the "Big Bear" from California failed to defeat Johnson, and a few white ministers even prayed from their pulpits for a Jeffries victory. So-called boxing "experts" weighed in with all types of assessments, many of them building upon

Figure 9.1 Defending champion Jack Johnson and challenger Jim Jeffries square off in a hastily constructed 20,000-seat outdoor arena in Reno under a blazing sun on July 4, 1910. This "fight of the century" attracted major attention because of its racial overtones and did much to move boxing into the mainstream of American sports. Special Collections, University of Nevada-Reno Library.

popular racial stereotypes that alleged that African Americans lacked the intelligence and courage to win such an important contest. In the days before the fight, Reno was overrun by an estimated 20,000 fight fans (and gamblers, pickpockets, prostitutes, and scam artists) most of whom arrived in specially chartered trains.

After the enormous build-up, the fight proved anticlimatic. As Johnson later wrote in his autobiography, when he entered the outdoor ring under a blazing sun and

surveyed the sea of white faces I felt the auspiciousness of the occasion. . . . I realized that my victory in this event meant more than on any previous occasion. It wasn't just the championship that was at stake – it was my own honor, and in a degree the honor of my race.[11]

There was only a sprinkling of black faces among the estimated 20,000 spectators who watched from temporary wooden bleachers that had been hastily erected on the east edge of town. They saw Johnson cruise to an easy victory over a former champion long past his time. Much too fast for his opponent, Johnson punished him with lightening-quick jabs and powerful counterpunches. During the middle rounds he seemed merely to toy with Jeffries, apparently unwilling to end the suffering of his opponent and his disappointed fans. The fight ended with a whimper when Jeffries did not leave his corner for the 15th round. While disappointed white fans walked quietly out of the arena and headed downtown to drown their sorrow at Reno's 60 taverns, across the nation a series of violent incidents occurred when white gangs took out their disappointment on innocent African Americans. These beatings reminded everyone that the status of African Americans had not changed, Johnson's compelling victory and retention of the heavyweight title notwithstanding. But Johnson had more than demonstrated his superb boxing skills for all to see. At the height of a virulent period of racism and racially inspired violence, he had successfully stood the test before an unfriendly audience. As Thomas Hietala observes, when Tex Rickard raised Johnson's hand in victory, he

> stood proudly at the summit, and symbolically, millions of African Americans stood beside him. For Johnson and his people, the championship seemed a partial but promising fulfillment of their collective hopes and dreams, a portent of a future brighter than their troubled past and present.[12]

Although no white or black fighter could wrest the championship from Johnson, the federal government was more than willing to bring him down. Law enforcement officials went after him with determination, and in 1913, Johnson was convicted of violating the Mann Act, a high-profile anti-prostitution law passed by Congress in 1910. The feds used Johnson's frequent train trips with willing white women to make their tenuous case. Johnson thereupon fled the country and defended his crown abroad several times. In 1915, his skills having diminished with the passing of the years, Johnson lost to the enormous 6' 6", 250-pound Jess Willard in Havana by a 26th round knockout. In 1920, his funds depleted, Johnson returned to the United States, surrendered to federal authorities, and served one year in the federal prison at Leavenworth, Kansas. Upon his release, he fought a few inconsequential bouts for much needed paydays, went on the vaudeville and carnival circuit, and died in 1946 in a car accident in North Carolina. Johnson was buried without fanfare, but his legacy of successfully challenging the nearly impenetrable wall blocking access of African Americans to the opportunities of sports was not forgotten by those who remembered that hot, sun-drenched Independence Day in Reno when he confounded boxing experts and racist Americans by humiliating the Great White Hope.[13]

Separate and Unequal: the Negro Leagues

The famed black scholar W. E. B. Du Bois once observed that for African Americans, "One ever feels his twoness – an American, a Negro, two souls, two thoughts, two unreconciled strivings; two warring ideals in one dark body, whose dogged strength alone keeps it from being torn asunder." As historian Jules Tygiel points out, this comment aptly summarizes the history of what has been termed the "Negro Leagues."[14] The unwritten "gentlemen's agreement" to exclude blacks from organized baseball that took effect in 1885, meant that African Americans had to play professionally in leagues of their own.[15]

The first sustained effort at an organized professional African American league was made in 1920 by Andrew "Rube" Foster, an exceptional pitcher in his own right (he won 54 games for the Cuban X-Giants in 1904), now owner and player-manager of the Chicago American Giants. In 1920, Foster organized the eight-team Negro National League (NNL) and dreamed of building it to the point where it would be considered a third major league. Much was made of the fact that his own team traveled first-class in their own private Pullman train car, prompting the prominent black newspaper, the *Chicago Defender*, to comment that Rube Foster was "the most successful Colored man in baseball, the only one that has made it a business."[16] But the NNL lacked franchises in the nation's two cities with the largest black populations – New York and Philadelphia – and two teams, the Kansas City Monarchs and his own Chicago Americans, dominated play and thereby reduced public interest. Foster wanted to demonstrate that African Americans could develop and operate a stable, viable league; only J. L. Wilkinson, owner of the powerful Kansas City Monarchs, was white. The league became well known among baseball fans for its special style of aggressive hitting and base-running, and sharp defensive play. However, the league suffered from the beginning from chronic instability, produced in large part by dependance upon a fan base comprised primarily of low-income African Americans who often could not afford a ticket. The league suffered from continued financial woes. White fans seldom turned out for a game unless it was an exhibition match against a white team. Foster repeatedly told his fellow owners that the league could survive only if everyone cooperated, but he apparently had difficulty following his own advice, and under criticism for his dictatorial ways, was forced to resign in 1925. In 1926, he suffered a mental breakdown, was institutionalized, and died in 1930. His league limped along briefly after his departure, but it folded under the duress of the Great Depression in 1931. In 1981, Rube Foster was admitted to the National Baseball Hall of Fame in Cooperstown.[17]

The NNL, however, had inspired an upsurge of interest in baseball among urban African Americans. One center of activity was Pittsburgh, where two semiprofessional teams had emerged as top-flight teams during the 1920s, the Pittsburgh Crawfords (named for a major thoroughfare that bisected the Hill neighborhood, heavily populated by African Americans), and the Homestead Grays, originally a steel-mill team from an industrial suburb. In 1933, Gus Greenlee, the owner of the Crawfords, created a new Negro National League and operated it for several years by bringing together teams from Eastern cities. Anyone who was anyone in Pittsburgh knew Greenlee, widely known in the Steel City as "Mr Big." He operated nightclubs, restaurants, and bars, was prominent in the local bootlegging trade, ran a stable of boxers, and was widely hailed for his support of local charities. He also had his hand in the lucrative Pittsburgh numbers racket. A major player in local Republican Party politics, Greenlee called the shots in the predominantly black Third Ward. Greenlee spent $100,000 to build a new baseball field in 1932 for his pride and joy, the Pittsburgh Crawfords. The Crawfords were one of a very few Negro League teams to have their own ballpark; most teams rented the venues of major or minor league teams.[18]

Although the Crawfords contended for honors with NNL teams now located in Newark, Philadelphia, New York, and Baltimore-Washington, their major competition was the cross-town Homestead Grays, owned and managed by Cumberland "Cum" Posey. While Greenlee, according to one of his veteran players, "looked like the racketeer he was" dressed in expensive suits, with a cigarette drooping from his lips and surrounded by an entourage, Posey was the picture of middle-class decorum, a businessman and civic leader who served on the local school board. He had earned a degree in chemistry from Penn State and studied pharmacy at the University of Pittsburgh. Posey's greatest achievement, however, was building the Grays into a nationally recognized African American baseball power. He added to his influence over the Pittsburgh sports scene by writing a column in the *Pittsburgh Courier*. Joining the Grays in 1911 as an outfielder, he soon was in control of both the team's baseball and financial operations. By 1920, he was able to attract top players from the Pittsburgh area and beyond, and he found ways to pay them so they did not have to hold another job. The Grays frequently played at Forbes Field when the Pirates were out of town. By the early 1920s, the Grays were taking on all comers and became well established as a national barnstorming team.[19]

In the 1930s and the 1940s, the two Pittsburgh teams competed fiercely for local bragging rights. The Grays featured many of the greatest African American players of the 1930s. Their speedy center-fielder, James "Cool Papa" Bell, was a sparkling lead-off batter who could spray hits to all parts of the field and was an accomplished base runner. The Grays also featured a home-grown Pittsburgh resident, the incomparable powerfully built catcher Josh Gibson, whose prodigious home runs were often compared to those of Babe Ruth. At first base was Buck Leonard, a native of North Carolina, whose sweet swing and graceful guardianship of first base inspired admiration. Between 1937 and 1945, Gibson and Leonard, often called the Babe Ruth and Lou Gehrig of the Negro leagues, led the Homestead Grays to nine consecutive NNL championships. During the hard-pressed Depression years, top players earned about $125 a month during the five-month season, scarcely adequate pay to support their families, which meant they spent the winters playing in the Caribbean or Mexico, or barnstorming through the segregated South, often playing top local white teams. Their pay increased substantially with the economic boom spurred by the Second World War, and in 1948 Leonard pocketed $10,000 for the entire year. Gibson's career ended tragically in 1947 when he suffered severe physical setbacks; he died at the age of 35 of a massive stroke.

While Gibson and Leonard powered Cum Posey's Grays, Greenlee's Crawfords countered with the incomparable pitcher Leroy "Satchel" Paige – at least some of the time, because the mercurial Paige and Greenlee often were at odds with each other, usually over the issue of Paige's salary. Paige's petulance often proved distracting, but he was worth the bother. Arguably one of the greatest pitchers of all time, Paige was blessed with a blazing fastball, a devastating curve, and several junk pitches to which he gave humorous names ("bee ball," "hesitation pitch," "jump ball," "trouble ball"). Born in 1906 in Mobile, he acquired his nickname "Satchel" when as a youth he worked as a baggage handler at the Mobile railroad

Figure 9.2 One of the greatest pitchers of all time, Satchel Paige, finally made the major leagues on July 19, 1948, at the age of 46 after a long and triumphant romp through the Negro leagues. Although many critics thought his signing by owner Bill Veeck was a publicity stunt, Paige played an important role in the close pennant race against the Yankees, helping the Cleveland Indians capture the pennant and the World Series. He won six games against just one loss as a starting pitcher, and appeared in relief in 14 other games. © Bettmann/CORBIS.

station. Tall and spindly, Paige began pitching for a Mobile semiprofessional team in 1924. Always on the alert for a better salary offer, Paige moved frequently from team to team. The best guess is that he played for eight different Negro league teams until he joined the Cleveland Indians in the American League in 1948 as a 42-year-old rookie. By his own estimate, Paige pitched 300 shutouts, 55 no-hitters, and won 2,000 games of the 2,600 or so in which he participated.[20]

Satchel Paige was undoubtedly the star attraction of the Negro leagues. Many think he was the second most popular baseball player of his era, second only to Babe Ruth. His appeal went far beyond his pitching skills, because he was a natural showman, often engaging in various on-the-field charades that delighted fans. Once, during warm-ups, he placed a burning candle on home plate and proceeded to put out the flame by whizzing a fastball just past the candle. He delighted crowds by fooling batters with his trick pitches. While playing against local teams during a barnstorming tour, he would intentionally walk the bases loaded, wave the outfielders into the infield, and proceed to strike out the next three batters. After the 1932 season, Paige and Dizzy Dean put together two teams – one black, one white – and barnstormed across the southern tier of states. Baseball executive Bill Veeck Jr recalled a 12-inning game in Los Angeles in which Paige bested Dean 1–0 as the greatest baseball game he ever watched.[21]

The Negro leagues filled an important void in the lives of African Americans. They helped create a sense of racial pride and were a major focus of the sports coverage of black newspapers. They provided an important sense of community during the trying years of the Great Depression. Financial instability, however, meant that between 1933 and 1948 the Negro National League had 18 different franchises, many lasting for just one or two seasons (including such long-forgotten teams as the Detroit Stars, Baltimore Black Sox, and the Bacharach Giants of Atlantic City). In 1938 the Negro American League began play, incorporating most of the top Midwestern and Southern teams. Both leagues were torn by conflict and turmoil internally, a situation only exacerbated by the rivalry between the two.

The Second World War produced a major increase in attendance because of the surging economy. With paychecks coming in regularly, fans flocked to the ballparks in historic numbers. Salaries went up across the league, and financially the war years were the most successful in league history. In 1942, it was possible to hold a meaningful Negro League World Series for the first time since 1927, in which the Kansas City Monarchs (bolstered by the pitching of Satchel Paige) defeated the Homestead Grays in an epic confrontation. The next two seasons, the Grays prevailed over the Birmingham Black Barons. By this time, however, pressures on major league baseball to drop its color ban were intensifying. Several leading journalists, including the influential black writers Wendell Smith of the *Pittsburgh Courier*, Frank Young of the *Chicago Defender*, and Sam Lacy of the *Baltimore Afro-American*, had for years campaigned vigorously for the integration of organized baseball. They pointed to the high caliber of play in the Negro leagues to buttress their argument. Their message was often echoed by prominent white sports writers, especially in New York City, but these arguments carried no weight with the one man who counted, commissioner Kenesaw Landis. This strong opponent to ending the organized baseball's ban on African American players, however, died as the war was winding down, and his replacement, the former governor of Kentucky, Albert "Happy" Chandler, held racial views that were much more progressive.

Negro league baseball had its most successful years financially during the later years of the Second World War. In 1944 the East–West All Star Game held in Comiskey Park drew 46,000 fans. But fans were fickle, and both leagues went into sharp decline in 1946. The departure of the top players to organized baseball proved fatal. By 1950, the major leagues had signed 150 players away from the two Negro leagues. Black fans much preferred to watch black players in an interracial setting. The NNL folded in 1948, and a few teams from the NAL limped on for a few years before disappearing. With the political winds filled with the talk of racial integration, by 1950 black baseball "offered little of value to African Americans," concludes historian Neil Lanctot. Sportswriter Harold Winston wryly observed, "With the various fights for integration going on, the aspects of an all-Negro anything is meeting with increasing opposition from the Negro people," or as NAL president J. B. Martin concluded in resignation in 1955, "Why maintain a Jim Crow baseball circuit?"[22]

Out of the Cotton Fields of Alabama: Jesse and Joe

One of the problems confronting the leadership of the Negro leagues was that black sports fans tended to identify primarily with individual black sports figures rather than with baseball teams, and with the exception of casual interest in Satchel Paige, the overwhelming percentage of white sports fans ignored the Negro leagues. But two exceptionally skilled African American athletes definitely captured the full and complete attention of both black and white Americans during the 1930s, in large part because their extraordinary achievements were accomplished against the backdrop of Nazi totalitarianism. However, the manner in which Jesse Owens and Joe Louis were perceived by white society indicated that racial attitudes had changed little from the late nineteenth century, if at all. Despite the fact that both men won important victories, white America nonetheless viewed them within a special context that indicated that racism was alive and well in the world's leading democratic society.

In 1936, Jesse Owens, a young African American from Cleveland, stunned the sports world with an extraordinary performance at the 1936 Berlin Olympics. Within the space of a few days, he won four gold medals, setting new Olympic records in the long jump at 26' 5.25" and a time of 20.7 seconds in the 200-meter dash. He tied the world record of 10.3 seconds in the 100-meter dash and won his fourth gold medal as a member of the 400-meter relay team. His incredible feat received enormous coverage in the press because it put the lie to Nazi dogma of the superiority of the "Aryan" race. During the early days of the Olympics, which the Nazis planned as a major propaganda opportunity, Adolf Hitler presented the medals to various track and field champions, but when the black American Cornelius Johnson won the high jump, Hitler abruptly left the stadium. He likewise was not present on the four occasions when Owens stood atop the victory stand, a fact that the American media reported in full.[23]

American journalists emphasized that Owens's life was the epitome of the American dream, reporting the story of his birth as one of 10 children to an impoverished Alabama sharecropping family. Joining the ranks of the "Great Migration" of African Americans from the rural South to the urban North, his family had relocated to Cleveland when Jesse was nine. In 1930, Owens led East Technical High School to a state track championship, and in a national meet he scored enough points himself to bring the national track and field team championship to Cleveland. He continued his spectacular athletic career at Ohio State University, where he refined his picturesque sprinting technique. His stride was so graceful that pictures of his running are still used by track coaches; he appeared to glide down the track, his feet seemingly never touching the ground. At the Big Ten track

and field championships held in May 1935, in a single afternoon Owens broke five American records (220-yard dash, long jump, 220-yard high hurdles, 200-meter dash and the 200-meter low hurdles) and he tied another record in the 100-yard dash with the time of 9.4 seconds.

Following his sensational 1936 Olympics performance, Owens found that fame was fleeting. He did whatever he could to earn a living for his wife and young daughters, appearing briefly as an inept song-and-dance man on the fading vaudeville circuit. He even stooped to such humiliating public exhibitions as racing against a horse and an automobile (he lost to both). His dry-cleaning business in Cleveland went bust in 1940 and he barely escaped prison on income-tax evasion charges. After the war, he found a niche as a public speaker and founded a small public-relations firm, playing upon his athletic fame as *entree* to white business audiences. In 1953, he was rewarded for his support of the Republican Party when he picked up a political appointment as head of the Illinois State Athletics Commission, whose major responsibility was overseeing professional boxing in Chicago. During the 1960s, he

Figure 9.3 Jesse Owens propels himself out of his starting position for a 100-yard dash. After winning four gold medals in Berlin in 1936, he became a public relations executive and popular motivational speaker. © Bettmann/ CORBIS.

became a spokesman for conservative Republican causes, was widely criticized by black leaders for his criticisms of civil-rights demonstrators, and in 1964 endorsed Barry Goldwater's presidential bid, one of few prominent African Americans to do so. His conservative political posture gave him access to corporate America, where he flourished as a motivational speaker at sales meetings because he blended athletic metaphors and conservative political and economic views. When a boycott of the 1968 Olympics by African American athletes loomed, Owens spoke out vigorously in opposition, further alienating himself from mainstream civil-rights activists. During his later years, Owens lived in Arizona, where he died of lung cancer in 1980 at the age of 67, the apparent victim of the pack-a-day cigarette habit he had picked up shortly after his return from Berlin in 1936.

While Owens became a national hero for a brief time because of his track and field exploits that the American press translated into a "humiliating public relations defeat" for Adolf Hitler, another son of an Alabama sharecropping family became the first black sports figure to achieve and maintain lasting popularity and fame among the dominant white population. Well before he won the world heavyweight championship, Joe Louis had already become a widely recognized public figure. His early success in the ring during the mid-1930s seemed to point to his capturing the heavyweight championship. Taking note of the heavy media attention Louis was receiving, sports columnist Damon Runyan commented, "It is our guess that more has been written about Louis in the past two years than any living man over a similar period of time, with the exception of Lindbergh."[24]

Louis remained on the front pages of newspapers for more than a decade and a half, winning the heavyweight championship in 1937 and holding it for 13 years. White America was absolutely fascinated by Louis. Journalists continually identified his skin pigmentation as a defining trait, revealing just how unusual it was for someone of his race to reach national prominence at the time. They did not simply refer to him by the accepted word of the time, "Negro," but instead had a field day creating race-laden alliterations such as "the tan tornado," "the sepia slugger," "the dark destroyer," and of course the one that stuck, "the brown bomber." It is instructive to note that of the 25 times Louis defended his crown, he fought 24 white challengers. As the first black who gained fame and fortune in the white sports world, he was embraced by the African American community as their hero when they had very few to cheer. After his victories, it was party time in black neighborhoods, especially when Louis knocked out German heavyweight Max Schmeling in 1938 in the pivotal bout of his career.[25]

The perception of Louis held by whites changed over the years. Initially he was viewed through the prism of well-established racial stereotypes, and reporters often quoted him in "darkie dialect," describing him as possessing large lips and curly hair, and implying that he lacked intelligence and suffered from laziness. That he was often called a "jungle killer," even in highly complimentary articles, was testimony to the powerful strength of existing racial stereotypes. However, that image changed when Louis lost to Schmeling in 1936, indicating to the public that he had vulnerabilities like other human beings. When he met Schmeling again in 1938, he carried with him the hopes and prayers of white

America, which then embraced him enthusiastically as the self-made American who had knocked out the great white hope of Adolf Hitler. That Louis was the anti-Jack Johnson – never seen escorting white women, deferential to the press and the public, married to a clean-cut black woman, modest to the point of deference after a knockout, never caught up in illegal or immoral situations – reassured white America. During the Second World War, Louis became enormously popular when he enlisted in the Army and was portrayed by the American propaganda machine as a symbol of national unity and sacrifice, easing white fears that aggrieved African Americans would sit out this fight for "democracy." After the war, most of the racial references regarding Louis largely disappeared, save for "brown bomber." Editorials and columns praised Louis's public-service record and his humanity. The word "dignity" appeared often.

Louis had moved to Detroit from rural Alabama with his mother in 1926, leaving his father behind in a mental institution. His mother worked at odd jobs and kept tight control over her son. She even insisted he take violin lessons, but he used the 50 cents she gave him for music lessons to take boxing lessons at a local gym instead. With his mother's reluctant endorsement, he entered Detroit's Golden Gloves amateur competition in 1932 and soon thereafter became the talk of the local boxing community as he compiled a 50–4 amateur record, 43 of the wins coming by knockout. In 1934, he signed on as a professional boxer with local numbers racketeer and political operative John Roxborough. Louis moved to Chicago, where he was trained by the experienced Julian Black and won his first professional bout on July 4, 1934, taking home a purse of $52. Starting his career at a time when most boxers were white, he learned early from his trainer Julian Black that white prejudice dominated the sport. He would be judged by white judges and referees:

> You can't get nowhere trying to outpoint fellows in the ring. It's mighty hard for a colored boy to win decisions. The dice is loaded against you. You gotta knock 'em out and keep knocking 'em out to get anywheres. Let your fist be your referee.[26]

Louis learned his lessons well and racked up an impressive string of knockout victories.

Both Roxborough and Black had witnessed how Jack Johnson has helped his own demise by flouting the established racial code. Roxbourgh cautioned Louis,

> To be a champion you've got to be gentleman first. Your toughest fight might not be in the ring but out in public. We never, never say anything bad about an opponent. Before a fight say how great you think he is; after a fight you say how great you think he was. And, for God's sake, after you beat a white opponent, don't smile.[27]

Louis was told not to stand leering over them when they hit the canvas, and he was careful never to be seen publicly in the company of a white woman. He always treated journalists deferentially, and purposely showed little emotion whenever before a camera. None of the arrogance and "uppitiness" that Jack Johnson had routinely exhibited was permitted to surface. To an approving white America, Louis was, in short, "a credit to his race," as one of his popular biographies was entitled. To African Americans, he was their top sports hero who handily defeated all comers, nearly all of whom where white.[28]

In 1935, Louis made his debut in New York City, knocking out former champion, gigantic (6' 6", 260 pounds) Primo Carnero in the sixth round at Yankee Stadium. His next big fight came on June 19, 1936, against another former champion, Max Schmeling, pride of the German Reich. The fight occurred in New York as Hitler was consolidating his power in Germany and preparing to host the Olympics. Louis had recently been declared the fighter of the year for 1935, and he had become overconfident. He did not train rigorously for this fight, and in round 12, Schmeling broke through Louis's defenses and tagged him with a series of right-hand blows, knocking him out. The Nazi propaganda machine quickly pronounced the result evidence that the Aryan was the "Master Race." Louis was humiliated and greatly disappointed because millions of his African American fans felt let down.

In 1937, Louis trained hard and won the world heavyweight title on June 22 when he knocked out James Braddock in the eighth round. Although he himself had been decked, Louis dominated the fight and at age 23 became the youngest man to win boxing's most important title. He would keep the title for a very long time – defend it 25 times in 12 years – before retiring undefeated in 1949. Although he was now world champion, the defeat to Schmeling still rankled, and he told the press, "I will not consider myself champion until I defeat him." The pre-fight hype was intense, reaching heights that even Tex Rickard would have appreciated. The Hitler propaganda machine cranked out its usual drivel as the Fuhrer anticipated an even-greater public relations coup. Before the fight, President Franklin Roosevelt called Louis to the White House for a photo opportunity and conversation. One of the photos that made the pre-fight front pages showed the President admiring the champ's powerful biceps. "Joe, we need muscles like yours to beat Germany," the President said, apparently anticipating the eventuality of war with the Nazi regime.[29]

This time a well-prepared Louis wasted no time extracting his revenge, nailing Schmeling with two vicious left hooks as the first round began and following up with a crushing right hand to the jaw as Schmeling's legs wobbled. Louis pressed his advantage and landed a right hand that referee Art Donovan said was powerful enough to "have dented concrete," then two shots to the body. Schmeling was down and out. At that precise moment, the live radio broadcast in Germany was cut off the air, and Joseph Goebbels's public information department spun the view that the result was "a disappointment but not a national disaster." In the United States, journalists took due note of German comments about "Aryan supremacy" that had followed the first Louis–Schmeling battle.

In 1942, Louis continued to make the right moves that enabled white Americans to feel comfortable with a black heavyweight champion. Within a month after Pearl Harbor, he enlisted in the US Army, but before he left for basic training, Louis fought Abe Simon and turned that purse over to the Army Relief Fund. Louis became a poster boy for the War Department, and photographs of him in

Figure 9.4 Joe Louis pins boxer Max Schmeling against the ropes in Yankee Stadium just prior to unleashing a barrage of blows that produced a spectacular round 1 knockout victory over the pride of the German Reich in 1938. The popular Louis became the first African American athlete to cultivate and receive the affection and admiration of white sports fans. © Bettmann/CORBIS.

uniform were frequently released showing him performing various soldierly tasks. However, Louis's major responsibility as a commissioned officer was to deal with public relations, primarily to box (for no extra pay) in a series of exhibition bouts as entertainment for the troops.

Louis defended his title 20 times between his defeat of James Braddock and entering the military in the spring of 1942, often against fighters of questionable ability. This series of bouts was dubbed the "palooka of the month" campaign by some writers, but on June 18, 1941, Louis struggled to keep his title against Billy Conn, a popular Irishman from Connecticut. Much quicker than Louis's typical opponents, Conn was winning the fight on points in the 13th round when he got reckless and went for a knockout; Louis saw an opening and floored his opponent with his powerful right hand. The public was anxious for a rematch, which occurred in June, 1946. Louis prevailed with an eighth-round victory. The champ was now well into his 30s, and cautious manager Mike Jacobs picked Louis's opponents carefully and spaced out his fights. Louis defeated a former sparring partner, Jersey Joe Wolcott, twice in close matches before retiring undefeated in 1949.

His finances, however, were a shambles, in part due to income tax problems, in large part due to a lack of attention to how the $5 million in prize money he had won was handled. Like many over-the-hill athletes, Louis attempted a comeback but lost to champion Ezzard Charles in 1950 by a decision. The following year he was ingloriously knocked through the ropes onto the main floor by an up-and-coming challenger, Rocky Marciano. The purses he won in these two depressing bouts did not solve his financial woes, and Louis ended up a sad, forlorn figure, trying to make a living as a professional wrestler, a boxing referee, investing modest sums in several failed business ventures. He eventually worked as a casino greeter at Caesars Palace in Las Vegas, before succumbing to heart trouble and dying in 1981. The night before he died he was given a long, loud standing ovation in Las Vegas before a championship fight between Larry Holmes and Trevor Berbick. The prominent black journalist Thomas Sowell wrote upon his death:

> What made Louis a unique figure was not simply his great talent as an athlete. He appeared at a time in America when blacks were not only at a low economic ebb – but were the butt of ridicule. In this kind of world Joe Louis became the most famous black man in America. What he did as a man could reinforce or counteract stereotypes that hurt and held back millions of people of his race. How he fared in the ring mattered more to black Americans than the fate of any other athlete in any other sport, before or since. He was all we had. . . . Joe Louis was a continuing lesson to white Americans that to be black did not mean to be a clown or a lout, regardless of what the image-makers said. It was a lesson that helped open doors that had been closed for too long.[30]

All America was pleased to know that Louis was to be buried with full military honors in Arlington Cemetery, a long way from the cotton patches of Alabama where his life had begun. His funeral expenses were paid by the prosperous German businessman, Max Schmeling.

Jackie

Wesley Branch Rickey stunned the baseball world on October 23, 1945, when he announced that he had signed Jack Roosevelt Robinson to a Brooklyn Dodgers' minor-league contract. When the 26-year-old Robinson appeared the following April in a Montreal Royals uniform, a new era had arrived that would greatly influence the future course not only of American sports but of American society. Rickey's decisive action capped a growing movement to challenge the unwritten "gentlemen's agreement" that had kept African Americans out of organized baseball since 1885. The black press, led by the *Chicago Defender* and the *Baltimore African American*, along with the Communist Party's *Daily Worker*, were the most outspoken, often making their case on the editorial page. Premier African American journalists, such as Wendell Smith and Sam Lacy, repeatedly hammered home the fact that the top players in the Negro leagues would elevate the quality of play in organized baseball. They were joined in their crusade by such leading white journalists as syndicated New York columnists Ed Sullivan and Damon Runyan. Additionally, such influential writers as Jimmy Powers of the *New York Daily News*, Shirley Povich of the *Washington Post*, Westbrook Pegler of the *Chicago Tribune*, and Dave Egan of the *Boston Record* weighed-in on the issue. Egan once wrote, "Do we, by any chance, feel disgust at the thought that Negro athletes, solely because of their color, are barred from playing baseball?" Despite this pressure, Commissioner Kenesaw Landis adamantly opposed lifting the ban, but he did issue a disingenuous statement: "Each club is entirely free to employ Negro players." He also privately hoped that all of the owners would maintain the racial status quo.[31]

As the Second World War was winding down, the pressures against the long-standing "gentlemen's agreement" mounted. Gunnar Myrdal's *An American Dilemma* had moved public opinion, especially among the educated classes, toward a recognition that the United States could not persist in its traditional racial patterns, and Rickey was very much aware of those shifting tides of opinion. In early 1945, baseball's new commissioner, Happy Chandler, created a Committee on Baseball Integration, but because of the hostile reaction by New York Yankees owner and general manager, Larry MacPhail, the group never met. Then New York Mayor Fiorello LaGuardia, apparently with an eye on the Harlem vote, appointed a committee to explore the issue, which put special pressure upon the three major league teams located in the nation's largest city. In spring 1945, New York sportswriter, Joe Bostic, brought two African American players to the gates of the Dodger spring training camp and demanded they be given a try-out, but to no avail; the resulting headlines, however, drove home his message. That same spring, the Boston Red Sox gave highly publicized tryouts to Jackie Robinson, Marvin Williams, and Sam Jethroe at Fenway Park because of political pressure brought by Boston councilman H. Y. Muchnick. "I'm telling you," he later recalled, "you never saw anyone hit The Wall the way Robinson did that day. Bang, Bang, Bang: he rattled it!" Afterward, Red Sox chief scout Hugh Duffy candidly admitted that the tryout had been for show only when he ruefully commented, "What a ballplayer! Too bad he's the wrong color."[32]

While all of this public posturing was taking pace, Branch Rickey quietly moved forward with his plan to put an African American in a Dodgers uniform. Rickey had left St Louis to assume control of the Dodgers in 1942, and he was determined to lay the foundation of a competitive team. Rickey's decision to sign Robinson grew out of a multiplicity of motives. Rickey's social consciousness, inculcated in him as a youth by his pious Methodist parents, clearly had been elevated by the growing pressure for reform, but he also wanted to tap a new pool of major league talent to help make the Dodgers a pennant contender.[33]

At the time, Robinson was well established as a talented infielder with the Kansas City Monarchs. When he was summoned to Rickey's office on August 15, 1945, he assumed he was going to be offered a contract with a new African American team Rickey had announced he was forming, the Brooklyn Brown Dodgers. Rickey had cleverly covered his tracks. He had little, if any, intention of actually putting a Brown Dodgers team on the field, but the concept gave his scouts cover as they scouted for the right candidate for what historian Jules Tygiel has called "Baseball's Great Experiment." Rickey wanted not only a player with undisputed major-league talent but also someone who had the personal traits to inspire support from the African American community, overcome well-known prejudices held by some of the Dodgers' players, and provide a role model as a family man and citizen who would appeal to white fans.[34]

Robinson met Rickey's criteria. During 1939–41, he had lettered in four sports at UCLA and would have graduated had he not departed for military duty in 1942. He had been a consensus All-American halfback and had led the Bruins basketball team in scoring. During the spring, he played baseball and ran track, sometimes on the same day. After receiving a medical discharge in 1945, Robinson joined the Monarchs. During his secret meeting with Rickey on August 28, Robinson was subjected to a combination three-hour lecture and questioning by a seasoned baseball man who loved to quote the Bible and Shakespeare. Rickey warned Robinson that he would be the target of relentless scrutiny and verbal attacks. He would see intimidating bean-ball pitches and hostile base runners who would test his courage with their spikes. Knowing Robinson's competitive nature, Rickey told him that he would have to have "enough guts not to fight back" when the inevitable physical or verbal assaults came. If he could not maintain his composure, he would not succeed. In his emotional commentary Rickey emphasized that "turning the other cheek" was good New Testament theology. Rickey cautioned Robinson that he would have to wear "a cloak of humility." Above all, he had to produce on the field. "You've got to do this job with base hits, stolen bases, and fielding ground balls, Jackie."[35]

Rickey's announcement of the signing two months later stunned the baseball establishment. Rickey's long-time rival, Yankees owner and general manager Larry MacPhail, predicted that if large numbers of African Americans came to see Robinson play, they would drive away white fans and produce a severe drop in ticket sales. He announced bluntly, "I have no hesitancy in saying that the Yankees have no intention of signing Negro players," and he issued an internal memorandum to other team owners that criticized Rickey for "exerting tremendous pressures on the whole structure of Professional Baseball."[36]

After an exceptional season in 1946 with Montreal, the Dodgers' top minor league club, Robinson was elevated to the parent team. For a time in spring training, a handful of veteran Dodgers with deep roots in the South, including star center-fielder Dixie Walker, talked of asking for trades, of a boycott, of a strike, of a signed petition of protest. The much-rumored protests fizzled, in part due to the support Robinson received from Kentucky native, shortstop Pee Wee Reese, and the adamant stand taken by manager Leo Durocher and Rickey. Nonetheless, it was a tense locker room into which the rookie walked.

After a slow start, Robinson began to play well in May. He had to adapt to a new position of first baseman, but the Brooklyn fans were enthusiastic in their support. His first major test came early on April 22 in Philadelphia, where manager Ben Chapman, a native of Alabama, fueled a racially charged verbal barrage from the Phillies' dugout. The abuse continued throughout the game, and as Robinson recalled, it was one of the most difficult days of his life. "I felt tortured and I tried just to play ball and ignore the insults," he later wrote in his autobiography,

but it was really getting to me. I was, after all, a human being. . . . For one wild and rage-crazed minute I thought, "To hell with Mr Rickey's noble experiment." . . . To hell with the image of the patient black freak I was supposed to create. I could throw down my bat, stride over to that Phillies dugout, grab one of those white sons of bitches and smash his teeth in with my despised black fist. Then I could walk away from it all.[37]

Of course he did not do so, but he scored the only run of the game, an effective response to the Phillies' racism. The Dodgers went on to sweep the Phillies in three games, and the heavy cloud of fear and doubt began to lift. Later, a composed Robinson calmly told a *Pittsburgh Courier* reporter, "The things the Phillies shouted at me from their bench have been shouted at me from other benches and I am not worried about it. They sound just the same in the big league as they did in the minor league." Robinson was lifted by the fact that the Phillies' dreadful conduct galvanized his own team behind him, Southerners included. Dixie Walker admonished his fellow Alabaman Ben Chapman, and Dodgers second baseman Eddie Stanky was reported to have shouted across the field, "Listen, you yellow-bellied cowards, why don't you yell at somebody who can answer back?" Branch Rickey had, of course, helped prepare Jackie for the ordeal, and he later said, "Chapman did more than anybody to unite the Dodgers. When he poured out that string of unconscionable abuse, he solidified and unified thirty men. . . . Chapman made Jackie a real member of the Dodgers."[38]

The pressure continued throughout the season. On the road he had to stay in private homes in several cities because hotels would not accept him where his teammates stayed. He was dismayed by the thousands of hate letters he received, many of them containing death threats, but these were more than offset by a tidal wave of letters and telegrams of encouragement. On the field, he was the target of many high and fast pitches; by July he had already set a league record for the number of times hit by pitches. Pitchers, of course, attempt to intimidate all rookies with inside pitches, but they discovered that if they hit Jackie, he would promptly make them pay by stealing second base. The inside pitches became less frequent as the season passed.

By the end of the 1947 season, Robinson had more than justified the trust displayed by Branch Rickey in selecting him from among many candidates for his historic role. He batted .297, scored 125 runs, and stole 29 bases, while fielding his position skillfully. He had helped his team win the pennant that preceded an epic seven-game World Series battle with the Yankees. He was named "Rookie of the Year" by the venerable *Sporting News*, edited by J. Taylor Spink, who had long been an outspoken opponent of the integration of organized baseball. As the Dodgers closed in on the pennant in late September, *Time* magazine put Robinson's picture on its cover. He had, by his quiet courage and resolute play, captured the hearts of a people who liked to root for the underdog. He was truly a historic figure, using the nation's most popular game as a means of breaking down racial stereotypes and taboos. As such, he did much to prepare the nation for the civil rights movement that would soon take wing.

Robinson did not join the Dodgers until he was nearly 28 years of age, but he enjoyed a decade of success with the team until he retired after the 1956 season. With Eddie Stanky traded after the 1947 season, Robinson moved to his

Figure 9.5 Jackie Robinson steals home with his usual flourish against Philadelphia on July 2, 1950. Star first baseman Gil Hodges backs away from the plate, while catcher Andy Seminick is late in applying the tag. The Phillies later won the pennant on the last day of the season, when Dick Sisler hit a home run in the 10th inning to beat star pitcher Don Newcombe and the Dodgers. © Bettmann/CORBIS.

natural position of second base and fielded at a Gold Glove level, often making spectacular diving catches. From 1949 through 1952, he led the league's second basemen in the number of double-plays turned. He helped propel the Dodgers to five more National League pennants, and in 1949 was named the league's Most Valuable Player after a season in which he batted .342, stole 37 bases, and batted in 124 runs as the Dodgers beat out the Cardinals on the last day of the season, then lost the World Series to the Yankees in five games.

Robinson continued to play at an All-Star level. When another African American player, Junior Gilliam, came up from the minors, Robinson moved to third base, where he continued to make dazzling defensive plays while batting above the .300 level. He was a perennial member of the All-Star team and was recognized as a team leader both on and off the field. In the 1952 World Series, he helped rally the Dodgers to tie the series at three games apiece, but they lost to the Yankees in game 7; the following year, they were again frustrated by the Yankees, but in 1955, the Dodgers finally broke through to take the World Series in seven games over the powerful Yankees. Showing his years,

Robinson missed 40 games that season due to injuries, his batting average fell to .259, and he retired after the following season. In 1962, Jackie Robinson was the first African American elected to the Baseball Hall of Fame, winning admission the first time that he was eligible for consideration.

Following his retirement, Robinson entered several business relationships, became politically active in support of liberal presidential candidates such as Nelson Rockefeller and Hubert Humphrey, and spoke out vigorously on civil rights. By the mid-1960s, his health visibly declined before an onslaught of diabetes. By 1970, he could barely walk and had lost the sight of one eye and most in the other. Losing weight but unable to control either his high blood pressure or his cholesterol levels, he suffered a series of strokes and a heart attack, and on October 24, 1972, at the age of 53, the brave and outspoken man who had broken the color line of baseball was gone, much too early. In 1997, baseball Commissioner Bud Selig announced on the 50th anniversary of Robinson's first season with the Dodgers that his number 42 would be retired by all baseball teams, a unique honor much deserved.

In the Shadow of Jackie Robinson

The appearance of Jackie Robinson in 1947 in a major-league uniform naturally drew the attention of the American people. At that time, professional baseball was beyond question the number-one sport in the country, and when Robinson trotted out to take his position at first base on April 15, 1947, America changed forever. He brought the issue of racial justice into sharp focus for the first time since Reconstruction. Even President Truman's creation of a Commission on Equal Rights, his bold step in ordering the desegregation of the military, and the strong civil rights plank in the platform on which he campaigned for re-election in 1948 did not affect the public consciousness as did Jackie Robinson. Bill Veeck Jr, now president of the Cleveland Indians, moved quickly in Branch Rickey's wake and signed another top Negro League player, shortstop Larry Doby, a crackerjack player whom the Dodgers had seriously considered before deciding upon Robinson. On July 5, 1947, Doby started in center field for the Indians, and by season's end five African Americans had appeared in major-league games. In 1948, Veeck signed Satchel Paige, making him a highly publicized 42-year-old rookie who pitched well enough to be named to the American League All-Star roster.

Despite the obvious boost Robinson gave the Dodgers, several clubs steadfastly refused to sign black players. For more than a decade, the Yankees did not aggressively pursue African American prospects, signing very few to minor league contracts. In late 1945, the Yankees lured one of the nation's best scouts, Tom Greenwade, away from the Dodgers. When he reported to work, team president George Weiss took him aside and told him, "Now Tom, I don't want you sneaking around back alleys and signing any niggers. We don't want them."[39] Greenwade, who had been heavily involved in Branch Rickey's search, thus was forced to pass on several top African American players he had identified as future major-leaguers, including future Hall of Fame shortstop Ernie Banks. Greenwade probably knew the pool of available black talent better than anyone else, and he would later speculate that the tailspin the Yankees experienced in the late 1960s was a direct result of the team's refusal to sign African American players.

The Yankees' racial policy was reflected in their handling of first baseman Vic Power. After Power led the American Association with a .349 batting average in 1953, the Yankees could no longer keep the talented Puerto Rican down on the farm, so instead the Yankees traded him and four other players to the Philadelphia Athletics for five journeymen. A stylish fielding first-baseman, Power would win seven Gold Gloves and have a career batting average of .284, while hitting with power for 12 major league seasons. (Power also was possessed of a good sense of humor. While appearing before a Southern justice of the peace on the grievous charge of jaywalking – not an unusual type of racially inspired Southern law enforcement pattern during this era – he told the judge: "I thought the 'Don't Walk' sign was for whites only. I've seen so many of those signs in this town.")[40] It was not until 1955 that the Yankees put Elston Howard in their outfield because his raw talent was so great they had no choice but to play him. Thus, only with great reluctance, did baseball's premier organization respond to one of the nation's most pressing social issues.

The National League moved much more rapidly than the American League in signing African Americans. As David Halberstam explains, what blacks brought to the game more than anything else was speed. On the base paths and in the field especially, their impact was immediately recognized. With the Dodgers signing several top young African Americans, other teams in the league followed suit, if for no other reason than self-defense. As a result, during the 1950s the National League moved well ahead of the American League in talent. Among those teams that would enjoy considerable success as a result were the St Louis Cardinals, New York/San Francisco Giants, and Cincinnati Reds. It was no mere coincidence that between 1960 and 1980 the American League would win only two All-Star games. The last major-league team to put an African American into their line-up was the Boston Red Sox, when Pumpsie Green joined its infield in 1959. By this time, 15 percent of the 400 major-league players were African American.[41]

Baseball's new racial policy doomed the Negro leagues. Never financially stable and beset by constant turnovers in ownership, franchise locations, and players, the two leagues now were confronted by a loss of talent that produced a swift decline in attendance. Thus the Negro National League folded after the 1948 season; the Homestead Grays, long the dominant team in the NNL, were suddenly gone. The rival Negro American League ended any pretense of being a major league operation in 1950, but it lingered on in obscurity for several years. The NAL's top franchise, the Kansas City Monarchs, its roster depleted of talent, continued to play exhibition games in the obscurity of small Midwestern towns into the mid-1960s before the team disbanded. Within three years after Jackie Robinson set foot on Ebbets Field, the Negro leagues were dead. "The big league doors suddenly opened one day and when Negro players walked in, Negro baseball walked out," Wendell Smith jubilantly wrote in the *Louisville Courier*; and fellow black journalist Frank

"Fay" Young informed his Cleveland readers, "far from being sorry . . . [African Americans] are glad."[42]

Racial progress was also occurring in other professional sports. In 1933, the fledgling National Football League, largely at the behest of Washington Redskins's owner George Preston Marshall, moved to an all-white policy, after permitting blacks to play since the league's inception in 1922. In 1946, however, a rival professional league, the eight-team All-American Football Conference, was formed. It lasted only four seasons before the top franchises were absorbed by the NFL, among them the conference's four-time champion Cleveland Browns. In the line-up that first season were two black players destined for the Hall of Fame, fullback Marion Motley and defensive lineman Bill Willis. At the same time, the Los Angeles Rams of the NFL signed two blacks as well, both of whom had played football at UCLA with Jackie Robinson: Woody Strode and Kenny Washington.[43]

Although the appearance of these four players in professional football occurred one year before Robinson joined the Dodgers, there was no controversy and little media attention. The apparent reason for this was that outside of the South, blacks had always played college football. Additionally, fans at football games are seated some distance from the field of play, and the helmets and padded uniforms tend to render the players more or less indistinguishable from each other. With professional football still a relatively small niche sport, these four players went about their business without the attention that engulfed Jackie Robinson. In 1946, the Rochester Royals of the even more-obscure Basketball Association of America, a forerunner to the NBA that was formed in 1949, added the first black to its roster without much fanfare, but in 1950, when the New York Knicks managed to lure Nat "Sweetwater" Clifton away from the showboating Harlem Globetrotters, the media made it into a major news story. That same year, the Washington Capitols signed West Virginia University star Earl Lloyd and the Boston Celtics added Duquesne University's All-American Charles Cooper to its line-up. Other teams soon followed suit, and the quality of professional basketball increased substantially. For several years, however, the NBA maintained an informal quota system that no more than two blacks would be starters and that no team would have more than four blacks on its 12-man roster.

Ever since its inception during the 1920s, professional basketball had limped through its seasons in relative obscurity. Salaries were low, and "major-league" franchises were located in such small venues as Syracuse, Sheboygan, Fort Wayne, and Rochester. Crowds were small, and many games were played in aging civic auditoriums and even in high school gymnasiums. The arrival of black players in the 1950s, however, changed all of that as the NBA moved into the mainstream of professional sports. In 1956, the Boston Celtics signed 6' 10" Bill Russell, one of the all-time defensive and rebounding greats, and the Philadelphia Warriors countered in 1959 with the 7' 2" scoring and rebounding dynamo, Wilt Chamberlain. Their titanic battles captivated basketball fans, and attendance soared and televison coverage became commonplace. Back-court stars such as Lenny Wilkins and Oscar Robertson entered the league in the early 1960s, bringing an abrupt halt to the popular myth that blacks lacked the discipline and intelligence to run sophisticated offensive patterns. By 1970, fully 50 percent of the NBA roster positions were filled by African Americans and the game continued to grow in popularity. The fears of some owners that this trend would alienate their primary fan base – affluent white males – proved unfounded.

Gentlepeople and Sanctimonious Hypocrites

Right from the start, tennis in the United States became the special province of the urban elite. The languid style of play, a conservative dress code that mandated all white clothing, the emphasis on good manners and court decorum, and a private club setting all pointed the game toward a deserved image of snobbish elitism. That tennis gave off an aùra of smugness cannot be denied. Mimicking the pattern set by private golf clubs, the United States Lawn Tennis Association (USLTA) did not accept African American members. Excluded from sanctioned tournaments, top black players could not earn the points necessary to qualify for the US National tournament held at Forest Hills, New York. That racial barrier came crashing down in 1950, largely as a result of a blistering article in *American Lawn Tennis* magazine written by former US Tennis Women's Open champion Alice Marble. She denounced the USLTA and its all-white membership for its "bigotry" in excluding African Americans from tournaments. In particular, she had in mind Althea Gibson, who was the perennial women's champion of the American Tennis Association (ATA), a small and struggling black tennis organization. "If tennis is a game for ladies and gentlemen," Marble wrote, "it's also time we acted a little more like gentlepeople and less like sanctimonious hypocrites."[44]

Later that year a chastened USLTA invited Gibson to enter the premier annual tournament at its exclusive digs in Forest Hills. In round 2, Gibson found herself on center court before several thousand curious fans with the recently crowned Wimbledon champion, Louise Brough, on the other side of the net. Brough swept through the first set 6–1 as Gibson seemed in a daze. Obviously nervous – a reporter wrote she looked "scared to death" – Gibson gained control of her emotions and unleashed her thundering ground strokes and pinpoint volleys to take the second set 6–3. Reporters in the bar got word of an enormous upset in the works and hustled back to the stadium to watch Gibson take a 7–6 lead in the final set (rules at the time required a two-game victory margin) when a large thunderstorm hit, forcing postponement of the match. The next day, just four points from an improbable victory, Gibson once again surrendered to nerves. She had all night to think about a potential upset victory. "The delay was the worst thing that could have happened to me," she recalled. She proceeded to lose the match 6–1, 3–6, 9–7.

That Althea Gibson was even playing tennis at Forest Hills was a personal triumph. She grew up in poverty-stricken Harlem during the Great Depression, and spent her time dodging public school truant officers while playing tennis on public courts. In 1946, she entered the ATA national tournament where she was observed by two Southern physicians who had a strong interest in tennis.

Figure 9.6 Althea Gibson shows her crisp backhand form in this mach at Wimbledon in the 1957 finals against fellow American Darlene Hard. In 1957 she became the first African-American woman to be selected as the Associated Press's Female Athlete of the Year. © Bettmann/CORBIS.

Doctors Hubert Eaton of North Carolina and Robert Johnson of Virginia took her under their wings and into their homes. They provided private tennis instruction and got her on an academic path that led to a belated high-school diploma and a scholarship at Florida A&M, from which she graduated in 1953.

In 1951, she became the first African American to be invited to play at Wimbledon but lost in the early rounds. With better coaching, her game improved and she joined a world tennis tour in 1956 that concluded at the French Open in Paris. The unseeded Gibson shocked the tennis world by winning the French singles title, and the following year won on the grass at Wimbledon, defeating Californian Darlene Hard in straight sets. At the grand concluding Wimbledon Ball, she was introduced to Queen Elizabeth. "Shaking hands with the Queen of England was a long way from being forced to sit in the colored section of the bus going into downtown Wilmington, North Carolina," she later recalled.[45] She received a ticker-tape parade upon returning to New York, and a month later reached the finals of the US Open before losing a close match to Shirley Fry. However, the following year she reeled off wins at Wimbledon and Forest Hills, a feat she would repeat in 1958. Althea Gibson had reached the pinnacle of the world of tennis.

Following the US Open in 1958, Gibson turned professional in order to earn a paycheck of $100,000 playing tennis exhibitions on basketball hardwoods as a preliminary to Harlem Globetrotters' games. Because the women's professional tennis tour had yet to be formed, her competitive tournament days were behind her. Attempting to find a new competitive outlet, not unlike Babe Didrikson Zaharias, Gibson turned to golf, earned her professional card, but did not do well on the tour. Nonetheless, she was once again a pioneer, being the first African American woman to earn a LPGA tour card. She died in 2003 after suffering a series of debilitating strokes, but late in life was able to appreciate the accomplishments of such black women tennis stars as Zina Garrison and Venus and Serena Williams. Unlike these ladies, she never earned the large purses and product endorsements that had become common, and she lived out her final years in near seclusion on limited income.

Virginia native Arthur Ashe was born 15 years later than Althea Gibson, and by the time he emerged in the mid-1960s as a nationally ranked men's player, the intense hostility and closed doors that she had confronted during the 1940s had receded. But he had encountered plenty of discrimination in his home town of Richmond, Virginia, where he was denied access to public tennis courts and junior tournaments. After graduating from UCLA which he attended on a tennis scholarship, Ashe became the first African American man to win the US Amateur (1968), the US Open (1968), and Wimbledon (1975).[46] Standing a slender 6' 1" and weighing only 155 pounds, Ashe did not look the part of a world-class athlete. The fact that he had to wear eyeglasses did not add to his physical appearance, but once he took the court he was a sight to behold. He possessed a complete tennis game, starting with a powerful serve that was complemented by a booming overhead and the ability to hit crisp volleys at sharp angles. His backhand was effective both down the line and cross-court; one amazed expert claimed he saw Ashe hit 17 different types of shots off his backhand during a single match. Ashe also was a master of finesse shots, hitting devastating lobs to the baseline, low-spinning chip shots, and tantalizing drop shots.

Ashe's emergence as a leading tennis player during the 1960s coincided with the high tide of the civil rights movement. Although strongly committed to the movement, he concentrated on his tennis because he felt it enabled him to make a statement about equality of opportunity as he took on the leading players of the world. In 1968, he reached the heights of the tennis world, reaching the semifinals at Wimbledon and winning the US Amateur and Open tournaments. In the Open final against Tom Okker, Ashe's serve was whistling into the service area at

115 mph. He hit 26 service aces, prompting the befuddled man from the Netherlands to ask, "What's the use? I can't see it anyway."[47] His powerful serving was an amazing feat because the small wooden racquet was still standard equipment. Oversized metal and composition racquets, which would produce serves in the 140-mph range, would not make their appearance until near the end of Ashe's competitive days.

Although he held strong personal views on racial justice, Ashe kept his thoughts to himself for many years. But in 1970, having turned professional, he found an appropriate means of combining his highly visible tennis stature with social justice, when as the world's number-one-ranked male player he applied for a visa and entrance into the South African Open Tennis Tournament, then a prestigious world-class tournament. He correctly predicted that he would be denied on both counts, and he called a press conference to protest the rigid apartheid policies of the white government of South Africa. His call for a boycott of the tournament was not honored by his white peers, but he had made his point. In 1973, however, both the visa and admission to the tournament were forthcoming. Increasingly involved in racial issues, Ashe came under criticism that he was not devoting himself sufficiently to his tennis game, but he quieted those critics when he defeated fellow American Jimmy Connors in the singles finals at Wimbledon in 1975 – yet another first for this modest man from Virginia.

As Ashe began to contemplate his post-tennis future, he suffered the first of three heart attacks. In 1979, he underwent open-heart surgery to open clogged arteries, and he was forced to retire from competitive tennis. He turned to writing tennis columns for the *Washington Post* and tennis publications, and served as captain of the American Davis Cup team. But in 1983 he had to undergo another heart operation, during which he received several blood transfusions. Five years later he was diagnosed as HIV-positive, undoubtedly having received tainted blood during his second heart surgery. He subsequently died from AIDS at age 49 in 1993. After his death, the new stadium at Flushing Meadows, home to the US Open, was named for him, but he undoubtedly would have taken great personal satisfaction when in 1996 the city of Richmond, where he had been denied access to public tennis facilities as a youth, erected a large statue of him – a tennis racquet in one hand, books in the other – on the city's famous Monument Row, which features several famous residents who served as Confederate generals.

The Baron and the Bear

The pace of racial integration in American sports intensified during the 1950s and the 1960s as one barrier after another came tumbling down. Sweeping social change produced high emotions and not infrequently, violence. One symbolic episode that focused the nation's attention upon the issue of racism occurred in 1951, when Drake University's football team traveled to Stillwater, Oklahoma, to play a Missouri Valley Conference game against Oklahoma A&M. The Drake Bulldogs were an upstart college football team that year, featuring flashy senior tailback

Johnny Bright, an African American whose previous season exploits had placed him on a short list of potential Heisman Trophy candidates. Possessing excellent quickness and agility, the muscular 215-pounder flourished in his coach's "BURP" offense ("Bright run or pass"). The senior was one of the most explosive offensive players in the country, a sure-fire first-round NFL draft pick.

On the first play from scrimmage against the Aggies, Bright casually trailed a run by a teammate, and as the whistle blew he was blind-sided by defensive tackle Wilbanks Smith, who flagrantly slugged him in the jaw. The vicious illegal hit was captured on film by two *Des Moines Register* photographers, and their sequential photographs indicated that Smith had delivered a deliberate cheap shot. In that one moment, Bright's Heisman hopes were shattered along with his jaw. *Life* magazine ran the pictures on its cover, and sports fans expressed outrage.[48] The question immediately arose: was Smith attempting to put out Bright because he was a threat, or because he was black? Or both? The talented tailback had to have a tooth removed so that he could take liquid nourishment through a firmly wired jaw. He returned later in the season but, having missed several games, he finished fifth in the Heisman voting, and later spurned the NFL to play professionally in Canada for several years.

The Johnny Bright incident highlighted the precarious state of race relations in college athletics. When the Missouri Valley Conference refused to take corrective action, Drake withdrew from the conference. In the South, the intersection of racial politics and sports roiled the waters of big-time college football. Political leaders expected colleges to maintain all-white teams, but also to play games only against lily-white opponents. During the 1920s, this posed little problem because college teams were invariable all-white. In 1934, seeking to enhance its national football reputation, Georgia Tech scheduled a game at the University of Michigan. When it was learned that the Wolverines had a starting black end, political leaders in Georgia demanded that he be withheld from the game or the Bulldogs would not take the field. The player in question, Willis Ward, was, in fact, the first black player on record at Michigan since 1892. Michigan students protested any effort to keep Ward on the bench, but Georgia officials were adamant that they not break the long-standing unwritten Southern "gentlemen's agreement" with their peer universites to restrict sports opponents to all-white teams. Ultimately a compromise was achieved that did little to enhance the stature of the University of Michigan. School administrators agreed to bench Ward, if Georgia Tech pulled its star end, All-American Hoot Gibson. Michigan won the game with the two ends sitting out the contest, but the fallout from this episode led Michigan, and many other Northern schools, to avoid scheduling Southern teams until the racial situation had changed. In most instances this informal boycott lasted until the 1970s.[49]

The issue of black opponents resurfaced again at Georgia Tech 21 years later. After the nationally ranked Ramblin' Wreck accepted a bid to the 1956 Sugar Bowl to meet the University of Pittsburgh, it was learned that Pitt's starting fullback was black. Georgia Governor Marvin Griffen demanded that Tech withdraw from the prestigious bowl game. Griffen had become a leader of the "massive resistance" movement against the US Supreme Court's order to desegregate public schools, and he apparently felt compelled to take an adamant stand:

> We cannot make the slightest concession to the enemy in this dark and lamentable hour of struggle. There is no more difference in compromising the integrity of race on the playing field than in doing so in the classroom. One break in the dike and the relentless seas will rush in and destroy us.[50]

A flood of protests from whites within his own state breached Griffen's racial dike. Several thousand students marched in protest on the State Capitol and governor's mansion, both of which were guarded by heavily armed state police. Frustrated, the students strung up an effigy of Griffen and stalled downtown traffic until midnight. The *Atlanta Constitution* published a hot editorial condemning Griffen's position, and even one staunchly segregationist newspaper said that the team should play to bring "fame and glory and prestige to the State of Georgia." These demonstrations occurred at the same time that headlines reported on the early days of the pivotal bus boycott in Montgomery, Alabama, that had been sparked by the brave action of Rosa Parks. A highly charged meeting led to a decision by the Board of Regents to defy the governor. In the football-happy South, football apparently edged-out segregation when national rankings were at stake. After the public controversy that swirled about in December 1955, the game itself was anticlimatic. Georgia won a tight 7–0 contest, and Pitt fullback Bobby Grier led all rushers that day as he broke the color line in one of the nation's leading bowl games. The following year a bill died in the Georgia legislature that would have prohibited public university teams from playing any contest that included African Americans. Within a few years the issue was swept away as racial integration occurred slowly, but surely, in Southern universities. If those schools wanted to earn national sports honors, their policy of playing only all-white teams was no longer viable. As the historian Charles Martin has shown, similar issues occurred in the Atlantic Coast Conference and Southwestern conferences with similar results, but only after much huffing and puffing by diehard segregationist forces, whose actions today seem silly and anachronistic, but at the time were central to the evolving civil rights struggle that consumed the American South.[51]

To the casual football fan, the seismic changes occurring in Southern big-time football schools was first recognized when the National Football League began blanketing the nation with television coverage during the late 1950s. Many star NFL players were identified as having attended, not big-time Southern white football schools such as Alabama and Louisiana State, but rather small and relatively unknown all-black colleges. Year in and year out, outstanding NFL players were identified as having come from such institutions as Jackson State, Grambling, Southern, Texas Southern, Alcorn A&M, South Carolina State, and Prairie View. These players, of course, had been systematically ignored during the college recruiting season by coaches from the Atlantic Coast, Southeastern, and Southwest conferences. With the civil rights movement gaining momentum during the late 1950s, and with their university administrators now actively seeking black students, coaches at Northern universities began extending their recruiting into the Deep South. Soon a sizeable migration of Southern black athletic talent to schools north of the Mason–Dixon Line commenced. This trend was highlighted in 1960, when the University of Minnesota won the Big Ten championship and played in the Rose Bowl, led by consensus All-American quarterback Sandy Stephens. A standout athlete from South Carolina, Stephens was the first black to play at the leadership position of quarterback at a major college university in modern times. In 1966, Michigan State tied for the national championship on the strength of several such players, including one of the best defensive linemen who ever played the game, Bubba Smith, a native of Beaumont who would have preferred to play his college ball in his native Texas.

During the early 1960s, the civil rights movement focused upon the historically all-white public universities. Governor George Wallace stood defiantly in the doorway of the admissions office at the University of Alabama in 1963 in a futile attempt to prevent the enrollment of a black student ordered enrolled by a federal court. The previous September, rioting and deaths resulted on the campus of the University of Mississippi in protest of the court-ordered enrollment of James Meridith. With sad memories of the bucolic Oxford, Mississippi, campus blanketed by smoke and tear gas still fresh in their minds, in March 1963 Mississippi residents found themselves facing another race-inspired issue at the other major state university. Bucking the domination by the University of Kentucky basketball team, the Mississippi State University Bulldogs had won the Southeastern Conference title, but Governor Ross Barnett sought to prevent the team from participating in the NCAA tournament because it would be matched against Northern teams with black players. With a sixth place national ranking in the final Associated Press poll, university officials wanted to play, and after much public discussion and in open defiance of the fuming governor, the State Board of Education voted to permit the team to travel to Michigan for its first tournament game against Loyola University of Chicago, which had four black starters. The pre-game handshakes became a media event, but the hard-played game won by Loyola that followed produced no incidents, and in its wake Southern universities quietly adopted a new policy that they would no longer avoid playing teams with African American members. Loyola, as it turned out, ended up winning the tournament.[52]

It was not long after this episode that once lily-white Southeastern Conference teams began to recruit blacks; coaches and knowledgeable fans understood that if they wanted to compete for national honors they had to recruit the best athletes. To permit a covey of future All-Americans to go North to score touchdowns and baskets now seemed a monumental oversight. One by one, Southern teams began to take on a multiracial hue, and by the mid-1970s the northward flood of black talent had slowed to a trickle. One ironic result of this change in policy was that the traditional black colleges saw their own sources of top athletic talent evaporate. Just as the integration of organized baseball inevitably meant the loss of baseball talent by the Negro leagues, so too did the integration of higher education greatly reduce the athletic talent level of the black Southern colleges.

The changes occurring during the 1960s in college athletics as a result of the civil rights movement were never more vividly highlighted than at the final game of the 1966 NCAA men's basketball tournament. Following the 1951 gambling scandals, the National Invitation Tournament held in Madison Square Garden lost most of its luster, and the NCAA-sponsored tournament gained in prestige. It came of age in 1957 as a significant national sporting event when North Carolina defeated a Wilt Chamberlain-led Kansas team 54–53 in three overtime periods. By the 1960s, the 16-team tournament had attracted a large television audience, but fear of gambler influence in major cities prompted the NCAA to play the tournament games on college campuses. Thus in 1966 the Final Four teams – Duke, Utah, Texas Western College, and Kentucky – assembled on a March weekend on the campus of the University of Maryland to determine the national champion.

Most experts expected the Wildcats of Kentucky to leave Cole Field House with their fifth national championship. Coaching the team was the already legendary "Baron of the Bluegrass," Adolph F. Rupp. When his team departed Lexington for Maryland, Rupp's teams had won 747 games during his 36-year tenure, racking up 22 Southeastern Conference championships, the 1946 NIT championship, and four NCAA championships. At one point during Rupp's reign they had won 129 consecutive home games. This was an especially intriguing team because it lacked a dominant center. Led by 6' 5" forward Pat Riley, this scrappy team was fondly dubbed "Rupp's Runts" by Kentucky fans. The Wildcats came into the tournament ranked number one in the nation and their coach had just added yet another "Coach of the Year" honor to his collection.

Rupp's reputation had been built playing in the segregated Southeastern Conference. Predominantly a football conference, the great majority of its member institutions viewed basketball as little more than something to pass the wintertime until spring football practice rolled around. Not so in Kentucky, a state that had a strong high-school basketball tradition. Many of Rupp's players came out of the hardscrabble mining towns of eastern Kentucky or the rolling farmlands of the western part of the state. The university was the northernmost member of the SEC, so Rupp upon occasion slipped across the Ohio River to pick up a few prize recruits from the neighboring basketball-rich states of Ohio, Indiana, and Illinois to supplement his annual Bluegrass harvest. None of his recruits, however, came from the basketball-rich African American neighborhoods of Louisville, Cincinnati, Cleveland, Indianapolis, or Lexington. His Wildcats had always been and continued to be an all-white team, and he had given no indication that this unwritten policy was about to change. But the racial landscape in America was undergoing a fundamental transformation, and unkind rumors about his racial views were now swirling around Rupp and his program. The racial glacier that was Southern athletics was beginning to melt under the pressures of national competition.

Although Rupp's defenders have since attempted to smooth over his racial views and practices, it seems that he was typical of his time, not malicious but simply grounded in the time-honored tradition of paternalism. He apparently believed that black players, while possessed of great natural skills, lacked the essential traits he emphasized in his coaching: discipline and intelligence in running complex offensive and defensive schemes. Clearly, Rupp upon occasion used crude racial stereotypes, which were commonly held and expressed by whites during his time. In one inadvertent slip of the tongue regarding the quickness of many black players, he told a radio interviewer "The lions and tigers caught all the slow ones."[53]

In any case, Rupp knew that as long as the SEC remained segregated the combination of his recruiting and coaching would enable the Wildcats to continue to dominate the conference. Instinctively conservative, set in his ways, and a dominant force in his state, the Baron of the Bluegrass was not about to be a force on behalf of equal opportunity. Even when the gambling scandals hit his program in 1951, Rupp was able to survive despite having to accept a one-year suspension of the program for the 1952–3 season. His Wildcats represented a state that had long endured a backward "hillbilly" image. On game nights, radios across the state were tuned in to the Wildcat Radio Network, where the soothing Southern inflections of popular announcer Cawood Ledford, a native of mining-town Harlan, filled the airwaves with his unique description of the action. Wildcat basketball was indeed an important Kentucky institution.

The scene was set for the 1966 NCAA finals at Cole Fieldhouse on the Maryland campus on Friday evening when Kentucky slipped by Duke by four points and the virtually unknown and certainly overlooked Texas Western College Miners upset Utah in the semi-final games. Texas Western – soon to be renamed the University of Texas at El Paso, or UTEP – lacked the great basketball tradition of its opponent in the finals. It also had an unknown young head coach who had been at the school only four years. The large, gruff Don Haskins, given the appropriate nickname of "The Bear," had quietly assembled a talented team in the sandy expanses of western Texas. Haskins had graduated from Oklahoma A&M in 1953, where he learned the intricacies of the game playing for Hank Iba, who coached the traditional controlled style of play that emphasized the importance of executing precisely accepted basketball fundamentals, methodically running patterned offenses, taking only high-percentage shots, and playing a tenacious man-to-man defense. The one thing that Iba's teams did not do was play without purpose or control; thus their fans seldom saw the Aggies run a fast break because too many mistakes could occur. This was precisely the style of play that Haskins taught his Texas Western team. Recognizing that football-crazy West Texas did not produce many top-tier basketball players, Haskins went on distant recruiting trips into predominantly black neighborhoods in Houston, Chicago, Detroit, and New York City. El Paso was considered a Western and not a Southern school, so it was exempt from the segregationist policies still in place in other Texas public universities.

It was thus a classic social confrontation when the two teams took the floor in Cole Field House before 14,000 spectators. Not only were the five starters for Texas Western black, but so were its two most frequently used substitutes. The Miners scored first and never trailed throughout the game as they played their typical disciplined offense and a sticky man-to-man defense, just as Hank Iba had taught Haskins. The final score was relatively close, 72–65, but the upstart team from Texas had won a decisive victory. Rupp and his squad were so stunned by their loss that they departed Cole Field House, leaving behind the runner-up trophy. At the time, the national media did not call attention to the racial implications of the game – neither the *New York Times* nor *Sports Illustrated* even mentioned the racial composition of the teams – but this game would later come to be viewed as a major milestone in race relations in the United States.[54]

A few weeks after the game, Vanderbilt University announced the signing of a black basketball recruit, and the racial barriers in the SEC began to crumble. It did not take long for other Southern coaches – eager to win, anxious to keep up with their peers – to join in the hunt for black talent. In 1969, Adolph Rupp signed his first (and only) black player, 7' 1" center Tom Payne out of Louisville. Rupp retired two years later, but his legend lives on as the Wildcats now play to sell-out crowds in the cavernous 24,000-seat Adolph Rupp Arena in downtown Lexington. At the time of this writing, the Wildcat head coach who has kept alive the winning tradition of Kentucky basketball, already with one national championship and a Coach of the Year award to his credit, was Orlando "Tubby" Smith, an African American.

10 Television Changes the Face of American Sports

The game was played in Yankee Stadium on December 30, 1958. The favored New York Giants met the upstart Baltimore Colts for the championship of the National Football League. Many football experts claim it was "the greatest game ever played." Whether that bold assertion is correct is subject to further review, and most certainly subject to continued impassioned across-the-generations dialogue at many a sports bar. What is beyond question, however, is that the game stands out as a turning point in the history of American sports because it established the NFL as a major professional sport, and revealed the vast potential the sport offered for commercial exploitation by televison.

Yankee Stadium bulged with 64,185 spectators that cold and damp day, and a national television audience estimated at between 30 and 40 million joined in the fun. At halftime, the underdog Colts held a surprising 14–3 lead, but in the second half the Giants roared to life and took the lead 17–14 late in the fourth quarter on a Charlie Connerly 15-yard pass to halfback Frank Gifford. Then the drama began. Taking possession on their own 38-yard line with just two minutes remaining, the Colts marched down the field on pinpoint passes from quarterback Johnny Unitas to Raymond Berry and Lenny Moore. With just seven seconds left and the Colts on the 13-yard line, Steve Myhra kicked a short field goal, and for the first time, an NFL championship would be decided in sudden-death overtime. The Giants won the coin toss and elected to receive the kickoff, but their offense sputtered and after a punt the Colts began their legendary drive on their own 20-yard line. Unitas once again led the Colts down-field, mixing running plays by fullback Alan Ameche and halfback Moore with passes to Berry and Moore. With a first down on the Giants' 8-yard line, head coach Weeb Eubank confounded everyone and ordered three consecutive offensive plays rather than kick an almost-certain field goal for the win. His strategy was rewarded when on a third down from the 1-yard line, Ameche crashed over tackle into the end zone. The final score read 23–17 as thousands of Baltimore fans rushed the field and ripped down the goal posts.[1]

That season NFL player salaries averaged about $10,000. One writer commented that prior to this game, the Baltimore Colts' players were "working men, tradesmen, glamorous only when compared to miners and factory workers," but after Ameche's deciding touchdown they were "legends, genuine folk heroes." Even seasoned sportswriters covering the game were caught up in its emotions. *Sports Illustrated*'s senior football writer Tex Maule proclaimed it the "greatest game ever played," and the *New York Times*' Arthur Daley called it "a wildly exciting and utterly mad affair." He continued, "The enthusiasm shows how completely pro football has arrived. Giants fans were as vociferous as their leather-lunged Baltimore counterparts." Even National Football League president Bert Bell was moved to comment that he had just witnessed "the greatest game I've ever seen."[2] On that overcast day in New York City, with an estimated 11 million television sets tuned in around the nation, sports television and professional football simultaneously came of age. The way in which sports influenced American culture had forever been altered.

The Formative Years of Sports Television

Even while commercial radio was in its infancy during the 1920s, scientists and engineers were already at work finding ways to transmit images over the airwaves. The first televised images were transmitted in England in 1926, and in 1936 an estimated 150,000 Germans witnessed the Summer Olympic Games in large halls in Berlin, Potsdam, and Leipzig. The following year, BBC telecast the Wimbledon men's finals between Don Budge and Frank Parker to some 3,000 British homes. Television in Germany and Great Britain moved forward more rapidly than in the United States because of government sponsorship and promotion. In the United States, decisions made at the end of the First World War had placed broadcasting in the hands of private commercial interests, and during the Great Depression even the largest electronics and broadcasting firms were cautious about investing in new technologies in an uncertain market. Nonetheless, television was on display in 1939 at the New York World's Fair, where 45 million visitors glimpsed the future on a nine-inch black-and-white screen.[3]

On May 17, 1939, the first American televised sports event took place when experimental station W2XBS set up two large, unwieldy RCA Iconoscope cameras at Columbia University's Baker Field and telecast the Columbia–Princeton baseball game. The cameras had difficulty picking up the small white ball, and viewers could follow the action only because of the narrative provided by veteran radio sports broadcaster Bill Stern. He worked without a monitor and had no idea what his viewers were seeing. What they witnessed, in fact, was mostly white spots on the screen and shadowy humanlike forms moving about. As Stern recalled, he spent a lot of time looking back at the camera to see where it was aimed. "I had no monitor. I had no idea where the damned thing was pointing. I never knew whether the thing could keep up with the play or not." Outfield play was unintelligible, and only plays close to home plate were clearly transmitted to confused viewers. The *New York Times* reported that the players seemed like "white flies" flitting about the screen. With that inauspicious beginning, a new era of televised sports had arrived, static, blurred screens, and missed plays notwithstanding. In autumn 1939, W2XBS telecast several other New York-area sports events as it worked on improving the quality of its telecasts – an Eastern grass court tennis championship match, a football game between Fordham University and Waynesburg College, a baseball game at Ebbetts Field between the Dodgers and the Reds, a heavyweight fight between Lou Nova and Maxie Baer, and a professional football game between the Brooklyn Dodgers and the Philadelphia Eagles. With only a few hundred television sets located in the New York area, commercial sports broadcasting remained a decade away.[4]

During the 1939 baseball game televised from Ebbetts, viewers got a glimpse of things to come when Dodgers radio broadcaster Red Barber sat in the upper deck near one of the cameras surrounded by fans as he announced the game. During one break between innings, he whipped out a box of Wheaties, filled a bowl, sliced up a banana, added milk, took a bite, and looked into the camera and proudly proclaimed, "Now, that's a Breakfast of Champions." That the future of American sports television was to be commercial-laden never seemed in doubt.[5]

In the immediate postwar years, the Federal Communications Commission issued hundreds of licences to local television stations and several manufacturers scrambled to produce receivers for the domestic market. For a time, the public was standoffish. Expensive and cantankerous, early television receivers were sources of both pride and immense frustration to their owners. By 1950, however, there were four million sets in operation that served 20 percent of the American population. In 1955, fully 75 percent of American homes were equipped with at least one set, a number that jumped to 90 percent in 1960. In that year, when voters elected John F. Kennedy president, more American families had television sets than indoor bathrooms.

As the preeminent professional sport, organized baseball was the first to take seriously the possible impact of television. After lengthy deliberation, its owners adopted a flawed policy that permitted each team to develop its own local radio and television markets and to keep the revenues thus generated. By 1960 the impact was already being felt; teams in large media markets were reaping far greater returns than those in small markets. The New York Yankees, for example, were generating annually $1 million in television revenues, while several competing clubs, such as the Washington Senators, received less than 10 percent of that amount. This disparity continued to grow exponentially during the next several decades and would become a major issue for baseball's critics. Essentially the same policy remains in place today and the criticism continues.

In 1953, CBS television launched the *Game of the Week* on Saturday afternoons. There had been network telecasts of the All-Star Game and the World Series for several years, but now regular-season games were made available.

Fans everywhere could watch the top teams and such stars as Ted Williams, Stan Musial, Mickey Mantle, and Jackie Robinson from the comfort of their own homes. And for free! In 1955, the network put former St Louis Cardinal pitcher Dizzy Dean behind the microphone. He became an immediate hit with his countrified accent, corny humor, and shameless self-promotion. Dean's convoluted syntax amused his audiences but became the bane of English teachers ("he slud into second"). When the action on the field dragged, Dean might break into dubious song, bellowing out his favorite country tune, "Wabash Cannonball." Dean became even more popular as a broadcaster than he had been as an All-Star pitcher and free-spirited leader of the Gas House Gang during the 1930s, giving an early indication of a phenomenon that would blossom during the 1960s and flourish thereafter – the sports announcer sharing the center of attention as a "star" in his own right, competing for public adulation with the athletes he was covering.[6]

While television ratings were soaring, attendance at the 16 major league ballparks fell from 21 million in 1948 to just 14 million in 1953, when it bottomed out and remained flat for the remainder of the decade. Minor league attendance plummeted 70 percent and the number of teams contracted from 488 to just 155. At the same time semiprofessional and "town ball," disappeared. Given a choice to watch major leaguers on television or the town nine stumble through a game, fans abandoned the locals.[7]

Television also changed the map of baseball. In 1953, major-league baseball was concentrated in the Northeastern quadrant of the country where it had existed for a half-century, but that was about to change. The Boston Braves moved to Milwaukee that year, where they drew a hefty 1.8 million fans and enjoyed a large media market in the vast region to the north and west, but the move of the Washington Senators to Minneapolis-St Paul in 1961 sliced their market in half, so the Braves moved again in 1966, this time to Atlanta, attracted by potential revenues of a seven-state television and radio network. In 1954, the St Louis Browns – after decades of performing miserably on the field and at the gate – relocated to Baltimore, assuming the historic name of Orioles. With the move of the Giants and the Dodgers to the West Coast in 1958 (with large television markets as a major lure) and the Braves to Atlanta, there was only one populous region in the country left unattended. That void in the Southwest was filled in 1965 by the creation of an expansion team in Houston, originally named the Colt-45s, and with the relocation of the expansion version of the Washington Senators (created in 1961 to appease irritated federal legislators when Clark Griffith took the original Senators franchise to Minnesota) to the Dallas-Fort Worth area where they became the Texas Rangers. When owner-manager Connie Mack retired at age 86, the hard-pressed Athletics moved from Philadelphia to Kansas City in 1954, then embarked for Oakland in 1968. Although many factors contributed to the movement of franchises and the creation of expansion teams – attendance, urban and regional boosterism, politics, the personalities and quirks of owners – at the bottom of this frenzied transitional era, television-market share provided the primary impetus.

Tale of the Tube: Boxing

The power of television to change a sport was readily evident in the changes that transformed boxing. Although the overwhelming percentage of American people had never seen a boxing match, they had nonetheless followed the sport for decades in newspapers, magazines, and on the radio. Everyone knew about the exploits of John L. Sullivan, Jack Dempsey, and Joe Louis, but relatively few persons had ever seen them throw a punch. Boxing and television seemed to be made for each other. During the early years of commercial television, with unwieldy cameras and primitive black-and-white technology, it was still possible to produce a tolerable picture of the action occurring in a 20 × 20-foot area blanketed in artificial light. As early as 1939, a writer for the *New York Times* had realized as much: "The roped arena is a perfect size for the camera to cover. The scene is packed with action and this is the life-blood of television. The colorful sounds punch realism into the picture. . . . Carnage is a dream of television."[8] Even before the arrival of national networks, local stations found that they could attract viewing audiences by producing boxing matches. Television executives greatly appreciated that boxing's three-minute rounds were separated by a one-minute rest period, thereby providing plenty of opportunities for producers to insert commercials.

In 1950, NBC-TV began to telecast the Friday night fights from Madison Square Garden. NBC radio had broadcast the Friday night feature bout from the Garden since the 1930s, with announcer Don Dunphy providing the blow-by-blow narration. The Gillette Company had long sponsored these radio broadcasts and it assumed the sponsorships of the televised bouts, proclaiming the wonders of its cheap safety razors and distinctive "blue blades" with a cartooned parrot chirping, "Look Sharp! Feel Sharp! Be Sharp!" Almost overnight, boxing became the most popular sport on television. Although many viewers had never before seen a live match and were oblivious to the game's "scientific" strategies and nuances, they became instant experts. By 1952, televised fights entered five million American homes each week – a hefty 31 percent of the market; by 1955, an estimated 8.5 million American homes regularly tuned into the fights.[9]

Professional boxing's roots lay in the small fight clubs located in cities large and small. There, in a dank environment reeking of liniment, cigar smoke, and sweat, young boxers learned the fundamentals of the manly art. They came primarily from the lower echelons of society – racial and ethnic minorities, recent immigrants, the poor – who had dreams of earning big purses and championships. The more promising were funneled into local amateur Golden Gloves tournaments, and if they showed professional potential, were signed to a contract by a manager who provided advanced instruction and professional guidance. Some of the more prominent clubs periodically offered a card of several bouts to give these fledgling fighters experience and exposure. It was a long and grueling process, with only a few survivors of the process eventually emerging to fight in bouts on a civic auditorium card offered by a local promoter. Before the advent of television, it was not unusual for a talented boxer to have fought 40 or 50 bouts before getting a shot at main events in large cities. Joe Louis, for example, a product of the fight clubs of Detroit and Chicago, did not enter the ring in quest of the heavyweight championship until his 47th bout. One of the all-time great light-heavyweights, Archie Moore, fought in nearly two hundred professional fights before getting a shot at the title. Along the way, it was not unusual for a young boxer to lose one or even several bouts but still rise to national contention. The American fight game, for all of its sleaziness, corruption, ties to organized crime, fixed fights, violence, permanent injuries, and occasional deaths, nonetheless provided opportunities for hopeful would-be champions to earn a big payday. In the process, they provided exciting action on fight cards at local clubs.[10] Gillette's televised Friday night fights were instant hits, generating large viewing audiences. Arthur Daley, sports columnist for the *New York Times*, observed in 1954 that

> the ring is small enough to always be in focus. The contestants are the absolute minimum of two. It's the ideal arrangement because every seat in front of a video screen is a ringside seat. And the price is perfect – free.[11]

But as would happen time and again in the highly competitive world of commercial television, whenever a popular program hit the market, another network would seek to emulate it, leading to over-saturation of the market and subsequent viewer indifference. Within a year after NBC launched its Friday night series, CBS-TV introduced its own *Wednesday Night Fights*, sponsored by another company seeking to target an adult male audience, Pabst Blue Ribbon Beer. Local stations added to the clutter by putting on their own "studio" bouts. After a few years of too many lackluster fights on too many channels on too many nights, with even championship bouts becoming all-too-routine, the once enormous television boxing audience tuned out. Ratings plummeted.

Long-standing boxing aficionados – those who had paid their dollar admissions to watch the local club fights – were dismayed by what television did to their favorite sport. They protested that the new television fight fans did not understand or appreciate the intricacies and nuances of the art of boxing, such as slipping punches on the ropes, forcing a clinch to regain one's composure, the slow process of wearing down an opponent, counter-punching, the short jab, throwing barely visible short body punches while in a clinch, even the tactic of moving backward and side to side to tire out an opponent. These many time-tested tactics – learned in the long hours spent training at local gyms – seemed tedious and boring to the untrained eyes of the johnny-come-lately television audience but were the stuff that hard-core fight fans understood and appreciated. The television camera best caught the long, looping overhead punch thrown by the slugger rather than the sophisticated tactics used by a skilled boxer. When the balletic featherweight champion Willie Pep easily defeated the wild-swinging challenger Ray Famechon in 1950, he did so by sidestepping the flailing Frenchman's errant blows while repeatedly landing clean, if light, counter-punches. It was, John Lardner said, "a classic exhibition of evasive skill and science." The judges voted Pep the fight by a whopping 12 rounds to three, but during the next several days the International Boxing Club and NBC were inundated with complaints that Famechon had been robbed; the television viewers had completely missed the fact that Pep had outmaneuvered and out-boxed his futilely flailing challenger. Jack Dempsey, himself not exactly a finesse fighter, agreed that the new fight fans were ignorant of the science and skill required: "There are millions of people who never saw a fight away from a televison set, but they talk about nothing else." Under the inexorable pressure of the television cameras, style, form, and technique were downgraded while simple power and the sensational knockout punch were emphasized for the unsophisticated newcomers perched in front of their television sets. Sportswriter John Einstein noted the change in the sport: "Today's fighter is primarily a slugger. The boxer, the hitter, the combination man is gone. The sponsor does not want him. The sponsor wants a man who'll sell his product, somebody popular, and colorful."[12]

In addition to being strongly encouraged to seek out boxers who would appeal to the new audience, promoters were also put under the gun by television executives to arrange bouts that had special appeal. In particular, they learned that bouts featuring fighters with several losses on their records were not attractive to television audiences. The need to match two undefeated fighters to attract good television ratings altered the traditional system whereby young fighters systematically worked their way up the ladder, perhaps absorbing a few defeats in the learning process. Television executives brought strong pressure on promoters to schedule main events with promising new fighters with undefeated records. This resulted in many young boxers being pushed too far, too fast.

This was the case with the undefeated Chuck Davey. He was attractive to television producers because he was white, college-educated, possessed of curly blond hair, and gave a good interview. In 1952, he became the darling of the television audience because of his fancy footwork and seemingly impressive record built against weak opponents; fans were delighted to learn that he had boxed at Michigan State College, where he earned bachelor's and master's degrees in education. Thus, well before he was ready for prime time, the pressures created by television executives put Davey into a Madison Square Garden ring with the defending welterweight champion, the veteran Kid Gavilan of Cuba. It was brutal, and 35 million Americans watched. The ring-savvy Gavilan systematically savaged the unprepared challenger, eventually knocking him out in the 10th round after administering the former college student a painful course in Boxing 101. A few weeks later, the devastated Davey announced his retirement from the ring. His fate was typical, wrote Arthur Daley in the *New York Times*: "There aren't that many good fighters any more. They are brought up before they are ready for that quick buck. They go down as fast as they rise."[13] Almost overnight, Chuck Davey had gone from being one of boxing's brightest attractions to a discarded also-ran.

The rise of televised boxing to high ratings was surpassed by the swiftness of its fall. One of the unintended consequences of television's exploitation of boxing was the demise of the hundreds of boxing gyms and clubs that for decades had prepared young fighters for the professional game. With featured bouts being telecast several times a week into the homes and taverns of America with no admissions charge, boxing fans abandoned the local clubs. Their subsequent closing reduced the flow of new talent into the sport. During the decade, the number of fight clubs had fallen from 300 to about 50, and the small-city boxing circuit, where over the years many top fighters had gotten their start, had virtually disappeared. By the end of the decade, the number of professional fighters had been reduced by a whopping 50 percent. Television also cut deeply into attendance of big city fight cards. In 1948, an average crowd of 12,000 would pay good money to see the Friday night card at Madison Square Garden; 10 years later, the audience averaged about 1,200. The vast Garden floor had become little more than a television studio. In 1951, one-third of the nation's television sets were tuned to the Friday night fights, but by 1959 that lofty figure had fallen to just 10 percent. Ratings-conscious television executives naturally looked elsewhere for new attractions with which to sell advertising.[14]

By 1959, most boxing had disappeared from the airwaves, and in 1960 NBC announced that it was dropping its traditional Friday night programming. ABC took over the show from Madison Square Garden, but dropped it in 1964 as ratings continued to decline. Boxing no longer captured the imagination of the casual television viewer. The sport moved into a new era, where it limped along on the fringes of respectability. The fight game now seemed to be more and more reliant on the heavily hyped heavyweight championship confrontations staged in Las Vegas, where hotel-casinos used high-profile boxing matches as a means of attracting "high-roller" gamblers to their green felt tables. But the traditional fight game had essentially ceased to exist, knocked down for the count by television.

Professional Football Comes of Age

It is not surprising that professional football, which today constitutes a multibillion dollar sports and entertainment enterprise, came into prominence with commercial television. Ever since its obscure origins in the Midwest in 1921, the National Football League had struggled to survive, its hardscrabble teams paying players a few hundred dollars a game at best, shifting thinly financed franchises like checkerboard pieces in and out of such small cities as Canton, Duluth, Marion (Ohio), Decatur (Illinois), Portsmouth (Ohio), Evansville and Green Bay. By the eve of the Second World War, however, the league had begun to mature with reasonably stable franchises in such cities as Philadelphia, New York, Detroit and Pittsburgh. It also had the good fortune to have star performers such as quarterbacks Sid Luckman and "Slingin'" Sammy Baugh, receiver Don Hutson, and running backs Red Grange and Bronko Nagurski to attract fans. The league championship game even was broadcast nationwide for the first time in 1940, but the anticipated close grudge match between the Chicago Bears and the Washington Redskins ended up with the lopsided score of 73–0 against the home town 'Skins.

Between 1945 and 1960, the NFL came of age. In 1946, NFL team owners selected Bert Bell as their new Commissioner. Reflective of the league's still-limited visibility, for several years this former owner of the Philadelphia Eagles actually ran the league out of his home, eventually moving to a small office in a suburban Philadelphia bank building. Bell took over the league at a difficult time, because in 1945 Chicago sportswriter Arch Ward had orchestrated the establishment of yet another new professional league – the All-American Football Conference (A-AFC).

His intent – at least his public statements so indicated – was to create a league equal to the NFL, with the two league champions squaring off in December for the national title. The A-AFC enticed several wealthy franchise owners who seemed willing to absorb losses if necessary in order to create a strong league.

The A-AFC's president, former Notre Dame Four Horseman Jim Crowley, attempted to find a way to avoid a bidding war for players and to get agreement on a post-season championship game, but he was unceremoniously rejected. The NFL was not in a mood to be of assistance. The A-AFC did quite well initially, signing 44 of the 60 college players selected for the All-Star Game, and luring away about a hundred established NFL players with attractive salaries in the $5,000 to $12,000 range. However, the A-AFC's biggest catch was Paul Brown, a 37-year-old coach who had built an 80–8–2 record while winning six state championships at Massillon High School in northeast Ohio, had gone on to Ohio State where he won a national championship in 1942, and then produced a powerhouse at the Great Lakes Naval Station while coaching many former college stars. After being turned down by Notre Dame's head coach Frank Leahy, Cleveland owner Arthur "Mickey" McBride named Brown his coach, and delighted fans voted to name the Cleveland franchise the "Browns." McBride lured Brown with an offer of a high salary of $25,000 plus 5 percent ownership of the team. McBride was well-known locally as a big-time sports gambler who was also very well-connected politically. Among his several financial interests was a contract that gave his taxi-cab company exclusive control of the local market.

Brown was undoubtedly an excellent coach on the field, but throughout his career he became best known for his many innovations that transformed the game. These included written play books for players to study, the use of game films to evaluate players and to analyze upcoming opponents, grading each player's performances by "breaking down" game film play-by-play, systematically scouting future opponents, and surreptitious use of hand signals to convey plays to the quarterback when coaching from the sidelines was deemed illegal. He continued to innovate when he took over the Browns. When unlimited substitution was legalized in 1949, he shuttled two offensive guards in and out after each play to communicate the next play to quarterback Otto Graham; in the 1950s, he even placed a radio receiver in the helmet of the quarterback to communicate directly, an innovation that proved technically unworkable but would later be implemented when better technology became available. Brown contributed greatly to enhancing the coach's control of the game, a trend that continues to the present. He called the offensive play signals and set the defense before each play. Brown also was one of the first coaches to put assistant coaches in the press box to get an overview of the game; they communicated with the coaches on the sidelines via telephone with their observations and suggestions.

Owner Mickey McBride liked to win, was willing to spend plenty of money to that end, and gave Brown a free hand in running the team. Brown became the first professional coach to hire full-time assistant coaches who worked year-around, not just during the season. When he announced that he was hiring five full-time assistants, shock waves reverberated throughout professional football. He had a built-in advantage over other teams when it came to stockpiling talent. With the team rosters limited to just 33 players, he convinced McBride to hire several reserves as taxi-cab drivers. Come practice time, a fleet of McBride's cabs would be seen parked outside the Browns practice facility. Brown thus had a group of replacements available to plug into his team in case of injury to a roster member.[15] That legacy lives on today. The NFL permits each team to keep eight players under contract beyond the 45-man regular roster; that supplemental group, of course, is known as the "taxi squad."

Brown assembled a talented team that would produce seven members of the Hall of Fame: quarterback Otto Graham, fullback Marion Motley, receiver Dante Lavelli, offensive lineman Frank Gatski, defensive lineman Bill Willis, defensive end Len Ford, and offensive tackle-place kicker Lou "The Toe" Groza. Brown's teams won the A-AFC championship four consecutive years, and the lack of competitive balance clearly hurt attendance. Even Browns fans became complacent, and by 1949 Cleveland's average attendance had fallen from 50,000 per game in 1946 to just 20,000. When the Browns defeated the San Francisco 49ers 21–7 in the fourth and final championship game, only 22,500 fans watched in Cleveland's mammoth 80,000-seat Municipal Stadium.

The NFL was also hurting in attendance, a result of the loss of talent to the rival league. Salaries had also escalated. A merger was the logical solution, and after much wrangling, the NFL agreed to accept three teams from what its leaders considered an inferior league: the Browns, the San Francisco 49ers, and the Baltimore Colts. Enmity lingered, however, and Bert Bell decided to teach Paul Brown a lesson – or at least to inaugurate a new era with high drama. He scheduled Cleveland to open the 1950 season at defending champion Philadelphia, but much to nearly everyone's surprise, the Browns dominated the Eagles in convincing style, 35–10. The vaunted Eagle offense was held to just 118 yards as 71,000 silent Eagles fans looked on in shock. The Browns proved that this game was no fluke and went on to a 10–2 season, capping it off with dramatic last-minute field goals by Lou Groza to win the divisional playoff with the Giants and the championship game against the Los Angeles Rams.

Throughout the 1950s, the NFL grew more stable despite several changes in franchise ownership. The value of a franchise hovered between $500,000 and $1 million during the decade, but unlike professional baseball, attendance grew steadily, jumping from an average of 25,300 to over 40,000 per game between 1950 and 1960. In part, this increase resulted from the improved quality of play. There were more and better players, and with the introduction of unlimited substitution they were able to concentrate upon refining specific skills, leading to a more exciting brand of play. Rules changes sought to stimulate scoring, including placing the goal posts on the goal line to encourage more field goal attempts. Specialization became the rule, and only a few players still went "both ways." By 1960, only the Eagles' Hall of Fame center/linebacker Chuck Bednarik did so with regularity.

The NFL's steady growth during the 1950s can be traced to an enlightened television policy that Bert Bell sold to the league's owners. Bell negotiated his first league-wide television contract with a network in 1951, a modest arrangement with the fledgling DuMont network that included local game blackouts. In 1953, federal district judge Allan K. Grim ruled that the NFL could black out games only within a 75-mile radius of the location where the game was being played. Although this did not give the NFL complete control over television, it provided the necessary protection for ticket sales. In 1956, CBS paid over $1 million in rights to televise selected games nationally, while several teams created their own regional networks. NBC paid in the six figures to carry the championship game. When Bell suffered a fatal heart attack on October 11, 1959, while watching the Eagles and Steelers play at Franklin Field in Philadelphia, an important transitional era in the history of the NFL came to an end. Bert Bell had guided the league to the point where it was about to embark on an extended period of expansion and prosperity – thanks in large part to the groundwork he had established with an enlightened television policy.[16]

Pete and Roone

Bert Bell's death came at a crucial time for the NFL. In 1959, yet another new rival league, the American Football League (AFL), had been created. Unlike several of the earlier incarnations of an AFL that made cameo appearances during the 1930s, this eight-team league placed all of its franchises in major cities, three of which already contained NFL teams. The premise of this new league, however, was that it could become viable solely with a lucrative national television contract; the selling of tickets would be of secondary importance. By this time, up-and-coming ABC-TV was anxious to get into the football business and prepared to fork over the princely sum of $2 million for the rights to the initial AFL 1960 season. The league was the brainchild of 27-year-old Texas oilman Lamar Hunt who, angry at being rebuffed by the NFL in his attempt to buy an existing franchise and move it to Dallas, decided to create a new league. He lined up such wealthy investors as Bud Adams in Houston, Bob Howsam in Denver, and Max Winter in Minneapolis, among others, to join in his enterprise as team owners. By November 1959 he had an eight-team league assembled.

Thus the new American Football League was definitely on the minds of the 12 NFL owners when they convened for their annual meeting in Miami Beach in January 1960. The selection of Bert Bell's successor was at the top of their agenda. But first they fired a shot across the bow of the new league by creating two expansion franchises, the Dallas Cowboys and, by luring Max Winter away from the AFL, the Minnesota Vikings. They then turned their attention to selecting a new Commissioner, but could not agree upon the top candidates. The politicking and arguing lasted for 10 long days before, in exasperation if not desperation, they finally named as their new Commissioner the young and inexperienced Los Angeles Rams general manager, Pete Rozelle. An exhausted group of owners could only hope for the best.[17]

Rozelle did not have a compelling football resume, coming to the game from a background in marketing and media relations. Raised in a small southern California town, he had earned a degree from the University of San Francisco and worked for a time for a public relations firm and as a Rams publicist. In 1957, he assumed the Rams general manager position, making a modest mark by introducing a popular line of merchandise carrying the Rams' horned logo – hats, sweatshirts, beer mugs, coffee cups, key rings. Soon all professional teams were in the team-paraphernalia business. Rozelle had acquired a solid grasp of the quirky television market of Los Angeles, and it would be Rozelle's expertise in dealing with the television industry that would propel the NFL to new heights of public support and wealth that the owners could not have imagined when they selected him. Unflappable, personable, seemingly always tanned in a surfy southern California way, Pete Rozelle was neither personally nor physically imposing. Labeled the "boy czar" by skeptical journalists, he looked like a short-timer.

Nothing could have been further from the truth. Beneath Rozelle's calm exterior, there existed a tough-minded negotiator who would brook little nonsense nor any challenge to his authority (soon after taking office, he had the temerity to discipline the recognized father figure of the NFL, the founding owner and coach of the Chicago Bears, George Halas). Rozelle's first substantive decision gave an indication of what he thought the NFL should be about. He moved the league's headquarters to a luxurious suite on Park Avenue in downtown Manhattan, just a stone's throw from the national headquarters of the major networks. Up until this point, Bert Bell had developed a television policy that left most decisions up to individual clubs, but with the all-important proviso that home games be blacked out. The new Commissioner's initial policy decision proved crucial to the league's future. He embarked on an audacious plan to convince his conservative, millionaire capitalistic owners of the many blessings to be gleaned from, of all things, socialism.

Just as Bert Bell had preached and practiced the gospel of maintaining a league of competitive teams, so too did Rozelle, but he extended that concept to the point of taking away millions of dollars from teams located in large media markets. Rozelle proposed to his owners that the league sell the television rights of all teams as a single package and that each franchise share in the income equally. He persuaded the owners that if this was not done, then the big media-market teams would most certainly dominate the league in the long run, creating a two-tier situation of haves and have-nots. In the long run, he argued, sharing revenues would generate more income for everyone. To pull this off, he had to make his case to the barons whose franchises were located in the nation's three largest media markets – Wellington Mara of the Giants, Dan Reeves of the Rams, and 66-year-old league patriarch, George Halas of the Bears. With the grudging acceptance of these three owners, who stood to give up the most by sharing all television revenues, Rozelle was off to Washington, DC, to lobby Congress for special legislation exempting the league from antitrust laws. After a summer of lobbying, Rozelle was rewarded in September 1961 with the Sports Antitrust Broadcast Act, which permitted leagues to pool their broadcast rights and sell them as a single entity. That was the end of contemptuous talk about a "boy czar." Rozelle would serve as Commissioner until poor health forced him into retirement in 1989.[18]

For the 1962 and 1963 seasons, Rozelle's hands were tied because nine of the teams already had signed agreements with CBS, but nonetheless he was able to secure a record-high contract of $4,650,000 per season, which amounted to $330,000 per team. But Rozelle was only warming up, and when the rights for 1964 and 1965 came up for renewal, he orchestrated a highly publicized secret bidding process by playing each network off against the others. Speculation abounded in advertising and sports circles as to which company would fork over the largest pile of money. With Rozelle presiding over the pre-bid rumors and hype, he made sure that it became a matter of pride for network executives to win. Upstart ABC saw the bidding as an opportunity to gain equal stature with its two much-larger rivals, while NBC and CBS were determined to protect their elite status. When Rozelle opened the sealed bids in a public ceremony, NBC came in with an unexpectedly high $10,750,00 for each of two seasons, and upstart ABC topped that with a shocking figure of $13.2 million. Rozelle then casually opened the final bid.

> I figured the CBS bid had to be anticlimactic. . . . So I opened their bid kind of lacka-daisically. The thing was two pages long – all that fine print. The number itself was sitting way down toward the bottom of the second page. I looked at it, and . . . "Good God," I thought, "it's for $14,100,000 a year!" [19]

The new financial reality of professional football's marriage with television was evident to ABC vice-president Ed Scherick, who thought, "Good Lord, I could not get it out of my mind. Here we had gone in with more than *twenty-six million bucks*. And we had been *rejected*! The whole damned *network* had cost only $15 million in 1951!"[20]

ABC's audacious bid, however, indicated that the network would become a big player in the sports business. The large but failed bid was largely the work of its youthful vice-president for sports, Roone Arledge, who brought imagination, energy and a willingness to take a chance to his new job. He arrived at ABC at a propitious time. The network had just signed on to broadcast the Saturday college football game of the week and also the new American Football League's games. Arledge brought to his position the conviction that if he offered casual viewers entertainment and drama that went beyond the game itself, they would tune in. Within a few years, Arledge had revolutionized the way television covered sporting events: "What we set out to do was to get the audience involved emotionally. If they don't give a damn about the game, they still might enjoy the program."[21]

Arledge's approach was radical. He instructed his lead announcers, such as the droll, down-home Southerner Keith Jackson, to describe the game in a manner that would keep the casual viewer glued to the set. His producers were instructed to capture not just the action on the field but the total atmosphere surrounding the game. Special hand-held microphones were placed on the field to pick up the "thud" of players smacking into each other, cranes provided overhead shots, and zoom cameras caught the action up close. His producers also blended in interviews with the coaches, the sounds of marching bands, and shots of anguished coaches prowling the sidelines cursing and screaming out instructions, of blood trickling down the face of a wounded warrior, and of inebriated (or at least excited) fans in the stands making fools of themselves. ABC became famous for its up-close images of attractive coeds in the grandstands, pretty cheerleaders doing their acrobatic routines, and leggy baton twirlers prancing in front of the band at halftime. By this time, new technology had made color television feasible, and Arledge gave his growing audiences a bright panoply of autumn colors from college stadiums, offset by sounds of football players grunting as they hit the ground. Arledge placed several cameras throughout the stadium to provide much greater coverage of the action on and off the field. Especially popular was the introduction of slow motion and instant replay that made it possible for viewers to see crucial plays over and over again. Arledge thus presented football not as just a game, but also as a human spectacle full of excitement, pathos, sometimes high drama. Ratings soared, and so did Roone Arledge's career.[22]

Within a year after moving to ABC, Arledge launched his weekend sports anthology *Wide World of Sports*. Using the catchy phraseology suggested by announcer Jim McKay, ABC "spanned the globe" to bring viewers "the thrill of victory and the agony of defeat." As McKay later recalled, the program was not "born out of a creative explosion. It was, as the old saying goes, born of necessity." Operating on a limited budget, Arledge found unique and inexpensive ways to fill those time slots. Only seldom, such as an occasional boxing match, did he present live events. Instead, he utilized the recent innovation of videotape to condense the action down to its essence. Thus his producers would compress a 26-mile marathon into a few minutes – showing the fresh pack of runners taking off from the starting line, their agonized faces as they slogged up a hill or struggled to keep going when "hitting the wall" at the 20-mile mark, and finally the exhausted leaders attempting to sprint to the tape after more than two hours of arduous effort. As ABC euphemistically put it, the shows were "shot live on tape." He sent his crews around the globe in search of anything remotely connected with sports that might prove entertaining to American audiences. In its first year *Wide World of Sports* reported on obscure rodeos from small towns in the West, track meets in Iowa, tennis in Mexico, soccer from London, auto racing from Le Mans, France, curling from Canada, hydroplaning from Seattle, mountain climbing in the Alps, and surfing from Maui. Lead announcer McKay, who usually did the voice-over in the New York studio after film crews brought in their tape, revealed a special talent for making even the most inconsequential event seem interesting by emphasizing underlying storylines – colorful personalities, danger to contestants, feuds between competitors, and the exotic location in which the event was held.[23]

Although initially *Wide World* tended to cover legitimate, if obscure, sports over the years the program tended to stretch things a little – and then some. During the years that Arledge had ultimate control over the program (until 1985), it was estimated that more than two hundred so-called "sports" had been given air time. His potpourri included jai-alai, badminton, wrist-wrestling, log-rolling, cat shows, dog shows, horse shows, truck pulls, horse polo, water polo, water skiing, figure skating, bobsledding, chess, ski races, bicycle races, motorcycle races, stock-car races, marathon races, and dog-sled races – and the list goes on and on. At times, the show went over the top with automobile demolition derbies, a climbing race up the Eiffel Tower, cliff divers falling several hundred feet into the Pacific Ocean at Acapulco, and high wire walks without a safety net. The most extreme moment came on January 1, 1968, when daredevil Evel Knievel attempted to jump the bubbling water fountain in front of Caesars Palace in Las Vegas on a 500-pound motorcycle. He landed in a heap, suffering a broken spine and a crushed pelvis, among other injuries. Knievel reappeared on *Wide World* 15 more times doing weird things – always to high ratings . . . and that was the name of the game.[24]

The NFL and the AFL Make Peace

Upon his arrival in 1960, Arledge and ABC found themselves in the middle of a bitter squabble between the NFL and the newly created American Football League. In its first year, the upstart league suffered low attendance, its eight teams losing an estimated $3 million despite the ABC contract. Contrary to broadcasts of college games where shots of the fans in the grandstands became common fare, ABC's cameramen had to be instructed to follow AFL games without showing the embarrassing vast stretches of empty seats. In 1963, the floundering AFL New York Titans franchise was purchased by multimillionaire David "Sonny" Werblin for $1 million. He hired Weeb Eubank, the former head coach of the 1958 champion Baltimore Colts, to lead the renamed New York Jets, moved home games to recently opened Shea Stadium, and stunned the sports world when he signed University of Alabama quarterback Joe Namath to a staggering $420,000 three-year contract in 1965. With Namath tossing passes, Jet attendance jumped from 22,000 per game to over 40,000, and the AFL had instant credibility. Namath's signing set off a bidding war for top talent that pushed up players' salaries.

In 1964 the AFL had signed a stunning five-year $42-million contract with NBC, more than five times what it received from ABC. Its survival was now assured by a television contract. With the AFL not going away, Pete Rozelle sought peace. A series of secret meetings led to an agreement to merge the two leagues. Rozelle would be the Commissioner of a greatly expanded National Football League, and a single draft would eliminate the bidding for players. Not only did the NFL agree to merge with all 10 AFL franchises, but Rozelle agreed to put an expansion franchise in New Orleans as a condition of gaining the critical support of Senator Russell Long and Congressman Hale Boggs of Louisiana for passage of an antitrust legislative exemption to the merger. That legislation quietly sailed through Congress as a rider to an appropriations bill, and three weeks later the establishment of the New Orleans Saints was announced to an unsuspecting world.[25]

Super Sunday and Monday Night

With Rozelle's greatly expanded 26-team empire now under one tent, it was only natural that a final championship playoff game be held between the American and National Football Leagues (changed to "conferences" in 1970). Although the owners wanted to call it the World Championship Game, Rozelle opted for the more regal title of "Super Bowl." In 1971, with the fifth Super Bowl approaching, Rozelle gave the upcoming Dallas–Baltimore game a distinctive touch by designating it with a Roman numeral, Super Bowl V. What was thus retroactively dubbed Super Bowl I, was played in spacious Los Angeles Coliseum on January 15, 1967, and slightly more than 35,000 fans paid the top ticket price of $12 to watch coach Vince Lombardi's Green Bay Packers run roughshod over the Kansas City Chiefs 35–10. The first game was telecast by both NBC and CBS, which sold advertising at $35,000 per 30 seconds; thereafter, the two networks alternated through 1984 as part of the ongoing contract with the league, at which point ABC joined in the fun.

The Super Bowl became one of the most important events on the American sports calendar, eclipsing even the World Series, Kentucky Derby, and New Year's Day college bowl games in importance. Super Bowl III, played on January 12, 1969, provided the turning point. According to Las Vegas bookmakers, the Baltimore Colts of the older league were a prohibitive 17-point favorite over the upstart New York Jets, led by "Broadway Joe" Namath, who had become a much-publicized celebrity member of the New York bachelor culture. A few days before the game, Namath brashly "guaranteed" a Jets victory. Much to the shock of the Vegas bookies and millions of sports fans, he delivered in dramatic fashion, engineering a 16–7 victory. On a rainy January day in Miami, he completed 17 passes, one for a touchdown, while the Jets' defense stifled the high-powered Colt's offense, still led by Johnny Unitas. Even Pete Rozelle, the master of public relations, could not have written a better script.

Thereafter, the Super Bowl became a national craze, complete with heavy network promotion, overblown media coverage, and a special crassness and outrageousness that no one could quite define. Super Bowl Sunday was not simply another day to watch a football game on television, but rather it became an informal national holiday. Each year, it seemed to grow ever more gaudy, ever more over-the-top. Several thousand media personnel assembled at the game site a week before kickoff to fill the airwaves and newsprint with the most trivial news and analysis of the upcoming game. In the host city, lavish parties were held for thousands of guests, invited or otherwise, with corporate sponsors attempting to outdo the others with their extravagance. Ticket prices accelerated each year, reaching $500 by Super Bowl XVIII in 2004, but scalpers could usually sell tickets for upwards of four times their face value. Across the country, the American people followed the hype, with an estimated 25 percent of the adult male population making some sort of bet on the game. Across the country millions of private parties were planned – newspapers even printed suggestions for Super Bowl buffet menus for struggling hosts – and vast amounts of alcohol were consumed.[26]

With half of the American people watching at least part of the game, advertisers lined up to buy air time. By 1980, the cost of commercials had reached $250,000 per 30 seconds, and $400,000 by 1985. In 2005, the half-minute rate had spiraled to the astronomical level of $2.5 million. Advertising agencies that designed the ads – largely for beer, automobile, and soft drink companies – even found themselves caught up in an informal contest for the most creative, humorous advertisements, which became part of the post-game media dissection. The importance of the Super Bowl to the television industry was driven home when Pete Rozelle admitted ABC to the network rotation for the 1985 game and charged a cool $18 million "admission fee" just for the privilege.

It was inevitable that two creative men such as Pete Rozelle and Roone Arledge would find a way to combine their talents. For several years, Rozelle had chafed under the limitations that confined NFL games to Sunday afternoons. He dreamed of putting his product on prime time, but both CBS and NBC continued to view sports with indifference. But what night? All three networks viewed Saturday nights as sacrosanct for their top-ranked programs, and Friday nights were unavailable because that night was traditionally reserved for high-school football. Except for the tradition of the Detroit Lions' Thanksgiving Day game, midweek seemed illogical. So what about Monday night? Rozelle was rebuffed by CBS for fear of losing its women viewers, who flocked to the network's popular Monday prime-time feature-movie presentation. NBC was interested but backed off when star Johnny Carson refused to push his *Tonight Show* back from its regular 11:30 p.m. time slot. That left ABC, which after some hesitation, decided to take the risk. When *Monday Night Football* (*MNF*) began in 1970, the Nielsen ratings went through the roof, jolting the entire television and advertising industries. While the cautious executives at CBS and NBC glumly contemplated their lack of imagination, their counterparts at ABC celebrated. Under Roone Arledge's magic touch, *Monday Night Football* became a national institution.[27]

Part of the magic was that Arledge pulled out all the stops in terms of modern television gadgetry. He flooded the stadiums with cameras, even mounted one on wheels that moved up and down the sideline to give close-up coverage of the line of scrimmage. Instant replays, isolation shots of individual players, and other special effects abounded. Special microphones picked up the sideline chatter, and cameras honed in on outrageously costumed fans (dressed like dogs in Cleveland, hogs in Washington) and homemade signs that were draped around the stadium carrying sometimes clever and (more or less) humorous messages that often incorporated the letters ABC.

But the real show was in the broadcast booth. Instead of the traditional two-man broadcasting team of football wonks, Arledge decided to put three wise men in the booth, including two "color" commentators who brought contrasting styles and personalities. One was Don Meredith, a former quarterback for the Dallas Cowboys. Possessed of a rural Texas wit that included a healthy skepticism about the essential importance of the game in which he had been a star, Meredith was capable of many an irreverent comment. On those occasions when he arrived in the broadcast booth, well fortified from a visit to the hotel bar, he might even break into an off-key country-western song. Meredith would leave the show in 1974 but return for another seven years in 1977. Opposite Meredith, Arledge placed a stereotypical embodiment of the arrogant New Yorker, Howard Cosell. After graduating from law school in 1940 and completing military service, Cosell practiced law for several years, building a practice that included several professional athletes as clients. He began dabbing in sports radio, eventually closing his law office in 1956 when he joined ABC radio. By 1960, he had emerged as an especially skilled

Figure 10.1 The three-man *Monday Night Football* broadcasting team poses before a game in 1971. On the left is the ever-loquacious Howard Cosell, while his sometimes friendly, sometimes not so friendly adversary, former Dallas Cowboy quarterback Don Meredith, is on the right. In the middle, where he often found himself during the frequent Cosell–Meredith dust-ups, is former New York Giants halfback, play-by-play announcer Frank Gifford. © Bettmann/CORBIS.

boxing commentator for ABC's televised fights, but he reported on all mainstream sports.[28]

Cosell became famous for his lucid, penetrating commentaries, which he did extemporaneously, thanks to his amazing facility for accurately recalling sports statistics and detailed information. Possessed of a massive ego, he was prone to making bold assertions about a particular player's capability or a coach's limitations as if he were expounding upon newfound truths soon to be etched in stone. His Brooklyn accent and palpable intellectual arrogance absolutely grated upon middle America. Well before his arrival on *MNF*, he had established his reputation for "telling it like it is" – that is, providing blunt and ofttimes critical commentary on the performance of athletes, coaches, and teams. Cosell's irreverent brand of sports broadcasting contrasted sharply with that of his peers, whose reporting was not all that far removed from the "Gee-Whiz" school of the 1920s. In the initial Monday night game, Cosell sparked a flurry of angry telephone and telegraph messages demanding his termination when he bluntly criticized Joe Namath for forcing a pass into heavy coverage that led to an untimely interception, and for stating that star Cleveland running back Leroy Kelly was "not having a compelling game." Fans were not used to such honest appraisals of their heroes.

Meredith and Cosell began their long stint on *MNF* by joking with each other, often trying to outdo the other with their critical insights into the game, but as the years rolled by their banter increasingly became laced with vitriol. Whatever their point of disagreement, their byplay often was more entertaining than the game on the field. Their relationship, rocky from the start and fired by personality differences and competition, quickly reached an adversarial level the first season on one cold November night in Philadelphia when Cosell, possibly suffering from the flu but definitely feeling the effects of several martinis, unceremoniously threw up on Meredith's fancy cowboy boots. The third man in the booth, Keith Jackson, had the responsibility of providing continuity by describing the flow of the game, but he was overshadowed by his jousting partners. After one season, Jackson happily returned to his first love of college football and was replaced by a former New York Giants star halfback, the telegenic Frank Gifford. This trio would make Monday nights an exciting time, drawing high ratings by enticing millions of viewers to their special show even if they cared not a whit for football. Announcers would come and go over the years, usually to considerable media comment, but never replicate the magic of the Howard and Dandy Don show. Nonetheless, *MNF* would remain a staple in the programming of ABC until it turned the event over to it corporate partner ESPN in 2006.

ESPN: All Sports, All the Time

Chet Simmons knew sports broadcasting. In the late winter of 1979, he stood astride the world of televised sports as President of NBC Sports. As a young television executive in the 1960s, Simmons had helped launch the *Wide World of Sports* at ABC, and more recently had made NBC the first among equals in the small, clubby world of network sports broadcasting. When asked his response to a recent announcement about the creation of a cable network dedicated exclusively to sports, Simmons confidently predicted, "Cable sports networks won't work. There are not enough people watching cable. I think this sports network is doomed, to be honest."[29]

Like Simmons, most established network executives viewed the idea as ill advised, if not simply goofy. The problems seemed daunting. How many viewers wanted to watch sports at 3 o'clock in the morning? Would over-saturation of the market drive down ratings? Where would the network get enough content to fill 168 hours of programming each week? With only 13 million homes connected to cable, just 18 percent of the total television market, how could it hope to attract serious advertising dollars? Would independent cable companies be willing to pay for the rights to carry its programs when nearly all cable networks provided their's at no cost? With American sports fans conditioned by 30 years of receiving their televised sports for free over the three major networks, how could a company convince viewers to pay for cable sports?

Three months later, Chet Simmons had learned enough to risk his career on the idea. He signed on as the new president of the cable network, giving it immediate credibility among independent cable company executives and advertisers. Simmons appreciated that the recently introduced 24-hour Cable News Network (CNN) had demonstrated that it could attract viewers. Why not one that catered to the American obsession for sports? Simmons thus changed his mind, and on July 18, 1979, it was announced that he was leaving his prime job at NBC for an untested, unknown and high-risk company located in the backwater town of Bristol, Connecticut. His decision stunned the communications industry. It would be only the first of many surprises that the new network would provide over the next quarter century.[30]

The oft-told company tale has it that the idea of an all-sports network originated with Bill Rasmussen and his 23-year-old son Scott while they were sitting in a Waterford, Connecticut, traffic jam during a steamy summer day in August 1978.[31] Recently fired from his position as public relations director and television announcer for the New England Whalers hockey team, the entrepreneurially inclined elder Rasmussen was contemplating his next career, and he turned to thinking big thoughts about the recent developments in the cable television field. While considering the possibility of creating a cable hookup for the Whalers, he had learned about the potential of satellites to transform cable television. Satellites had already proved they could receive and reflect back to earth sharp images with incredible speed, precision and reliability, and it was this capability that had prompted some two thousand local cable companies to spring up across the United States during the 1970s. Informed that he could rent a transponder on an RCA satellite that could blanket the entire United States 24 hours a day for just $35,000 a month, he signed the contract although he had little money in the bank.

Certain of the prospects, Rasmussen gambled that he could find willing investors. After being repeatedly rebuffed, Rasmussen found the financing he needed when Getty Oil executive Stuart Evey agreed to invest $10 million, in return for 85 percent control of what would be called the Entertainment and Sports Programming Network (ESPN). Rasmussen had located his company in the small city of Bristol, Connecticut, because of a good deal offered by a city government eager to unload a vacant lot. In summer 1979, a satellite dish and a foundation for a studio appeared on the lot. But even as President Rasmussen sought to turn his dream into reality, he found himself being pushed out the door. Evey viewed Rasmussen as unpredictable and lacking the ability to control a large organization. He muscled him aside, hiring Chet Simmons to get the project under professional control. With the launch date set for early September 1979, Simmons frenetically hired a group of writers, producers, technicians and announcers, including a youthful

Chris Berman, whose booming voice, corny humor, and unabashed enthusiasm would make him the network's most recognizable icon.[32]

At 7 p.m. on September 7, 1979, ESPN hit the airwaves with a brief promotional announcement, bouncing its signal to 650 affiliates across the United States and to their two million subscribers via RCA's Satcom I. The first live telecast began promptly at 7:30. It was an inauspicious start for such an ambitious sports network – a slow pitch softball game between the Kentucky Bourbons and the Milwaukee Schlitzes. The latter nickname caused Chet Simmons heartburn every time the announcer repeated it because he had just signed Anheuser-Busch and Budweiser to a much-needed $1.4 million advertising contract. The softball game was followed by live wrestling and a half-hour live studio-based "Sports Recap" show. Reruns of the softball game and a taped tennis match from France kept the station on the air until 4 a.m. The next morning those who tuned in saw a game of munster hurling from Ireland, a variety of field hockey in which grown men in short kilts ran around a large field wacking at a ball and each other with wooden sticks.

This type of eclectic, even oddball programming would characterize ESPN for many years. The network broadcast what it could get cheaply, or even better, for free. On the second day, ESPN aired live a college soccer match between Connecticut and UCLA, a taped volleyball match between teams from Korea and Japan, a documentary about marathon racing, and ever more wrestling. The initial reception of fans – "sports junkies" in particular – was positive, but Wall Street and Madison Avenue remained skeptical. Media investment analysts said the new station was a novelty and the viewing public would soon lose interest. One financial analyst noted that the three major networks broadcast 18 hours of sports a week between them, and who could want more than that? *Newsweek* predicted, tongue in cheek, that the network would contribute to marital discord because husbands would sprawl on the couch to watch a meaningless soccer match previously taped in a distant land rather than clean out the basement. *Sports Illustrated* more presciently suggested that the new station "may become the biggest thing in TV sports since *Monday Night Football* and nighttime World Series games."[33]

The hometown *Bristol Press* saw much that was promising:

> It would be premature to say that ESPN represents a threat to the existing big three television networks, but the possibilities are clear. An independent station with the right to beam its programs through a communications satellite can offer alternative programming without affiliating with one of the major networks. The potential now exists for decentralization of television broadcasting, dominated by ABC, CBS, and NBC for three decades. Stations such as the local ESPN are among the first to test the new options opened by the proliferation of communications satellites. They are trailblazers and it will be interesting to monitor their progress.[34]

By spring 1980, ESPN had reached its goal of 24-hour broadcasting, but it had to rely heavily upon taped reruns and a wide range of inconsequential contests it could broadcast live at little or no cost. Thus the viewer was inundated with sports events he or she had probably seldom, if ever, seen: college lacrosse, Australian football, marathon races, college baseball, wind surfing, water skiing, European professional soccer, volleyball, swimming and diving, fencing, track and field, plus an inordinate number of pseudo-sports that the major networks had never considered: karate, rodeo, mud-wrestling, tractor pulls, demolition derbies, bicycle racing, checkers and chess, roller derby, and semiprofessional women's softball. It its first year ESPN offered up 65 different sports for its viewers. And, many of its events were aired – thanks to the miracle of videotape – several times.

On September 7, 2004, ESPN celebrated its 25th anniversary.[35] Its Bristol headquarters had grown to a massive complex of seven large interconnected buildings and its employees numbered over 2,500. The company had gone through several corporate owners, including Capital Cities and (in 1997) Walt Disney. It had become an enormously profitable enterprise, earning an estimated $100 million a year. When Disney purchased Capital Cities, a holding company that included ESPN and ABC, Disney chairman Michael Eisner said that the cable company was "the crown jewel" in this mega acquisition. Its number of subscribers approached 80 million and the small town of Bristol had improbably become the *de facto* capital of the burgeoning world of American sports.[36]

ESPN succeeded because it was able to fill the niches that the three networks left open. Or ineptly fumbled away. In 1981, ESPN thrilled college basketball fans with its coverage of the early rounds of the NCAA tournament, switching from one game to another to show upsets in the making or exciting overtime games. It gradually increased its coverage of major league baseball as the seasons rolled by, and in 1987 finally obtained rights to broadcast a small number of NFL games live – introducing the Sunday night game. After the NCAA lost its monopolistic control of college football in 1983, college games became a major staple, not just on Saturday afternoons and nights; "mid-major" conferences found that they could get considerable national exposure by agreeing to play games during midweek. ESPN also became the normal venue for weekly club boxing, as well as an occasional championship fight that did not go the route of pay-for-view. During the long winter months, an endless procession of college basketball and professional hockey went out over the airwaves. The problem of over-saturation and of lack of material were long forgotten, although the healthy use of re-runs continued to fill the long late night and early morning hours.[37]

ESPN succeeded because of the high quality of reporters, writers, and behind-the-scenes producers it lured to Bristol. Dick Vitale became a national icon for his over-the-top hysterics describing college basketball. Chris Mortensen and John Clayton excelled in reporting on the National Football League, as did Peter Gammons with major league baseball, and Brent Musburger with professional basketball. Sal Marchiano elevated greatly the quality of reporting on boxing, a tradition of excellence that Charlie Steiner carried on during the 1990s. Tom Mees excelled in reporting hockey. Roy Firestone created a special niche with his sensitive and revealing interviews with leading sports figures, many of whose playing days had long since ended. Chris Berman made NFL predictions as the silly "Swami," gave clever nicknames to athletes, and described home runs and long football runs with his patented rat-a-tat "back-back-back-back" or "stumblin' bumblin' rumblin'." Unlike many of his contemporaries at ESPN,

Berman remained loyal to the network and did not depart for a major network gig. Over the years he became a living icon for the network.

Although ESPN steadily increased its live coverage of major events, it was the late evening "SportsCenter" that became its daily, rock-solid foundation. Introduced in 1979 as "Sports ReCap," over the years the hour-long show grew its audience with generous use of video game clips with dual anchors providing commentary and analysis – along with plenty of laughs thrown in for good measure. It became a daily staple for millions of sports fans. Berman became an early host favorite, but he went on to focus on professional football and special assignments. During the early 1990s, the "tag team" pair of Dan Patrick and Keith Olbermann took "SportsCenter" to new heights of popularity with their pungent writing, candid analysis of controversial issues, and irreverent and sparkling spontaneous humor. "SportsCenter" became one of the nation's most watched nightly news shows, the unquestioned source of the nation's best sports coverage. Ultimately, personality conflicts between the tempestuous Olbermann and ESPN executives led to a parting of the ways, but the show retained its high ratings as new talent found its way to Bristol.[38]

ESPN's search for top talent included minorities and women. Greg Gumbel joined the network in 1981 and many African Americans followed and distinguished themselves. The first woman to anchor "SportsCenter" was Brooklyn-born Gayle Gardner, whose sharp writing and controlled on-camera skills made her an instant hit in 1981; soon thereafter other talented women arrived as anchors and reporters, their professional work giving the lie to the assumption that women could not understand and interpret sports at a high professional level. Among these pioneers were Robin Roberts, a former college basketball star whose knowledge of the sport was unequaled, Linda Cohn, Suzy Kolber, Lesley Visser, Bonnie Bernstein, and Karie Ross. Many women were employed as off-camera producers, writers, researchers, and technicians. Although the seldom-told underside of ESPN was replete with allegations of sexual harassment, these women and many others persevered and built strong reputations as professional journalists.

During the 1990s, with the assurance of financial stability provided by an ever-increasing profit stream, ESPN flexed its muscles and expanded into many new enterprises. Various efforts by rival networks to supplant ESPN – Rupert Murdoch's effort in 1999 to connect nine regional sports networks into a national competing network, in particular – proved futile, largely because ESPN had become so firmly established. ESPN demonstrated an ability to continue to innovate and reinvent itself. It also preempted the intentions of its potential rivals by launching ESPN-2 in 1993. Dubbed "The Deuce," it was originally intended to appeal to younger sports fans, with hard-hitting commentary and emphasis upon such offbeat sports as women's beach volleyball, skate boarding, outdoor fishing and hunting, "X-treme" skiing and snow boarding, along with other alternative sports, but over the years ESPN-2 tended to morph into a pale imitation of the parent company, with its live sports featuring such events as "mid-major" football games from Conference USA and the Western Athletic Conference, and a flood of college basketball games not deemed worthy to run on the primary network. ESPN-2 proved an instant financial success, adding millions of dollars to the company's coffers each year, and proving once again that the American people had a seemingly insatiable thirst for anything the resembled sports on the tube. In 1992, it inaugurated a 24-hour radio network that quickly had 250 affiliate stations. In 1996, the company moved into print journalism, launching *ESPN: The Magazine*. Edited in a flashy manner designed to set it apart from the increasingly staid *Sports Illustrated* and appeal to the age demographic of 18–34, its trendy design layout tended to offend older readers (such as this author), who had difficulty separating advertising from the articles, found the garish computer-designed graphics offensive, and who rebelled at the frequent avant garde subject matter and chic writing style. *ESPN: The Magazine*, however, proved an immediate success, cutting into the readership and advertising of *Sports Illustrated*, a fact highlighted by several wars fought by the two magazines over top editorial talent. By 2004, circulation exceeded 900,000.

Not content merely to report upon sports events, ESPN also created its own. In imitation of the annual motion picture Academy Awards, it created the "ESPY" awards at which time individual athletic achievements during the previous year were recognized. In 1995, ESPN launched the *Extreme Games*, soon dubbed the *X-Games*, which provided hours of television footage for the Deuce. The summer *X-Games* featured dangerous high flying competitions of skate boarders and bikers and the winter games outrageous ski jumps and snow boarding bravado. To fill the long summer months, the *Outdoor Games* were created and included contests of wood sawing, tree climbing, log rolling, fly fishing, trap shooting, and hunting dogs racing over and under barriers. Sports fans were also lured to enormous glitzy ESPN sports bars and restaurants in Baltimore, Washington, DC, New York and other cities, where the standard fare was oversized burgers and spicy chicken wings served awash with large schooners of high-priced designer beers with scores of television sets naturally tuned into ESPN. What insiders now called Planet ESPN had become the cash cow for the Disney corporation, producing an estimated 25 percent of the company's profits by the early twenty-first century. In 2004, one Wall Street analyst estimated that ESPN was generating in excess of $500 million in profits on revenue of $1.5 billion. The venerable Wall Street firm of Sanford C. Bernstein estimated the company's market value at $15.5 billion.[39]

11 College Sports in the Modern Era

Writing in 1929, Henry Pritchett of the Carnegie Foundation summarized the dilemma confronting college athletics:

> It takes no tabulation of statistics to prove that the young athlete who gives himself for months, body and soul, to training under a professional coach for a grueling contest, staged to focus the attention of thousands of people, and upon which many thousands of dollars will be staked, will find no time or energy for any serious intellectual effort.[1]

As the Carnegie Report established, big-time programs had already crossed the line from amateurism to a quasi-professional model. In one way or another, institutions found ways to pay their athletes. Journalist John Tunis, in commenting on the Carnegie Report a month after it appeared, aptly summarized the issue:

> The colleges of the country make money out of intercollegiate sports. The colleges take the money and use it. If their presidents really desired to clean up the athletic situation, they could do so and they would find an amazing number of alumni behind them. But alas, in that event no money would be made.

Tunis concluded that the presidents "will probably do nothing" about the problem. "If it did nothing else," he glumly concluded, "the Carnegie Report brought to light the intellectual dishonesty of the American college."[2] With huge stadiums to fill and high-priced coaches to pay, big-time intercollegiate athletes was already well along the road to becoming, as Murray Sperber would later describe the multi-billion-dollar commercial enterprise, "College Sports, Inc."[3]

As the decades went by, the problems that the Carnegie Commission had identified were magnified many times. Walter Byers served as executive director of the

NCAA from the pivotal year of 1951 until 1987. One would assume that this executive would be among the staunchest defenders of the system he helped create. But after his retirement, Byers published a surprising *mea culpa*, confessing his sins and turning upon his former employer with surprising vengeance. Ascribing the treatment of "student-athletes" by the collegiate athletic system to a "neoplantation" mentality, Byers denounced the very programs he had helped build over his long career. Intercollegiate athletics, he said, were "biased against human nature and simple fairness."[4]

On the eve of the Second World War, intercollegiate athletics remained firmly under the control of individual schools and, in some instances, conferences. The guiding principle was "home rule." This meant that each institution was responsible for supervising itself in the matters of recruitment, academic eligibility, and financial aid. The NCAA had no significant enforcement powers and was little more than a national clearing house that established game rules and conducted a few national championships. In 1940, its largest source of income was a $10,000 profit made on the eight-team national basketball tournament. Its second source of income was the annual dues of $25 paid by each institutional member, which numbered about 250.

During the 1930s, big-time football found itself on the defensive. The echoes of the Carnegie Report resonated, and several motion pictures presented football in an unfavorable light. Influential journalists – including John Tunis, Sol Metzger, Francis Wallace, and Paul Gallico – published articles in popular magazines detailing abuses. For example, in 1939 Gallico wrote that college football was "one of the last strongholds of genuine old-fashioned hypocrisy . . . the leader in the field of double-dealing, deception, sham, cant, hambug, and organized hypocrisy."[5]

The Sanity Code Is Scuttled

Between 1939 and 1948, NCAA membership responded to the drumbeat of criticism with an ongoing discussion about the role of intercollegiate athletics and the policies under which it should exist. Finally, in 1948, the so-called Sanity Code was formally adopted. The Code was a noble effort to find a middle ground between pure amateurism and crass professionalism. Under the Code, the NCAA recognized the right of member institutions to provide full tuition (but no living expenses) to athletes, but *only if* they met the same academic standards required of other students and *only if* financial need existed. Athletes could also hold legitimate jobs, on or off campus, to pay for living expenses.[6] The Sanity Code was a notable effort to establish as policy the traditional ideal of amateurism. It also created an enforcement committee with the power to investigate violations and impose sanctions, including to recommend in extreme cases expulsion from the NCAA, which would require a two-thirds vote by the membership.

Not surprisingly, within a year the NCAA found itself in crisis. Many institutions complained long and loud, with the University of Virginia leading the way. They argued that the Sanity Code would devastate their football programs and they openly defied the NCAA and its policy. The NCAA responded by announcing that seven schools were in violation and recommended expulsion. Most were members of the Southern Conference: Virginia, Virginia Military Institute, Virginia Polytechnic Institute, the University of Maryland, and the Citadel. In addition Boston College, and Villanova were on the list of the "Sinful Seven." Faced with the possibility of the breakup of the association, the NCAA blinked and ingloriously retreated. At its national convention in 1950, the motion failed to get a two-thirds majority, although more than one-half of the members voted in favor. The Sanity Code was then quietly scuttled.

Almost immediately, the NCAA moved in the opposite direction, voting in 1952 to authorize full scholarships based solely on athletic ability, stripping from its policy book any academic achievement or financial need requirement. As the debate on this fundamental shift took place, the wisecracking head coach of Michigan State College, Duffy Daughterty, made it clear that in one way or another coaches would find a way to funnel monies to their players: "Our grants-in-aid are based on academic achievement and need. By academic achievement, we mean the boy can read and write. By need – well, we don't take a boy unless we need him."[7] During the next few years, under its first full-time executive director, former Big Ten associate commissioner Walter Byers, the NCAA tinkered with its new financial-aid policy and in 1956 adopted an "Official Interpretation" that allowed each institution to provide an athlete with educational expenses covering tuition and fees, books, room and board, and $15 a month for incidental living expenses. Byers instructed all members that they were now to refer to the individuals receiving the so-called "full ride athletic scholarship" as "student-athletes."[8]

Creation of a Cartel

During the 1950s, the NCAA was transformed from a weak, ineffectual national coordinating body into a powerful economic cartel. This occurred, not surprisingly, during a time of crisis. Just as the shock of the basketball points-shaving scandals of 1951 were receding from the headlines, a series of academic fraud cases took their place, beginning with expulsion of half the high-ranked West Point football team for academic cheating just before the 1951 season was to begin. Then it was revealed that officials at William and Mary College, which was seeking to attain status as a major football power, had engaged in massive fraud that included forged and altered high-school transcripts, coaches giving grades of "A" to players for physical education courses they did not attend, and the approval of pay slips for campus jobs not done. In 1953, Michigan State, recently admitted to the Big Ten, was hit by revelations that it made an estimated $50,000 of illegal payments from a "slush fund" to football players. On the West Coast the premier Pacific Coast Conference simultaneously had placed four of its eight members – California, UCLA, Southern California, and Washington – on probation for flagrant violations in recruiting; each of the four schools was found to be paying star football players out of secret accounts established from booster donations.[9] This flurry of negative publicity fueled the demand that the NCAA develop a strong rules-enforcement division.

The NCAA had actually demonstrated its power to discipline a member institution in 1952, when Byers and his executive committee worked behind the scenes with the Southeastern Conference to force a recalcitrant University of Kentucky to cancel its 1952–53 basketball season as a result of player involvement with gamblers over a series of years. This bold move greatly enhanced the prestige and power of the NCAA, or as Byers put it, "it gave a new and needed legitimacy to the NCAA's fledgling effort to police big-time college sports."[10] Big Ten Commissioner Wayne Duke recognized the new power that the NCAA had assumed: "the Kentucky action just indelibly stamped on the public that the NCAA meant business. It was first thing out of the box . . . and it gave the NCAA clout."[11]

The NCAA also sought economic clout by taking control of the sale of rights for televising football games. During the 1940s, the University of Pennsylvania had pioneered in the development of television technology, and its cooperation with the DuMont Laboratories led to a contract with the fledgling (and ill-fated) DuMont network to televise its games. During the late 1940s, Notre Dame had signed an exclusive contract with NBC for national coverage, and Oklahoma, USC, Michigan, and Tulane had made agreements with local stations. Most college sports programs had shied away from television, however, fearing it would cut into ticket sales. By 1951, several conferences had adopted policies prohibiting the televising of any games.

Thus, in a major step toward establishing itself as a cartel, in 1951 the NCAA national convention voted overwhelmingly 161–7 that the association would control the televising of *all* college football games. According to historian Ronald Smith, the NCAA's bold move put it "on its way toward national control . . . and reigning in a future dominant entity."[12] The plan was to permit the national telecast of one game per week, with an occasional set of regional games being offered about once a month. The University of Pennsylvania, with a three-year $850,000 contract in hand, was not about to give up its television income without a fight. Its president, the former youthful Governor of Minnesota and presidential hopeful Harold Stassen, decided not to abide by the NCAA policy, thinking that his position would be supported in federal court under antitrust law (in 1984 his position was affirmed by the US Supreme Court). He also hoped that Notre Dame would persevere with its own ambitious television plans, but its new president, the Reverend Theodore Hesburgh, decided that Notre Dame did not need potential bad publicity and cut a deal with Walter Byers that informally guaranteed Notre Dame at least two television appearances a year in return for canceling its deal with NBC. Stassen soon learned that his adversary was a foe to be reckoned with. The NCAA declared Penn a member "not in good standing" and threatened expulsion; five of Penn's upcoming football opponents informed Stassen that they would not play unless Penn abided by the new NCAA television policy. Stassen surrendered, decided not to take the case to the federal courts, and the Quaker football team fell from its lofty perch as a national power.

The leadership of the NCAA had learned how to wield its power. It established a policy of offering the highest-bidding network eight national games and five regional games each football season. The NCAA received $1,250,000 in 1955, with the revenues shared among the participating teams and other members of the NCAA, and an unspecified amount being retained by the NCAA to cover its growing operational costs. The value of the rights rose to $3 million by 1960. The NCAA's enforcement division learned that a threat to exclude an institution from appearances on television was a powerful club by which to keep wayward institutions in line.

Emphasis and De-Emphasis

In 1960, college sports stood on the eve of a period of enormous growth. Although much of public scrutiny was directed at major college basketball and football, in fact the NCAA was becoming a large, sprawling, and diverse organization that embraced a wide variety of missions. The great majority of the members of the NCAA were small institutions that fielded a variety of teams with no pretensions of athletic grandeur. In 1973, the NCAA created a three-tiered grouping of schools. In Division III were several hundred small colleges that offered no athletic scholarships. Division II schools were permitted to offer a restricted number of athletic grants-in-aid, while Division I schools could provide a larger number of "full-ride" grants-in-aid.

The main focus of intercollegiate athletics, however, was on big-time football and basketball. Football, even at many institutions with national ambitions, continued to pose a dilemma because of its high costs. Consequently, between 1945 and 1960, more than sixty once-hopeful big-time football schools either dropped the sport altogether or opted to "de-emphasize" it by reducing financial aid and slashing staff and operations budgets. Several institutions had canceled football during the war, and some, such as Mercer University in Georgia, and Gonzaga University in Washington, chose not to revive it. Many schools that had held high football aspirations before the war cut back their programs to affordable proportions. Included in this group were Washington University of St Louis, Western Reserve University, and Carnegie Tech, all of which had once enjoyed their moments in the national pigskin spotlight.

The flurry of canceled programs was reason for concern among football enthusiasts. In part, the trend was a residual effect of the anti-football movement of the 1930s, but the main culprit was the more immediate financial distress caused by falling attendance. A large number of private urban Catholic universities were among those leading the de-emphasis movement. The University of San Francisco stunned the football world when it dropped the sport on the heels of an undefeated, untied, nationally 10th-ranked season in 1951. Despite the heroics of All-American running back Ollie Matson, the Dons nonetheless produced a $75,000 deficit along with their spotless record. The most prominent university to drop football during this period was Georgetown University, which in the late 1930s had won 43 consecutive games. Its president cited football's lack of educational value in an article in the *Saturday Evening Post*, commenting that the sport provided nothing besides public entertainment. Other Catholic institutions followed suit, among them St Bonaventure, Duquesne, Villanova, Fordham, Detroit, Xavier (of Cincinnati), and Marquette.

The most significant change in football occurred ironically on the East Coast on campuses where the sport had originated. One-time football giants Yale, Princeton, and Harvard decided to end any pretensions of competing for national football honors. These fiercely independent private institutions had resisted granting any control over their internal operations to any external body, such as an athletic conference. In 1945, eight elite institutions signed the first Ivy Group Accord, which placed heavy emphasis on unsubsidized football and the maintenance of high academic standards for athletes. But one member of the group, Pennsylvania, continued to aspire to national recognition and in 1948 fielded one of the strongest teams in the nation. Between 1938 and 1948, the Quakers had gone 34–5–5 against Ivy opponents. When the NCAA forced Penn to abandon its lucrative television contract with the DuMont nework, its big-time football aspirations were doomed. By then, the institution was more than ready to de-emphasize football and was welcomed back into the good graces of its Ivy peers.

Between 1952 and 1956, the Ivy Group formalized itself into the Ivy League and instituted a series of reforms aimed directly at the excesses of big-time football. The League's membership included Princeton, Columbia, Yale, Dartmouth, Harvard, Brown, Cornell, and Pennsylvania. For starters, the new league banned a leading symbol of commitment to big-time football – spring practice, which had long been a contentious issue that divided faculty and coaching staffs. Off-campus recruiting was sharply curtailed, and no student could play whose tuition and fees were paid by someone not closely connected to his own family, thereby eliminating a long-standing practice whereby an alumnus or booster "adopted" a potential athlete and paid his expenses. Special admission policies for athletes were abolished. So too were post-season bowl game appearances, training tables, financial subsidies to athletes (although they could compete for academic scholarships), athletic slush funds, cushy on-campus jobs, and clinics for high school coaches (another recruiting subterfuge). Beyond doubt, the Ivy League schools took the position that they no longer had any interest in seeking national football fame. The storied days of Walter Camp were history.

Although many alumni screamed to high heaven, the new Ivy League became a model for the practice of amateur athletics in an academic environment, and within a short time it became the source of alumni pride as healthy rivalries developed on a level field of competition. These eight institutions thus assured themselves that they would not have the ignominy of a football scandal blemishing their reputations, and each set out to develop for their students broad-based athletic programs that were funded within the general institutional budget. The programs were designed to be "independent of won-loss or competitive record" by "approaching athletics as a key part of the student's regular undergraduate experience." Ivy League football teams compete at the Division I-AA level (but do not participate in the national playoffs) while its other teams compete in Division I-A.

Upon occasion, its basketball champions have won NCAA tournament games, with Princeton in 1965 and Pennsylvania in 1979 reaching the Final Four. The Ivy League has remained an eight-school operation, and today it supports competition in more than 30 separate sports for men and women, with many teams excelling and winning national championships in lacrosse, rowing, swimming, tennis, squash, and handball. The Ivy League also prides itself on its "rigorous academic standards" that year in and year out have produced the highest graduation rates of any athletic conference in the country. As other Division I programs opted for a professional model designed to enhance commercial opportunities, the Ivy League became a lonely beacon adhering to values that college administrators and coaches had long talked about but never quite got around to establishing.

Woody and the Bear

With the NCAA established as the central authority, those schools pursuing big-time football established a commercial, professional model of intercollegiate athletics. Over the years, the big-time football schools exerted their power to move the major conferences further and further away from the amateur ideal, leaving the Ivy League increasingly isolated as an anomaly, a curious island of integrity in a rising sea of rampant commercialism, cheating, and hypocrisy. With football producing the great bulk of sports revenue, head football coaches naturally demanded that their needs be met first. Between 1955 and 1965, long-time restrictions on substitutions were removed. This led to the development of specialized defensive and offensive players, accompanied by a host of other "specialists" such as punter, place-kicker, and kick-off and punt returner. Where teams were usually restricted to less than 50 players, coaches now assembled squads reaching 150. Free substitution contributed markedly to a much more exciting, if specialized, type of game. It also meant that football budgets had to be increased substantially. Coaches now routinely signed 30 to 40 new players to grants-in-aid each recruiting season. The size of travel squads increased from 35 to more than 60, all justified by the new imperatives established by free substitution.

Time and again, the NCAA convention acceded to the demands of coaches. In 1972, the NCAA convention voted to permit freshmen to play, a major policy change that most academics deplored because they believed it essential for freshmen to have an opportunity to adjust to college life without having to prepare for and compete in high-pressure games. At the same time, the NCAA annual convention voted to reduce grants-in-aid from a four-year commitment to just one year. This meant that an athlete who was not playing at an acceptable level could be dropped and a new athlete given his grant-in-aid. In 1973, under intense pressure from coaches, the NCAA lowered eligibility requirements for a grant-in-aid to the point that nearly any high-school graduate could meet minimum standards.

High paid coaches were expected to produce winning teams and annual trips to post-season bowl games. They responded by increasing the size of the coaching staffs, demanding the construction of new training facilities, athletic dormitories, and other amenities. The argument for these enhancements was always that football paid the cost of "non-revenue" sports and were necessary to keep pace with the opposition. In reality, most football programs actually lost money each year and required subsidy from the institution's general fund. Economists who have attempted to make sense of athletic budgets confess that there is no way to determine actual bottom lines. Smith College economist Andrew Zimbalist has examined the issue extensively and concludes that only a handful of, if any, big-time programs actually operate in the black. To balance their budgets, in cooperation with compliant university administrators, athletics program managers shift costs to other university budget lines, tap into campus buildings and grounds budgets to maintain their facilities, and offload salaries to instructional and administrative budgets. Longtime critic Murray Sperber has even argued that the deficits created by athletic programs have negatively impacted academic programs because of stealth transfers of funds from instructional budgets to cover athletic department deficits. One of the unrecognized ironies of commercialized college athletic programs is that they have been able to shield themselves from the Internal Revenue Service by claiming to be non-profit educational programs.[13]

Establishing this model for the major football program as a commercial enterprise were two men who dominated the game from the 1950s until the late 1970s, Woodrow Wayne "Woody" Hayes and Paul "Bear" Bryant. Their programs set the standard that competing schools tried to replicate, thereby driving up the expenses of competitors who sought to stay even. They also became powerful political figures within their home states and their influence extended well beyond their campuses to the entire states of Ohio and Alabama.

The long coaching career of Woody Hayes encompassed the many changes in college football that occurred during the mid-twentieth century. A 1935 graduate of Denison College, Hayes first coached in Ohio high schools, taught social studies, and then served in the US Navy during the Second World War. When he returned from serving in the South Pacific in 1946, he assumed the head-coaching position at his alma mater, and then moved on to Miami University of Ohio in 1949. After producing a 10–1 record and a Salad Bowl upset win over Arizona State in 1950, Hayes was selected as head coach at Ohio State following an emotionally charged, highly publicized search process in which many fans sought to have Paul Brown brought back to campus. Hayes had impressed the search committee with his strong recruiting skills, and was named to replace Wes Fesler, who had produced three consecutive winning seasons, a Big Ten championship, and a Rose Bowl victory, but had committed the unforgivable sin of losing four consecutive times to arch-rival Michigan.[14]

Possessed of a fiery temper and committed to a philosophy of football that emphasized raw physical power and a simplistic play book, Hayes also had a rare touch for recruiting. To be certain, he had the advantage of coaching the only major-college team in talent-rich Ohio, where some 40,000 high school boys played on 800 teams. A continuum of skilled players to the Columbus campus enabled him to field a nationally ranked team every season after his initial 4–3–1 debut. In 1954, the Buckeyes went undefeated and stomped Southern California in the Rose Bowl. A national championship that year greatly enhanced his status in football-crazed Columbus, and in 1957 he won another national title. His teams became famous for his "three yards and a cloud of dust" offense, in which his bevy of powerful running backs ran a conservative offense behind a massive offensive line. His defenses became known for their punishing, aggressive play, but he perhaps was most famous for his disdain for the forward pass, stating that "three things can go wrong when you pass, and two of them are bad" – an incomplete pass or an interception.

Hayes became the most popular resident of Ohio, much in demand as an entertaining after-dinner speaker, the confidant of Republican governors and senators, appreciated for his knowledge of military history (from which he often drew analogies that he applied to football situations), admired for his inability to accept defeat graciously, and well known for his emotional outbursts on the sidelines. His hard-nosed style of play was reflective of Ohio's hard-working factory workers and small farmers. On fall Saturday afternoons his teams played before 90,000 scarlet-clad fans in the famed "horseshoe" Ohio Stadium that had been erected as a war memorial in 1921, and millions of Ohioans listened in on a state-wide radio network. Hayes became the epitome of the controlling, demanding, domineering coach. He prowled the sidelines in a state of near-constant fury during games, often smashing equipment, turning his rage equally on referees and his own players. Off the field he oversaw an elaborate recruiting network of booster and alumni euphemistically called "the committee."

For more than a century, the Ohio State–Michigan rivalry has been one of the most intense in all of college football. Representing neighboring Midwestern states, the two universities first played in 1897. When Ohio State joined the Western Conference (later renamed the Big Ten) in 1912, the rivalry intensified. Coaches at both schools ultimately kept or lost their jobs based on their record against their rival, always the final game of the regular season. Although Hayes lost his first Michigan game, he proceeded to win 11 of the next 15 games, earning the unquestioning affection of Buckeye fans.

The rivalry grew white-hot in 1969 when Glenn "Bo" Schembechler stunned Hayes by accepting the Wolverines' head-coaching position. Hayes viewed it as a personal betrayal by one of his top students. Often called "Little Woody," Schembechler had played tackle for Hayes at Miami of Ohio, and he was Hayes's offensive-line coach from 1959 through 1963, at which time he returned to Miami as head coach. Schembechler was Hayes's equal when it came to emphasizing the fundamentals of fierce blocking and tackling. He also exhibited the same inner fury and drive, accepting nothing but victory. Pugnacious and defiant, on one notable occasion while a Buckeye assistant, after Hayes, in normal form, angrily tossed a chair across the room, Schembechler casually picked up the chair and threw it back at him. These two friends, both fierce competitors who could not abide defeat, turned the traditional rivalry into a personal no-holds-barred street fight. The stakes were raised even higher when Schembechler did the unthinkable by invading Ohio during recruiting season to pick off some of Ohio's top prospects. Hayes, however, disdained recruiting players from "that state up north" (he was not known to utter the word "Michigan"). Within short order, nearly one-third of Schembechler's squads were comprised of Ohio high school graduates, adding additional spice to the annual November bloodbath. During the ten years that these two men competed against each other, the Big Ten became known as the "Big Two and the Little Eight," as either Michigan or Ohio State won the Big Ten championship each year.

Hayes's frequent, well-publicized public eruptions on the sidelines were an embarrassment to the university – breaking yardstick markers, pushing cameras into the face of photographers, confronting officials at midfield – but tolerant, perhaps fearful, administrators took no action. Winning, the old saying goes, covers a multitude of sins. It was thus fitting that Hayes's famous temper led to a premature end to his coaching career. Near the end of a close game in the 1978 Gator Bowl against Clemson, with the Buckeyes marching to take the lead, Tiger linebacker Charlie Bauman picked off an errant Ohio State pass in front of the Ohio State bench, ensuring Clemson's victory. As Bauman ran out of bounds, Hayes slugged him in the face, an instinctive act that television cameras picked up and repeatedly showed on instant replay. Such an egregious act could not go unpunished, even at Ohio State and even by the now-legendary Woody Hayes. The next day, he was fired by athletic director Hugh Hindman, bringing an abrupt end to his 28-year career at Ohio State. His well-oiled and well-financed football machine had produced a record of 205–61–10, including 13 Big Ten championships, and after his death a main street through campus was named Woody Hayes Drive.

If Woody Hayes was idolized in Ohio, his many peccadillos notwithstanding, Paul "Bear" Bryant was immortalized in Alabama. More than two decades after he retired, head coaches of the Crimson Tide were still compared – and found wanting – to the Bear. Born the eleventh of 12 children to a poor sharecropping family in Fordyce, Arkansas, at the age of 13 young Paul gained his nickname when he accepted a challenge to wrestle a live bear at a carnival for one dollar. He reckoned that he could earn a dollar for a minute's effort as opposed to working 12 hours picking cotton for 50 cents. Bryant found an escape from rural poverty in the midst of the Great Depression when he accepted a football scholarship to attend the University of Alabama. He played end opposite one of the greatest pass receivers ever to play the game, Don Hutson. In 1945, he became head coach at Maryland, but resigned after one year when the president overturned his decision to boot a player off the squad for violating team rules. He moved on to the University of Kentucky, where his teams compiled a 60–23–5 record at a school that had never before enjoyed much gridiron success. Bryant, however, realized that basketball would remain king in bluegrass country, and after eight seasons accepted the head coaching position at Texas A&M. Before the first season in 1954, he took his 111-member squad to a remote camp at Juction, Texas, where he conducted a "brutal boot camp" in searing heat. Sixty players quit the team before it returned to College Station, and the decimated team won but one game. However, he had put his personal stamp on the team and recruits flooded to College Station. In 1956 the Aggies won the Southwest Conference championship with a 9–1 record.[15]

In 1957 Bryant returned to his alma mater to resuscitate the once-proud Alabama program that had fallen on hard times. His initial salary as coach and athletic director was an astronomical $57,000 – Alabama might have been a financially hard-pressed university with bottom-tier faculty salaries, but finding booster support to secure the services of a winning football coach was no problem. Bryant's teams more than satisfied his financial backers. His first team won five games, one more victory than had been won in the three previous seasons, and in 1959, his team went 7–2–2 and ranked 10th in the nation. That team went to a bowl game, beginning a 24-year string of consecutive post-season appearances. But that was only the prelude to a record-setting run. Under Bryant, Alabama won six national championships (1961, 1964, 1965, 1973, 1978, and 1979). Utilizing the support of a large and generous group of alumni and boosters, Bryant had the resources to build state-of-the-art facilities and to out-recruit his Southeastern Conference foes, in-state rival Auburn in particular. His squads included 125 players on grants-in-aid and several dozen other "walk-on" hopefuls. His enormous coaching staff included 17 full-time assistants, supplemented by a cadre of graduate assistants and other support personnel.

In 1963, his career was threatened when the *Saturday Evening Post* published an article alleging that he had conspired with the Athletic Director at the University of Georgia to obtain the game plan of the University of Georgia team prior to the season-opening game. According to the convoluted story, Georgia Athletic Director Wally Butts had been removed from his head football coaching position against his will, and in retaliation sought to sabotage the coach who had replaced him. The alleged scheme that the *Post* reported had Butts, deeply in debt and facing a forced retirement, seeking to assure that the Crimson Tide would cover the points spread of 17 so he could make a killing through a Chicago bookie. The evidence hinged upon allegations made by an Atlanta insurance agent who claimed that while making a long distance telephone call he was somehow patched into a conversation between Butts and Bryant in which he listened for 15 minutes while they discussed the Bulldogs' game plan. Both Butts and Bryant denied these sensational allegations and sued the magazine. At trial in an Atlanta federal court the allegations were not proven and the *Post* was ordered to pay Butts over $400,000 in damages. Bryant proved to be a star witness against the magazine. Shortly thereafter Bryant and the *Post* settled out of court. Former Notre Dame football player, Attorney James Kirby, who observed the trial for the Southeastern Conference, later wrote a book about the case and contended that while the *Post* had acted unprofessionally and that its allegations were weak, nonetheless concluded that important questions about the telephone conversation (which records showed did occur) between Bryant and Butts went unexplored at trial. While stopping short of accusing Bryant of wrongdoing, Kirby nonetheless says that the episode was closed with many key questions left unanswered.[16]

Although this bizarre episode for a time threatened Bryant's career, it was soon forgotten, as the Bear proceeded to win championships. Bryant had long chafed under the "white only" gentlemen's agreement that precluded the recruitment of black players. But working in a state where the rabid segregationist George C. Wal-

lace was governor, Bryant had to bide his time. But when desegregation did occur in Deep South universities, he led the Southeastern Conference in recruiting African American players. By 1973, he had black captains leading his Crimson Tide teams which now numbered 40 percent African American. When Bryant retired he had amassed a career record of 323–85–17, breaking Amos Alonzo Stagg's all-time winning record. He had been named national Coach of the Year three times by Associated Press. After his death in 1983, the NCAA's Coach of the Year award was named in his honor. The weird story of the alleged conspiracy to obtain a rival team's secrets had long since been forgotten, and Bryant's harsh treatment of his Texas A&M players in 1954 became the subject of a warm and fuzzy made-for-television movie in 2002.

Figure 11.1 University of Alabama coach Paul "Bear" Bryant is carried from the field on November 14, 1981, after his record-setting 314th career coaching win against Penn State. At Alabama he took the Crimson Tide to 29 consecutive bowl games and won five national championships. He often said that his entire life was coaching, and he died in January, 1983, just 28 days after he announced his retirement from coaching. © Bettmann/CORBIS.

Deceit and Deception: the NCAA and Gender Equity

In 1972, when Congress enacted its annual Education Act, few persons took notice of an amendment – labeled Title IX – offered by Congresswoman Edith Green of Oregon, which stated, "No person in the United States shall, on the basis of sex, be excluded from participation in, be denied the benefits of, or be subjected to discrimination under any education program or activity receiving Federal financial assistance." Women's groups, however, took close notice and soon had lawyers for public school districts and colleges and universities examining the law. The attorneys told administrators that the law clearly stated that any school receiving federal funds had to establish athletic programs for females at a level consistent with those for males. If schools failed to do so, they faced the possibility of the loss of all federal funding. At the public-school level, compliance occurred relatively quickly and with limited opposition. Budgets were adjusted, locker rooms built, coaches hired, schedules arranged, and interscholastic competition was soon underway. At the secondary school level the major source of conflict was access by boys and girls team to courts, fields, and pools for practice. If a school administrator or school board member might have wanted to slow down the process of compliance, he ran into the political reality that parents were determined that their daughters have the same opportunities for sports competition as their sons.

Strong parental support for competitive girls' programs reflected a seismic change in thinking regarding the impact of competition and vigorous physical exercise for girls. At the time Title IX was enacted, most public and private schools offered little or no sports programs for junior and senior high-school girls. There were exceptions to this rule, of course, such as Iowa and Texas where girls' basketball had survived the budget cuts of the 1930s, and private prep schools located primarily on the East Coast, where a wide range of sports was offered. Well into the 1960s, prevailing attitudes toward gender roles assumed that young boys played with balls and girls played with dolls, and that by the time girls reached high school their proper place was on the sidelines as cheerleaders or drill squad members. If a young girl exhibited strong interest in sports, she was labeled a "tomboy," and if that interest persisted into her teenage years, she was advised to find other activities. Rigorous exercise, it was commonly believed, would make them "muscle-bound" and unladylike.

Given these widely accepted social standards, girls tended to avoid sports and concentrate their energies on activities deemed acceptable. Peer pressure and parental guidance meant that few girls spent time to develop their athletic skills, thus confirming widespread beliefs that girls lacked the coordination and strength to compete. It became a vicious cycle. Since girls did not spend time developing athletic skills, did not receiving coaching, and only rarely were encouraged by parents to develop their skills, they consequently did not develop athletically. Few fathers ever thought to invite their daughters to shoot baskets or toss a ball as they did their sons. Consequently, on the few occasions when girls were called upon to perform athletically, they usually looked inept, or worse.

Such attitudes and behaviors, however, were now falling out of favor. The development of the women's rights movement during the 1960s meant that traditional stereotypes were being seriously challenged. Title IX – a notable product of that widespread movement – sparked a compelling new question: if, as its spokesmen contended, sports teach important values and attitudes believed essential to success in the business and professional worlds – teamwork, perseverance, dedication, setting and reaching goals, preparation, sportsmanship, responding positively to setbacks, performance under pressure – then why should those experiences be denied to girls? If, as was often said, the lessons learned in the locker room lead to success in the corporate board room, then young women were being given short shrift. Educational psychologist David Auxter placed the issues created by Title IX in such a context:

> We value athletics because they are competitive. That is, they teach that achievement and success are desirable, and that they are worth disciplining oneself for. By keeping girls out of sports, we have denied them this educational experience. Better athletic programs will develop more aggressive females, women with confidence, who value personal achievement and have a strong sense of identity. I think that would be a good thing for us all.[17]

The response of the NCAA to Title IX was complex. Executive Director Walter Byers had often conferred with women athletic administrators and coaches, even making public statements indicating that at some time the NCAA would become involved in sponsoring women's championships. But in 1965 the annual convention adopted a resolution prepared by its executive committee that, "The games committee conducting any NCAA event shall limit participation to eligible male student-athletes." With the NCAA not showing any substantial interest, in 1971 a group of women interested in developing an intercollegiate women's sports program banded together to form the Association for Intercollegiate Athletics for Women (AIAW). This new organization clearly was philosophically close to the anti-competition orientation that had taken control of women's sports during the 1920s, and its program was designed to foster healthy competition on an educational model, not the professional, competitive model embraced by the NCAA. The AIAW forbid the granting of athletic scholarships, coaches could not recruit off campus nor pay for a prospect's trip to campus, and did not establish a rules enforcement committee. Compliance would be the responsibility of participating institutions. All in all, the AIAW was designed to protect female students from institutional exploitation and to avoid the many problems that men's programs routinely encountered.[18]

Such naivety, however, did not last for long. Within a few years it was apparent that the leadership of the AIAW – women coaches and athletic administrators – were out of touch with the rising tide of the feminist movement. The requirements of Title IX ultimately opened up a serious division within the ranks of women coaches and athletic directors, leading inevitably to a major fissure within the AIAW. Could an institution meet the federal standard of equal protection if it gave athletic scholarships to men but not to women? Feminists argued that women deserved equal opportunity for financial aid, while the leadership of the AIAW countered that it would debase women's programs. Leading the challenge to the educational model was the women's athletic director at the University of New Mexico, Linda Estes, who argued long and vociferously for equal treatment of women athletes, including full scholarship aid and the opportunity to compete for national championships. As Walter Byers of the NCAA recalls in his memoirs, "Women's athletics leaders discriminated against themselves through the years by

Figure 11.2 One of the early beneficiaries of Title IX was guard Nancy Lieberman, shown here in 1979 driving toward the basket against Queens College during her All-American season with the Lady Monarchs of Old Dominion University. © Bettmann/CORBIS.

refusing to accept competitive athletics as a proper pursuit for teenage women."[19] In 1973, the hierarchy of the AIAW reluctantly agreed to permit athletic grants-in-aid, but with male athletic directors controlling university athletic budgets, the amount of financial aid available to women proved inconsequential.

While women sports administrators argued about philosophical issues, the more pragmatic male-dominated NCAA callously attempted to subvert Title IX. The men controlling intercollegiate athletics viewed Title IX as a serious threat to the economic foundation of their programs. Although Title IX did not specifically mention sports and compliance guidelines had yet to be adopted by the Department of Health, Education, and Welfare, the bottom line seemed to indicate that women and men would have to be treated equally. The male athletic establishment viewed Title IX as a major threat. Walter Byers recalled that the AIAW was now pressuring HEW to establish guidelines that stipulated 50 percent of the resources of a college budget devoted to intercollegiate athletics should be allocated to female sports and women's athletics should be operated separately from men's. Their theme was "equal numbers and equal dollars," a position that he and the thousands of men he represented viewed as completely unacceptable. Suddenly, men's athletic budgets were in play, in particular gargantuan football budgets. Contending that so-called "revenue-producing sports" (i.e. football and basketball) should be exempt from Title IX, Byers derisively dismissed the claim that "football and women's field hockey immediately deserved the same per capita expenditures" as "financial lunacy."[20]

The NCAA leadership developed a three-pronged strategy. One was to exploit the many close connections between coaches and athletic directors and their friends in Congress to overturn Title IX, and failing that, to put a maze of legal roadblocks in the way of implementation. If that failed, the back-up strategy was to take over the women's programs by destroying the AIAW.

The first NCAA move was to support the amendment offered in 1974 by conservative Republican Senator John Tower of Texas, which would have exempted intercollegiate athletics from the purview of Title IX. When that failed in committee, leading football schools launched an extensive lobbying effort in Congress to delay the issuance of compliance guidelines. President Gerald Ford, himself a former All-American center at Michigan, received a barrage of letters from across the land and even granted an interview to coaches Bear Bryant and Barry Switzer of Oklahoma, who urged him (without success) to exempt football from Title IX calculations. An NCAA-hired law firm filed suit in federal court contending that if an athletic program did not receive direct federal aid, then it should be exempt from compliance reviews. The argument was that because athletics were not specifically mentioned in Title IX, HEW had exceeded its rightful authority by applying it to college athletics. The federal district court in Washington, DC, summarily dismissed the case in 1978. Therefore, the opportunistic Walter Byers and NCAA declared war on the AIAW by offering a large range of championships for women at the Division II and III levels in 1981 and in Division I in 1982. Then it used its vast resources to induce AIAW members to switch to the NCAA by including women in its new national basketball television contract and by offering to accept transfers from AIAW-affiliated schools by waiving membership fees. NCAA spokesmen also gently raised the possibility that if schools did not abandon the AIAW, their men's programs might be given special scrutiny by the rules enforcement committee. By 1982, more than 150 AIAW members, primarily those with men's programs affiliated with the NCAA, made the switch. With its financial resources dwindling, the AIAW gambled on a lawsuit against the NCAA, alleging antitrust violations. Legal costs from pursuing the suit depleted the organization's remaining financial reserves. After its case was summarily dismissed in June 1982, the AIAW quietly folded. The NCAA not only had eliminated a financial rival, but one that embraced a different philosophy.

Among women athletic administrators, Linda Estes of the University of New Mexico and Alice Hill of San Diego State, were in the forefront in scuttling the AIAW. Byers praised them for their embrace of the professional-competitive model of the NCAA: "Right or wrong, [they] sought high-level competition, and national exposure for women's college sports. They were committed to the NCAA's philosophy – to the winner belongs the spoils."[21] A different perspective was held by

Peg Burke, a former president of AIAW: "I think it is interesting that an organization that has been so active in fighting equal opportunity for women now wants to offer championships for them," she said in 1980. "This is not the consent of the governed. In certain circumstances involving men and women, lack of consent is classified as rape."[22]

The consolidation of women's and men's athletic programs changed the nature of the struggle, but the battle was far from over. On campuses, women's program administrators were appointed to posts clearly subordinate to the male athletic director, who retained control of budgets. Suddenly many aspiring male coaches found that they could achieve a personal professional goal of becoming a college head coach – of a women's team. During the 1980s, the percentage of women head coaches actually declined by 50 percent because men were appointed to fill vacancies as new women's teams were initiated. A new type of guerrilla warfare raged within athletic departments over a wide range of issues: access to facilities, recruiting budgets, travel budgets (often men went by air, women by van), coaches' salaries, the number of scholarships, and, as in the case of Temple University, even the difference in quality and quantity of game and practice uniforms provided to men's and women's teams. It would not be until the mid-1980s that the first female athletic director – Judith Sweet of the University of San Diego – would be appointed with control over men's programs. As late as 2004, only five women had been appointed to the post of Director of Athletics of Division I programs, the most prominent being Deborah Yow of the University of Maryland, and Barbara Hedges at the University of Washington.

While embittered battles over gender-equity issues were fought on many campuses, the struggle also continued at the federal level. With the NCAA now responsible for women's programs, the organization ironically found itself in the position of attempting to prevent Title IX from being undercut by social conservatives, a 180-degree reversal from its position in the 1970s. The administration of Jimmy Carter had staunchly supported Title IX, but the administration of Ronald Reagan showed scant enthusiasm, and the pace of compliance reviews slowed markedly in the early 1980s. In 1984, the US Supreme Court dropped a bombshell on women's athletics when it agreed with the NCAA's legal position of 1978 in *Grove City College v. Bell*, that Title IX applied *only* to programs receiving direct federal financial aid and that unfunded programs, such as intercollegiate athletics, were exempt even if a university received federal assistance for other programs.

For a time it seemed that *Grove City* had put women's programs back to a pre-1972 status, but momentum for women's programs had been building for more than a decade and would not be stopped by a mere Supreme Court ruling. The grass-roots development of high school and college programs had produced a new outlook among the American public that assured that women's programs would not be scuttled. Budgets for women's programs continued to improve, although the Reagan Administration halted more than 800 compliance reviews and related investigations. Many university presidents, now under intense pressure from women faculty and community leaders, made clear to their athletic departments that long-term plans for achieving compliance with Title IX would continue to be implemented no matter what the courts had ruled. The hiring of many women professionals by the NCAA placed them within that organization's decision-making bureaucracy where they exerted authority. The issue was finally resolved for good in 1988, when Congress passed over President Reagan's veto the Civil Rights Restoration Act, which restored the original intent of Title IX. Any gender discrimination in public schools or higher education, including sports programs, was once again in violation of federal law.[23]

By the early years of the twenty-first century, women's sports had come of age as an integral part of a university athletic program. The pipeline of athletes was surging, as young girls now had many opportunities to perfect their skills prior to entering college. That they had opportunities in sports that were not available to their mothers and grandmothers probably seemed somehow arcane, if not irrelevant to them. They now could develop skills in summer camps, play competitive softball, volleyball, and soccer in organizations and leagues affiliated with national associations, and in junior and senior high school have a wide range of team sports from which to choose. The more individualistic sports – golf, tennis, swimming, track and field, gymnastics – were also available for girls to develop skills and compete. By the time young girls reached junior high school, competent coaching had become available. Competition became as intense as what had long existed among boys, and arduous practice and physical conditioning was no longer considered un-feminine. For exceptional female athletes, like their male counterparts, a "full-ride" university "athletic scholarship" could be the reward.

Title IX at all levels exerted a revolutionary force on American sports. A young girl in today's society has a wide vista of opportunities that her mother did not enjoy. Resistance to women engaging in competitive sports still is occasionally revealed in corners of American society, but the main battle has been fought and gender equity has controlled the field. Mopping-up skirmishes remain to be fought, but a new world of opportunity now exists for females of all ages. If long-term trends are any indication, the gap between funding and opportunities for women as compared to men will continue to narrow, but important social and psychological implications remain. The quest for equality of opportunity for women, however, does not simply entail requiring men to make room for the women. It also means that men have to abandon their once-unique masculine identification. As women continue to improve as athletes, they will narrow the gap between men's and women's performance levels, thereby assuming many of the traits once identified as masculine: strength, agility, speed, skill. These traits, as Susan Cahn explains, will "become human qualities and not those of a particular gender." Noting that historically sports had enabled boys to become men possessed of the qualities needed to assume leadership roles in society, now girls are being presented with the same opportunities. This will ultimately lead, she suggests, to the reformulation of traditional models of masculinity and femininity, undercutting "the social hierarchies that have historically granted men greater authority in political, economic, religious, family, and athletic matters."[24] If Cahn is correct in her analysis, women's expanding role in sports will ultimately lead to a transformation of gender roles and relationships in America.

Criticism of Major College Sports

In 1990, Indiana University professor Murray Sperber published *College Sports, Inc.*, a book that the NCAA and big-time college sports departments wished had never been written. Marshaling a vast array of data to support his view that the NCAA had become a powerful, multibillion-dollar cartel, and that athletic departments had become essentially for-profit economic enterprises that, while located on college campuses, were for all intents and purposes independent, Sperber painted an uncomfortable picture of overpaid coaches and athletic directors; of exploited athletes; of fearful presidents quaking before the powerful network of boosters, donors, and trustees. In particular, he contended that even the most successful athletic programs were "awash in a sea of red ink" and routinely found ways to subvert money from instructional and research budgets to bail out irresponsible spending in athletic programs. A decade later, Sperber returned to the attack in *Beer and Circus*, in which he accused educational leaders of abandoning their responsibilities of corralling out-of-control athletic departments that had continued their wastrel ways, paying themselves outlandish salaries and providing themselves with myriad perks and supplemental income. At the same time, these self-indulgent coaches and athletic directors used their influence within the NCAA to enact and enforce policies that prevented athletes from receiving a portion of the monies they helped generate, even to the point of creating policies that made it more difficult for athletes to avail themselves of a genuine college educational experience.[25]

Sperber's critique, of course, has never connected with the general public or the sports fans whose only interests lie in entertainment and rooting for their favorite teams. Throughout Sperber's informed and revealing books, the words "corruption," "fraud," and "hypocrisy" resonate. During the Watergate scandal of the early 1970s, Indiana University basketball coach Bob Knight commented, "When they get to the bottom of Watergate, they'll find a basketball coach." He spoke with an ironic bite, of course, but he gave expression to the fact that his profession had more than its share of serious ethical lapses. During the half century that the NCAA had maintained its enforcement division, at any one time programs at about 20 percent of Division I institutions were either on probation or under investigation. Over the years, a high percentage of the most prominent big-time colleges were exposed for major violations, many of them so flagrant as to defy the imagination. The reason for this was quite simple – it takes outstanding (so-called "blue chip") athletes to win championships, and it takes several to make a team "number one" and win a national championship. In addressing the issue of the importance of recruiting, back in 1951 the head football coach at Wake Forest, Douglas "Peahead" Walker, laconically noted, "You don't go bear hunting with a switch." The successful football coach at Iowa, Forest Evashevski, told a reporter in 1957 that the only objective in college football was "to go out and win." He confessed,

> At most colleges the pressure is on the coach from the president on down. The
> coach enters into a tacit understanding with the president that he will recruit good

Figure 11.3 Between 1964 and 1975, under Coach John Wooden, the Bruins of UCLA won 10 NCAA national men's basketball championships. One of the many outstanding players who made this feat possible was 7' 2" center Lew Alcindor, shown dunking against Georgia Tech in 1967. Before his senior year he announced his Muslim faith and changed his name to Kareem Abdul-Jabbar. He later played 19 seasons in the NBA with the Milwaukee Bucks and Los Angeles Lakers, setting scoring and rebounding records, and being named the league's Most Valuable Player six times. © Bettmann/CORBIS.

ball players by any means short of larceny. And if the coach doesn't come through with good recruiting, out he goes.[26]

According to many critics, the greatest fraud in the entire college sports enterprise has been the lip service given to "academics." Such commitment is *de riguer* during the interview process when a new coach is hired and during the pat speeches that coaches deliver to alumni and boosters. But the coach knows that athletic graduation rates are of minor consideration in the grand scheme of things. Players have long been counseled into "snap" courses to maintain eligibility and are required to put in long, grueling hours at conditioning and practice that leave them too exhausted to do serious study. Increased scheduling of midweek games means they miss many classes. Although in recent years the pressures of television upon money-strapped schools to schedule midweek games has produced some criticism, there has been little, if any, criticism of college spring baseball and softball schedules that call for teams to play 50 games or more.

The coach's priorities have to be on winning, and winning consistently. Coaches know that athletic directors, with their eyes constantly on ticket sales, booster donations, post-season invitations with lucrative payoffs, and the number of television appearances, have always been ready to change coaches if the number of losses mounts. With the number of football bowl games reaching 25 during the 1990s, it was not unusual for an athletic director to budget as income a future bowl game, thereby placing enormous pressure upon the coach. Thus, in 2005, it was a most unusual event in intercollegiate sports when Nancy Zimpher, president of the University of Cincinnati, fired the school's most successful men's basketball coach in history, Bob Huggins, specifically for the sorry academic record and criminal rap sheet of his players. In 16 seasons, Huggins had erected an enviable 399–127 record and taken the Bearcats to 14 NCAA post-season tournaments, but his graduation rates were abysmal. As one angry Bearcat booster said about the decision: "Fans have forgiven players for suspensions and arrests because the program was so successful. We knew what kind of players Huggins recruited. But who cared?"[27]

The recruitment of athletes has always been a major source of unethical practices. Many coaches have said in unguarded moments that they find the system degrading and humiliating. But it is an essential skill for the coach who is to be successful in the won–lost column. The history of college recruiting is filled with stories that make a mockery of the goals and standards that the NCAA has set for its programs. Over the years, a once-slender NCAA manual on rules enforcement grew to more than 500 pages as the organization struggled to keep pace with the cheaters in an effort to provide "a level playing field" for all members. Whenever a new twist to the old recruiting game was uncovered, the compliance manual was amended and expanded. Many a faculty representative to the NCAA, charged with overseeing rules compliance on each member campus, has confessed that the rules became so complex that some violations, however "minor" they might be, are almost inevitable. Coaches have long complained that enforcement is highly selective and that the established winning programs are given a free pass, a charge that NCAA executives have denied emphatically. However, even taking into consideration journalist Don Yaeger's tendency toward sensationalism, his book *Undue Process* establishes many inconsistencies in the NCAA's enforcement policies.[28] Because the NCAA is a private entity, its enforcement officials lack the power to subpoena witnesses and must rely on individuals voluntarily testifying. Over the years, many investigations have fizzled due to a lack of willing witnesses. Even when it was able to prove violations, the punishment meted out seems not to have had its intended deterrent effect. The typical punishments that the NCAA imposed on a wayward program proved insufficient to stop cheating – being placed on probation, a reduction in the number of available scholarships, a ban on post-season games, loss of television revenues, limits on recruiting. But it seemed that most everyone seemed to accept them as a price for doing business and the intended embarrassment to a university seldom had significant impact. Besides, the standard response went something like this: "Our opponents are cheating and we simply have to keep up with the competition. We just got caught."

By 1985, the frustration – if not desperation – of NCAA officials with their inability to curb rules transgressions led the organization to hold an "integrity convention." That convention authorized a get-tough policy that included the power to terminate a program if it repeatedly and egregiously engaged in improper conduct. The press dubbed this the "death penalty," which in fact the NCAA had utilized de facto in 1952 when it cooperated with Southeastern Conference officials to force a defiant University of Kentucky to shut down its basketball program for one season. The new penalty called for the suspension of a program for two years if it were demonstrated that a university administration did not exert proper "institutional control" over its athletic program and that a consistent pattern of major wrongdoing were found that included egregious repeat offenses.

It did not take long for the death penalty to be invoked. NCAA investigators uncovered a massive scam at Southern Methodist University that essentially put many football players on salary. Payments ranged from free airline tickets up to cash payments of many thousand dollars a year. The total cost of these illegal payments, funded by wealthy alumni and boosters, probably exceeded $100,000 a year. Not that the university had not been warned – it had been the most punished institution in history of the NCAA, being hit with probations in 1958, 1974, 1976, 1981, and 1985. It was found that not only did the university athletic director make monthly payments to players, but that boosters associated in the recruiting process provided recruits with free apartments, automobiles, and cash. The crucial witness was a Pennsylvania high school recruit who was given $5,000 in return for his signature on a national letter of intent. Incredibly, the monthly payroll payments continued even after the institution was informed that an official NCAA investigation was underway. These payments were specifically authorized by the chairman of SMU's board of trustees, William Clements. Apparently, Clements and other officials believed that, should they halt the illicit payments, angry players would tell all to NCAA investigators. That Clements had served Presidents Nixon and Ford as a deputy Secretary of Defense and had been elected Governor of Texas (and was in the midst of launching another campaign for that office) provides ample evidence of the extent to which university and community leaders would go in order to enjoy the bragging rights of a winning football team.[29]

This church-affiliated university suffered greatly for the sins of its athletic program and boosters. SMU's governing board, including Governor Clements, was fired by an angry Council of Bishops. President Donald Shields resigned, citing health reasons, as did the recently hired football coach and athletic director, who had inherited the mess but attempted to cover it up. However, the coach under whom the payroll system had apparently originated, Ron Meyer, had already left for the head coaching position of the professional New England Patriots and escaped punishment. To be certain, he denied any knowledge of the payoffs, but his role in the scandal is unquestionable according to NCAA Executive Director Walter Byers, who cites instances where Meyer would show a prospective recruit a $100 bill with the comment, "Young man, this is my calling card." The message was clear – the recruit would soon be contacted by a Mustangs booster with checkbook open. When Meyer was starting his tenure at SMU, one of the leading high school running backs in the country was Eric Dickerson, who lived with his grandmother in a ramshackle one-bedroom house in a small town 60 miles west of Houston. Well before he committed to SMU, high school student Dickerson was seen driving a new $15,000 high-performance automobile, which he claimed his grandmother had purchased for him. According to Byers, it had actually been the gift of a Texas A&M booster; and when Dickerson elected to attend SMU, apparently for a better deal, he kept the car. The snookered Aggie booster could not complain or the NCAA enforcement staff would have paid a visit to College Station.[30]

The entire enforcement mechanism of the NCAA is predicated upon the cooperation of member institutions. It is based upon an informal set of policies and procedures. The NCAA does not have subpoena power and it cannot compel individuals to testify. This raises an intriguing question: what happens when a member institution decides *not* to cooperate with the NCAA enforcement officers? What happens when a coach refuses to cooperate with the NCAA, when he is supported in that defiant stance by the university president, the athletic director, boosters, and trustees, indeed by the entire power structure of a state, including the legislature and state court system? Can he thumb his nose at the enforcement officers and the NCAA? The long-running feud that lasted for almost three decades between the NCAA and high-profile basketball coach Jerry Tarkanian is therefore most instructive.

Ever since he emerged as a talented coach at Long Beach State in the late 1960s, after compiling an enviable won–lost record at two California junior colleges, Tarkanian and the NCAA seemed to be on a collision course. Tarkanian followed a simple formula throughout his 40-year coaching career that saw him win 778 games and have an unequaled winning percentage of 83 percent. He could identify and recruit top talent, often unpolished players overlooked by other programs, and turn them into talented players with his coaching skills. One of the principal reasons many of Tarkanian's recruits were "overlooked," however, was that they often had dubious academic credentials. Tarkanian loved to play the role of "Father Flanagan," giving young men who had faced social and economic obstacles an opportunity to escape their past. His willingness to take a chance on players whom other schools passed over – high academic risks, unpolished but promising athletes, the poor, and especially the inner city black athlete – enhanced his reputation in serious basketball circles. Between 1968 and 1973, he turned a mediocre Long Beach State program into one that enjoyed national rankings and appearances in the 16-team NCAA tournament – much to the irritation of nearby basketball power UCLA. He compiled a 122–20 record at the upstart state college, and in the process attracted the attention of the NCAA – his supporters contend that UCLA athletic director J. D. Morgan blew the whistle – leading to 23 violations charges and two years of probation for Long Beach.[31]

By the time the penalties were handed down, however, Tarkanian had already departed for Nevada's recently opened state university in Las Vegas. Within a week after his appointment was announced, the NCAA indicated that it was reopening a dormant investigation of the UNLV basketball program. To Tarkanian, this move was clear evidence that he had been targeted by executive director Walter Byers and director of enforcement David Berst. He believed that a comment he made in a Long Beach newspaper in 1973 was responsible. In that article, he charged the NCAA with something that many coaches believed but wisely elected not to say publicly, that the organization followed selective enforcement policies that protected the prestigious programs while punishing those which sought to reach a higher level. He wrote,

> It's a crime that Western Kentucky is placed on probation. The University of Kentucky basketball program breaks more rules in a day than Western Kentucky does in a year. The NCAA just doesn't want to take on the big boys.

The UNLV officials readily said that they were using basketball to give the new institution national visibility. Tarkanian delivered on his promises and turned the UNLV basketball team into a popular Las Vegas extravaganza. The "Runnin' Rebels" provided an exciting high-scoring machine that reached the Final Four of the NCAA tournament in 1976. That same spring, however, the NCAA levied new allegations about improprieties in the UNLV basketball program that had been committed since Tarkanian's arrival. Instead of meekly accepting the informal justice system of the NCAA, however, UNLV and Tarkanian counter-attacked, denying all charges. UNLV Vice President Brock Dixon conducted an in-house investigation and concluded that the evidence presented by David Berst was "clearly in doubt" and that it lacked a "standard of proof and due process" that was "inferior to what we might expect." Dixon told the press, "In almost every factual situation delineated by the NCAA, the university's own investigation has been able to find a substantial body of conflicting evidence."

Tarkanian complained that he was being judged by the same persons who brought the indictment and that the informal disciplinary procedures of the NCAA prevented him from confronting his accusers, thus denying him the right of due process. For the first time in its history, the NCAA's relatively informal enforcement mechanism – an essential part of its power – was being openly challenged. Economists who have studied the behavior of economic cartels have frequently noted that they do not tolerate contrarian behavior, and this was the case in 1977 when the organization slapped UNLV with probation. Most significantly, for the first time in its history, the NCAA took the dramatic step of demanding that the school suspend its head coach for two years without pay. This was indeed an unprecedented penalty. Subsequent developments indicate that Tarkanian had plenty of reason to suspect that he was being singled out for special attention.

Tarkanian – carrying an alliterative nickname that could be interpreted many ways, "Tark the Shark" – responded just as he would as a coach when an opponent threatened to upset the Rebels. He went on attack with the legal and political equivalent of a full-court press, suing the NCAA, launching a media backlash through his journalist friends in Las Vegas, denouncing the NCAA for attacking him with "lies, distortions, and half truths," in a "Star Chamber" environment. He called into play many of the political leaders of Nevada, marshaling key members of the legislature, the Board of Regents and the UNLV administration behind him. A series of lawsuits were filed that stopped the suspension in its tracks, and the prolonged process of litigation that ensued bought him a delay of 20 years. To say that the hierarchy of the NCAA was perturbed by his response is an understatement. In the meantime, Tarkanian's Runnin' Rebels were dominating the Big West Conference, enjoying high national rankings and – much to the dismay of Berst and Byers – appearing every year in the NCAA post-season tournament, making it to the Final Four in 1987 and winning the championship in 1991 with an unprecedented 30-point blow-out victory over Duke in the final game. The following year, the team went undefeated throughout the regular season, led by a bevy of players soon to make their way to the National Basketball Association, but lost to Duke in a major upset in the semi-finals of the Final Four. Tarkanian never served his two-year suspension.

Just at the time Tarkanian's teams crested at the top of the college basketball world, his audacious behavior caught up with him. He had received strong criticism, even in friendly Las Vegas, when it was revealed that he had gone into a California medium security prison to sign one special recruit to a letter of intent, and when one of his prize junior college recruits, Lloyd Daniels, whose academic record was highly suspect, was arrested by an undercover police team while purchasing cocaine in North Las Vegas. Daniels never played for the Rebels, but he did have a modest career as a reserve forward in the NBA. These revelations moved UNLV president Robert Maxson to begin the process of forcing accountability on the coach for the image of his program.

In June 1991, the bottom fell out of Tarkanian's program when the *Las Vegas Review Journal* published front-page pictures of three members of the national championship team sitting in a hot tub drinking beer at the posh Las Vegas home of the infamous sports gambler, Richard "The Fixer" Perry. He had been convicted of fixing harness races in Massachusetts during the 1970s and of bribing Boston College basketball players to shave points in 1984. By 1991, Tarkanian had become engaged in a power struggle with president Maxson, who feared that the Runnin' Rebels were creating an image that undercut his efforts to upgrade the academic reputation of UNLV. With the damning pictures appearing on page one of the city's largest newspaper, Tarkanian's support within the Las Vegas community began to crumble. When he resigned under pressure shortly thereafter, the community was bitterly divided. Maxson was subjected to death threats by angry Rebel boosters and was shortly thereafter forced out of the presidency, whereupon he accepted, ironically, the presidency of Long Beach State.

Tarkanian would go on to a brief 20-game coaching career in the NBA and then return to his alma mater, Fresno State, where many of his players became ensnared in various scrapes with law enforcement. Charges of gamblers influencing the outcome of some Bulldog games were even leveled at the program, but never proven. In 1998, Tarkanian won perhaps the greatest victory in his coaching career when the NCAA decided to settle without admission of guilt a lawsuit that Tarkanian had brought against the organization in 1992 for harassment and fabrication of evidence. The shockingly large settlement of $2,500,000 was the first in the NCAA's history and was viewed by many observers as evidence that Tarkanian had been unfairly treated by the NCAA. "They've never paid money to anybody [before]," he told the press, "I feel vindicated. They beat the hell out of me for twenty-five years."[32] Nonetheless, the renegade image of "Tark the Shark" continued to cloud Tarkanian's image even after he had retired. Perhaps that explains why he was never elected into the Basketball Hall of Fame, despite his lofty won–lost record and many championships that spanned four decades of college coaching.

Television and the Triumph of Commercialized College Sports

Much of college athletics' contemporary problems can be traced to the huge amounts of money available from the sale of television rights for football and basketball. This began innocently enough in 1953, when the NCAA secured control of football television revenues. As the revenue stream increased with the passing of the years, the great majority of NCAA member institutions were pleased with the arrangement because it not only provided a large percentage of monies to the football programs that were featured on the Saturday telecasts, but also distributed some funds to other members. In 1968, the NCAA signed its first national contract for televising the national basketball tournament – a $2 million deal with NBC. The popularity of this event grew steadily during the 1970s, climaxing with the 1979 championship game between Michigan State and Indiana State, which featured two of the most exciting players of the century, Earvin "Magic" Johnson and Larry Bird. The tournament, now labeled "March Madness," filled a void in the annual sports calender, setting off a frenzy of gambling based largely on "bracket" predictions and pools conducted in offices and sports bars. In 1985, the NCAA expanded the field from 32 to 64 teams, overnight doubling the number of games to be televised. The men's basketball tournament became a cash cow for the NCAA, by the mid-1980s funding over 80 percent of its total operations. In 1989, CBS signed a seven-year $1 billion contract for the broadcast rights, and in 2002 the network agreed to an 11-year, $6.2 billion deal.

The basketball windfall came at a propitious time because in 1982 the NCAA lost control of its football television monopoly. When the NCAA established its absolute control in the early 1950s, Notre Dame had reluctantly gone along with the restrictive plan. But Notre Dame's president, Father Theodore Hesburgh, believed that the program was "socialistic" and denied the Fighting Irish millions of dollars of additional revenue each season. Behind the scenes, Hesburgh worked with like-minded university presidents to return to the "home rule" days that preceded 1952.[33]

In 1982, Father Hesburgh's efforts were rewarded when the presidents of two major football institutions, William Banowsky of the University of Oklahoma and Fred Davison of the University of Georgia, filed suit in federal court in Oklahoma City alleging that the NCAA was operating in a monopolistic fashion by restraining free trade by preventing members from pursuing their own television deals. Federal district judge Juan Burciaga agreed with the presidents, and ruled that the NCAA was in direct violation of antitrust laws by its "presumptuous seizure" and "commandeering" of television rights. The NCAA's television policy and controls on member institutions were "unreasonable, naked restraints on competition" that were motivated by "rank greed" and "a lust for power." In short, the NCAA no longer could control the televising of football games of member institutions. Judge Burciaga's sharply worded decision made it clear that the NCAA was not the educational association it claimed to be, but rather a commercial entity that was operating in the manner of a powerful cartel by fixing prices, restricting access, and restraining the free flow of commerce.[34] In 1984 the US Supreme Court upheld the decision by a 7–2 vote. The NCAA had suffered a major setback.

With the loss of its football television package, the NCAA looked to basketball for its financial future. By the 1990s, it could be reasonably argued that basketball was threatening to surpass football as the premier college sport. "March Madness" – the 64-team post-season tournament – had become the most popular college sports event on television, much more so than post-season bowl games. By 1989, the basketball tournament was drawing more viewers than the 25 bowl games, a trend that continued into the twenty-first century.

Unlike all other sports sponsored by the NCAA, only its top football division of some 115 institutions did not have a national championship playoff system. It was the only sport that had its "national champion" determined by the vote of coaches and/or journalists in two separate polls. On the surface, resistance to a playoff for Division I-A seemed strange, especially when it was estimated that the television rights for a playoff would generate $100 million a year. The stock response given by university presidents for their refusal to create a 16-team – or even eight-team – playoff was that it would adversely affect the academic welfare of student-athletes because it would occur near the time of final examinations. That of course was pure hypocrisy, because the presidents had frequently and routinely supported policies that adversely affected the academic welfare of athletes. And, advocates of a playoff pointed out, the NCAA offered 16-team playoffs for schools playing football at Division I-AA, II and III.

In reality, the big-time football schools were opposed to a playoff for several reasons. Because bowl games are held in warm-climate locations, over the years Southern and Southwestern schools have benefited handsomely from the informal invitation process; close "good-old-boy" relationships developed between athletic directors, coaches, and bowl directors, and these persons were loath to cut those sentimental and often personal ties. In likelihood, a playoff system would soon kill most bowl games. Further, the bowl payoffs were substantial and 50 teams got to participate. A playoff would reduce that to a small number. Several bowls also were steeped in football tradition. The Big Ten and Pac-Ten had enjoyed their lucrative Rose Bowl rivalry since 1947 and were reluctant to abandon that tradition. Bowl executives, their own livelihoods on the line, became ardent lobbyists against a playoff system whenever the idea reached the NCAA Presidents' Council. The great majority of head coaches, already under enormous pressures to produce winning teams, did not want the additional stress of a playoff system wherein all but one coach would end the season with a loss. It would be much better to have an opportunity to win one of 25 bowl games. It was widely rumored that some university presidents, overshadowed on their own campus by a popular football coach, seemed unwilling to give the coaches an even greater opportunity for publicity that a national playoff would engender.[35]

The national media, however, demanded that a national playoff system be established. This pressure eventually led to the creation of the Bowl Championship Series (BCS). The unstated purpose was to preserve the bowl system and quiet the critics demanding a playoff. The BCS was organized outside the NCAA. It placed the conference commissioners of the six most prestigious football conferences in control. The plan was to use a complicated formula that included won–lost records, "strength of schedule," traditional polls, so-called "quality wins," and computerized "power rankings" to select the top two teams to play in one of the four BCS bowls for the national championship. The three other BCS bowl games would have the pickings from among other top-ranked schools. All six conference champions had to be included in the four games, with the faint possibility being held out to non-BCS programs that they could be included for consideration if a team finished high enough in the BCS-designed computer ratings. Not surprisingly, in the first six years of operation, this did not occur, although after the 2004 season the undefeated and highly ranked University of Utah from the Mountain West Conference was named to play in the Fiesta Bowl where it easily defeated a BCS team, the University of Pittsburgh.

The BCS system was a transparent effort to preserve the traditional bowl system and enable the six self-appointed BCS conferences – Big Ten, Big East, Southeastern, Atlantic Coast, Pac-Ten, and Big Twelve, along with independent Notre Dame – to control large chunks of television revenue outside the purview of the NCAA. The result was widespread dissatisfaction. By effectively excluding several Division I conferences – Western Athletic, Mid-America, Mountain West, and Conference USA – the BCS created a two-tiered pecking order within the ranks of Division I-A football, re-enforcing the perception that the rich were getting much richer while leaving the excluded schools out in the cold. The computer ratings designed to select the top two teams proved to be a major joke. The two teams selected to square off for the national championship sometimes conflicted with the national polls, thereby angering fans of those teams overlooked. Each year controversy reigned when the computer spit out its final numbers. Although the teams were determined by a previously adopted statistical model, the computer-generated results revealed serious oversights on the part of the human beings who created the rating formula. Each year, the formula was revised to respond to the most recent glitches and criticisms, indicating that the entire concept had inherent flaws that could not be solved. As the BCS encountered continued criticism from many quarters, the likelihood of some form of national playoff system for Division I-A being sponsored by the NCAA seemed to increase each year, but its proponents realized that the major obstacle presented by the BCS schools had to somehow be circumvented.

The Knight Commission Report

In 1989, the Knight Foundation funded an extensive examination of the state of big-time college athletics. The Knight Commission was reminiscent of the Carnegie Commission of 1929 and its findings were hauntingly similar; so too was its impact on changing the culture of major college athletics – negligible.[36] The commission's concerns were aptly expressed by *Time* magazine at the time of its creation: "an obsession with winning and moneymaking that is pervading the noblest ideals of both sports and education in America." The Commission's report, issued in 1991, was replete with indignation and frustration over the debasement of higher education by athletic departments. More than 50 percent of the Division I programs had been sanctioned or put on probation during the 1980s, and Southern Methodist had suffered the ignominy of having its football program shut down for two seasons. The news media produced a never-ending barrage of negative publicity about tutors taking examinations and writing papers for athletes, avoidance of standardized admissions requirements, widespread criminal acts committed by male athletes, often against women, illegal payments to players, unethical and even bizarre behavior by coaches, and embarrassingly low graduation rates (especially among football and men's basketball squads). A random survey of former and current professional football players indicated that one-third of them had received illicit payments while in college, and most significant, that they saw nothing wrong with that fact.

The commission identified the monies generated by television broadcasting contracts as the main culprit because these relationships "moved colleges and universities into the entertainment business in a much bigger way" that attracted a primary viewing audience not associated with the campus or its alumni – "people who valued winning more than they did the universities' underlying purposes." Thus "the thrill of victory, sports as spectacle, sports for gambling – these were their lodestones." The solution, the Commission concluded, rested not with the NCAA because it was a willing partner in maintaining the status quo, but with campus presidents who were "directed toward academic integrity, financial integrity, and independent certification."

A cursory examination of the names of the members of the Knight Commission, however, indicated that these self-appointed reformers had been major players on their campuses in helping to create or at least to permit the existence of the problems they now decried. Their reform recommendations, tightly wrapped in lofty academic language, merely sought to shift some control of sports programs away from the athletic departments to central administration, not to diminish the size of the programs or return to a truly amateur system. Although written in compelling language, the report's recommendations would have done little to change the underlying assumptions or *modus operandi* of intercollegiate athletics. To the issue that critics of college athletics have frequently raised, that the athletes did not share in the vast pool of revenues they helped generate, the Knight Commission was strangely mute. As one critical book by several prominent economists concluded, "Until this is done, the rest of the so-called reform movement can be seen for what it is: a bunch of people shedding crocodile tears for the young men and women on the playing field."[37]

At the time the Knight Commission issued its initial report, Bo Schembechler, former coach and athletic director at the University of Michigan, derisively dismissed the report with the comment that while the reforms would attract a great deal of initial attention, "by the turn of the century, things will return to their normal state. The hubbub will pass, as will the so-called reformers." His cynical comment was, of course, absolutely correct. When the Commission reassembled on its 10th anniversary in 2001 to assess its impact, it had to conclude that nothing had changed for the good, that "the problems of big-time college sports have grown rather than diminished." Academic dishonesty had produced several high-profile scandals, the money being spent on athletics programs had greatly accelerated as institutions increased stadium seating capacities, added luxurious boxes, built enormous basketball arenas and indoor football practice facilities, and sought to attract recruits with ever-more lavish locker rooms, study areas, weight-training rooms, and athletic "halls of fame" that proclaimed the glories of past athletic triumphs – a sure stop during every recruit's visit to campus.

Perhaps most egregious was the fact that salaries for high-profile coaches, always a problem, had now escalated out of all proportion, with 30 coaches making more than one million dollars a year, and twice that number approaching seven-figure incomes (in 2004, in the wake of winning the national championship, Louisiana State University head football coach Lou Saban signed a contract calling for $2.7 million a year, making him, at least for one season, the champion of the salary race). All of this, the Commission intoned, meant that it had found vast "evidence of the widening chasm between higher education's ideals and big-time college sports." The problem was "money-madness." Drawing upon the ideas of long-time critic Murray Sperber, the Commission concluded, "What we have now is a separate culture of performers and trainers, there to provide bread and circuses but otherwise unconnected to the institution that supports them." The reassembled Knight Commission, in reality, held out little hope for substantive reform in the years to come.

At the heart of the problem, the Commission gently conceded, was that the NCAA was incapable of living up to its written role statement of maintaining intercollegiate athletics as "an integral part of the educational program, and the athlete as an integral part of the student body, and to return a clear line of demarcation between intercollegiate athletics and professional sports." The 2001 interim report concluded that "its [NCAA's] dual mission of keeping sports clean while generating millions of dollars in broadcasting revenue for member institutions creates a near-irreconcilable conflict."[38] The two reports, separated by 10 years, issued by the Knight Commission were but many in a long line of well-intentioned critiques that have fallen off of the shoulders of those in charge of America's institutions of higher education like so much water off a duck.

From the Carnegie Commission to the Sanity Code to the Knight Commission, and with library shelves stocked full of books and articles providing a mountain of compelling documentation of the same essential story of greed and chicanery, reform-minded individuals could hold out little hope for the future. When it comes to big-time intercollegiate sports, the more things change, it seems, the more they remain the same.

12 Play for Pay

Professional sports came of age with television. Prior to the age of television only professional baseball had gained widespread acceptance with the American sports fan. Ironically it would be television that would undercut "America's Pastime" to the point where its popularity fell behind professional football and was seriously challenged by NASCAR as the nation's primary spectator sport. It was also challenged, but never surpassed, by professional basketball during the 1980s and the 1990s, and even for a time hockey enthusiasts thought that with nationwide expansion their sport would also flourish. Those hopes were never realized, as hockey never caught on outside of Canada and a few Northeastern American cities. The story of professional sports is much more than the games played, because they became enmeshed in a continuum of labor disputes and aggravating strikes, the movement of franchises from city to city by owners seeking sweeter financial deals, and endless jousting with television networks for extended coverage and higher broadcasting rights. Although the sports fans focused on game scores and championships won and lost, those running the professional teams were businessmen making hard-headed business decisions.

A Tale of Two (Football) Cities

Cleveland is a hard-nosed football town. Its population is largely descended from the immigrants who came to work in its bustling mills, foundries, wharves, factories, and refineries during the two great human migrations out of Eastern Europe and the rural American South that transformed the United States between the Civil War and the Second World War. From the moment the Cleveland Browns played their first games in the new All-American Football Conference in 1946, residents of the city and the surrounding region enthusiastically supported the team. On autumn Sundays, 70,000 fans flocked to aging and decrepit Municipal Stadium – the much-criticized "Mistake by the Lake" – to root for their team. More popular than the baseball Indians, the orange, brown, and white-clad Browns epitomized this blue-collar city and its people. After an extended championship-filled run under innovative coach Paul Brown, the fortunes of the team began tailing off in the mid-1960s, mirroring the sagging industrial economy of this prototypical Rust Belt City.

In 1963, new owner Art Modell fired coach Brown for petty reasons, and a long period of decline soon set in. The Browns won its last NFL championship in 1964 on the strength of the running of Jim Brown, and the talented squad Paul Brown left behind. That championship brought temporary hope and pride to a city that had become the butt of television comedians' jokes, the city that had declared bankruptcy, the city divided by the Cuyahoga River, which was so polluted with industrial waste that it would actually catch fire in 1969 (the evening news showed the improbable picture of city firemen squirting water on a river to put out ugly toxic flames).[1] From the perspective of 2001, Cleveland native Joe Posnanski recalled the heyday of the team:

> The old Browns were the heartbeat of old Cleveland. Lives were built around those Browns. All week long, they were the pulse that kept the town going. Monday you reviewed the game, Tuesday you argued who should be quarterback, Wednesday you wondered why they were not getting sacks, Thursday you called into the radio station to be the ninth caller and win those tickets, Friday you were in love. . . . And the games on Sunday were like nothing else. It was always 25 degrees colder inside old Cleveland Stadium and . . . you screamed against the wind. Cleveland Browns football was everything. Everything.[2]

Even the futility of enduring mediocre teams and losing seasons and of watching hated Pittsburgh enjoy its extended championship run during the 1970s did not deter the Browns' faithful. In the 1980s, on three agonizing occasions, the Browns were defeated in a play-off game just short of the Super Bowl: in 1980, Oakland intercepted a Brian Sipe pass deep in Raider territory, in 1987 Denver Broncos' quarterback John Elway engineered a last-minute 98-yard drive to tie the game and set up a Denver overtime victory, and the following year Browns' running back Ernie Byner was heading for the tying touchdown when Broncos' backup corner back Jeremiah Castille stripped him of the ball at the two-yard line. After that disaster, Browns fans had good reason to believe their team was suffering from a diabolical jinx. "In Cleveland, in those days," Posnanksi recalls, "there was desperation. When the Browns won, you felt alive. When they lost, you were left with snow piled halfway up your window and potholes the size of Olympic swimming pools and a million gray days and a million Cleveland jokes."[3]

This close relationship between a blue-collar town and its blue-collar football team came to a sudden, embittered end on November 6, 1995. On that day, Modell announced at a press conference called by the Governor of Maryland that he was moving the Browns to Baltimore, citing the offer by the Maryland Stadium

Authority of $65 million up-front money to cover transition costs, the construction of a modern new 70,000-seat stadium that his team would use rent-free, and the substantial supplemental income he would receive from the rental of luxury boxes, sale of licenses for the right to purchase "stadium seats," concessions, and stadium advertising. Modell was peeved that a new baseballpark had been built for the Indians and a modern new arena for the basketball Cavaliers, but that his demands for similar treatment had gone unheeded.[4]

The incredulity and shock that initially swept through Cleveland and northern Ohio soon gave way to a flood tide of angry recriminations and pure, unadulterated hatred aimed at the villain. The son of working-class New Yorkers, Modell was 34 years old in 1961, possessed of little wealth but plenty of ambition when he convinced a Cleveland bank to loan him $4 million to buy the Browns. Over the years, he became a popular community figure, but that affection ended abruptly that traumatic day in November 1995. Radio talk-show lines lit up as fans excoriated the pariah. Death threats were dispatched by mail, fax, telegraph, and telephone. Newspaper editorials denounced Modell's greed and perfidy. Politicians from the city council to the US Senate gave fiery speeches and hustled a team of lawyers into court in a futile effort to stop the move. Resolutions came streaming out of the city government, clergy preached sermons about community well-being and personal trust, and conversations at local watering holes were animated. What Modell failed to grasp, Posnanski lamented, was that "the Cleveland Browns weren't a football team. They were religion and family and history and the only pride of a city that had taken too many punches."[5]

By early 1996, the smoke had cleared. The NFL agreed to put a new expansion team in Cleveland by 1999, and Modell agreed to permit the new Cleveland franchise to retain the old team colors and name, even to adopt its 50 years of team records. Following a public contest in Baltimore, he renamed his franchise the Ravens in a tip of the hat to the city's brooding poet and novelist, Edgar Allan Poe. While Cleveland fans felt terribly violated, giddy football fans in Baltimore felt vindicated for the loss they had suffered when their Colts – the storied franchise that in 1958 had ridden the powerful right arm of legendary Johnny Unitas to the NFL championship in the "greatest game ever played" – had literally left town in the middle of the night in 1984. For several years, Colts' owner Robert Irsay had been demanding that the taxpayers of Maryland build him a new stadium, complete with the requisite luxury boxes and other financial concessions, and when a grouchy Maryland legislature passed a bill that permitted the state to use its power of eminent domain to wrest control of the team away from the irascible owner, Irsay decided to take the best offer. When he learned of impending legal action by the Maryland attorney general that would have tied his team up in court for years, he literally accepted overnight an offer from Mayor Thomas Hudnut of Indianapolis, who was seeking a tenant for the still-unfinished 65,000-seat Hoosier Dome. So, in the dead of night, to avoid a possible court injunction the next day, workers loaded office files and equipment, film and projectors, team uniforms, even weight-training equipment, onto a fleet of 12 Mayflower moving vans. Not until the last yellow-and-green van had cleared the state lines did Mayor Hudnut announce that the Baltimore Colts were now the Indianapolis Colts. In response to irate Maryland fans inquiring about his loyalty, Irsay snapped, "This is my team. I own it, and I'll do whatever I want with it."[6]

It was more than a decade before Baltimore again became the proud host city of an NFL team. In 1995, a journalist checked the number of professional team franchises and discovered that 37 of the existing 113 teams "came from somewhere else." Noting that over 33 years Art Modell had become a symbol of stability in the NFL, and had even openly opposed giving an expansion franchise to Baltimore just two years previously, another journalist concluded, "What makes the Modell move so galling [is that] Modell is so mainstream in the league . . . the thinking goes that if Modell goes, anybody will go."[7] While Modell became the toast of the town in Baltimore, he wisely never returned to Cleveland. Ten years after his shocking decision, it still was not deemed safe for him to show his face anywhere in town. But life goes on, and the new Browns, owned by locals who (of course) pledged never to move the team, began play in 1999 in a magnificent newly-constructed stadium, courtesy of Cuyahoga County taxpayers, just as big and as spiffy as the stadium that lured Art Modell to Chesapeake Bay. Somehow, though, it was not quite the same.

Urban Rivalry, Redevelopment, and Promotion

The triangular Baltimore–Indianapolis–Cleveland fast-shuffle was but one of a long continuum of franchise relocations. The year after Art Modell took the money and ran, the Houston Oilers announced that the failure of their city to build them a new stadium (to replace the 30-year-old Astrodome) had forced its move to Nashville, where city leaders, eager to be recognized as a "major-league" city, had promised the construction of a modern stadium. Today, the St Louis Rams play in a new domed stadium built along the banks of the Mississippi River, financed by taxpayers. The Rams arrived in the River City in 1994, having moved there from Anaheim, California, the sprawling suburb best known as the smoggy home of Disneyland, to which it had moved a decade earlier from the 100,000-seat Coliseum in downtown Los Angeles, which team officials had deemed inadequate. In 1994, Southern California not only lost the Rams to St Louis (which had previously lost its football Cardinals to Phoenix in 1988), but also the Los Angeles Raiders, who decamped for Oakland, a city from which they had originally moved in 1982 in search of larger crowds and the tantalizing but not-forthcoming prospects of pay-for-view cable telecasts. The sudden departure of the Rams and the Raiders left the nation's second largest metropolis without professional football, a void that the owner of the Seattle Seahawks Kenneth Bearing, eagerly sought to fill. That move was stopped by a flurry of lawsuits, threats of political retaliation, and the ultimate location of a new buyer (retired multibillionaire Microsoft executive Paul Allen) who promised to keep the team in the Pacific Northwest. Allen, however, extracted from the Washington State Legislature a special tax to pay for the 67,000-seat

Seahawk Stadium to replace the dim and dank King Dome, which was uncere-moniously imploded one quiet Sunday morning to make way for the new football stadium and a large parking lot. Nearby stood the recently constructed Safeco Field and its retractable roof, built by taxpayers in 1999 for $517 million to keep the baseball Mariners in town.

Such stories were common in the frenetic world of professional sports, where greed and urban rivalries and boosterism produced a continuum of franchise movement. Although economists have repeatedly concluded that the existence of a major-league franchise does not add measurably to the economic health of a city, community leaders everywhere have nonetheless been willing to spend mas-sive sums of taxpayers' money on that dubious premise. The growth in the number of major-league professional franchises in the past half century has reflected the near-doubling of the American population, from 150 million in 1950 to 280 million in 2000. In 1950, there were 44 major-league football, baseball, basket-ball and hockey franchises in the United States, along with two Canadian hockey teams. By 2005, that number had increased to 113 American and eight Cana-dian franchises. Rapid population growth in the South and West was reflected in the establishment of a flood of franchises into those areas. Although hockey was a game that originated and thrived in Canada and a few Northern American cities, the NHL expanded rapidly and without much thought; by 2005 only six of 30 franchises were located in Canada. Although such Northern American cities as Detroit, Chicago, New York, and Boston had storied hockey traditions stretching back to the 1920s, recent expansion carried the league improbably to commu-nities located in Sun Belt cities where there was absolutely no hockey tradition: Charlotte, Atlanta, Nashville, Dallas, Phoenix, Anaheim, and San Jose, even the subtropical environs of Tampa and Miami. In 1950, all major league franchises were located east of the Mississippi River and north of the Mason–Dixon Line. A half century later teams are spread across the continent. Only a handful of cities of over 1.5 million population were not represented by at least one major league franchise (the largest such city, rapidly growing Las Vegas, suffered in its bid for a franchise by unmerited fears of the influence of gamblers).

The recent history of professional sports has been intricately tied to the abil-ity of privately owned teams to extract enormous bounties from their host cities, which fear losing them to rival urban locations. The construction of these modern-day sports palaces was often tied to efforts to revitalize declining central cities. In 1996, Cincinnati voters agreed to foot the bill to build separate stadiums for the football Bengals and the baseball Reds along the Ohio River as the hub of an inten-sive effort at downtown renewal. Both teams, playing the usual extortion game, had threatened to move to other cities if new facilities were not forthcoming. Con-struction of the mammoth Super Dome in New Orleans in the mid-1970s provided a major boost to the Crescent City's effort to lure tourists, setting off a boom in hotel construction and during the 1990s. Atlanta's construction of a new base-ball stadium, a domed stadium for football, and an arena for hockey and basketball provided the centerpiece of a grand urban redevelopment effort. Coors Field for the baseball Rockies, built in a dilapidated warehouse district of Denver, stimulated a remarkable surge in upscale business and residential development. One of the most oft-cited examples of downtown revitalization is Oriole Park at Camden Yards in Baltimore, completed in 1992 as part of the larger Inner Harbor redevelopment project that transformed an industrial slum into an upscale tourist and business core. When the Ravens were secured, a new 70,000-seat stadium was built adjacent to Oriole Park so that parking facilities could be shared.

While the focus of new stadium and arena construction has often been in the older inner cities – as in Seattle, Oakland, Cleveland, Boston, Minneapolis, Cincinnati, Columbus, and Denver, to name just a few – other cities decided to locate their new facilities in the suburbs along major freeways to accommodate affluent suburban ticket buyers. In the early 1970s, the Harry S. Truman Sports Complex was constructed 15 miles from downtown Kansas City at the confluence to two major freeways; it featured separate stadiums for the baseball Royals and football Chiefs. Had the Chiefs not upset the Minnesota Vikings in the Super Bowl after the 1969 season, it is doubtful that Jackson County voters would have been so forthcoming. Detroit, suffering from the heavy blows of major race riots in 1967 and a severely deteriorating inner city, saw the football Lions move to suburban Pontiac some 20 miles north of downtown with the construction of the Silver Dome in the mid-1970s. This structure featured an innovative inflated Teflon fabric roof over 80,000 seats. In 1988, the basketball Pistons followed the Lions out of inner city Detroit when they moved into the Palace in suburban Auburn Hills. Early in the twenty-first century, however, the Lions returned downtown to the new domed Ford Field, located near the baseball Tigers' new Comerica Park in the refurbished central city neighborhood of Foxtown.

In nearly every city that professed major-league aspirations, bitter political fights occurred over the public financing of facilities; the sweetheart deals awarded to teams as incentives often aroused a citizens' protest and various legal and ballot initiative measures. Seldom did opponents to new athletic facilities succeed. Economist Michael Danielson has concluded, "The purported benefits in terms of jobs, tax revenues, and general economic development are overstated and the costs understated. ... [E]conomic benefits have become harder to realize." Increasingly, professional sports enthusiasts have attempted to sell the latest new stadium on intangible factors, such as community spirit, civic pride, and the "quality of life," rather than on direct economic benefits.[8] The mayor who pushed hard for the redevelopment of Camden Yards, Kurt Schmoke, repeatedly talked about the Orioles "as the glue. . . to help hold the community together." A city official in St Petersburg, Florida, where an indoor stadium was built in the early 1980s in hopes of attracting a major-league baseball team, spoke of the ability of professional teams to bridge the yawning gaps in the urban social fabric: "Sports is one of the few things in life that transcends all strata of the community. It is one of the few things left in society that ties us together, regardless of race, economic standing or gender."[9] With the eventual tenant, the expansion Tampa Bay Devil Rays spending most of their time in the American League East's cellar year after year, some residents had to wonder about the magic of sports as a community bonding agent.

The Travails of Baseball

The central theme of the history of baseball in recent decades has been expansion of the two major leagues, and an ongoing battle between owners and players. Between 1953 and 1998, 12 new teams were created and nine franchises relocated. Despite increased attendance and revenues, the game was disrupted several times by embittered labor disagreements between the owners and the Players' Association. Four major strikes disrupted play, the last leading to the unprecedented and severely damaging cancellation of the 1994 World Series – something that even the Second World War could not accomplish. Inept management decisions and shrewd legal maneuvering by Players' Association executive director Marvin Miller led to the end of the restrictive reserve clause during the mid-1970s, setting off a new era dominated by free agency that permitted players to offer their services to the highest bidder after four years under contract. The result was an escalation of salaries that made the pre-free agency pay scales seem minuscule by comparison. Unlike the NFL and NBA, where reasonable constraints on players' salaries and mechanisms for the sharing of revenues were in place, organized baseball proved unable to establish even a modicum of revenue-sharing while efforts to restrain outrageous salaries proved futile. Disparity in the income that teams received from radio and television contracts further exacerbated the competitive balance of the two leagues. Vast differences in club income meant that in 1999 the New York Yankees were able to spend $77 million more than the Montreal Expos on players; by 2005, the Yankees had a payroll of $215 million (for a roster of 25 players), as compared to the $29 million spent by division rival Tampa Bay.

After 50 years of stability, in 1953 major league baseball permitted the relocation of two financially strapped teams whose attendance had fallen to below 300,000: the St Louis Browns went to Baltimore and the Boston Braves to Milwaukee. In 1954, 86-year-old Connie Mack sold his Athletics to financier Arnold Johnson, who relocated the team to his hometown of Kansas City. These moves, however, did not reflect the rapidly changing demographics of postwar America, which saw most population growth occurring in the Sunbelt stretching from Florida to California. California now seemed the most attractive to baseball executives. The introduction of commercial jet fleets in 1957 meant that teams could fly nonstop coast to coast in six hours.

The face of baseball changed dramatically in 1957 when the New York Giants and the Brooklyn Dodgers announced they were relocating to the West Coast. Giants' owner Horace Stoneham took the leap first. His announcement that his team was San Francisco-bound was greeted with disappointment by New Yorkers, but everyone knew that the dilapidated Polo Grounds no longer constituted a major league venue – baseball writer Robert Creamer aptly called it "an antiquated museum." San Francisco's savvy mayor, George Christopher, had orchestrated the deal, promising Stoneham the construction of a new publicly financed 40,000-seat stadium to be built at Candlestick Point 12 miles south of the city, located hard by a major freeway and with parking for 10,000 automobiles. This deal would be the beginning of a trend the required local governments to pay for stadiums to attract (or keep) major league franchises.

Although Stoneham was given a pass by the people of New York, the owner of the Brooklyn Dodgers was viewed as a heinous traitor when he announced that his team was also California-bound. In the long tradition of baseball owners, Walter O'Malley viewed the Dodgers not as a civic treasure that belonged to Brooklyn, but as his personal cash cow. By the time the cheers had faded from the Dodgers' seven-game World Series triumph over the Yankees in 1955, O'Malley was already contemplating relocating the Dodgers. Forty-five-year-old Ebbetts Field, with a capacity of less than 35,000 and located on the edge of a declining neighborhood with a rising crime rate, had become hopelessly outdated. In a new era in which the automobile had become the standard form of transportation, Ebbetts Field had only 700 parking places, and despite the exciting teams led by such stars as Jackie Robinson and Duke Snider, Brooklyn's fans stayed away in droves. New York politicians did not take O'Malley seriously when he threatened to move if the City of New York did not provide him with an accessible plot of land sufficient for the construction of a privately funded 40,000-seat ballpark with 12,000 parking places. He did not demand that the city taxpayers foot the bill for building a new stadium; he just wanted a plot on which to build the modern stadium he envisioned. City planner Robert Moses also stipulated that the city build and operate the ballpark.[10]

Negotiations languished and Walter O'Malley turned his attention to Los Angeles where mayor Norris Poulson made available 300 acres of prime urban land near downtown Los Angeles. In late September 1957, the Los Angeles City Council voted 10–4 to issue a formal invitation to the Dodgers to make their new home in Chavez Ravine and the Dodgers were bound for Los Angeles. The reaction throughout the five New York boroughs was the verbal equivalent of a firestorm. O'Malley was accused of high treason, of Machiavellian manipulation, of greed, even of piracy. Even today, a half-century later, his name is anathema in the city he abandoned.

Until Dodger Stadium could be constructed in Chavez Ravine – its construction was delayed by several law suits opposing the city's deal with O'Malley – the team played in the Los Angles Coliseum, which had been designed for football and track and field, but definitely not for baseball. The dimensions of the baseball field that were superimposed on this Los Angeles sports landmark were weird, with the right-field fence a monumental 440 feet from home plate, but the left-field fence stood just 251 feet away down the foul line. Even a 40-foot high screen could not prevent a flood of cheap pop-fly-home runs. In 1959, journeyman Wally Moon, batting left-handed, developed a peculiar in-to-out slicing swing that enabled him to loft the ball over the left-field screen 19 times; the press dubbed these dubious home runs "Moon Shots."

Despite a dismal seventh-place finish in their initial season, the Dodgers drew 1.8 million fans, and the following year they thrilled the city by winning the National League pennant over the Milwaukee Braves in extra innings in the third and final playoff game, and then subdued the Chicago White Sox in the World Series. More than 90,000 fans watched each game from the Coliseum bleachers

PLAY FOR PAY
291

Figure 12.1 Two of baseball's biggest stars during the 1950s and the 1960s were outfielder Willie Mays of the San Francisco Giants and shortstop Ernie Banks of the Chicago Cubs. They are shown visiting before a game at Wrigley Field in 1965. Both were voted into the Hall of Fame the first year of their eligibility. © Bettmann/ CORBIS.

during the playoffs and World Series. "Who will have the effrontery to tell us now – the several million of us – that the movement to supply the Dodgers with a decent playing yard was against the public interest?" the *Los Angeles Times* editorialized. Taking note of the widely dispersed population in the sprawling Southern California metropolis, the *Times* suggested that the cost of bringing major league baseball to the region was worth every penny:

> Their triumph is that they have created one of those centers of attachment that the metropolitan area of Los Angeles has needed so desperately. The team has made the people for a couple of hundred miles around aware that they have a common interest. A major league baseball team does not a city make, but in our agglomeration of Southern California communities any joint enterprise which excites a wide interest serves as a sort of civic glue.[11]

In 1962, the Dodgers opened the season in spiffy new Dodger Stadium, and attendance for the next three decades hovered annually near the three million mark.

The success of the Giants and the Dodgers encouraged 78-year-old

Branch Rickey to start a new league, the Continental, with the foundation being a new team located in Queens. Memories of the costly Federal League challenge were dusted off, and organized baseball soon cut the Continental League off at its knees when it announced plans to expand both leagues from eight to ten teams, with the American League expanding in 1961 and the National League the following year. The Dodgers and the Giants would be replaced in New York by the Metropolitans (Mets), and cowboy-movie star Gene Autry was given an American League franchise that he named the California Angels, which would be located down the street from Disneyland in Anaheim. Calvin Griffith was permitted to move his bottom-feeding Washington Senators to Minneapolis-St Paul, where he bridged the urban rivalry by renaming his team the Twins, and an expansion franchise was placed in the nation's capital to placate fussy congressmen. The other new National League team was located in rapidly growing Houston; the team played under the name of the Colt-45s for a few years before adopting the name Astros in honor of the city's new Johnson Space Center and the heroism of the American astronauts. These expansion teams were not competitive for many years, with the Mets under 73-year-old manager Casey Stengel (who upon occasion fell asleep during games) setting the major-league record for the most losses in a season (122) as New York fans made light of the bonehead plays, multiple errors, and flailing swings of inept first baseman "Marvelous Marv" Throneberry. In 1969, the "Miracle Mets" under manager Gil Hodges, the former star Dodgers first baseman, and young pitcher Tom Seaver jumped from a ninth-place finish the previous season to upset the Atlanta Braves in the play-offs and ambush the powerful Baltimore Orioles in the World Series.[12]

When it opened on April 3, 1962, Dodger Stadium became an icon of excellence as a sports venue. It was everything – and more – that Walter O'Malley had wanted for Brooklyn – 52,000 thousand seats with unobstructed views of the field, 24,000 parking places in a city that set the standard for automobility. It was unfortunate that the many other new stadiums built in the following decade did not emulate stylish Dodger Stadium. In an attempt to placate taxpayers, architects sought to design facilities that would accommodate both football and baseball, but in so doing, they adequately accommodated neither sport. The resultant multipurpose circular stadiums, almost cookie-cutter in design, were nearly all torn down within 40 years, many being "imploded" by explosives with thousands of fans cheering their obliteration. The multipurpose stadiums that appeared in San Francisco, Pittsburgh, Cincinnati, Philadelphia, New York, Oakland, St Louis, and Anaheim seemingly were near-images of each other. When football was played, the field was laid out from home plate to center field, leaving many fans seated far from the field of play; during the baseball season the circular configuration led to vast swaths of foul territory. Built of gray precast concrete, the dull, unremarkable architectural features would have made the best Soviet architects of the Stalin era proud. To reduce the cost of maintenance and to encourage the holding of rock concerts and other large events, management of these public facilities installed artificial turf that led to a rash of knee injuries for football players and to weird bounces of the baseball that warped the integrity of the game. Two major deviations from this dreary pattern were the Houston Astrodome, opened in 1965 at a cost of $40 million, with an initial glass ceiling that made it impossible to see or catch a fly ball during day games but whose air-conditioned and mosquito-free environment delighted long-suffering Houston fans; and the well-designed 80,000-seat Arrowhead Stadium for the football Chiefs and the 41,000-capacity Royals Stadium for baseball in Kansas City.

By the early twenty-first century, only a few of the venues built in the 1960s were still in use. Beginning in the early 1990s, they were replaced by ballparks designed for baseball only, which featured a "retro" style that sought to capture the ambience of older, more intimate baseballparks coupled with all the modern amenities, including enormous electronic scoreboards and luxury boxes. This new "retro" trend was begun with Orioles Park at Camden Yards in Baltimore in 1992, which had an ambience reminiscent of the ballparks built early in the twentieth century, complete with dark green seating and non-symmetrical fences, but containing many new features for the comfort of spectators. Despite its great popularity upon opening, Camden Yards had been strongly opposed by local social activists and was only approved by nervous city officials when they came to fear that the Orioles would fly the coop just as the Colts had done. Soon new baseball-only stadia with seating capacities in the 40–50,000 range appeared in Cleveland, San Francisco, Arlington, Detroit, Atlanta, Denver, Houston, Philadelphia, Seattle, Cincinnati, Pittsburgh, and San Diego. However, baseball traditionalists remained of the opinion that the three surviving parks of a much-earlier era – Fenway Park in Boston, Wrigley Field in Chicago, and Yankee Stadium (having been given a $100 million remodeling in 1976) in the Bronx – remained the architectural crown jewels of baseball.[13]

In 1950, only the Cleveland Indians (and Browns) played in a publicly financed stadium. But the construction of Candlestick Park in San Francisco began a new and powerful trend. Soon, team owners and politicians were singing the same chorus: a professional team is a major economic stimulant to a city, attracting tourists, creating jobs, revitalizing depressed neighborhoods, creating millions of dollars of "free" publicity. These claims have been scrutinized by economists who have almost universally concluded that there is no demonstrable economic benefit to be derived by local governments or their taxpayers from the costly construction (and sometimes operation) of a modern stadium. Andrew Zimbalist is a leading critic of this line of argument: "The overwhelming conclusion of studies that have tried to estimate the economic benefit of a football or baseball stadium is that there isn't any."[14]

Managers of most of the new sports venues have sought to extract additional monies from advertisers, permitting corporations to place their name on the ball-park with instructions given to broadcasters that they had to specify that the games was being played at such places as Comerica Park in Detroit, Bank One Park in Phoenix, Safeco Field in Seattle, Cinergy Field in Cincinnati, Petco Park in San Diego, Coors Field in Colorado, Citizens Bank Park in Philadelphia, or Pac Bell Park (renamed SBC Park in 2004 following a corporate realignment, and then ATT Park in 2006) in downtown San Francisco. The selling of the name not only led to weird names for sports venues – Qualcomm Park in San Diego or Monster Park at Candlestick Point come readily to mind – but also to embarrassment. When the new, strangely configured $250 million baseball park in Houston opened in 1999, it was named Enron Field after the high-flying Houston energy company, but when Enron went bankrupt in 2002 in one of the greatest corporate scandals in American history, the name was quickly changed to the more prosaic Minute Maid Field, where among other things, fans could participate in a so-called "squeeze play" sponsored by the fruit drink company.

Baseball's Labor Disputes

By the 1970s, major-league baseball players might have been playing in larger ballparks before much larger crowds, but they were not sharing much in the increased revenues. Ever since the shake-out following the Federal League fiasco of 1915, players had tended to defer to management at contract time. An occasional star might hold out for a few extra bucks but for the most part players were content to earn about twice the annual salary of skilled industrial workers. In 1965, the average major-league salary was $12,000, with superstar salaries hovering around $100,000. In spring 1966, however, the somewhat vague uneasiness that seemed to exist over salary scales began to meld into a growing sense of militancy when the Players' Association hired Pittsburgh labor lawyer Marvin Miller. Within a short period, Miller had won the hearts of his constituents and the everlasting enmity of the owners. In 1968, hinting at a work stoppage, he got the owners to sign a new "Basic Agreement" that increased the minimum salary from $7,000 to $10,000 and guaranteed players the right to be represented by an agent. In 1969, Miller called for a boycott of spring-training games when the owners balked at tying rising television revenues to increased contributions to the players' pension fund, but when the opening of the season was imperiled, the owners crumbled. In 1972, a unified union delayed the start of the season for three weeks with a strike over a myriad of contractual issues, including demands for increased playoff shares and pension contributions. Under Miller, the players became united, while the owners became bitterly divided among themselves. In 1973, the Basic Agreement was modified by incorporating the right of a player with two or more years of major-league experience to seek independent arbitration of his salary; fears of losing arbitration hearings led management to offer higher salaries and to negotiate multi-year deals, all of which tended to increase salaries. By 1975, Miller renegotiated the minimum players' salary up to $16,000.[15]

Miller might have been able to obtain substantial increases in pay and fringe benefits at the negotiating table, but the owners still held all the trump cards in the sacrosanct reserve clause. By 1975, however, with a mixture of skillful legal maneuvering and pure luck, Miller had killed the reserve clause, and a new era of free agency was at hand. Players' salaries soon soared to seemingly astronomical heights, then they went much higher. The death of the reserve clause had its beginnings in 1969 with the courageous leadership of St Louis center fielder Curt Flood, who refused to accept a trade to Philadelphia and brought suit against organized baseball challenging the legality of the reserve clause as a "vestige of slavery." In 1972, the case was decided by a split US Supreme Court, which ruled 5–3 against Flood. The majority of justices said that they were loath to overturn a prior decision in 1922 that exempted organized baseball from antitrust laws, while the minority suggested that the Court should do precisely that. The failure of Congress to act on the issue, the three dissenting justices wrote, "should not prevent us from correcting our own mistakes," and the *Washington Post* correctly editorialized that when it came to the reserve clause, "tradition had once more won out over logic."[16]

The decision proved to be but a temporary victory for the owners, because Miller and the players tightened the screws in future negotiations. Their major break came in 1974, when the cantankerous owner of the Oakland Athletics, Charles O. Finley, refused to make good on a deferred annuity clause in pitcher Jim "Catfish" Hunter's contract. Arbiter Peter Seitz ruled that Finley's action had voided the contract, and he declared Hunter a free agent and ordered Finley to pay the $50,000 in question. Because of Finley's obstreperousness, the first player in history was freed from the reserve clause and had the unique opportunity of discovering his real market value. The result was startling. Hunter, who had won 161 games over 10 seasons, learned that he was worth $3.75 million over five years; whereas he had earned $100,000 for his 25 victories the previous season. He would now make $750,000 a season from the Yankees. The new owner of the Yankees, Cleveland shipping magnate George Steinbrenner, was castigated by his fellow owners for signing Hunter, but as subsequent baseball history revealed, he was just beginning a pattern of purchasing top players at high prices to make his Yankees a perennial championship contender.[17]

In 1975, Marvin Miller once again outsmarted the owners and the plodding Commissioner, Bowie Kuhn. His careful examination of the standard player contract revealed a gaping hole in the reserve clause as it was written. It stated that if a player refused to sign a contract, he could be renewed for one year without his signature, but the reserve clause policy was silent on anything beyond that time. Miller got two established pitchers, Andy Messersmith of the Dodgers and Dave McNally of the Montreal Expos, to play that season without a contract. Owners had assumed – erroneously it turned out – that they could continue a player *ad infinitum* under the reserve clause without a new contract. Arbiter Peter Seitz ruled on behalf of the players, saying that the standard contract stipulated one year and one year only. The contract was, the owners were told, what it said. Seitz declared the two men free agents, in effect killing the reserve clause. Messersmith signed for $1.7 million a year with the Atlanta Braves, and McNally, suffering from arm problems, retired with the satisfaction of having opened the door to great wealth for those who would follow. A new day had dawned for organized baseball, with the pendulum of power having swung decisively in favor of the players.[18]

For the first time in baseball history, the players held the upper hand in salary negotiations, and their pay rates jumped spectacularly. Miller negotiated an agreement whereby players would be eligible for free agency after four years under the new standard contract. By 1980, the average player pay was $144,000, and by

1991 it reached $891,000. When the 2004 season opened, player salaries had sky-rocketed to an average of $2.7 million, while top stars, and many mediocre players, were making between $8 and $15 million annually. In 2001, the ultimate potential of free agency was realized when the Texas Rangers signed Seattle Mariners shortstop Alex Rodriquez, widely believed to be the best all-around player in baseball at the time, to a 10-year, $252 million contract.[19]

After the arrival of free agency the level of play on the field proved exciting, with many hard fought pennant races; attendance grew in response. The owners, however, were not happy campers as they repeatedly sought to regain control of salaries, but each time their heavy-handed plan of attack backfired. An effort in 1981 to abolish the free-agency market led to a mid-season strike that saw the players unified (they forfeited more than $30 million in salaries). When the owners' strike insurance ran out, they surrendered, but not before 713 games had been canceled with the loss of an estimated $72 million in ticket sales.

Under new Commissioner Peter Ueberroth in 1985, the owners were informally advised to control salaries by not pursuing players eligible for free agency. For three years, there were no significant free-agent signings, while owners piously professed that they had no interest in building their teams other than through their own minor-league systems or by trades. An appeal to an independent arbitrator by the Players' Association led to a finding that the owners had engaged in a massive conspiracy of collusion, and they were ordered to make payments to former free agents totaling a whopping $280 million.[20] A new round of free agency signings by the wealthy clubs ensued, and soon salaries for star players had reached $10 million or higher, with even utility players making well into the seven figures.

Most owners complained about escalating salaries but they were essentially criticizing themselves. In the early 1990s, several owners expressed their desire to establish some form of salary restraint (or "salary cap"), as existed in professional basketball and football, but now they faced a unified and strong union headed by Miller's former assistant, attorney Donald Fehr. In 1993, a season in which Toronto defeated the Philadelphia Phillies in an exciting six-game World Series, season attendance figures reached a record 70 million. Although baseball probably had never been in a better overall financial position, the owners were determined to take back much of what the players had gained over the previous two decades. The 1994 season began under a heavy cloud: the Basic Agreement had expired, but talks between the two sides continued with both staking out extreme bargaining positions. Ultimately, the Players' Association decided to strike on August 12, hoping to force concessions before the playoffs and World Series drew near. Acting Commissioner Bud Selig, a former automobile dealer and now owner of the Milwaukee Brewers, threatened to cancel the playoffs and the World Series unless an agreement was reached by September 9, apparently thinking that this deadline would force the players to capitulate. However, they did not blink and the season was canceled. For the first time in 89 seasons, there would be no World Series.[21] The "fall classic" had somehow survived throughout two world wars, but now a dispute among millionaire owners and millionaire players abruptly ended the season in August.

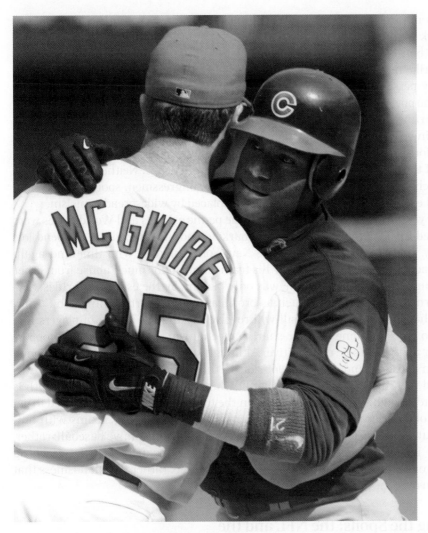

Figure 12.2 After the disastrous strike that led to the cancellation of the 1994 World Series, organized baseball suffered through several difficult seasons as many fans went "on strike." They returned with enthusiasm in 1998 when Sammy Sosa of the Chicago Cubs and Mark McGwire of the St Louis Cardinals went on a home run hitting binge that saw both eclipse the record of 61 set in 1961 by Roger Maris. Their friendly competition thrilled even the most jaundiced of baseball fans, although that enthusiasm was later dimmed by the shadows cast over baseball by allegations of widespread use of steroids. © Gary Hershorn/Reuters/ CORBIS.

The strike continued well into spring training in 1995. Finally, the National Labor Relations Board issued a preliminary finding which concluded that the owners had conspired to abolish free agency and impose a salary cap. The players had won again, and the season began a week late. Angry fans retaliated: attendance fell by 20 million from the 1993 season and remained depressed the following two seasons. Fans put the blame on both owners and players, believing that neither side could be counted on to protect the sacred trust of America's Game. The strike broke the game's continuity with the past; records and statistics were forever disrupted, and the fans' emotional connection to the game was seriously jarred. Only the most naive persons could look at the game and not see that it was no longer the special "National Pastime" that connected generations – baseball was now just another business.

It was not until the season of 1998 – when Sammy Sosa of the Chicago Cubs and Mark McGwire of the St Louis Cardinals went on a home-run hitting binge that saw both surpass Roger Maris's record – that fans returned to the ballparks in pre-strike numbers. The two sluggers enjoyed the competition and engaged in a friendly personal duel that helped erase the many bad feelings created by the strike. The powerfully built McGwire ultimately won the duel with a record-setting 70 home runs, while Sosa settled for 66.[22] In 2005, however, a series of congressional hearings led to revelations that many major league players had for years used various forms of steroids and human growth drugs, and the images of the two heroes of the slugfest of 1998 were linked to steroid usage. Neither men admitted using such substances, much to the disbelief of congressmen, sports writers, and fans, and even the magic of 1998 had been replaced by widespread cynicism.

In the years since the debacle of 1994, the pennant races and World Series were dominated by teams with large media markets and owners willing to spend lots of money. George Steinbrenner of the New York Yankees, who time and again signed leading free agents to bolster his team, came in for much abuse from other owners and sports writers. But he was only playing by the established rules. Several informed commentators, such as broadcaster and sports savant Bob Costas, argued that the future of baseball will revolve around the ability of players and owners to agree on some revenue-sharing mechanism that will provide an opportunity for all teams to be competitive. Although some teams with limited revenue have won divisions and competed for slots in the World Series – the Oakland Athletics and the Minnesota Twins fit that bill during the early 2000s – the truth is that few teams whose payrolls were not in the top 25 percent have managed to get to the World Series since the great strike of 1994. Increasingly, teams with limited resources are no longer in the business of playing competitive baseball: rather, they are in the entertainment business. As Costas argues, such far-reaching reform would enable fans to view baseball "as a game, rather than a business that has taken over the game."[23]

Reaping the Spoils: the NFL and the World of Parity

For complex reasons, the leadership of baseball proved unable to emulate the successful policies designed to assure financial parity of all franchises that have enabled the National Football League to achieve economic success in the front office and competitive balance on the field. Attendance for nearly all NFL games approached sellouts, and television ratings remained high despite heavy saturation of college and professional games. When Pete Rozelle became Commissioner of the NFL in 1960, he preached the doctrine of competitive balance and implemented it effectively with sharing of television fees, gate receipts, and even from the sale of NFL-franchised paraphernalia. This competitive balance has meant that between 1967 and 2004, 24 teams have played in at least one Super Bowl. No team has come close to dominating the NFL as the Yankees have baseball. That

did not mean, however, that certain well-managed and well-financed teams did not enjoy extended periods of success, such as the Green Bay Packers during the 1960s; nor did it mean that parity could overcome the inept family stewardship of the St Louis-Arizona Cardinals that condemned that woeful franchise to just two division championships and not a single appearance in a conference championship game or a Super Bowl between 1970 and 2004.

During the 1970s, the Packers were replaced by two teams that prematurely had the word "dynasty" applied to them – the Dallas Cowboys and the Pittsburgh Steelers. In 1933, Pittsburgh's man about town Art Rooney bought a new NFL franchise for $2,500, named the team the Pirates, and watched them suffer through seven consecutive losing seasons. Renamed the Steelers in 1940, the team finally enjoyed its first winning season in 1942. It was not until 1952 that the Steelers – as blue-collar and traditional a team as one could find – abandoned the single-wing formation for the chic passing-friendly T-formation. Finally, in 1962, the Steelers made it to a playoff game, but the team's losing ways continued throughout the 1960s. Despite the losing seasons, Rooney remained positive, continued his quest for success, operating his team as if it were a community trust and not a personal business.

Figure 12.3 Green Bay Packers coach Vince Lombardi is shown along the sidelines during the initial Super Bowl played in Los Angeles against the Kansas City Chiefs on January 15, 1967, a game won by the Packers 35–10. With him are three star players who helped him win five NFL championships: fullback Jim Taylor (31), halfback Paul Hornung (5), and quarterback Bart Starr (15). © Bettman/ CORBIS.

At a time when many owners sought to extort their communities for new stadiums and other amenities, Rooney never mentioned moving the franchise: "Pittsburgh is my home. The Pittsburgh Steelers are my team."[24] In 1969, he finally hit upon the right person to take the Steelers to the top when he hired Chuck Noll, a young coach who had played at the University of Dayton and learned the intricacies of the professional game as an offensive lineman for Paul Brown at Cleveland. Noll used the draft wisely, building a powerful aggregation of young players through four successive drafts, four of whom would become future Hall of Fame members. In 1972, Noll led his rebuilt team to an 11–3 record and then won one of the most memorable of all playoff games against the Oakland Raiders when fullback Franco Harris made the seemingly impossible "immaculate reception" for a touchdown on a tipped pass late in the game. The Steelers defeated the Minnesota Vikings in Super Bowl IX. It would be the first of four such championships that the Steelers would win during the 1970s; they capped off their magnificent ride through the 1970s with an eighth-straight central division crown and six consecutive AFC championships with a decisive 31–19 victory over the Los Angeles Rams in Super Bowl XIV. Aging players and low draft opportunities – Pete Rozelle's parity – caught up with the Steelers during the 1980s, but they remained competitive, making the playoffs three times. In 1991, Chuck Noll, headed for the Hall of Fame, retired with an overall record of 209–156–1.

The Steelers' emphasis on a crunching defense and a disciplined offense was an apt reflection of the industrial city they represented. The Dallas Cowboys, however, were marked from their initial season as a finesse team, one that was representative of the new service and high-tech environment of modern Texas. In 1960, New York Giants' defensive coordinator Tom Landry was hired by owner Clint Murchison to coach his Dallas expansion team; Landry remained at the helm for 29 seasons. The Cowboys were winless in their initial season and were only 13–38–3 after four losing seasons, at which time Murchison awarded Landry a 10-year contract extension. The maturing team went on a 20-year run of winning seasons that included four Super Bowl appearances (with victories over Miami in 1972 and Denver in 1978), 18 playoff appearances, and 13 division titles. Under Landry and general manager Tex Schramm, the Cowboys became a model of efficiency and computer-age competence in the front office and on the field. Landry introduced new strategic concepts that included the "flex" defense, a "multiple-set" offense, a "shotgun" offensive formation, and extensive man-in-motion formations designed to confuse defenses. Schramm's complex player-evaluation computer programs led to many an astute selection on draft day. Wearing their classic silver and metallic-blue uniforms, the Cowboys became known as "America's Team," enjoying unusually high ratings on nationally televised games. Part of the Cowboys' image was the synchronized sideline dancing of the scantily clad and perpetually smiling Dallas Cowboy Cheerleaders, who became the prototype for exploiting "wholesome" sexuality as part of the overall NFL entertainment package. Close-up television shots made the Cheerleaders America's favorites along with the team on the field. Soon most teams had created their own version of the famous Dallas Cowboy Cheerleaders.[25]

During the 1980s, the Cowboys locked horns with the San Francisco 49ers of cerebral Bill Walsh, a coaching protege of Paul Brown, whose innovative offensive system created a revolution in the concepts of offensive football. Called the "West Coast" offense, Walsh's system featured the importance of a quarterback quick of foot and even quicker of mind, who could "read" the defense before the snap of the ball, audibly calling an appropriate play to exploit the weakness detected. The West Coast system emphasized finesse blocking on complex running plays and intricately executed pass patterns that involved three to five receivers, precision timing between quarterback and receiver, utilization of running backs as pass-receivers, and meticulous pre-game planning that included the scripting of the first 25 offensive plays to be run based upon intensive analysis of the opposing team. Hired away from his head coaching position at Stanford University in 1979 by free-spending owner Eddie DeBartolo, Walsh assembled a talented group of athletes, led by Hall of Fame quarterbacks Joe Montana and Steve Young, whose abilities fit his unique system. He had a special knack for player evaluation, springing big surprises – many proving to be prescient – on draft day by his unconventional approach to the art of player selection. Using DeBartolo's very deep pockets, Walsh assembled the "Team of the Eighties" in part simply by outbidding other teams for top free-agent talent.[26]

Although the National Football League enjoyed success since its merger with the upstart American Football League in 1966, the road nonetheless was often rocky. During the 1980s, the league endured two devastating strikes, both of which resulted in alienation (temporarily, to be certain) of fans and serious disruption of two seasons. In 1982, the league played only a nine-game regular season as play was interrupted from mid-September to almost Thanksgiving. In 1987, the owners hired "replacement" players (players' union officials called them "scabs") for three games before the complex economic issues were settled with neither side able to claim a clear victory. Although the two strikes faded into the background, they underscored that, with increased success and rising revenues, the stakes for owners, players, and host cities had risen dramatically.[27]

The financial success of the NFL after it merged in 1966 with the American Football League stimulated two rival leagues, both of which sought to take advantage of television. In 1974, Los Angeles businessman Gary Davidson announced the formation of the World Football League (WFL). It featured teams with such exotic names as the Shreveport Steamer, the Philadelphia Bell, and the Chicago Fire. Although the 12 teams managed to stir a few ripples in the waters of professional football, the anticipated big television contract was not forthcoming and the WFL disappeared after two desultory seasons. Ten years later, the United States Football League made its appearance, and with such high-profile owners as financier Donald Trump, it initially seemed to pose a substantial threat to the NFL. The USFL played its first season in the spring and early summer months and attracted an average attendance of over 20,000. However, it decided to move its games to the fall and challenge the NFL in several cities. The NFL naturally fought back, and its retaliatory actions stimulated a $600 million antitrust suit by the new league charging the NFL with attempting to prevent its securing a major television contract. The NFL faced possible treble damages of $1.6 billion. After two months of trial, the jury agreed with the USFL and found the NFL guilty, assessing it the magnanimous amount of $1 in damages. When that was tripled, in accordance with the law, the USLF walked away with a check for $3. Shortly thereafter, the new league vaporized. The jury apparently felt that the NFL had conspired to restrict the USFL from access to the networks, but that the new league, by deciding to change its original philosophy of playing its games between spring and fall, had broken faith with fans and had demonstrated bad business judgment.[28]

The USFL's most significant decision was to break the NFL's unwritten agreement with college football not to draft or sign college players until their four years of eligibility had expired. The NFL, which had refused to establish any form of costly minor-league developmental teams, preferred to let the colleges do that work for them; in return, the league had not drafted college players until they had exhausted their eligibility. However, the USFL recognized that there was no legal basis to deny playing opportunities to underclassmen. In 1983 Donald Trump, signed junior running-back and Heisman Trophy winner Herschel Walker to a New Jersey Generals contract off the campus of the University of Georgia for $4 million, a seemingly astronomical salary for professional football at the time. Several other top under classmen were drafted thereafter. The Los Angeles Express stunned the sports world when it signed Brigham Young University All-American quarterback Steve Young to a 10-year $40 million contract, with much of the money tied up in post-retirement annuities, deferred payments, and other exotic forms of creative financing. The USFL also signed such future NFL star quarterbacks as Doug Flutie and Jim Kelly, but the lack of a solid financial basis, a mediocre product on the field, and the prestige and popularity of the NFL combined to doom the new league to oblivion in 1985 after just three seasons.

While the two rival leagues caused occasional heartburn at NFL headquarters, it was issues that surfaced within the league that were of greater import. The most significant of these distractions were the work of the brilliant but obstreperous Al Davis of the Oakland Raiders. Ever since the merger of the AFL and the NFL in 1966, Davis had demonstrated his fiery independence, accentuated with his penchant for filing lawsuits. In 1963, he became the head coach of the struggling Oakland Raiders of the American Football League and produced a 10–4 record in his first season, and in 1966, became the Commissioner of the AFL. He was instrumental in conducting the extended negotiations that led to the merger with the NFL, but when that deal was consummated, he apparently was upset by the "indemnities" that the NFL extracted from AFL teams, as well as by the decision that Pete Rozelle, and not he, would become commissioner of the merged league.[29]

In Oakland, Davis encouraged the development of the image of the Raiders as a renegade outfit, often signing players who had previously encountered discipline problems with other teams, as well as some whose encounters with law enforcement, raucous behavior, drug use, and heavy drinking were legendary. The Raiders lost to Green Bay in the 1968 Super Bowl, but under youthful coach John Madden they won the 1977 Super Bowl XI over the Minnesota Vikings and the 1981 Super Bowl over the Philadelphia Eagles. When the Los Angeles Rams began exploring the possibility of leaving their long-time home in the Los Angeles Coliseum in 1979, Davis expressed interest in moving the Raiders to heavily populated Southern California. He knew, of course, that NFL polices would require approval by the other team owners, but he forged ahead and dared the league to stop him. When he signed the first legal papers with Los Angeles officials, law suits flew fast and furious. In 1982, a federal court in Los Angeles ruled that Davis was correct in charging the NFL with antitrust violations in denying the Raiders' right to move to Los Angeles, and in April 1983 a second jury not only upheld the original verdict but assessed the NFL $35 million in damages. It was the biggest setback in Rozelle's 29 years at the NFL helm.[30]

Rozelle and most NFL owners thereafter treated Davis as a pariah in their midst, a role that he seemed to relish. When the USFL sued the NFL for antitrust violations, Davis and the Raiders were excluded as defendants in return for his testimony against his own league! San Diego Chargers' owner Gene Klein perhaps most eloquently described the team owners' feelings about Davis:

> He's an egomaniac! He loves to bitch and complain and throw smokescreens. He loves to hear himself talk and tries to get the spotlight at our meetings. He loves to expound about everything. The son of a bitch has been trying to take power ever since I've been in the League.[31]

In January 1984, the Los Angeles Raiders won Super Bowl XVIII over the Washington Redskins, but then slowly sank into mediocrity; the franchise would have to wait two decades before it made another Super Bowl appearance. With 100,000 seats to fill in the rambling Los Angeles Coliseum, and with the team barely winning half of its games, attendance did not come close to approaching projections. Consequently, most Raiders home games were blacked out in Southern California's huge television market, and the team never connected with the fans in the sprawling megalopolis. When various new stadium proposals fizzled and Davis's demands for extensive remodeling of the Coliseum were rebuffed, he cut a sweetheart deal with the Alameda County Commissioners and moved the Raiders back to Oakland in 1995. Shortly thereafter, when ticket sales did not produce sellouts in the hideously remodeled Oakland Coliseum (seating expansion being part of the deal to lure the Raiders back to Oakland), Davis promptly sued the county for various alleged misdeeds. Finally, following the 2002 season, the renegade team that Davis had long touted as having "Pride and Poise" and "Commitment to Excellence" finally returned to the Super Bowl, only to be soundly trounced 48–21 by the Tampa Bay Buccaneers, now coached by Jon Gruden, a bright and promising young head coach who had left the Raiders just 10 months earlier because of his difficulties in working under the aging and increasingly cranky Al Davis.

One of the lasting legacies of Pete Rozelle was his commitment to the proposition that all teams should have an opportunity for success. Five years after Rozelle retired, new Commissioner Paul Tagliabue, fittingly an attorney by profession, added to Rozelle's legacy by working with the NFL Players' Association to maintain a highly competitive environment. In the new General Bargaining Agreement concluded in 1994, the NFL took a major step to address an imbalance that many critics had come to believe threatened Rozelle's equity policy. The target was the free-spending owner of the San Francisco 49ers, Eddie DeBartolo. Determined to have a winner at any cost, DeBartolo opened his own deep pockets and apparently drew upon funds available through the family's privately owned DeBartolo Corporation, a leader in shopping mall development and management. It was widely said around the league that the 49ers had better back-up players than many of their opponents had starters. For DeBartolo, winning was far more important than showing a mere profit:

> It wasn't a disregard for dollars and cents. That wasn't it. Show me a good loser and I'll show you a loser. . . . You either win and give it your all – physically, emotionally, spirit, and dollars or get the hell out, you don't belong in sports.[32]

Following that spendthrift philosophy, DeBartolo enjoyed five Super Bowl victories and several division titles under Walsh and his successor, George Seifert. DeBartolo's freewheeling days came to an end when the new Collective Bargaining Agreement established a firm salary cap that limited the total amount that a team could spend on its 45 regular and eight reserve squad members. The owners were not only tired of DeBartolo's willingness to buy championships, but they also acutely recognized that his pursuit of free agents was driving up salaries across the league. The new salary cap was linked to a complicated computer-driven formula based upon anticipated league revenues from television contracts and ticket sales, with 63 percent of the amount reserved equally for players' compensation for all teams. In return for agreeing to such a cap, the players received the right to free agency after four years under contract to a team. The players also received a guaranteed minimum salary. In 1994, when the new agreement went into practice, each team was limited to $35 million for player compensation, a figure that grew with inflation, increased television revenues, and higher ticket prices to $85 million for the 2005 season. The impact of the salary cap was immediate. All teams were permitted to spend the same amount for player salaries, which meant that the expertise of the front office in drafting college players and signing free agents, and the skill of the coaching staff, could turn a losing team into a winning team very quickly. It also seemed to mean that the likelihood of one team dominating the league for any extended period of time was highly unlikely, an assumption that the New England Patriots challenged with three consecutive Super Bowl wins in 2003–4–5.

The Wondrous World of Magic, Larry, and Michael

The National Basketball Association has deep roots in East Coast seaboard cities such as Boston, Philadelphia, and New York. Professional basketball was played during the 1920s and the 1930s in the Eastern League and American Basketball League but teams came and went with frequency; however, such teams as the New York Original Celtics and the Philadelphia SPHAs (named for the South Philadelphia Hebrew Association) enjoyed a loyal local fan base, often playing games

before 4,000 or more. The Original Celtics once played 205 games in one season on a national barnstorming tour. In 1949, the small and unstable nature of professional basketball began to change when the National Basketball Association (NBA) was formed. The NBA developed slowly with franchises located in such small venues as Syracuse, Rochester, and Fort Wayne. During the 1950s, the Boston Celtics emerged as an exciting team that captured national attention, thanks in large part to the behind-the-back and no-look passes of guard Bob Cousy and the up-tempo style coached by Arnold "Red" Auerbach. The fortunes of the team skyrocketed in 1956 when 6' 10" center Bill Russell joined the team after leading the University of San Francisco to two NCAA championships. The slender, long-armed Russell was a defensive and rebounding standout, and the team began a run of eight consecutive NBA championships. In 1966, Auerbach turned over the coaching duties to Russell – making him the NBA's first African American coach – who won two of the next three titles as a player-coach. Russell's play virtually revolutionized the game, as he turned his blocked shots and rebounds into quick outlet passes to such speedy teammates as K. C. Jones or John Havlicek, producing one of the most effective fast-break offenses in the history of the game.

Figure 12.4 Two of professional basketball's great centers, Wilt Chamberlain (13) of the Philadelphia Warriors and Bill Russell (6) of the Boston Celtics, are captured in this picture during a game at Boston Gardens on November 7, 1959. Their titanic rebounding and defensive battles near the basket, often televised nationally, helped make the National Basketball Association a major professional sport. © Bettmann/CORBIS.

When 7' 2", 275-pound Wilt Chamberlain joined the Philadelphia Warriors in 1959, the titanic battles between this new high-scoring center and the great defender in Celtic Green became the stuff of hoops legend. The seemingly slender "Wilt the Stilt" had enormous speed and agility. In 1960, Chamberlain scored 100 points in a game against the last-place New York Knicks, and during the 1961–62 season he averaged 50 points a game, a record that no one has even approached since. During his 14 years in the league, Chamberlain set a record of 23,928 rebounds that remains on the books. He helped the Philadelphia 76ers win the 1967 NBA championship, and in his final year in the league in 1972, became a defensive specialist to help the Los Angeles Lakers, led by guard Jerry West, win a championship. Chamberlain's many critics liked to point to Russell's 11 championship rings during essentially the same time, but Chamberlain rightfully contended that Russell was surrounded by a much better group of players on the dynastic Celtics.[33]

During the 1960s and the 1970s the league expanded into the south and west, adding 21 franchises in all. The success of the NBA, and the potential of television revenues, naturally spawned an imitator. In 1967, the American Basketball Association (ABA) made its appearance in 12 cities, featuring a red, white, and blue ball, with shots from beyond 21 feet counting for three points. The league was plagued by franchise failures when the anticipated lucrative television contract failed to materialize, but it managed to last for nine years. During that time, 31 franchises came and went, and at the end there were only 12 still standing. The ABA at one time or another included such long-forgotten teams as the Memphis Tams, Pittsburgh Pipers, Minnesota Muskies, and Anaheim Amigos. Several outstanding players played in the ABA, but no player approached the skills of Julius "Dr J" Erving, who entered the league in 1971 with the Virginia Squires and ended up playing for the New York Nets. Known for his soaring drives to the basket and an incredibly soft touch off the glass, Erving went on to star in the NBA with the Philadelphia 76ers. Throughout its nine years, the ABA was colorful and exciting. In 1976, the NBA agreed to absorb four of the best franchises – the New York Nets, Denver Nuggets, Indiana Pacers, and San Antonio Spurs – while such teams as the Kentucky Colonels and Spirits of St Louis disappeared.[34]

The demise of the ABA came during a down period for the NBA. With the great stars of the boom years of the 1960s now retired, the league lacked star appeal. That changed in 1980, when Earvin "Magic" Johnson and Larry Bird entered the league. The two had attracted high television ratings when their college teams, Michigan State and Indiana State, met in the 1979 NCAA championship game – many say this was the game that turned "March Madness" into an American sports phenomenon – and they would continue their intense, if friendly, rivalry for more than a decade. Their popularity turned NBA basketball into a major spectator sport. In Bird's first season in 1979–80, the Boston Celtics won 61 games, reviving memories of the great Boston teams of the 1960s. However, it was Magic Johnson, teaming with center Kareem Abdul-Jabbar, who helped transform the Lakers from a lackluster team into NBA champions. The following season, Bird proved to be the catalyst for a championship run as he teamed with center Robert

Figure 12.5 Many sports experts believe Michael Jordan to have been the greatest male athlete of the twentieth century. Shown here making a spectacular dunk in an NBA playoff game against the Detroit Pistons in 1988, Jordan not only became a power on the basketball court, but his endorsements and business ventures created a financial empire that made him one of the wealthiest men in America. © Bettmann/CORBIS.

Parish and forward Kevin McHale to form one of the most formidable front lines in NBA history.

The rivalry between the two superstars reached its crescendo between 1983 and 1988, when one of their teams captured the NBA title each year.[35] The style of play between the two was a study in contrasts. The 6' 8" Johnson was a dynamo of speed and incredible balance and agility, at times leading fast breaks, making no-look sleight-of-hand passes, driving for an acrobatic lay-up, at times playing the point-guard position to set up his teammates for easy baskets, at others posting himself in the pivot to take advantage of a smaller defender. Bird was markedly slower and less athletic. He relied upon his determination to master fundamentals and to take advantage of every slight lapse by his opponent. Bird became famous for his ability to block out opponents to get a crucial rebound, and his ability to make passes around or through several defenders to set up a teammate for an easy basket became legendary. By the time Bird retired in 1992, the Celtics had won three NBA titles and finished second twice; Johnson's Lakers had won five championships while losing in the finals four times.

As the magisterial competition between Bird and Johnson began to wane in the late 1980s, league officials feared that the game would fall into another trough as in the post-Celtic heyday of the 1970s. That did not occur because of the emergence of Michael Jordan. The son of middle-class parents from Wilmington, North Carolina, as a freshman Jordan led the University of North Carolina to the NCAA championship in 1982, when he sank a last minute 15-foot jump shot to defeat the favored Georgetown Hoyas by one point. After earning All-American honors for the next two seasons, he declared himself available for the NBA draft after his junior year.[36] In 1984, he was drafted third by the long-struggling Chicago Bulls (leading to the all-time top sports trivia question: Who were the two players drafted in front of Michael Jordan?).[37]

Biographer David Halberstam contends that although he possessed incredible natural ability, the key to Jordan's success was his enormous personal pride, which pushed him to work harder than his competitors. During his first NBA season in 1984–85, Jordan averaged 28.2 points a game and was named to the All-Star Team and as Rookie of the Year. He become known for his spectacular, even artistic crowd-pleasing slam-dunks in which he seemed to hang above the basket as if suspended from the ceiling. Rival coaches and players also recognized that he played defense better than almost anyone in the league. Jordan's shining personality helped make him a media favorite, and coupled with his superior athletic talent prompted the smallish but growing Nike sportswear company to make him its surprising choice to endorse a new brand of basketball shoe that had a pocket of air in the heel. Soon fans everywhere were calling both the player and his shoe "Air Jordan."

Despite Jordan's personal heroics, the Bulls struggled for several years, but then, in 1989, the Bulls hired Phil Jackson as coach and bolstered the players' roster with forward Scotty Pippen and center Horace Grant. The Bulls lost in a seven-game series against the Detroit Pistons in the Eastern Conference finals, but the following year, the Bulls won 61 regular-season games, deposed the defending champion Pistons in the conference finals, and took out the Los Angeles Lakers in five games to win the NBA championship. Jordan took time out in summer 1992 to spark the "Dream Team" to an easy victory in the Barcelona Olympics, the first time the United States sent professional athletes to compete in the Olympics.

By fall 1993, due to his sophisticated Nike commercial appearances and his exceptional level of play, Jordan had become one of the most famous persons in the world – his ubiquitous red Number 23 jersey being observed even on the remote plains of Outer Mongolia. He was undoubtedly the most recognizable and most popular American. In his television and magazine commercials, Jordan's sparkling personality connected with his audience as almost no other athlete had done since Babe Ruth. He became a national icon for the American world of commercial entertainment, in a culture obsessed with celebrity and in awe of superior athletic achievement. He did this at a time when African American athletes had previously been given only limited opportunities to cash in on product endorsements. When Jordan retired from playing in 1998, *Fortune* magazine estimated that he had generated $10 billion in revenues. Michael Jordan, Inc. was larger than many Third World countries.[38]

Always Turn Left: NASCAR Takes the Checkered Flag

As the twentieth century wound down, the most rapidly growing sport in the United States was stock car racing. Controlled by the privately owned National Association of Stock Car Automobile Racing (NASCAR), by the mid-1980s the sport's major races were drawing crowds of 150,000. Although NASCAR only first appeared on national television in 1979, by the mid-1990s its annual television revenues had exceeded $1 billion and its total viewing audience was second only to professional football. In 2001, NASCAR signed a six-year $2.8 billion contract with a combine of FOX, NBC, and Turner Cable, and its ratings continued to soar.

Until the breakthrough decade of the 1990s, NASCAR had a distinctly rural, white, southern "redneck" flavor. Its fan base was originally overwhelmingly white working-class males who lived in former Confederate states. At the race tracks, the down-home culture of barbeque, beer, pick-up trucks, and country music predominated. Confederate flags were in much in evidence. The origins of NASCAR can be found in the 1930s, when hard-pressed drivers sought to make a few dollars during tough economic times delivering moonshine whiskey from illicit mountain stills to urban distributors. These "whiskey trippers" were hounded by tax agents of the federal government and often had to put the pedal to the metal to outrun the "revenuers." The risks to these drivers were great, but the profits irresistible – a typical load of 25-gallon jugs of "white lightening" would bring $250 at a time when jobs were scarce or even nonexistent.[39]

Soon the more audacious drivers sought local bragging rights by racing their fellow whiskey trippers along back roads. Before long, they were testing their skills on crude dirt tracks cut out of red-clay hillsides, with local rules prevailing and races often ending in beer-drenched brawls. When these small tracks began making their appearance in the 1940s, "chaos and confusion" reigned in the emerging sport. As one observer recalls,

> There were too many conflicts of interest. The rules weren't uniform, they weren't fair and the promoters couldn't be trusted. This wasn't news. Everybody who'd been

in racing longer than a week knew about getting cheated out of a win, swindled out of a purse, or tricked in one way or another.[40]

Track owners often neglected the safety of the spectators and drivers. Spectators were not well protected from wayward careening cars, and some oval tracks were not banked on the curves and their dirt surface was dangerously rutted.

One of the many drivers who became infatuated with the racing of cars taken from the show lot stock of any automobile dealer was William France, owner of an automobile repair shop in Daytona Beach, Florida. On the weekends, he raced his 1935 Ford on the ocean beaches, and in 1938 he took over the promotion of local races. After the war, "Big Bill" (he stood 6' 5" and weighed 240 pounds) decided that stock-car racing had a viable financial future if it were properly organized, regulated, and promoted. He intuitively understood that America's fascination with automobiles could be converted into a spectator sport. "We need to have races for the most modern automobiles available. Plain, ordinary working people have to be able to associate with their cars. Standard street stock cars are what we should be running." France envisioned an annual national championship built upon a series of sanctioned races. As Scott Crawford writes, "He had a dream of creating a national organization that would transform a rough, informal, redneck activity into a structured, formal sport."[41]

In 1948, France established NASCAR by bringing together several regional competing circuits and organizations. At the planning meetings that he called and over which he presided, France made certain he would be in complete control. On many occasions Big Bill was accused of being a "dictator." His patented response was, "Well, let's make that a benevolent dictator."[42] His successor, son Bill, Jr., would continue that domineering style and operate a national program in which the participant-owners had little, if any, say or control over the operation of a multi billion dollar entertainment and sporting enterprise. NASCAR was and remains a private family-owned enterprise. The advantages the Frances have offered to race-car owners and their drivers and pit crews were more than sufficient to preclude any insurrection.

France established his full authority during the first year of operation. At the 1949 "strictly stock" Grand National Championship held in Charlotte – NASCAR's first major race – he disqualified apparent winner Glenn Dunnaway for using a system of wedges in his 1947 Ford spring shock absorbers (a trick, incidentally, that whiskey trippers had often used to keep firm control on the sharp curves on hill-country roads). Ironically, it was later determined that Dunnaway's car had actually been used the previous week to transport moonshine! The owner went to court to get France's decision overturned, but he was slapped down by a judge's ruling that upheld NASCAR's power to set the rules for its own races. Thus France's formula for success was in place: the races would be conducted on a level field with owners and drivers held to rigorous standards. The result was that many races would be decided by a few seconds with less than a car length often separating the front runners after several hundred miles of circling the oval track. Such finishes, France knew, would produce suspense and excitement and bring the spectators back for more. He had hit upon an appealing formula.

Figure 12.6 Contemporary NASCAR fans would scarcely recognize the popular sport of stock-car racing from this 1953 photograph of a multi-car pile-up on the then dirt track at the Daytona Speedway. Over the years, the France family financial empire that operated NASCAR, built Daytona into an ultra-modern racing venue. © Bettmann/CORBIS.

Not that France was unwilling to change. In the 1950s, he began a process of permitting the substantial modification of race cars to the point that they only *looked like* vehicles off the showroom floor. The "stock" vehicles that fans saw were, in fact, hand-built, custom-made engineering marvels modified in every way possible to enhance speed and safety. During the 1960s, many heated arguments occurred as France forcefully established the power of his organization to control every tiny part of the vehicles on the track, which looked from afar like nothing more than the neighbor's Mercury. By the mid-1960s, speeds approaching 200 mph were recorded.

In 1959, France opened the Daytona International Speedway. With its 31-degree banked corners and wide racing configuration that permitted several cars to race side by side, he created a new environment for stock-car racing. The Daytona Speedway was designed to encourage both safety and high speeds, a sure formula for creating excitement. Over the years, the Speedway was transformed into a 480-acre venue of museums, shops, restaurants, vast public parking lots, and an amphitheater that could seat 165,000 fans. It is the site each February of the first of the many NASCAR point-system races. (Unlike other sports, NASCAR holds its premier event as the first of the season, not the grand finale.) In 1961, France's control of NASCAR was threatened by an effort by several discontented drivers to join the Teamsters Union, but he managed to halt the effort, at one point threatened to "plow up" his Daytona racetrack if the Teamsters became part of stock-car racing, and he later banned for life those drivers he believed were behind the union movement.[43] In a classic "the end justifies the means" rationalization, racing journalist Steve Waid had this to say about the organization of NASCAR in 1996:

> It is a dictatorship, pure and simple. Let's make that a benevolent dictatorship. It makes the rules; calls the shots. As a result, everyone might not agree, but everyone does what they are told – and the positive results have become obvious.[44]

As NASCAR gained steadily in popularity during the 1950s and 1960s, the regionalism of the sport became one of its major strengths – and weaknesses. The ties to moonshine running – a game of "cops and corn" as one writer put it – became a nostalgic part of stock-car racing lore. In 1965, journalist Tom Wolfe published "The Last American Hero is Junior Johnson. Yes!" in *Esquire* magazine. It was a romanticized story of Robert "Junior" Johnson, a "country boy" who delivered moonshine to city folk from his father's large copper still located in the heart of Wilkes County, North Carolina, then widely considered the "moonshine capital" of America. At one point the authorities caught Johnson red-handed, and he served 10 months in a federal detention center. Upon his release he focused his attention on stock car driving. In 1963, he won more than $100,000 on the NASCAR circuit. This felon-turned-racing-star had become, according to Wolfe, "a famous driver, rich, . . . respected, solid, idolized in his home-town and throughout the rural South."[45]

Over the years, the informality and Southern small-town ambiance of stock-car racing inexorably waned, replaced by images of corporate America with all the bureaucratic organization, computer-driven efficiency, top-down regimentation, and rigid regulation that was the norm of modern American corporations. In 1969, under pressure from anti-smoking groups, the federal government banned all cigarette advertising on radio and television, so cigarette manufacturers not only had plenty of money for advertising but needed to find new ways to spend it. The Phillip Morris Company responded to this challenge by sponsoring the Virginia Slims Women's Professional Tennis Tour. Taking a cue from its larger competitor, R. J. Reynolds opted to sponsor the 31-race NASCAR championship series. Thus was born the Winston National Championship Cup, a year-long event in which each driver was awarded points in a complex scoring system based upon the finishing place, the number of laps led, etc. At season's end, the driver with the highest points total was declared the champion. In 2005, NASCAR incorporated a late season series of races restricted to the top ten ranked drivers to add more suspense to the championship competition.

The connection between cigarettes and auto racing proved to be profitable for both sides as the Winston Cup became a bigger event with each passing year. As anti-smoking groups fumed, in 1979 the Winston label would be seen on national television when CBS carried the Daytona race live on a February Sunday afternoon. In 1982, the Turner cable network signed a $450,000 contract to broadcast several races, a contract that expanded to $1 million in 1990. However, the promoter of each NASCAR race had the right to negotiate its own television contracts, so viewers were forever channel-surfing. In 1999, however, emulating the centralized NFL approach, NASCAR officials negotiated a uniform contract with a combination of three networks for six years and a cool $2.8 billion.

Ever since the sport's early days, stock-car racing owners had willingly cut sponsorship deals with various manufacturers. Many such contracts called for bonus payments for victories, Winston Cup rankings, and other memorable achievements. Most race cars looked like an advertising montage with individual sponsors' logos affixed on the body. In the early days, sponsorship was pretty much small-time stuff and as late as the early 1980s automobiles carried the symbols of such companies as South Hill Texaco, Lo Law Automotive, Mountain Truck Stop, Beldon Asphalt Service, and Stone's Cafeteria. In 1972, the popular driver Richard Petty signed the first national sponsorship deal with the STP oil-additive company, while rivals David Pearson and Davey Allison signed on with Purolator and Coca-Cola. National television exposure, however, made it desirable for many major corporations to sponsor race teams: these soon included automobile manufacturers, oil companies, automobile-parts companies, tobacco firms, and of course, beer companies. Perhaps taking note that more than 60 percent of NASCAR fans were males, in 2001 the Pfizer drug company sponsored an entry, plastering driver Mark Martin's blue Number 6 automobile with their sexual performance-enhancement medication, Viagra.[46]

One of the allures of stock-car racing was that fans could identify with a particular automobile maker, and several auto manufacturers readily cooperated with team owners to produce a specially engineered automobile that only looked like the auto on the showroom floor. Fans were also attracted to the different personalities of the drivers, and the sale of personalized merchandise became a major source of revenue. The first major star of NASCAR was Richard Petty, whose father Lee had been a pioneering stock car driver. During the 1960s, the native of Level Cross, North Carolina, won a series of major races and two Grand National Championships. In 1967, he won 27 consecutive races, becoming one of the fans' favorites; his many public appearances were designed to create a special persona. They featured his flowing mustache, cowboy hat, and dark shades. In 1971, he was the first driver to surpass $1 million in prize money, and during the 1970s he won five Winston Cup Championships as well as four Daytona International races. In 1984, Petty won his 200th, and, as it would turn out, his last victory. As with many top NASCAR drivers, family heritage was important because racing constituted a year-around immersion. Thus Lee Petty's son Richard passed on to his son Kyle the opportunities for success, who in turn prepared his son Adam to follow in the family tradition. Adam began racing go-karts at age 6 and while still a teenager qualified for the Winston Cup series. All did not unfold according to family plans, however, because at age 19 Adam was killed at the New Hampshire International Speedway when he smacked into a retaining wall during a practice run on May 12, 2000.

Richard Petty – who enjoyed the nickname of "The King" – dueled with many top drivers who also won more than their share of races – Darrell Waltrip, Cale Yarborough, Bobby Allison, and "The Intimidator," Dale Earnhardt. Like so many who rose to the top of the NASCAR world, this often surly man came to the sport as part of family tradition. His father, Ralph, had won more than 350 races, had often taken his son with him to the races, and so it was natural that young Dale would follow in his father's "profession". He won his first major race at Bristol, Tennessee, in 1979, and the following year captured the Winston Cup. He drove with little apparent concern for his personal safety, was often criticized for bumping rivals out of his path, displayed a reckless determination that contributed to many a smash-up, and in the process received many reprimands and an occasional suspension. By 1994, he had won his seventh Winston Cup and was averaging more than $3 million annually in prize money. Befitting his "Intimidator" image, Earnhardt wore black racing gear and his famed Number 3 Chevrolet was painted the same supposedly ominous color.

Earnhardt became an icon for a new form of individuality and rebelliousness in a sport that was, in fact, now dominated by corporate money and beholden to national television networks. Earnhardt's image was reinforced when he was killed on the fourth and last turn of the final lap of the 2001 Daytona as he typically attempted to fight through several cars to gain the lead; instead, he brushed another car and drove headlong into the concrete restraining wall at 180 mph. His neck was broken and he died almost instantly. As in many other racing families, the beat went on as Dale Jr took his father's place as the Earnhardt crew's top driver, winning several races and pushing himself toward the top of the annual Winston Cup standings. Like father, like son, like grandson. So it goes in the close-knit, family-bound world of NASCAR.

Television and corporate sponsorships dictated that NASCAR move beyond the comfortable Southern cultural cocoon in which it had for so long existed. National television networks quietly removed the Confederate flags that had once dotted the racing grounds. The fact that early in the twenty-first century fewer than 10 percent of NASCAR fans were nonwhite became an important issue among its image-makers, who now had every intention of making it a national sport. That meant increasing the commitment to racial diversity and quietly and subtly diminishing the redneck image. That there had been only one African American ever to race on the NASCAR circuit said much about its racial and cultural origins. Wendell Scott of Virginia raced for 13 years on the NASCAR circuit, but he never obtained the sponsorships required to compete in the top rankings. With limited funds, he was forced to do much of his own mechanical work and lacked the support staff of many of his competitors. Journalist Joe Menzer writes that during the 1960s, Scott was often forced to enter race grounds by the back entrance, was denied service at food stands, and even had his car sabotaged more than once. It was widely believed that his car was often targeted for unnecessary bumps during races. In 1963, at the Jacksonville Speedway, Scott surprised everyone by crossing the finish line well ahead of the pack, beating Buck Baker by two full laps, but the race official somehow neglected to drop the checkered flag and the victory was awarded to the second-place finisher. In fact, track officials were so fearful of having an African American publicly declared the winner that they did so quietly two hours after the race had ended when they allegedly discovered their "mistake."[47]

Scott never won another race and retired in 1973 after suffering serious injuries in a crack-up at Talladega. His racing career – including a brief stint as a moonshine runner early in his adult life – became the stuff of racing legend when it served as the basis for the 1977 motion picture *Greased Lightning*, starring actor Richard Pryor. Scott's difficult time on the circuit more than supported Menzer's commentary in his history of stock-car racing:

> NASCAR was a white man's sport in a white man's world, and there was little or no sympathy for Scott when his NASCAR effort met with resistance. A handful of drivers accepted him for what he was – a man, like them, with a burning passion for driving race cars and possessing the physical skills to do it at unusually high speeds. However, many hated him because of his skin color and tried to make his life miserable whenever he showed up at a racetrack.[48]

Recognizing the economic bonanza to be reaped from converting NASCAR into a national sport led to many changes, including an effort to attract black spectators. However, as late as 2004, Scott had been the only regular black driver on the circuit. In 2001, the France family gave up direct control of their private business, and long-time executive and close family friend Mike Helton took control as 67-year-old Bill France Jr. went into semi-retirement as he battled serious illness. Helton's challenge was to continue the growth of the sport, and his focus was on moving NASCAR into the mainstream of the nation's sports fans. Already major tracks outside the South hosted Winston Cup races in New Hampshire, Delaware, California, Nevada, Arizona, and Michigan, with new facilities being planned outside Chicago and on Long Island. A nagging concern for the image-makers of NASCAR was the 30-year-old sponsorship by the R. J. Reynolds Tobacco Company (now RJR) as the anti-smoking movement continued to gain momentum. In 1998, the cigarette industry's $206 billion settlement with 46 state attorneys general created new problems relative to adhering to their pledge to stop all advertising aimed at individuals under the age of 18. Not surprisingly, in 2003 the company asked to be released from its $50 million annual Winston Cup sponsorship. The new sponsor seemed to fit well with NASCAR's efforts at broadening its appeal and attracting a diverse national audience. The giant utility Nextel, a major manufacturer and distributor of wireless telephones, fitted the high-tech image that Helton was seeking. Nextel's sponsorship removed the stigma of smoking, while appealing to individuals of all ages, races, and classes. When the Nextel Cup competition began at Daytona in February 2004, it was clear that NASCAR had come

a long way from the days of dirt tracks in small Southern towns and the screech-
ing of tires as whiskey trippers sped away from a revenuer's road block.

Struggling To Be Major League

The rise of NASCAR was one of the most significant aspects of professional sports
in the latter decades of the twentieth century. As it gained popularity in relationship to traditional sports, it became evident that public tastes were subject to many
influences, but particularly to the persuasive reach of network and cable television.
By the turn of the century, NASCAR had developed a fan base that challenged professional basketball and baseball, while marginal "major" team sports such as
professional hockey and soccer were left far behind the curve. Despite the location
of hockey teams in many Southern and Western states during the heyday expansion in the 1980s, this indigenous Canadian sport never caught on in the United
States except as a niche sport with a small but loyal fan base. It is often said that
hockey is one of the greatest of all spectator sports if watched in person, but hockey
could not translate that excitement to the typical American television viewer who
had little experience with the game. The speed and agility of the skaters did not
translate well onto the television screen, the distinctive swishing sound of the
skates as they cut through the ice did not resonate across the airwaves, and the
small black puck zooming at speeds above 100 mph was difficult for the camera to
follow and for viewers to see. Such superstars as Wayne Gretzky of the Las Angeles
Kings could temporarily stimulate widespread interest; it could not be sustained
when he retired. With player salaries soaring but ticket sales flat and television
revenues in jeopardy, hockey faced many difficult challenges as the twenty-first
century began; the future of the game seemed further imperiled when a season-
ending lockout occurred during the 2004–05 season as owners sought to impose
a salary cap at a much lower pay scale on a unified players union. More than two
hundred players ended up in Europe playing for a fraction of their former salaries.
When the National Hockey League resumed play in fall 2005, the owners had their
new salary model in place, the players were frustrated and upset with their union
leaders, and most American sports fans did not care. They were, in fact, hardly
aware that the NHL had foregone the entire 2004–05 season.

While hockey struggled to maintain its place as a niche professional sport,
efforts to build soccer into a professional sport fizzled spectacularly. Although
youth soccer became a rage in the United States during the 1980s and thereafter, and although the success of the American women in winning the Women's
World Cup in 1999 generated momentary interest, the upswing in public interest in soccer was not sustained. The men's eight-team Major League Soccer circuit
received virtually no national media attention; the women's United Soccer Association even less, and soccer's future as a professional sport remained problematical.

13 Do You Believe In Miracles?

The President's wife, Rosalynn Carter, called it a "national malaise." Others had even less charitable things to say about the mood of the nation as the decade of the 1970s wound down. The decade had seemingly been the one of the worst in the nation's history, right behind those of the Civil War and the Great Depression.

It had begun with the rising tide of protests over the war in Vietnam that saw four students shot and killed and 13 others wounded by the Ohio National Guard on May 5, 1970, on the normally placid campus of Kent State University. In the aftermath, hundreds of campuses erupted in protests and rioting, and classes, even spring commencements, were canceled. In 1973, the Organization of Petroleum Exporting Countries (OPEC) of the Middle East shut off oil shipments to the United States, producing severe shortages at the gasoline pumps and near-panic among automobile-dependant Americans. Late that same year, it was revealed that Vice-President Spiro Agnew had long been on the take, accepting hundreds of thousands of dollars in bribes from road contractors with whom he had done business while a county commissioner in suburban Baltimore and as Governor of Maryland. He had even accepted sacks full of large bills in his vice-presidential offices in the Executive Office Building.

The wave of scandal also engulfed President Richard M. Nixon when revelations of the June 16, 1972, Watergate burglary of the Democratic Party national headquarters incrementally piled up to the point where he had to resign on August 8, 1974, or suffer the ignominy of being impeached. What began as a "third-rate burglary," as Nixon once described it, revealed an administration that had engaged in systematic criminal behavior, including illegal telephone taps, breaking and entering, bribery, and using the FBI and other government agencies to obstruct justice. As the American people grappled with the fact that their President and his top aides had committed felonies and systematically lied about them, they also saw their purchasing power suffer from rapidly rising inflation. The loss of millions of jobs in the industrial sector, including the near-collapse of the once-dominant American automobile industry before the onslaught of better engineered and less-expensive foreign vehicles, raised serious questions about the future of the American economy.

As the decade neared its conclusion, the news did not get any better. Another serious oil shortage in 1979 again produced anxiety and long lines at service stations, and the Three Mile Island nuclear-power generating station in central Pennsylvania was crippled by a malfunction that for a time threatened a catastrophic meltdown. With annual inflation at 10 percent and interest rates at times reaching 20 percent, the American people began discussing the possibility that the United States had entered an ominous period of decline and decay. Finally, as if to bring a coup de grâce to American confidence and pride, in November 1979 a group of angry Iranian students stormed the US embassy in Teheran to protest the Carter Administration's decision to protect the Shah of Iran, now living in exile in New York. The students took 53 Americans hostage and held them prisoner for more than a year. As the news media reported nightly on their plight – some keeping tally of the number of days of the ordeal – Americans felt both angry and helpless. The crisis generated by the Iranian hostages came to symbolize the sense that America had lost its way, that its leadership position in the world was imperiled, that a serious decline had set in. President Carter correctly summarized American opinion when he commented that a "crisis of confidence" had enveloped the nation, striking "at the very heart and soul of our national will."

On February 22, 1980, however, the fog began to lift as the American people were given an unexpected emotional boost. That evening, they watched with incredulity as a supposedly hopelessly out-manned collection of college hockey players pulled off one of the biggest upsets in American sports history when they defeated a veteran Soviet Union team 4–3 in the Olympic Games. Even ABC had no premonition that an American victory was in the offing or it would have shown the game live rather than on a tape-delayed basis. The 1980 Winter Olympics was held in Lake Placid, New York, with the rivalries and tensions of the cold war ever present. Journalists from both sides of the Iron Curtain kept medal counts and wrote of the games as an extension of cold war power politics. The outcome of individual matches was viewed as an integral part of the ideological conflict between the forces of communism and democratic capitalism. Although the Olympic leadership still maintained the fiction of amateurism, that myth had long since been revealed as a sham. The American hockey team members were, of course, paid to play the game through their college scholarships, and although technically amateurs they were in fact professionals receiving thousands of dollars in benefits each year from their university athletic departments. Six members of the team would later play in the National Hockey League. The Soviets were considered by the International Olympic Committee to be "state amateurs," a clever euphemism that accepted they were members of the Soviet military and spent their time working at nothing other than their profession of hockey. The Soviet national team that took to the ice at Lake Placid was widely recognized as the best team in the world, amateur or professional. The previous year, the Soviets had handily defeated a National Hockey League all-star aggregation by a decisive 6–0 score, and had dominated the World Championship with an easy 5–2 victory over the Canadian national team in the finals.

The American team was young and overmatched, but it nonetheless had plenty of talent. With an average age of 22, it was the youngest team in the Games. Coach Herb Brooks, whose University of Wisconsin teams had won three NCAA championships, spent nearly 18 months preparing his team. He held several try-out camps, put several hundred candidates through psychological tests and grueling workouts before culling them down to a team of 20. He then worked them unmercifully, recognizing that the only way they could compete with the world's best teams was through speed, endurance, conditioning, and disciplined play. His players nearly rebelled more than once as he drove them to physical exhaustion and emotional distress. "He messed with our minds at every opportunity," one player recalled, and team captain Mike Eruizone later commented, "If Herb came into my house today, it would still be uncomfortable."[1] As the Winter Olympics approached, the political fires were stoked when the Soviet Union invaded Afghanistan on Christmas Day, 1979. World tensions mounted, and speculation about an American boycott of the Olympics in protest of the invasion began to circulate. Thus world politics once more enveloped an event that was self-proclaimed as a major force to promote world understanding and peace. Just one week before the Games opened, in the last pre-Olympic exhibition game, the Soviet team destroyed the United States team in Madison Square Garden by an embarrassing 10–3 score. Things did not look good for the Americans.

In the preliminary round the Americans had to come from behind to tie Sweden, then they defeated a strong Czechoslovakia team 7–3 and proceeded to win games over Norway, Romania, and Germany. Entering the four-team medal round, the Americans were considered no match for the powerful Soviets. Among other things, they had to find a way to get the puck past goalie Vladislav Tretiak, arguably the world's best net man. Late in the first period the score stood 2–1 in favor of the Soviets, but signs that this was the Americans' day began to appear. American goalie Jim Craig somehow managed to stop a barrage of shots on goal – he turned away 39 during the game – and with only seconds remaining in the first period, American forward Dave Christian fired a 25-foot shot that Tretiak easily turned away. However, the Soviet defenders, thinking the period had ended, did not provide cover, and Mark Johnson stormed the net and slapped the puck past a surprised Tretiak. An instant-replay review indicated that Johnson had scored with less than a second remaining.

As the second period began, angry Soviet coach Viktor Tikhonov inexplicably benched Tretiak – a horrendous strategic mistake – but the Soviets continued to dominate play; the Americans managed only two shots on goal and were happy that the period ended with them trailing only 3–2. Despite completely dominating play, the Soviets clung to only a tenuous lead. In the final period, Herb Brooks's emphasis on speed and conditioning began to pay off. While Tikhonov kept his veteran players on the ice, Brooks substituted frequently; the tiring Soviets no longer

320

Figure 13.1 Joyous US Olympic hockey players celebrate their improbable gold medal victory over Finland at Lake Placid, New York, in 1980. This victory came only after their "Miracle on Ice," a 4–3 victory over the heavily favored Soviet team. The plucky American hockey team did much to stimulate a surge of nationalist pride as the difficult decade of the 1970s ended. © Bettmann/ CORBIS.

could skate with the wave after wave of fresh collegians, who kept up the pressure. Johnson tied the score off a fumbled puck, and with 10 minutes left in the game captain Mike Eurizone stole a pass, outskated surprised defenders, and flipped a shot past the reserve Soviet goalie – a shot that Tretiak could have stopped in his sleep. The Soviets made a final charge, but Craig made several key stops and as the last seconds counted down, an excited ABC announcer Al Michaels screamed into the microphone, "You got ten, nine, eight . . . five seconds left! Do you believe in miracles? Yes!" As the American team celebrated, their fans waved American flags and chanted "USA! USA!"

The next day, newspapers across the United States blared the news in large headlines and television news programs led with the surprising story. All across the country, flags flew in front of homes and from the aerials of automobiles. An upsurge in nationalistic sentiment – a veritable outpouring of pure unadulterated patriotism – swept the nation. The team's victory was right out of American mythology – the overmatched underdog persevering against all odds to pull off a dramatic and improbable triumph. David had slain Goliath, and the victory in fact seemed to regenerate the American national mood. The gold medal game against Finland seemed anticlimactic. Brooks worked his team hard in practice to prevent an emotional letdown, and once again the

Americans came from behind to win 4–2. Pictures of goalie Jim Craig skating exuberantly around the rink draped in an American flag were on front pages across America.

A new decade seemed to bring new promise, perhaps what Ronald Reagan, elected President over a resolute Jimmy Carter in November, would call "Morning in America." As Reagan took office on January 20, 1981, the hostages were released in Iran, interest rates soon began to fall, a revitalized high-tech economy, fueled by the computer revolution, began generating new jobs, and as Reagan's second term wound down a tenuous detente with the Soviets took hold, leading to a significant reduction in nuclear arms in 1987. Shortly thereafter, the cold war would dissolve along with the Soviet Union. Although it is a stretch to credit any of these events to a single hockey game, nonetheless the "Miracle of Lake Placid" would be viewed as the time when the "long national ordeal" had finally bottomed out. If nothing else, the hockey triumph proved to be a classic example of how politics and sports had become intricately intertwined.

The Cold War Shapes the Olympics

Two major forces influenced the evolution of the Olympic Games after the Second World War. The cold war inevitably became an underlying issue as the United States squared off against the Soviet Union and other Soviet bloc nations. Beginning in 1968, commercial television became a major factor as it exploited the cold war tensions to create profits. The quest for gold medals led inevitably to the erosion of the original amateur conception of the Olympics, and with the International Olympic Committee anxious to collect millions of dollars for the sale of television rights, the inevitable pressure to make the Games another forum where professional athletes performed and reaped large monetary rewards transformed the Games into a quadrennial capitalistic orgy.

The founder of the Olympics would have been appalled. Frenchman Baron Pierre de Coubertin had conceived of the modern Olympic movement in the pristine image of British elite athletic amateurism. His world was that of the European aristocracy, where one's station in life truly mattered. Deeply impressed with the English upper class and its casual, almost indifferent approach to athletics, Coubertin conceived of an international competition between gentlemen who would strive to represent themselves and their countries in an atmosphere of comradery and good sportsmanship. Gentlemen of good breeding would not stoop to play games for remuneration, but only for the intrinsic rewards to be derived from the spirit of fair play. Just as Americans of the Victorian era had looked down their noses at professional ballplayers and pugilists, so too did their European counterparts view professional athletes with disdain.

Baron de Coubertin believed that the amateur sportsman should play the game purely for the joy of participation: "The most important thing in the Olympic Games is not winning but taking part; the essential thing in life is not conquering but fighting well."[2] Victory was a worthy goal, but so too was the healthful, joyful pursuit of that worthy objective. At one point, the amateur ideal even excluded men who worked with their hands, as the rules for the Henley Regatta stated in 1878: "No persons shall be considered an amateur oarsman or sculler . . . Who is or has been by trade or employment for wages, a mechanic, artisan, or laborer."[3] The elitists who wrote such ridiculous rules sought to justify them by suggesting that working-class men were not inclined to play by the rules. Such snobbery, of course, could not survive even in class-ridden Victorian England, so when the Olympics was organized it was permissible for members of the working classes to take part, but only if they did not attempt to gain financially from their efforts.

In 1894, Coubertin assembled a group of like-minded men in Paris, and the International Olympic Committee (IOC) was formed. Its essential philosophy was pure Coubertin. Every four years strictly amateur male athletes would meet to compete in track and field, gymnastics, and swimming – the number of events would grow over the next century to nearly two hundred – in an atmosphere of fair play and international goodwill. So that the Games would be free from politics and international rivalries, each participating nation would have its own privately organized national Olympic committee that could not be controlled by its government. In 1914, Coubertin created the official Olympic flag of five interlocking colored rings on a white background. As he liked to say, at least one of those colors – red, green, black, orange, and blue – was found in every national flag in the world. "The Olympic Games are for the world and all nations must be admitted to them," he said, but with the caution that the Games were not designed to intensify nationalist sentiments but instead existed, "for the exaltation of the individual athlete." Although Coubertin was emphatic about reviving the ancient Greek Olympics, he conveniently ignored the fact that the Greeks had lavished booty upon their sports heroes, and in fact many of the best ancient athletes were essentially full-time professionals who trained for competitions and expected to be rewarded for their efforts. The modern Olympics were a product of the values of a Western European elite of the late nineteenth century, not ancient Greece.[4]

Coubertin served as president of the IOC until 1925 and for the most part managed to maintain his major ideals, although he lost the battle to keep women from taking part. He fought hard to keep the Games an all-male event, but by the 1920 women competed in swimming and gymnastics; it was not until 1928 that they were permitted to compete in track and field. Coubertin and his like-minded committee members believed that track and field was too strenuous a sport for females, a myth that Babe Didrikson emphatically put to rest in 1932 at Los Angeles. The Olympics that occurred just before Coubertin's death must have disturbed him immensely. When the 1936 Games was awarded to Germany in 1929, the Nazi Party was only a slight blip on the political screen of European politics. Adolf Hitler assumed power in 1933, however, and by 1935 the malevolent goals of his regime had become all too evident. As the Games approached, many factions urged their cancellation. In the United States, Jewish leaders especially urged a boycott and for a time this seemed a distinct possibility, but the chairman of the United States Olympic Committee, Chicago millionaire businessman Avery Brundage, maneuvered adroitly to assure that the United States would participate. The 1936 Berlin

Figure 13.2 Bob Mathias of Tulare, California, is shown here completing a discus throw during the decathlon competition that he won for a second time at the 1952 Olympics in Helsinki. Mathias commented that the games were overshadowed by the intense competition that existed between cold war rivals United States and the Soviet Union. © Bettmann/CORBIS.

Olympics were awash in the rising tide of German nationalism that Adolf Hitler's regime had unleashed; Berlin set the tone for the Games that would occur after the Second World War, each of which had a sharp political edge to it until the end of the cold war.[5]

Worldwide war caused the cancellation of the 1940 Games scheduled for Tokyo and the 1944 Games, but the IOC was determined to celebrate the end of the war by holding the Games, however limited they might be, in war-ravaged London in 1948. Everywhere spectators and participants went in London, burnt-out buildings and piles of rubble provided grim reminders of the Nazi bombings. Little new construction was attempted as the financially strapped British held the Games in Wembley Stadium and other existing venues. Even the provision of food for the athletes was a public issue. Instead of housing the athletes in a specially constructed Olympic Village, army barracks were pressed into service. The Americans dominated the major events, with a teenager from Tulare, California, Bob Mathias winning the decathlon, while 30-year-old Fanny Blankers-Koen of Holland won the hearts of spectators as she captured four gold medals in the 100-meters, 200-meters, 80-meter hurdles and 400-meter relay. As a teenager, she had competed in Berlin.[6]

The biggest story of the London Olympics, however, was the fact that the Soviet Union did not compete. During the previous three years, the wartime alliance of the United States, Great Britain, and the Soviet Union had disintegrated as traditional political and cultural issues resurfaced. Only the common enemy of Hitler's fascist regime had held together the tenuous wartime coalition of capitalistic democracies and the authoritarian communist Soviet Union. Eastern European nations had been pulled into the Soviet orb, and pro-Soviet "puppet" governments established; in March 1946, former Prime Minister Winston Churchill had angrily denounced the "Iron Curtain" that now divided Europe. In retaliation for perceived aggressive Soviet policies, the United States had launched its containment policies against the Soviets and their "satellites" with the Truman Doctrine and Marshall Plan. As the London Games began, West Berlin was under a Soviet blockade and the civil war in China was not going well for Chiang Kai-shek's forces in their battle against the communist forces of Mao Zedong.

The cold war was the controlling factor of the 1952 Olympics, held just 30 miles from Leningrad, in Helsinki, Finland. As he was leaving office, the president of the IOC, Sigfrid Edström of Sweden, had to deal with several difficult political questions. The first was whether to permit the Soviets to participate. Although the Olympic ideal demanded that the communist countries be permitted to compete, IOC leaders also understood that the existence of a Soviet Olympic Committee operating independent of the Kremlin was fantasy. Additionally, it was already widely understood that Soviet athletes were employees of the state – most were officers in the Red Army – and that they were paid to concentrate on developing their athletic skills. Members of the IOC thus understood that the Soviet Union violated two of the Games' most sacred concepts – a free and independent national committee, and unpaid amateur athletes – but they were also dedicated to the concept of inclusion rather than exclusion. All things being equal, the IOC decreed, athletes from all countries should be permitted to participate.[7] Consequently, the IOC conveniently ignored its fundamental policies and agreed to permit the participation of the Soviets' professional state-employed athletes whose careers were directed by a committee controlled by the Kremlin.

Edström also had to deal with two delegations that wanted to represent China – a one-man team from Chiang Kai-shek's Nationalist China now in quasi-exile on the island of Taiwan, and a larger delegation of athletes from the People's Republic of China (PRC). Eventually, the IOC decided, in a most curious decision, not to recognize either committee but to permit both teams to participate. Nationalist China promptly withdrew its solitary athlete (team), and the PRC team inexplicably did not arrive in Helsinki until the Games were in their final days of competition. Finally, there were the dilemmas posed by a divided Germany; both the Democratic Republic of Germany (East) and the American-backed Federal Republic of Germany (West) had created their own requisite national committee and sought to be recognized for the Helsinki Games. In theory, both governments were temporary until a reunited Germany could be formed, but the divisions between what the media referred to simply as East Germany and West Germany were already firmly established and would not disappear until the collapse of the Soviet Union in 1991. The IOC attempted to merge the two committees and form one team, but ideological and political realities made that effort impossible. Eventually, the West German Olympic Committee was recognized because it had been formed first, but in 1956 the East German team would compete, with a determined resolve to prove the athletic superiority of its political and social system.

The competition at Helsinki in 1952 reflected the cold war, which now included a nuclear-arms race between the United States and the Soviet Union (which tested its first weapon successfully in 1949) and was seriously exacerbated by the American development of a thermonuclear hydrogen bomb in 1952, a technological and scientific accomplishment soon matched by the Soviets. The Korean War – the first of many military confrontations that the cold war would spawn – had settled into a dreary but bloody stalemate just north of the 38th parallel. The American people were about to elect an heroic military figure, Dwight D. Eisenhower, as their new President, on the presumption that he understood the military and ideological threat posed by the communist bloc. High-ranking Soviet officials had already made many public comments about the importance of Soviet athletes demonstrating their superiority against the representatives of the soft "bourgeois" capitalist countries. Andrei Zhdanov, a cultural spokesman, made this clear in 1949 when he said, "Each new [athletic] victory is a victory for the Soviet form of society and the socialist sports system; it provides irrefutable proof of the superiority of socialist culture over the decaying culture of the capitalist states."[8] That the Soviets were on a serious mission was reflected by the decision not to house their athletes at the Olympic Village but keep them free from Western influence just across the nearby Finnish–Soviet border at Otaniemi, near the Soviet Porkkola naval base. Everywhere Soviet athletes went in Helsinki, they were accompanied by chaperones to prevent their contact (perhaps defections to the West) with other athletes.

Americans quickly perceived the political importance of the Games, and a national fund-raising drive to "support our athletes" was launched to put the bite on corporate America; even school children were urged to donate their coins in special receptacles. The USOC arranged for a special television fundraiser starring Bob Hope and Bing Crosby. During the show, Hope cracked,

> I guess Joe Stalin thinks he is going to show up our soft capitalist Americans. We've got to cut him down to size. This is the best thing I've ever undertaken and, brother Bing and I are going to throw our best punches.[9]

The tension during the Helsinki Games was palpable, as repeat decathlon champion Bob Mathias related:

> There were many more pressures on American athletes because of the Russians than in 1948. They were in a sense the real enemy. You just loved to beat 'em. You just had to beat 'em. It wasn't like beating some friendly country like Australia. This feeling was strong down through the entire team, even [among] members in sports where the Russians didn't excel.[10]

To the irritation of IOC officials, journalists from both the East and the West created a point scale to measure overall team results (based on the number of medals won), each equation designed to give their side an advantage. The Americans won a total of 76 medals to the Soviets' 71, although the United States captured twice the number of gold medals. For all intents and purposes, it was a standoff, and as the Games came to an end both sides were already gearing up for the next confrontation in Melbourne.

Perhaps the most significant event at Helsinki was that the IOC, after much maneuvering, posturing, and 25 secret ballots, elected wealthy Chicago building contractor Avery Brundage as its new president. Brundage had been a track star as an undergraduate at Illinois, had competed in the decathlon at the 1912 Olympics, coming in sixth behind winner Jim Thorpe, and had won several AAU championships. He competed in American track and field events well into his thirties, when he became a world-class handball player. As Olympic president he devoted himself to maintaining the spirit of Baron de Coubertin. Brundage had long been active in the American Athletic Union and was elected the head of the American Olympic Committee after the 1924 Paris Games. He immediately threw himself into his duties with messianic zeal, essentially making the Olympics his life's work. It became, for him, a personal religion: "Sport is recreation, it is a pastime or a diversion, it is play, it is action for amusement, it is free, spontaneous and joyous – it is the opposite of work."[11] At the heart of Brundage's convictions was an abiding disdain for professionalism: "The amateur code, coming to us from antiquity, contributed to and strengthened by the noblest aspirations of great men of each generation, embraces the highest moral laws. No philosophy, no religion, preaches loftier sentiments." The fundamental distinction between the amateur and the professional, he felt, "was a thing of the spirit" because it "exists in the heart and not in the rule book." Condemning professional sports as "as a branch of the entertainment business," Brundage believed that amateurs, by rejecting materialism in their sporting efforts, play "for the love of the game itself without thought of reward or payment of any kind."[12] Unrelenting in his beliefs, Brundage would always push the argument that if an individual became a professional in one sport, he forfeited his amateur status in all sports. Behind the bureaucratic scenes, it was apparently Brundage who made certain that Jim Thorpe, who lost his 1912 track and field gold medals because he had earned a few dollars playing minor-league baseball, would remain an object lesson for future athletes to contemplate.

Time and again, Brundage found himself in delicate situations where common sense or political realities forced him to parse the truth, to make deals that revealed him to be, in the eyes of his legions of critics, a shameless hypocrite. His opposition to an American boycott of Berlin led to charges that he was anti-Semitic; his willingness to bend the rules to permit the Soviets to compete at Helsinki led to charges that he was a communist sympathizer; his efforts to include apartheid South Africa produced angry accusations that he was a white supremacist. His first Olympics as president of IOC – 1956 in Melbourne – was challenging on the political front. The two Germanies again argued over which was the legitimate representative of the German people, and a crisis in the Middle East led to military action when the British and French invaded Egypt to protect the Suez Canal, which had been seized by the Egyptian government; meanwhile, Israel attacked Egypt at the instigation of the French and British. The Soviets backed the Egyptians, and Iraq, Egypt, and Lebanon boycotted Melbourne in protest of the Israeli military adventure. Then things got even more complex when in October, just three weeks before the Games were to open, the Soviet Union brutally put down a revolution in Hungary when it sent tanks and troops into Budapest. The deaths of thousands of heroic Hungarians was front-page news, and now threats of boycott blended with demands that the Games be canceled. Believing that the Olympics transcended international politics, Brundage ordered the Games to proceed, blandly commenting,

> Every civilized person recoils in horror at the savage slaughter in Hungary, but that is no reason for destroying the nucleus of international cooperation and good will we have in the Olympic Movement. The Olympic Games are contests between individuals and not between nations.[13]

Tensions naturally ran high at Melbourne. In one widely reported event, a water polo match between the Soviets and Hungary deteriorated into a full-scale brawl with plenty of blood in the water, much of it Soviet. The referee was compelled to cancel the match (other reports say the Soviets conceded to prevent further mayhem), and afterward spectators had to be restrained by police from attacking the Soviet team. So much for the Olympics generating international goodwill.

The Melbourne Games, however, proved to be a decisive athletic triumph for the Soviets as they won 98 medals to the Americans' 74. Their victory was even more convincing in those sports that attracted considerable media interest and tested strength and speed, thereby taking on a quasi-military symbolic significance: track and field, boxing, wrestling, and weightlifting. The US men's track team won 15 of 24 events, but the Soviets demonstrated a much-improved quality that anticipated future Olympic track and field glory. The Soviet women were clearly superior to the Americans in track and field, and with female medals counting equally to those won by males in the now all-important informal medal count, a reconsideration of the "play nice" approach to physical education and competitive sports for girls and women began in earnest in the United States. In the wake of the medal-count deficit at Melbourne, American Tobacco Company heiress Doris Duke gave the US Olympic Committee $500,000 to begin a training program for women athletes. Lacking a national developmental program in the high schools and universities, it would take more than two decades for American women to begin to compete across the board on an equal footing with the Eastern bloc women.

For the 1960 Olympics at Rome, the USOC found a stop-gap solution to the chasm separating the Americans from the Eastern bloc women in the form of Tennessee State's Tigerbelles track team. Nearly all of the 1960 American women's track team came from this small black college in Nashville. Leading the Tigerbelles was one of the most improbable track stars in history, the lithe 5' 11" Wilma Rudolph. Born prematurely, one of 22 children that her father produced with two wives, she was raised in near-poverty and forced to spend many years of her childhood in bed suffering from debilitating childhood diseases. At age six, she contracted polio and was confined to bed for more than a year, then had to wear a heavy metal brace on her withered left leg. Determined to live a normal life, she underwent therapy, exercised relentlessly, and by the time she was in her teens had overcome her disability to become an outstanding basketball player. While still in high school, she began to train as a sprinter with a sociology professor who also was the unpaid women's track coach at Tennessee State, Ed Temple. Wilma developed into a world-class sprinter and won a bronze medal – one of the few won by an American woman – at the Melbourne Games at age 16. At Tennessee State, she continued to improve under Temple's coaching. At the Rome Olympics in 1960, Rudolph demonstrated that American women could compete with the professionals from behind the Iron Curtain as she became the first American woman to win three gold medals in one Olympics – the 100- and 200-meter sprint races and as anchor on the 400-meter relay team. She set world records in all three events, although her 11.0 seconds in the 100-meter was set aside due to wind; despite a bad hand-off of the baton in the 400-meter relay, she overtook the German anchor and the American (Tennessee State) team won a gold at 44.5 seconds; the previous day in the semi-finals they had set a world record of 44.4 seconds. Proclaimed by the media as "the fastest woman in the world," Rudolph returned to Tennessee a genuine sports hero. Governor Buford Ellington was anxious to bask in her fame and lead the local celebration, but upon learning of the celebration plans, Rudolph politely declined, saying that she would not participate in a racially segregated event. Ellington and local politicians quickly relented, and the first truly integrated public event ever held in her hometown of Clarksville took place – a parade and a banquet in honor of a young African American woman who was the best sprinter in the world.[14]

By 1960, even the cold war standoff had become passe, with the athletes from both sides of the Iron Curtain frequently becoming friendly rivals. Following the Melbourne Games, the major track and field powers met each summer, and international soccer and hockey matches were also played annually. Thus the world-class athletes became familiar with each other, friendships blossomed, and even before crucial Olympic events the athletes were frequently seen wishing each other "good luck" and shaking hands. Emotional embraces between rivals often occurred after a hard-fought competition. Although the cold war became less and less important to the athletes during the 1960s, it remained important to nationalistic politicians and the media. However, other emotional issues now pressed to the fore, especially issues related to racial discrimination in America and apartheid in South Africa.

Television Transforms the Olympics

Except for the drama created by the standoff of the cold war powers during the Olympiads at Helsinki and Melbourne, most Americans paid scant attention to the Olympics. Television coverage in the United States was minimal, limited to brief newsreel-type capsules shown 24 hours or more after the event took place. The first Olympic Games that Americans saw live was the 1960 Winter Olympics at Squaw Valley in eastern California. CBS was able to obtain the rights for those Games for just $50,000. With the action taking place high above Lake Tahoe in the Sierra, it was possible to show a limited number of events to American audiences live. The coverage was primitive at best. Anchorman Walter Cronkite reported on the action from a mobile set-up located in the back of a Chevrolet station wagon. That summer, CBS covered the Rome Summer Games – for which it paid only $500,000 – by sending videotape by jet aircraft to studios in New York, from which highlights were shown 24 hours after the winners had already been identified on radio or in local newspapers. Although CBS managed to convey the human drama of the Games – especially in the sparkling performances by Wilma Rudolph – the coverage of the two events was spotty, and most Americans paid scant attention. However, ABC's new director of sports, Roone Arledge, was a most interested viewer, and he determined that his fledgling company could turn the Olympics into a major prime-time American television event. Thus ABC paid $500,000 for the rights to the 1964 Winter Games at Innsbruck, Austria, and Arledge threw himself into planning a major breakthrough in television coverage.[15]

He faced tremendous technical problems, with different events being held at remote mountain locations. However, he and his crews had three years of experience of covering events on-site for *Wide World of Sports*, and they tackled the challenges with confidence. Austria was six time zones ahead of New York City, so Arledge's producers air-expressed four-hour black-and-white videotapes to ABC headquarters in time for them to be edited for prime-time showing the next day. Arledge built large audiences by unashamedly focusing only on the top American athletes, to the detriment of the others. He not only featured the performance of Americans, but his cameras and microphones also picked up the high-flying drama of ski-jumpers, the incredible speed of the bobsledding teams, and the beauty and grace of the figure skaters. Americans stayed glued to their television sets even though only one American won a gold medal – Terry McDermott in the 500-meter speed-skating. American skiers Billy Kidd and Jimmy Heuga, however, won a silver and bronze in the exciting downhill slalom. The highlight of the coverage at Innsbruck was a technical preview of things to come: the use of an orbiting satellite made it possible to show about 15 minutes of the closing ceremony live before the satellite moved out of range. American interest in the Tokyo Summer Games of 1964 was low; the fact that NBC delayed the showing of the opening ceremonies until 1 a.m. after the *Johnny Carson Tonight Show* had ended suggested the level of national interest, although the stirring gold medal performances of swimmer Don Schollander, heavyweight boxer Joe Frazier, and sprinter Bob Hayes created a brief stir.

With his coverage at Innsbruck a commercial as well as technological success, Arledge focused upon 1968, and ABC won the bids for both Games; the cost had escalated, however, and the network paid a total of $6.5 million for the rights. Twenty years later, that seemingly enormous sum would jump to $309 million! The sophisticated coverage that ABC provided in 1968 turned the Olympics into a major television event for the American people. To cover the Winter Games in the tiny French Alps town of Grenoble, ABC inserted 250 staffers who produced fascinating personal stories about the trials, tribulations, and triumphs of the leading athletes – a television convention that became a popular device for many Olympiads to come – and exciting pictures of some of the action. Always, the focus was upon Americans, with non-Americans appearing largely within the context of competition with Yanks. The Americans did their part with solid performances, led by the incredible beauty and skill of figure skater Peggy Fleming, who won the only American gold medal of the Games. The well-placed ABC cameras caught the excitement of ski-jumpers, downhill racers, and ice-skating racers. Instant replay and slow motion captured many a skier tumbling dangerously down the treacherous Casserousse run after a fall. Strategically placed microphones even transmitted the unique sound of speeding skis and skates into the living rooms of infatuated American audiences. Arledge demonstrated that television coverage, expertly conceived, could transform a sporting event into a mass spectacle in which millions became involved. The Olympics had become a major event that both entertained and captivated.[16]

Encouraged by the rave reviews he received for covering Grenoble, Arledge sent 450 workers to Mexico City in September for the sprawling Summer Games. In fact, the ABC "team" was larger than all but three of the Olympic teams sent by participating nations. ABC produced an astounding 48 hours of prime-time coverage via color videotape that spanned 10 days of competition. Fifty cameras caught the action simultaneously from 13 scattered venues. Arledge even rented a 250-foot crane to hang a camera over the running track. Throughout the Games, he and his top producers sat in an enormous control room, switching deftly from one event to another in anticipation of catching a particularly compelling bit of action. It was a long, long way from the time when Walter Cronkite stood in the snow with his frosty breath swirling around his head as he described a few events at Squaw Valley.

The politics of race became the lead storyline at Mexico City. After Americans Tommie Smith and John Carlos had finished first and third in the 200-meter dash, Arledge captured them on camera as they stood on the victors' stand, their black-gloved fists raised in a Black Power protest salute. As the flag was raised and the "Star Spangled Banner" played, these two African American athletes from San Jose State University lowered their heads away from the flag. ABC captured the moment perfectly, as did many newspaper photographers, and the images kicked up an instant furor in the United States. Immediately after the incident, ABC's Howard Cosell interviewed the gold medal winner and asked Smith pointedly if he was proud of his American citizenship; Smith's evasive answer only exacerbated the situation. Carlos later commented,

Figure 13.3 American sprinters Tommie Smith and John Carlos raised their gloved fists in a Black Power salute at Mexico City as the American flag was being raised and the Star Spangled Banner played. They were suspended from the US team and sent home, but in 2005 their alma mater, San Jose State University, dedicated a permanent statue on the campus that cast Smith and Carlos in bronze just as they were captured in this famous 1968 photograph. © Bettmann/CORBIS.

Tommie and I were just telling them that black people and minority people were tired of what was taking place in the US and all over the world. . . . The press and TV blew it all out of proportion. They made it a huge harmful thing, like some kind of fire-spitting dragon.

Would the athletes have made a statement if they had known the television cameras were not aimed at them? Probably not. As Carlos said, "Ours was not a political act, it was a moral act, and that is all right. When else can you do something like that? Only at the Olympics or when you land on the moon. Then everyone is looking at you."[17] The next day, Avery Brundage and the United States Olympic Committee reprimanded the two athletes, expelled them from the team, and sent them home; Brundage made certain the International Olympic Committee banned them from taking part in future Games.[18]

Photographs of the Black Power salute became one of the most famous moments in the history of the Olympics. This incident was the almost-logical conclusion to a lengthy period of racial discord that occurred within the higher echelons of the Olympic hierarchy as well as an important development of the struggle against racial discrimination within the United States. In 1960, the Soviet Union had raised the issue of the apartheid policy of the white minority governments of South Africa and Rhodesia, which had previously sent all-white teams to the Olympics. Clearly, the Soviets were seeking political advantage in Africa. Most black governments in Africa soon joined in the chorus of protest. The issue placed the United States on the defensive because of its own widespread racial-segregation laws and practices, a fact not lost on the Soviets. After a great deal of political infighting, the IOC banned South Africa from the 1964 Games in Tokyo but urged the besieged government to petition for readmission for Mexico City. On the basis of little more than false hopes – Brundage seemed willing to grasp at straws to get South Africa readmitted – the IOC lifted the ban in February 1968. Thirty-two predominantly black African nations promptly announced that they would boycott the Games. The protests continued, and finally the IOC reversed itself again, revoking its invitation to South Africa on the flimsy pretext that it would be dangerous for the South African team to travel abroad. Once again, major international political issues had stripped the IOC of its idealism, and Brundage and the IOC looked inept and out of touch.

Within the United States, the forces protesting discrimination and racism found in sports a useful way to publicize their issues. Leading this movement was Harry Edwards, a former basketball and track star at San Jose State University. Late in 1967, he began a campaign among premier black track and field stars to boycott the Mexico City Olympic Games as a means of protesting racial conditions in the United States. As Edwards toured the country, he met with mixed reactions. While many black athletes were sympathetic to his message, they also understood that they would more than likely have no other opportunity to take part in an Olympics; they did not want to waste years of training and preparation for a protest that did not seem to relate directly to issues within the United States. Besides, the star of the 1936 Olympics, sprinter and long-jumper Jesse Owens, was also touring the country at the behest of the USOC, urging that there was nothing to be gained by a boycott and much to be lost. The boycott fizzled, but the issues still simmered as the Americans embarked for the 7,000-foot elevation of Mexico City.

Just before the Summer Games were to begin, an outpouring of anger by thousands of Mexican college students almost led to their cancellation. Mexico was not a wealthy country, and the cost of hosting the event was enormous. Poverty was a fact of life for most Mexican citizens, and within the country questions about the advisability of hosting the Games had become a staple of political dialogue. College students in Mexico City were in the forefront of the questioning and protests, and several brushes with law enforcement occurred in the months leading up to the Games. Their grievances were many, but the Olympics provided the necessary catalyst. In the resulting violent confrontation between thousands of protestors and the Mexican military and police, approximately three hundred protesting students were killed, although many observers said the actual number was much higher. The American news media gave scant coverage to the incident, failed to connect it to the larger economic and social issues surrounding the forthcoming Olympics, and tended to agree with unsophisticated and misleading State Department analyses that the riots were communist-inspired. A subdued Avery Brundage bravely told the press after the massacre in the plaza of the Tlatelolco neighborhood of Mexico City that the Games would proceed, that violence would not prevent the holding of "a friendly gathering of the youth of the world in amicable competition."[19] As of 2005, the Mexican government continued to refuse to release its files on the massacre.

When sprinters Tommie Smith and John Carlos held their clenched fists covered by black gloves high and their eyes low, they created a firestorm of protests across white America. Brundage dismissed the two men as "warped mentalities and cracked personalities," comments that engendered charges by Harry Edwards that Brundage was racist. Brundage's narrow view of the situation was that the Olympics stood for equality and international brotherhood, and by suggesting otherwise Smith and Carlos were using the Games to advance a cause that lay outside of the Olympic realm. When the Mexican Olympic organizing committee later included the protest in its official film of the games, Brundage was aggrieved:

> The nasty demonstration against the United States flag by negroes . . . had nothing to do with sport, [and] it was a shameful abuse of hospitality and it has no more place in the record of the games than the gunfire [at Tlatelolco].[20]

The stark image of the Black Power salute thereafter became the most recognized symbol of the Mexico City Games. It unfortunately overshadowed stunning athletic achievements. Americans Lee Evans and Bob Beamon, both African American, set world records in the 400-meter and long-jump events. Beamon's feat was one of the most amazing in all of Olympic history. Between 1935 and 1965, the world's record for the long-jump had increased incrementally by just eight inches, with the world record being set by American Ralph Boston in 1965 at 27' 4¾". In just a few seconds, that record was obliterated by New York City native Bob Beamon, when he took off and seemingly flew through the thin Mexico City air, actually landing beyond the reach of the electronic measuring instrument. He had exceeded Boston's record by almost two feet with a leap of 29' 2½" – a record that would not be broken (by 2 inches) until 1991. Although Beamon's wondrous jump received its deserved share of publicity, the gold medal victory by boxer George Foreman was given even greater attention in the American media when he joyfully danced around the ring waving an American flag after winning the championship. This black man's patriotic display seemed to mute the sting to mainstream America produced by Smith and Carlos, although Foreman later said that his star-spangled victory dance had nothing to do with the sprinters and that he regretted his display was interpreted by the American media as a rebuke of his friends.

Thus ABC got much more than it had bargained for when it signed on to broadcast the Mexico City Olympics. International politics, apartheid, the bubbling-over of American racial tensions, a massacre of protesting students – all contributed to an unfolding drama in which television was much more than just a passive bystander.

The Games Must Go On

The experience that ABC gained from handling the various protests and issues surrounding the Mexico City Games proved useful when the Munich Games unfolded in 1972. The IOC had awarded the Games to Munich as a symbolic recognition of welcoming Germany back into the fold of civilized nations. The Games were intended to be, among other things, a means of extirpating memories of Nazism. The local committee had done itself proud in building the 700-acre Olympic venue, with modern athletic facilities built around a massive translucent canopy covering the 80,000-seat stadium and the swimming and fencing halls. A plush Olympic Village was erected, featuring luxury apartments complete with swimming pools and other upscale amenities, which would be converted into condominiums at the completion of the Games. The carefully manicured grounds featured a multitude of bright flowers, set off by several hundred recently planted trees, all arranged in neat symmetrical patterns. New hotels and restaurants had sprung up around town, with new expressways and a subway connecting them to the dazzling Olympic venue. German efficiency was once again on display, although without the heavy propaganda of the 1936 Berlin Games.[21] Anticipating major economic benefits, Munich mayor Hans Jochem Vogel proudly said, "Obtaining the Olympics has brought advantages of immediate benefit for the future. It has accelerated achievements which otherwise would have taken at least twice the time to be gained."[22] Clearly, the Munich Olympics were seen by the local planners as bringing money – lots of it – into local coffers. But from the point of view of the IOC, it was putting a stamp of approval upon post-Nazi Germany, assisting the German people to move beyond their recent tragic history.

In his comments at the official opening of the Games, German Chancellor Willy Brandt proclaimed them to be the "Olympics of Joy." Spectators and participants alike seemed to share in the spirit of moral and spiritual uplift as the heavy cloud of Hitler's regime faded into the past. The skies were crystal blue, the sunshine sparkled brightly, and even the smiling security forces wore colorful pastel uniforms. An ABC producer, Doug Wilson, got caught up in the spirt of the Games when he focused attention upon a small, young Russian woman gymnast, Olga Korbut, whose sprightly personality and fierce determination made for a good storyline. That ABC was featuring the appealing human qualities of a Soviet athlete was itself somewhat surprising – a reflection of the goodwill that the Games were generating around the world. When Korbut fell from the uneven bars late in the gymnastic competition, the images of her tearful eyes produced an outpouring of empathy across the United States. Up until this point, women's gymnastics was considered one of the lesser Olympic sports; hereafter, it would be one of the featured events by American television.

About 5:00 a.m. on September 5, however, the feel-good atmosphere suddenly dissolved when eight members of the radical Palestinian Black September terrorist organization forced their way into the Olympic Village apartments in Building 31, occupied by the athletes, coaches, and officials from Israel. The Israeli wrestling coach, Moshe Weinberg, attempted to block the door; while shouting to others to flee, he was gunned down by automatic rifle fire. Two other Israelis also died in the first moments of the attack. Most of the Israeli delegation managed to escape in the confusion, but nine members were taken hostage, and a 24-hour standoff ensued. In an incredibly bitter irony, with the notorious Nazi death camp of Dachau standing only nine miles away, once again Jews were dying in Germany at the hands of hate-filled individuals. The terrorists, wearing black head masks that gave off the grim visage of hangmen, presented a list of demands that included freeing some 234 Muslims currently incarcerated in Israeli prisons; the freeing of several terrorists held in various other countries, including the notorious German terrorists Andreas Baader and Ulrike Meinhof; and safe passage by air for the terrorists and their prisoners to an unnamed Middle Eastern country. They threatened to execute two hostages each hour beginning at noon, but then postponed their deadline several times. To emphasize their demands, they unceremoniously tossed the body of Moshe Weinberg into the street. Israel's Prime Minister Golda Meier promptly reiterated her nation's policy of not negotiating with terrorists and deferred to German authorities to handle the crisis.[23]

The ABC Middle East correspondent Peter Jennings somehow managed to gain access to a hidden balcony of a nearby building from which he provided detailed descriptions of the tragic events. ABC's cameras showed grotesque pictures of one hooded terrorist holding high an automatic rifle. On orders from Avery Brundage, however, a limited schedule of Olympic events went forward as hostage negotiations continued. His decision met with widespread criticism in the Western world. Red Smith of the *New York Times* wrote, "Walled off in their dream world, appallingly unaware of the realities of life and death, the aging playground directors who conduct this quadrennial muscle dance ruled that a little blood must not be permitted to interrupt play."[24]

After a long, tense day, at 9:00 p.m. three helicopters landed near the compound and the hostages, the terrorists, and three German security personnel were flown to nearby Furstenfeldbruck airport where a Lufthansa 727 jet awaited. German officials had no intention of permitting the aircraft to take off, however; in fact, no flight crew members could be found who were willing to volunteer to fly the hostages out of Germany. It was later revealed that Chancellor Brandt had wanted the inevitable shoot out to occur away from the Olympic Village, and therefore several German sharpshooters waited at the airport. As two of the Palestinians walked out of a helicopter toward the airplane, the sharpshooters fired, killing them instantly; chaos reigned. Several Israelis were shot and killed by their terrorist guards, and the others died when a hand grenade was tossed into their helicopter. ABC anchor Jim McKay, who had provided a coherent narrative throughout the long ordeal, tearfully said, "They're gone. . . . My father once told me, that our greatest hopes and our worst fears are rarely realized. Tonight, our worst fears have been realized."[25]

The next day, Brundage postponed the competition so that a memorial service could be held, but many in the audience expressed their displeasure. They had come expecting to watch track and field events, not a memorial service. Even in the midst of this tragedy, politics intruded. Around the stadium where the service was held, the flags of most participating countries flew at half-mast. However, Arab delegations insisted that their flags fly atop the poles in the normal manner. The Soviets ignored the memorial; as the service proceeded within the stadium, just outside the Soviet soccer team practiced for an upcoming match. The final speaker at the memorial service was the 84-year-old Avery Brundage, his entire life's mission of promoting the Olympics as a means of increasing international understanding having essentially been shattered by the events of the previous day. He revealed his innate stubborn adherence to a romanticized Olympic ideal when he interpreted the terrorist attack as one upon his beloved Olympic Games, not upon the 11 dead Israelis.

> Every civilized person recoils in horror at the barbarous criminal intrusion of terrorists into peaceful Olympic precincts. . . . Sadly, in this imperfect world, the greater and the more important the Olympic Games become, the more they are open to commercial, political and now criminal pressure.[26]

Then Brundage made one of the most callous and insensitive statements of his career – and he had made many over the years – when he compared the deaths of the Israelis to a simple political effort by the government of Rhodesia when it had threatened to boycott the Games:

> The Games of the XX Olympiad have been subject to two savage attacks. We lost the Rhodesian battle against naked political blackmail. We have only the strength of a great ideal. I am sure that the public will agree that we cannot allow a handful of terrorists to destroy this nucleus of international cooperation and good will. . . . The Games must go on.

Some observers were critical of Brundage's decision to resume the competition; others were angered at his linking the hostages with the threatened boycott. However, some persons thought it was his "finest hour" as he upheld an ideal that he had pursued for more than 60 years. To those defenders, canceling the Games would have meant that the terrorists had won.

The "Munich Massacre" ended whatever idealism any thoughtful person still held about the Olympics. That the Games would become enmeshed in the realities of international politics was inevitable, but for the most part the actual athletic competition at Munich had been free from acrimony. Unfortunately for such American athletes as swimmer Mark Spitz, who won seven gold medals and with each victory setting a new world record, and Frank Shorter, who was the first American to win the premier traditional Olympic event of the marathon since 1908, the hostage situation overshadowed their notable efforts. The 1972 Games would also be remembered as the time that the United States lost its first Olympic basketball game – ingloriously to the Soviet Union in the gold medal game – in a close match that ended in near-chaos as two referees demonstrated either anti-American bias or gross incompetence, perhaps both. With the United States leading 50–49 and three seconds remaining in the game, a Soviet pass from beneath the American basket was knocked out of bounds at mid-court; under unprecedented orders from the head of the International Basketball Federation (not one of the floor referees), the game officials reset the clock at three seconds, thereby giving the Soviets another opportunity. A referee from Bulgaria curiously ordered the Americans not to guard the player making the in-bounds pass, which went to a Soviet player illegally camped (by international Olympic rules) in the three-second lane, whereupon he knocked down two American defenders before catching the ball and scoring unmolested. All of this supposedly happened in three seconds. According to international basketball experts, five major officiating errors occurred during these waning moments; to make matters worse, when American coach Hank Iba pushed his way through the milling crowd to lodge a protest, a pickpocket swiped his wallet and $370. Everything that could go wrong for Iba and his team apparently did. Both the scorekeeper and a referee from Italy refused to sign the score book in protest, but an appeals panel then voted to uphold the 51–50 USSR victory; the panel included jurors from Cuba, Poland, and Hungary who outvoted non-communist bloc jurors. The US team felt so strongly about the bizarre circumstances of their loss that they refused to accept the silver medal, and the ongoing controversy surrounding the game led to major reforms in the training and selection of officials in future international play.[27]

American athletes did not compete well with the Soviet Union and other Eastern bloc countries at either Munich or Montreal. The Soviet Union clearly swept the medal competition, and in 1976 at Montreal small East Germany won 90 medals to the 94 of the Americans. The American Olympic effort had long been hamstrung by intense rivalries between various sports governing bodies. At the highest level, the Amateur Athletic Union has long been at odds with both the National College Athletic Association and the United States Olympic Committee. In 1976, President Gerald Ford appointed a blue-ribbon committee of private citizens to review what could be done. The President's Commission on Olympic Sports submitted its final report in late 1977, and the following year Congress passed the Amateur Sports Act that granted much more power to a reconstituted USOC, and the AAU was left out in the cold. The USOC raised private funds to develop a national training center in Colorado Springs, and rules governing the financial support of amateur athletes were relaxed. The USOC now operated intensive training programs to produce future American Olympic athletes. However, athletes still had to receive their monies indirectly, with appearance fees and generous travel allowances being channeled through the USOC or designated individual sports federations.

To Boycott or Not To Boycott

To read a detailed history of the Olympics beginning with the 1936 Berlin Games is to read an endless tale of the manipulation of the Games by governments and their politicians to achieve their political agendas. None of the Olympiads held after the Second World War until the end of the cold war took place without issues of international politics, social dogma, or religion impacting the participation of nations. With the closing of the Munich Games, Avery Brundage retired from the IOC presidency at age 84, to be replaced by a genial Irishman, Lord Killanin, who introduced a more relaxed and pragmatic approach to dealing with intractable issues. "I try to deal with things as they are, not as we'd like them to be in a more perfect world," he said in a veiled commentary about his dogmatic predecessor. He introduced new policies that permitted athletes to accept financial support during their training, helping prepare the way for the admission of professional athletes in 1988. He also would have liked to eliminate the element of nationalism by banning flags and national anthems, but he bowed in this matter to traditions long established and not easily changed. Killanin's leadership, however, can best be described as casual and uninspired. The disastrous Montreal Olympics were the result: the stadium was not completed on time, the local organizing committee lost $1 billion, most African countries boycotted the Games because, curiously, New Zealand's soccer team had played a pre-Olympic match in South Africa, and the intractable issue of steroids unexpectedly surfaced. The head of the IOC proved incapable of handling these many complications. One exasperated Olympic official exclaimed, "Explaining something sensible to Lord Killanin is akin to explaining something to a cauliflower. The advantage of the cauliflower is that if all else fails, you can always cover it with melted cheese and eat it."[28]

When the IOC announced that the 1980 Games would be held in Moscow, many leading American conservatives, such as columnists William F. Buckley and George Will and soon-to-be President Ronald Reagan, expressed dismay, urging that the United States boycott. Although many observers believed that the IOC had acted in good faith by deciding to hold the Games in a country other than a Western democracy, thereby indicating that the Olympics were above politics, conservative critics felt otherwise and demanded that the American athletes stay home. Given President Jimmy Carter's idealist approach to international affairs, however, such a prospect seemed highly unlikely. That changed dramatically when the Soviet Union invaded neighboring Afghanistan on Christmas Day, 1979, executed the popular prime minister Hafizullah Amin, and installed a rival friendly to the USSR. Civil war soon erupted and President Carter demanded the Soviet's withdraw from the country, but the Soviets under Premier Leonid Brezhnev were adamant about not permitting an unfriendly government to exist on their southern border. Previously they had invaded Hungary in 1956 and Czechoslovakia in 1968 to prevent the overthrow of communist governments beholding to Moscow. Carter faced a major political dilemma. With his re-election campaign about to begin, he felt the pressure to improve his low public approval ratings. The recent taking of 53 American hostages in Tehran had raised questions about his toughness, and gasoline shortages brought on by another OPEC embargo, along with persistent double-digit inflation, had undermined his support at home. To compound his political problems, the liberal wing of the Democratic Party felt that he had abandoned their policy objectives and Senator Ted Kennedy of Massachusetts announced he would challenge Carter in the primaries. Carter believed he had to advance an image of statesmanship and firm resolve in order to fend off the Kennedy challenge in the spring primaries, as well as to defeat his yet unnamed Republican challenger in November. The Moscow Olympics gave him that opportunity.

As the pivotal year of 1980 began, Carter contemplated the possibility of boycotting the Moscow Games, but he carefully refrained from taking action until after the Winter Games in Lake Placid, New York, had been completed in February. The American people had too much money invested to call them off; to boycott our own Winter Olympics seemed unrealistic. In the spring, Carter's heavy-handed efforts, including dispatching Muhammad Ali to Africa as a goodwill representative, to get African nations to join in a boycott of the Moscow Games fizzled; African leaders were still upset that the United States had not joined in their own boycott of the Montreal Games in 1976. In March, Carter ordered an embargo of shipment of American-manufactured athletic equipment to the Soviet Union in an effort to undercut Olympic preparations. Finally he used his presidential influence to persuade the United States Olympic Committee to announce that it would not send a team to Moscow; he also required NBC to withdraw from its contract to televise the Games. American athletes, most of whom had only a small window of opportunity to compete in the Olympics given its quadrennial schedule, and who had spent years in training, were angered by Carter's move. Public opinion polls revealed that a majority of Americans opposed a boycott, but Carter's pressure led to 65 national Olympic committees refusing to send a team to Moscow, including West Germany, Japan, Republic of China, and Canada. Nonetheless, Carter's objective of forcing the Soviets and/or the IOC to cancel the Games failed. Significantly, France and Great Britain sent their teams and ultimately some 80 countries took part. Several world records fell as the East German and Soviet athletes dominated the Games.[29]

Olympic diplomacy as practiced by Jimmy Carter proved counterproductive, ultimately serving only to alienate leading American athletes and sports fans who had come to believe that the Games should transcend politics. It also triggered a

Soviet boycott of the upcoming Los Angeles games in 1984. One Soviet official told the American businessman Peter Ueberroth, designated to organize the Los Angeles Olympics, "You sometimes call us the bear, the big bear. This time you can call us the elephant because we don't forget."[30] As the United States prepared for the 1984 Games, it soon became apparent that the Soviets were seriously considering ordering a boycott by Eastern bloc nations. For three years the Soviets indicated that they would send their team, but the death of premier Yuri Andropov, who had worked to reduce tensions with the United States, meant that hardliner Konstantin Chernenko was now in charge. He had been a close associate of Brezhnev, who had taken the American snub in 1980 as a personal affront, and so on May 8, 1984, with the Games scheduled to begin in less than three months, the Soviets cited "security problems" in Los Angeles and withdrew. It clearly was payback time.

Even the efforts of the new IOC president, Juan Samaranch of Spain, who at one point had been the Spanish ambassador to the Soviet Union, failed to persuade the Kremlin to send a team to Los Angeles. The withdrawal of 14 Eastern bloc countries meant that not only many of the world's leading track and field performers were absent, but also wrestlers, weightlifters, boxers, gymnasts, and swimmers. Nonetheless, teams from 140 counties did show up and the allure of the Olympics still produced high ratings for ABC, which made money despite forking over $400 million for television rights. With more than 200 hours of coverage, ABC managed to show nearly every American's performance if it generated a medal, while top athletes from other countries were generally treated minimally, if at all. Despite the lack of a Soviet foil for the blatant nationalism ABC's coverage demonstrated, the network managed to attract record viewing audiences. The Olympics had become as much a made-for-television spectacle as a major sports event.

With many of the world's top athletes remaining in eastern Europe, the Americans won a lopsided number of 83 gold medals and an additional 93 silver and bronze. In 1976, going head-to-head with the Eastern bloc, the Americans won only 94 medals. Romania ignored the boycott, however, and its athletes won 53 medals. The People's Republic of China also ignored the Soviet-inspired boycott, and made its Olympic debut a good one, with gymnast Li Ning winning six medals. But it was "USA!" all the time on ABC. Of course, ABC had plenty to crow about in two Americans, Carl Lewis and Mary Lou Retton. Lewis, a 23-year-old native of New Jersey who had been groomed from early childhood by his parents for track and field excellence, performed spectacularly by equaling the accomplishment of Jesse Owens at the 1936 Olympics, actually winning the same events: the 100- and 200-meter sprints, the long jump, and anchoring the 4 × 100-meter relay team. Lewis, however, was a difficult sell as a likeable sports star, despite ABC's best efforts. A much-publicized $65,000 shoe deal with Nike had created an image of greed – although most world class athletes had similar deals despite rules prohibiting them – and at Los Angeles he came across as arrogant and selfish. Despite his spectacular performances, he was roundly jeered by American fans when, after wrapping up the long jump with a 28-foot leap on his first jump, he refused to take the next two in order to save his strength for upcoming events; the American fans wanted to see him go for a world record. Controversy would continue to dog

Figure 13.4 West Virginia native Mary Lou Retton exults because she knows that she has captured the gold with a perfect 10 score in the vault at the 1984 Olympics. She won the All-Around Gymnastics competition in Los Angeles, the only American women ever to do so. Retton's exploits did much to create a large increase in the number of young girls who entered gymnastic instructional programs. © Bettmann/CORBIS.

his career, especially when he "named names" of other American athletes whom he alleged used illegal steroids. He would appear in the next three Olympiads and when he formally retired in 1997 was the possessor of nine gold medals.[31] But his personal popularity never equaled his substantial athletic accomplishments.

Such was not the case of a muscular young lady with a made-for-television smile from Fairmont, West Virginia. Mary Lou Retton came into the Los Angeles games with 14 consecutive all-around titles in international competitions, but a few weeks before the Olympics suffered a torn knee cartilage. She persevered in her training, postponed recommended surgery, and thrilled the American television viewers when she scored a perfect 10 in the all-around competition, including a dramatic concluding vault. Her gold medal in the all-around competition was a first for an American woman, and she won four other silver and bronze medals to become the athlete with the most medals at Los Angeles – an amazing feat to be certain, but one that she more than likely would not have achieved if the stable of world-class gymnasts from behind the Iron Curtain had been present. But to the American media, the United States had an answer to the 1972 performance of Olga Korbut, and Retton was credited with stimulating an upsurge in the number of young American girls who enlisted for serious gymnastics training.[32]

The real star of the Los Angeles Olympics, however, was the heretofore unknown 41-year-old California businessman who in 1980 assumed the role of heading up the local organizing committee. Peter Ueberroth's challenge was to put on the Los Angeles games without government subsidy. The near-disastrous Montreal Games of 1976 ended with a $1 billion deficit, and none of the Games since 1936 had turned in a profit. Many skeptics predicted that Ueberroth would fail in his mission. His effort was a model of good old-fashioned American hype and promotion. His charismatic leadership produced an avalanche of sponsor dollars that not only paid for the staging of the two-week event, but also left the organizing committee with a $222.7 million profit on revenues totaling $718.5 million. When the contract between the IOC and the Los Angeles Olympic Organizing Committee was signed in 1978, one new stipulation included was that the local organizing committee would retain any profits. Because not one cent of profit had been made in the previous 50 years, the IOC did not give this matter much thought. Thereafter no such provision would be included – the IOC would make certain it got its cut. Ueberroth put together a paid staff of 1,750 to handle the massive project. Domestic and international television rights brought in $260 million, while 30 major sponsorships produced another $130 million from such corporations as Coca-Cola, IBM, Levi's, Snickers, and Anheuser-Busch. Sponsorships were sold for each of the competition venues, and a long list of corporations paid good money to be recognized as the "official" Olympic product. McDonalds sold the official Olympic burger nationwide, and Coca-Cola the official soft drink. General Motors provided the official automobile for Olympic dignitaries, and so forth. Ueberroth's staff also flooded the markets with T-shirts, hats, key chains, beach towels and other items that tourists were likely to purchase.[33]

A major factor in the financial success was that Ueberroth and his associates decided that they would avoid the large expense of building new facilities. The competition venues were scattered along a 100-mile range of southern California. The Los Angeles Coliseum, constructed for the 1932 Games, received a modest $10 million face-lift and seated 100,000 for track and field. Dormitories at the University of Southern California were converted into a serviceable Olympic Village. The University of Southern California also provided the swimming and diving pools, while UCLA hosted tennis and gymnastics. Field hockey was held at East Los Angeles City College, the soccer finals were staged in Pasadena at the Rose Bowl. Ticket sales were pushed nationwide by travel agencies, and a heavy public relations campaign encouraged Los Angelenos to rent their homes to visitors as a means of preventing over-booking at hotels. Locals also were urged not to drive near the major venues, which helped prevent the much-predicted traffic snarls. Even the weather cooperated; cooler-than-normal temperatures for August prevailed, which meant that smog level was below normal.

The Triumph of Professionalism

Ever since that day in 1913 when the United States Olympic Committee stripped decathlon gold medalist Jim Thorpe of his gold medals, the issue of professionalism at the Olympics had been an issue. Under the presidencies of Pierre de Coubertin and his American disciple, Avery Brundage, the IOC had steadfastly adhered to the quaint but unrealistic code of amateurism. American athletes found ways to support themselves – and their families – through a wide variety of subterfuges. Many were, of course, college athletes who received academic scholarships that included food and housing, not a munificent income to be certain, but substantial financial support nonetheless. Other athletes were employed by companies supportive of the American Olympic effort, and were provided plenty of time in which to do their training. That the Eastern bloc of nations sent professional teams to the Olympics was widely recognized but Avery Brundage was determined to have the Iron Curtain nations participate in order to approximate Coubertin's ideal of representation from five continents and all countries. Thus the American teams tended to be comprised of college-aged men and women who had to compete against mature adults who had devoted many years to perfecting their skills. This fact is what made the "miracle" of the American hockey team at Lake Placid truly miraculous.

It was inevitable that the Olympics would become the province of professional athletes. The unique case of decathlon star Bruce Jenner is illustrative. In 1972, after coming out of obscurity to win a spot on the American team that went to Munich where he finished a disappointing 10th, Jenner devoted himself full-time to training for Montreal. This handsome, muscular native of Newtown, Connecticut, had told anyone who cared to listen that he intended to become a famous Olympian in order to convert his fame into financial rewards. No illusions about patriotism or dedication to the competitive amateur ideal here; Jenner clearly viewed sports as his entrée to wealth. Whereas Bob Mathias had won the decathlon in London in 1948 after only a few months of practice, Jenner worked to prepare for four years, gambling that the effort would produce a gold medal along with fame and fortune. His wife supported him as a flight attendant while he trained with near-fanaticism, averaging about seven hours a day, six or seven days a week. At Montreal his four-year regimen paid off. He won the decathlon 110 hurdles, javelin throw, pole vault, and 1,500-meter run, ultimately leaving his opponents in the distant dust as he compiled an Olympic record 8,618 points. In the process he defeated former gold medalist Nikoli Avilov of the Soviet Union and a strong competitor from West Germany, Guido Kratchsmer. He not only won the gold medal but also was widely proclaimed to be the world's greatest athlete. But Jenner's victory left many with questions, if not disappointment. When the decathlon competition was over, before leaving the track with his gold medal firmly in hand, he announced his retirement, and as if to make a statement about his love for the sport he had just dominated, left his vaulting poles on the field as he walked away. True to his plans, he soon had signed several product endorsement contracts, went on the paid lecture circuit, made cameo appearances in motion pictures and television shows, and at various times did televison sports commentary. He and his second wife – he divorced the spouse that had supported his training – later launched a company that produced fitness and self-defense tapes and marketed a line of exercise equipment.[34]

Perhaps it was Jenner's cynicism (or was it realism?) that made it possible for the new president of the IOC, Juan Samaranch of Spain, to get the rules changed so that professionals could perform at the quadrennial Games. In 1988, professional athletes openly competed in Seoul. Samaranch believed their presence would make the Games more attractive to international television audiences, and provide sports fans everywhere an opportunity to see the unquestioned top athletes of the world compete. Besides, it would end the transparent myth of amateurism that had long been mocked by athletes and journalists alike. The 1988 Games in Seoul saw the USOC send it last collection of presumed amateurs, but the 82–76 loss by the men's basketball team – a collection of college players – to an experienced Soviet team ended any pretext that the USOC would not end its holdout against professionalism.

The 1992 Barcelona Games were notable for two reasons. The collapse of the Soviet Union in 1991 meant that the once powerful Unified USSR team that incorporated the top athletes from 14 independent states, was no longer present. The quadrennial competition between the capitalists and the communists was now a relic of an earlier era. Consequently, much of the drama of the summer Games was drained away, and American television coverage focused more than ever upon telling the tales of American athletes who had overcome various obstacles – however contrived by televison writers – to become an Olympian. The mini-biographies were intended to create dramatic human interest stories to attract viewers who otherwise had little interest in the athletic competition itself. The televised Olympics thus became part soap opera and part athletic competition; the medal count competition was now of minor significance, although from time to time the audience would be reminded by a television commentator of how many medals the Americans had captured.

Fortunately for the television producers in 1992, the appearance of the American basketball "Dream Team" provided American viewers with something novel. In fact, the entire world had fixated upon the much-ballyhooed aggregation led by three of the best professionals ever to play in the National Basketball Association – Magic Johnson, Larry Bird, and Michael Jordan. This formidable triumvirate was surrounded by other top NBA players, including Charles Barkley, Patrick Ewing, Clyde Drexler, John Stockton, David Robinson, and Karl Malone. The only collegiate player was Christian Laettner of Duke University. Coached by Chuck Daley, whose Detroit Pistons had won two National Basketball Association titles, the "Dream Team" was criticized in some circles for making a mockery of the Games, but at Barcelona the teams that lost to the Americans by an average of 44 points a game did not seem to care. Many players were simply proud to be on the same floor as the Americans. At one point, a star-struck player guarding Magic Johnson was seen waving to a teammate on the bench carrying a camera, urging him to be sure to get a picture of that special moment. Although observers felt that the Americans did not extend themselves in many of the games, they did not have to because they were far superior to their opposition. Only Lithuania, which previously had provided top talent for unified Soviet teams and had sent several players to the NBA, presented a potential threat to the Americans, but in the semi-final round the Americans jumped to a quick 34–4 lead and coasted to a lopsided 127–76 victory. Croatia was no match in the championship game, losing to the uninspired Americans who waltzed to victory 117–85.

The presence of a collection of NBA stars in Barcelona signaled that a distinct new era in Olympic history had arrived. Coach Chuck Daley was both magnanimous but prescient in his post-game comments about future Olympic opponents after his team captured the gold:

> They knew they were playing the best in the world. They'll go home and for the rest of their lives be able to tell their friends they played against Michael Jordan, and Magic Johnson and Larry Bird. And the more they play against our players, the more confident they're going to get. Finally there will come a day – it's inevitably going to happen – that they will be able to complete with us on even terms. And they'll look back on the Dream Team landmark event in that process.[35]

That inevitable day came much sooner than Daley or any overconfident American basketball fan might have realized. For one thing, after 1992, many of the very best NBA players no longer wanted to represent their country – they were professionals and there was no pay for Olympic participation. Further, after playing a very long NBA season that stretched upwards to nine months, they needed a vacation from basketball. So the quality of successive "dream teams" tailed off, but not all that much. The 2000 American team included Jason Kidd, Kevin Garnett, Gary Payton and Alonzo Mourning, who discovered that the teams that they now faced were catching up, and rapidly. At Sydney in 2000, Lithuania came within a whisker of upsetting the Americans in the semi-finals before losing 85–83; only a failed three point attempt at the buzzer prevented the third American basketball defeat in Olympic history. France trailed by only four points in the final minutes of the gold medal game before falling 85–75. Chuck Daley's day of reckoning had arrived much sooner than he most likely expected.

Athens and Beyond

The return of the Olympics to the historic land of Greece where it began in ancient times and the site for the first modern Games in 1896, seemed like a good idea at the time, but as the Games approached in summer 2004, second-guessing became a new gold medal sport. Would the Greeks be able to afford the cost of constructing the facilities? Would they get the construction done on time? Would the traditional hot summer days put a damper on the ability of athletes to perform? And, with the grim visage of the destruction of the World Trade Center in New York City still uppermost in the minds of many Americans, would the Olympics become the target of a major terrorist attack? Although the Summer Games left the Greek people with a $10 billion deficit, due in part to very low attendance from Western countries largely attributed to fear of terrorism, the Games went off without a hitch and the much-maligned lackadaisical approach that seemed to characterize the Greek organizing committee and its construction contractors proved unfounded. The venues were completed in time and the Games were run efficiently and without serious controversy. And unlike the 1996 Summer Games in Atlanta, where a bomb killed one woman and injured 111 in Centennial Olympic Plaza, no terrorist attacks occurred. The highly publicized extensive (and expensive) security measures put in place by the Athens organization committee may or may not have kept any possible terrorist attack from occurring.

After the many anticipated problems, none of which came to pass, the games themselves were almost anticlimactic. More than 21,000 media personnel assembled to report the Games (and possible terrorism), outnumbering the athletes by a 2:1 ratio. A record 202 countries sent teams but the biggest record was established in providing security from the much-anticipated terrorists. Estimates of the number of security personnel (the actual number was not revealed for security reasons) who covered the city of Athens like a blanket ranged between 45,000 and 70,000 and the official budget figures set security costs at a whopping $1.2 billion. NBC television paid a record $793 million for the rights to televise the Games in the United States. Although ratings were generally high, especially for the ever-popular gymnastics and track and field events, the focus of the American media was upon the exploits of 19-year-old swimmer Michael Phelps of Baltimore, who entered the Games saddled with predictions that he would eclipse the record seven gold medals of Mark Spitz in 1972. That he failed to do so was perhaps not surprising. He withdrew from one event so that a teammate could capture a gold. Phelps paddled away from Athens, however, with five gold and two bronze medals – not a bad haul for a week's effort.

It was not the dominant Phelps, however, who received the greatest amount of attention from American sports fans. Rather, it was the lackluster (by traditional standards) US basketball team. The predictions of 1992 Dream Team coach Chuck Daley came crashing home. The team was coached by the enormously successful long-time college and professional coach, Larry Brown, fresh from guiding the Detroit Pistons to the 2004 NBA championship. His team was filled with young NBA stars, because several leading NBA players were tellingly absent. Among those who opted not to participate were Kobe Bryant, Shaquille O'Neal, Tracy McGrady, Kevin Garnett, and Jason Kidd. Several of the national teams that appeared in Athens had played together for years; their rosters included a sprinkling of NBA players and the others were veterans of many years of international competition. The young American squad never found a chemistry and discovered much too late that the convoluted committee-dominated selection process had neglected to include one good outside shooter. The primary point guard, Allen Iverson, had a notoriously bad time shooting over tight zone defenses, and he could seldom penetrate them for his patented athletic drives to the basket. Center Tim Duncan found himself surrounded by collapsing defenders, while youngsters Carmelo Anthony and Lebron James found that they could not slash to the basket for easy dunks. Puerto Rico – ironically a small island territory of the United States – set the stage for the dreary American showing with a 92–73 pasting of the Americans in the preliminary rounds as the rest of the world exulted over only the third American loss in Olympic history.

That stinging defeat proved to be a sign of things to come as the Americans lost two more games in decisive fashion – to eventual gold medalist Argentina, and Lithuania. Facing mature and well-coached teams that clearly had mastered the fundamentals of the game, this youthful version of the "Dream Team" suffered through a nightmare of an Olympics, ultimately salvaging a modicum of self-respect by defeating Lithuania for the bronze medal, 104–96. America's domination of the world of international basketball had come to an end. Apologists noted that several top veteran NBA players had elected not to play for their country, and emphasized that decades of American State Department goodwill programs, in which top coaches taught the game in clinics around the world, had eventually produced international parity. Others, such as commentator Dick Vitale, noted that the team had little time to practice together, suggesting that future US squads should be the most recent NBA championship team. More incisive comments noted that the opposition played a much more fundamentally sound style of basketball that emphasized team strategies rather than the showboating one-on-one style that had come to dominate the American college and professional games. America's individual stars, they said, had been sidetracked by teams that played as a team and not as a bunch of individuals seeking to make a sensational slam-dunk intended to get them on television highlight shows.

That the American women, playing much more as a team, won their third straight gold medal did nothing to assuage the loss by Larry Brown's squad of individual but undisciplined talents.

These comments, however, were largely heard only by a small circle of passionate American basketball fans. Rather, the American people as a whole seemed to have developed a blase attitude toward the Olympics in general and the success of the American athletes and teams specifically. Televison ratings remained high, notably buoyed by high ratings among women viewers of the women's gymnastics and high diving swimming events during the Summer Games, (and the ice skating during the Winter Games). The super-critics, however, dismissed even those high ratings, pointing out that the Games took place during the late summer season when anything new and fresh would draw a large viewing audience that had tired of network reruns. That the colorful opening ceremonies of Salt Lake Winter Games in 2002 received the highest ratings of the two-week extravaganza, not the actual sports competitions, suggested that the lack of an Evil Empire against which to compete had deprived the Games of much of its allure for the American people. That said, somehow it was still difficult to become nostalgic about the good old days when the Olympics was a battlefield of the cold war.

14 The Persistent Dilemma of Race

Passage of the Civil Rights Acts of 1964 and 1965 brought to a conclusion the first stage of an ongoing struggle against discrimination and segregation by African Americans that had begun during the late nineteenth century. Between 1945 and 1965, American society was consumed by an intensifying drive to overturn the most visible vestiges of discrimination and segregation. Forces on behalf of racial equality utilized many strategies and tactics, highlighted by public demonstrations and marches, forceful pursuit of constitutional issues in the federal courts, and intense political activity to mobilize public opinion and secure changes in discriminatory laws in state legislatures and the United States Congress. The major breakthrough occurred on May 17, 1954, when the United States Supreme Court ruled that the "separate but equal" doctrine established in 1896 was unconstitutional and ordered the desegregation of public schools throughout the country. The civil rights movement then increased in momentum with the Montgomery bus boycott, passage of the limited (but still symbolically important) Civil Rights Act of 1957, the emotional struggle over the integration of Little Rock Central High School in 1957, and confrontations between local law enforcement and civil rights activists at drugstore lunch counters, in Greyhound Bus stations, at voting registration offices, and on college campuses. The enormous public demonstration by civil rights supporters on the Washington Mall on August 28, 1963, set the stage for passage of important federal legislation.

By 1965, the Civil Rights Acts shepherded through a resistant Congress by President Lyndon Johnson produced a new day in America, a day when a hotel or restaurant owner could no longer deny service to someone because of skin pigmentation, when voting booths were opened to African Americans across the South, and when the Department of Justice could and would defy segregationist forces. Once segregated Southern universities now admitted African American students and despite violent opposition at times, local public schools had, in general, complied with the rulings of federal courts. None of these accomplishments came easily; the evening television news and morning newspapers frequently featured the dramatic story of confrontations between civil rights activists and embittered segregationists. Schools and churches had been bombed, civil rights leaders threatened, physically attacked, and sometimes killed, and across the South the smell of smoke and tear gas had became all too familiar.

The civil rights movement transformed American sports. Of course, sports had always reflected America's tortured history of race relations. When the pall of segregation spread across American society in the 1880s, organized baseball readily joined in and excluded African Americans. The unwritten but effective exclusionary policy that went into effect in 1885 lasted until Jackie Robinson came on the scene in 1946. During that same period, throughout the South and border states, black college students were excluded from taking part in intercollegiate athletics except at all-black colleges. In other parts of the country, economic and social forces kept to a very small number those African Americans who were able to participate in intercollegiate contests. To look at the team photos of college football or basketball teams from the Western Conference (Big Ten) or Pacific Coast Conference (Pac-Ten), for example, from the 1920s and the 1930s is to see virtually all-white squads.

Prior to the Second World War, whenever African American athletes did rise to the top of their sport, such as Jack Johnson and Joe Louis in professional boxing, Rutgers All-American Paul Robeson in college football, or Jesse Owens in track and field, they invariably attracted an unusual level of national attention. The media treated them almost as an abberation. Newspaper accounts of their achievements invariably focused upon their race as much as their athletic achievements, with commentary heavily laden with the prevailing discriminatory attitudes of the day.

During the 1950s, the issue of race remained alive and well in American sports. Administrators at Southern universities had to confront the fact that whenever their all-white teams ventured into the North or West that the chances now were that they would be matched against increasing numbers of African American athletes. During the 1960s, the once all-white Southern teams began to recruit African Americans. At the professional level, teams found that they could seldom win without availing themselves to talented black athletes; if they did not their opponents certainly would. However, in both college and professional sports, the ranks of coaches remained lily-white and black athletes often found that they were the target of new forms of subtle but nonetheless telling forms of discrimination. Many college teams engaged in "position stacking," whereby certain positions (i.e., quarterback and middle line-backer in football, point guard in basketball) were informally but definitely declared off-limits to blacks. Young men recruited to predominantly white campuses to play sports often found that the campus social life was off-limits to them, and complained that their athletic department academic advisors routinely advised them into "snap" courses so as to keep them eligible rather than into curricula that led to a college diploma. Thus when a dominant athlete emerged on the scene during the 1960s, who was unwilling to acquiesce to established racial conventions, and even had the temerity to exercise his constitutional rights as an American citizen, the result was a classic confrontation that captured the nation's attention.

"I'm the Greatest"

No single individual better captured the cultural conflicts and contradictions of the 1960s than Muhammad Ali. He burst upon the American scene with a grand flourish just as the American military was gearing up for war in Vietnam and the civil rights movement was cresting, about to begin to lose its focus and spin off in several disparate directions. In his prime, Ali was indeed one of the "greatest" of all time. Tall and willowy, fighting at a trim 210 pounds, he used speed, quickness, and ring savvy to frustrate his more powerful but less agile opponents. He possessed the cunning and guile of Gene Tunney, the punching power of Joe Louis, and the charisma of Jack Dempsey. When he refused induction into the US Army in 1967, the reaction of the boxing establishment was sure and swift. He was summarily stripped of his title and boxing licence, and for three years unable to pursue his livelihood. Ali's opposition to the Vietnam War made him an ironic public figure, an enormously talented professional fighter who embraced the doctrines of pacifism.[1]

When Cassius Marcellus Clay Jr burst upon the professional boxing scene following his gold medal victory in the light-heavyweight division at the 1960 Rome Olympics, most sports writers and fans enjoyed his brash behavior, writing it off as merely a new wrinkle on an old theme of hyping fights. In 1961, at age 19, Clay turned professional. He was initially financed by a consortium of Louisville businessmen. Under the tutelage of veteran trainer Angelo Dundee, he quickly developed into a leading heavyweight. His penchant for making audacious prefight comments – often drawing upon the rhetorical tradition of simple rhythmic verse that was popular with young urban black males – gave reporters something to write about ("Archie Moore will go down in four," or "At the sound of the bell, Terrell will catch hell," etc., etc.). He first employed this shtick as a professional in 1962 when pitted against a seemingly formidable foe, Sonny Banks. At a pre-fight press conference, he told a laughing, if disbelieving, group of reporters: "The man must fall in the round I call. Banks must fall in four." True to his prediction, Clay knocked out his opponent in the specified round, and the resulting publicity thrust him into the national spotlight. At one point, he correctly predicted the round in which he would dispatch his opponent in seven of eight fights.[2]

With decisive victories over such opponents as former light-heavyweight champion Archie Moore and British heavyweight champion Henry Cooper, Clay found himself at age 22 preparing to take on the formidable reigning heavyweight champion, Sonny Liston. The imposing champion had a long police rap sheet, having served hard time for armed robbery. Violent, sullen, even frightening, Liston seemed to be much more than the youthful Clay could handle. Liston had won the championship with a stunning round 1 knockout of Floyd Patterson in Chicago in 1962, and six months later in Las Vegas, once again dispatched Patterson with a

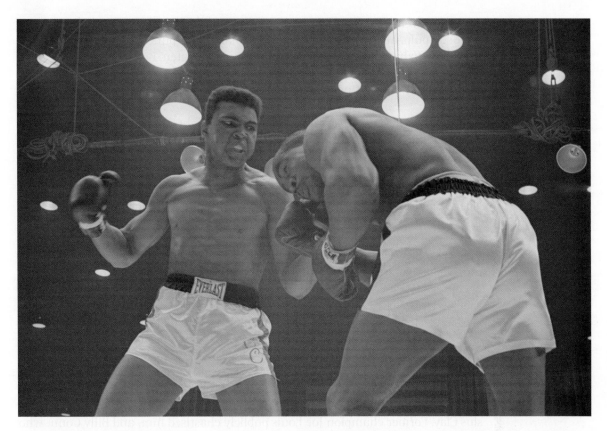

powerful first-round punch. This brooding, uncommunicative champion seemed invincible. Many boxing experts feared that young Clay
risked a severe beating, even permanent injury. Despite Clay's 19 consecutive victories since turning professional, the boxing commission
in California refused to sanction the fight with Liston, taking seriously Rocky Marciano's warning that Liston would likely inflict serious
damage. The fight was eventually scheduled for Miami.

During the pre-fight weigh-in, Clay seemingly went berserk, screaming and shouting at Liston as he bounded about the room. "I'm going to
whup you so baaad," he shouted. "You're a chump, a chump!" Stunned
reporters concluded that young Cassius had lost his senses and was
consumed with fear, but Dundee quietly smiled as Clay worked his
psychology on the impassive Liston. To those who knew him well,
the performance, while more extreme, was one they had seen before.
During Clay's training sessions, he and Dundee had invoked a new
mantra, "Float like a butterfly, sting like a bee." And that is precisely
what Clay did, as he out-maneuvered his plodding opponent, who never
could get set to throw his best punches. Clay peppered his opponent
with stinging left jabs – contrary to some negative pre-fight punditry
his jab indeed did possess plenty of wallop – and by the fourth round

Figure 14.1 A young Cassius Clay unleashes his lightning-fast fists against the heavily favored champion Sonny Liston in their title bout in Miami on February 25, 1964. The next day Clay informed the media that he had converted to the teachings of Muslim faith, setting off a controversy that would envelop his subsequent boxing career. Several weeks later he announced that he had changed his name to Muhammad Ali. © Bettmann/CORBIS.

it was apparent that a new champion was about to be crowned. Liston's face was a bloody pulp, and he seemed incapable of landing a punch on his much-quicker opponent. Exhausted, frustrated, and thoroughly beaten, Liston did not respond to the bell for round 7. As Liston slumped in his corner, the new champion bounced around the ring shouting to the stunned press row, "I told you! I told you! I'm the greatest!"[3]

The shocking outcome of the championship fight was but a prelude to what proved to be the main event. At a press conference the next day, the new champion informed reporters that he had converted to the little known, but highly suspect, Black Muslim religion. The charming, dashing, even poetic Cassius Clay became an instant pariah to much of white America. The Nation of Islam stood far outside the mainstream of the civil rights movement as a religion with Middle Eastern and African roots that was primarily known for its embrace of black nationalism, its denunciation of whites as evil, and repudiation of the central tenet of contemporary liberalism: racial integration. When it was later learned that Clay's conversion had been facilitated by the militant Malcolm X, public indignation intensified. "I believe in the religion of Islam," the new champion said, "which means I believe there is no God but Allah, and Elijah Muhammad is his Apostle."[4]

His insistence that the press refer to him as Cassius X exacerbated the situation. A few months later, he changed his name to Muhammad Ali, as suggested by Elijah Muhammad (Muhammad meaning "one worthy of praise," and Ali after an ancient general who was related to the Prophet Muhammad). Nearly all media outlets, even the progressive *New York Times*, ignored Ali's request and for several years continued to call him by what he now referred to as his "slave name," Cassius Clay. Former champion Joe Louis publicly chastised him, and Billy Conn, who nearly took the championship away from Louis in 1946, said, "He is a disgrace to the boxing profession. I think that any American who pays to see him fight after what he has said should be ashamed."[5]

The champion, however, was not moved by such criticisms. Instead, he talked about his religion's emphasis on marital fidelity, pre-marital chastity, and a lifestyle that shunned the use of alcohol and drugs while emphasizing personal responsibility and lawfulness. But white America only saw the policies of racial exclusion, black pride, and the justification of using force in self-defense. When white reporters reminded Ali that Joe Louis had been a "credit to his race," the new champion bluntly silenced them: "I don't have to be what you want me to be. I'm free to be who I want."[6] With that powerful declaration of independence from traditional expectations of heavyweight champions, much of black America exulted as white America recoiled in dismay.

Between that momentous night in Miami in February 1964 and spring 1967, Ali successfully defended his championship nine times. In a rematch, he knocked out Liston in the first round (the decisive punch was delivered so fast that many ringside observers did not see it). The most memorable of his early title defenses occurred in November 1965, when Ali defeated former champion Floyd Patterson in a technical knockout in round 12. During the pre-fight build-up, Patterson became mainstream white America's great hope in a symbolic battle between "the

Crescent and the Cross." Patterson was a conservative Catholic who was appalled by Ali's embrace of the Nation of Islam. In pre-fight comments, the former champion repeatedly referred to his opponent as "Cassius Clay" and at one point drew parallels between the Black Muslims and the Ku Klux Klan:

> I have nothing but contempt for the Black Muslims and that for which they stand. The image of a Black Muslim as the world heavyweight champion disgraces the sport and the nation. Cassius Clay must be beaten and the Black Muslim scourge removed from boxing.

He repeatedly told reporters he was going to "take back" the heavyweight title "for America," saying at one point stating that Ali (or Clay) was "disgracing himself and the Negro race."[7]

Such pre-fight braggadocio notwithstanding, Ali easily defeated Patterson in a technical knockout, but Patterson's comments had connected with mainstream America. The criticism that Ali's membership in the Nation of Islam engendered proved to be merely a prelude to the angry public reaction to his refusal to be inducted into the United States Army in 1967. Like many Americans, he did not support the American war aims in Vietnam. As he said in an oft-quoted comment, "I ain't got nothing against those Viet Congs." Various veterans and patriotic organizations – recalling the decision of Joe Louis to volunteer for the army shortly after Pearl Harbor – contended that Ali was either a coward or the dupe of a radical religious sect. Ali's position, however, was based upon his deeply felt religious beliefs. Had he been cynically using his religion as a means of escaping military service, he could easily have accepted an offer to serve in the army in a noncombatant role, giving exhibition fights to entertain the troops just as Joe Louis had done during the Second World War. He rejected this option, and his serious public demeanor and private comments to associates gave credence to his sincerity: "I have searched my conscience, and find that I cannot be true to my belief in my religion in accepting [induction]." Thus on April 28, 1967, in Houston, Texas, when his name was called he refused to take the symbolic step forward to repeat the oath signifying his acceptance of induction into the armed forces. He was thereupon arrested.[8]

With the exception of anti-war activists who applauded his stand, Ali was roundly condemned by white America. His decision came at a critical juncture of the war when thousands of new troops were being inserted into the beleaguered small southeast Asian nation and American bombs were raining down on its civilian countryside. Ali thus confronted the American people with the courage of his convictions. Americans were not prepared for a serious statement of faith from a professional boxer, especially one who was a member of the Nation of Islam. The press, with the notable exception of ABC announcer Howard Cosell, was swift to condemn him, demanding that he be jailed. The New York Boxing Commission, without even the pretense of holding a hearing, stripped him of his title in less than three hours after he refused induction, and other state commissions followed in short order. Moving with incredible speed, in just 10 days the Justice Department indicted him and proceeded to trial in a Houston federal court six weeks later. Judge Joe Ingraham gave the jury precise instructions that virtually assured Ali's conviction, then threw the book at him with the maximum sentence permitted by law: five years in federal prison and a $10,000 fine. The judge also ordered Ali's passport seized, so the former champion would be unable to earn money fighting abroad.[9]

Public response to these developments depended upon one's point of view. The predominant view of white America was neatly summarized by Congressman Robert Michael of Illinois, who angrily declared,

> I cannot understand how patriotic Americans can pay for pugilistic exhibitions by an individual who has become the symbol of draft evasion. While thousands of our finest young men are fighting and dying in the jungles of Vietnam, this healthy specimen is profiteering from a series of shabby bouts. Apparently Cassius will fight anyone but the Vietcong.[10]

Urban working-class blacks, however, found in Ali a new hero who was not afraid to challenge the white establishment, as he did in a press conference a few days prior to his appearance before the draft board in Houston:

> Why should they ask me to put on a uniform and go ten thousand miles from home and drop bombs and bullets on brown people in Vietnam while so-called Negro people in Louisville are treated like dogs? If I thought going to war would bring freedom and equality to twenty-two million of my people, they wouldn't have to draft me; I'd join tomorrow. . . . I either have to obey the laws of the land or the laws of Allah. . . . So I'll go to jail."[11]

While lawyers appealed his conviction, Ali worked the college lecture circuit, where he talked about his religious beliefs and his refusal to serve in the military. Initially, his anti-war position went counter to public opinion, but by 1970 the war's support had dwindled to almost 50 percent. Public criticism became muted, and many persons now spoke about Ali's brave stand for a principle. The swing in public opinion led the New York Boxing Commission to reissue Ali's boxing license, and on June 21, 1971, the United States Supreme Court, apparently also reading public opinion, unanimously overturned his conviction by citing an obscure legal technicality while studiously refusing to rule on the issue of whether his religious beliefs made him a bona fide conscientious objector in the eyes of the law. Ali thereupon resumed his boxing career. He regained his championship in 1974 by defeating champion George Foreman, and he successfully defended it 10 times (including his fabled 1975 TKO victory over Joe Frazier in the "Thrilla in Manilla") before losing to Leon Spinks in 1979 at the age of 38.[12]

Ali's public persona had originally played a crucial symbolic role in the widening chasm in American life during the 1960s, but during the 1970s he became a symbol of healing and reconciliation. After his retirement (and a brief unsuccessful comeback attempt in 1980), he became a popular, beloved public figure. His seriously deteriorating physical condition caused by Parkinson's disease, likely brought on by the many blows to the head he had absorbed during his 25 years of amateur and professional boxing, further endeared him to the American people. Despite his shocking physical deterioration, Ali maintained a public presence and enjoyed immense public popularity. He had transformed himself from a despised draft dodger into a beloved American icon.

Boycott, Backlash, and Beyond

Muhammad Ali's problems with the United States government occurred during a time of growing protest against racial discrimination by top black athletes. Their tactic of choice was the boycott. In part, the movement was inspired by the spirit of the times, which saw the nonviolent strategies of the civil rights movement challenged by militant calls for confrontation. The boycott movement included specific grievances by African American collegiate athletes against coaches, athletic governing boards (the NCAA, the United States Olympic Committee), and college and university administrations. At the center of this movement was a young college instructor, Harry Edwards, a former basketball and track star at San Jose State University. In 1967, Edwards assumed a position in the Department of Sociology at San Jose State. Before the start of the fall semester, Edwards and several black athletes approached the university's administration with a list of demands that included the abolition of racial discrimination in all campus organizations and activities, including the traditionally segregated fraternities and sororities. They also demanded a major overhaul of practices and policies in the athletic department, which they viewed "as racist as any of the other areas of college life." After Edwards met with senior administrators about his concerns, he became frustrated: "They literally laughed in my face – they took my concerns as a joke." He reported that Dean of Students Stanley Benz "made it crystal clear that, where the interest and concerns of the majority whites were concerned, the necessities of black students were inconsequential."[13]

Those experiences prompted Edwards to organize a protest demonstration to force the cancellation of the first football game of the season against the University of Texas at El Paso. The national media jumped on the story: would a student protest lead to the cancellation of a college football game? Governor Ronald Reagan offered to send in the National Guard to put down any demonstration, but the university administration decided to cancel the game to avoid the possibility of violence between would-be demonstrators and counter-demonstrators. UTEP not only got a victory by forfeiture but also a check for $12,000 under a cancellation clause in the game contract.

Encouraged by the success of his first boycott effort, Edwards turned his attention to the 1968 summer Olympic Games scheduled for Mexico City. Edwards later recalled, "We found out that those black athletes who were being shafted on the campuses were the same athletes the nation depended on as part of its Olympic contingent." For a time, the idea of a boycott gained momentum, getting its share of newspaper space along with urban riots, anti-war demonstrations, and the assassinations of Martin Luther King Jr and Robert F. Kennedy. By bringing national attention to the grievances of black athletes at San Jose State, Edwards had sliced open a hornets' nest of latent anger and frustration among black athletes on college campuses across the United States, and wherever he went he received a warm welcome from them. He organized the Olympic Project for Human Rights to spearhead a boycott, which he saw as one small component of "the broader civil rights movement. ... We wanted to establish an organic link with the struggle of Dr. King, the struggle of Malcolm X, the struggle of SNCC, the struggle of CORE, the struggle of the [Black] Panthers." During a visit to New York City, he said,

> We're not just talking about the 1968 Olympics. We're talking about the survival of society. What value is it to a black man to win a medal if he returns to be relegated to the hell of Harlem? And what does society gain by some Negro winning a medal while other Negroes back home are burning down the country? ... I think the time has gone when the black man is going to run and jump when the white man says so, and then come back home and run and jump some more to keep from being lynched.[14]

Edwards believed the Olympic Games made a perfect target because it was an international stage where "athletes had become soldiers in a global struggle between East and West." Ultimately, the boycott fizzled because very few black athletes actually refused to take part in the Mexico City Olympics – the most notable defections were several college basketball players, including Lew Alcindor (Kareem Abdul-Jabbar), Bob Lanier, Elvin Hayes, and Wes Unseld, who passed on tryouts for the American Olympic team. Most athletes had been in training for several years and were reluctant to pass over the competition; they also realized that they would be past their athletic prime by 1972. A few of the dissidents decided to compete but to use the Olympic stage to exhibit their discontent. Most of those who actually did so were closely identified with San Jose State: including Tommie Smith and John Carlos of the famed Black Power salute protest. Looking back on his organizational efforts for a boycott from the perspective of 30 years later, Edwards felt that it failed because most athletes decided "to put their individual aspirations first." That the US Olympic Committee pulled out all stops to undercut the boycott – including dispatching such prominent black athletes as Willie Mays and Jesse Owens to talk to potential boycotters – helped persuade some athletes to put aside their grievances and compete.[15]

Nonetheless, the spirit of protest spilled over to American college campuses. Sports pages were dotted with stories of confrontations between coaches and their athletes, who expressed grievances ranging from segregated housing, team rules against interracial dating, position "stacking," even team dress codes that forbade "Afro" hairdos. Between 1967 and 1972 confrontations embroiled prominent football and basketball programs at such universities as Washington, California, Iowa, Michigan State, Oklahoma, Princeton, Western Michigan, Oklahoma City, Kansas, and Marquette. However, it was the boycott of athletic competitions with Brigham Young University that attracted the most attention.

At issue was the policy of the Church of Jesus Christ of Latter-Day Saints (the Mormon Church) which prohibited African Americans from entering its priesthood.

In spring 1968, the UTEP track team refused to compete against BYU, and prior to a home game against BYU on October 18, 1969, all 14 black members of the University of Wyoming football squad sought approval from coach Lloyd Eaton to wear black armbands during the game to protest the church policy. Eaton refused, citing unwritten team rules, and dismissed all 14 from the team when they appeared in the football office wearing the armbands. When the university president and the Governor of the State of Wyoming sought to mediate the standoff on the eve of the game, the athletes firmly stated that they would never again play for Eaton, whom they accused of making racially offensive comments. The Governor and university president backed the coach, although news reports pointed out that no rules could be found in team manuals that would have prohibited the armbands. It was clear that the major offense committed by the "Wyoming Fourteen" was to challenge the authority of their coach.[16]

The Wyoming incident led to several other protests during BYU basketball and football games, most notably at the universities of Arizona, Colorado State, New Mexico, and Washington. At one point, the BYU team hotel in San Jose was subject of a bomb threat. More serious, however, were the decisions by Stanford University and the University of Washington to discontinue playing BYU. The demonstrations faded into obscurity by the end of 1970, most likely because across the United States the number of protests had begun to ebb. The anti-war movement faded rapidly, and the civil rights movement moved from the streets into the nation's courts and legislative chambers. At BYU, faculty members plaintively pointed out that the issue of membership of minorities in the Mormon priesthood had originally been raised by members of the church itself; soon thereafter, a small number of black athletes began to appear on Cougar team rosters. In 1978, the First Presidency of the LDS Church announced that a "revelation" had been received that men of African descent could in fact be admitted to the priesthood. The idea of boycott, a red-hot issue that captured front-page headlines for a brief period, disappeared almost as quickly as it had appeared.[17]

A New Era in Race Relations

By the mid-1970s, a new era of race relations in American sports was at hand. After the tragic killing of four students and wounding of 13 others by Ohio National Guardsmen at Kent State University on May 5, 1970, a sense of introspection inevitably set in. Compromise and conciliation became more prevalent, confrontation much less so. The anger that had characterized the 1960s began to seep out of public discourse. Quiet returned to the college campuses, and the streets of major cities were no longer the scenes of protests and demonstrations.

Racial attitudes and public policy changed. Most whites now accepted, or at least accommodated themselves to, the idea of equality. The most egregious symbols of discrimination and segregation disappeared as polling places, restaurants, churches, theaters, public restrooms, universities, and public schools were opened to members of all races. A viable and growing black middle class was now in evidence. African Americans were increasingly portrayed on television and in motion pictures as intelligent and sensitive individuals; the demeaning stereotypical images of Stepin Fetchit and Amos n' Andy were replaced by Sidney Poitier and Bill Cosby.

The process of social healing was readily evident in sports, although in many instances change came slowly and not without resistance. But change was definitely in the air. The once lily-white professional golf circuit opened up to pioneering players Lee Elder and Charley Sifford; in a symbolically important moment, Elder played in the 1974 Masters Tournament at the ultra-exclusive, all-white National Golf Club in Augusta, Georgia. Prior to that moment, the only appearance of blacks in the tournament had been as caddies carrying the bags of white players. In another sport long associated with racial discrimination, Virginia native Arthur Ashe knocked down racial barriers in tennis, enjoying a lengthy run as a top-ranked international player.

Throughout the South, once-segregated universities began to recruit local black players where previously most had opted for Northern schools or Southern black colleges. By the early 1970s, nearly all major Southern university basketball and football teams had been integrated. A long-time barrier in professional baseball was finally breached in 1975 when Frank Robinson was named manager of the Cleveland Indians; Larry Doby was introduced as the manager of the Chicago White Sox in 1978.

However, the number of minority managers remained small for the next quarter-century, although such talented individuals as Robinson, Dusty Baker, Cito Gaston, and Don Baylor were viewed with high respect as managers. Gaston became the first African American manager to win a World Series when his Toronto Blue Jays edged out the Atlanta Braves and the Philadelphia Phillies in 1992 and 1993.

By the turn of the new millennium, the racial composition of college and professional teams had changed drastically from a half-century earlier. Blacks now constituted slightly more than half of professional and major college football teams; basketball teams in the National Basketball Association and those in the major college division exceeded 70 percent African American. Major league baseball, however, saw the number of black players slip from 17 percent in 1970 to less than 10 percent in 2005, but the influx of players from Latin America was large, with 20 percent of players now having come from the Caribbean or South America. The arrival of several top-notch baseball players from Japan as the new millennium began – including the multi-talented outfielders Ichiro Suzuki of the Seattle Mariners and Hideki Matsui of the New York Yankees – gave an indication that the racial and ethnic composition of future teams would continue to show increased diversity. By the early twenty-first century, more than two dozen foreign countries were represented on the rosters of NBA teams. After the fall of the Iron Curtain in 1991, the influx of players from such countries as Croatia, Russia, Lithuania and Ukraine provided ample evidence of the high quality of basketball being played in eastern Europe. Additionally, athletes from Spain, Italy, Argentina, and Puerto Rico also added to the multinational mix of professional basketball. Although such stellar players as Vlade Divac and Peja Stojakovic of Serbia-Montenegro, and Kirk

Nowitzki of Germany were standout players, the greatest attention was focused upon the multi-talented 7' 6" center Yao Ming of China who found a home as an All-Star performer with the Houston Rockets.

Racial stereotypes die hard. American sports fans learned that in 2003, when conservative radio talk-show host turned football commentator Rush Limbaugh created a front-page incident as an "analyst" on the ESPN *Countdown* Sunday football show. He blithely suggested that All-Pro Philadelphia Eagles quarterback Donovan McNabb was overrated, saying that he was the creation of a fawning liberal white media more eager to extol the talents of a black quarterback than to report upon his deficiencies. Limbaugh was heavily criticized for his comments. He denied that his comments were "racist" and stoutly defended his comment, but he nonetheless resigned amid a flurry of criticism. Skeptics contended that Limbaugh had fulfilled ESPN's hidden objective: namely, to generate a larger viewing audience by creating a racially charged issue. McNabb had the last laugh: after the season ended, he was named to the Pro-Bowl for the fourth time and led the Eagles to the National Conference championship game. Two seasons later he led his team to the Super Bowl and was selected to the post-season All-Star team. No other network gave Limbaugh a second opportunity to try his hand at football commentary.

Despite the increasing number of black athletes, management was reluctant to entrust head coaching positions to experienced and obviously well-qualified African Americans. It was not until 1989 that a nationally prominent college football program appointed a black head coach, when Stanford University named Dennis Green as its leader. In 1992, Green moved on to the National Football League when he assumed command of the Minnesota Vikings and enjoyed a successful 10-year run with a 101–70 record. Green was only the second African American coach in the league's history (the first was former All-Pro lineman Art Shell, who was named head coach of the Oakland Raiders in 1989, the same year he was inducted into the NFL Hall of Fame). In 2004, there were only three black head coaches in the NFL (one of them Dennis Green, now with the Arizona Cardinals), four managers in the major leagues, and eight head coaches in the NBA. Only five of 117 Division I-A college football teams that same year were headed by African Americans. For years the Black Coaches Association had expressed its frustrations even in getting qualified black candidates interviews for college openings. When Notre Dame hired Tyrone Willingham away from Stanford as its head coach in 2002, many observers thought that his appointment to lead the nation's legendary football program would help other blacks to get opportunities. Despite a 21–15 record, in a highly controversial decision involving a new Notre Dame president who had not yet even taken office, Willingham was summarily fired after only three seasons. He was not even permitted to remain in the job long enough to coach the first group of his recruits in their senior year. As the 2005 recruiting season began, only three blacks, Sylvester Croom of Mississippi State, Karl Dorrell of UCLA, and Willingham (who moved to the University of Washington) held head coaching positions at high-profile college programs.

College basketball had a better record of providing minority candidates opportunities than other sports because of the large number of blacks who dotted the rosters of college teams beginning in the 1960s; they thus constituted a large pool of potential coaching talent but also were in demand because of the perception that they could recruit top black players more easily than white coaches. An important pioneer in college basketball was George Raveling. After playing at Villanova during the 1960s, Raveling became the first black assistant coach in the Atlantic Coast Conference in 1970 (at Maryland), and in 1972, he became head coach at Washington State in the Pac-Ten, moving on to Iowa in 1983 and to Southern California in 1986. Recognized as a leading spokesman for his profession, Raveling took USC to four consecutive NCAA tournaments and was voted the national College Coach of the Year by his peers in 1992. Also in 1972, Georgetown University named former Boston Celtics backup center John Thompson to head its then-woeful program; by 1979, Thompson had led the Hoyas to a Big East Conference championship, and in 1982 his team lost in the final 15 seconds of the NCAA finals to North Carolina on freshman Michael Jordan's jump-shot. In 1984, Georgetown won the NCAA tournament with a 10-point victory over the University of Houston.

By 1990, black basketball head coaches had become commonplace and their appointment no longer produced perceptible public comment. However, the appointment of Nolan Richardson as head coach at Arkansas in 1985 and of Rob Evans at Mississippi in 1992, were important breakthroughs in the Deep South. Both coaches enjoyed successful careers. Evans brought respectability to the Ole Miss basketball program, winning the school's first road game against powerhouse Kentucky since 1927, and turning in two consecutive 20-game winning seasons (something the Rebels had not done since 1937–38) before moving on to Arizona State in 1998. In 1990, Richardson guided the Arkansas Razorbacks to a Final-Four appearance, and in 1994 his team won the national championship, utilizing a swarming full-court pressing defense and a high-octane fast-break offense that Razorback fans termed "forty minutes of hell".

During the 1960s "position-stacking" became a point of contention as the number of African American players on college team rosters increased substantially. It was seen by civil rights advocates as a subtle device whereby college coaches "stacked" several black players at the same position, thereby ensuring that other positions could be filled by whites. This was designed to assuage racist fans who feared that their once all-white teams would be heavily dominated by black starters. Evidence for the charges of stacking were manifold. Clearly, certain positions seemed to be reserved for blacks – running back, defensive back, wide receiver in football – while they were excluded from positions demanding leadership or decision-making skills – quarterback, offensive center, middle linebacker. In basketball, whites tended to dominate at the point-guard position. Charges of stacking, however, dwindled rapidly during the 1970s because coaches, understanding that they had to win games in order to keep their jobs, decided to play the best players at all positions, no matter their skin pigmentation. The issue disappeared, although it was kept alive in sociology of sports textbooks. By the 1980s, black point-guards abounded, and the naming of a starting black quarterback no longer created a stir. On New Year's Day in 1991, when Colorado and Notre Dame met in the Orange Bowl with the national championship on the line, black quarterbacks Darian Hagen and Tony Rice lead their teams into battle (Hagen's Buffalos prevailed 10–9).

The racial transformation of American sports during the 1970s and the 1980s was truly revolutionary. By 1980, the typical major college football team was composed of about 50 percent blacks, and college basketball teams substantially more. No one blinked any more when a professional or college basketball team started five African Americans. Major league baseball teams were 30 percent black by 1980 (a figure, however, that would shrink to 15 percent by 2000 as elite African American athletes opted for other sports); NFL football teams were 40 percent black in 1980, but that number would rise to 70 percent by 2000. In that same year, NBA squads were 80 percent black. A large majority of the Most Valuable Players in all three professional sports, year in and year out, were African American. Between 1960 and 2000, 25 of the 40 individuals receiving the Heisman Trophy, awarded annually to the nation's best college football player, were black. Beginning with Ohio State running-back Archie Griffin in 1974, 10 consecutive winners of the trophy were African American, but it was not until 1989 that the first black quarterback was so honored (André Ware of the University of Houston). The NBA has honored a Most Valuable Player ever since 1956, and through the 2003–04 season the award went to a white player only eight times. (Larry Bird alone won three MVP awards during the mid-1980s.) The MVP awards for the NFL and for baseball were not quite so dramatically skewed toward blacks, but nonetheless, ever since the mid-1950s, the MVP awards in the two leagues went to a nonwhite 60 percent of the time.

Arguably the two most popular athletes – of any racial or ethnic background – of the last two decades of the twentieth century were basketball player Michael Jordan and golfer Tiger Woods. Whenever they competed, television ratings soared and their smiling faces were a constant on television and in newspapers and magazines. Jordan and Woods transcended racial barriers to become two of the most popular figures in American life – not just in sports – and were symbolic of a much different outlook on the part of black athletes. Whereas sports pioneers such as Jackie Robinson, Arthur Ashe, Curt Flood, Muhammad Ali, and Hank Aaron were outspoken in their criticism of racial discrimination in America, a new generation of black athletes emerged who were more likely than not to be indifferent to racial and social issues. Frequently conservative and Republican in their politics, they assiduously avoided using their star appeal to advance social causes, including race relations. During the 1990s, Jordan came under strenuous attack from various liberal groups for his endorsement of Nike products. He shrugged off allegations that the high-priced "Air Jordan" basketball shoes that carried his name were made in grimy sweatshops in the Far East that exploited women and child labor, implying that Asian working conditions were not his responsibility nor something about which he need concern himself.[18] Woods also skirted the issue during his long and remunerative relationship with Nike, and blithely went about his business of winning golf tournaments and never became identified with political or social issues. That he lived in a posh gated community of large mansions near Orlando, complete with a private golf course and other upscale amenities, seemed only natural for this superbly talented, young, good-looking, incredibly popular multimillionaire.

Thus, in the sports world of the last quarter-century, performance tended to overwhelm once-pervasive racist attitudes. Along with Woods and Jordan, the new generation of prominent black sports stars, such as Barry Bonds, Bo Jackson, Kobe Bryant, Shaquille O'Neal, Deion Sanders, and Jerry Rice (to name a few prominent figures at random), seemed to care little about those early pioneers who had fought bravely against entrenched racism so that their successors could have access to extraordinarily lucrative multimillion-dollar players' contracts and hefty product endorsements. "Today's black athlete is very different," sociologist Harry Edwards noted in 1998 on the 30th anniversary of the boycott movement that he had once spearheaded:

> Their identify is different – they live in a rich, largely white world, a world where black individuality is tolerated so long as it is without reference to the black community. If you ask them about the history of the black athlete, many couldn't tell you much. They don't find that history relevant to their world.

Edwards recalled a conversation with a leading black NBA star whom he asked about the pioneering racial role played by NBA guard Oscar Robertson; the stunning response he received was, "Don't know, don't care, and don't take me there!" Unfortunately, Edwards said, contemporary black athletes

> don't care about whose shoulders they stand on. They have no idea about who set the table at which they are feasting. And the worse part about it is not that they are ignorant of this history, but they are militantly ignorant.[19]

Conversely, that this new generation of black athletes did not feel the sting of racism suggests that at least for black sports stars the most egregious forms of racism and discrimination have indeed been banished from American life. Jackie Robinson, his uniform Number 42 permanently retired by all major-league teams in 1997 on the 50th anniversary of his first appearance in a Brooklyn Dodgers uniform, was definitely of an earlier and much different era.

Hank Aaron Catches the Babe

In 1961, American sports fans carefully followed New York Yankee outfielders Roger Maris and Mickey Mantle as they zeroed-in on Babe Ruth's season record of 60 home runs. When it was recognized that one or both might catch the Babe, Commissioner Ford Frick announced in mid-season that, should the record be broken, the new mark would be placed in the record books with "a distinctive mark," indicating that the new record was set in a 162-game season rather than the 154 that Ruth played. The issue of the number of games in the season created the only real controversy as Ruth's record was eclipsed by Maris. His home run total stood at 59 after his 154th game, and on the last game of the season –

number 162 – he hit the record-breaking number 61. His record was thereupon accompanied by an asterisk (*) to preserve the Ruthian achievement of 1927. A very private individual, Maris did not handle his new-found fame well. He suffered from injuries and personal problems that curtailed his career, was traded to St Louis in 1966, and when he retired two years later with a career 275 home runs, no one paid much attention. The only significant public display memorializing his baseball career is located in a corner of a shopping mall in his home town of Fargo, North Dakota.

That was not the case a decade later when Henry ("Hank") Aaron of the Atlanta Braves began to creep close to the Babe's career home-run number of 714. Born in Mobile in 1934, Aaron first entered the major leagues in 1954 with the Boston Braves and launched a long, productive career as an outfielder and power hitter. In May 1970, he banged out his 3,000th base hit, but because he never hit more than 50 home runs in any season, no baseball expert anticipated that when he reached his late thirties that this slender, lithe athlete would unleash a sustained home-run barrage that would put Ruth's career record in jeopardy. Aaron ended the 1970 season with 592 home runs, placing him third all-time behind Ruth and Willie Mays. In the next three seasons, he smacked 47, 34, and 40 homers, and at the end of the 1973 season stood at 713, just one behind the Babe. Over the winter, baseball writers speculated endlessly about the implications of the feat that Aaron would surely accomplish early in the 1974 season.

Many white fans did not take kindly to the possibility that an African American would surpass the Babe. During the season of 1973, as he approached the magic number of 714, Aaron was flooded with nasty, crude, even life-threatening letters. During the 12 months before he broke Ruth's record, according to the US Post Office, Aaron received 930,000 pieces of mail, more than any person in the United States other than the Watergate scandal-ensnared President Richard M. Nixon. The threats made against Aaron were sufficient to justify an ongoing FBI investigation, and the hiring of personal bodyguards.[20] On opening day in 1974, Aaron tied Babe Ruth with a line drive over the left field fence at Riverfront Stadium in Cincinnati, and on April 8 in Atlanta, he hit the record-breaking number 715 off of Al Downing of the Los Angeles Dodgers. Baseball Commissioner Bowie Kuhn was conspicuously absent that historic day, and during the midst of a congratulatory telephone call that Aaron received in the locker room from President Nixon, the line suddenly went dead.

Hank Aaron thus found himself in a bittersweet mood. As he later wrote in his autobiography, "It should have been the most enjoyable time of my life, and instead it was hell." The angry letters and death threats took their toll. He had discovered that the only tangible way he could respond to his many hate-filled correspondents was to go for the record.

> I kept feeling more and more strongly that I had to break the record not only for myself and for Jackie Robinson and for black people, but also to strike back at the vicious little people who wanted to keep me from doing it. All that hatred left a deep scar on me. I was just a man doing something that God had given me the power to do, and I was living like an outcast in my own country.[21]

Aaron retired from baseball after 23 major league season in 1976 with a grand total of 755 home runs. His career number of runs batted-in of 2,297 is also a record, and he is ranked third in total career hits with 3,771. In 1982, he received the second-highest percentage of votes in history (behind Ty Cobb) upon his election to the Baseball Hall of Fame. He was later quoted that he hoped that "some kid, black or white," would exceed his record. "I will be pulling for him." However, when that person turned out to be Barry Bonds of the San Francisco Giants in 2005, a power hitter whose use of anabolic steroids was widely rumored, Aaron rightfully spoke out in protest of players enhancing their natural skills with banned substances.

Can White Men Jump?

During the early 1970s, as black athletes became much more prominent in American mainstream sports, a red-hot debate broke out. Speculation about the role of race in explaining sports prowess had long bubbled beneath the surface of American sports (fostering such myths as blacks were poor swimmers because of heavy muscle mass, were good boxers because of thicker skulls, were speedy runners due to longer legs). In 1971, however, speculation about racial differences moved beyond such mindless speculation when a well-respected senior writer for *Sports Illustrated* published a lengthy essay that drew heavily, and selectively, on a substantial body of scientific evidence to argue that black athletic success resulted from a combination of special physiological and psychological factors attributable directly to race.[22] In this explosive article, Martin Kane took notice of the recent upsurge of successful black athletic performance since the end of racial segregation in American sports, especially in those popular spectator sports where strength, agility, and speed were essential. "Twenty-six years ago there were no blacks on any of the big-league basketball, football or baseball professional teams," Kane noted, but by 1971 nearly 50 percent of the athletes in these sports were African American. He concluded that "the black community in the US is not just contributing more than its share of participants to sport, it is contributing immensely more than its share of stars." Noting that at the 1968 Olympic Games in Mexico City, all eight Olympic records set by the American track and field team were the result of performances by blacks, he quoted a European coach, "If not for the blacks, the US team would finish somewhere behind Ecuador."[23]

Although Kane was careful to identify many contributing social, economic, and environmental factors, including access to playing facilities (hence the small number of elite black golfers, swimmers, or tennis players), he nonetheless came down hard on the side of racial characteristics as a determining factor. Kane, in fact, identified three areas for examination: race-linked physiological and physical characteristics, race-linked psychological characteristics, and race-linked historical factors. He cited several physiological studies that he contended demonstrated that, as a racial group, black athletes had more flexibility, longer legs and arms, narrower hips, less body fat, greater bone density, more tendon, and less muscle, all of which produced individuals with greater speed, power, and dexterity. Additionally, Kane curiously cited "a distinctive ability to relax under pressure," a trait which he attributed to "the suppressed life of the black man in America," which had enabled him to endure and survive the indignities of slavery and segregation. "White kids haven't had to live under an oppressive burden," he said. Thus blacks had an inherited ability to "relax" during times of intense stress, as well as a deep-seated subconscious motivation "to exceed whites athletically" whenever given the opportunity.

Kane emphasized the struggle of African tribesmen to survive captivity by slave hunters in Africa, the brutal and deadly Middle Passage across the Atlantic Ocean, and the inhumane time of "seasoning" or "breaking-in" that prepared survivors for backbreaking labor in the sugar cane fields of the Caribbean and in the tobacco, rice, and cotton fields of North America. He contended that contemporary blacks were the products of "natural selection" resulting from an unforgiving Darwinian "survival of the fittest" history that stretched back to the 1600s. He even went so far as to suggest that black athletic ability was further enhanced by selective breeding by white masters of female slaves with the strongest and biggest males. Thus the opening of the door to organized sports, Kane concluded, meant that

> every black child, however he might be discouraged from a career with a Wall Street brokerage firm, knows he has a sporting chance in baseball, football, boxing, basketball or track. . . . He has the examples of Willie Mays and Bill Russell, of Frank Robinson and Lew Alcindor to inspire him.

Kane thus concluded that the black athlete's unique psychological and physical characteristics enabled him to outperform his white competitors.

Kane's article, coming as it did on the heels of the assertions by two well-known scholars, psychologist Arthur Jensen and Nobel Prize-winning physicist William Shockley, that lower academic achievement by African Americans was attributable to genetics rather than social and cultural factors, set off a heated public controversy. Among those taking up the challenge was Harry Edwards, the leader of the 1968 Olympics boycott, now holding a professorship in sociology at the University of California, Berkeley. He responded with a blistering article in *The Black Scholar* and in a much more detailed analysis in his textbook, *Sociology of Sport*. Edwards feared that Kane's argument "opens the door for at least an informal acceptance of the idea that whites are intellectually superior to blacks." He pulled no punches, bluntly attributing racist assumptions to Kane's article. "The argument that blacks are physically superior to whites as athletes or as a people is merely a racist ideology camouflaged to appeal to the ignorant, the unthinking, and the unaware in a period heightened by black identity." Summarizing the widely shared academic viewpoint on the issue, Edwards emphasized, "The simple fact of the matter is that the scientific concept of race has no proven biological or genetic validity. As a cultural delineation, however, it does have a social and political reality."[24]

Edwards made certain that his readers understood that Kane's article was a melange of folk tales, pseudoscience, and unproven assertions, all premised on racist assumptions. Drawing on an extensive body of sociological and anthropological research, he noted that even the concept of *race* was not well established: "typically, there has been little success in any effort to derive consistent patterns of valid relationships between racial categories and meaningful social, intellectual, or physical capabilities,"[25] and that one scholar had clearly demonstrated

> it is quite obvious that Black athletes differ from each other physically quite as much as Whites do. . . . [W]hat physical characteristics does Kareem Abdul-Jabbar have in common with Elgin Baylor, or Wilt Chamberlain with Al Attles? The point is simply that Wilt Chamberlain and Kareem Abdul-Jabber have more in common physically with Mel Counts and Hank Finkel, two seven-foot tall white athletes, than with most of their fellow black athletes.[26]

Edwards also emphasized that Kane drew upon only a small subset of black Americans – a few elite black athletes – and not the general population of 20 million individuals, who, he noted, came in all shapes and sizes, and about whom it was meaningless, if not absurd, to generalize about a commonality of musculature or bone structure. He pointed out that the great percentage of African Americans lacked special aptitude for sports, just like their white counterparts. A few black athletes, he said, excelled only in those sports to which they had access and ample opportunity to hone their skills. Thus inner-city basketball courts, city streets, and parks provided opportunities to learn basketball, football and baseball. At best, black youngsters could excel in games offered by public-school systems. Private golf courses, segregated swimming pools, private tennis clubs, and remote ski resorts obviously contributed to the dearth of black success in these sports. Additionally, these sports have other features that limit black access: the importance of expensive private lessons, costly club memberships, and equipment priced far beyond the reach of most African Americans. America's pervasive system of racial discrimination, not racially determined physical traits, explained black success in a few sports and lack thereof in others. Kane's polemic, he said, even did the most successful of black athletes no favors by emphasizing natural talent over hard work and dedication. He quoted Bill Russell to the effect that he had become a superior basketball player because of the intensive effort he put into his craft: "Russell once stated that he had to work as hard to achieve his status as the greatest basketball player of the last decade, as the president of General Motors had to work to achieve his position."[27]

Although Edwards's erudite dismantling of Martin Kane's hypothesis tended to satisfy the academic world, his powerful analysis apparently did not reach the average sports fan or even prominent sports figures who should have become better informed. In 1987, the general manager and president of the Los Angeles Dodgers, Al Campanis, appeared on the *Night-line* television show for an interview with ABC's Ted Koppel on the 40th anniversary of Jackie Robinson's first appearance in a Brooklyn Dodgers uniform. At one point, Campanis shocked Koppel when he attributed the relatively low number of black managers in baseball to a lack of mental acuity, asserting that they "may not have some of the necessities to be, let's say, a field manager, or perhaps a general manager." When Koppel attempted to provide Campanis a chance to rephrase his insensitive comments (at one point Koppel asked incredulously, "Do you really believe that?" and then after a commercial break, "I'd like to give you one more chance to dig yourself out"), the Dodgers executive instead continued to affirm his initial comments, going on to state that blacks also were not good swimmers because they "don't have buoyancy." For his candor, Campanis was fired by the Dodgers two days after his infelicitous remarks.

Just nine months after the Campanis debacle, another leading sports figure, sports handicapping guru and CBS television personality, Jimmy "The Greek" Snyder, stepped onto the same landmine. While waiting for a table at a Washington, DC restaurant, he casually responded to a query by a reporter about the reason African American athletes had become so successful. It was, he said, due to selective breeding during slavery:

> I'm telling you that the black is the better athlete, and he is bred to be the better athlete, because this goes back all the way to the Civil War. . . . The slave owner would breed his big black to his big woman so that he could have a big black kid, you see. I mean that's where it all started.

Where it would end, he predicted, was the total domination of American sports by the genetically advantaged black athlete: "They've got everything, if they take over coaching like everybody wants them to there's not going to be anything left for the whites. I mean all the players are black." Just as the Dodgers terminated Campanis for his remarks, CBS wasted no time in firing "The Greek" amid a brief but raucous national debate over the merits of his comments and the correctness of CBS's decisive action.[28] Four years later, actors Wesley Snipes and Woody Harrelson entertained American movie goers with a humorous treatment about the quirks and vagaries of black and white athleticism as they portrayed a pair of playground hustlers playing two-on-two basketball for high stakes; when black opponents saw the scrawny white kid (Harrelson) come onto the asphalt, they were prime for picking by he and his black co-conspirator.

In the years that followed the Campanis and Snyder debacles, various efforts were made by writers who lacked scientific credentials to reprise the race-performance connection. Although these efforts produced the expected mixed reaction from those who read their books, articles, and internet postings, for the most part sports fans and journalists paid little or no attention, and the authors were soundly critiqued for their lack of scientific rigor by academics from the fields of anthropology, sociology, and biology who took their writings seriously. Their efforts to attribute the success of a few elite athletes to racial traits were soundly debunked from a wide spectrum of scientific perspectives. The noted sports sociologist Jay Coakley aptly summarized the underlying issue when he writes,

> When it comes to using racial classification in our personal lives, we should recognize that the human race contains many combinations of changing physical similarities and differences and that racial categories are based on social meanings given to those similarities and differences, not biology.[29]

Tiger

The difficulty in attributing success in sports specifically to racial traits was well exemplified by the unprecedented success enjoyed by golfer Eldrick "Tiger" Woods. Proud of his mixed heritage (Native American, African American, Asian, Eurasian), he once suggested that journalists refer to him as "Cablinasian." Rising swiftly to the very pinnacle of the world of professional golf – long the province of white men – Woods baffled those who clung to racial evidence to explain mastery in sports. That he had a natural aptitude for the sport was obvious, but Woods' success clearly resulted from his intense personal drive coupled with strong parental support and guidance that provided extensive exposure learning and playing the sport from an early age. At the age of 21 and having turned professional just six months earlier, this dynamic young athlete stunned the sports world when he did the seeming impossible by winning the prestigious Masters Tournament on his first try in 1997 by a record-setting 12 strokes, establishing a new tournament record with a score of 270. He drew enormous galleries as he routinely boomed his tee shots over 300 yards, controlled his fairway woods and irons with precision, and pitched and chipped onto the lightening fast greens with uncanny precision. As putt after putt unerringly dropped into the hole, his putter seemed at times to have been transformed into a magic wand. During the four-day tournament, Woods captivated an entire nation, turning millions of non-golfers into ardent Tiger fans. Televison ratings soared as viewers were transfixed by his incredible performance. The fact that Woods shot a 4-over-par 40 on the front nine holes the first day of the tournament (he rallied to blister the back nine in 30) made his record-setting accomplishment all that more incredible. By the end of his first full season on the PGA tour, Woods had added another five wins and had pocketed more that $2 million in prize money.

Woods burst upon the relatively staid world of professional golf like a thunderbolt. His feats in national junior and amateur competition – including several near-miraculous comebacks in major tournaments – had drawn serious attention even before he turned professional in August 1996. Recognizing that he was something special, in anticipation of what he might bring to the world of sport even before he won his first Grand Slam tournament, *Sports Illustrated* named him its "Sportsman of the Year" for 1996. Senior writer Gary Smith hypothesized that Woods was the "Chosen One," a special person who would forever banish racial prejudice from American golf. Pointing toward Woods's multiracial heritage, Smith predicted that Woods would help reduce the intense racial chasm that had for so long preoccupied America.[30]

Indeed, Woods did prove to be the "Chosen One," transforming the image of American golf with his superb talent and the sheer joy with which he embraced the game. His personal magnetism, projected by his winsome smile and his composure during press conferences, won him millions of fans and made him an instant celebrity. Within a year on the tour, he had become one of the most popular and acclaimed men in the United States, traits that made him a sought-after

Figure 14.2 Tiger Woods celebrates sinking a long putt on the 16th green at Pebble Beach during his unprecedented 15-stroke victory in the 2000 US Open tournament. At age 21, Woods stunned the world of golf by winning the Masters by 12 strokes over runner-up Tom Kite, his first Grand Slam victory as he set out upon a personal quest to eclipse the record of 18 Grand Slams held by Jack Nicklaus. © Reuters/ CORBIS.

spokesman for commercial products. Sensing his uniqueness, the Nike sporting goods company signed him to a long-term $40 million endorsement contract at the time he announced he was turning professional, a sum previously unheard of for a golfer, especially one without a single professional tour victory. At the age of 21, Tiger Woods was already in the rarified endorsement league of Michael Jordan.

After his initial success, Woods tailed off in 1998, winning only one tournament. Determined to improve, he undertook an intensive program of weight and aerobics training – highly unusual at the time for professional golfers, who perhaps practiced several hours a day but were prone to retire to the 19th hole for relaxation and reflection rather than hit the weights or run five miles at day's end. By the start of the 2000 tour, Tiger had added 20 pounds of muscle, and many of his top rivals undertook similar regimens, if for no other reason than in hopes of keeping within hailing distance of golf's new phenomenon. After his lackluster 1998 season, Woods rebuilt his already powerful swing under the tutelage of coach Butch Harmon, attempting to create even more distance and improve his accuracy. Thus in 1999, after falling short at the Masters, he won nine tournaments, including the PGA.

His play in 2000 was the stuff that makes golfing legends for the ages. At the US Open played at the famed Pebble Beach course in California, Woods eclipsed the field by an almost incomprehensible 15 strokes, despite having his concentration and continuity of play interrupted by rain delays. Watching Woods leave the world's best professionals far behind, 1982 US Open champion Tom Watson could only mutter, "Tiger has raised the bar to a level that only he can jump over."[31] Woods then proceeded to win the two remaining "majors," outdistancing the British Open field by eight strokes and defeating Bob May in a dramatic three-hole playoff to claim the PGA for a second consecutive time. In spring 2001, Woods made it four majors in a row with a two-stroke victory in the Masters at Augusta National over David Duval. No one in history, not even Jack Nicklaus, Ben Hogan, or Bobby Jones, had such a comparable run. It was easy to overlook the fact that Tiger accomplished this feat by the age of 25, when most professional golfers have yet to reach their potential. Journalist Frank Deford asked, "Has anybody in any sport been this much better than everyone else?" After Woods won his third Masters in 2002, critics, more serious than flippant, began to speculate whether the hidebound traditionalists who run Augusta National should redesign the course to make it "Tiger-proof."[32]

By the end of the 2005 season, Woods had won 10 major tournaments (four Masters, two US Opens, two British Opens, and two PGA tournaments) and 45 PGA tournaments despite playing in only about 20 events a year. In one unprecedented streak he retained his ranking as the world's top professional golfer for 264 consecutive weeks – more than five years – a record, eventually relinquishing the top spot to Vijay Singh, a native of the island nation of Fiji, in September 2004. But he won it back in 2005. Just 29 years of age that year, he could look forward to 20 more years on the PGA tour, providing him ample opportunity to achieve the personal goal he set for himself of exceeding Jack Nicklaus's record of 18 major titles and 70 tour victories. Woods publicly stated many times that Nicklaus was the greatest golfer in history and that his goal was to surpass the "Golden Bear" before he retired. It was at the age of 13, in fact, when most boys are contemplating making their junior high school baseball team or earning a Boy Scout merit badge, that young Tiger had already memorized Nicklaus's major achievements, knew the story of his career backward and forward, and matter of factly told his parents that it was a benchmark he someday planned to surpass.

Born the only child of middle-class parents in 1975, Woods was nicknamed "Tiger" by his father, after a military buddy, Vuong Dang "Tiger" Phong, a South Vietnamese lieutenant colonel whose bravery in battle earned him the nickname.

One important facet of Woods's enormous popularity was that his heritage made him a veritable walking American melting pot. It was commonplace for the media and fans to consider him to be African American, but Woods pointed out that his mother Kultida, is Asian – in fact, she is one-half Thai, one-quarter Chinese, and one-quarter white. "I don't want to be the best black golfer ever," Tiger once told a *Sports Illustrated* writer. "I want to be the best golfer ever." He said that whenever he has to fill out a form inquiring about his ethnicity, "I always fill in Asian." His mother met Tiger's father during the Vietnam War and they were married in 1969. Father Earl Woods was a graduate of Kansas State University, where he played baseball; he played low-handicap golf as an adult. After graduation, he pursued a military career, became a Green Beret, and saw serious action in Vietnam. He also was multiracial, being one-half African American and one-quarter American Indian and one-quarter Asian. Woods's unique racial heritage, as *Sports Illustrated* predicted in 1996, only added to his public appeal.[33]

If ever there was a child prodigy, it was young Tiger Woods. When he was two, he would sit for hours in a high-chair watching his father hit practice golf balls into a net at the family home in Anaheim. One day he climbed down from the high-chair and picked up a plastic toy club and took a swing that was almost a mirror image of his father's – except that he did it left-handed. At the time, he could barely walk. As his biography recounts, "A few days later, he stepped around the ball, correctly reversed his grip, and made an equally precocious swing from the opposite side. At that moment, Earl realized he was the steward of an extraordinary talent."[34] At the age of three, Tiger amazed a television audience on the *Mike Douglas Show* as he putted efficiently against famed comedian (and capable golfer) Bob Hope. By age five he could hit golf balls with power and control, much to the amazement of a national audience of *That's Incredible*. By age six, he had scored two holes-in-one. As he matured, his parents encouraged his development as a golfer but did not demand that he do so. Rather, it was young Tiger who insisted that he wanted to spend hours each day practicing and playing a local public course. His mother found maintaining discipline easy: she would simply deny him an opportunity to practice his golf when he broke the rules.

His father and mother sacrificed to support Tiger's development. In addition to private lessons and greens fees several times a week, he played intensely competitive matches with his father. Earl would attempt to distract him, suddenly talking as he started his down swing, or jingling the change in his pocket as he prepared to putt – even clapping his hands or whatever he might do to distract his son. Earl and Tiger later said that this psychological testing helped Tiger learn to control his nerves and concentrate on the shot at hand while completely shutting out extraneous distractions. Unlike some notorious parents who push and prod their children to become a top junior athlete, Earl and Tida merely encouraged their son in his quest by providing opportunity. He practiced with ferocity because of his love of the game; in grade school, when other children drew pictures of animals, he was drawing trajectories of his golf shots. His dedication to long hours of daily practice marked his childhood and continued throughout his professional career. His determination to excel was noted by his coach at Stanford, who was surprised to see him on a practice driving range, dripping wet, resolutely hitting balls into heavy wind-blown rain. Tiger explained that he wanted to take advantage of the opportunity to learn how to hit balls with accuracy in a driving rain.[35]

At age 15, Woods won the 1991 United States Junior Amateur Championship and proceeded to win it the next two years as well. He emulated his "three-peat" by winning three consecutive United States Amateur titles in 1994–95–96. In 1994, Woods won his first United States Amateur tournament in grand style, defeating Oklahoma State star Trip Kuehne at Pontra Vedra Beach in Florida in a 36-hole final pairing. This tournament is played under match-play rules, in which paired opponents play one-on-one with the winner being whoever wins the most holes, not the lowest number of strokes. With 12 holes left to be played, Kuehne led by five and merely needed to tie eight of the remaining holes or win just four. Then Tiger began one of his famous comebacks. Playing with intense concentration on the crucial par-three 35th hole, an island target surrounded by water that swallows tens of thousands of balls a year, he calmly went for the flag located perilously near the water's edge. His ball landed three feet from disaster, and he calmly sank the fourteen-foot putt to avoid defeat. At that moment, Kuehne knew that the match had been lost, as indeed it had.

Heavily recruited by top college golf programs, Tiger selected Stanford, where he became the nation's top collegiate player as a freshman. He took a heavy course load with a major in economics, and after his sophomore year, realizing that there were no challenges left in college golf, turned professional in fall 1996. Six months later, he sat atop the world of golf after his shocking dismantling of the famed Augusta National course as he donned the famed green jacket, emblematic of his first Master's championship.

Woods was unique. Blacks saw in him someone who dominated a traditionally all-white sport. White Americans found redemption from the longstanding critique that golf was a game that practiced and encouraged racism. As David Owen writes,

> When white golfers do think about Woods' racial background, it's often with a sense of relief: his dominance feels like an act of forgiveness, as though in a single spectacular career he could make up for the game's ugly past all by himself.

And for young African Americans

> outside America's cultural mainstream, Woods has meant incalculably more. He is the fearless conqueror of a world that has never wanted anything to do with them . . . He inspires them to do well and be great in whatever it is that they want to do.[36]

Sister Act: Venus and Serena

They burst upon the staid white world of professional tennis like a stage-five hurricane, leaving in their wake a checkered record of contentiousness and triumph, ultimately producing awe and astonishment at their skill level and domination of women's tennis. Unlike most top men and women players, they did not come from financially comfortable white families that lavished upon their precocious children expensive tennis lessons, tuition at high-powered year-round tennis schools, and expensive travel to play a formidable junior tennis tournament schedule in preparation for moving on to the United States Tennis Association tour. Instead, sisters Venus and Serena Williams learned their tennis from their father on the pocked blacktop public courts in the downscale, gang-infested city of Compton in the Los Angeles Basin. Richard Williams, who supported his family as part-owner of a security-guard firm, had little interest in tennis until he watched on television when a check for $30,000 was presented to a tournament winner. He thereupon taught himself to play the game by reading tennis manuals and watching instructional videos, with the specific intent of producing at least one professional champion from among his five daughters. The two youngest showed the most potential, and from age five he put them through hours of practice six days a week. By the time they were 10, both dominated junior tennis tournaments in the Los Angeles area. In 1990, the older, Venus, won the 12-and-under Southern California title and sister Serena the 10-and-under. Part promotions whiz, part conniving huckster, Richard launched a shrewd marketing blitz that attracted the attention he wanted: several tennis equipment manufacturers came calling, armed with offers of endorsement contracts. In 1991, Richard moved his family to Florida, where he placed the girls under the guidance of professional instructors, who honed their skills to the point that they were prepared for international junior competition.[37]

At this juncture, with plenty of offers of lucrative endorsements, Richard surprised the tennis world by pulling his daughters out of all junior tournament competition, insisting that they were to concentrate upon their studies, but the intense practice regimen continued. Unlike many parents of tennis prodigies who turned their children professional at an early age, Richard decided to postpone that decision. Although confidently predicting that his "ghetto Cinderella," as he called Venus, would someday dominate women's professional tennis, he had his own time-plan.

> I'm sick of looking around tennis and seeing these poor kids making a living for their parents, seeing these parents drive around in their Mercedes and Rolls Royces. . . . That's like the parents turning against the kids and prostituting them.[38]

To facilitate their tennis progress, his wife home-schooled the girls, who eventually earned diplomas with honors from a private high school.

Perhaps it was not too surprising that Richard gave in to the money and permitted Venus to turn professional when she was 14. But he restricted her play to only a few events each year, insisting that she focus on her studies. She won her first professional match in a California tournament in 1994 against the world's 59th ranked player, but lost in the second round to second-ranked Arantxa Sanchez Vicario. After winning the first set, her game fell apart as she succumbed to a healthy case of tournament jitters. Clearly Venus's lack of extensive junior tournament experience showed in her match against Vicario, and for the next three years

Figure 14.3 Sisters Serena and Venus Williams enjoy their doubles victory at the 2002 Wimbledon tennis championships. After often-contentious initial seasons on the women's professional tour, they became fan favorites as they transformed their personal images, and in the process raised the level of women's tennis with complete games that featured power as well as finesse. © Reuters/CORBIS.

Venus played sporadically. Despite a rocky start in her professional career, the Reebok Company was convinced of her future and signed her to a five-year, $12 million contract in 1995. Richard's improbable dream had paid off. Despite his early protestations about the exploitation of youngsters, he was not hesitant to take the money.

Still, Venus's first three years on the tour were difficult. At the end of the 1996 season, she was ranked 212 in the world. Then she broke through in 1997, methodically working her way up the rankings. She entered the US Open unseeded with a ranking of 66 and powered her way to the finals before losing in two sets to the top seed and number-one-ranked Martina Hingis. Venus's game was strikingly different from typical women players, most of whom preferred to play a cautious game from the baseline. Instead, Venus stunned the tennis world with her powerful ground strokes; her serves routinely were timed at 120 miles per hour. She tore around the court smashing overheads, volleying with a vengeance, striking her ground strokes with a ferocity that became the talk of the tennis world. As she moved into the top rankings, her confidence – some said arrogance – grew and she appeared on court in dramatic skin tight outfits, her hair often bedecked with cornrows and colorful beads. Sportswriters wrote admiringly of her power, physical strength, speed, and endurance, creating a new image that coupled racial imagery with masculinity. The *New York Times* observed that Venus had a "wide receiver physique" and her younger sister Serena a "running back physique."[39]

But Venus Williams's sudden rise to prominence was replete with racial overtones. On the positive side, *Sports Illustrated* called her "a brilliant new talent – witty, intelligent, and charismatic – a streetwise child of gang-plagued Compton, Calif., who could be sports' next Tiger Woods." Venus agreed, noting, "Tiger's different from the mainstream, and in tennis I also am. I'm tall. I'm black. Everything's different about me. Just face the facts." That reality was not lost on several of her fellow players. Resentment against Venus and her outspoken father – who was quick to play the race card – surfaced at the 1997 US Open as she mowed down her opponents with her blistering game. During her semifinal match, the 11th-seeded Irina Spirlea intentionally bumped into Venus during a changeover between games, and afterward said she did it purposely because of Venus's allegedly arrogant "in your face" attitude. Richard, however, charged that the motivation was blatant racism, telling the press that he and Venus had both heard players refer to her as "that nigger." Although Richard denounced Spirlea's intentional collision as racially inspired, he in turn told the press that the Romanian was "a big, ugly, tall, white turkey." The 17-year-old Venus sought to calm the waters in a press conference, invoking the names of Althea Gibson and Arthur Ashe, as white reporters sought unsuccessfully to elicit from her a controversial racially tinged comment. Following this incident, Venus took her 6–0, 6–4 defeat to top-seeded Martina Hingis in the finals in stride, and while *Sports Illustrated* predicted that while she possessed "spectacular gifts" that would "energize" women's tennis, at the same time her aloof demeanor and the antics of her outspoken father/coach would also "provide plenty of freewheeling, and damaging, distractions." Tennis insiders now talked about a sensation-seeking father and a standoffish, seemingly arrogant daughter. Undeterred, Richard retorted, "We couldn't care less what people think of us."[40]

The following February, at the 1998 Australian Open, women's tennis got a glimpse of the future when Venus met her 16-year-old sister Serena in the second round and came away with a 7–6, 6–1 victory. But Serena gave every indication that in the long run she might surpass her sister, a prediction their father had already made. A confident Serena told the press afterward, "What you saw was something for the future." Venus concurred, "Seeing her across the net was a little bit odd, but it's to be expected and in the future it'll be the same." So it was. In 1999, Venus lost a long, exhausting three-set match against top-seeded Hingis at the US Open, then had to watch her younger sister defeat the obviously weary world's top-ranked player in the finals in two close sets. Serena, at age 17, was the first African American to win a Grand Slam event since Althea Gibson in 1958. Both sisters were now ranked among the top five in the world.[41]

Venus and Serena became not only top-ranked rivals who frequently met in the finals of major tournaments but also, much to the surprise of most observers, they remained close friends. Apparently their several years of working long hours on the court under their father's demanding glare had brought them very close, something that even face-offs at Grand Slam championship tournament finals could not erode. They often entered doubles tournaments as a team, winning championships at the 1999 US Open and the 2000 Wimbledon Championships, even knocking down a gold medal at the 2000 Sydney Olympic games. Both enjoyed their moments in the spotlight of Grand Slam finals, with Venus winning Wimbledon in 2000 and 2001 and the 2000 and 2001 US Open championships. For a time, Serena emerged as the more successful of the two – however slightly – as she defeated her sister in five Grand Slam finals: 2002 French Open, the 2002 US Open, Wimbledon in 2002 and 2003, and the 2003 Australian Open. But then Venus revived her game to win the 2005 Wimbledon, winning a three hour marathon three-set match from American Lindsay Davenport. And the money rolled in. Beyond their substantial prize monies, Venus capitalized on her fame with a $40 million renewal of her Reebok contract, while Serena enjoyed a multimillion deal with Puma.

Financially secure beyond even their father's wildest dreams, both women expressed interest in life beyond the cloistered and often inhibiting world of women's tennis. Both studied fashion design at the Art Institute of Florida, and Venus opened her own design company. Bright and confident young women, the sisters unobtrusively moved away from the shadow of their domineering father. His often racially tinged comments no longer shocked or interested tennis fans. (When in 2003 he told a reporter that tennis was replete with racism and that he hoped his daughters would quit the game and take up ice-skating, Serena calmly changed the subject when it came up in a press conference.) With winning came confidence, and the icy reserve with which they had early on reacted to their peers on the circuit, melted away. They no longer isolated themselves from other top women players, no longer refused to talk to them in the locker room or in public venues, as once was their wont (or their father's orders). At the same time that they reshaped their public images, they also went their own individual ways. Serena, enjoying the limelight, was not afraid of making bold statements, but also refused to engage in false modesty ("When I lose a match it is usually because of how I played"). Venus remaining her more reserved self, seeking new outlets outside of tennis, noting at one point, "Tennis was my father's dream, not mine. Winning, losing, money, riches, or fame don't make you happy." As she reduced her number of tournament appearances, she found pleasure in her interior design company. Thus the hostility that Venus, especially, had initially encountered on the tennis circuit faded away. Both women clearly had modified their behavior as they moved into adulthood and away from the control of their father, but what once was seen as "arrogance" was now interpreted as "confidence," their "brute strength" had somehow morphed into "sleek power," and the tight-fitting, shocking tennis garb that writers had once denounced as "lapses in good taste" had become "bold and provocative."[42]

The celebrity and fortune that the Williams sisters enjoyed became the harbinger of a new era of race relations in American sports. Although early in Venus's and Serena's professional careers writers frequently made mention of their humble origins (e.g., "two ghetto-raised African Americans"), with the passage of time and their rise to top rankings the significance of their race receded to the distant background as appreciation of their talent and sparkling personalities grew. That they were the first black women to dominate professional tennis since Althea Gibson in the late 1950s was perhaps lost on most sports fans, but the substance of their accomplishment can hardly be overstated. Their total game forced other women to elevate their own. The widow of Arthur Ashe got it right when she commented after the sisters' historic meeting in the finals of the US Open in 2001 – the first time that siblings had met in the finals since Maud Watson defeated her sister Louise in three sets at the first Open in 1884: "Tennis has come to a different level now – these girls have raised the bar." Indeed, and they found that other top women players were ready for the challenge.

Their success had helped move American sports forward toward a new era, hopefully an era in which an athlete's race will be of little or no consequence no matter the sport. They also had helped elevate public perception of women as athletes equal in their accomplishments to men (during their reign at the top, women's tennis ratings on television regularly exceeded those of the men). One close observer of their careers, tennis writer Julianne Cicarelli, correctly concludes,

> Their ascendency in tennis and in corporate sponsorships has helped to change the way Americans view African American women, women athletes, and women in general. The sisters, young, spirited, intelligent, fun-loving, confident, strong, and beautiful, were seen as role models for women in the new century.[43]

White or black.

15 "Only in America!"

When the Soviet Union fired *Sputnik 1* into orbit around the earth in September 1957, the shock to the American people and its leaders was palpable. Overnight, the United States seemed vulnerable. It seemed to be far behind its arch-enemy in those areas which mattered most to national security in a nuclear age – engineering, science, and especially rocket capability. In short order, Congress established major programs to stimulate the teaching of science and mathematics in the public schools, created an ambitious program to support research and teaching in engineering and science at its universities and colleges, accelerated funding for the recently established National Science Foundation, and established the National Aeronautics and Space Administration (NASA) to oversee a concerted effort to catch the Soviet Union in the seemingly all-important "space race." Determined to put the United States into the lead in this race, early in his presidency, John F. Kennedy announced the audacious goal of placing an American on the moon and returning him safely to earth by "the end of this decade." Kennedy thus placed American prestige on the line in the depths of the cold war, and the American people responded enthusiastically.[1]

The nation's attention focused upon the seven men selected for the moon-bound Mercury program. The "astronauts" became instant American heroes, even before they traveled in space. The American people could not learn enough about them – their biographies, their families, their daily training routines, the dangers they anticipated in space – with the result being an incredible saturation of news about their every exploit. The expectations the American people held for these seven men were immense. The stakes were raised on April 5, 1961, when Soviet cosmonaut, Yuri Gagarin, became the first human to orbit the earth. His single trip around the planet in *Vostok I* gave the Soviets a major propaganda triumph. Three weeks later, however, NASA responded by sending astronaut Alan Shepard hurtling across the

Caribbean on a 15-minute suborbital flight from Cape Canaveral, and astronaut Virgil "Gus" Grissom made a slightly longer flight in July. Although these brief missions confirmed the reliability of the technology and rocketry, neither came close to equaling the Gagarin trip around the Earth. Pressure on NASA mounted, especially as several rocket tests – carried live on network television – fizzled with the rockets exploding on the launching pad or lifting only a short distance before thrashing wildly out of control and collapsing ignominiously to earth in a fiery heap. In August 1961, the Soviets upped the ante when *Vostok II* carried a cosmonaut for a 25-hour flight that included 16 rotations of the Earth.

The United States was clearly behind the Soviets in the space race. Adding to the grief was the fact that the Americans were not doing all that well in the sports world either. During the 1956 and 1960 Olympics, as well as at other international competitions, the Soviet and Eastern bloc men and women clearly were, as a group, superior to the athletes from the United States, especially in the all-important track and field competitions. That Eastern bloc athletes were essentially full-time professionals, and that the US Olympic Committee rigorously enforced the amateur regulations of the International Olympic Committee did not register with most Americans. President Kennedy captured headlines when he said that the American people were not in good physical condition and urged them to exercise regularly. The President's message was blunt – the American people had gone soft and flabby, and that would not do at a time when the nation was confronted by a resolute Soviet Union. Kennedy established a presidential advisory committee on physical fitness, and his family set an example by engaging in aggressive touch-football games that the press covered as if they were post-season bowl games. Several of Kennedy's cabinet members responded to the fitness challenge and participated in highly publicized 50-mile fitness walks.

These two seemingly disparate issues – the space race and physical fitness – came together when test pilot turned astronaut, John Glenn, was selected to be the first American to ride a Mercury capsule in an orbital flight around the Earth. Glenn appeared to be the perfect incarnation of fictional Jack Armstrong, the "All-American Boy." The son of middle-class parents, born and raised in the small eastern Ohio town of New Concord, Glenn married his high-school sweetheart and in 1942 dropped out of Muskingum College to join the Navy Air Corps. He flew 59 fighter missions in the South Pacific, and during the Korean War flew another 63 missions, shooting down three enemy aircraft, earning five Distinguished Flying Crosses and many other commendations. After the war, he became a Navy test pilot, and in 1957 set a transcontinental record by flying from Los Angeles to New York City in three hours and 23 minutes. In 1959 he was one of the seven men selected out of 110 candidates to become an astronaut.

When his selection for the first orbital mission was announced, Glenn immediately became a household name. Reporters readily discovered that this trim, athletic 41-year-old kept fit by running several miles each day. Glenn had discovered that the aerobic exercise of distance running was instrumental to his physical conditioning. He was an early student of US Air Force physician Kenneth Cooper, whose research into heart disease and its prevention had led him to advocate lengthy periods of moderate exercise that would elevate the heart rate. Cooper found that aerobic exercise that elevates the heart rate to 130 beats per minute, three times a week, for a 25-year-old person over a long period of time substantially reduces the heart rate, lowers blood pressure, increases the likelihood of a good night's sleep, stimulates mental acuity, reduces the chances of depression, enhances one's sexual appetite and performance, and in general creates a happier, healthier individual.

When Glenn's Mercury capsule, *Friendship 7*, successfully left the launch pad and pushed beyond the Earth's gravitation pull to a height of 192 miles on February 20, 1962, most activity in the United States came to a halt. With all three national television networks covering the event live, the American people collectively held their breath through the dicey "lift off," and listened attentively as Glenn chatted with "Mission Control" from outer space and calmly took over flying the capsule when a computer failed. After making three orbits of the earth and spending nearly five hours aloft, *Friendship 7*, tethered to a large parachute, gently splashed down right on target into the Atlantic Ocean near the West Indies. When NASA announced that a navy ship had picked up Glenn safe and sound, the American people exulted. Because Glenn's life was thought to be endangered due to a loose heat shield designed to prevent incineration during re-entry into the Earth's atmosphere, his mission seemed even more heroic.

Safely back on Earth, Glenn resumed his daily regimen of long-distance running, and millions of Americans joined in. All across America, men and women took to streets and roads to enjoy the same health benefits that John Glenn and his fellow astronauts had achieved through aerobic exercise. "Jogging" became a national craze. In 1968, Dr Cooper's book *Aerobics* hit the market and became an instant best-seller, going through several printings. Cooper emphasized that running was only one means of achieving good cardio-vascular results – they could just as easily be accomplished by other exercises including swimming, squash, racquetball, aerobic dancing, even speed walking. The evidence urging Americans of all ages to become physically active was overwhelming. At a time when most Americans did not do heavy physical labor, it was now believed important that they adopt an active lifestyle that included regular, vigorous physical activity.[2] If an adult had taken to the streets to run several miles each day during the 1950s, he would have been laughed out of town as some kind of nut.

Triumph of the Swoosh

Thus did the American people plunge headlong into a new era where physical activity for all ages was encouraged, even demanded. Millions opted for John Glenn's choice of distance running and set out on personal training programs that included several long runs a week. Naturally, the competitive instinct kicked in. By the early 1970s, in cities large and small, charitable organizations held weekend 10,000-meter (6.2-mile) races or shorter "fun runs" that drew hundreds to thousands of runners (and walkers). In the spirit of the 1960s phenomenon of large outdoor rock concerts, race organizers introduced the weekend mass run. In Boulder, Colorado, the Memorial Day "Bolder Boulder" 15-kilometer run attracted upwards of 50,000 runners, and in Phoenix, a local restaurant held an annual springtime 10-kilometer race that saw 20,000 entrants resolutely chugging along the banks of irrigation canals. For many decades in San Francisco, a handful of runners had annually raced across the city on a May Sunday morning, beginning in the shadows of the Bay Bridge and traversing the city's hills, ending up at the oceanfront in Golden Gate Park. A local newspaper took over the inconsequential event, and soon the "Bay to Breakers" race was attracting upwards of 100,000 runners, joggers, and walkers – of all sizes, shapes, and ages – many of whom ran in crazy costumes or tethered together in a unique "centipede" competition. The festive atmosphere surrounding the race had the feeling of a mobile rock concert, and it became the largest annual community event in the City by the Bay. On a more serious level, the historic Boston Marathon grew to the point where qualifying times had to be submitted and the number of entries limited to 20,000. The New York Marathon became a popular annual event, drawing 20,000 runners in 1980 and more than 50,000 in 2000. In 1961, the year in which President Kennedy first prodded the American people to get off their couches and into serious exercise, less than two hundred runners had shown up for the 26-mile (and 385 yards) ordeal.

The initial jogging and running craze did not run its course, as many predicted, but sustained itself as an important form of exercise for millions of Americans. Its advantages were simple – it could be done at any time of the day, it could be incorporated into business or vacation trips, it was inexpensive, and it worked. Aerobic-style running was assimilated into the lifestyle patterns of millions of Americans. Many would sustain that commitment well past middle age, and stories often made the newspapers of individuals in their seventies or eighties completing long-distance races to the cheers of onlookers. Runners flocked to sporting-goods stores to buy the latest innovation in running shoes, purchased stylish running gear, carried a digital heart monitor while they ran, kept a daily log of their times and distances, invested in specially crafted wristwatches to time their runs, and planned their day's activities around workouts. Conversations around the office water-cooler, at lunch, or at weekend cocktail parties (where white wine or a designer beer increasingly replaced strong spirits as the beverage of choice) frequently included not-so-subtle braggadocio: "I only got in 40 miles this last week," or "I'm in training to do my first marathon next fall." Those conversations also were replete with knowing references to the benefits of "carbohydrate loading," the positive effect of the release of "endorphins" that produced a "runner's high," the value of "interval-training" and "cross-training," how to ward off aggressive dogs (and an occasional petulant automobile driver) during runs, the relative merits of competing running shoes on the over-saturated market, the proper vitamin and herbal supplements, and the advantages of this or that new miracle diet.

Aerobic running was the spearhead of a much-wider fitness movement that followed in its wake. This phenomenon might have been initiated by the imperatives

of the cold war and a determined young President who called upon a generally
sedentary people to adopt a more vigorous lifestyle, but it quickly expanded in
ways that no one could have imagined. It was only natural that in the world's leading capitalist nation, entrepreneurs would take note that Americans were ready to
invest substantial sums of money in their quest for health and fitness. During the
1970s, a new business appeared in American towns and cities – the private health
club. Offering a wide range of activities – racquetball, squash, indoor swimming,
weight-lifting, aerobic dance classes, stationary exercise bicycles, electronic tread-
mills, and stair-climbing machines – the clubs also provided the upscale amenities
of steam baths, whirlpools, saunas, stylish locker rooms, massage therapy, and a
restaurant with a juice bar and vegetarian entrees. The new profession of "personal trainer" emerged, providing one-on-one counseling by a "certified health
professional" regarding diet and workout strategies – for a hefty hourly fee.

These trends reflected the pioneering work of two men who had preached much
the same message, but clearly were well ahead of the nation's physical fitness
curve. Born in rural Missouri in 1868, Benarr McFadden willed himself to survive
a "sickly" childhood by rigorous physical exercise and a diet heavy in fruits, nuts,
and vegetables. By the turn of the century he had built onto his 5' 6" frame a mass
of rippling muscles by a weight-lifting regimen and had launched a publicity crusade to sell his lifestyle to the American people, founding and operating various
institutes and fitness camps. Not hesitant to promote himself and his message of
"physical culture," McFadden was part health educator and part carnival huckster.
By the 1920s, his personal fortune, derived largely from his many publications,
was estimated at $20 million, but as he aged McFadden engaged in increasingly
bizarre behaviors. His public advocacy of the joys of sex and his publications that
featured men and women scantily attired (so as to facilitate strenuous physical
activity) alienated middle America, and his repeated renunciations of the medical
profession amounted to nothing more than ignorance compounded by stubborn-
ness. The one-time fitness advisor to presidents died in 1955 at the advanced age
of 87, but not before he had attracted national attention in 1949 at age 81 by safely
parachuting from an airplane – his first of two such publicity-seeking plunges.[3]

Beset by increasing criticisms of his personal life and public behavior, McFadden's lost his public relations edge during the 1930s to body-builder Charles Atlas,
a man whose imposing physique – often portrayed in cartoon format – appeared
with regularity in men's magazine advertisements touting his line of barbells and
vitamins. In 1936, a young bodybuilder by the name of Jack La Lanne opened the
nation's first health club in Oakland, California, and in 1951 began a 33-year stint
on daytime television demonstrating exercises and urging his viewers to join in his
workout routines, and (of course) to purchase his assorted exercise equipment and
famous "juicer." La Lanne liked to proclaim that he was the first physical fitness
expert who publicly urged women to lift weights as a regular component of their
exercise program, and he devoted his life to promoting good health through vigorous exercise and a controlled diet. In 2005 at the age of 92, still deriving much
of his daily nutrition from the fruit and egg white concoctions he squished in his
personal "juicer," La Lanne was still doing serious weight lifting and perform-

ing demanding exercises two hours each morning before spending another hour swimming laps.[4] That both McFadden and La Lanne lived to advanced age with a minimum of serious health problems, gave credence to their basic message of proper diet and vigorous exercise. That same message, tweaked and slightly modified, would be advanced by an army of health advocates during the latter years of the twentieth century.

Both McFadden and La Lanne sought to make money from their lifestyle crusade. In so doing they walked a heavily traveled American entrepreneurial highway. As the fitness craze swept the United States in the 1960s and the 1970s, old-line athletic apparel and equipment companies attempted to respond to the burgeoning new market. However, the enormous profit potential naturally attracted aggressive new competition in the form of specialized companies armed with new products and compelling advertising strategies. The firm that proved to be the most agile and adept and set the standard for the new fitness age began in the Oregon college town of Eugene during the 1960s. Year after year coach Bill Bowerman's University of Oregon track team was one of the nation's best, and the coach was forever experimenting with equipment as well as the accepted techniques of running and jumping. He had long believed that the conventional spiked leather track shoes were harmful to his runners' feet and that better design and more flexible materials could improve the times of his world-class distance runners. In one inspired moment, he used his wife's waffle iron to create a revolutionary "waffle" composition sole to which he attached light leather and fabric shoes. Bowerman hooked up with one of his former Oregon track athletes, Phil Knight, and together they created a small shoe-manufacturing company, Blue Ribbon Sports. Knight had originally conceived of the shoe company in a term paper he had written as a college business major and in which his imagined company followed a plan to challenge the world sports shoe leadership of the German company Adidas. In the late 1960s, Bowerman and Knight changed their company's name to Nike, the Greek goddess of victory, and for a mere $35 commissioned the design of the soon-to-be ubiquitous "swoosh" as their company logo. In 1972, they sold $3 million-worth of their innovative waffle-sole running shoes, and new and more colorful models began to appear with unerring frequency. Nike fortuitously entered the athletic shoe market at the same time the running craze was enveloping the nation. The niche market of running shoes provided the platform for building a Fortune 500 company that would branch out into many sports and leisure activities.

In 1980, Nike went public with a stock offering and immediately became a darling of Wall Street. By this time, Nike had eclipsed the staid traditional athletic shoe manufacturers, and it now launched an audacious advertising campaign that reflected new trends of modern society. CEO Phil Knight tapped into the American penchant for athletic prowess, its love of heroes, and its obsession with status, style, and innovation, and he tied Nike's expanding line of products to charismatic athletes who either flaunted or at least challenged society's norms. When Knight selected the 21-year-old, unproven NBA player Michael Jordan in 1983 to be its spokesman for a revolutionary new form of basketball shoe – the "Air Jordan" with its cushioned pocket of air in the heel – his competitors scoffed. But Jordan's infectious smile, bubbly public personality, and growing stature as an NBA star made the clunky red basketball shoe a runaway best-seller. Nike aggressively expanded its product line to encompass a wide range of leisure and sports clothing and equipment. The company likewise hit pay dirt in 1996 when they signed the highly touted 21-year-old Tiger Woods to a lucrative endorsement contract, and 10 years later they took the same risk with the 16-year-old female golf phenomenon from Hawaii, Michelle Wie. In 1996, Nike reported net profits of over $550 million on $6.5 billion in revenues; in 2004 their net revenues had increased to $14 billion and their profits had grown accordingly. Not bad for a company that began in a small-town Oregon kitchen with a waffle iron and a dream.

Nike readily expanded into other ventures – a full line of golf equipment, leisure clothing, a complete line of soccer equipment and clothing as a vehicle to expand internationally, the eye-popping postmodern Nike Town stores – and naturally encountered criticism as its success mounted. During the 1990s, Knight and Nike were hammered for outsourcing much of the shoe manufacturing to Indonesia, where wages were low and working conditions allegedly poor. Its highly successful "Just Do It" advertisements were blamed by various critics for contributing to a highly publicized series of murders of teenage boys who refused to turn over their expensive Air Jordans when confronted by violence-inclined thugs. But those problems proved to be little more than a nagging nuisance, and Nike continued to dominate the athletic shoe and apparel markets – a powerful Fortune 500 testimony to the role and influence of fitness and sports in modern American life.[5]

The World of Jimmy the Greek

In 1951, the subterranean world of sports gambling burst into the American public consciousness, and the picture it presented of itself was not a pretty one. The far-reaching college basketball points-shaving scandals ripped at the heart of the credibility of competitive sports, and the heavily publicized concurrent hearings conducted by Senator Estes Kefauver on the influence of organized crime drew close connections between sports gambling and urban crime organizations. Although Kefauver focused attention upon a dying institution – the illegal horse betting parlors that were tied to distant race tracks by telegraph lines – he also brushed up against the rapidly growing phenomenon of betting on college and professional football, basketball, and baseball. The connections between these crime organizations and sports gambling seemed all the more ominous because they both were linked to local political organizations. There still existed, of course, legal betting on the horses at state-licensed tracks, but interest in that gambling venue was leveling-off at this time and it never regained its once-prominent role. Younger gamblers, especially, were turning to wagering on team sports due to the immense popularity of the points spread system that turned every game into a potentially profitable opportunity.

Nearly all of this multibillion dollar gambling enterprise, however, was illegal, operating beyond the purview of tax collectors and law enforcement authorities. By 1960, federal officials estimated that some 250,000 illegal bookmakers handled wagers that exceeded the annual income of the nation's largest corporation, General Motors. Clearly, the traditional negative view of gambling was giving way to one that viewed it as an acceptable leisure activity. The traditional perception of gambling as a sin was aptly summarized by a Methodist minister in 1963 when he wrote, "Gambling is a moral and social evil that tends to undermine the ethical teachings of our churches and glorifies the philosophy of getting something for nothing."[6] By 1963, however, his traditional view was rapidly losing its appeal; already 30 states had given their approbation to gambling by legalizing *pari-mutuel* horse racing – actually, a slick trick by which politicians could increase government revenues without raising taxes. Gambling on other sports, however, had been illegal throughout the United States until the economically troubled State of Nevada legalized wide-open casino gambling in 1931 as a Depression-bred move to increase tourism and raise much-needed state tax revenues.

Legalized sports gambling in Nevada might have begun on a modest basis but by the 1980s it had become a powerful economic force that exerted strong, if often overlooked, influence upon college and professional sports. The enterprise began almost imperceptively in a few undistinguished buildings in Las Vegas and Reno. These modest "turf and sports clubs" squeezed out small profits by booking bets on horseraces conducted at tracks around the country. Reeking with cigar smoke and stale beer, these clubs also accommodated clients who wished to bet on baseball, basketball, and football. However, at the behest of the Kefauver Committee in 1951, Congress imposed a 10 percent tax on sports wagers other than horseraces. This tax had the potential of ending legal sports gambling in Nevada because the high tax rate made it impossible for a bookmaker to turn in a profit. However, several turf club managers used various subterfuges to get around paying the federal tax while accommodating their customers' desires to wager on professional and college team games.[7]

That charade ended in 1974, when Congress lowered the prohibitive rate to 2 percent. It was now possible for a well-run book to make a modest profit. Two years later, the Nevada Gaming Control Board, attempting to increase state revenues, voted to permit sports wagering within casinos; soon, plush sports books appeared in the largest casinos, complete with banks of television sets for bettors to watch the fate of their investments being determined at stadia and ballparks around the country. The days of the small, grimy turf clubs were numbered. In 1983, Congress further encouraged Nevada's sports books by reducing the federal tax on sports bets to just one-quarter of 1 percent. By 1986 every large hotel-casino in Nevada offered a full-service sports book to their customers.

One result of the sensational Kefauver hearings was that federal and local law-enforcement launched an all-out assault upon sports gamblers. Thus, with the heat on in Eastern and Midwestern cities, professional gamblers headed to Las Vegas. At the same time, television coverage of important games encouraged increased betting levels. Many sports fans discovered that they enjoyed watching games in which they had a financial interest in the outcome, while others watched games to scout future investments. Television became, in effect, an electronic version of the traditional published racing forms that had helped guide horseplayers for decades. As the sports-gaming industry grew, hundreds of tout sheets appeared, in which self-appointed professional handicappers "released" their predicted winners to subscribers willing to pay hundreds of dollars each week for such advice. Analyses of these tout sheets indicated that the great majority of them were often sold under false pretenses – often distorting or even simply fabricating past won–lost records – and that the ability of their editors in picking winners was seldom better than that of the average weekend bettor By 2000, an estimated one-thousand such tout services operated during football and basketball seasons.[8]

The popularity of sports gambling was reflected in the daily sports pages, where game stories often mentioned the pre-game point spread, and most published the daily (and fluctuating) "Las Vegas Line" as a service to their readers. The Las Vegas Line replaced the famous *Green Sheet* that had carried the dominant "Minneapolis Line" set by handicapper/publisher Leo Hirshfield during the 1940s and the 1950s. As Las Vegas boomed as a new vacation destination, state legislatures took note of the advantages that gambling afforded them. Governors and legislators, wary of raising the hackles of voters by raising taxes, opted instead to increase state revenues by embracing gambling. The first step was taken in New Hampshire in 1963, when a state lottery, the winning numbers determined by a horserace, was instituted; by the mid-1980s, 37 states had established lotteries, and several states, over the outraged opposition by religious organizations, authorized casino gambling.

The national embrace of state lotteries and casino gambling, however, did not extend to sports wagering. Even today it remains legal only in Nevada. The stigma of possible scandals involving games tampered with by gamblers seeking a sure thing has helped prevent its widespread legalization. In 1993, Congress passed legislation that essentially gave Nevada a monopoly on legalized sports action by forbidding other states to enter the field. That did not mean, however, that sports fans elsewhere could not get down a bet. Illegal "bookies" operated in cities large and small, unregulated and untaxed. Most college campuses even had their own student bookies operating out of campus hangouts. These individuals, contrary to popular myth, were seldom associated with crime syndicates; rather they were small- to medium-sized operators handling their own cluster of customers. Emulating the Nevada sports books, they adjusted the odds or points spread to generate equal amounts of money bet on both sides of a contest so that they could earn a profit of about 4 to 5 percent on the money wagered (often called the "juice" or the "vigorish"). With the advent of the world wide web during the 1990s, several hundred offshore Internet sports books were established in the Caribbean, Mexico, England, and Australia, and these posed major competition to the neighborhood bookie; gamblers could now use their credit cards to place bets from their laptop computer.

In 1976, CBS took note of the fact that the National Football League had become a favorite of gamblers. Football was a natural venue for gamblers. A carefully set points-spread made every game attractive to bettors, and the fact that a team played only one game per week intensified interest, giving gamblers time to analyze, ponder, and reflect upon the relative merits of the two teams relative to the points-spread. Many die hard fans of particular teams blindly bet on their team each week as part of their pre-game ritual. Television sports shows, talk radio, and Internet sites intensified interest. With an eye toward an emerging trend among football fans, in 1976 CBS-TV added the nation's most famous gambler, Demetrius Synodinos, a.k.a. Jimmy "The Greek" Snyder, to its expert panel on the popular Sunday afternoon *NFL Today* show that preceded the professional games of the day. The weekly appearance of the most famous Las Vegas sports handicapper brought an immediate legitimacy to his craft. That his presence encouraged fans to bet on NFL games was routinely denied by CBS and the NFL, but his weekly "picks" certainly did nothing to discourage wagering. Each Sunday "The Greek" "released" predictions on the upcoming afternoon games, complete with seemingly prescient details and crisp analysis. As Snyder's segment segued to a commercial, gamblers all across America rushed to their telephones to get down a bet; nervous bookies monitored the show and made adjustments in their betting lines to compensate for the response to Snyder's opinions.[9]

Snyder began his gambling career as a teenager during the Depression years of the 1930s in his hometown of Steubenville, Ohio. Before the Second World War, he moved to Florida, where he showed proficiency in picking horses. During the 1940s, he relocated to New York City, where he became known as a "high-roller," someone who bets heavily on sporting events. His high profile led to police and FBI surveillance and attention by the Kefauver Committee; consequently, like many East Coast professional gamblers, he relocated to gambler-friendly Las Vegas in the late 1950s. In 1963, he began writing a weekly sports-betting column for the *Las Vegas Sun* that became syndicated. He formed a handicapping service and a public relations firm, all the while energetically and shamelessly promoting himself as the nation's top odds-maker and handicapper, a claim that many of the Las Vegas professional sports gambling fraternity, the so-called "wise guys," found amusing – they reportedly responded to his newspaper column and CBS picks by betting the other side with considerable profit. Contrary to popular myth, Snyder's handicapping skills were not the best in the business, according to Las Vegas insiders.

The rapid growth of sports wagering contributed substantially to the growing popularity of mainstream team sports in contemporary America, and Snyder rode that cresting wave to national prominence and celebrity. Sports gambling grew exponentially during the late twentieth century. In 1980, it was estimated by federal officials that somewhere in the neighborhood of $8 to $10 billion were wagered illegally each year, but with the growth of televised sports and the decline in anti-gambling sentiment, that figure rose to $90 billion by 1995. The biggest single sporting event for gamblers was the Super Bowl. In 2000, federal officials estimated that the American people bet more than $1 billion on the Super Bowl. Of that amount about $80 million – or less than 10 percent – was channeled through the legal sports books in Nevada; the rest was wagered in defiance of federal and state anti-gambling laws, much of it in small office and bar pools. In Nevada, Super Bowl Sunday was the single largest-volume event at the state's approximately one hundred sports books when they booked about $75 million in bets; over the year they handled more than $3 billion in sports wagers. The four-week NCAA men's basketball tournament produced the second-largest betting event. However, the sports books cranked out a profit on a daily basis with off-track horse racing and the daily flow of games throughout the year. In fact, there was only one day each year in which sports books did not have a new contest upon which gamblers could get down a bet – the Monday before the annual July All-Star baseball game. Even on Christmas Day, in Las Vegas and on the streets of American cities, there were bookmakers eager to take their action on basketball and football games.

The Tragedy of Pete Rose

The fact that even experienced sports gamblers can and do lose money – lots of it – was made patently clear by the example of star Cincinnati Reds player and manager Pete Rose. When he looped a soft single to left field on September 11, 1985, for his 4,192nd base hit, eclipsing the record set decades earlier by Ty Cobb, Rose seemed to be on the fast track to the Hall of Fame. Rose's insatiable quest to bet on sports, however, derailed his express trip to Cooperstown. A blue-collar player who drove himself to succeed, Rose's frenetic style of play, highlighted by his furious head-first slides, had earned him the popular nickname of "Charlie Hustle." But when baseball Commissioner A. Bartlett Giamatti announced in August 1989 that Rose had agreed to a lifetime ban due to allegations that he had broken organized baseball's cardinal rule prohibiting anyone associated with a major-league team from betting on baseball, the sports world was stunned. By placing Rose on baseball's Ineligible List, Giamatti observed that he could not be nominated for membership in the Hall of Fame.[10]

It was a most curious agreement, because its pages did not contain an admission that Rose had bet on baseball. However, he had accepted a severe punishment as if he had. In announcing the agreement, Giamatti proceeded to inform a press conference that while he was relieved the agreement had brought "a sorry end to a sorry episode" that was "a disgrace to the game," he nonetheless believed that Rose had broken baseball's cardinal rule against gambling. Referring to a 1,200-page report by private investigator John Dowd that had guided his decision, the Commissioner left no doubt as to his take on the situation:

> In the absence of a formal hearing and therefore in the absence of evidence to the contrary, I am confronted by the factual record of Mr Dowd. On the basis of that, yes, I have concluded he [Rose] bet on baseball.[11]

Rose and his lawyer were blind-sided by Giamatti's unexpected statement, and apparently had been led to believe that Rose would be barred from the game for only a year or so. When that assumption, and a likely serious misperception or miscalculation on their part, proved in error, baseball's all-time hit leader proceeded to campaign vigorously to have Giamatti's decision reversed, proclaiming at every opportunity that he had never bet on baseball. He continued his plea of denial for the next 15 years – telling anyone who would listen that he had been

railroaded. However, skeptics asked why had Rose agreed to such a settlement if he was innocent? Ultimately, the truth came out. Apparently,
after years of futility, Rose came to believe that if he confessed and apol-
ogized, Commissioner Bud Selig would lift the suspension and he could
once more seek employment in baseball as a coach or manager and
have his name placed on the Hall of Fame ballot. Thus, in early 2004,
Rose published a slapdash memoir in which he recanted his denials,
although positing a series of dubious physiological and psychological
problems to explain away his betting problem and his subsequent campaign of lies and deception. To read Rose's version of events, he was
possessed by demons beyond his control. Everyone, it seemed, was
to blame but himself. But after three hundred tortured pages in his
soap-opera written *mea culpa*, Rose finally admitted that he had been
persistently lying about his gambling problem for almost two decades.
Now, he confessed that during the time he managed the Reds he bet on
major-league games "about four or five times a week," in defiance of
baseball's best-known rule. As if it mattered, he self-righteously emphasized that he had never bet against the Reds and that "I never made any

Figure 15.1 Pete Rose was
headed for the Hall of Fame
until he was derailed by his
gambling habit. Throughout
his entire career as a baseball
player he was a fans' favorite
for his high-energy style of
play as seen in this 1980
photograph, sliding head-first
into home plate. In that year
Rose helped the Philadelphia
Phillies capture their only
World Series championship.
© Bettmann/CORBIS.

bets from the clubhouse." Sports journalists overwhelmingly condemned Rose's duplicity, and his millions of fans who had believed his version of the truth, felt betrayed, or worse. Contrary to his hopes in releasing the book, his Hall of Fame hopes took on even greater odds.[12]

Rose's self-serving book did little to rehabilitate his image with sports fans. Now, the nickname of "Charlie Hustle" had taken on a new and distorted meaning, and Rose's hopes of being reinstated into baseball's good graces remained firmly stuck on "hold." When, or if, Commissioner Selig would lift the ban remained one of baseball's mysteries. Rose certainly did not enhance his chances by making his confession in a superficial "autobiography." It seemed to his growing band of cynical critics that Pete Rose had elected to write the book as a means to come clean primarily to hustle a few book royalty checks.

Rose's gambling problems, however depressing, nonetheless underscored the fact that organized baseball had in fact been successful in eliminating the scourge of fixed games following the debacle of the 1919 World Series. College basketball had not been so lucky. After the devastating revelations of point shaving in 1951 that saw 33 players arrested, the NCAA and college officials claimed that the problem had been solved. But in 1961 a second scandal was identified by New York district attorney Frank Hogan, which actually took on larger dimensions than the initial scandal. This time, Hogan indicted 49 players from 27 colleges. At least 67 games had been subject to point-shaving efforts during 1957–1961. The central figure was a product of the streets and playgrounds of New York City and a former Columbia University All-American forward, Jack Molinas, who had become a budding star in the NBA until he was banished for life in 1954 for gambling on his own team, the Fort Wayne Zollner Pistons. In 1963, Hogan nailed Molinas – now possessed of a law degree and a member of the New York State Bar – when Molinas instructed an accused player, Billy Reed of Bowling Green State University, on how to lie to the grand jury. Reed, however, had already cut a deal with Hogan and was wearing a recording device. Molinas went to jail for four years for suborning perjury and – just like 10 years earlier – college basketball's newest scandal faded into the background with incredible speed. Sportswriters, it seemed, were not interested in keeping the story alive; perhaps they, like basketball fans, were weary of scandal and wanted to move on.[13]

During the 1980s, gambling problems once again hit the headlines when former Ohio State All-American quarterback Art Schlichter was kicked out of the National Football League for repeated violations of its anti-gambling policies. Schlichter, it seemed, was unable to overcome his desire to bet heavily on football and other sports, his life ultimately being ruined by what *Sports Illustrated* called "a textbook case of a man's promise destroyed by gambling." Long after leaving football, he ended up in prison on various charges of credit card fraud, writing bogus checks, and theft, crimes that all stemmed from his massive gambling debts.[14] In 1985, scandal once again touched college basketball when it was revealed that a top Tulane University player had shaved points in return for drugs – a modern twist on an old story. That same year it was revealed that in 1979 a notorious New England-based gambler, Richard "The Fixer" Perry, who had been convicted of fixing horseraces, had also bribed a Boston College basketball player to dump games. In 1994 a Northwestern running back even fumbled near the goal line to make certain that his team would not cover a points spread, upon which he had personal money wagered.

It was not surprising, with the early rumors about Pete Rose hitting the streets along with a flurry of other gambling issues, that the leading sports magazine of the time, *Sports Illustrated*, would feel compelled to examine the noxious influence of gambling on sports. In 1986, it weighed in with a lengthy issue devoted to sports gambling in which the editors made clear that they believed the practice posed a major threat to the integrity of the entire enterprise:

> Most Americans tend to view such wagering as a naughty-but-nice diversion. Yet from the Black Sox scandal of 1919 to the Tulane basketball fixes of last season, nothing has done more to despoil the games Americans play and watch than wide-spread gambling on them. As fans cheer their bets rather than their favorite teams, dark clouds of cynicism and suspicion hang over games, and the possibility of fixes is always in the air.[15]

The Demise of Boxing

As the debate over sports gambling unfurled during the late twentieth century, it was curious that the sport long reputed for nefarious influence by gamblers was virtually ignored. That oversight suggests that the "manly art" of pugilism, which had always existed on the fringes of respectability, had fallen into such public disfavor that it was in danger of becoming of complete irrelevance. Except for a few high-profile championship bouts, few sports fans paid much attention. That was because by the late twentieth century, it had become little more than the mind-numbing burlesque and charade that was professional wrestling. Controlled by three rival international organizations of questionable origin and authority, beset by conniving and untrustworthy promoters, dogged by professional medical demands that it was too dangerous to be labeled a sport, beset with a welter of such strangely named and confusing weight classifications as "cruiser weight" and "junior heavyweight," boxing had careened close to becoming a caricature of its former self. Additionally, boxing had long existed under the cloud of suspicion that fighters would "take a dive" at the behest of influential gamblers. Actually, this state of affairs was not much out of the ordinary for boxing, because the enterprise had always been viewed with suspicion as a brutal blood sport that debased the human condition and was run by individuals of dubious virtue.

Although he was arguably the first bona fide sports star in America, heavyweight John L. Sullivan often had to ply his craft in out-of-the-way places to avoid the long arm of the law. At the turn of the twentieth century, the only state that permitted legalized prizefighting was Nevada. The negative image of boxing changed substantially with the legalization of the sport in many states during the 1920s, a time when Jack Dempsey and Gene Tunney stirred widespread excitement during the new age of spectator sports. Million-dollar gates, national radio broadcasts live from ringside, and heavy attention by the media created a new and more-positive image for the sport. During the next half-century, boxing enjoyed its heyday, as leading boxers such as Joe Louis, Sugar Ray Robinson, Rocky Marciano, Kid Gavilan, Joe Frazier, and Mohammad Ali provided plenty of excitement and newsworthy action in and out of the square "ring." Even then a distasteful aura still hovered over the sport. Allegations of fixed fights, of close connections between fight promoters and organized crime syndicates, and an occasional death in the ring tended to remind observers that boxing had never quite escaped its questionable legacy.

The demise of the sport began in the 1950s, when the game's heart was ripped out by the machinations of commercial television, but that fact was overlooked due to the excitement produced by the charismatic Muhammad Ali during the 1960s and the 1970s. But Ali's powerful presence and huge box-office draw merely masked the problems confronting the sport, and when he departed in 1980, the game fell into a prolonged decline. The lack of a strong, ethical organization to monitor the fight game lay at the heart of boxing's problems. The United States Congress refused to establish a national regulatory body despite repeated calls by boxing's critics for such a body. State boxing commissions were typically run as tight little political fiefdoms and demonstrated a greater interest in assisting promoters arrange profitable fights than in monitoring the integrity of the sport. Consequently, over the years several different international bodies claimed they were the legitimate organization to supervise the business and to monitor the physical health and financial well-being of professional boxers. The result was that the casual fan was confused by a proliferation of weight divisions and by multiple champions claiming titles, his interest dulled by a lack of charismatic fighters.

Not surprisingly, money lay at the root of boxing's evils. Most young men who opted for a professional boxing career were poor and minimally educated; many had experienced encounters with law enforcement. They saw the sport as their main opportunity to earn money and escape difficult social and economic circumstances. But even those few who managed to rise to the top of the profession more often than not found themselves somehow shorn of their large payoffs by unscrupulous managers and promoters. News reports that a prominent ex-boxer was broke and simultaneously in trouble with the Internal Revenue Service were not uncommon.

Boxing's image always suffered from its sheer brutality. It is the only sport in which the basic intent is to inflict serious physical harm upon one's opponent. The most exciting moment is the knockout, which results when a boxer suffers a concussion sufficient to render him unconscious. Over the years, comedians have made light of the "punch-drunk" ex-pugilist, but such a condition is a very real and very serious medical problem. Officially called "chronic encephalopathy," it results from the brain absorbing small injuries over an extended period of time, with the end result being a loss of memory, uncontrollable tremors, and general physical debilitation; that Muhammad Ali exhibited precisely those symptoms within a few years after retiring following a 20-year professional career should have come as no shock to anyone closely associated with the dark side of boxing.

But merely one well-placed punch can be lethal. There is always the danger that a knockout punch will rupture the blood vessels that surround the brain. Such a blow can cause a dangerous build-up of blood that expands into the narrow space between the skull and the soft tissue of the brain. Called a hematoma, this process can result in the brain being squeezed to the point where death will occur.[16]

This has been known as an incontrovertible medical fact for more than a half-century, but all efforts by the American Medical Association to prevent such injuries have failed – that would have required abolition of the sport, a decision with big dollar figures attached that elected public officials have been unwilling to make. Between 1945 and 2005, some 120 Americans died from blows received in the ring. Most of these deaths occurred in low-profile situations, but a few instances produced considerable negative publicity. Among these was the death of Charlie Mohr, a University of Wisconsin middleweight who died in the spring of 1960 while defending his NCAA championship. In this instance, the required protective headgear did not prevent massive bleeding, and Mohr's death led to the banning of boxing as an intercollegiate sport. In 1962, a popular welterweight, Benny "The Kid" Paret, was killed by the punches of Emile Griffith in a championship bout. Known for his ability to absorb punishment, Paret had been knocked out twice the previous year, a fact that many believed made him susceptible to a fatal punch even though an electrocardiogram before the fight revealed no brain damage. In 1963, a club fighter by the name of Davey Moore was killed in a Los Angeles bout, but it was revealed that, desperate for money, he had lied to authorities about underlying health problems. Moore's death emphasized the need for a strong federal oversight commission that would, among other things, monitor the condition of all boxers and prevent their lying about health problems or even fighting under different names in different states to avoid detection of medical problems.[17]

On November 13, 1982, in a lightweight championship bout in Las Vegas, an overmatched Korean boxer, Duk Koo Kim, never regained consciousness after absorbing a horrendous beating for 14 rounds at the hands of champion Ray "Boom Boom" Mancini. Showing enormous fortitude, if not good sense, Kim had gained the admiration of the ringside television announcer, who said as the final and fatal round began, "Duk Koo Kim. You may not have heard of him before – but you will remember him today. Win or lose." Obviously, as it turned out. Kim never regained consciousness after falling to the canvas in that round, and he died four days later in a Las Vegas hospital of cerebral edema – swelling of the brain. Promoters paid his pregnant widow his guaranteed purse of $20,000. Kim's death occurred at a time when several other boxers of lesser fame also died, including 13-year-old, 71-pound Harlan Hoosier, who died in 1980 after fighting three times without headgear in a three-day youth boxing tournament in Lenore, West Virginia.[18]

The fact that Kim died from injuries sustained in a nationally televised championship fight brought considerable, if fleeting, attention to the brutality of the sport. State boxing commissions went into a defensive mode, reviewing their policies amid a flurry of critical magazine articles and newspaper opinion columns. Ultimately, the congressional Subcommittee on Commerce, Transportation and

Tourism conducted the obligatory hearings. Congressman James J. Florio of New Jersey, who chaired the hearings, stated,

> Our ultimate conclusion is that there has to be some degree of uniformity with regard to boxing across the nation. We have to spell out Federal standards that have to be adhered to by the states in order for boxing to take place.

Pledging himself to introduce legislation to require a national database on boxers' physical condition (which subsequently was shelved), Florio said, "People keep saying, 'What does the boxing profession think of the controversy?' Well, the answer is: There is no boxing profession. It's not a system, it's a non-system, and it's getting worse."[19]

Congressman Florio's comments were indeed accurate, but not even he could anticipate the subsequent descent of boxing that would further blemish the sport. Nothing came from the demands for reform because boxing meant big money for promoters and sponsors of major championship fights, especially hotel-casinos in Las Vegas and Atlantic City, which used these highly publicized events to lure "high rollers" to their gaming tables. In September 2005, Las Vegas witnessed another death in the ring – incredibly its sixth death since 1994 – when 35-year-old International Boxing Federation lightweight champion, Leavander Johnson, lost his title to challenger Jesus Chavez. Videotape analysis of the bout revealed that Johnson had absorbed an estimated 400 punches, including two dozen unanswered blows to the head in the round 11, after which the fight was called off. He left the ring on his own power, but fell unconscious while walking to the dressing room and died of massive damage to the brain in a hospital a few days later. While the state boxing commission promised the inevitable investigation, promoter Lou Di Bella was sanguine: "I don't think there is anything to blame other than circumstances. He's a victim of his own courage."[20] The national sports media gave this event brief coverage, the Nevada boxing commission promised a report in nine months, and within days all was forgotten.

Central to this long period of boxing's decline as a respected sport was a Cleveland-born promoter and publicity guru, Don King. His meteoric rise to international boxing prominence began shortly after he was released in September 1971 from the Ohio Correctional Institute in Marion, where he had served four years on manslaughter charges. Within four years after leaving prison, King had shrewdly finagled himself to the top of the boxing promotion business where he reigned for the next quarter-century. As head of Don King Productions, he wheeled and dealt with sponsors, fighters, managers, and boxing commissions as he amassed hundreds of millions of dollars in profits.

Born in Cleveland in 1931, King grew up on that city's tough east side. By the time he was in his early twenties, he had become a leading numbers (or policy) operator, using a small tavern as cover for his illegal but lucrative business. In 1954, he shot and killed a man in an altercation over a numbers payoff but successfully pleaded self-defense. In 1966, he killed his second man, a small-time Cleveland gambler and racketeer, during an altercation over $600 that King said the man owed him from a wager. According to witnesses, the 240-pound King brutally beat Sam Garrett to death outside a tavern in broad daylight, repeatedly kicking the much smaller and sickly man (who had recently undergone kidney surgery) long after he had lost consciousness.[21] King was convicted of second-degree murder, a crime punishable with up to life in prison. The presiding judge, however, with no one present in his office and without informing the prosecutor, inexplicably reduced the sentence to manslaughter. King served what most observers felt was a very light sentence – four years.

Just three years after leaving prison, King thrust himself upon the world when he promoted the famous "Rumble in the Jungle" championship fight in 1974, between Muhammad Ali and George Foreman. By capitalizing on the potential of making the fight available to cable television subscribers, King was able to offer a historic (for the time) $1 million purse that the two fighters split. In 1975, he followed up with the "Thrilla in Manila," the epic brawl between Ali and Joe Frazier. During the late 1970s, Ali was the central player in King's domination of the sport, but when age took its toll on Ali, King quickly moved to sign top heavyweight prospects Larry Holmes, Ken Norton, and the Spinks brothers, Leon and Michael, to contracts that gave him exclusive rights to promote their fights. In addition, his stable of fighters included one of the most popular of all fighters of the time, the handsome, flashy welterweight Sugar Ray Leonard. Within a decade, King had magically transformed himself from convicted felon to one of the most famous and richest men in America.

The question of race never was far from the surface throughout King's career. He was the first African American to become a successful fight promoter, and it was widely perceived that many white reporters and boxing officials were hopeful that his promotions would fail. Perhaps with reason, because whenever criticized or placed under legal scrutiny, King was quick to brand his critics as "racist." Clearly, King's business success rested in large part upon his ability to gain the confidence of black fighters at a time when boxing commissions, ring officials, managers and promoters were virtually all white. Given to wearing his lengthy hair in a distinctive style that stood straight up as if he had just been hit by a bolt of lightning, King also was known for his preference for gaudy clothes and expensive, ostentatious diamond-laced gold jewelry. His appearance merely reinforced the fact that Don King had an innate sense of how to exploit his natural flamboyance into creating an image of himself as black America's version of Horatio Alger. He loved to talk about himself and his financial success using the phrase, "Only in America," and his publicity machine repeatedly related how he had vowed while in prison to become a law-abiding and hard-working citizen.[22]

In 1985, a promising new boxer appeared on the scene, to whom King was ineluctably drawn, 19-year-old Mike Tyson. Born to an unmarried New York City welfare recipient, Tyson grew up in one of the nation's most notorious slums, the Brownsville section of Brooklyn. Raised amid pervasive poverty, crime, drugs, and violence, Tyson grew into a powerful and angry young man who was quick to use his fists. By age 12, he had experienced ample amounts of drugs and alcohol and had been arrested 40 times; eventually, he ended up in a juvenile detention

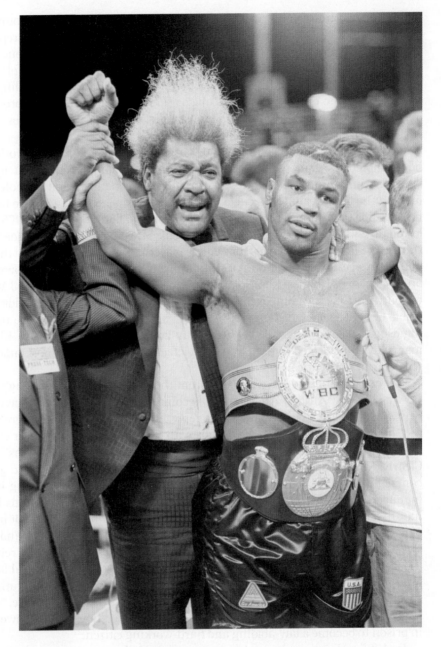

Figure 15.2 Mike Tyson is congratulated by Don King in this March 7, 1987 photograph following a unanimous decision in a heavyweight championship fight with James "Bonecrusher" Smith in Las Vegas. King dominated the professional fight game as a promoter ever since he staged the famous "Rumble in the Jungle" between Muhammad Ali and George Foreman in Kinshasa, Zaire in 1974. Tyson's many personal problems became a metaphor for the decline of boxing as the twentieth century wound down. © Bettmann/CORBIS.

center in upstate New York, where a counselor and physical-education instructor sought to control his rage and elevate his poor self-image by teaching him to box. By 1979, Tyson had shown so much promise that he was introduced to the famed manager/trainer of former heavy-weight champion Floyd Patterson, Cus D'Amato, who proceeded to prepare him for the professional ranks. In 1981, Tyson won the Junior

Olympics, a program structured for boys under the age of 16. His powerful blows and seething anger quickly became legendary in the boxing circles of New York City. He won his first professional fight in 1985 over Hector Mercedes in a 91-second knockout and proceeded to win 14 more consecutive fights by knockout. At the age of just 22, on November 22, 1986, he won the World Boxing Commission's version of the heavyweight title over Trevor Berbick, and early in 1987 defeated James "Bonecrusher" Smith for the World Boxing Association title. Later that same year, he won a unanimous decision over Tony Tucker in Las Vegas to take the International Boxing Federation title, thereby consolidating his domination of all three versions of the title. The following year, he knocked out Michael Spinks and walked away with the largest purse up to that time in the history of boxing, $21 million.[23]

Don King envisioned Tyson as his key to unprecedented large gates and even larger closed-circuit television revenues. But Tyson was forever teetering on the edge of self-destruction. His reputation for violent behavior spiraled out of control in September 1988. He was involved in a brutal late-night fight outside a nightclub, and then it was reported in New York newspapers that he had attempted suicide by intentionally driving his late-model BMW into a tree; at the time, it was reported in the media that Tyson was under psychiatric treatment for manic depression. Later that same month, while in Moscow with his wife of several months, actress Robin Givens, he reportedly physically attacked her and then attempted to commit suicide by downing a hefty combination of an anti-depressant drug and vodka. At one point, he chased Givens screaming through the hotel lobby, then stood atop a hotel balcony and threatened to jump off. To casual observers, Tyson had become a bona fide sociopath with powerful fists.[24]

Tyson's erratic behavior continued. He also approached his training lackadaisically, and his development as a boxer essentially stopped. In February 1990, King sought an easy payday by promoting a championship fight in Tokyo with journeyman Buster Douglas. It seemed like a typical Don King promotion, a terrible mismatch that he promoted shamelessly and from which his company would earn millions of dollars in pay-for-view television rights. The fight was considered such a mismatch that several Las Vegas sports books refused to put it on their board, and those that did offered it at the staggering odds of 42–1. The overconfident Tyson barely went through the motions in training and never seemed to realize that he was in a championship bout when the bell rang. From round 1, Douglas controlled the fight. In round 10, the challenger caught the champion on the jaw with a flurry of punches – Tyson went down, wobbled to his feet, then pitched forward again for the count. It was, to say the least, a stunning upset.[25]

Things continued to go downhill for Tyson, and along with him the tarred image of boxing. In 1992, Tyson was accused of raping an 18-year-old beauty-pageant contestant, Desiree Washington, in an Indianapolis hotel, and following a sensational and controversial trial, an Indiana jury found him guilty. Trial watchers could scarcely believe the inept defense put on by Tyson's lawyer. As the steel doors of the Indiana State Prison swung shut, it was reported that Tyson was nearly broke; somehow he had managed to divest himself of the estimated $77 million he had earned during his seven-year professional career. As writer Jack Newfield, well-known for his antipathy for Tyson's manager, commented, "Under Don King's tutelage, Mike Tyson lost his crown, lost his money, and lost his freedom."[26]

Within two years following his release from prison in 1995, Tyson had regained the WBC and WBA crowns with technical knockout wins over Bruce Seldon and Frank Bruno. Then, on November 9, 1996, his skills now obviously diminishing and the effects of his frenetic lifestyle catching up with him, Tyson lost his WBA crown in an 11-round TKO to Evander Holyfield in Las Vegas. The following June, King arranged a lucrative rematch, but Holyfield dominated the bout from the beginning. It was clear that Tyson no longer was the powerful, much-to-be-feared fighter. What unfolded that evening in Las Vegas shocked everyone present and would become a bizarre part of boxing lore. The demons that afflicted Tyson were obviously at work that night when in a first-round clinch he chomped down on Holyfield's ear. After receiving a stern warning from referee Mills Lane, in the third round Tyson proceeded to bite off a one-inch chunk of Holyfield's ear. The stunned veteran referee summarily disqualified Iron Mike. Sportswriters, few of whom had any affection or respect for this deeply troubled man, excoriated him for weeks. More importantly, the Nevada Boxing Commission fined him $3 million and suspended him for a year. Whatever respect Tyson still enjoyed was lost, and the reputation of boxing as a legitimate sport sunk to an all-time low.

In 1999, Tyson's problems continued when he got into a fracas along a Maryland highway with two men whose car had collided with his; as a result he spent another nine months in prison. Upon his release, the aging boxer vainly attempted to put together several big paydays, but his boxing skills had been seriously diminished. In 2001, he filed for bankruptcy, and his boxing career ended in the fourth round at the hands of journeyman Danny Williams in Louisville in June 2004, with the once fearsome champion sprawled unconscious on the canvas. Undeterred by his break with his biggest meal ticket, Don King continued to promote fights. Despite an avalanche of complaints by his former clients that he had ripped them off, promising young boxers continued to sign on with Don King Productions, eager to earn one of the million-dollar payouts for which King was famous. As former heavyweight champion Larry Holmes once put it so succinctly: "I make more money with Don King stealing from me than from 100 other promoters."[27] Such was the sorry state of boxing. As the man who had killed two men, spent years in prison, operated a lucrative numbers racket, and allegedly bilked his business partners and fighters of millions of dollars was wont to exclaim, "Only in America!"

Whatever It Takes

In 1973, Harold Connelly, the 1956 American Olympic gold medalist in the hammer throw, told a US Senate committee, "The overwhelming majority of athletes I know would do anything, and take anything, short of killing themselves to improve athletic performance."[28] Connelly spoke at a time when sports administrators and fans were just beginning to perceive the impact of performance-enhancing substances used by athletes to improve body mass and strength. Originally, the controversy focused on the use of anabolic steroids to increase muscle mass, but as the years passed a large and varied number of substances were developed by clandestine scientists who were in cahoots with trainers and athletes to enhance athletic performance. The science of identifying and determining illegal sports "doping" required the expertise of research scientists and physicians, and even those individuals who devoted their careers to finding ways to determine when an athlete had violated clearly established rules had to admit that they believed the use of some sophisticated substances could be "masked" to avoid detection, while other newly developed drugs were immune to identification because no one except a few conspirators even knew of their existence.

The term "doping" is derived from the Dutch *dop*, which was a special type of brandy that had a stimulating effect and which was made from grape skins found only in South Africa. By the late nineteenth century the term *dope* was used to describe substances given to race horses and racing greyhound dogs – normally a narcotic mixture of opium – intended to impair their performance so that gamblers betting on a long-shot could enjoy a big payday. During the latter part of the twentieth century, "doping" came to connote the generic term used to describe the use of any substance that would improve performance in the world of sports.[29] Although leaders in the world of international sports competition first became concerned in the 1950s when female athletes from several Iron Curtain countries exhibited unusual strength and masculine traits such as heavy musculature development, deep voices, and facial hair, the use of performance-enhancing substances can be traced to the late nineteenth century, when Belgian bicycle racers were found to be taking a potion of sugar tablets soaked in ether, French riders quaffed heavy doses of caffeine, and British cyclists inhaled pure oxygen while using brandy to wash down a frightening mixture of strychnine, heroin and cocaine. By 1900, boxers in England and America were believed to drink a combination of strychnine and alcohol before, and during, a bout. As early as the 1904 Olympics, evidence of doping startled officials when an American marathon runner, Thomas Hicks, nearly died mid-race after he downed a mixture of egg whites and large amounts of strychnine. Following the Second World War, stimulants such as amphetamines became popular, especially with cyclists. In 1960, at the Rome Olympics, several cyclists had to be given emergency treatment following their excessive use, and a Danish rider died. The victims had reportedly suffered extreme dehydration brought on by the presence of massive quantities of amphetamines in their system. In 1967, one of the world's leading cyclists, Tommy Simpson of Great Britain, died during the Tour de France. An autopsy revealed that he died from an overdose of amphetamines.[30]

The widespread popularity of recreational drugs during the rebellious years of the 1960s fused with a growing awareness by world-class athletes that certain substances improved their performances. As sports physician Robert O. Voy wrote in 1991, "There are probably gold medal winners and world record holders from the United States who would never have even come near the winner's podium had it not been for their use of performance enhancing substances."[31] As usage became increasingly widespread, many athletes came to the conclusion that in order to keep pace with their competition – whether to win an Olympic medal or simply to make the starting lineup of a college football team – they had to endanger their health and reputation by using banned substances to enhance performance. As Dr Voy observes, "What's worse, I also know, after working elbow-to-elbow with elite-level athletes, that many drug users do not *want* to use drugs but feel they *have* to stay even with everyone else."[32] An American Olympic weightlifter, Ken Patera, laconically commented to the press in 1971, after he lost to a Russian superheavy-weight-lifter at the Pan American games, "The only difference between me and [Vassili Alexeev] was that I couldn't afford his drug bill. When I hit Munich, I'll weigh in at about 340, or maybe 350. Then, we'll see which are better – his steroids or mine."[33] In Munich, Patera apparently learned that Alexeev's druggist was better – the Russian took the gold.

During the late twentieth century, as understanding about the use of steroids became commonplace, most sports executives and fans were bewildered by the news. The names of the substances were foreign to nearly everyone, their dangers unknown, and their users protected by various player union contracts. Colleges and high schools found that testing was prohibitively expensive and that various legal protections – including a constitutional ban on unwarranted search and seizure – made a comprehensive prohibition against their use impossible. The typical response by fans, coaches, and athletic directors was to ignore the problem, hoping it would take care of itself and simply go away. Unfortunately, this "see no evil, hear no evil" policy placed many athletes at risk. This was especially true of potent anabolic-androgenic steroids and other substances that were popular among average citizens as recreational substances.

Initially, there was a great deal of disagreement about the actual ability of steroids to produce muscle mass and strength. It was not until the mid-1980s that a sound body of positive scientific evidence had been developed. By then, scientists had not only confirmed what users had known for years, but could also now say with certainty that heavy usage over a period of time could result in serious physical harm. On one level, chemically induced growth produces greater stress by placing increased muscle weight on joints and limbs, creating muscle tightness and thereby the potential for injury (such as recurring pulled hamstring muscles). Male athletes who took popular substances such as Dianabol (popularly called "D-bol") exposed themselves to many serious health risks, including arterial sclerosis, high blood pressure, liver cancer, heart disease, prostate cancer, sterility, and – as often emerged as the first symptom of heavy usage – psychological changes that sometimes encouraged violent behavior. Women risked damage to their reproductive organs, high blood pressure, irregular menstruation, severe depression, and irreversible physical changes that included masculine features, excessive hair growth on the body and face, and a deepened voice.

The athletes were far ahead of athletic administrators in their knowledge of steroids. By the mid-1960s, the use of anabolic steroids – synthetic male hormones – became almost a *sine qua non* for world-class weightlifters and among weight throwers in track and field. Leading American weight throwers identified as users included 1956 hammer-throw gold medalist Harold Connelly, 1964 shot-put gold medalist Dallas Long, and 1968 shot-put champion Randy Matson. The team physician for the 1968 American Olympic track team was later quoted as saying,

> I don't think it is possible for a weight man to complete internationally without using anabolic steroids. . . . All the weight men on the Olympic team had to take steroids. Otherwise they would have been out of the running.

Sprinters also learned that a steroid such as Dianabol enhanced their explosiveness off the starting blocks. At the Mexico City Games in 1968, insiders discovered that the debate over steroid use by Americans and athletes from other countries was not over the moral issue of taking such drugs but about which substances were the most effective. The 1968 American decathlon gold medalist and the recipient of the prestigious Sullivan Award by the American Amateur Union, Bill Toomey, readily admitted to using drugs to enhance his performance at Mexico City.

As a result of the subsequent rise in new world records, news of the doping epidemic could not be contained. John Hendershott, editor of *Track and Field News*, sarcastically commented that anabolic steroids were the new "breakfast of champions,"[34] and journalist Bil Gilbert published a revealing series in *Sports Illustrated* in 1969 in which he described widespread usage and called for their prohibition.[35] However, it would not be until 1980 that the International Olympic Committee began to impose prohibitions on the use of performance-enhancing substances and instituted modest testing procedures. The American Olympic Committee and the NCAA, two primary guardians of the integrity of American sports, were likewise lethargic in their response.

Professional football players, especially linemen and linebackers, were quick to take note. Although it was not commonly known until the late 1980s, the use of anabolic steroids became rampant in the National Football League during the 1970s. Various estimates indicated that at least 50 percent of all players at least experimented with their use and that 75 percent of linemen and linebackers were regular consumers. Gilbert's 1969 articles had intimated widespread usage encouraged by strength coaches and team physicians. In 1991, Steve Courson, an offensive lineman for the Pittsburgh Steelers and Tampa Bay Buccaneers from 1977 until 1984, stunned the league officials and football fans with his candid recollection of heavy steroid use that began when he was a freshman at the University of South Carolina in 1973. Of his days in Pittsburgh, Courson commented that not only did half of his teammates use steroids but that "an even greater number" took amphetamines on Sunday before a game. These powerful stimulants were readily available in the Steelers locker room in large cookie jars, from which "interested players could scoop up however many pills they wanted." Courson later recalled that the combination of steroids and amphetamines greatly increased his and his teammates' aggression, and they would seek to "take an edge off" the "roid rage" after games and practices by the use of marijuana.[36]

Courson recalled that locker room talk frequently revolved around the relative merits of the many drug combinations available to them. "We sounded like a bunch of pharmacists talking shop," he recalled.[37] The strongly worded warnings by physicians about the dangers of steroid use were not exaggerated. By age 36, Courson's career came to a crashing halt when he was diagnosed with a serious heart condition complicated by other serious maladies. After he became the first NFL player to speak openly about steroid usage, the NFL sought to use damage control, issuing a flurry of conflicting and self-serving press releases. Courson's head coach at Pittsburgh, Chuck Noll, testified to a congressional committee that he had never ordered, authorized, or even recognized any use of such substances during his 30 years in the NFL.[38]

Many athletes in the 1980s apparently took to using various drugs for both performance enhancement and recreation. These included heroin and especially cocaine. During the late nineteenth century, cocaine was considered a medical miracle and was often prescribed by physicians for a variety of ailments. Some cigarettes were laced with cocaine, and initially it was one of several secret ingredients in the popular soft drink Coca-Cola (hence its name). It did not take long, however, for the negative effects of "coke" to become apparent, and the drug was made illegal in the Harrison Anti-Narcotic Act of 1914. During the 1960s, a wide variety of drugs hit the streets, including powerful mind-altering substances such as LSD. Marijuana had long been popular within segments of the urban culture, and during the rebellious sixties it grew enormously in popularity. By the 1970s, cocaine became the drug of choice among serious users because it produced a euphoric "high" that encouraged users to believe they could perform difficult tasks at a high level. Usage apparently was tacitly encouraged by many coaches who simply chose not to know. At the same time, team physicians, trainers, and coaches encouraged the belief that the use of drugs was acceptable by encouraging, even insisting upon, the use of powerful (and legal) painkillers so athletes could compete despite suffering from severe injuries. The locker room culture was seemingly awash with medications and injection needles.

Although subject to occasional news stories, these developments occurred largely without the knowledge of the American public. That changed, however, in June 1986, when two high-profile athletes died within three days of each other of cocaine overdoses. Len Bias was a talented All-American basketball player at the University of Maryland, and after his senior year was the first-round draft choice of the Boston Celtics, a championship team that envisioned him as the player who would eventually replace forward Larry Bird as the team's superstar. General Manager Red Auerbach believed he had secured the most promising player of the decade, and many basketball experts believed that the 6' 8" forward had the potential to equal Michael Jordan as an all-around performer. Auerbach firmly believed that by drafting Bias he had ensured the continued Celtic domination of the NBA well into the 1990s.

The circumstances surrounding Bias's death remain unclear, but he apparently used cocaine the night he returned from Boston after signing a lucrative Celtics contract and being introduced by an exuberant Red Auerbach to the New England media. Back in College Park, Maryland, he visited with friends in a dormitory and then left for an unknown destination. About 6 a.m., he returned to the campus, where he suffered a massive seizure and shortly after died in a nearby hospital emergency room. The sports world was stunned by his death, even more so when the cause of death was reported to have been a heart attack brought on by an overdose of cocaine. Subsequent investigations revealed that this was not a case of a first-time user as some believed (or hoped) but rather that Bias had been living with a drug problem for several years. Although he had nothing directly to do with Bias's death, Maryland head basketball coach Lefty Driesell was forced to resign, the implication of university officials being that he should have known of Bias's problem and taken corrective action.[39] Two days after Bias died on the East Coast, Cleveland Browns defensive back Donald Rogers died from a heart attack in Sacramento. An autopsy indicated that the attack was brought on by cocaine. Together, the two tragedies on the nation's two coasts forced a major reassessment of drug education at both the college and professional sports levels.

The deaths of these two elite athletes also stimulated massive media attention to the issue. Sports pages were filled with anguished columns, and many popular sports figures were seen on television urging young athletes to "just say no" to drugs. But as the furor over the two deaths receded into the background, repeated stories of top professional athletes and their drug usage indicated that "just say no" was not working. The flame-throwing Los Angeles Dodgers left-handed pitcher Steve Howe became almost a poster boy for the problem when he was arrested seven times for violating drug laws and suspended four times from organized baseball, including two "life suspensions." Dexter Manley, star defensive tackle of the Washington Redskins, and New York Knicks star forward Michael Richardson were suspended permanently by their leagues for repeat offenses. The gold medal winner of the 100-meter sprint at the 1988 Seoul Olympics, Canadian sprinter Ben Johnson, had surprised track experts when he blew by the favored American Carl Lewis to set a world record that prompted the press to call him "The World's Fastest Human." But fame is often fleeting, and in Johnson's case extremely so. He had his gold medal taken away and his record time erased from the record books when he tested positive to the use of Stanozolol after the race. Johnson not only had his career end in shame but lost an estimated $15 million in potential product endorsements. In 1993, the sports investigative reporters Don Yaeger and Don Looney published an expose of Notre Dame football, in which they implicated a heralded head coach: "First Lou Holtz arrived at Notre Dame. Then a lot of steroids did. The connection is inescapable. It also has been devastating. The football team quickly became awash in anabolic steroids, starting in 1986."[40]

Football, because of its emphasis upon speed, strength, and bulk, became the center of attention. Ambivalence characterized much of the reaction by college and professional teams. After all, the hard-hitting 240-pound linebacker or the hole-opening blocker were often singled-out by sports writers for their raw physical power. The implications of steroid use, however, were brought into sharp focus in 1992, with the agonizing death of former All-Pro defensive end Lyle Alzado. Near death from a rare form of cancer of the brain, Alzado went public and attributed his disease to more than 20 years of taking steroids and human-growth hormones. He had begun his college football career as an undersized defensive lineman at Yankton College in South Dakota in 1969, but after being introduced to anabolic steroids his weight zoomed to 240 pounds. When he played professionally, however, he possessed a powerful physique of 300 pounds of muscle. Not only did he put on immense muscle mass, but his strength and speed also increased markedly. His growth in physical strength was accompanied by a simultaneous growth in his penchant for aggressive behavior. He began taking steroids at Yankton, and throughout his professional career he would spend about $30,000 a year for this ticket to the All-Star team. "I outran, outhit, outanythinged everybody," he recalled. I was taking steroids and I saw that they made me play better and better." His ferocity and fearlessness on the field made him a fourth round draft choice with the Denver Broncos. He spent 15 years in the National Football League, receiving several All-Star team recognitions, and concluded his career with the Oakland Raiders. In 1984, he was the defensive star when the Raiders handily defeated the Washington Redskins in the Super Bowl. But his steroid-driven career exacted an enormous price. At age 41, he suffered from severe depression and had to deal with periodic dizziness, fainting spells, and intense headaches. In 1991, he was diagnosed with an unusual form of brain lymphoma. Although his physicians would not categorically state that his illness resulted from steroid use, Alzado flatly told the world in a *Sports Illustrated* article a few weeks before his death that in his own mind, this was the case:

> I started taking anabolic steroids in 1969 and never stopped. It was addicting, mentally addicting. Now I'm sick, and I'm scared. Ninety percent of the athletes I know are on the stuff. We're not born to be 300 lbs or jump 30'. In all the time I was taking steroids, I knew they were making me play better. I became very violent on the field and off it. I did things only crazy people do. Once a guy sideswiped my car and I beat the hell out of him. Now look at me. My hair's gone, I wobble when I walk and have to hold on to someone for support, and I have trouble remembering things. My last wish? That no one ever dies this way.[41]

Although much of the news regarding steroids revolved around football, cycling, weightlifting, and track and field, organized baseball encountered a serious public-relations dilemma following the 1998 season in which Sammy Sosa of the Chicago Cubs and Mark McGwire engaged in a home-run derby that saw McGwire ultimately hit 70 home runs and Sosa 66. Both sluggers exceeded Roger Maris's record of 61 set in 1961. Fans thrilled to their exploits, and as the season evolved they packed the stadiums to watch McGwire and Sosa swing for the fences. Their competition resulted in a friendly rivalry between the two men that the media loved, and their exploits did much to bring fans back to the game of baseball after the disastrous strike of 1994. However, reports that McGwire was using androstetenedione – a form of testosterone supplement popularly called "andro" – caught the attention of baseball writers. At the time, the supplement was not banned by the federal government or by organized baseball, but its ability to increase muscle mass and strength was well established. It was also rumored, but never proven, that Sosa's sudden-found extra power also resulted from something more than good diet and weight training.

McGwire never attempted to hide the fact that he was taking "andro" and large containers of the substance were visible on his Busch Stadium locker shelf. The active ingredient androstenedione is a natural chemical substance found in the human body. It enables the body to produce more testerosterone than normal. The chemical can also be isolated in some meats and even in plants. It is not by scientific or legal definition a steroid but rather an "androgen" – a steroid precurser – that produces a change of chemical reactions in the body that promote the production of testerosterone. At the time McGwire was taking andro and swatting 70 balls out of major-league ballparks, it was a legal substance according to the Federal Drug Administration. But when reporters began to explore McGwire's use of andro, many fans and most baseball experts took exception, arguing that he was unfairly setting a major-league record with a substantial boost from chemicals that was not available to Babe Ruth and Roger Maris. McGwire was candid in his response, noting that the substance was purchased legally and that it was not banned by organized baseball. He was playing within the rules. "Everything I've done is natural," he plaintively said. And, more ominously, "Everybody that I know in the game of baseball uses the same stuff I use."[42]

Family physicians everywhere were appalled, however, because they knew that some of the known side effects included changing testosterone to the female hormone estrogen in some (but not all) males, the complete shutting down of the production of testosterone, baldness, severe acne, a dangerous lowering of "good" cholesterol levels that could lead to heart disease, and perhaps most ominous of all, the stunting of growth in adolescents. That McGwire's sudden fame encouraged a heavy increase in the over-the-counter sale of andro among teenagers only heightened concerns. The comments of Boston Red Sox slugger Mo Vaughan did nothing to assuage fears: "Anything illegal is definitely wrong. But if you get something over the counter and legal, guys in power hitter positions are going to use them."[43]

It was not until 2003 that the FDA issued a ruling making androstenedione a banned substance. Ever since its introduction to the market in the mid-1990s, as a steroid precursor and not the steroid itself, drug and health-food companies had marketed andro as a dietary supplement. In April 2003, when the head of the major-league players' union, Donald Fehr, refused to support a ban on andro before a Senate subcommittee, US Senator John McCain threatened punitive legislation. A visibly upset McCain told Fehr that he and his union were "aiding and abetting cheaters" and that if organized baseball did not act swiftly, Congress would. That the NFL had banned the substance in 1999 only added to baseball's besmirched image. Baseball finally made its ban effective for the 2004 season.

Thus American sports officials at all levels wrestled, often inconclusively and uneasily, with the many legal and scientific vagaries of performance-enhancing substances. Nefarious chemists were ever ready and able to produce new substances that could escape detection by existing testing measures, and athletes seeking an edge would continue to use them. In fall 2004, the *San Francisco Chronicle* published a front-page exclusive story that reported on sealed federal grand jury testimony taken a year earlier, at which time the leading All-Star slugger and first baseman of the New York Yankees, Jason Giambi, admitted to taking a new generation of steroids for which there was no test. That Giambi had gained an estimated 30 pounds of muscle between 2000 and 2003 had not been lost on reporters, but until the story leaked to the press he had adamantly denied using any illegal substance. That he had fallen victim to a mysterious severe stomach ailment that sidelined him for the latter half of the 2004 season seemed to indicate that he was victim of the use of some form of steroids. His leaked grand jury testimony confirmed those suspicions.[44]

Like many athletes before him, Giambi had willingly and knowingly risked his health, perhaps his life, in the quest for an edge on his competition – or, given the widespread perception that many other baseball players were also clandestine users, perhaps he was merely attempting to stay even with his competition. America's penchant for winning at all costs was once more on the front page for all to contemplate.

Under a Cloud: Barry Bonds Chases Hank Aaron

The dilemma posed by steroids and drugs heightened the public perception of the obsession that Americans had come to place upon winning. When Jason Giambi was forced to tell the truth to a grand jury, he was assured that his comments would be kept sealed and that, in return for his testimony against a San Francisco drug company, he would be exempt from federal prosecution. But someone leaked the testimony, and Giambi had to confront the reality of his problem in public, having to face fans and reporters to whom he had lied. Giambi had developed serious digestive problems and benign tumors on his pituitary gland that had severely weakened him to the point where he could not play in the second half of the 2004 season, a condition now believed by the media as resulting from steroid use. The ethical dilemma that Giambi faced, however, was not as complex as that which confronted Barry Bonds, one of baseball's all-time great players who also was caught up in the same grand jury investigation. Giambi frankly admitted steroid use over a three-year period, including injecting himself with the steroid Deca Durabolin as well as administering a new and undetectable synthetic steroid, THG (tetrahydrogestrinone) which is absorbed through the skin. However, Bonds, as of 2001 the holder of the all-time season home-run record of 73, attempted to deflect all allegations. In his testimony to the same grand jury, the San Francisco Giants outfielder admitted to using substances provided by his personal trainer but strongly contended that he thought the substances identified to him as "the cream" and "the clear" were merely harmless herbal compounds (flaxseed oil and a balm for arthritis he blandly told the grand jury), not new designer steroids undetectable by even the most sophisticated testing laboratories. Bonds may have felt that his tortured testimony gave him some cover in the suddenly raging steroids controversy, but his version of the truth told under oath produced profound skepticism, if not downright incredulity.[45]

The son of prominent slugger Bobby Bonds, who played for the Giants and six other major league teams over 14 seasons, Barry entered the National League in

1986 after being drafted out of Arizona State University by the Pittsburgh Pirates. He established himself as a talented contact hitter and left-fielder and became a perennial All-Star. Acquired by the Giants in 1993 as a free agent, Bonds signed one of the most lucrative contracts in baseball history up to that time and proceeded to establish unquestioned Hall of Fame credentials. At the end of his 15th major-league season, he had a career batting average of slightly over .300 and 494 home runs. In only four seasons up to this point had Bonds hit more than 40 home runs, with his career high of 49 being set in 2000. Then, at the age of 37, when professional ball players are normally well into their declining years, Bonds unleashed a burst of unusual power for someone his age. Playing in the new Pac Bell Park in San Francisco in 2001, where the distances to the outfield fence are long and the winds often favor pitchers, Bonds proceeded to eclipse the single-season 70 home run record established in 1998 by Mark McGwire, ending the season with 73. Many fans and journalists were prone to comment upon his new appearance. The one-time relatively slender, lithe athlete had become the possessor of a large, imposing, powerful frame that enabled him to launch tape-measure home runs into McCovey Cove in San Francisco Bay beyond the distant right field bleachers. Bonds attributed his increased size and strength to his year-around physical conditioning program that featured exhaustive weightlifting and aerobic workouts, complemented by a carefully regimented diet and consumption of dietetic supplements provided by his personal trainer, Greg Anderson. Widespread whispers that Bonds had transformed himself by the use of steroids and human growth hormones were brushed off.

During the next three seasons, Bonds continued his home-run barrage as he moved past the 40 years of age mark. By the end of the 2005 season, he had hit a career 703 home runs, just 11 behind Babe Ruth's record, and well within hailing distance of the 755 set by Hank Aaron in 1973. While Bonds hit 45 home runs the year he turned 40, Aaron had struggled to hit 16. Bonds had somehow managed to hammer 209 home runs between his 37th and 40th birthdays – a feat that produced incredulity. Then came revelations of his testimony to the Grand Jury admitting use of "the cream" and "the clear," designer steroids allegedly produced by the Bay Area Laboratory Company (BALCO). The grand jury had opened its investigation into BALCO – leading to the secret testimony of Giambi, Bonds, and several other premier athletes – only after the testing laboratory in Los Angeles used by the United States Olympic Committee had received anonymously a syringe filled with a substance unknown to all testing laboratories. It apparently had come from an unknown track and field coach who had reason to suspect that new and unknown synthetic steroids were being used by world-class track athletes.

For years, the leadership of the baseball players union and the leaders of organized baseball had danced around the issue of performance enhancements. Now, faced with an angry US Senate committee headed by Senator John McCain and buffeted by the startling revelations of the BALCO investigation, a new drug-testing policy was rushed into being for the 2005 season, calling for year-round unannounced testing with a 10-day unpaid suspension for an initial offense leading to a year's suspension after four positive tests. While sports commentators felt that this was a positive development, given the prior years of relentless stone-walling by the players' union, most journalists and public officials contended that it was too little, much too late. The initial 10-day suspension drew caustic commentary and many a cynic pointed to the fact that both the NFL and the NBA had passed more stringent policies years earlier, and that the US Olympic Committee was routinely banning athletes from competition for two years or more if they tested positive for the first time.

The BALCO episode was clearly the most direct and damaging hit that any American professional sport took on the steroid issue up to that time. Its biggest star – arguably one of the greatest players in the history of the game – had become implicated. Dr Charles Yesalis, a Penn State professor of health policies and co-author of the authoritative book, *The Steroids Game* (1998), placed the BALCO development into an ironic but compelling context: "I haven't seen anything that shows me the fans really care," he told a reporter. "Baseball just had a stellar year, and if your IQ was at or near room temperature you didn't need to hear Jason Giambi's testimony to know these guys are using drugs." In comparing the recent exploits by Mark McGwire, Ken Caminiti, Gary Sheffield, Sammy Sosa, and Barry Bonds, among the most notable sluggers, Yesalis conceded, "they are breaking records, but I'm outraged." But he sadly acknowledged that most fans did not share his anger. In an all-consuming entertainment age, he said with a heavy dose of sarcasm: "Why should you draw a distinction between athletes who do and don't use drugs? Using drugs makes the athletes more entertaining. The ball goes out of the park more often."[46]

Journalist David Wallenchinsky, who specialized in covering the Olympics, noted that when McGwire hit his record 70 home runs in 1998, fans everywhere cheered and packed the stadiums. In St Louis, McGwire became the city's most popular resident, and even a major freeway was named in his honor. But everyone knew that he had taken andro; the media had made all knowledgeable sports fans aware that McGwire was using the steroid precursor. Noting that in 1996 the elite American shot putter Randy Barnes had been banned from track and field competition for life for using the same substance, Wallenchinsky said: "Randy Barnes was given a lifetime ban for using it. McGwire got millions of dollars and became an American hero, and he was taking the same drug." Like many observers, Wallenchinsky concluded that "people want their heroes. They don't want a drug scandal. They want to look the other way."[47]

In spring 2005, the US House of Representatives held public hearings on steroid use. McGwire's non-responsive comments, much of which involved invoking the Fifth Amendment that protects a witness from self-incrimination, severely damaged his public image. Only the most generous did not come away from his depressing testimony believing he had not taken substances far more powerful than andro while he was assaulting baseball's home run records. At those same hearings, one of only seven major league players in history to make 3,000 base hits, 40-year-old Baltimore Orioles first baseman Rafael Palmeiro, emphatically told the congressional committee under oath, "I have never used steroids. Period." He dramatically jabbed his finger in the air for additional emphasis. Four

months later Palmeiro was suspended by major league baseball for testing positive to a "serious steroid." Pundits now were forced to question just how many hits
this discredited, potential Hall of Fame player, might have made if he had not used
illegal substances. Was this a first-time situation, or had he used them for years? A
cloud of suspicion hovered over the long-time popular player, and it seemed likely
to remain there long into his post-baseball life.

In spring 2006, Barry Bonds continued his home run drive under a very dark
cloud, created by a devastating book written by two highly respected investigative journalists. This presented what most knowledgeable observers believed to be
overwhelmingly conclusive evidence that his late-in-career home run bonanza
was the result of a heavy use of steroids. Although his hometown fans in San Francisco cheered his 715th run, which on May 28 eclipsed Babe Ruth's career mark,
Bonds was roundly denounced by baseball fans everywhere else he played. Among
serious baseball fans and journalists, his achievement produced an ambivalence
that was palpable.[48]

American sports reeled under the continuum of allegations about steroid use at
the college and professional levels. It was only a matter of time until the public dialogue reached down into the high school. Several state athletic associations issued
press releases that they were looking into the problem that steroids might pose for
young athletes. Perhaps the fact that several teenage athletes had died from their
steroid use within the year, as reported in a national news magazine on Christmas
Eve, might have gotten their attention.[49] Even as their anguished parents pleaded
with Congress and sports leaders to take decisive action to prevent further abuse,
politicians ducked and sports executives called for more studies. That the issue
would continue to plague American sports into the distant future seemed a safe
prediction.

16 The Democratization
of Sports

Following the Second World War, as the years melded into decades, the United States enjoyed a sustained and unparalleled time of economic growth and expansion. Powerful scientific and technological forces transformed American life. Life expectancy increased substantially, and improved healthcare contributed to almost a doubling of the population, from 140 million in 1940 to nearly 300 million in 2005. Most Americans gravitated toward the sprawling metropolitan areas, with the South and West showing the largest gains. Although industrial production remained high – despite strong competition from modern Asian and European countries – the greatest increase in economic activity occurred in the service and high-tech areas. Following a sobering downturn in traditional "rust belt" heavy industry during the 1970s, a stunning "new economy" took hold during the 1980s, spurred by biotechnology and computer science. Social changes accompanied those in the economy, highlighted by the transformation of the role of women in the culture as they assumed new leadership roles in the professions, business, and politics. New patterns of immigration led to a significant increase in racial, ethnic, and religious diversity. All of these forces contributed to a growing tenor of equalitarianism and democracy in the ebb and flow of everyday American life; those sensibilities were played out in the recreational activities and games in which the American people took part, and the sporting contests that they watched.

Community Cauldron: High School Sports

The growth of organized youth sports during the years after the Second World War was one important manifestation of the nation's growing affluence. Families not only had more time and more money to devote to recreation and organized sports, but they also believed that they were essential for the healthful develop-ment of children and that they taught lessons that would contribute to success in their personal and professional lives as adults. During the early decades of the twentieth century, the teachings of Luther Gulick and his followers established the importance of competitive sports in helping young people to grow and develop into healthy, physically fit young adults who also understood the importance of good citizenship and moral leadership. The underlying role played by the tenets of what was once called "Muscular Christianity" should not be minimized. The YMCA movement and development of physical-education programs in the public schools gave ample testimony to this movement. Competitive interscholastic athletic com-petition had its origins in Gulick's health and fitness philosophy.

Not surprisingly, within a society in which competition provided the essential framework for an aggressive capitalist economy, winning in sports usually took precedence over merely competing and learning to be "good losers." Americans, tempered by frequent wars and ongoing economic struggles to keep ahead of the competition, often seemed to forget that in the world of sports, 50 percent of the teams (or individual competitors) lose every time out. Winning was not the only thing, of course, but losing on a regular basis was unacceptable. Thus the foun-dation of the large and pervasive American sports culture of recent years – youth and public school sports programs – was naturally based upon the competitive, winning model. Proper attention was paid, of course, to the importance of good sportsmanship, but the primary lesson that went with losing was the importance of fighting back, of not giving up, of keeping the ultimate goal of victory in mind.

In American society, the importance of winning naturally took precedence. In the competitive world of high school sports, league standings, post-season tourna-ments, and championships took precedence over health and physical education. By the 1920s, state athletic associations were conducting statewide champion-ships in basketball, track and field, and baseball. Various systems were devised to determine state champions in football, including statewide ballots by coaches or journalists and sometimes playoff systems. High-school sports were of great impor-tance everywhere, but they seemingly took on the greatest importance in small cities and towns where a strong sense of community pride prevailed and commu-nity affairs were heavily focused around the only high school in town. Intense political and economic rivalries that had developed over the passing of the years between neighboring towns were naturally played out when their high school teams met on the field or court.

The power of a high-school team to galvanize a community has been dem-onstrated in many settings over the years. One of the most dramatic examples occurred in 1954 in Indiana, where basketball held a particularly powerful sway. For reasons rooted in its early history, the state athletic association did not divide schools into several divisions based on enrollment; instead, all schools, large and small, competed in a single division. Over the years, in the closely followed state tournament held in February, a few "miracle" teams from small rural schools had won a few early round tournament games, even pulling-off an improbable upset over a large urban school. However, come state finals time, the finalists invariably represented urban schools with substantial enrollments. Nineteen fifty-four, how-ever, proved to be a special year, when the tiny high school from the small farming town of Milan (pop. 987), located in the rolling hills of the southeastern corner of the state, powered its way through the sectional and regional tournaments to reach the "Final Four" played in cavernous Butler University Field House in India-napolis. It was truly a David versus Goliath story – there were 773 teams entered in the tournament – and the state's intense basketball fans were enthralled. The tallest player on the team was 6' 1" center Gene White, and the team's leader was sharp-shooting 5' 11" forward Bobby Plump. Like thousands of boys across the state's rolling prairie land, Plump had spent countless hours perfecting his game, practicing his favorite jump shot on a hoop nailed above the barn door at his family farm. Although the Milan Indians came into the tournament with a 20–2 record, statewide ranking polls did not give them any mention. At Indianapolis, the Indi-ans encountered one of the state's top-ranked teams, the powerful Tigers from Crispus Attucks High School in Indianapolis, a team from the segregated school led by future All-American and NBA Hall of Fame player Oscar Robertson. But Plump hit nine of 13 shots before a frantic crowd of 15,000 to lead Milan to a 13-point victory, and on Saturday night the "little team that could" squared off for the state championship against top-seeded and heavily favored Muncie Central.[1]

The Muncie Bearcats represented a school with a rich basketball tradition that boasted of a starting five averaging 6' 4" and they towered over their improbable challengers. With an estimated two million people watching on a statewide televi-sion network, Milan coach Marvin Wood employed a slow-down offense he called the "cat and mouse." The Indians refused to run with the bigger and faster oppo-nents, passed the ball for minutes before taking a wide-open shot, and as the game unfolded the teams traded the lead several times. The score was tied at 26–26 as the fourth quarter began, and following Wood's daring instructions, Plump stood improbably at mid-court holding the ball for more than five minutes. The cautious Bearcats refused to come out of their zone defense as time ran down. The teams traded baskets, and with just 18 seconds remaining in the game, the score was tied at 30–30. With the Bearcats now in a man-to-man defense, Plump moved off a screen, dribbled into the key, and calmly put up a 15-foot jump-shot, gently releasing the ball just as he had thousands of times in his barnyard. As the buzzer sounded the ball nestled softly into the net. In that very instant, one of Indiana's greatest sports legends was born. "Bobby Plump overwhelmed Indiana," the India-napolis Star reported. "No other high school player ever had a season like the one he has just completed. He completely captured the heart of Indiana's basketball fans, a discriminating audience, which chooses its heroes carefully and treasures them forever."[2] The "Milan Miracle," became the basis for the popular 1986 motion pic-ture, Hoosiers, although Indiana basketball purists were quick to point out many discrepancies between reality and the Hollywood version.

The Milan story, however heartwarming, proved to be a short-lived story. Coach Wood moved on to a larger school, Plump and his teammates graduated and went their separate ways, and the Indians team never again approximated what had been done that special year.

Larger, well-organized and sharply focused communities, however, have taken special pride in producing a winning tradition that has extended over many decades. As has occurred in many a small town over the years, a winning high school basketball could temporarily energize small towns during tournament time. Larger communities, however, have tended to focus their attention upon football. An early prototype of a perpetually successful program emerged in the mill town of Massillon, Ohio. In 1932, Paul Brown, a young graduate from Miami University in Oxford, Ohio, took over the head-coaching duties at Massillon's only high school. Between 1935 and 1940, his Massillon Washington High teams won 58 of 60 games and claimed six consecutive state championships. Brown established a tradition that continues to the present day. He created the Tiger Booster Club to raise funds and provide community support, and he introduced coaching innovations that he would later use with the Cleveland Browns. He installed his offensive and defensive systems through a coaching network that extended downward to the junior varsity, freshman and junior-high teams, even to the touch-football games played between elementary schools. He controlled the appointment of all coaches throughout the school system, required that they follow his system, so that when players arrived at Washington High from the city's three junior-high schools they were already well versed in his offensive and defensive schemes.

A typical mill town located in the industrial belt that stretches across five states from Chicago and Detroit to Pittsburgh, Massillon in the 1950s was a company town of 30,000 dominated by a Superior Steel Company plant. It was the epitome of the tough blue-collar town, and its attitude was revealed through the tenacity of its football teams. Over the years, the Tigers claimed 23 state football championships, sent hundreds of players off to major college teams, 16 of whom became All-Americans, and several of whom starred in the National Football League. Over the years, six of its head coaches left to take major-college head-coaching positions, and as the winning seasons piled one upon another, community commitment intensified. The booster club grew to 3,000 paying members by 1980, and 22,000-seat Paul Brown Stadium, complete with sparkling orange and black seats, dominated the school grounds. When artificial turf became the rage, Massillon was among the first high schools to have it installed, the money raised by a special campaign. When year-round weight training became an integral part of the college football scene, Massillon Washington High soon had its own weight-training facility that was equal to those at most colleges. When college sports public information officers began producing gargantuan pre-season press books highlighting the upcoming season and the team, Massillon's was the biggest and most professional to be found among Ohio high schools.

On game days, the town's main streets were lined with orange and black flags and banners, and handwritten signs urging the team on to victory were posted in store front windows. Young boys in Massillon were raised with the expectation that they would contribute to the team; each new baby boy left the local hospital with his first worldly possession – an orange and black miniature football, a gift of the Tigers Boosters. Parents frequently held their boys back one year in elementary school so they will be more fully developed physically for their senior season. For girls, positions on the cheer squad and drill team were the focus of intense competition, and the Tiger Swing Band was considered one of the most accomplished in the state. Visitors to town can tour the Tiger Football Museum. One local mortuary even offered a festive tiger-striped orange and black casket to provide a spirited send-off for the most dedicated of fans.

In 1985, Washington High won its 600th game, becoming the first high school team in the United States to achieve that level, and at the end of the 2004 season the Tigers' overall record stood at 750 wins, 214 losses, and 35 ties. Between 1921 and 2004, the school had endured only four losing seasons, with two back-to-back 4–6 seasons occurring in 2003 and 2004. Competition apparently had caught up with the Tigers, with rival schools such as Cincinnati Moeller, Canton McKinley, and Cleveland St Ignatius mounting their own well-funded and aggressive year-round football developmental programs.

In 1999, Massillon football was the topic of a documentary film shown as a feature in many American theaters. *Go Tigers! A Team's Fate, A Town's Future* revealed a community obsessed with its football team, where sagging Rust Belt economic woes had led voters to turn down three consecutive bond issues to bail out an educational system that was bordering on bankruptcy. Nonetheless, the team had sparkling new uniforms, nine assistant coaches, a full-time trainer, and a sports information director. As the season's final regular-season game against traditional arch-rival Canton McKinley High loomed, the film's director indicated that unless the 17- and 18-year-old boys won the big game, the fourth tax-levy vote was probably doomed. They won, however, and the bond issue passed by a narrow majority. The observation of a visiting journalist in 1965 still rang true in 2005: "If you are a member of the solid blue collar class in Massillon the odds are that you are also an official booster of football." He also noted that, "visiting teams are crushed before the kickoff by the Tigers' record, confidence, spirit, the town's booster pride and noise, their conditioning and training." Back-to-back losing seasons apparently did little to dampen the town's enthusiasm. Everywhere in town as the year 2005 approached, a curious visitor (this author) heard a familiar mantra as he visited with locals: "Wait till next season."[3]

Observers have long believed that similar patterns of obsession with high school football could be found in Pennsylvania, Texas, and in fact, throughout much of the South. In 1990, the special obsession produced by high school football in Texas was revealed when *Philadelphia Inquirer* reporter, B. G. "Buzz" Bissinger, published his best-selling book based upon a full year spent in Odessa, Texas, observing the community-wide obsession with Permian Basin High School football. In his best-selling book, *Friday Night Lights*, Bissinger reported an "intensity more than I could have imagined."[4] He described a classic scenario where the pressure to win was inexorable, extravagant football expenditures and minimal academic budgets were accepted, and players skated through their academic courses with little effort. The Panthers played in a modern 20,000-seat stadium, complete with artificial turf, a large press box, bright lighting, and a modern scoreboard. For distant games, the team traveled by chartered jet. The team basked in the adulation of the adults in the community, and within the social structure of the school, players were the exalted ones. Bissinger described impressionable teenagers being subjected to intense community pressure to "win state," with their coaches under siege to win every game. When an upset defeat occurred early in the season, the head coach came home to find a flock of for-sale signs stuck in his front yard. Bissinger also reported that the few black players on the team were viewed through a different lens than whites; his description of the impact of a torn knee cartilage on the team's top running back, Boobie Miles, reveals how the young man went from being a top-recruited prospect by major colleges to a useless object of little worth, forgotten by college recruiters and rejected by the community. Boobie's hopes for a college scholarship were dashed, and because the educational system had betrayed him, he was forced to attend a modest junior college from which he did not graduate. Lacking discernable skills, Boobie Miles faced an improbable future where his once vaunted football skills would not prove of value.

Bissinger's candid narrative shocked many readers. "It became obvious that these kids held the town on their shoulders," he wrote, and quoted one disillusioned parent:

> Athletics lasts for such a short period of time. . . . But while it lasts, it creates this make-believe world where normal rules don't apply. We build this false atmosphere. When it's over and the harsh reality sets in, that's the real joke we play on people. . . . Everybody wants to experience that superlative movement, and being an athlete you can have that. It's Camelot for them. But there's life after [football].[5]

And that life afterward, Bissinger reported, was often fraught with disappointment.

It was inevitable that high-school athletics would take on a more national outlook as a result of the increased media attention devoted to sports. During the 1920s, the University of Chicago had held a short-lived national high-school basketball tournament, but in the 1980s, the trend toward national orientation intensified when the recently introduced national newspaper *USA Today* thrust high-school sports into a national context when it began to publish national rankings of the "top 25" high-school football, baseball, and basketball teams. Powerful high school football programs began adding a game or two to their fall schedules that included top-ranked teams from out-of-state. Massillon played comparable schools from the Washington, DC area and Pennsylvania. De La Salle High School, located in the northern California suburban community of Concord, played games in Hawaii and Los Angeles during its unprecedented 151-game winning streak that began in 1991. In 2003, ESPN-2 picked-up high national television ratings when it carried a game in which the De La Salle Spartans handily defeated Evangel High School, a perennial Louisiana powerhouse from Shreveport. The Spartans' unprecedented winning streak finally came to an end in September 2004 on a visit to the Seattle area, where they were beaten by Bellevue High 39–20.

The increased profile of high-school football and basketball was greatly intensified by national recruiting efforts of major college teams, encouraged by a host of state and regional publications that described the talents of top high-school players for the benefit of interested coaches/recruiters. The emergence of the Internet added a plethora of web sites devoted to recruiting, turning the recruiting season into another competition followed intently by dedicated fans. The pressure on top prospects to "commit" to a particular institution became intense, but some of these hot high-school commodities found that they could have their moment in the sun by holding a press conference announcing their decision that attracted local and even national television coverage.

College football recruiting necessarily dealt in large numbers, with up to 25 players being signed by each college to a binding national "letter of intent" early in February. The basketball recruiting process, however, was much different. Because just one or two top players could turn a so-so college basketball team into a contender for national honors, the recruiting process for star high-school players became hopelessly intense. It is estimated that a major college team will spend $25,000 simply recruiting one player during a multi-year process that often begins when a hot prospect is a high school freshman or sophomore. During the summer months, high-profile "all-star" or "blue-chip" camps are held in several locations, often sponsored by basketball shoe manufacturers, to which top players are invited and where they can showcase their skills before a small army of college recruiters. During the Christmas break, top high school teams from around the country convene on such cities as Las Vegas where large, extravagant tournaments are held, sponsored by shoe companies. These tournaments are considered convenient recruiting venues where college recruiters can watch a bevy of top prospects.

Not only do parents and high-school coaches become involved in the recruiting process, but often summer team coaches and even "street agents," with their own agendas that often include making money one way or another, seek to insinuate themselves into the players' decision-making process. In 1990, two journalists, Alexander Wolff and Armen Keteyian, described the excesses and corruption in the recruitment process in *Raw Recruits*, describing how college coaches and talented high school players are caught up in a crass and corrupt system, with illegal payoffs rampant, that brings only shame upon the lofty values ascribed to intercollegiate athletics. If the continued high number of NCAA investigations and penalties are any indication, the nasty business of recruitment has only gotten worse since this revealing book was published. Those who have looked closely at high school sports programs have noted that many ethical ambiguities exist, and that many of the oft-mentioned ennobling benefits are little more than self-serving hokum.[6]

Conflicting Views of Youth Sports

Increased emphasis on channeling young boys and girls into structured youth sports programs – with the tendency to force a young athlete to concentrate upon one sport very early in his or her development – has generated considerable attention in the past few decades. The issues are many and complex, but essentially millions of parents have apparently come to believe that such programs are important for their youngsters' development. As of 2005, an estimated 12 million youths between the ages of eight and 13 currently take part annually in adult-supervised team instructional and competitive team-oriented programs in football, basketball, softball, hockey, soccer, and baseball. In addition to this, hundreds of thousands of preteens and teenagers are enrolled in instructional programs for individual performance sports, such as gymnastics, ice-skating, skiing, swimming, golf, and tennis, and for-profit instructional programs have emerged in many cities that offer youngsters individualized instruction in basketball and baseball. Structured developmental programs for children began to appear in large numbers immediately following the Second World War, and in recent decades have become increasingly prominent. During the presidential election of 2000, the political predilections of "soccer moms" became a source of considerable speculation; that there were sports-oriented mothers in such large numbers was in and of itself significant.

The standard rationale for the existence of these youth programs is that they provide a wholesome activity supervised by caring adults who teach youngsters the fundamentals of a sport and supervise games in a manner that is believed to provide a wholesome learning experience. These programs, often with a national affiliation to a parent umbrella organization, claim to teach the values of good sportsmanship, teamwork, and wholesome competition along with the fundamentals of a sport.

Organized team play for youths was virtually unheard of until the YMCA began to field teams early in the twentieth century, but those programs never gained substantial traction. Following the Second World War, however, conditions were right for the growth of youth programs. Postwar prosperity put discretionary income in the hands of middle- and upper-middle-class parents who wanted to provide their children with opportunities that they had been denied by exigencies of depression and war. Lurking behind the youth movement were cold war fears of communist subversion, as well as the informal social and economic power exerted within American society by large corporations. Parents wanted to instill in their offspring the values they deemed necessary to survive and succeed in this conflicting time: competition, patriotism, acceptance of authority, discipline, and the importance of cooperation and teamwork. In the age of "organization man", it seemed that parents wanted to instill in their children the values of working within a group, interacting effectively with others, and accepting authority – precisely those interpersonal skills that they believed would enable them to succeed as adults within large corporate or governmental organizations. It has often been said that in America access to the boardroom of major corporations is a journey that begins in the locker room. Whether consciously or unconsciously, parents of the postwar era sought a controlled environment in which their children would learn the skills that would enable them to succeed as adults – long after their youth playing days were over. For them, future professional and business success indeed would grow out of the many lessons learned in youth sports.

The result was a series of programs, such as Bobby Sox Softball, Pop Warner Football, and Little League Baseball, whose agendas were set on a national (or even international level). Little League Baseball set the standard. Founded in Williamsport, Pennsylvania, in 1939 by a local factory worker, Carl Stoltz, the program added franchises throughout the United States during the immediate postwar years, and by the 1950s more than a million boys ages nine to 12 participated. The organization soon had leagues in Canada, Europe, Latin America, and the Far East. In 1948 it held its first Little League World Series in Williamsport, and in 1953 the championship game was described on ABC radio by Howard Cosell; 10 years later, Roone Arledge televised the finals on his *Wide World of Sports* on ABC-TV. Growth continued, and by 1980 there were more than 16,000 local leagues serving some 2.5 million youths. The pattern of growth leveled out during the late twentieth-century, but more than three million young boys (and a sprinkling of girls) participated each year in Little League.[7]

Emphasis throughout was upon adult (mostly parental) control, with each local league governed by a commissioner who enforced the rules and policies established at the international administrative offices in Williamsport. The emphasis was upon emulating the atmosphere in which major league baseball operated. Before the season began, players "tried out," were evaluated by team coaches, and "drafted" to teams. Players not drafted were deemed "free agents" and could be signed by any team willing to take them on. Standardized uniforms were issued, with teams normally assigned names emulating the major leagues (Tigers, Cubs, Twins, Astros, etc.); practices were conducted several times a week; team strategies were taught by the coaches; and games played in miniature stadiums complete with outfield fences, manicured grass infields, dugouts, scoreboards, a public-address announcer, and bleachers from which parents and siblings could watch. At season's end, a league "all-star" team was selected to enter a district tournament with the distant goal of being one of a handful of teams to move through state and regional tournaments in order to qualify for the Little League World Series in August.

While various informal polls taken by this author over the years indicate that a vast majority of Little League graduates look back on their experience as positive, the idea of establishing adult supervision over youthful play produced many skeptics. The litany of criticisms are familiar: the preteen years, it is frequently said, are a time when children should learn to organize their own play and not have the spontaneity of play subverted by meddling, if well-meaning adults. Although Little League literature emphasizes the primary goals of participation and learning, in reality many team adult "managers" play the best players in the most important positions, stationing the least adept for the humiliating minimum number of required innings in right field where few balls are likely to be hit. The pressure to win sometimes places players under emotional stress, and parents and other onlookers often exhibit antisocial behavior, loudly criticizing the umpires, the coaches, even the young players. The national news occasionally reports a physical attack by an angry parent upon an umpire, and many leagues have had to deal with brutal verbal assaults on the coach by an irate parent who felt the coach did not recognize his/her child's athletic ability. Although some obsessive parents seem determined to revel in athletic achievement through their children, some apparently envision their child's experience in Little League (or other youth sports) as leading to a college scholarship, perhaps a professional career. These expectations – clearly those of a distinct but nonetheless recognizable minority of

parents – sometimes leads to unrealistic expectations and hypercritical comments toward their children, especially after they strike out with the bases loaded or drop a pass in the end zone. Over the years, some leagues have had to make as a condition for a child to participate that parents attend a pre-season clinic that teaches the basics of good sportsmanship and proper fan behavior.

Former major-league pitcher Jim Brosnan, writing in 1963, summarized the case against Little League and implicitly, other adult-supervised youth programs. He complained that the organization "is rapidly becoming a status symbol replete with too much aggressiveness, competitiveness, and emphasis upon winning. It is not a world the kids make." He found the spring "draft" and the declaring of non-drafted players as "free agents" repulsive. "Putting a price on a boy's ability is obviously adult business." He found from personal observation that many coaches did more damage than good: the coaches "are usually on the lower part of the sociological curve, guys who can't quite make it in their business, marriage, or social life. So they take it out on the kids." That Little League required the maintenance of team won–lost records and standings, selected post-season "all-stars," and sponsored a set of elimination tournaments resulting in a World Series,

Figure 16.1 Little Leaguers emulate the professionals with a "high five" after a game on a Harlem field in New York City in 1990. Founded in Williamsport, Pennsylvania, in 1939, Little League grew rapidly in popularity after the Second World War. Despite its many critics, Little League expanded worldwide and its August Little League World Series attracted teams from Latin America, Europe, and Asia. © Robert Maass/ CORBIS.

Brosnan contended, was an absurdity that contradicted the organization's professions about the primacy of participation rather than victory. "Preadolescents are immature and can't be expected to live up to the physical and emotional guidelines of older children – parents included. Winning games should not be given the importance that exists in the Little League age group."[8] Brosnan's critique, and others like it, had no discernable impact, and parents found in the program much to like. Some parents even envisioned that their youngsters would someday be like Joey Jay, a pitcher who was the first of many Little Leaguers to progress to playing for a major league team. In 1955, Jay signed a contract with a hefty $20,000 signing bonus with the Milwaukee Braves and enjoyed a lengthy major-league career, complete with All-Star Game appearances. A visitor to the Little League Museum in Williamsport is confronted with a large exhibit that features former Little Leaguers who became major-league stars.

Pop Warner Football has never approached the size or impact of Little League, but it nonetheless offers a national program including post-season tournaments. Its critics are even harsher than those of Little League, contending that pre-adolescent boys, in the midst of their important growth phase, are not prepared to handle the physical shocks of tackling and blocking. Critics are especially harsh in their treatment of coaches who revel in the physical aspect of the game and conduct ruthless practice sessions, supposedly in emulation of well-known college or professional coaches. Pop Warner games, of course, include young boys in full pads knocking each other around while coaches direct the action from the sidelines. Uniformed referees blow their whistles and cheerleading squads of young girls lead parents and siblings in organized cheers. Each December, teams from around the country that have won their regional tournaments convene in Florida for championship "bowl games."

The motivation of parents in providing their youngsters with intensified sports opportunities run the gamut – hoping to provide an enjoyable and educational experience, learning the values of good sportsmanship, fostering an appreciation of the importance of teamwork, creating an ability to confront challenges, dealing with both success and defeat, and overcoming awkwardness and lack of coordination. Clearly, the great majority view the games in a healthy manner, but virtually every league each year has to deal with some unfortunate situation involving adult behavior or attitude. One embarrassing problem has been aggressive coaches who seek out overage players and slip them onto their squad. On occasion, a few parents visualize in their offspring potential dollar signs and future headlines: All-American college players, Olympic champions, professional players. Such parents might enroll a seemingly talented child in a local clinic run by former coaches or players who provide individual instructional sessions and even year-round intensive training programs as a supplement to team activities.

With parents willing to spend substantial sums on their child's athletic development, a cottage industry has developed in urban areas that features year-round instructional programs in many sports, including basketball, baseball, softball, volleyball, tennis, and gymnastics. Among the most extensive were programs for young girls in gymnastics, ice-skating, and swimming. Over the years, the more adept girls are encouraged to move into intensive advanced programs, complete with regional and national competitions that lead, in some instances, to college scholarships. It was out of this structured program that America's women Olympic gymnasts emerged – highly skilled athletes often no more than 15 or 16 years of age. In order to achieve this pinnacle of success, parents sometimes have to neglect their daughter's education and social development and have her live apart from her family to be near a nationally acclaimed coach. There she is expected to adhere to rigid diets, put in many hours of arduous training each day, and generally not have the opportunities of a normal teenage social life. Many promising gymnasts, of course, also suffer severe injuries in the process.

In her revealing book on the training of America's elite gymnasts and figure-skaters, journalist Joan Ryan describes the heavy sacrifices required of elite women athletes who have aspirations of Olympic and international acclaim. Because of the influence of television, American viewers focused on the American gymnasts during the Summer Olympics and on figure-skaters during the Winter Olympics. For those few athletes who win gold medals, the reward is great – product endorsements, speaking engagements, special exhibitions, television talk-show appearances, all of which produce substantial income.[9]

But the long trail leading to such heights is fraught with dangers and littered with disappointed, disillusioned, even clinically depressed young women. Ryan's book is a chilling revelation of a system in which young girls are subjected to manic coaches who demean and berate them, seeking a psychological edge to spur them on to greater achievements. Ryan details a sordid story of eating disorders brought on by expectations that women gymnasts must weigh well below 100 pounds in order to perform at the highest level. This expectation has to be achieved by following a near-starvation diet of 1,000 calories a day, sometimes supplemented by forced vomiting and the indiscriminate use of laxatives and diuretics. If the girls were permitted to develop naturally into young women, their breasts and hips would preclude their performing the physical tasks demanded of Olympic champions. In 1976, the average age of the American Olympic gymnastics team was 18 and the girls averaged 106 pounds; by 1992, the team average had fallen to 16 years of age and the girls averaged just 83 pounds each.

Such unrealistic and debilitating demands, Ryan charges, result in stunted growth, the postponement of puberty, weakened bone structure, and psychological disorders. She concludes that "our national obsession with weight and our glorification of thinness, have gone completely unchecked in gymnastics and figure skating." The result, Ryan charges, is nothing less than "child abuse," with much of the blame falling

> on the coaches and parents. . . . There is no safety net protecting these children. . . . Child labor laws prohibit a thirteen-year-old from punching a cash register for forty hours a week, but that same child can labor for forty hours or more inside a gym or an ice skating rink without drawing the slightest glance from the government.

Unfortunately, her exhaustive research into the two sports revealed a serious problem:

There have been enough suicide attempts, enough eating disorders, enough broken bodies, enough regretful parents and enough bitter young women to warrant a serious re-evaluation of what we're doing in this country to produce Olympic champions. . . . It is time the government drops the fantasy that certain sports are merely games and takes a hard look at legislation aimed at protecting elite child athletes.[10]

Ever since it became a sport of importance during the 1970s, women's professional tennis has seen many a child prodigy rise rapidly to the top of the ratings, only to suffer from debilitating injuries or psychological burn-out. Despite the demise of such outstanding players by the time they reach voting age – Andrea Jaeger and Tracy Austin come readily to mind – parents have repeatedly enrolled their sons and daughters in programs designed to produce national junior champions, with an eye toward major professional prize money. Capitalizing upon that instinctive parental urge to encourage their prodigy children to national fame and fortune was former Marines officer Nick Bollettieri. In 1980, he opened his elite Bollettieri Tennis Academy in Bradenton, Florida, and soon top teenage players were living away from home in order to perfect their tennis skills. His several hundred students, average age 15, moved to Bradenton and lived in dormitories, taking their high-school courses on site and practicing several hours each day under the supervision of teaching professionals specially schooled in the Bollettieri method. The several hours of tennis instruction each day were supplemented by vigorous physical conditioning and diet counseling. Bollettieri's objective was to make each student who completed his program capable of competing for a college scholarship; his publicity even held out the possibility of a professional tennis career.[11] Among his former star pupils were high-profile tour professionals André Agassi, Monica Seles, Anna Kournikova, Tommy Haas, Jim Courier, and Maria Sharapova.

During the 1990s, Bollettieri merged his program with the growing sports management behemoth IMG, which expanded the curriculum to several sports. By 2000, the campus in Bradenton offered specialized instruction all year round in baseball, basketball, soccer, and golf, as well as tennis. In fall 2004, IMG academies had some 650 full-time students enrolled at an annual cost of $40,000. When individualized instruction was added – especially for aspiring tennis players and golfers – the annual cost approached $70,000. From September through May, the students worked at their individual sport at least four hours a day, six days a week, engaged in rigorous physical conditioning, and attended classes at the International Performance Institute, which taught sports psychology concepts to improve individual performance.[12]

The IMG program merely took to a sophisticated level the trend across the United States whereby prospective top athletes at an early age are channeled by parents and coaches into concentrating their efforts on a single sport. The theory is that competition for team slots is so intense at large high schools that only a year-round commitment can assure a place on the team. The result often is that as early as the seventh or eighth grade, prospective high-school athletes select one sport upon which to concentrate, spending much of their free time working on their skills in various privately sponsored leagues and under the supervision of tutors or clinic instructors. Summers for these aspiring athletes (and their parents) are given over to attending specialized camps and playing on club teams in competitive leagues. The pressure for excellence has even led to youth sports teams – hockey, soccer, softball, volleyball, basketball, wrestling, for example – hiring professional coaches rather than relying on the varying skills of volunteer parents. Teams in the 10–16 years age bracket might enter several tournaments each year, entailing long trips, even by airplane, to compete in high-level competitions that bring together teams from many states. In many instances, the young athletes find themselves devoting much of their free time to one particular sport.

This trend has raised many questions about forcing young teenagers into making sports choices much too early. The pressure to specialize in one sport, of course, is a by-product of the emphasis placed on winning. Such pressure has naturally been interpreted by various experts as both good and bad, depending on the psychological makeup of the individual. What cannot be disputed, however, is that organized play has replaced unorganized, spontaneous play by youngsters. Instead, the organizing, coaching, and specialized athletic tutoring of young athletes has become a profitable new industry in the United States. IMG is only the most visible example of what has become a substantial enterprise. Left to their own devices, children are natural cross-trainers, dabbling in many sports and related activities. But the growth of organization and adult supervision has undercut spontaneity. Many experts decry the overemphasis at an early age upon concentration on one sport. "We've got tennis kids who can't hop, skip or jump," laments David Donatucci of the IMG Performance Institute.

> We've got golfers who if you threw them a ball, they'd duck – basketball players who can't swing a baseball bat. We've got some kids who are really good at their sports, but if you looked closer, you'd be surprised at how unathletic they really are.[13]

Golf's Golden Age: Arnie, the Super Mex, and the Golden Bear

The importance parents placed upon getting their children into the "right" sports program in part reflected the growth of televised sports and the big dollar signs it dangled before the sports viewing public. Not only did traditional team games grow in popularity in the latter half of the twentieth century, but other sports did so as well. This led to the emergence of celebrity status for standouts in sports that heretofore received only limited attention. Golf and tennis, for example, underwent fundamental changes in their images, becoming new examples of how the democratizing spirit of sports was taking hold. After the spectacular reign of Bobby Jones during the 1920s, professional golf went into the doldrums during the Great Depression and languished during the Second World War. During the postwar years it slowly began to nudge its way back onto the sports pages. Babe Didrikson Zaharias went on a tear on the limited women's circuit, but only the most dedicated of golf fans paid much attention. Men's golf was largely dominated by Ben Hogan and Sam Snead, who had become promising new figures on the tour during the late 1930s but had to put their game on the shelf for military duty. Over the years, they conducted several epic duels in major tournaments. "Slammin' Sammy" was known for his long, straight drives off the tee, and between 1942 and 1955, he won seven grand-slam events while compiling a career number of 81 PGA tournament victories. Famous for his graceful, natural golf swing, Snead is unfortunately remembered as one of the all-time great golfers who never managed to win the US Open. Throughout his lengthy career, Snead played in 37 Opens, and although he came close several times, never closed the deal.

Ben Hogan was born in Texas in 1912 and raised in near-poverty by his widowed mother. He began caddying at age 12 to help with family finances. A self-taught golfer, he was naturally left-handed, but could not afford the more expensive left-handed clubs, so he taught himself to play from the right side. The slender 5' 7", 135-pound Hogan joined the PGA tour in 1938 and by the eve of the Second World War had become a player who exhibited every indication of future greatness. After returning from military service, "Bantam Ben" became the leading golfer of his era on the strength of his dedication and endless practice. Not a natural golfer – he frequently said there was no such thing – he simply willed himself to become better through hard work. At a time when most top golfers practiced lackadaisically between tournaments, Hogan hit balls daily until his hands bled; at night he took his putter home and practiced on a rug. When his finely honed swing was called "natural" by admirers, he muttered, "There is nothing natural about a golf swing."[14] In 1948 Hogan won the US Open and seemed destined for the same golfing pantheon as Bobby Jones.

That potential was almost snuffed out on February 2, 1949, when his automobile was hit head-on by a Greyhound bus along a foggy West Texas highway. He saved his wife's life by throwing his body across hers at impact but suffered life-threatening injuries, including broken ribs and a crushed pelvis. Rushed to an El Paso hospital, he nearly died from blood clots that formed following surgery to repair his broken bones; doctors had to tie off veins in his legs to prevent clots from reaching his heart.[15]

Golfing experts believed that he would never play professionally again, but Hogan was determined to return to the tour. He played his first tentative round in December of the same year as the accident, and the following summer, his painful legs wrapped in elastic stockings, he won another US Open in dramatic fashion in a three-way playoff with George Fazio and Lloyd Mangrum. In 1951, he made it two straight Open championships at the fabled Oakland Country Club in Michigan. Despite having to fight constant leg pain and numbing fatigue as a result of the accident, in 1953 at the age of 41 he enjoyed his best year, winning his only British Open and Masters along with his fourth and last US Open.[16]

Although Hogan is considered one of golf's greatest players, his reserved personality and lack of charisma never made him a popular champion. All business on the course and withdrawn off it, Hogan was greatly respected as a skilled golf craftsman, but he never received public adulation. Hogan approached his golf with analytical precision, played round after round without a smile erasing the steady grim visage of concentration, and changed golf forever with his intense approach

THE DEMOCRATIZATION OF SPORTS

that combined endless practice with a seriousness of purpose and attention to even the most minute nuances of the game. Even his books on how to play the game (especially *Five Lessons: The Modern Fundamentals of Golf*, 1957) were laden with detailed, highly technical language that left most weekend-golfing readers more confused than enlightened. For this intense man born and raised in poverty, golf was a tough business, never a game.

Perhaps the distance Hogan maintained between himself and the press and the fans explains the enthusiastic, even exuberant embrace with which they greeted a young, brash golfer whose enthusiasm for the game was infectious. Arnold Palmer burst upon the close-knit world of professional golf just as Hogan and Snead began the inevitable slide as they approached the age of 50. A native of the small town of Latrobe, located 30 miles east of Pittsburgh, Palmer grew up working and playing on a nine-hole golf course where his father was combination greens-keeper, teaching professional, and clubhouse manager. Palmer carried 175 pounds on a husky 5' 11" frame appropriate for a college halfback. He smacked the ball with unusual ferocity out of a cramped, unconventional swing that probably made the stylistic Snead and perfectionist Hogan cringe. He lunged at the ball with a curious swipe that was part home-run swing and part hockey slap-shot; nonetheless, Palmer hit the ball with a raw power seldom seen on the tour. After punishing the ball long off the tee, he characteristically walked at a rapid pace down the fairway, hitching up his pants, which always seemed about to fall to his knees, puffing on a cigarette, talking rapidly, and gesturing to his caddy. He then quickly lined up his next shot, tossed his cigarette aside with a flourish, and with a minimum of pre-shot ritual, exuberantly smacked his next shot. Once on the green, unlike many professionals, he spent a minimum time reading the line. Then he awkwardly hunched over the ball in a uniquely familiar but unorthodox style, his body language indicating he was superbly confident that the ball was going into the cup. [17]

Palmer's every motion and expression told the gallery that he loved to play the game and that he especially relished a situation where he had to make a difficult shot under extreme pressure on the last day of a major tournament. His come-from-behind "charges" became a thing of golfing legend. One of his hallmarks was hitting almost impossible shots out of difficult lies onto the green to save a par or make an improbable birdie – going around or through trees, cutting across long and treacherous out-of-bounds territory as a shortcut to the green, or blasting out of high rough. Palmer brought an air of excitement to the game that it had never before witnessed, and in so doing, he did more to popularize golf with the American people than any other individual in the history of the game.[18]

Palmer came late to the professional tour. After playing collegiate golf for three years at Wake Forest College and serving three more in the Coast Guard, he did not turn professional until 1955 at the relatively advanced age of 25. He immediately became a favorite of the gallery. Between 1955 and 1973, Palmer won 60 PGA events including seven majors, and during the 1980s he won 10 more tournaments on the Seniors Tour. Although his overall record falls somewhat short of other top players, he undoubtedly was the most popular golfer of the twentieth century, if one considers Tiger Woods to be primarily a twenty-first century golfer. Very long (if not always straight) off the tee and sensational on the green, especially in pressure situations, Palmer popularized the game for the average American. Good-looking and personable, a small smile curling his lips, he brought a sense of excitement to the game that even Bobby Jones did not accomplish. His charisma was infectious, and the galleries that followed him were enormous. Unlike the staid, reserved crowds of an earlier day, his fans were loud and exuberant, urging him onward. "Charge!" they'd shout as he began one of his patented final rounds seeking to overcome the targeted leader. Dubbed "Arnie's Army," his legions of fans transformed the culture of American golf, stripping away its elitist pretensions. In 1981, when Palmer left the PGA circuit to join the Seniors Tour, one close observer attempted to pinpoint the Palmer mystique.

> There's no word or phrase that quite describes what it is that Palmer transmits to the galleries. He is one of a kind – different and special. He keeps reinventing the game of golf. Maybe someday he will invent a way to describe himself and what he does to the multitudes of people who come out to watch him.[19]

Some like to say that Palmer's long-time run saved golf from stultifying boredom, while others argue that he changed it forever by democratizing a sport that had for so long been associated with the upper strata of American society. Beyond question, one of Palmer's most important contributions was that he lured to the game millions of fans who had never before paid much attention. Wherever he played, thousands of fans, many of whom had never even played the game, came out to watch and cheer as part of the volunteer "army." After Palmer appeared on the scene, television ratings for golf events soared, especially when he was in contention on the last two days of a big tournament, which was more often than not.

Arnold Palmer popularized golf for middle-class and even blue-collar America, and as a result of his widespread fame, millions decided to take up the game. Just as Palmer's game began to slip slightly in the late sixties, he had to make room at the top of the heap for a stocky Mexican-American from Dallas, Lee Trevino. The exuberant, seemingly carefree Trevino arrived at the top echelon of professional golf in a way that simply shouted: "The American Dream." Born to a single parent in 1939, he was raised by his mother, who worked as a domestic, in a small wooden shack that had a dirt floor and lacked electricity or plumbing. Even as a youngster, Trevino found a way to take advantage of his circumstances. His family's modest dwelling stood near a suburban Dallas golf course, and he learned to scavenge for errant balls for resale along the course's perimeter and by diving in a small lake. By the time he was 16, playing on public courses, Trevino carried a handicap of two. When he returned to Dallas in 1960 after a four year stint in the Marines, he hustled games at public courses and earned a decent income on side bets. He learned that players better than he would often choke when money was on the line. Possessed of excellent feel for a golf club, he began to challenge (and distract) opponents by promising to play right-handed with left-handed clubs. Then he taught himself to play an entire course with a taped quart-size Dr Pepper bottle; he later claimed that he never lost a bet during a three-year stint playing with the taped bottle.[20]

Self-taught and super confident in his skills – "I'll tell you what pressure is," he once remarked. "It's playing a big guy for five bucks and you only have two in your pocket" – in 1966 he entered and won the Texas Open and then began to play on the PGA tour, winning $20,000 his first year. Encouraged by that seemingly enormous income, Trevino played well in 1967 and was named PGA Rookie of the Year. In 1968 he won $50,000 in early tournaments and was marked as a future star, a promise that he fulfilled at the US Open in Rochester in June when he blistered the course to tie the course record of 275 while holding off challenges from Jack Nicklaus and Bert Yancy. He gladly pocketed the $30,000 winner's check. He also set a new Open mark by shooting under 70 in all four rounds. His greater triumph, however, was the bond he established in that tournament with the fans, who cheered his every shot and engaged in continuous back-and-forth commentary with the animated golfer that prompted many a laugh. Shouts of "Whip the Gringo!" came out of the predominantly Anglo gallery, and indeed he did. With Arnold Palmer shooting an uncharacteristic 301 for a 59th place finish, Arnie's Army seemed to morph into "Lee's Fleas." Still, many sportswriters considered Trevino's victory a lucky moment, at least until he won the Hawaiian Open later in the year. Trevino pocketed $132,000 that year. He went on to have a solid year in 1969 by winning the Tucson Open and more than $100,000, and in 1970, although winning just one tournament, nonetheless ended the year as the leading money winner on the tour with $157,000 in prize money. With those hefty purses deposited in his bank, Tevino cracked, "You can call me a Spaniard now. Who ever heard of a rich Mexican?"[21]

In 1971, Trevino was at the top of his game, and in a space of just 23 days he won three tournaments – the US Open for a second time, the British Open, and the Canadian Open. At season's end, the awards came pouring in to the man who made galleries laugh and shout, including being named PGA Player of the Year. Long before the word "diversity" had entered the American political lexicon, the gifted sportswriter Dan Jenkins had early captured the importance of Trevino as a symbol of racial and ethnic achievement. Touching upon the cultural significance of Trevino's arrival at the top of the leader board, Jenkins lauded the "Super Mexkin":

> There he was out in the midst of all of that US Open dignity with his spread-out caddy-hustler stance and his short, choppy public-course swing, a stumpy little guy, tan as a tamale, pretty lippy for a nobody, and, yeah, wearing those red socks.

In naming him its "Sportsman of the Year" for 1971, *Sports Illustrated* noted that Trevino had "added a new dimension" to the staid sport of golf because he was "a common man with an uncommon touch."[22]

While Palmer and Trevino made golf fashionable among the American working and middle classes – the number of weekend hackers increased during the 1960s and the 1970s by several million – the greatest golfer of the era never quite connected with the general public, at least not until the autumn days of his playing career. Jack Nicklaus's achievements, however, clearly overshadowed Hogan,

Figure 16.2 During the 1960s, Arnold Palmer and Jack Nicklaus dominated men's professional golf. Their many duels made for great drama and drew millions of new fans to the game. Here the Golden Bear watches Palmer tee off to start an 18-hole playoff in the 1962 US Open held at Oakmont near Pittsburgh. The two had ended the regular four rounds tied at 283. Nicklaus won the playoff by three strokes. © Bettmann/CORBIS.

Palmer, Trevino, as well as the best of the foreign players, Gary Player. In a career that spanned four decades of serious competition – he won his last major at the 1986 Masters at the age of 46 – Jack Nicklaus won a record-setting 18 major tournaments among the 70 tour championships he captured. His career average was 71 strokes per round, and he was the leading money winner on the tour eight times and runner-up six times. The PGA named him its Golfer of the Year on five occasions. He won each of the four major tournaments at least three times; no other golfer has ever won each twice. Nicklaus was known for his length and accuracy off the tee, his ability to hit his irons with the accuracy of a Ben Hogan and, once on the green, for his unerringly accurate putting, especially in clutch situations.[23]

From the time Nicklaus appeared on the national scene, he demonstrated a rare combination of brute strength and incredible finesse. A cautious player who always played the percentages, Nicklaus crafted each shot with the intent of minimizing errors and maximizing his opportunity to score. When compared to the electrifying Palmer and Trevino, his cautious, calculated, cerebral style of play never resonated with fans. Early in his career, as he began to challenge Palmer for golfing's supremacy, he was frequently criticized by fans for his aloofness and detached style of play.[24]

Over the years, Nicklaus learned to ignore the many sharp comments, even boos, that came from Arnie's Army, who disliked him for knocking their hero off his pedestal. As Frank Deford wrote long after the chill between the two highly competitive men had waned, "No matter how badly Nicklaus beat Palmer, he didn't win affection. Esteem, respect, admiration – yes. But affection? No."[25] His consistently excellent play slowly won over the fans, who began to call him the "Golden Bear" after his blond mop of hair and large physique. When he stomped the field at the Open in 1965 and won by a shocking nine strokes, even Bobby Jones could only watch in awe: "He plays a kind of game with which I am not familiar," the former Grand Slam champion ruefully commented.[26]

Born and raised in Columbus, Ohio, Nicklaus had access to the venerable Scioto Country Club at an early age. Nicklaus was an all-around athlete in high school, starring in basketball, football and track, but his major talent was smacking a golf ball long and straight – he was routinely driving 275 yards from the tee when he entered his teens. At age 13, he scored a 69 from the back tees at Scioto, a distance of 7,095 yards. His parents poured substantial money into his golfing education, and at age 16 he rewarded them by shooting a 64 in the first round of the Ohio Open and went on to win the tournament over a field of top adult amateurs and professionals. As a junior and senior high school student in Columbus, he won 15 junior tournaments, including the Trans-Mississippi Championship. At age 17, he qualified for the US Open, and in 1959 he became the youngest player in 50 years to win the US Amateur Championship. In 1960, while still an amateur, he finished just two strokes behind Arnold Palmer at the memorable US Open tournament at Cherry Hill.

Although Lee Trevino correctly observed that the one iron was the bane of most golfers, it was one of Nicklaus's favorite clubs, especially in crunch time. At Balustrol in the 1967 British Open, he hit his one iron into a brisk wind 238 yards onto the green, close enough to sink his putt. That magnificent shot under extreme pressure enabled him to eclipse the 276 course record set in 1948 by Ben Hogan. In 1972, he assured his US Open victory at Pebble Beach when he hit the ball 250 yards onto the 17th green, and at the 1975 Masters he drilled the ball 246 yards to the 15th green to give him a one-stroke advantage over Tom Weiskopf and Johnny Miller. Many golf experts considered this the single best shot of his career. While all of the great names of golf up to this time had won less than 10 major tournaments during their careers, Nicklaus won 18. It was thus only fitting that he won his final major – the 1986 Masters – by exceptional shot-making, shooting an eagle on the 15th hole and birdies on the next two to edge Greg Norman and Tom Kite by a single stroke.[27] In a fitting testimony to Nicklaus's lifetime achievement, Tiger Woods has frequently said that his major career goal is to exceed Nicklaus's 18 major championships. At a celebration of the first one hundred years of American golf in 1988, a distinguished panel of journalists and golf figures voted the Golden Bear the "Golfer of the Century." That Nicklaus beat out Bobby Jones, Ben Hogan, and especially Arnold Palmer, was a tribute to his excellence if not to his popularity.

Billie Jean Sparks a Revolution

It was inevitable that the gathering social and political storm that came to be called the women's rights movement would spill over into the major professional sports in which women prominently participated. The drive for equal treatment by the Ladies Professional Golf Association and within the United States Tennis Association (USTA) was a long, difficult struggle. By the dawn of the twenty-first century, the battle was not yet won, but the distance yet to be traveled was substantially shorter than it was three decades earlier.

In the early years of the twenty-first century, women's professional tennis in many ways had outstripped the men's tour in popularity among serious tennis fans. With the men now hitting the serve at 140 mph and higher, their game was largely reduced to blazing service aces or serves weakly returned for a put-away volley. Major technological advances in racquet design put a weapon in the hands of the men that enabled them to hit powerful, precise ground strokes as well as thunderous serves. During the 1970s and the early 1980s, however, men's tennis enjoyed its pinnacle of popularity, with such exquisite American shot-makers as Arthur Ashe, Jimmy Conners, and John McEnroe taking on the best of the world. The 1980 finals at Wimbledon, when McEnroe lost in a close match to Sweden's Bjorn Borg, was a classic test of delicate shot-making and court strategy that lasted for over three hours. It was decided in a dramatic, extended fifth set, 8–6. Borg still used a wooden racquet and the tempestuous McEnroe an early version of the aluminum racquet, but those racquets were soon rendered obsolete by oversized styles made of various exotic fibers and high-tensile metals that encouraged the power game. During the 1990s, southern Californian Pete Sampras dominated men's tennis – many experts consider him the greatest American male player of all time – but upon his retirement the American tennis contingent faded. Although Las Vegas native André Agassi won his share of championships, and was still playing at a high level at age 35, he never quite became the dominant force that Americans had come to expect. Consequently, interest in the men's game faded along with the decline of the American men before a host of challengers from South America and Europe.

Such was not the case for the women's tour, which saw several Americans ranked at the highest levels – the Williams sisters, Jennifer Capriatti, Lindsay Davenport, and emigres to America Martina Navratilova and Monica Seles. Although these women faced many challenges from talented Europeans, they nonetheless competed with frequent success. More importantly, they played a much more interesting and compelling game than the men. Although the women's game revealed much greater emphasis upon power than had previously existed, it nonetheless produced many superbly played, competitive matches with long and arduous rallies and breathtaking shot-making that made for an exciting spectacle.

These women not only played superb tennis, but they received television ratings comparable to the men. Tennis fans flocked to their matches. As a consequence, prize money become comparable between men and women, and the top women were rewarded with lucrative endorsement opportunities. The complaints of unequal treatment that had been commonplace during the 1960s and the 1970s were seldom heard anymore in the women's locker rooms. They had essentially reached a point where they were as important, if not more so, to the health of the game of professional tennis as the men.

Such certainly was not always the case. During the 1960s, the male-dominated United States Tennis Association held tournaments for both men and women, but the women were given short shrift. Fewer tournaments were held for women than for men, and at those major tournaments, such as the US Open, where men and women both competed for championships, the prize money for the men was four or five times higher than for the women. Seldom did the women get to play on center court, except for semifinal and final matches, and even their locker rooms were smaller and less well appointed. Most women players accepted this discriminatory situation, but not the top woman player of the era, Billie Jean King. Born in 1943 to working-class parents, King grew up in Long Beach where she learned to play tennis on the city's public courts. After she won several junior tournaments, she received instruction from Alice Marble. At age 18, she had already enjoyed top junior rankings and won her first match at Wimbledon.[28]

By 1965, King was the top-ranked American women, popular with tennis fans for her aggressive, attacking style. In 1966, she defeated Maria Bueno for the Wimbledon title and followed up in 1967 with her first of four US Open championships. During more than a decade as a leading player, King won 72 tournaments, and despite the relatively low prize money, she managed to win more than $2 million during her professional career. She won six Wimbledon singles titles, along with 14 other Wimbledon championships in doubles and mixed doubles. Her career was all the more remarkable because of several surgeries she had to endure to repair chronic knee problems. During the 1970s, the intense battles she had with the rising young star Chris Evert did much to stimulate widespread interest in women's tennis.

King was never shy on or off the court. She assumed the leadership of the women professionals, and during the late 1960s began to criticize the male-dominated USTA for its discriminatory policies toward women. In 1970, she created headlines when she called a press conference to denounce the fact that as the Italian Open champion she received a prize of just $1,500, while the male champion earned $12,500. In 1972, Australian Stan Smith walked away from Wimbledon with $12,500 and King just $4,800, and later that same year, she earned $10,000 by winning the US Open, but her male counterpart, Ilie Nastase, cashed a check for $25,000. Such discrimination, King charged, was unacceptable. As president of the new organization she had helped establish, the Women's Tennis Association, King suggested a boycott was the likely solution. But her outspoken leadership had its effect, and the disparity in prize money was steadily reduced. Throughout 1973, the total amount of prize money paid to women on the tour totaled $900,000, but 20 years later that amount had grown, along with the popularity of the women's game, to more than $25 million.[29]

King's dual role as the top woman player in the world and the outspoken advocate of improved conditions for women's tennis made her the logical target of self-styled tennis hustler Bobby Riggs. Born in 1918, Riggs had enjoyed considerable success in his tennis career, including winning the 1939 Wimbledon and US Open titles. What should have been his best years were wiped out by tournament cancellations during the war; in the late 1940s, he played many exciting matches with the best of the day – Don Budge, Pancho Gonzales, and Jack Kramer – losing far more than he won. Long after his skills had faded, Riggs continued to earn a living by promoting exhibition tennis matches, often placing a large bet on himself in the process. Always known as a brash, outspoken hustler, Riggs drew national attention to himself when he announced that the demands by King and other women for equal treatment were a sham, stating that he could easily beat any of the top-ranked women despite his 55 years. This was preliminary to his announcement that he had conned some California promoters into putting up $10,000, winner take all, for a match between himself and the outstanding Australian, Margaret Court. Although most experts thought Court, at the top of her game and in great physical condition, would easily defeat Riggs, she played tentatively and permitted a good case of nerves to undercut her normal power game. She lost in straight sets, and Riggs crowed long and loud.

Riggs then set his sights on King, who had earlier rejected his challenge. Once Court had been decisively beaten, however, King felt she had no alternative but to respond. She had come to believe that not to play Riggs would hurt the stature of women's tennis. *Time* magazine noted that King was "the personification of the professional female athlete that Riggs loves to taunt." Once the match was scheduled for the Houston Astrodome, the hype machine went into high gear. ABC-TV Sports agreed to dispatch Howard Cosell to cover the match, and the newspapers were filled with pre-match hyperbole. Riggs told the press,

> Hell, we know there is no way she can beat me. She's a stronger athlete than me and she can execute various shots better than me. But when the pressure mounts and she thinks about 50 million people watching on TV, she'll fold. That's the way women are.

He even added, for good chauvinistic measure, that his forthcoming victory would "put Billie Jean and all other women libbers back where they belong – in the kitchen and the bedroom."[30] Many experts agreed and picked Riggs to win the match of the "libber vs. the lobber." Jimmy the Greek set the odds with Riggs an 8–5 favorite. Gene Scott, a ranked tennis player at the time, concurred, giving expression to the many sexist emotions current at the time:

> You see, women are brought up from the time they're six years old to read books, eat candy and go to dancing class. They can't compete against men. They're not used to the competition. Maybe it'll change some day. But not now.[31]

On the evening of September 20, 1973, some 35,000 people paid their way into the Astrodome, and ABC estimated its television audience at 50 million. It would be one of the most significant sporting events of the era. *Sports Illustrated* senior correspondent Curry Kirkpatrick aptly described the scene as having "all the conflicting tones of a political convention, championship prizefight, rock festival, tent revival, town meeting, Super Bowl and sick joke." As soon as the match began, however, it was evident that the joke was on Riggs. From the first few points, King took charge, easily handling the many lobs, drop shots, and other assorted sliced-and-diced trick shots that Riggs threw at her. She pounded the ball deep to the corners, took to the net to put away easy volleys, and won in three easy sets, and – much to the anguish of hustler Riggs – she claimed the winner-takes-all $100,000 prize. "Seldom has there been a more classic example of a skilled athlete performing at peak efficiency in the most important moment of her life," Kirkpatrick concluded. The "battle of the sexes" ended with King noting, "It helped women stand taller."[32]

This bizarre spectacle might have proven little, if anything, but it gave women's tennis a terrific boost in credibility. As King's career faded over the next several years, she was replaced in the limelight by Chris Evert, a stellar baseline player, and the hard-hitting left-handed Martina Navratilova, who defected at the age of 18 from communist Czechoslovakia in 1974 and became a US citizen in 1981. Throughout much of the 1970s and the 1980s, the names of "Chris and Martina" evoked instant images of their many closely contested matches, especially in Grand Slam tournament finals. The contrast in their style of play tantalized tennis fans; Evert seldom rushed the net, preferring to hit her crisply placed shots from the baseline for winners, while Navratilova's high-energy game of serve and volley provided startling contrast.

Navratilova played almost 20 years at the highest level, her ranking never falling below number four. Her dedication to physical fitness set a new standard for women tennis professionals, one that would inspire the Williams sisters among others: she ran several miles a day and worked out in a gym as well as subjecting herself to hours of intense tennis practice. Her regular traveling entourage included a physical trainer and a nutritionist as well as a tennis coach. Navratilova won a total of 18 Grand Slam events and 167 singles tournaments overall, a number that almost surely will never be topped. Evert, possessed of a classic two-handed backhand shot, which she could zip down the line or cross-court with stunning accuracy, won 101 tournaments, of which 16 were Grand Slams (including seven at Roland Garros Stadium outside of Paris where the red clay was to her particular liking).

Their competition provided jaded sports fans with a rare view of what true sportsmanship could and should be: fierce competition on the court, mutual admiration and friendship off it. "Martina revolutionized the game by her superb athleticism and aggressiveness, not to mention her outspokenness and candor," Evert said upon Navratilova's retirement.

> She brought athleticism to a whole new level with her training techniques – particularly cross-training, the idea that you could go to the gym or play basketball to get in shape for tennis. She had everything down to a science, including her diet, and that was an inspiration to me. I really think she helped me to be a better athlete. And then I always admired her maturity, her wisdom and her ability to transcend the sport. You could ask her about her forehand or about world peace and she always had an answer. She really is a world figure, not just a sports figure.[33]

The Comeback Kids

When it comes to real-life stories of individuals overcoming extreme hardship or misfortune to accomplish great things, the American people cannot hear enough. This alone helps explain the surge in popularity of cycling during recent years. For nearly a century, serious bicycle racing was one of the least popular of America's many so-called minor sports. No one paid much attention to the few stage races that were held each year – such as the Coors International Bicycle Classic or the World Professional Road Race – until two Americans surprisingly came to dominate a sport that the French take as seriously as Americans do their baseball and football. Not only did the amazing exploits of Greg LeMond and Lance Armstrong reveal inner strength and determination to overcome life-threatening crises, but they also came to dominate the sport and the event that the French have long considered to be their own national sports passion – the Tour de France.

Greg LeMond, born in California and raised in Reno, made headlines in 1986 when he became the first American ever to win the Tour de France. LeMond began his riding career as a teenager in Reno in 1976 and became so wrapped up in his training that he withdrew from Wooster High School; one of his favorite stories is of a teacher who admonished him for skipping class to train on the vast open expanses of Nevada highways: "Greg, you'll never make anything of yourself riding a bike." Ultimately, he earned his high-school diploma via correspondence while establishing himself in international racing events, winning the world championship in Buenos Aires in 1979, the youngest person ever to do so. He turned professional in 1981 and became a leader on the European circuit, finishing third in his first Tour de France in 1983, the first American ever to finish in the top three. In 1985, he finished the 2,500-mile race in second place. When he defeated Frenchman Bernard Hinault the following year, his victory produced a nasty personal disagreement between one-time friends and teammates. Thereafter, the more than 20 million Frenchmen who lined the roads for the 23-day Tour did not know whether to cheer or jeer the American. After all, this upstart American was winning their equivalent of the Super Bowl.[34]

His victory in 1986 was cheered, of course, but more than anything else it was considered a rare anomaly. A freak accident, when he was accidentally riddled by a shotgun blast by his brother-in-law while hunting wild turkey in northern California, prevented him from defending his crown in 1987. Emergency surgery saved his life, but several pellets remained in his abdomen. During his slow recovery, he had to undergo an emergency appendectomy and then leg surgery for a serious infection. While knowledgeable cycling people conceded that his racing days were over – no sport is more demanding on the body for such an extended period of time than multi-stage, multi-day road racing – LeMond returned to his vigorous training regimen in 1988 and surprised the world when he won the 1989 Tour de France. He did so in dramatic fashion, taking the lead in the 2,000-mile race only in the final moments of the last stage through the streets of Paris, edging out the home-country favorite and two-time champion Laurent Fignon. Only a supreme effort bolstered by fierce determination enabled the 28-year-old American to make up a seemingly insurmountable 50-second lead on the final stage into Paris. Riding at a record speed averaging 34 miles per hour, the fastest ever for a time trial stage in the Tour, he edged out Fignon by a mere eight seconds. It was the closest finish in the history of the tour. LeMond repeated as champion again in 1990, but then his body began to give out on him and, suffering from a rare disease that reduces the ability of the muscles to burn sufficient protein, he retired from active racing in 1994.[35]

The ambivalent feelings the nationalistic French people evidenced when the American hijacked their national sport turned into downright obnoxious behavior when a brash, blunt, and arrogant Texan, Lance Armstrong, began his almost incomprehensible feat of winning seven straight Tour de France races in 1999. This amazing feat proved to be too much for French cycling fans, who not only saw their top racers fall far behind the powerful American, but also suffered the terrible embarrassment of having one of their best, Richard Virenque, disqualified for doping. As Armstrong piled up his impressive string of victories, French fans insinuated that he had to be benefiting from drugs. Otherwise, how could he sustain his incredible charges up the steep mountain roads where he picked up valuable minutes on the *peloton* (the pack)?[36] Even after he retired in 2005 after victory number seven, various French publications sought in vain to besmirch his incredible achievement.

The truth was simply that Armstrong's unprecedented domination of the world's greatest stage race was a combination of personal determination, a passion for exhaustive workouts, and the miracles of modern medicine. Born in Plano, Texas, in 1971, Armstrong became a local legend as a teenager for his domination of triathlons, winning at age 17 the national sprint triathlon (1,000-meter swim, 15-mile bike ride, 3-mile run). He then decided to concentrate on biking full time, moved to Austin, and soon achieved international notice. In 1991, he won the US National Amateur and in 1993, having turned professional, won $1 million by capturing the American triple crown; that same year, he also won a stage of the Tour de France, reputedly the youngest rider ever to do so. His dedication to long, punishing workouts had already become the talk of the international racing set, but so too was his expressive personality that contrasted with the traditional bland personalities that had dominated European racing.

Armstrong was incredibly blessed with inherent physical attributes that contributed to his success as a cyclist: tests taken when he was 16 at the Cooper Clinic in Dallas, home to the aerobics movement, revealed that he had an almost superhuman capacity to absorb and utilize oxygen, and that his propensity for producing lactic acid – the substance that produces the burning sensation in one's lungs and legs when winded or fatigued – was incredibly low. Journalist Alan Shipnuck summarized Armstrong's public persona after he captured the Tour du Pont: "Armstrong's bionic legs, savvy in the saddle, and steel will may have dazzled his competitors, but it is his charisma and matinee-idol good looks that charmed the two-million plus fans."[37]

On the first day of October, 1996, everything seemingly was breaking his way. He had signed a $1 million endorsement deal with Nike and a $2 million contract to ride with the French Cofidis cycling team. As he looked forward to the 1997 Tour de France, Armstrong seemed destined for fame and fortune. He had purchased a large villa in a gated community in Austin and plotted his months of workouts in preparation. Incredibly strong and with unmatched endurance, Armstrong now set his sights on winning the big one – the Tour de France – exuding all of the confidence of a 25-year-old athlete possessed of enormous strength and endurance:

> "I was a world-class athlete with a mansion on a riverbank, keys to a Porsche, and a self-made fortune in the bank. I was one of the top riders in the world and my career was moving along a perfect arc of success." He felt "bullet proof."[38]

That euphoric, even cocky, attitude changed quickly the next day. On October 2, 1996, Armstrong was diagnosed with an advanced stage of testicular cancer. He immediately underwent surgery to remove a cancerous testicle, but a few days later further tests revealed that the disease had metastasized to his lungs and brain. The oncology team at Indiana University told Armstrong that he had 14 tumors that threatened his life and that he had no better than a 40 percent chance of survival. His physicians put him on a debilitating program of aggressive chemotherapy and radiation that stretched over three months. During this grueling ordeal, he lost 15 pounds of muscle (his body fat was measured at just 2 percent), but between treatments in the hospital, despite his weakened condition, he continued to ride his bike, often struggling to complete just a few miles. His treatments, however, proved effective, and by the summer of 1997 tests revealed no signs of malignancy. Armstrong returned to riding. By January 1998, he was once more riding between six and seven hundred miles a week at his typical frenetic pace. The loss of weight, he discovered, had made him both leaner and lighter, a body perfectly suited for the steep climbs of the French Alps that are a crucial part of each Tour de France. An exercise physiologist who tested Armstrong found that he had gained 6 percent of power despite the loss of 15 pounds of muscle. The reason was simple: he spent many months preparing for the Tour de France by riding between five and seven hours a day up and down the steep Pyrenees, always putting in a minimum of 30 hours of these arduous workouts each week. Physiologist Ed Coyle put Armstrong's superior strength into stark perspective when he noted that Armstrong could ride a bike at the high rate of 32 mph for a full hour's time; the average well-conditioned college-age male can keep up that pace for only 45 seconds. "For the first 10 seconds they're great. After about 20 seconds they think they're gonna die. After 40 seconds they throw up."[39]

When Armstrong's illness was first announced, the Cofidis team coldly refused to renew his contract, and so the once-again healthy Armstrong signed with a team sponsored by the United States Postal Service. His return to the Tour was vindication of his bravery in fighting his cancer with the most aggressive treatment possible and a vivid testimony to his tenacity in regaining a level of competitive fitness. When he won the first stage of the race, the short eight-kilometer Prologue time trial, leaving the Cofidis team in his wake as he proudly donned the *maillot jaune* – the yellow jersey that signifies the Tour leader – he readily admitted that he enjoyed immensely that moment of personal revenge. He then proceeded to stun the world with his endurance, and in the crucial mountain stage where even the greatest of riders have been reduced to absolute exhaustion, Armstrong pulled ahead of the *peloton* by an incredible six minutes. His performance was almost beyond comprehension, prompting one journalist to write in awe, "It was so remarkable that everything we thought we knew about human athletic achievement needs to be reconsidered."[40]

Armstrong's achievement naturally produced suspicions that he was doping. As he sped through the mountains in 1999, eclipsing long-established records, the speculation and insinuation in the French press began. Some articles even speculated that his chemotherapy, which had produced severe nausea for three months and shrunk his muscular body by 15 pounds, had somehow mysteriously given him some secret drugs that enhanced performance! He has flatly denied ever using such substances and has been tested hundreds of times with always a negative result. French racing officials, frustrated that an American – of all foreigners! – dominated their national sport, have gone the extra mile in attempts to implicate Armstrong for using drugs; of course, the sport has been rife with such activities for years and those allegations were to be expected. Not that Armstrong has not attempted to meet his skeptical French critics halfway – he learned to speak French and purchased a house in the French countryside to facilitate his pre-race training. During races, he was constantly barraged by angry cries from French fans hollering "Dope! Dope," but he said such taunts only inspired him to pedal faster.[41]

In retrospect, Armstrong realized that the attacks were part of the larger cultural and political divide between the American and French cultures: "I lived in France, and I love the country." He took special note of the fact that after a massive drug scandal during the 1998 Tour, in which he did not participate, many top non-French riders did not train in France for fear of police surveillance:

> Not me. While other riders were afraid of being harassed by the police or investigated by the governmental authorities, I trained there every day. France was the most severe place in the world to be caught using a performance enhancer, but I did all my springtime racing in France, and conducted my entire Tour preparation there. Under French law, the local police could have raided my house whenever they wanted. They didn't have to ask, or knock. . . . If I was trying to hide something, I'd have been in another country.

But even his residency did not assuage the criticism. "Nothing works," he once sighed. "They told me to speak French. Told me to smile, sign autographs. Didn't work. It's just not going to happen."[42]

Although Greg LeMond and Lance Armstrong became famous Americans, treated like conquering heroes when they returned from their triumphs in France, the sport of bicycle racing enjoyed only a moderate boost among Americans. Significantly, *Sports Illustrated* selected LeMond for its prestigious Sportsman of the Year award in 1989 and Armstrong in 2001. But for deep-seated cultural reasons, bicycle racing never became more than a niche sport in the United States, attracting a relatively small but enthusiastic number of participants. Although the Tour de France received substantial coverage when the Americans were in contention, bicycle racing within the United States normally existed far below the radar screen of the media. Nonetheless, an estimated 12 million Americans, mostly between the ages of 18 and 50, had taken up biking in a serious fashion by the onset of the twenty-first century, donning the festive outfits, shaving their legs (to prevent painful treatment if the rider should fall and scrape the skin), wearing aerodynamic helmets, and riding long distances with their local biking clubs, perhaps entering races on weekends. Perhaps some have been inspired by the example of LeMond and Armstrong, but most have taken up the sport as an enjoyable and effective means of physical conditioning. One seldom sees an overweight biker whiz by.

Viva America! America's Soccer Women

Football for Americans means heavy pads, grunting linemen, artistic quarterbacks and slippery ball carriers. Football for the rest of the world means, of course, a free-flowing game in which scoring is low and the cultural significance high. Soccer is a game that most Americans have long ignored, even scorned as dull. Few Americans ever bothered to learn the intricacies of soccer: deft footwork, precise timing, and complex defensive and offensive maneuvering. Thus, the spectacular rise to an improbable World Cup by the American women's national soccer team in 1999 gave sports fans everywhere reason for good cheer and hope. That the United States had a women's team competing at this rarified level was viewed by most observers as a vindication of the passage of Title IX 27 years earlier. What that legislation did was produce a groundswell of youth programs that slowly developed a large and strong pool of talented women athletes from which to build a world-class competitive team. In 1972 when Title IX slipped virtually unnoticed through Congress, only one in every 27 girls participated in any form of organized athletic team activity. By 1999, one in every three girls had such an opportunity. Not only did Title IX create a large pool of skilled athletes to stock college and professional teams, but those athletes in turn spawned an enormous base of young female athletes who sought to emulate their achievements. As Donna Lopiano, executive director of the Women's Sports Foundation and formerly athletic director for 16 years at the University of Texas, commented, "People don't realize it takes ten to fifteen years to make a professional athlete."[43]

The march of the American women to the title was followed closely by the American people, feeding off of the heavy media coverage provided for the first time for an American soccer team. That the final rounds of the competition were held in major American venues added to the interest, of course, but a quarter-century of youth soccer programs had led to the formation of an American team with the talent to challenge the world's best. Major corporate sponsors helped ignite interest, and 79,000 wildly enthusiastic fans turned out at the Meadowlands near New York City for the Americans' trouncing of Denmark in the opening round; observers noticed that the lines of young girls at the ice-cream stands were much longer that those of adults at beer concessions. Fans came with their faces painted red,

Figure 16.3 Mia Hamm's triumphant soccer career inspired a new generation of young girls to take up the game. In 1999, she and her fellow teammates won the World Cup in dramatic fashion over China, greatly elevating the importance of women's sports and soccer in the eyes of the American public. She is pictured here on the attack in the 2003 World Cup against Sweden in a match at RFK Stadium in Washington, DC. © Paul J. Sutton/Duomo/CORBIS.

white, and blue, carrying homemade banners and waving American flags. National television coverage was intensive, and late-night host David Letterman repeatedly talked about the team as it moved toward the finals in Pasadena.

That the team had won the gold at the 1996 Olympics in Atlanta had stirred public interest. But now, public attention was focused upon the team's self-effacing star, forward Mia Hamm. The daughter of a military family, Mia had moved many times as a child but had always demonstrated a penchant for sports; at age 14 she attracted national attention for her play on an Olympic developmental soccer team. When the US National team coach Anson Dorrance first saw her outmaneuver older and more experienced players with her deft dribbling and lightning-quick moves, he was stunned: "This skinny brunette took off like she had been shot out of a cannon," he later commented. At 15, she became the youngest player ever named to the national team, and then she followed Dorrance to the University of North Carolina, where he was the head coach. She led the women's team to four consecutive NCAA championships from 1989 through 1992, and by the time she was 25 was recognized as the world's best woman soccer player.[44]

At 5' 5" and 125 pounds, Hamm was not the most imposing player on the field, but her fierce determination and superb coordination and quick reflexes enabled her to rise to the top of her sport. At age 19, she was the youngest player on the US national team that won the world championship in 1991 in China. Hamm emerged as a youthful star on the team, adept at dribbling and ball handling with either foot, using her strength and speed, together with a low center of gravity, to barrel past unsuspecting defenders. But she was also blessed with the innate gift of being able to decoy defenders and goalies when she got near the net. She had the extra sense of how to get the ball past defenders into the net. As she explained,

> A great finisher can analyze in a split second what the goalie is doing, what surface of the ball to use, and then put the ball in exactly the right spot. It's an ability to slow down time. You don't actually shoot any faster than other players do, but you process a lot more information in the same time.

But after saying that, she added her usual self-effacing caveat: "I'm still working on that."[45]

That unexpected world championship in 1991 marked the arrival of the United States as a world soccer power, but when the team returned home they were met by an apathetic nation. Only a few people – family, friends, and a few US Soccer Federation members – met the airplane. No televison cameras, no crowd of cheering fans welcomed the team home. *Sports Illustrated* gave the triumph one brief paragraph notice, and David Letterman and Johnny Carson neglected to call. "No one offered us endorsements, money, or fame," Hamm wrote in her autobiography, but "that is not why we play. . . . Look back at the pictures of all the young faces on that 1991 team, awash with smiles, the glow of a world championship, and athletic glory in its purest form, and it becomes obvious why we play."[46]

By 1999, however, that apathy had turned into national acclaim. Hamm and her teammates had become the center of vast media coverage. By the time they powered their way to the final match against China in Pasadena, the American people were following their games closely. Forty million persons watched the game on television, and a capacity crowd of 92,000, including President Bill Clinton, filled the Rose Bowl, the largest crowd in history to watch a women's athletic event. By this time, Hamm was the world-record holder for the number of goals scored in international competition and she had become the symbol for the emergence of the American woman athlete, her name and picture now proudly used by such heavyweight companies as Gatorade and Nike. But unlike so many top male athletes, Hamm refused to talk about herself and her achievements, insisting instead that she was merely part of a great team composed of many star athletes. "People don't want to hear that I'm no better than my teammates," she once groused to a reporter. "They want me to say, 'I'm this or that,' but I'm not. Everything I am I owe to this team."[47]

The championship game against China proved to be all that those who paid up to $1,000 to scalpers hoped for. It was a defensive struggle marked by a relentless Chinese defense pitted against the attacking Americans. Midway through the second half, Michelle Akers, the 33-year-old midfielder, had to be taken to the locker room suffering from extreme dehydration and a minor concussion that had exacerbated her ongoing battle with chronic fatigue syndrome. After the 90-minute regular time had expired, the two teams battled through two 15-minute overtime periods, setting up the dramatic penalty-kick shootout anticlimax. It is the type of situation that soccer players hate – the goal tender now confronted by five free kicks from just 12 yards out from the goal. The American goalie, Briana Scurry, guessed right on the third Chinese kick and made a leaping fingertip stop, setting up the winning goal by Brandi Chastain. When her kick zipped into the corner of the net giving the United States an improbable 5–4 victory, the large crowd erupted in cheers and the triumph was proclaimed across the land the next morning with front-page headlines.

Although there were plenty of heroes to go around – Chastain, Akers, Scurry, Julie Foudy – it was Hamm who captured the public's imagination. She was soon seen flipping Michael Jordan in a judo move in a popular Nike advertisement to the musical accompaniment of "Anything You Can Do, I Can Do Better." Nike soon thereafter named the largest building on its sprawling Portland campus after her. As Nike CEO Phil Knight explained, "We've had three athletes who played at a level that added a new dimension to their games. That's been Michael Jordan in basketball, Tiger Woods in golf, and Mia Hamm in soccer." Hamm continued to play the game for five more years with the same ferocity and intensity that had propelled her to the top of the sports' world. She increasingly devoted her time to her foundation, which supported programs to create opportunities for young women in sports and to foster research in bone-marrow disease (which had tragically taken her older brother Garret's life at age 28). Some of the funds that she contributed to her foundation came from her endorsement of a Soccer Barbie doll, which was programmed to say, "I can kick and throw like Mia Hamm." As Hamm explained, "When I was little Barbie rode around in a red Corvette and lived in a mansion. I sure didn't relate to that. Soccer Barbie is a lot more realistic."[48]

The fact that Mia Hamm and her fellow soccer players had captured the imagination of the American people and helped lure hundreds of thousands of youngsters into youth soccer programs was a strong indication of the changes that had occurred within the structure of American sports. Although the enormous power of television kept a national focus on the major men team sports of basketball, football, and baseball, beneath the surface the popularity of participant sports continued to grow. No one person and no team better symbolized that democratic spirit than Mia Hamm and the US national women's soccer team's capturing of the World Cup before an exulting nation.

Epilogue

During the latter half of the twentieth century the American people expanded and refined their roles as participants, dedicated fans, and casual spectators. New forms of mass media greatly expanded the seeming importance of sports. Television extended to the American public unprecedented opportunities to watch college and professional games. New customs and rituals naturally took hold – health clubs and city recreational programs encouraged participation of people of all ages in a myriad of individual and team activities. Sports betting, fostered by the influence of Las Vegas and the Internet, grew to an immense (but unknown) size and influence, and in a new twist to the American penchant for gambling, fantasy leagues attracted millions of weekend wannabe "sports executives" who created their own dream teams, drafting, buying and selling players at will. Sports bars and restaurants, mixing alcohol and casual food fare with a bank of television sets, became entertainment fixtures in communities large and small. ESPN and its several imitators provided national and regional sports coverage in repetitive and excessive detail, while national radio network gossip and sports talk shows fanned the fires with news, analysis, and commentary, information and ideas that were turned into white heat by local stations devoted exclusively to sports talk. By the twenty-first century, these more-traditional forms of communications were further supplemented (or subverted) by an endless array of Internet sites providing tidbits of sports information that featured endless rounds of second-guessing, rumors, and wild speculation.

Americans are not just spectators; millions are also fans of their favorite professional or college teams. Spectators watch sports for their entertainment value, sometimes in person but much more often by clicking their television remote control. When the game is over the casual spectator moves on to other entertainment, but the true sports fan – passionately committed to the fortunes of one team – is left either consumed with a sense of elation or dejection. Fan(atic)s have their own special personal bond with one team; more often than not it is the team that they embraced as a child because that was the team their father rooted for. Being a true lifelong fan is much like belonging to a political party – it is almost tribal in its meaning, the bonds are often strained but never broken, and loyalty is unquestioned even during the depressing depths of the inevitable losing seasons. In my native state of Ohio, for example, an estimated 25 percent of the 13 million residents on a given autumn Saturday closely monitor the fate of the Ohio State University Buckeyes on television or radio. On home-game days, 100,000 ticket-holders, bedecked in their scarlet and gray outfits, jam Ohio Stadium located along the picturesque Olentangy River on the edge of the sprawling Columbus campus. Coaches at Ohio State have come and gone over the years, but the one true mea-surement of their tenure has been how many times they defeated rival Michigan in the Big Game, a tradition that began in 1897 and one that shows no indication of ending anytime in the new century. During the days leading up to game-day Sat-urday, Buckeye fans follow the latest injury reports and news bulletins regarding the team's practices. Journalistic assessments of the opposition are read with the utmost seriousness. Internet sites are probed for even more detail, along with con-fident predictions and the wildest of rumors. Everyone in Ohio, it seems, is smarter than the coach, especially when it comes to picking the starting quarterback or second-guessing a crucial play call. Sundays are given over to a detailed review of the previous day's game; blow-out victories produce little joy but plenty of criti-cisms for style points; defeats lead to anguished wailing and infinite criticism of the head coach, even of the university president for picking such a dumb lout. Follow-ing the near-inevitable trip to a post-season bowl game after yet another winning season, OSU fans intently follow the news of the mid-winter recruiting wars, and 40,000 turn out for the annual inter-squad game that ends the ritual of spring practice. By June, Buckeye fans are awaiting the arrival of the annual college foot-ball pre-season magazines and their assessments of the college teams. Opening game kickoff is just around the corner.

Every major college football and basketball team has its diehard loyal fans, and the same is true of professional teams. In certain instances, as with the Green Bay Packers, the team becomes not only a community treasure, but one that is shared with the entire state of Wisconsin. Fans everywhere worry before each upcoming contest, cheer loudly during the game, grouse about every fumble and incom-plete pass, and suffer temporary depression after the inevitable losses. Defeat at the hands of the traditional rival in the Big Game – e.g.: UCLA–USC, Florida–Florida State, Oregon–Oregon State, Alabama–Auburn, Ohio State–Michigan – is unthink-able but somehow the dejected fans manage to live to cheer another day.

Journalist Warren St John explored the phenomenon of the super-fan in his book about the dedicated thousands who travel far and wide in an unorganized armada of crimson-bedecked recreational vehicles that converges upon the site of the University of Alabama football game each autumn weekends for 48 hours of serious tailgating. The dedication to the Crimson Tide cause of these individuals is striking. During the 1999 season, St John encountered many Alabama fans who had seldom (if ever) missed a game for 25 years or more. During the season, St John came across a funeral parlor director who offers (with many takers) specially designed Crimson Tide caskets, tastefully bedecked in crimson and white (complete with the block A letter inscribed inside the lid. Another fan, carrying an electronic pager linking him to a Nashville hospital where he hoped to receive a heart transplant, defied instructions and traveled far beyond prescribed distances to watch his favorite team play. He would rather risk missing his transplant than miss the Tide's game! St John also related one conversation with a quiet gray-haired couple in their sixties who proudly confessed they had not missed an Alabama game for 15 years:

> So the reporter idly asks what sort of things they've given up in pursuit of the Tide. Let's see, the man said in a soft Southern drawl. We missed our daughter's wedding. You what? We told her, just don't get married on a game day and we'll be there, hundred percent, and she went off and picked the third Saturday in October which everybody knows is when Alabama plays Tennessee, so we told her, hey, we got a ball game to go to. We made the reception – went there soon as the game was over.[1]

Studies by psychologists and sociologists have contributed to our understanding of the dedicated sports fan.[2] These studies suggest that the decline in the durability of the American family and the rise of a mobile population has prompted many Americans to seek a new form of social and community identification by closely associating themselves with a particular team. Urbanization, technology, and geographical mobility have undercut traditional societal bonds, and so many individuals have found it reassuring to align themselves with a group of strangers who also accept the same symbols – logo, mascot, coach, players, fight song, team colors. Most often that allegiance is to a single team, but it can also be a statewide identification with a sport, such as high school basketball in Indiana or football in Texas. In a few instances the phenomenon has extended to the entire United States, as evidenced by the widespread adulation expressed over the 1980 US Olympic hockey team and the 1999 women's World Cup soccer team. Although academics have posited many theories, often couched in humanist, Marxist or feminist perspectives, the truth is that even the most dedicated ("rabid") fan puts his or her team loyalty into a healthy perspective. For the great majority of fans, as Warren St John discovered in the makeshift RV city that magically coalesces for Alabama football games, the pleasure gleaned from the process temporarily removes the individual from the daily pressures of everyday life, providing an emotional "time out." Individuals get an opportunity for personal renewal by immersing themselves in a pleasurable social activity with like-minded individuals who come from a wide variety of backgrounds (many are not even Alabama alumni). Victory, of course, is eminently better than defeat, but everyone knows that after every loss there is always another game to be played, another season around the corner that promises glorious victories yet to be cherished.

Over the years, many students and friends have asked my predictions on what the future of American sports holds in the twenty-first century. Historians, perhaps, are not good prognosticators since their eyes are firmly set upon the past, but they are good readers of long-term trends, and the prominent trends that I foresee have been discussed in detail in the preceding pages. It seems likely that participation in games and sports will increase among people of all ages in the future. In an effort to reverse the distressing national trend toward obesity, more and more Americans will join in the exercise phenomenon, encouraged not only by government agencies, employers, and their personal physicians, but also by the vast amount of monies spent on advertising by health clubs and sporting goods companies. The popularity of youth sports will continue to provide an important facet in the lives of most families with children, especially those with parents who understand the importance of exercise and competition in the physical and social development of their children. In particular, the number of girls and women who compete in organized sports will continue to grow, demonstrating that Congress's enactment of Title IX in 1972 was a fortuitous act of statesmanship.

Because of the pervasive influence of television, the most popular spectator sports will remain as they are today: football, baseball, and men's basketball will constitute the "big three." Those games have such a long and rich tradition that it would take cataclysmic events to reduce their importance in the grand scheme of things. Big-time college athletics has become an enormous economic dynamo that will not shrink. Renewed efforts at reform (emulating the Carnegie and Knight commissions) will come and go, but have little impact upon the well-entrenched power structure that controls the enterprise. It is altogether likely that the number of universities and colleges willing to pay the high cost of competing in Division 1-A football will slowly dwindle. Several "mid-major" football conferences, such as the Mid-American, Sun Belt, and Western Athletic, may be forced to retreat to a lower division, or perhaps create their own version of the Bowl Championship Series, so that they can realistically compete for a national championship. Despite its inherent inequities and failings, the current Bowl Championship Series, dominated by six self-anointed conferences, will continue in some form, preventing the establishment of a post-season playoff that nearly every football fan wants. Professional baseball will continue to attract plenty of attention and attendance, but the game's relative lack of action makes for bland television fare, and that will prevent it from ever regaining its perch as the most popular sport in America. Stock car racing, which has enjoyed a significant rise in popularity in the past 30 years, will continue to increase the size of its national audiences as it builds additional new racetracks outside the South. NASCAR will continue to grow unless it proves unable to control its internal operations and cannot prevent defections or the creation of a rival circuit. The so-called niche sports – hockey, soccer, tennis, golf – will continue to enjoy their current levels of popularity with small segments of the population, but will never rise to challenge the big three (or big four if NASCAR can sustain its current growth rate).

Sports at all levels will have to deal with repeated threats to their integrity. The growth of Internet sport gambling sites poses a serious problem that seems impervious to government regulation; the potential for fixed games will increase as a result. In some instances, the interest in gambling (such as with the fantasy leagues) can supersede the importance of the games themselves. Similarly, the ability of illicit drug makers to stay ahead of the testing laboratories will mean that the integrity of games will be increasingly compromised unless effective measures are mounted to counter the rise in steroid use. The recurring incidents of lawlessness by male athletes – heavily reported by the national media – will remain a nagging problem for sports officials. Violent and antisocial behavior by leading athletes produces dramatic headlines that are usually soon forgotten, but until American society can find ways to curb similar behavior among the population in general, the news media will continue to report upon a tedium of physical assaults, the occasional use of firearms, and drug abuse by athletes. I have little hope that the shame of intercollegiate athletics – especially recruiting violations, academic fraud, and financial excesses – will end. The NCAA and its campus clients – the athletic directors and coaches – have created a lucrative, closed world unto themselves within the realm of higher education; the overweening influence of money generated from the box office and television rights will prove too great an obstacle for any substantive reform effort to be successful. With the pots of money getting ever larger, the incentives to cheat in recruiting and in determining eligibility are likely to increase proportionately.

Such weighty matters, however, pale in comparison to the many benefits sports provide the average American. During the past decade my wife and I have taken to the roads of America, ostensibly in search of information for my other academic research interest in the history of the evolving role of the American small town, but our travels have also impressed upon me the pervasive influence of sports. Visits to hundreds of college and university campuses reveal the centrality of sports to those educational institutions, with large football stadiums and basketball arenas dominating the campus landscape. At an upscale restaurant in Columbus in May, the band regularly breaks out into the Buckeye Fight Song, "Across the Field," and in New England, it seems that every other child and adult is wearing a Red Sox hat or shirt. In rural Florida, while enjoying a leisurely lunch at a local spot festooned with stock car memorabilia, we witness a near-brawl break out among several young men, seemingly over differing opinions on the right carburetor settings. All across the land, in the Dakotas or in Texas, in Oregon or in Tennessee, the local newspapers and radio air waves are filled with local sports news and information, and in the evenings the skies are alive with the lights of adult softball and youth baseball fields. Far into the night the quiet of our downtown St Louis hotel in February is punctured by the raucous sounds of several hundred Detroit Red Wing fans who arrived en masse on Thursday in preparation for a Sunday afternoon face-off with the St Louis Blues, and a revisit to that same hotel in June found us surrounded by thousands of red-shirted Cardinal fans in town for the weekend intra-league series with the Yankees; most of those happy folk with whom we talked had driven in excess of 150 miles to take in a mid-season game.

And so it goes today throughout the United States, where sports have become an integral aspect of the daily ebb and flow of American life. As has oft been written, America is truly a land of many contrasts and cultures. From Miami to Seattle, from San Diego to Boston, sports provide a common thread, even a common language, for a diverse people and a far-flung nation made up of many peoples, cultures, regions, and locales. To understand America, as the French scholar and writer Jacques Barzun once wrote, foreigners must first learn the language and culture of baseball. His oft-quoted observation was an exaggeration undoubtedly, but he was definitely onto something. To paraphrase and expand his comment, to understand modern America, it would be wise to understand and appreciate the influence of sports.

Notes

Preface

1 See the *Journal of Sport History*, published by the North American Society for Sport History since 1973. For the early histories and related studies of the broad expanse of American sports history and America's embrace of sports, see Foster Rhea Dulles, *America Learns to Play: A History of Popular Recreation, 1607–1940* (New York: Appleton-Century, 1940); John R. Betts, *America's Sporting Heritage, 1850–1950* (Reading, MA: Addison-Wesley, 1974); John R. Lucas and Ronald A. Smith, *Saga of American Sports* (New York: Lea and Febiger, 1978); James A. Michener, *Sports in America* (New York: Random House, 1976); Benjamin G. Rader, *American Sports: From the Age of Folk Games to the Age of Televised Sports* (Englewood Cliffs, NJ: Prentice Hall, 1983, 5th edition, 2003); Douglas N. Noverr and Lawrence E. Ziewacz, *The Games They Played: Sports in American History* (Chicago: Nelson-Hall, 1988); Elliott J. Gorn and Warren Jay Goldstein, *A Brief History of American Sports* (New York: Hill and Wang, 1993), and Steven A. Riess, *Major Problems in American Sport History* (Boston: Houghton Mifflin, 1997). Richard D. Mandell, *Sport: A Cultural History* (New York: Columbia University Press, 1984), provides a global perspective on the history of sports from the ancient Greeks to the modern Olympics. Students might begin their study of the phenomenon of American sports with Michael Mandelbaum's thought-provoking *The Meaning of Sport: Why Americans Watch Baseball, Football, and Basketball and What They See When They Do* (New York: Public Affairs Press, 2004).

1 Games the Colonists Played

1 Richard Holt, *Sport and the British: A Modern History* (Oxford: Clarendon Press, 1989), p. 15.
2 Nancy L. Struna, *People of Prowess: Sport, Leisure, and Labor in Early Anglo-America* (Urbana: University of Illinois Press, 1996), pp. 17–20.
3 Winton U. Stolberg, *Redeem the Time: The Puritan Sabbath in Early America* (Cambridge, MA: Harvard University Press, 1977), p. 48; and Robert W. Malcolmson, *Popular Recreations in English Society, 1700–1850* (Cambridge: Cambridge University Press, 1973), p. 10.
4 Stolberg, p. 48.

5 Malcolmson, p. 45.

6 Holt, p. 17.

7 Malcolmson, p. 48.

8 Holt, p. 30.

9 Malcolmson, p. 43.

10 Holt, p. 20.

11 Malcolmson, p. 43.

12 Holt, p. 18.

13 Dennis Brailsford, *Sport and Society: Elizabeth to Anne* (London: Routledge, 1969), pp. 53–8; Malcolmson, pp. 34–40.

14 Malcolmson, p. 41.

15 Ibid., p. 34.

16 Elliott J. Gorn and Warren Jay Goldstein, *A Brief History of American Sports* (New York, Hill and Wang, 1993), pp. 9–10; Struna, p. 21; Malcolmson, p. 11.

17 Malcolmson, p. 11.

18 Struna, pp. 28–9.

19 Malcolmson, pp. 6–7.

20 Bruce C. Daniels, *Puritans at Play: Leisure and Recreation in Colonial New England* (New York: St Martins Press, 1995), pp. 163–72.

21 Malcolmson, p. 7.

22 Gorn and Goldstein, pp. 11–12; Struna, pp. 24–33.

23 See Daniels for a detailed study of the complex Puritan view of the relationship of work, leisure, and entertainment.

24 Ibid., p. 167.

25 Ibid., pp. 168–9.

26 T. H. Breen, "Horses and Gentlemen: The Cultural Significance of Gambling Among the Gentry of Virginia," *William and Mary Quarterly* (1977), pp. 239–57.

27 Breen, pp. 242–7.

28 For a useful summary of the southern sporting life, see Gorn and Goldstein, pp. 17–30; Struna, pp. 96–164.

29 Gorn and Goldstein, pp. 17–37.

30 Breen, p. 245.

31 Ibid., pp. 241–54.

32 Ibid., p. 251.

33 Elliott J. Gorn, "'Gouge and Bite, Pull Hair and Scratch': The Social Significance of Fighting in the Southern Back Country," *American Historical Review* (February, 1985), pp. 21–2.

34 For a detailed analysis of the powerful social role that taverns played in colonial America, see Struna, pp. 143–64.

35 Ibid., p. 159.

36 Gorn, p. 42.

37 Ibid., p. 20.

38 Struna, p. 163.

39 Jefferson to J. Bannister, October 15, 1785, reprinted in Henry Steele Commager, *Living Ideas in America* (New York: Harper and Row, 1964), pp. 557–8.

2 The Emergence of Organized Sports, 1815–60

1 Elliott Gorn and Warren Goldstein, *A Brief History of American Sports* (New York: Hill and Wang, 1993), pp. 53–4.

2 Melvin L. Adelman, *A Sporting Time: New York City and the Rise of Modern Athletics, 1820–70* (Urbana: University of Illinois Press, 1986), pp. 42–3.

3 "Rules and Regulations Approved and Adopted by the New York Jockey Club" (September 13, 1842). *American Periodicals Series Online, 1740–1900*, pp. 586–92.

4 Gorn and Goldstein, p. 54.

5 Adelman, pp. 34–8.

6 Ibid., p. 37.

7 Ibid., pp. 32–6.

8 Ibid., pp. 43–4.

9 Peter Levine, *American Sport: A Documentary History* (Englewood Cliffs, NJ: Prentice Hall, 1989), pp. 18–26.

10 Dwight Akers, *Riders Up: The Story of American Harness Racing* (New York: Putnam, 1938), p. 30.

11 Akers, p. 93.

12 Adelman, pp. 55–73.

13 Adelman, p. 61; Akers, pp. 30–2.

14 Gorn and Goldstein, p. 77.

15 Akers, pp. 48–53.

16 Steven Riess, *City Games: The Evolution of American Urban Society and the Rise of Sports* (Urbana: University of Illinois Press, 1989), p. 40; A. D. Turnbull, *John Stevens* (New York: Century Books, 1928), p. 510; Adelman, p. 212.

17 Adelman, pp. 213–14.

18 Ibid., pp. 214–20.

19 Ibid., pp. 189–93.

20 Ibid., pp. 192–7.

21 Ibid., pp. 197–8.

22 John Dizikes, *Sportsmen and Gamesmen* (Boston: Houghton Mifflin, 1981), p. 106.

23 Dizikes, pp. 106–10; Adelman pp. 197–8.

24 Dizikes, p. 114.

25 Ibid., p. 117.

26 Elliott J. Gorn, *The Manly Art: Bare-Knuckle Fighting in America* (Ithaca, NY: Cornell University Press, 1986), pp. 60–4.

27 Ibid., p. 77.

28 Ibid., pp. 71–81.

29 Ibid., p. 79.

30 Ibid., p. 79.

31 Ibid., pp. 81–97; Adelman, pp. 231–2.

32 Jon Sternglass, *First Resorts: Pursuing Pleasure at Saratoga Springs, Newport and Coney Island* (Baltimore, MD: Johns Hopkins University Press, 2001), pp. 147–55.

33 Harold Seymour, *Baseball: The Early Years* (New York: Oxford University Press, 1960), pp. 8–11; Albert Spalding, *America's National Game* (New York: American Sports Publishing, 1911), pp. 19–26.

34 John P. Rossi, *The National Game: Baseball and American Culture* (Chicago: Ivan Dee, 2000), pp. 5–7; George B. Kirsch, *The Creation of American Team Sports: Baseball and Cricket, 1838–72* (Urbana: University of Illinois Press, 1989), pp. 58–73.

35 Seymour, pp. 6–8; David Q. Voigt, *American Baseball: From the Commissioners to Continental Expansion* (Norman: University of Oklahoma Press, 1970), pp. 15–17.

36 Seymour, pp. 15–20; Voigt, pp. 16–17; Benjamin Rader, *Baseball: A History of America's Game* (Urbana: University of Illinois Press, 1992), pp. 2–5.

37 Rossi, pp. 3–10.

38 Melvin J. Adelman, "The Early Years of Baseball," in S. W. Pope, ed., *The New American Sports History* (Urbana: University of Illinois Press, 1997), pp. 58–87.

3 "This Noble and Envigorating Game"

1 Jules Tygiel, *Past Time: Baseball as History* (New York: Oxford University Press, 2000), pp. 4–14; Allen Guttmann, *From Ritual to Record: The Nature of Modern Sports* (New York: Columbia University Press, 1978), pp. 96–7; Kenneth S. Robson, ed., *A Great and Glorious Game: Baseball Writings of A. Bartlett Giamatti* (Chapel Hill, NC: Algonquin Books, 1998), p. 7; Geoffrey C. Ward and Ken Burns, *Baseball: An Illustrated History* (New York: Alfred A. Knopf, 1994), provides an excellent overview of baseball's 150-year history that includes several compelling essays and excellent and often rare photographs.

2 S. W. Pope, *Patriotic Games: Sporting Traditions in the American Imagination, 1876–1926* (New York: Oxford University Press, 1997), p. 79; Allen Guttmann, *A Whole New Ball Game: An Interpretation of American Sports* (Chapel Hill: University of North Carolina Press, 1988), pp. 52–5.

3 Edward Pessen, "Life, Baseball and Intellectuals," *Reviews in American History* (March, 1992), p. 112; Charles Alexander, *Our Game: An American Baseball History* (New York: Henry Holt, 1991), pp. 3, 112.

4 Harold Seymour, *Baseball: The Early Years* (New York: Oxford University Press, 1960), pp. 8–11; Albert Spalding, *America's National Game* (New York: American Sports Publishing, 1911), pp. 19–26.

5 Alexander, pp. 11–12.

6 Voigt, p. 18; Stephen Gelder, "Their Hands are All Playing: Business and Amateur Baseball, 1845–1917," *Journal of Sport History* (spring, 1984), pp. 5–27.

7 Joseph Amato, *The Decline of Rural Minnesota* (Marshall, MN: Crossings Press, 1993), pp. 49–55; Lewis Atherton, *Main Street on the Middle Border* (Bloomington: Indiana University Press, 1954), pp. 200–2.

8 Guttmann, p. 97.

9 Melvin L. Adelman, *A Sporting Time: New York City and the Rise of Modern Athletics, 1820–70* (Urbana: University of Illinois Press, 1986), pp. 165–6.

10 Alexander, p. 14; Adelman, pp. 170–72; Rossi, pp. 15–17; Seymour, pp. 56–8.

11 Rader, pp. 25–8; Alexander, p. 19.

12 Seymour, p. 58.

13 Ibid., pp. 56–8; Alexander, p. 23.

14 Alexander, p. 23.

15 Seymour, p. 61.

16 Tygiel, p. 17.

17 Alexander, p. 10.

18 Tygiel, pp. 18–19.

19 Ibid., p. 23.

20 Ibid., p. 23.

21 Ibid., p. 19.

22 Adelman, pp. 175–6; Tygiel, pp. 15–34.

23 Warren Jay Goldstein, *Playing for Keeps: A History of Early Baseball* (Ithaca, NY: Cornell University Press, 1989), pp. 35–7.

24 Rader, pp. 18–20; Ian Tyrell, "The Emergence of Modern American Baseball, 1850–80," in Richard Cushman and Michael McKenna, eds., *Sport in History* (Brisbane: University of Queensland Press, 1979), p. 219.

25 Richard O. Davies and Richard G. Abram, *Betting the Line: Sports Wagering in American Life* (Columbus: Ohio State University Press, 2001), pp. 18–20; Rader, pp. 19–20.

26 Tyrell, p. 222.

27 Stephen Freedman, "The Baseball Fad in Chicago, 1865–1870," *Journal of Sport History* (summer, 1978), pp. 42–64.

28 Rader, p. 29.

29 Pope, pp. 64–5; Rader, p. 43.
30 J. E. Findling, "The Louisville Gray's Scandal of 1877," *Journal of Sport History* (summer, 1976), pp. 176–87.
31 R. Jake Sudderth, "Albert Goodwill Spalding," *Scribner Encyclopedia of American Lives: Sports Figures* (New York: Charles Scribner's Sons, 2002), vol. 2, pp. 382–4.
32 Alexander, pp. 35–45; Rader, pp. 41–52.
33 Ronnie D. Lankford, Jr., "Michael Joseph "King" Kelly," *Scribner Encyclopedia of American Lives: Sports Figures* (New York: Charles Scribner's Sons, 2002), vol. 1, pp. 509–11.
34 Alexander, p. 47.
35 Rader, pp. 32–4; Alexander, pp. 48–9.
36 Seymour, pp. 135–88; Rader, pp. 47–52.
37 Alexander, pp. 36–58.
38 Alexander, pp. 49–52; Rader, pp. 51–2.
39 Seymour, pp. 334–5; Rossi, pp. 34–5; Alexander, pp. 49–52.
40 Seymour, pp. 221–39; Alexander, pp. 53–8.
41 Spalding, p. 280.
42 Ibid., p. 281.
43 Seymour, p. viii.

4 The Formative Years of College Football

1 Michael Oriard, *Reading Football: How the Popular Press Created an American Spectacle* (Chapel Hill: University of North Carolina Press, 1993), pp. 44–5.
2 Oriard, pp. 45–6; John Stuart Martin, "Walter Camp and His Gridiron Game," *American Heritage* (October, 1961), pp. 50–5; Elliott J. Gorn and Warren Jay Goldstein, *A Brief History of American Sports* (New York: Hill and Wang, 1993), pp. 154–62.
3 John Sayle Watterson, *College Football: History, Spectacle, Controversy* (Baltimore, MD: Johns Hopkins University Press, 2000), pp. 18–25.
4 Martin, pp. 77–9.
5 Oriard, pp. 25–56.
6 Scott A. McQuilkin and Ronald A. Smith, "The Rise and Fall of the Flying Wedge," *Journal of Sport History* (spring, 1993), p. 59.
7 Ronald A. Smith, *Sports and Freedom: The Rise of Big-time College Athletics* (New York: Oxford University Press, 1988), pp. 88–98; Watterson, pp. 13–14.
8 Watterson, pp. 58–60.
9 Robin Lester, *Stagg's University: The Rise, Decline, and Fall of Big-Time Football at Chicago* (Urbana: University of Illinois Press, 1995), p. 72; Watterson, p. 114.
10 Watterson, pp. 27–63.
11 Ibid., pp. 28, 36.
12 Lester, pp. 7–14.
13 Ibid., pp. 18–19.
14 Ibid., p. 26.
15 Ibid., pp. 125–63.
16 Oriard, pp. 57–8.
17 Murray Sperber, *Shake Down the Thunder: The Creation of Notre Dame Football* (New York: Henry Holt, 1993), pp. 23.
18 Source: University of Missouri Alumni Affairs Office.
19 Sperber, pp. 79–81.
20 Martin, p. 51.
21 W. Bruce Leslie, *Gentlemen and Scholars: College and Community in the Age of the University* (University Park: Pennsylvania State University Press, 1992), p. 109.
22 "President Eliot's Report," *Harvard Graduate Magazine* (1895), p. 869.

23 Ibid., p. 869.
24 Watterson, pp. 27–9.
25 Ibid., p. 28.
26 Ibid., pp. 27–31.
27 Lester, p. 65.
28 Watterson, pp. 64–9.
29 Ibid., pp. 68–74.
30 Ibid., pp. 68–74.
31 Ibid., pp. 120–40.

5 Sports and the Emergence of Modern America, 1865–1920

1 Frank Luther Mott, *A History of American Magazines* (Cambridge, MA: Harvard University Press, 1938), pp. 331–7.
2 Gene Smith, "A Little Visit to the Lower Depths Via the National Police Gazette," *American Heritage* (October, 1972), pp. 65–73.
3 Guy Reel, "Richard Fox, John L. Sullivan, and the Rise of Modern American Prize Fighting," *Journalism History* (summer, 2001), p. 73–86.
4 Michael T. Isenberg, *John L. Sullivan and His America* (Urbana: University of Illinois Press, 1988), pp. 102–13; James A. Cox, "The Great Fight: 'Mr Jake' vs. John L. Sullivan," *Smithsonian* (December, 1984), p. 158; Reel, "Richard Fox, John L. Sullivan and the Rise of Modern American Prizefighting."
5 Cox, pp. 153–68.
6 Isenberg, pp. 271–80; Cox, pp. 164–6.
7 Jeffrey T. Sammons, *Beyond the Ring: The Role of Boxing in American Society* (Urbana: University of Illinois Press, 1988), pp. 10–12; Isenberg, pp. 276–9.
8 Isenberg, pp. 281–99.
9 Elliott J. Gorn, *The Manly Art: Bare-Knuckle Fighting in America* (Ithaca, NY: Cornell University Press, 1986), pp. 238–47; Arnold Fields, *James L. Corbett* (Jefferson, NC: McFarland, 2001), pp. 53–63.
10 *New York Times* (November 15, 1922), p. 19.
11 James M. Mayo, *The American Country Club: Its Origins and Development* (New Brunswick, NJ: Rutgers University Press, 1998), pp. 7–13.
12 Bob Considine and F. R. Jarvis, *The First One-Hundred Years: A Portrait of the NYAC* (New York: Macmillan, 1969).
13 Quoted in *Sports Illustrated* Fiftieth Anniversary Insert (July 14, 2003); see also Elliott J. Gorn and Warren Jay Goldstein, *A Brief History of American Sports* (New York: Hill and Wang, 1993), pp. 136–7.
14 Benjamin G. Rader, *American Sports: From the Age of Folk Games to the Age of Televised Sports* (Upper Saddle River, NJ: Prentice Hall, 2004), p. 79.
15 Mayo, pp. 63–4.
16 Ibid., pp. 65–87.
17 Robert J. Moss, *Golf and the American Country Club* (Urbana: University of Illinois Press, 2001), p. 3.
18 Mayo, pp. 83–4.
19 Ibid., p. 85.
20 Catherine Beecher, "Letters to the People on Health and Happiness," in Steven A. Riess, ed., *Major Problems in American Sport History* (Boston: Houghton Mifflin, 1987), p. 172.
21 Susan K. Cahn, *Coming on Strong: Gender and Sexuality in Twentieth-Century Women's Sport* (New York: Free Press, 1994), p. 7.
22 Patricia Marks, *Bicycles, Bangs, and Bloomers: The New Woman in the Popular Press* (Lexington: University of Kentucky Press, 1990), p. 193.

23 Richard O. Davies, *Main Street Blues: The Decline of Small-Town America* (Columbus: Ohio State University Press, 1998), p. 110.

24 Agnes Rogers, "The Undimmed Appeal of the Gibson Girl," *American Heritage* (December, 1957), pp. 80–98; Frederick Platt, "The Gibson Girl," *Art and Antiques* (November, 1981), pp. 112–17.

25 Gail Bederman, *Manliness and Civilization: A Cultural History of Gender and Race in the United States, 1880–1917* (Chicago: University of Chicago Press, 1995), pp. 14, 84–8.

26 Gorn and Goldstein, p. 90.

27 Thomas W. Higginson, "Saints and Their Bodies," in Riess, pp. 82–95; Gorn and Goldstein, p. 91.

28 Clifford Putney, *Muscular Christianity: Manhood and Sports in Protestant America, 1880–1920* (Cambridge, MA: Harvard University Press, 2001), pp. 64–72.

29 Ibid., pp. 153–61.

30 Ibid., pp. 99–126.

31 Roosevelt to Camp, March 11, 1895, in H. W. Brands, ed., *The Selected Letters of Theodore Roosevelt* (New York: Cooper Square Press, 2001), p. 99.

32 Gorn and Goldstein, p. 146.

33 Roosevelt, "The American Boy," in *The Strenuous Life: Essays and Addresses* (New York: Century Company, 1902), pp. 155–64.

34 Joseph B. Oxendine, *American Indian Sports Heritage* (Champaign, IL: Human Kinetics Books, 1988), pp. 203–37; Robert W. Wheeler, *Jim Thorpe: The World's Greatest Athlete* (Norman: University of Oklahoma Press, 1979).

35 Kate Buford, "Jim Thorpe," in Arnold Markoe, ed., *Scribner Encyclopedia of American Lives: Sports Figures* (New York: Charles Scribner's Sons, 2002), vol. 2, p. 428.

36 Quoted in Riess, *Major Problems in American Sport History*, p. 283.

37 Grace Naismith, "Father Basketball," *Sports Illustrated* (January 31, 1955), p. 65.

38 John Devaney, *The Story of Basketball* (New York: Random House, 1976), p. 12.

39 Alexander Wolff, "The Olden Rules," *Sports Illustrated* (November 25, 2003), insert; Keith Myerscough, "The Game with No Name," *International Journal of the History of Sport* (April, 1995), pp. 137–52.

40 Mike Douchant, *Encyclopedia of College Basketball* (New York: Gale Research, 1995), p. 5.

41 Gorn and Goldstein, pp. 169–77.

6 Baseball Ascendant, 1890–1930

1 Charles Alexander, *Our Game: An American Baseball History* (New York: Henry Holt, 1991), pp. 58–83; Benjamin G. Rader, *Baseball: A History of America's Game* (Urbana: University of Illinois Press, 1992), pp. 61–9; John P. Rossi, *The National Game: Baseball and American Culture* (Chicago: Ivan Dee, 2000), pp. 51–8; Charles Alexander, *John McGraw* (Lincoln: University of Nebraska Press, 1988), pp. 32–81.

2 Rossi, p. 56; Alexander, *Our Game*, pp. 68–9; Eugene C. Murdock, *Ban Johnson: Czar of Baseball* (Westport, CT: Greenwood Press, 1982), pp. 26–7.

3 Rossi, p. 57.

4 Murdock, pp. 18–48.

5 Alexander, *Our Game*, pp. 76–83; Murdock, pp. 43–66. By 1903 the American League had franchises in Boston, New York City, Philadelphia, Washington, DC, Cleveland, Detroit, Chicago and St Louis.

6 Harold Seymour, *Baseball: The Golden Age* (New York: Oxford University Press, 1971), pp. 8–14; Alexander, *Our Game*, pp. 76–83; Murdock, pp. 43–66.

7 Rader, 70–81; Harold Seymour, *Baseball: The Early Years* (New York: Oxford University Press, 1960), pp. 307–24.

8   Louis P. Masur, *Autumn Glory: Baseball's First World Series* (New York: Hill and Wang, 2003), p. 220.

9   Murdock, pp. 82–98.

10   Rossi, pp. 77–9.

11   Reed Browning, *Cy Young: A Baseball Life* (Amherst: University of Massachusetts Press, 2000).

12   Ty Cobb, *My Life in Baseball: The True Record* (Lincoln: University of Nebraska Press, 1993), p. 65.

13   Charles Alexander, *Ty Cobb* (New York: Oxford University Press, 1984), pp. 5, 240.

14   Seymour, *The Early Years*, p. 290.

15   Frank Deford, "Giants Among Men," *Sports Illustrated* (August 25, 2002), p. 61.

16   Alexander, *John McGraw*, pp. 7–8.

17   Deford, p. 64.

18   Rossi, pp. 61–81; Rader, pp. 90–1; Connie Mack, *My 66 Years in Baseball* (Philadelphia: Winston Publishers, 1950).

19   William C. Kashatus, "Connie Mack," *Scribner Encyclopedia of American Lives: Sports Figures* (New York: Charles Scribner's Sons, 2002), vol. 2, p. 90.

20   Jules Tygiel, *Past Time: Baseball as History* (New York: Oxford University Press, 2000), pp. 35–63; Rader, pp. 90–1.

21   Rader, p. 101.

22   Murdock, pp. 108–18; Alexander, *Our Game*, pp. 102–7; Seymour, *The Golden Age*, pp. 169–234.

23   Alexander, *Our Game*, pp. 102–7; Murdock, p. 118.

24   Rader, pp. 110–11; Alexander, *Our Game*, p. 135.

25   Seymour, *The Golden Age*, pp. 235–55; Murdock, pp. 119–31.

26   Rader, pp. 102–3; Alexander, *Our Game*, pp. 108–13.

27   Much has been written on the 1919 World Series. The best single source is Eliot Asinof, *Eight Men Out: The Black Sox and the 1919 World Series* (New York: Henry Holt, 1987). See also the detailed narrative by Seymour, *The Golden Age*, pp. 274–310, and Alexander's concise summary in *Our Game*, pp. 115–29. For a perspective from the business of sports gambling, see Richard O. Davies and Richard G. Abram, *Betting the Line: Sports Wagering in American Life* (Columbus: Ohio State University Press, 2001), pp. 18–28.

28   Murdock, pp. 188–9.

29   Alexander, *Our Game*, pp. 123–9; Seymour, *The Golden Age*, p. 293.

30   Leo Katcher, *The Big Bankroll: The Life and Times of Arnold Rothstein* (New York: Da Capo Press, 1994), pp. 144–5.

31   Asinof, p. 280.

32   Seymour, *The Golden Age*, p. 330.

33   The two best biographies of Ruth are Robert W. Creamer, *Babe: The Legend Comes to Life* (New York: Simon and Schuster, 1974), and Marshall Smelser, *The Life that Ruth Built* (Lincoln: University of Nebraska Press, 1975).

34   Creamer, p. 273.

35   Tygiel, p. 85.

36   Smelser, p. 440.

37   Creamer, pp. 366–7.

38   Ibid., p. 397.

39   Murray Polner, *Branch Rickey: A Biography* (New York: Atheneum, 1982); Tygiel, pp. 87–115.

40   Tygiel, p. 94.

41   Alexander, *Our Game*, pp. 143–5; Tygiel, pp. 93–4.

42   Murdock, p. 207.

43   Seymour, *The Golden Age*, p. 460.

7 "An Evil to be Endured": Sports on Campus, 1920–50

1 Walter Byers, *Unsportsmanlike Conduct: Exploiting College Athletes* (Ann Arbor: University of Michigan Press, 1995), pp. 44–5.
2 Andrew Zimbalist, *Unpaid Professionals: Commercialism and Conflict in Big-Time College Sports* (Princeton, NJ: Princeton University Press, 1999), p. 3.
3 Robin Lester, *Stagg's University: The Rise, Decline, and Fall of Big-Time Football at Chicago* (Urbana: University of Illinois Press, 1995), p. 191.
4 Ronald A. Smith, *Sports and Freedom: The Rise of Big-Time College Athletics* (New York: Oxford University Press, 1988), pp. 172–4.
5 Smith, p. 171.
6 Andrew Miracle and C. Roger Rees, *Lessons of the Locker Room: The Myth of School Sports* (Amherst, NY: Prometheus Books, 1994), pp. 29–55.
7 John Sayle Watterson, *College Football: History, Spectacle, Controversy* (Baltimore, MD: Johns Hopkins University Press, 2000), p. 157.
8 Watterson, p. 157.
9 Lester, pp. 128–31.
10 Red Grange and Ira Morton, *The Red Grange Story: An Autobiography* (Urbana: University of Illinois Press, 1993).
11 Watterson, pp. 152–5.
12 Charles Fountain, *Sportswriter: The Life and Times of Grantland Rice* (New York: Oxford University Press, 1993), p. 209.
13 Watterson, p. 154.
14 Murray Sperber, *Shake Down the Thunder: The Creation of Notre Dame Football* (New York: Henry Holt, 1993), p. 185.
15 Ray Robinson, *Rockne of Notre Dame: The Making of a Football Legend* (New York: Oxford University Press, 1999), pp. 39–48; Sperber, pp. 37–42.
16 Robinson, p. 62.
17 Sperber, pp. 105–13.
18 John A. Lucas and Ronald A. Smith, *Saga of American Sport* (Philadelphia: Lea and Febiger, 1978), p. 316.
19 Sperber, p. 182.
20 Ibid., pp. 282–8.
21 John R. Thelin, *Games Colleges Play: Scandal and Reform in Intercollegiate Athletics* (Baltimore, MD: Johns Hopkins University Press, 1994), pp. 90–6.
22 Elliott J. Gorn and Warren Jay Goldstein, *A Brief History of American Sports* (New York: Hill and Wang 1993), p. 232.
23 Watterson, p. 161.
24 Ibid., pp. 162–4.
25 Howard J. Savage, *American College Athletics* (New York: Carnegie Foundation, 1929); Watterson, p. 165; Gorn and Goldstein, p. 232.
26 Thelin, p. 94.
27 Susan K. Cahn, *Coming on Strong: Gender and Sexuality in Twentieth-Century Women's Sport* (New York: Free Press, 1994), pp. 7–82.
28 Allen Guttmann, *Women's Sports: A History* (New York: Columbia University Press, 1991), pp. 113–14.
29 Guttmann, pp. 85–105.
30 Cahn, pp. 84–109; Senda Berenson, *Basketball for Women* (New York: American Sports Publishing, 1903), pp. 36–9.
31 Berenson, p. 39.
32 Ibid., p. 162.
33 Guttmann, pp. 135–42.

34 Ina Gittings, "Why Cramp Competition?" *Journal of Health and Physical Education* (January, 1931), pp. 10–12ff.

35 Gittings, p. 54.

36 Murray Sperber, *Onward to Victory: The Crises That Shaped College Sports* (New York: Henry Holt, 1998), pp. 285–6.

37 Sperber, *Onward to Victory*, p. 286.

38 Sperber, *Onward to Victory*, pp. 294–326; Richard O. Davies, *America's Obsession: Sports and Society Since 1945* (Fort Worth, TX: Harcourt Brace, 1994), pp. 18–27.

39 Richard O. Davies and Richard G. Abram, *Betting the Line: Sports Wagering in American Life* (Columbus: Ohio State University Press, 2001), pp. 51–60; Charles Rosen, *The Scandals of '51: How The Gamblers Almost Killed College Basketball* (New York: Seven Stories Press, 1999), p. 26; Sperber, *Onward to Victory*, pp. 286–7.

40 Davies, pp. 24–5.

41 *New York Times* (March 29, 1996), p. B 22.

42 Clair Bee, "I Know Now Why They Sold Out to Gamblers," *Saturday Evening Post* (February 2, 1952), pp. 26–7; Davies, p. 22.

8 Sports in an Age of Ballyhoo, Depression, and War, 1920–45

1 The literature on the causes and impact of the Great Depression is extensive, but the classic study remains, John Kenneth Galbraith, *The Great Crash: 1929* (Boston: Houghton Mifflin, 1954). The many and varied impacts of the economic collapse are cogently summarized in David M. Kennedy, *Freedom From Fear: The American People in Depression and War, 1929–1945* (New York: Oxford University Press, 1999).

2 John Tunis, "Changing Trends in Sports," *Harper's Magazine* (December, 1934), pp. 75–86.

3 Mark Inabinett, *Grantland Rice and His Heroes* (Knoxville: University of Tennessee Press, 1994), p. 14.

4 Inabinett, p. 3.

5 Lynn Dumenil, *The Modern Temper: American Culture and Society During the 1920s* (New York: Hill and Wang, 1995), p. 78. Murray Sperber, *Onward to Victory: The Crises That Shaped College Sports* (New York: Henry Holt, 1998), p. 30.

6 Inabinett, p. 2.

7 Ibid., p. 42.

8 Ronald A. Smith, *Play-by-Play: Radio, Television, and Big-Time College Sport* (Baltimore, MD: Johns Hopkins University Press, 2001), pp. 25, 42–6; Charles Fountain, *Sportswriter: The Life and Times of Grantland Rice* (New York: Oxford University Press, 1993), pp. 195–6.

9 Smith, pp. 24–8.

10 Robert Warren Wind, *The Story of American Golf* (New York: Alfred A. Knopf, 1975), pp. 70–82.

11 Ibid., pp. 118–32.

12 Ibid., pp. 133–64.

13 Inabinett, p. 57.

14 Ibid., p. 61.

15 Frank Deford, *Big Bill Tilden: The Triumphs and the Tragedy* (New York: Simon and Schuster, 1975), pp. 13–58; Al Silverman, *Sports Titans of the Twentieth Century* (New York: Putnam, 1968), pp. 136–53; Inabinett, pp. 63–73.

16 Deford, pp. 17–18.

17 Susan K. Cahn, *Coming on Strong: Gender and Sexuality in Twentieth-Century Women's Sport* (New York: Free Press, 1994), pp. 32–6; Will Grimsley, *Tennis: Its History, People, and Events* (Englewood Cliffs, NJ: Prentice Hall: 1971), pp. 140–50.

18 Joseph Severo, "Obituary of Gertrude Ederle," *New York Times* (December 1, 2003), p. A23.

19 Cahn, pp. 32–3.

20 Charles Samuels, *The Magnificent Rube: The Life and Times of Rex Rickard* (New York: McGraw-Hill, 1957).

21 Randy Roberts, *Jack Dempsey: The Manassa Mauler* (Baton Rouge: Louisiana State University Press, 1979).

22 Ibid., p. 189.

23 Ibid., p. 143.

24 William Nack, "The Long Count," *Sports Illustrated* (September 22, 1997), pp. 72–84; Roberts, pp. 212–35.

25 Nack, "The Long Count."

26 Paul Gallico, *Farewell to Sport* (New York: Alfred Knopf, 1938), pp. 208, 221.

27 Susan E. Cayleff, *Babe: The Life and Legend of Babe Didrikson Zaharias* (Urbana: University of Illinois Press, 1995); Gene Schoor, *Babe Didrikson: The World's Greatest Woman Athlete* (New York: Doubleday, 1978); William O. Johnson and Nancy P. Williamson, *"Whatta Gal": The Babe Didrikson Story* (Boston: Little, Brown, 1977).

28 Cahn, p. 215.

29 Gallico, p. 233; Schoor, p. 96.

30 Schoor, p. 96.

31 Cahn, p. 216.

32 Ibid., p. 216.

33 Cindy Himes, "The Female Athlete in America, 1860–1940," quoted in Cayleff, p. 261.

34 This section relies heavily upon Charles Alexander, *Breaking the Slump: Baseball in the Depression Era* (New York: Columbia University Press, 2002). Also useful are John P. Rossi, *The National Game: Baseball and American Culture* (Chicago: Ivan Dee, 2000), pp. 21–44; and Benjamin G. Rader, *Baseball: A History of America's Game* (Urbana: University of Illinois Press, 1992), pp. 136–40.

35 Alexander, p. 89.

36 Lynn Hoogenboom, "Jay Hanna 'Dizzy' Dean," *The Scribner Encyclopedia of American Lives: Sports Figures* (New York: Charles Scribner's Sons, 2002), vol. 1, p. 221.

37 Alexander, pp. 94–6.

38 Ibid., p. 183.

39 Lou Cannon, *Governor Reagan: His Rise to Power* (New York: Public Affairs Press, 2003), p. 45.

40 Alexander, p. 101.

41 Ibid., p. 271.

42 Ibid., p. 93.

43 Laura Hillenbrand, *Seabiscuit: An American Legend* (New York: Random House, 2001).

44 Ibid., p. 33.

45 Ibid., p. 324.

46 Rossi, p. 142.

47 Gia Ingham Berlage, *Women in Baseball: The Forgotten History* (Westport, CT: Praeger, 1994); Susan E. Johnson, *When Women Played Hardball* (Seattle: Seal Press, 1994).

48 Susan Cahn, "No Freaks, No Amazons, No Boyish Babes," *Chicago History Magazine* (spring, 1989), p. 30.

9 America's Great Dilemma

1 Gunnar Myrdal, *An American Dilemma* (New York: Harper & Row, 1944), pp. lxxi, 1004.

2 Patrick B. Miller and David K. Wiggins, eds., *Sport and the Color Line: Black Athletes and Race Relations in Twentieth-Century America* (New York: Routledge, 2004), p. xi.

3 Michael E. Lomax, "Black Entrepreneurship in the National Pastime," in Miller and Wiggins, *Sport and the Color Line*, pp. 24–43.

4 David K. Wiggins and Patrick B. Miller, eds., *The Unlevel Playing Field: A Documentary His-*

tory of the African American Experience in Sport (Urbana: University of Illinois Press, 2003), pp. 58–63.

5 Wiggins and Miller, pp. 63–6.

6 Michael T. Isenberg, *John L. Sullivan and His America* (Urbana: University of Illinois Press, 1988), p. 301.

7 Randy Roberts, *Papa Jack: Jack Johnson and the Era of White Heroes* (New York: The Free Press, 1983), pp. 3–35.

8 Roberts, p. 18; Wiggins and Miller, pp. 66–8.

9 Jeffrey T. Sammons, *Beyond the Ring: The Role of Boxing in American Society* (Urbana: University of Illinois Press, 1988), pp. 34–40; Thomas R. Hietala, *The Fight of the Century: Jack Johnson, Joe Louis, and the Struggle for Racial Equality* (Armonk, NY: M. E. Sharpe, 2002), pp. 29–39; Roberts, pp. 54–84.

10 Roberts, pp. 85–101.

11 Wiggins and Miller, p. 74.

12 Hietala, p. 46.

13 Roberts, pp. 124–230.

14 Jules Tygiel, *Past Time: Baseball as History* (New York: Oxford University Press, 2000), p. 117.

15 For the Negro Leagues, see Robert Peterson, *Only the Ball Was White: A History of Legendary Black Players and All-Black Professional Teams* (New York: Oxford University Press, 1970); and Neil Lanctot, *Negro League Baseball: The Rise and Ruin of a Black Institution* (Philadelphia: University of Pennsylvania Press, 2004).

16 Eric Enders, "Rube Foster," in Arnold Markoe, ed., *Scribner Encyclopedia of American Lives: Sports Figures* (New York: Charles Scribner's Sons, 2002), vol. 2, p. 292.

17 Peterson, pp. 103–15; Enders, pp. 291–3; Charles Alexander, *Our Game: An American Baseball History* (New York: Henry Holt, 1991), pp. 151–5; Benjamin G. Rader, *Baseball: A History of America's Game* (Urbana: University of Illinois Press, 1992), pp. 142–50; Wiggins and Miller, pp. 92–5.

18 Charles Alexander, *Breaking the Slump: Baseball in the Depression Era* (New York: Columbia University Press, 2002), pp. 204–38.

19 Peterson, pp. 91–5.

20 Peterson, pp. 129–49; Alexander, *Breaking the Slump*, pp. 211–38; Wiggins and Miller, pp. 95–8.

21 Alexander, *Our Game*, p. 181.

22 Lanctot, pp. 365, 395.

23 William J. Baker, *Jesse Owens: An American Life* (New York: Free Press, 1986).

24 Chris Mead, *Champion: Joe Louis, Black Hero in White America* (New York: Charles Scribner's Sons, 1985), p. x.

25 Hietala, pp. 150–90; Joe Louis with Edna and Art Rust, Jr., *Joe Louis, My Life* (New York: Harcourt Brace Jovanovich, 1978).

26 Mead, p. 6.

27 Ibid., p. 6.

28 Gerald Astor, *". . . And a Credit to His Race": The Hard Life and Times of Joseph Louis Barrow, a.k.a. Joe Louis* (New York: Putnam, 1974).

29 Mead, pp. 128, 134; David Margolick, *Beyond Glory: Joe Louis vs. Max Schmeling, and a World on the Brink* (New York: Alfred A. Knopf, 2005).

30 Mead, p. 295.

31 Arnold Rampersad, *Jackie Robinson: A Biography* (New York: Alfred A. Knopf, 1997), p. 120.

32 Rampersad, p. 120.

33 Jules Tygiel, *Baseball's Great Experiment: Jackie Robinson and His Legacy* (New York: Oxford University Press, 1983), provides the most authoritative and detailed account of the role of Branch Rickey and Jackie Robinson in breaking the baseball color line. See also Joseph

Dorinson and Joram Warmund, eds., *Jackie Robinson: Race, Sports, and the American Dream* (Armonk, NY: M. E. Sharpe, 1998).

34 Harvey Frommer, *Rickey and Robinson* (New York: Macmillan, 1982), pp. 80–130.

35 Joseph Dorinson, "Jack Roosevelt Robinson," in Arnold Markoe, ed., *Scribners Encyclopedia of American Lives: Sports Figures* (New York: Charles Scribner's Sons, 2002), vol. 2, p. 290.

36 Tygiel, *Past Time*, p. 111.

37 Rampersad, pp. 172–3.

38 Ibid., p. 173.

39 David Halberstam, *October 1964* (New York: Fawcett, 1995), p. 55.

40 www.baseballlibrary.com/power

41 Tygiel, *Baseball's Great Experiment*, pp. 285–302.

42 Tygiel, *Baseball's Great Experiment*, p. 302.

43 Richard O. Davies, *America's Obsession: Sports and Society Since 1945* (Fort Worth: Harcourt Brace, 1994), pp. 35–42.

44 Will Grimsley, *Tennis: Its History, People and Events* (Englewood Cliffs, NJ: Prentice Hall, 1971), p. 165.

45 Ibid., p. 161.

46 Arthur Ashe and Arnold Rampersad, *Days of Grace* (New York: Alfred A. Knopf, 1993).

47 Grimsley, p. 124.

48 *Life*, November 5, 1951.

49 Charles H. Martin, "Racial Change and 'Big-Time' College Football in Georgia: The Age of Segregation, 1892–1957," *Georgia Historical Quarterly* (fall, 1996), pp. 532–62.

50 Martin, "Racial Change and 'Big-Time' College Football in Georgia," p. 554. See also Martin, "Integrating New Year's Day: The Racial Politics of College Bowl Games in the American South," *Journal of Sport History* (fall, 1997), pp. 358–77.

51 Charles H. Martin, "The Rise and Fall of Jim Crow in Southern College Sports: The Case of the Atlantic Coast Conference," *North Carolina Historical Review* (July, 1999), pp. 253–84.

52 Charles H. Martin, "Jim Crow in the Gymnasium: The Integration of College Basketball in the American South," *International Journal of Sport History* (April, 1993), pp. 68–86.

53 Randy Roberts and James Olsen, *Winning Is the Only Thing* (Baltimore, MD: Johns Hopkins University Press, 1989), p. 45.

54 "Texas Western Tamed Wildcats in NCAA," *New York Times*, March 21, 1966, p. 44; Frank Deford, "Go-Go With Bobby Joe," *Sports Illustrated* (March 28, 1966), pp. 26–9.

10 Television Changes the Face of American Sports

1 Tex Maule, "The Best Football Game Ever Played," *Sports Illustrated* (January 8, 1959), pp. 8–11.

2 Randy Roberts and James Olson, *Winning Is the Only Thing* (Baltimore, MD: Johns Hopkins University Press, 1989), p. 111; Arthur Daley, "Overtime at the Stadium," *New York Times*, December 29, 1958, p. 25; Robert W. Peterson, *Pigskin: The Early Years of Pro Football* (New York: Oxford University Press, 1997), pp. 202–3.

3 Phil Patton, *Razzle Dazzle: The Curious Marriage of Television and Professional Football* (Garden City, NY: Dial Press, 1984), pp. 7–16.

4 William O. Johnson, *Super Spectator and the Electric Lilliputians* (Boston: Little, Brown, 1971), pp. 39–46; Benjamin G. Rader, *In Its Own Image: How Television Has Transformed Sports* (New York: Free Press, 1984), pp. 17–18.

5 Ron Powers, *Supertube: The Rise of Television Sports* (New York: Coward-McCann, 1984), pp. 31–2; Ronald A. Smith, *Play-by-Play: Radio, Television, and Big-Time College Sports* (Baltimore, MD: Johns Hopkins University Press, 2001), p. 51.

6 Rader, p. 79; Charles Alexander, *Our Game: An American Baseball History* (New York: Henry Holt, 1991); pp. 222–3; Powers, pp. 70–6.

7   Charles Alexander, *Our Game*, pp. 217–45; Rader, pp. 47–64; Neil J. Sullivan, *The Minors* (New York: St Martins Press, 1990), pp. 235–55; Johnson, pp. 97–105.

8   Patton, p. 29.

9   Jeffrey T. Sammons, *Beyond the Ring: The Role of Boxing in American Society* (Urbana: University of Illinois Press, 1988), p. 149.

10   Daley, "Is Boxing on the Ropes?" *New York Times Magazine* (January 31, 1953), pp. 19ff; John Lardner, "So You Think You See the Fights on TV!" *Saturday Evening Post* (May 2, 1954), pp. 144–6.

11   Daley, p. 19.

12   Johnson, pp. 91–6; Roberts and Olson, pp. 103–8; Lardner, pp. 145–6; Sammons, p. 150.

13   Daley, p. 22.

14   Sammons, pp. 151–77.

15   Peterson, pp. 151–63.

16   Rader, pp. 83–90; Marc S. Maltby, "Bert Bell," in Arnold Markoe, ed., *Scribner Encyclopedia of American Lives: Sports Figures* (New York: Charles Scribner's Sons, 2002), vol. 1, pp. 68–9.

17   Tex Maule, "The Infighting Was Vicious," *Sports Illustrated* (February 8, 1960), pp. 50–2.

18   David Harris, *The League: The Rise and Decline of the NFL* (New York: Bantam Books, 1986), p. 14.

19   Johnson, p. 124.

20   Ibid., pp. 125–6.

21   Roberts and Olson, p. 113.

22   Powers, *Supertube*, pp. 145–6; Smith, *Play-by-Play*, pp. 105–6.

23   Bert Randolph Sugar, *The Thrill of Victory* (New York: Hawthorn Books, 1978) pp. 86–130.

24   Ibid., p. 121.

25   Rader, p. 93; Harris, pp. 16–17.

26   Patton, pp. 113–19; Rader, pp. 96–9; Richard O. Davies, *America's Obsession: Sports and Society Since 1945* (Fort Worth, TX: Harcourt Brace, 1994), pp. 93–4.

27   Powers, pp. 182–7; Patton, pp. 105–12.

28   Marc Gunther and Bill Carter, *Monday Night Mayhem: The Inside Story of ABC's Monday Night Football* (New York: Beech Tree Books, 1988); Howard Cosell, *I Never Played the Game* (New York: Morrow, 1985).

29   Michael Freeman, *ESPN: The Uncensored History* (Dallas: Taylor Publishing, 2000, p. 80.

30   "An All-Sports Network," *Newsweek* (November 12, 1979), p. 124; Freeman, p. 80.

31   Bill Rasmussen, *Sports Junkies Rejoice! The Birth of ESPN* (Hartsdale, NY: QV Publishing Company, 1983), pp. 76–82.

32   Freeman, pp. 70–90; Rasmussen, pp. 122–215.

33   Freeman, pp. 94–5.

34   Ibid., pp. 95–6.

35   "Happy Birthday to Us," *New York Times* (September 7, 2004), p. 31.

36   "Disney's ESPN Unit Buying Classics Sports Programmer," *New York Times* (September 4, 1997), p. D7; Freeman, pp. 213–36.

37   Freeman, pp. 111–94; William O. Johnson, "High on Cable," *Sports Illustrated* (August 17, 1981), pp. 28–40; "ESPN's 10-Year Journey to the Top," *New York Times* (September 18, 1989), p. D8.

38   "At ESPN, the Revolution Was Televised," *New York Times* (September 7, 1999), p. D1; Freeman, pp. 195–212.

39   Freeman, pp. 269–92.

11 College Sports in the Modern Era

1   Allen L. Sack and Ellen J. Staurowsky, *College Athletes for Hire: The Evolution and Legacy of the NCAA's Amateur Myth* (Westport, CT: Praeger, 1998), pp. 99–100.

2 John Tunis, "Dying for Dear Old Mazuma," *The Outlook* (November 27, 1929), p. 506.

3 Murray Sperber, *College Sports, Inc.: The Athletic Department vs the University* (New York: Henry Holt, 1990).

4 Walter Byers, *Unsportsmanlike Conduct: Exploiting College Athletes* (Ann Arbor: University of Michigan Press, 1995).

5 Gallico quoted in John Sayle Watterson, *College Football: History–Spectacle–Controversy* (Baltimore, MD: Johns Hopkins University Press, 2000), p. 199; see also Paul Gallico: "Hero Poison," *American Magazine* (November, 1934), pp. 55ff, and "Beware of Athlete's Head," *Reader's Digest* (October, 1936), pp. 11–14; John Tunis, "Whose Game Is It?" *The Outlook* (November 3, 1929), pp. 424–5, "What Price College Football?" *American Mercury* (October, 1939), pp. 267–72, and "Dying for Old Mazuma"; Francis Wallace, "This Football Business," *Saturday Evening Post* (September 28, 1929), pp. 10–11ff; "I Am a Football Fixer," *Saturday Evening Post* (October 31, 1936), pp. 16–17ff; and Sol Metzger, "The Football Fallacy," *Saturday Evening Post* (November 8, 1930), pp. 28–30ff.

6 John R. Thelin, *Games Colleges Play: Scandal and Reform in Intercollegiate Athletics* (Baltimore, MD: Johns Hopkins University Press, 1994), pp. 101–3.

7 Thelin, p. 169.

8 Byers, pp. 69–76.

9 Thelin, pp. 98–154.

10 Byers, p. 61.

11 Don Yaeger, *Undue Process: The NCAA's Injustice for All* (Champaign, IL: Sagamore Publishing, 1991), p. 13.

12 Ronald A. Smith, *Play-by-Play: Radio, Television, and Big-Time College Sport* (Baltimore, MD: Johns Hopkins University Press, 2001), p. 67.

13 Andrew Zimbalist, *Unpaid Professionals: Commercialism and Conflict in Big-Time College Sports* (Princeton, NJ: Princeton University Press, 1999), pp. 149–72; Murray Sperber, *Beer and Circus: How Big-Time College Sports is Crippling Undergraduates* (New York: Henry Holt, 2000), pp. 71–80.

14 The best biography is Robert Vare, *Buckeye: A Study of Coach Woody Hayes and the Ohio State Football Machine* (New York: Harpers, 1974), which unfortunately was published before Hayes's career ended. See also Steven Geitschier, "Woodrow Wayne 'Woody' Hayes," in Arnold Markoe, ed., *Scribner Encyclopedia of American Lives: Sports Figures* (New York: Charles Scribner's Sons, 2002), vol. 1, pp. 400–1.

15 Journalist Mickey Herskowitz has written a laudatory biography, *The Legend of Bear Bryant* (New York: McGraw-Hill, 1987). See also James Smallwood, "Paul 'Bear' Bryant," in Arnold Markoe, ed., *Scribner Encyclopedia of American Lives: Sport Figures* (New York: Charles Scribner's Sons, 2002), vol. 1, pp. 127–8.

16 James Kirby, *Fumble: Bear Bryant, Wally Butts, and the Great Football Scandal* (New York: Dell Books, 1986).

17 Richard O. Davies, *America's Obsession: Sports and Society Since 1945* (Fort Worth, TX: Harcourt Brace, 1994), p. 171.

18 Sack and Staurowsky, pp. 111–16. For an overview of the history of women's intercollegiate sports, see Ying Wushanley, *Playing Nice: The Struggle for Control of Women's Intercollegiate Athletics, 1960–2000* (Syracuse, NY: Syracuse University Press, 2004).

19 Byers, p. 243.

20 Ibid., p. 243.

21 Ibid., p. 245.

22 Sperber, p. 322.

23 Sack and Staurowsky, pp. 111–26.

24 Cahn, pp. 278–9.

25 Murray Sperber, *Beer and Circus: How Big-time College Sports Is Crippling Undergraduate Education* (New York: Henry Holt, 2000).

26 For example, see Thelin, *Games Colleges Play*; Yaeger, *Undue Process*; Rick Telander, *The Hundred Yard Lie: The Corruption of College Football and What We Can Do to Stop It* (New York: Simon and Schuster, 1989); Charles Thompson and Allan Sonnenschein, *Down and Dirty: The Life and Crimes of Oklahoma Football* (New York: Carroll and Graff, 1990); David Whitford, *A Payroll to Meet: A Story of Greed, Corruption, and Football at SMU* (New York: Macmillan, 1989), David Wolf, *Foul! The Connie Hawkins Story* (New York: Holt, Rinehart, 1972); Alexander Wolff and Armen Keteyian, *Raw Recruits: The High Stakes Game Colleges Play to Get Their Basketball Stars – and What It Costs* (New York: Pocket Books, 1990); Davies, *America's Obsession*, p. 203.

27 Associated Press, August 24, 2005.

28 Yaeger, *Undue Process*.

29 Whitford, *A Payroll to Meet*.

30 Byers, pp. 18–36.

31 For different perspectives on Tarkanian, see Richard O. Davies, "Jerry Tarkanian: Nevada's Special Rebel," in Davies, *The Maverick Spirit: Building the New Nevada* (Reno: University of Nevada Press, 1998), pp. 248–70; Byers, pp. 204–11; Jerry Tarkanian and Terry Pluto, *Tark: College Basketball's Winningest Coach* (New York: McGraw-Hill, 1988); and Don Yaeger, *Shark Attack: Jerry Tarkanian and His Battle with the NCAA and UNLV* (New York: HarperCollins, 1992).

32 Davies, "Jerry Tarkanian: Nevada's Special Rebel," p. 269.

33 Zimbalist, pp. 96–7; Smith, pp. 145–52.

34 Smith, pp. 162–76.

35 Smith, pp. 191–204, provides a cogent summary of the bowl fixation and the possibilities of the creation of a national play-off system.

36 "Report of the Knight Commission," March, 1991.

37 Arthur Fleisher et al., *The National Collegiate Athletic Association: A Study in Cartel Behavior* (Chicago: University of Chicago Press, 1992), p. 160.

38 Knight Commission, "A Call to Action; Reconnecting College Sports and Higher Education," June, 2001.

12 Play for Pay

1 *Time*, August 1, 1969, p. 41.

2 Posnanski, "Modell Doesn't Get It." *Kansas City Star*, January 22, 2001.

3 Posnanski, "Modell Doesn't Get It."

4 Mark S. Rosentraub, *Major League Losers: The Real Costs and Who's Paying For It* (New York: Basic Books, 1997), pp. 242–81; Michael N. Danielson, *Home Team: Professional Sports and the American Metropolis* (Princeton, NJ: Princeton University Press, 1997), pp. 3–6.

5 Posnanski, "Modell Doesn't Get It."

6 Danielson, pp. 67, 120–5; Dave Anderson, "Twelve Vans to Indianapolis"; *New York Times*, March 30, 1984, p. 23.

7 *New York Times*, November 26, 1995, p. F6.

8 Danielson, pp. 105–8.

9 Ibid., p. 110.

10 Neil Sullivan, *The Dodgers Move West* (New York: Oxford University Press, 1987), pp. 20–106.

11 Sullivan, p. 188.

12 Charles Alexander, *Our Game: An American Baseball History* (New York: Henry Holt, 1991), pp. 246–79.

13 Andrew Zimbalist, *Baseball and Billions* (New York: Basic Books, 1992), pp. 123–46.

14 *New York Times*, May 2, 2004, p. B6.

15 Benjamin G. Rader, *Baseball: A History of America's Game* (Urbana: University of Illinois Press, 1992), pp. 189–97.

16 Marvin Miller, *A Whole Different Ball Game* (New York: Birch Lane Press, 1991), pp. 174–202; Zimbalist, pp. 18–22; Rader, pp. 189–97; Richard O. Davies, *America's Obsession: Sports and Society Since 1945* (Fort Worth, TX: Harcourt Brace, 1994), pp. 129–43.

17 Gerald Scully, *The Business of Major League Baseball* (Chicago: University of Chicago Press, 1989), pp. 37–9; Zimbalist, pp. 21–2.

18 Scully, p. 37.

19 Zimbalist, pp. 75–104.

20 Scully, pp. 39–43; Zimbalist, pp. 23–7.

21 Tom Verducci, "In the Strike Zone," *Sports Illustrated* (August 1, 1994), pp. 26ff; "Brushback," *Sports Illustrated* (August 10, 1994), pp. 60–7.

22 John P. Rossi, *The National Game: Baseball and American Culture* (Chicago: Ivan Dee, 2000), pp. 205–8.

23 Bob Costas, *Fair Ball: A Fan's Case for Baseball* (New York: Broadway Books, 2000), pp. 91–104.

24 Randy Roberts and James Olson, *Winning Is the Only Thing* (Baltimore, MD: Johns Hopkins University Press, 1989), p. 71.

25 Bob St John, *The Landry Legend: Grace Under Pressure* (Dallas: Word Publishing, 1989); Skip Bayless, *God's Coach: The Hymns, Hype, and Hypocrisy of Tom Landry's Cowboys* (New York: Simon and Schuster, 1990).

26 Glenn Dickey, *49ers: The Rise, Fall, and Rebirth of the NFL's Greatest Dynasty* (Roseville, CA: Prima Press, 2000); Richard O. Davies, "Bill Walsh," in Arnold Markoe, ed., *Scribner Encyclopedia of American Lives: Sports Figures* (New York: Charles Scribner's Sons, 2002), vol. 2, pp. 476–77.

27 David Harris, *The League: the Rise and Decline of the NFL* (New York: Bantam Books, 1986), pp. 542–8.

28 Ibid., pp. 554–5.

29 Glenn Dickey, *Just Win, Baby: Al Davis and His Raiders* (New York: Harcourt Brace, 1991).

30 Harris, pp. 413–594.

31 Ibid., p. 574.

32 www.knbr.com

33 Richard P. Harmond, "Wilt Chamberlain," in Arnold Markoe, ed., *Scribner Encyclopedia of American Lives: Sports Figures* (New York: Charles Scribner's Sons, 2002), vol. 1, pp. 161–4.

34 Terry Pluto, *Loose Balls: The Short, Wild Life of the American Basketball Association* (New York: Simon and Schuster, 1990).

35 Stephen Fox, *Big Leagues: Professional Baseball, Football, and Basketball in National Memory* (New York: William Morrow, 1994), pp. 430–2.

36 David Halberstam, *Playing for Keeps: Michael Jordan and the World He Made* (New York: Random House, 1999), pp. 3–107.

37 Centers Akeem Olajuwon of the University of Houston by the Houston Rockets, and Sam Bowie of the University of Kentucky by the Portland Trail Blazers.

38 Halberstam, p. 417; Walter LaFeber, *Michael Jordan and the New Global Capitalism* (New York: W. W. Norton, 2002).

39 Mark D. Howell, *From Moonshine to Madison Avenue: A Cultural History of the NASCAR Winston Cup Series* (Bowling Green, OH: Bowling Green State University Press, 1997), p. 15.

40 Howell, p. 15.

41 Scott Crawford, "William France," in Arnold Markoe, ed., *Scribner Encyclopedia of American Lives: Sports Figures* (New York: Charles Scribner's Sons, 2002), vol. 1, pp. 298–300; Joe Menzer, *The Wildest Ride: A History of NASCAR* (New York: Touchstone, 2001), pp. 57–76.

42 www.hickoksports.com/biograph/francebill.shtml

43 Howell, p. 32.

44 Ibid., p. 13.

45 Tom Wolfe, "The Last American Hero is Junior Johnson. Yes!" *Esquire* (March 1965), pp. 68ff.
46 Menzer, pp. 197–200.
47 Ibid., pp. 160–3.
48 Ibid., p. 161.

13 Do You Believe in Miracles?

1 Jamie Fitzpatrick, "Miracle on Ice," at www.proicehockey.com
2 At www.brainyquote.com/decoubertin
3 Allen Guttmann, *The Olympics: A History of the Modern Games* (New York: Columbia University Press, 1992), p. 12.
4 Ibid., p. 12.
5 Allen Guttmann, *The Games Must Go On: Avery Brundage and the Olympic Movement* (New York: Columbia University Press, 1984), pp. 62–81. Guttmann, *The Olympics*, pp. 53–71.
6 Ibid., pp. 73–84.
7 Guttmann, *The Olympics*, pp. 85–102.
8 Randy Roberts and James Olson, *Winning Is the Only Thing* (Baltimore, MD: Johns Hopkins University Press, 1989), p. 13.
9 William O. Johnson, *All That Glitters Is Not Gold: The Olympic Games* (New York: Putnam, 1972), pp. 223–4; Benjamin G. Rader, *In Its Own Image: How Television Has Transformed Sports* (New York: Free Press, 1984), p. 158.
10 Richard Espy, *The Politics of the Olympic Games* (Berkeley: University of California Press, 1979), p. 38.
11 Guttmann, *The Games Must Go On*, pp. 82–131.
12 Ibid., p. 116.
13 Ibid., p. 162.
14 Wilma Rudolph, *Wilma: The Story of Wilma Rudolph* (New York: New American Library, 1977); Katharine Britton, "Wilma Glodean Rudolph," in Arnold Markoe, ed., *Scribner Encyclopedia of American Lives: Sports Figures* (New York: Charles Scribner's Sons, 2002), vol. 2, pp. 308–10.
15 Ron Powers, *Supertube: The Rise of Television Sports* (New York: Coward-McCann, 1984), p. 18; Jim Spence, *Up Close and Personal: The Inside Story of Network Television Sports* (New York: Atheneum, 1988), p. 42.
16 Powers, pp. 204–20; Rader, pp. 157–63.
17 Johnson, pp. 262–3.
18 Guttmann, *The Olympics*, pp. 130–2; Guttmann, *The Games Must Go On*, pp. 243–5.
19 "La Noche Triste" (A Sad Night), *Time* (October 11, 1968), p. 33.
20 Guttmann, *The Games Must Go On*, p. 245.
21 Johnson, pp. 264–73.
22 Ibid., p. 270.
23 Guttmann, *The Olympics*, pp. 138–40; John Kiernan, Arthur Daley, and Pat Jordan, *The Story of the Olympic Games, 776 BC to 1976* (Philadelphia: Lippincott, 1977), pp. 378–80; Roberts and Olsen, *Winning Is the Only Thing*, pp. 190–3.
24 Thomas Lowitt, "Terrorists Turn '72 Munich Olympics into Bloodbath," *St Petersburg Times*, December 29, 1999.
25 Powers, *Supertube*, p. 214.
26 Guttmann, *The Games Must Go On*, p. 254.
27 Guttmann, *The Olympics*, pp. 127–8; Kiernan et al., pp. 484–6.
28 Guttmann, *The Olympics*, p. 142.
29 Ibid., pp. 149–56.
30 Randy Roberts and James Olson, *Winning Is the Only Thing* (Baltimore, MD: Johns Hopkins University Press, 1989), p. 205.

31 David Marc, "Carl Lewis," in Andrew Markoe, ed., *Scribner Encyclopedia of American Lives: Sports Figures* (New York: Charles Scribner's Sons, 2002), vol. 2, pp. 39–41.

32 Adriana Tomasino, "Mary Lou Retton," in Arnold Markoe, *Scribner Encyclopedia of American Lives: Sports Figures* (New York: Charles Scribner's Sons, 2002), vol. 2, pp. 262–3.

33 Kenneth Reich, *Making It Happen: Peter Ueberroth and the 1984 Olympics* (Santa Barbara, CA: Capra Press, 1986).

34 Rader, pp. 156; Kiernan et al., pp. 518–19; Sabine Louissaint, "Bruce Jenner," in Arnold Markoe, ed., *Scribner Encyclopedia of American Lives: Sports Figures* (New York: Charles Scribner's Sons, 2002), vol. 1, pp. 467–8.

35 At www.nba.com/dreamteam

14 The Persistent Dilemma of Race

1 David W. Zang, "The Greatest: Muhammad Ali's Confounding Character," in Patrick Miller and David K. Wiggins, eds., *Sport and the Color Line* (New York: Routledge, 2004), pp. 289–303.

2 Muhammad Ali, with Richard Durham, *The Greatest* (New York: Random House, 1975), pp. 17–19.

3 Thomas Hauser, *Muhammad Ali: His Life and Times* (New York: Touchstone, 1991), pp. 56–80.

4 Hauser, pp. 81–112; Jeffrey T. Sammons, *Beyond the Ring: The Role of Boxing in American Society* (Urbana: University of Illinois Press, 1988), pp. 193–7.

5 Hauser, pp. 104, 147.

6 Randy Roberts and James Olson, *Winning Is the Only Thing* (Baltimore, MD: Johns Hopkins University Press, 1989), p. 170.

7 Hauser, pp. 139; Roberts and Olson, pp. 173–4.

8 Sammons, pp. 200–4; Hauser, pp. 171–202.

9 *New York Times* (April 30, 1967), p. 190; "Muhammad Ali Loses His Title to the Muslims," *New York Times* (April 20, 1967), p. F-8; "As the Judge Threw the Book at Muhammad," *Sports Illustrated* (July 3, 1967), pp. 18–19; "Decision for Allah," *Newsweek* (July 12, 1967), pp. 61–3; Roberts and Olson, pp. 171–2.

10 Hauser, p. 166.

11 Ibid., p. 167.

12 Sammons, pp. 207–19; Hauser, pp. 463–515.

13 Harry Edwards, *The Revolt of the Black Athlete* (New York: Free Press, 1969), p. 43.

14 Harry Edwards, "What Happened to the Revolt of the Black Athlete? 1968 and Today," *Colorlines* (summer 1998), pp. 12–15; *New York Times*, December 16, 1967.

15 Edwards, "What Happend to the Revolt of the Black Athlete?"

16 Roberts and Olson, p. 175.

17 Newell G. Bringhurst, *Saints, Slaves, and Blacks: The Changing Place of Black People Within Mormonism* (Greenwich, CT: Greenwood Press, 1981), pp. 181–3.

18 Douglas Kellner, "The Sports Spectacle: Michael Jordan, and Nike," in Patrick Miller and David K. Wiggins, eds., *Sport and the Color Line* (New York: Routledge, 2004), pp. 305–26.

19 Edwards, "What Happened to the Revolt of the Black Athlete?"

20 Hank Aaron, with Lonnie Wheeler, *I Had a Hammer: The Hank Aaron Story* (New York: HarperCollins, 1991), pp. 315–20.

21 Ibid., p. 328.

22 Martin Kane, "An Assessment of 'Black is Best'," *Sports Illustrated* (January 18, 1971), pp. 73–83.

23 Ibid., pp. 39–40.

24 Harry Edwards, "The Sources of the Black Athlete's Superiority," *The Black Scholar* (November, 1971), pp. 39–40.

25 Harry Edwards, *Sociology of Sport* (Homestead, IL: Dorsey Press, 1973), p. 194.

26 Edwards, *Sociology of Sport*, p. 194. See also Edwards, "The Myth of the Racially Superior Athlete," *Intellectual Digest* (March, 1972), pp. 58–60.

27 Edwards, "The Sources of the Black Athlete's Superiority," pp. 39–40.

28 Richard O. Davies and Richard G. Abram, *Betting the Line: Sports Wagering in American Life* (Columbus: Ohio State University Press, 2001), pp. 132–7.

29 Jay Coakley, *Sport in Society* (New York: McGraw-Hill, 2001), 7th edition, p. 246.

30 Gary Smith, "The Chosen One," *Sports Illustrated* (December 23, 1996), pp. 28–52.

31 John Garrity, "Open and Shut," *Sports Illustrated* (June 26, 2000), p. 63; Martin Sherwin, "Eldrick 'Tiger' Woods," in Arnold Markoe, ed., *The Scribner Encyclopedia of American Lives: Sports Figures* (New York: Charles Scribner's Sons, 2002), vol. 2, p. 516.

32 Steve Rushin, "Grand Slam," *Sports Illustrated* (July 31, 2000), pp. 52–61; Frank Deford, "Better than Imagined," *Sports Illustrated* (December 18, 2000), p. 91.

33 David Owen, *The Chosen One: Tiger Woods and the Dilemma of Greatness* (New York: Simon and Schuster, 2001), pp. 11–90.

34 Ibid., p. 61.

35 Ibid., p. 69.

36 Ibid., p. 194.

37 Julianne Cicarelli, "Venus Ebone Starr Williams," in Arnold Markoe, ed., *The Scribner Encyclopedia of American Lives: Sports Figures* (New York: Charles Scribner's Sons, 2002), vol. 2, pp. 503–5.

38 "Never Too Young for Tennis Millions," in *New York Times*, November 10, 1993; S. L. Price, "Venus Envy," *Sports Illustrated* (September 15, 1997), pp. 35–6.

39 *New York Times*, September 10, 1999, p. D4.

40 Price, pp. 35–6.

41 *New York Times*, March 1, 1999, p. D1; S. L. Price, "Father Knew Best," *Sports Illustrated* (September 20, 1999), pp. 40–3.

42 L. Jon Wertheim, "The Serena Show," *Sports Illustrated* (May 26, 2003), pp. 38–41; Wertheim, "Go in Style," *Sports Illustrated* (March 22, 2004), pp. 113–15.

43 Cicarelli, p. 504.

15 "Only in America!"

1 Patrick J. Walsh, *Echoes Among the Stars: A Short History of the US Space Program* (Armonk, NY: M. E. Sharpe, 2000), pp. 16–20.

2 For an informative overview of the impact of the space exploration program on American fitness, see Tom Wolfe, *The Right Stuff* (New York: Farrar, Straus, and Giroux, 1979).

3 Robert Ernst, *Weakness Is a Crime: The Life of Benarr McFadden* (Syracuse, NY: Syracuse University Press, 1991); Mary McFadden and Emile Gauvreau, *Dumbells and Carrot Strips* (New York: Henry Holt, 1953); Clement Wood, *Benarr McFadden, A Study in Success* (New York: Beekman Publishers, 1974).

4 Patrick Perry, "Jack La Lanne: Fit For Life," *Saturday Evening Post* (November, 2000), pp. 38ff.

5 H. W. Brands, "Just Do It," in *Masters of Enterprise: Giants of American Business* (New York: Free Press, 1999), pp. 256–66; "The Swoon of the Swoosh," *New York Times*, September 13, 1998; Aaron Frisch, *The Story of Nike* (North Makato, MN: Smart Apple Media, 2004).

6 Quoted in Jimmy Breslin, "In Defense of Gambling," *Saturday Evening Post* (January 5, 1963), p. 12.

7 Richard O. Davies, "Only in Nevada; Nevada's Unique Experiment with Legalized Sports Gambling, 1931–2000," *Nevada State Historical Society Quarterly* (spring, 2001), pp. 3–19.

8 Richard O. Davies and Richard G. Abram, *Betting the Line: Sports Wagering in American Life* (Columbus: Ohio State University Press, 2001), pp. 140–2.

9   Richard O. Davies, "The Age of Jimmy the Greek: Sports Wagering in Modern America," *Nevada State Historical Society Quarterly* (spring, 1999), pp. 21–45.

10 Michael Y. Sokolove, *Hustle: The Myth, Life, and Lies of Pete Rose* (New York: Simon and Schuster, 1990).

11 James Reston, Jr., *Collision at Home Plate: The Lives of Pete Rose and Bart Giamatti* (Lincoln: University of Nebraska Press, 1991), pp. 306–8.

12 Pete Rose, *Pete Rose: My Prison Without Bars* (Emmaus, PA: Rodale Company, 2004), p. 316; Pete Rose with Roger Kahn, *Pete Rose: My Story* (New York: Macmillan, 1980).

13 Charles Rosen, *The Wizard of Odds: How Jack Molinas Almost Destroyed the Game of Basketball* (New York: Seven Stories Press, 2001).

14 "Unartful Dodger," *Sports Illustrated* (May 29, 2000), pp. 28–9.

15 Editorial, "The Biggest Game in Town," *Sports Illustrated* (March 10, 1986), pp. 30–1.

16 David Noonan, "Boxing and the Brain," *New York Times Magazine* (June 12, 1984), pp. 40ff.

17 Robert H. Boyle and Wilmer Ames, "Too Many Punches, Too Little Concern," *Sports Illustrated* (April 11, 1983), pp. 44–67; Charles Leerhsen, "The AMA Tries to KO Boxing," *Newsweek* (December 17, 1984), p. 67.

18 Fred Bruning, "Shake Hands and Come Out Killing," *Maclean's* (December 13, 1982), p. 13.

19 Noonan, p. 42.

20 At www.FightNews.com (September 25, 2005).

21 Jeffrey T. Sammons, *Beyond the Ring: The Role of Boxing in American Society* (Urbana: University of Illinois Press, 1988), pp. 219–21.

22 Gloria Cooksey, "Don(ald) King," in Arnold Markoe, ed., *The Scribner Encyclopedia of American Lives: Sports Figures* (New York: Charles Scribner's Sons, 2002), vol. 2, pp. 519–20.

23 For several perspectives on Tyson's career, see Daniel O'Connor, ed., *Iron Mike: The Mike Tyson Reader* (New York: Thunder's Mouth Press, 2002).

24 Jack Newfield, *Only in America: The Life and Crimes of Don King* (New York: William Morrow, 1995), pp. 266–72.

25 Ibid., p. 288.

26 Joyce Carol Oates, "Rape and the Boxing Ring," *Newsweek* (February 24, 1992), pp. 60–1; William Nack, "A Crushing Verdict," *Sports Illustrated* (September 22, 1992), pp. 22–3; Newfield, p. 293.

27 Newfield, pp. 132–8.

28 Tom Donahoe and Neil Johnson, *Foul Play: Drug Abuse in Sports* (New York: Basil Blackwell, 1986), p. 1.

29 Robert Voy, *Drugs, Sport, and Politics* (Champaign, IL: Human Kenetics, 1991), pp. 3–7.

30 Ibid., pp. 16–18.

31 Ibid., p. xv.

32 Ibid., p. xv.

33 Steve Courson, *False Glory: Steelers and Steroids* (Stamford, CN: Longmeadow Press, 1991), p. 150.

34 Michael S. Bahrke and Charles E. Yesalis, *Performance-Enhancing Substances in Sport and Exercise* (Champaign, IL: Human Kenetics, 2002), pp. 7–8.

35 Bil Gilbert, "Drugs in Sports," *Sports Illustrated* (June 23, 30 and July 7, 1969.

36 Courson, pp. 49–55.

37 Ibid., p. 55.

38 Ibid., pp. 55–9.

39 C. Fraser Smith, *Lenny, Lefty, and the Chancellor: The Len Bias Tragedy and the Search for Reform in Big-Time College Basketball* (Baltimore, MD: Bancroft Press, 1992).

40 Don Yeager and Douglas S. Looney, *Under the Tarnished Dome: How Notre Dame Betrayed Its Ideals for Football Glory* (New York: Simon and Schuster, 1993), p. 48.

41 Shelly Smith, "I'm Sick and I'm Scared," *Sports Illustrated* (July 8, 1991), pp. 20–4.

42 David Markel, Noah Kaplan, and Michael Fishel, "The Andro Debate," (no date) at www.angelfire.com/tx2/andro

43 Ibid.

44 Bill Saporito, "How Pumped Up Is Baseball?" *Time* (December 13, 2004), pp. 34–5.

45 For example, see Rick Reilly, "No Doubt About It," *Sports Illustrated* (December 13, 2004), p. 118.

46 "Drug Free Sports Might Be a Thing of the Past" Associated Press (December 27, 2004).

47 Ibid.

48 Mark Fainaru-Wada and Lance Williams, *Game of Shadows: Barry Bonds, BALCO, and the Steroids Scandal that Rocked Professional Sports* (New York: Gotham Books, 2006).

49 Jerry Adler, "Toxic Strength," *Newsweek* (December 20, 2004), pp. 45–52.

16 The Democratization of Sports

1 Richard O. Davies, *America's Obsession: Sports and Society Since 1945* (Fort Worth, TX: Harcourt Brace, 1993), pp. 103–9.

2 Mary Pieratt and Ken Honeywell, *Bobby Plump: Last of the Small-town Heroes* (Indianapolis, IN: Good Morning Publishing, 1997).

3 Christopher Davis, "Go Massillon Go!" *Esquire* (December 1965), pp. 206–7.

4 H. G. Bissinger, *Friday Night Lights: A Town, a Team, and a Dream* (Reading, MA: Addison-Wesley, 1990), p. xiii.

5 Bissinger, p. xiv.

6 Alexander Wolff and Armen Keteyian, *Raw Recruits: The High Stakes Game Colleges Play to Get Their Basketball Stars – and What It Costs* (New York: Pocket Books, 1990); for a harsh critique of the underside of high school sports programs see Andrew Miracle and C. Roger Rees, *Lessons of the Locker Room: The Myth of High School Sports* (Amherst, NY: Prometheus Books, 1994).

7 Lewis Yablonsky and Jonathan Brower, *The Little League Game: How Kids, Coaches, and Parents Really Play* (New York: Times Books, 1979); Bill Geist, *Little League Confidential* (New York: Macmillan, 1992); Lance and Robin Van Auken, *Play Ball! The Story of Little League Baseball* (University Park: Pennsylvania State University Press, 2001).

8 Jim Brosnan, "Little Leaguers Have Big Problems – Their Parents," *Atlantic* (March, 1963), pp. 117–20.

9 Joan Ryan, *Little Girls in Pretty Boxes: The Making and Breaking of Elite Gymnasts and Figure Skaters* (New York: Doubleday, 1995).

10 Ibid., pp. 13–15.

11 See Davies, pp. 124–6, for a detailed description of the tennis academy philosophy.

12 Michael Sokolove, "Constructing a Teen Phenom," *New York Times Magazine* (November 28, 2004), pp. 80–5.

13 Ibid., p. 84.

14 Sandra Redmond Peters, "(William) Ben Hogan," in Arnold Markoe, ed., *Scribner Encyclopedia of American Lives: Sports Figures* (New York: Charles Scribner's Sons, 2002) vol. 1, p. 422.

15 James Dodson, *Ben Hogan: An American Life* (New York: Doubleday, 2004), pp. 237–51.

16 "A Champion Proves They Can Come Back," *Life* (January 23, 1950), pp. 21–3; "Little Ice Water," *Time* (January 10, 1949), pp. 52–6; "Out for Greatness," *Newsweek* (July 20, 1953), pp. 80–1.

17 Ray Cave, "Arnold Palmer, Sportsman of the Year," *Sports Illustrated* (January 9, 1961), p. 25.

18 Martin Sherwin, "Arnold Daniel (Arnie) Palmer," in Arnold Markoe, ed. *Scribner Encyclopedia of American Lives: Sports Figures* (New York: Charles Scribner's Sons, 2002), vol. 2, pp. 220–2; Cave, pp. 23–31.

19 Alfred Wright, "The Trouble with Leading an Army," *Sports Illustrated* (June 25, 1962), pp. 16–20; "Win or Lose, Arnie Draws," *Sports Illustrated* (July 27, 1981), p. 47.

20 "The Man and the Myth," *Time* (June 28, 1968), p. 76; Martin Sherwin, "Lee Buck Trevino," in Arnold Markoe, ed., *Scribner Encyclopedia of American Lives: Sports Figures* (New York: Charles Scribner's Sons, 2002), vol. 2, pp. 438–9.

21 Dan Jenkins, "Lee Trevino, Fleas and All," *Sports Illustrated* (June 8, 1970), pp. 70–1; "Lee Trevino: Cantinflas of the Country Clubs," *Time* (July 19, 1971), p. 48.

22 Jenkins, p. 71; Curry Kirkpatrick, "A Common Man with an Uncommon Touch," *Sports Illustrated* (December 20, 1971), pp. 34–9.

23 Martin Sherwin, "Jack William Nicklaus," in Arnold Markoe, ed., *Scribner Encyclopedia of American Lives: Sports Figures* (New York: Charles Scribner's Sons, 2002), vol. 2, pp. 188–90.

24 "Prodigious Prodigy," *Time* (June 29, 1962), pp. 38–42.

25 Frank Deford, "Still Glittering After All These Years," *Sports Illustrated* (December 25, 1978), p. 34.

26 Sherwin, "Jack William Nicklaus," p. 189.

27 Rick Reilly, "Day of Glory for a Golden Oldie," *Sports Illustrated* (April 21, 1986), pp. 18–25; Pete Axthelm, "From Fat Boy to Legend," *Newsweek* (April 28, 1986), p. 80; Deford, pp. 26–32.

28 Billie Jean King, *Billy Jean* (New York: Harper and Row, 1974); Karen Gould, "Billie Jean Moffit King," in Arnold Markoe, ed., *Scribner Encyclopedia of American Lives: Sports Figures* (New York: Charles Scribner's Sons, 2002), vol. 1, pp. 517–19.

29 Deford, "Mrs Billie Jean King!" *Sports Illustrated* (May 19, 1975), pp. 71–82.

30 *New York Times*, August 3, 1973, p. 61; Pete Axthelm, "The Battle of the Sexes," *Newsweek* (September 24, 1973), pp. 82–5.

31 *New York Times*, July 12, 1973, p. 41.

32 Curry Kirkpatrick, "There She Is, Ms America," *Sports Illustrated* (October 1, 1973), pp. 30–2.

33 Curry Kirkpatrick, "The Passion of a Champion," *Newsweek* (November 14, 1994), p. 58; S. L. Price, "Hail and Farewell," *Sports Illustrated* (July 11, 1994), pp. 16–21.

34 Samuel Abt, *LeMond: The Incredible Comeback of an American Hero* (New York: Random House, 1990); Franz Lidz, "Vive LeMond!" *Sports Illustrated* (July 31, 1989), pp. 12–17; Alexander Wolff, "Tour de Courage," *Sports Illustrated* (August 5, 1991), pp. 2–31.

35 E. M. Swift, "An American Takes Paris," *Sports Illustrated* (August 4, 1986), pp. 12–17; Greg LeMond, *Greg LeMond's Complete Book of Bicycling* (New York: G. P. Putnam's, 1987), pp. 9–40.

36 Austin Murphy, "Magnifique!" *Sports Illustrated* (August 6, 2001), pp. 34–9; Kelli Anderson, "King of the Hill," *Sports Illustrated* (August 5, 2002), p. 38.

37 Alan Shipnuck, "Tour de Armstrong," *Sports Illustrated* (May 20, 1996), pp. 48–50.

38 Lance Armstrong, *It's Not About the Bike: My Journey Back to Life* (New York: Berkeley Books, 2001), p. 4.

39 Rick Reilly, "Sportsman of the Year: Lance Armstrong," *Sports Illustrated* (December 16, 2002), p. 56.

40 Timothy Kringen, "Lance Armstrong," in Arnold Markoe, ed., *Scribner Encyclopedia of American Lives: Sports Figures* (New York: Charles Scribner's Sons, 2002), vol. 1, p. 41; Richard Hoffer, "Tour de Lance," *Sports Illustrated* (July 26, 1999), p. 27.

41 Anderson, p. 38.

42 Armstrong, p. 248.

43 Sara Hammel and Anna Mulrine, "They Got More Than Just a Game," *US News and World Report* (July 12, 1999), p. 54.

44 Mark Starr, "Keeping Her Own Score," *Newsweek* (June 21, 1999), p. 60; Mia Hamm, *Go for the Goal: A Champion's Guide to Winning in Soccer and Life* (New York: HarperCollins, 2000), pp. 3–24.

45 Starr, p. 62.
46 Hamm, pp. 208–9.
47 Mark Starr and Martha Brandt, "It Went Down to the Wire . . . and Thrilled Us All," *Newsweek* (July 10, 1999), p. 53.
48 Starr, p. 61.

Epilogue

1 Warren St John, *Rammer Jammer Yellow Hammer: A Trip Into the Heart of Fan Mania* (New York: Three Rivers Press, 2004).
2 For a useful evaluation of the studies of spectator and fan behavior and attitudes, see Daniel L. Wann, Merrill J. Melnick, Gordon W. Russell, and Dale G. Pease, *Sports Fans: The Psychology and Social Impact of Spectators* (New York: Routledge, 2001).

Index